D1708932

COLLECTED WORKS OF ERASMUS

VOLUME 13

Phillips

THE CORRESPONDENCE OF
ERASMUS

LETTERS 1802 TO 1925

March–December 1527

translated by Charles Fantazzi

annotated by James K. Farge

University of Toronto Press

Toronto / Buffalo / London

The research and publication costs of the
Collected Works of Erasmus are supported by
University of Toronto Press.

© University of Toronto Press 2010
Toronto / Buffalo / London
Printed in Canada

ISBN 978-0-8020-9059-1

Printed on acid-free paper

Library and Archives Canada Cataloguing in Publication

Erasmus, Desiderius, d. 1536
[Works]
Collected works of Erasmus.

Each vol. has special t.p. ; general title from half title page.
Translation of: Opus epistolarum Des. Erasmi Roterodami.
Includes bibliographies and indexes.

Contents: v. 13. Correspondence of Erasmus, letters 1802–1925.
ISBN-10: 0-8020-2831-4 (set). – ISBN-13: 978-0-8020-9059-1 (v. 13)

1. Erasmus, Desiderius, d. 1536 – Collected works. I. Title

PA8500.1974   199'.492   C740-06326-x rev

University of Toronto Press acknowledges the financial assistance to its
publishing program of the Canada Council and the Ontario Arts Council.

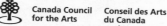 

University of Toronto Press acknowledges the financial support for its
publishing activities of the Government of Canada through the Book Publishing
Industry Development Program (BPIDP).

Collected Works of Erasmus

The aim of the Collected Works of Erasmus
is to make available an accurate, readable English text
of Erasmus' correspondence and his
other principal writings. The edition is planned
and directed by an Editorial Board, an Executive Committee,
and an Advisory Committee.

*This volume was published with the financial assistance of the late
John Simon Gabriel Simmons OBE, Slavonic bibliographer and librarian,
associated both with the Bodleian Library, Oxford, and the Russian State
Library, Moscow, sometime Fellow Librarian of All Souls College, Oxford,
and a dedicated friend and supporter over many years
of the Collected Works of Erasmus.*

Contents

Illustrations

Preface

This volume makes available for the first time the English translations of the first 124 letters in volume VII of P.S. Allen's *Opus epistolarum Des. Erasmi Roterodami*. Included with them are five additional letters: Ep 1806A, which came to Allen's attention in time to be tipped into the volume by the printer; Epp 1807A, 1837A, and 1895A, which were discovered after the publication of volume VII; and an unnumbered letter that Allen placed at the head of Ep 1902. Of these 129 letters, 85 were written by Erasmus and 42 were addressed to him. Ep 1846 (from Pope Clement VII to Alonso Manrique de Lara) and a letter in French (from King Francis I to the University of Paris, which appears at the head of Ep 1902), were considered by Allen to be so integral to the events of this period in Erasmus' career that he included them with Erasmus' own correspondence. The identity of two correspondents in this volume escaped Allen; we have been able to make positive attribution of one of them (Ep 1827). All the translations are the work of Charles Fantazzi, with the single exception of the French letter at the head of Ep 1902. It was translated by the annotator.

All 129 letters were written during the nine months between 28 March and the end of December 1527. Erasmus addressed his 85 letters from Basel, from where he was not to depart until April 1529. He chose to publish 59 of them in his *Opus epistolarum* (Basel 1529), which appeared after he had moved his residence to Freiburg-im-Breisgau. Another seven (Epp 1841, 1844, 1853, 1855, 1856, 1879, and 1895A) are dedicatory epistles to works that he published, or was preparing to publish, during this time. Ep 1900 constitutes Erasmus' eulogy for his favourite printer and close friend Johann Froben, who died on 27 October of this year. It includes two epitaphs that Erasmus composed for him.

Erasmus' continuing frustration with his critics, both Catholic and reformist, is the overriding issue in the present volume. It was his personal dilemma that neither the conservative Catholic theologians nor the religious reformers saw him as an ally or friend. In one of the longest of the letters here (Ep 1804 to Thomas More) Erasmus reflects upon the irony of the divisions within the Catholic side: while his Catholic enemies consider his works to favour the spread of heresy, his Catholic friends see him as the best person to refute the heretics. In the very next letter (Ep 1805 to the young Spaniard Juan Maldonado) he dwells on the hatred that the Spanish 'pseudomonks' manifest for his works.

In Ep 1875 Erasmus confides to Juan de Vergara that the books of Luther contain 'such a great quantity of imprecations, sneers, invective, boasting, insults, ovations, and triumphs that I was well nigh overcome with disgust' (lines 4–5). By that time he had acceded to the wishes of his Catholic friends and completed the second book of *Hyperaspistes* (CWE 77). In the preface to it (Ep 1853), we find the clearest and strongest affirmation of the definitive break with Luther that Erasmus had resisted for several years but had first begun to make clear in *De libero arbitrio* and in *Hyperaspistes 1* (CWE 76). Indeed the language is so strong that the reader could credibly expect this work to have satisfied Erasmus' Catholic critics, but it brought neither a reconciliation nor even a truce with them. Instead, the polemic between Erasmus and his Catholic critics would continue at the same pitch as prior to his three books against Luther.

The twenty-two letters exchanged with Spanish correspondents show that the opposition to Erasmus in Spain, already an ominous threat as the letters in CWE 12 make clear, emerged at this time as his most critical preoccupation. His Spanish friends provided him, as they do us, with valuable insight into the background and events leading up to the inquisition into his orthodoxy that convened on 27 June 1527. Juan de Vergara (Ep 1814) singles out the Spanish translation of the *Enchiridion* as the principal cause for the 'implacable war' declared against Erasmus by the Spanish theologians. Vergara also names and gives his appraisal of the theologians commissioned to sit in judgment against Erasmus. Because Vergara was a vehement critic of anyone who had reservations about Erasmus, and because his facts do not always coincide with those provided by other sources, his letters – like so many of the letters concerning this affair, both to and by Erasmus – must be read judiciously.

In regard to the Valladolid inquisition we should take note that Ep 1846 (from Pope Clement VII to Grand Inquisitor Alonso Manrique) authorizing the inquisition was not dispatched until 1 August 1527, five weeks after it was convened and just thirteen days before it suddenly ended. The prorogation *sine die* of those proceedings, when only four of the twenty-one items on the agenda had been considered, was a victory that would protect Erasmus and his followers in Spain for only several years. Some of Erasmus' Spanish supporters, fully aware that the inquisition might be resumed again, implored him to moderate the expression of his views and to refrain from answering his Spanish critics (Ep 1907). This was the kind of advice that Erasmus could not abide and did not follow.

The account of events in Spain given by Juan Luis Vives (Ep 1847), who was living in Bruges at this time, complements that of Juan de Vergara. It also informs us of two other narratives, neither of them extant, which had been sent to Erasmus by Alonso Ruiz de Virués and Alfonso de Valdez. We know that similar letters, also lost to us today, reached Erasmus – a reminder that the treasury of letters included in the present volume would have been even richer had those and other lost letters survived. We can nevertheless appreciate how such letters spurred Erasmus to prepare an initial, if incomplete, refutation of the charges brought against him: Ep 1877 to the inquisitor-general Alonso Manrique de Lara. Just as *Hyperaspistes 1* had been produced as a hurried answer to Luther's *The Enslaved Will*, Ep 1877 can be regarded as a hasty preview of Erasmus' longer and more considered *Apologia adversus monachos quosdam Hispanos*, the preface to which is published here as Ep 1879.

The conflict with Erasmus' French critics is no longer centre stage in 1527 as it was in 1526, but it continues nevertheless. Ep 1906 to Noël Béda, the syndic of the Paris faculty of theology, is the last in a long and increasingly bitter exchange of letters between them. Erasmus' concern for the safety of his French translator Louis de Berquin appears several times, notably in Ep 1875 to Juan de Vergara. After having abjured his errors in 1523, Berquin was accused of recidivism and brought to trial again in 1526. Erasmus' efforts to win over the Parlement of Paris to his own cause and that of Berquin (Ep 1905) would have no success at all. In voicing the same concerns to the cardinal of Lorraine (Ep 1911), Erasmus would have received a better hearing, but the cardinal was more successful in promoting Erasmus' friend Gervasius Wain than in protecting Berquin or Erasmus himself. On 16 December 1527 the Paris faculty of theology formally condemned 112 propositions drawn from Erasmus' works. This would lead to a censure of Erasmus' *Colloquies* by the whole University of Paris in June 1528, although the text of all the Paris condemnations would not be published until 1531.

The favour of rulers had always constituted an important source of patronage and protection for Erasmus. Now, in an increasingly dangerous climate of censure and in a Europe torn by war and breaking apart into religious confessionalism and regionally organized churches, that royal or imperial favour became more important than ever. Erasmus' own sovereign, Emperor Charles v (Epp 1873, 1920), extended his protection through, and perhaps at the bidding of, his chancellor Mercurino Gattinara (Epp 1815, 1872) and his councillor Jean (II) de Carondelet (Ep 1806). Erasmus would sometimes boast of such imperial favour, but he would later complain of being thrown to the 'beasts' by Charles (Ep 1888) – an accusation that proved to be without foundation. In Ep 1869 we see him plead with Duke George of Albertine Saxony, the ruler with whom he corresponded most frequently, that 'if rulers do not lend me their support, I fear I cannot hold my position, not so much because of the Lutherans as of those who call themselves Antilutherans but are in fact the most fanatical of Lutherans, and who are attempting to arrogate to themselves the victory owed to Christ' (lines 10–14).

In his need to cultivate the protection of well-placed churchmen Erasmus was careful to maintain the long-standing good will of William Warham, archbishop of Canterbury. In Epp 1828 and 1831 we see him make the rare admission to Warham that, in retrospect, some parts of his early works might well have been phrased more judiciously. But he also tries to convince Warham that his enemies are less concerned with his putative heterodoxy than with obstructing his promotion of 'humane letters' – the success of which threatens their prestige and their outmoded scholastic method. Yet at this same time some of Erasmus' close English friends like Cuthbert Tunstall and Thomas More were growing increasingly worried about the spread of heresy in England and generally in Europe. Perhaps in recognition of this changing climate in England Erasmus addressed the longest letter in this volume – a treatise defending his theology of the Holy Spirit – to a young English friend, Robert Aldridge (Ep 1858).

Erasmus' friendship with the Polish nobleman Jan (ii) Łaski, who had stayed with him in Basel during the spring of 1525, produced an increasing number of letters to and from correspondents in Eastern Europe. This had political implications, because many of those correspondents (like Łaski himself) were not friends of Erasmus' Hapsburg patrons. One of the chief points of contention in the East was the dispute over the title of king of Pannonia (Hungary) that followed the death of King Louis ii on the battlefield of Mohács (1526). Łaski and his entourage denied the Hapsburg claim to Hungary and recognized the Hungarian nobleman John Zápolyai as king. At Łaski's urging and that of the royal physician Jan Antonin, Erasmus addressed Ep 1819 to King Sigismund i of Poland. In this letter, which constitutes a short treatise on kingship, Erasmus referred to Zápolyai as king of Hungary. This naturally offended Erasmus' correspondents who were clients of the Hapsburgs (Ep 1917) to the point that in 1529, when Erasmus published that same letter for wider consumption in the Opus epistolarum, he changed the phrase 'John, the king of Hungary' to read 'John, who has usurped the title of king' (153).

Prior to residing in Basel Erasmus had made his home in Louvain (c July 1517–May 1520), where for a time he had been an adjunct lecturer in the university. From Basel he remained in contact with friends in Louvain like Jan Becker of Borsele, Conradus Goclenius, Jacobus Ceratinus (Jacob Teyng), Maarten Lips, Rutgerus Rescius, and Nicolas Wary. Erasmus especially maintained a keen interest in the well-being of Louvain's Collegium Trilingue, and in his letters of 1527 he freely offers advice to officials there about curriculum and staffing problems. But he had a number of determined, vociferous enemies in Louvain as well. The recent deaths of his two most strident critics there (the Carmelite Nicolaas Baechem and the Dominican Vincentius Theoderici) had no sooner reduced the level of criticism in Louvain than another Flemish antagonist, the Franciscan Frans Titelmans, appeared in 1527. As a young man Titelmans had attended the Louvain college founded by Jan Standonck, where (like Noël Béda at the Collège de Montaigu in Paris) he embraced Standonck's ideal of combining scholastic learning with piety and asceticism for the purpose of reforming the church. Titelmans later joined the Franciscan order and, later, its Capuchin branch. Only one exchange of letters between him and Erasmus is extant. Titelmans proved to be a more intelligent and prolific polemicist than Baechem. Like Pierre Cousturier in Paris, Titelmans was particularly concerned to defend the Vulgate translation of the Bible against humanist textual criticism and commentary. Although denigrated by Juan Luis Vives and Erasmus, Titelmans was respected as a serious theologian and opponent by many of his Protestant enemies, and his polemic against Erasmus did not cease when the correspondence between them stopped.

Throughout all this controversy over religion Erasmus repeatedly protests that the sole aim of his life's work is to promote the study of the humanities for the profit of both knowledge and religion – goals that even some of his friends failed to understand. As for those who oppose him, he writes, 'Their only motive is that the reflowering of good letters and the efforts of a new, spiritual Christianity to regain its primitive vigour detract from their privileges and authority' (Ep 1909:6–9). But even with his friends Erasmus can brook no criticism of his method of study and his programme to reform education. We see this in letters exchanged with long-time correspondents like Guillaume Budé (Epp 1812, 1840) and Juan Luis Vives (Epp 1836, 1847). Ep 1912, an encouraging letter, totally free of servile flattery, from Johann von Vlatten, a young German friend, must have come as a great relief (Erasmus would dedicate his *Ciceronianus* to Vlatten in 1528). The very next letter in sequence, from a well-meaning young Spaniard, carried a message that Erasmus may have been prepared to hear: 'From the beginning it was ordained that in this perverse world the good man would undergo persecution' (Ep 1913:12–13). But the disconcerting fact that this correspondent drew his biblical examples not from the Bible but from the

Historia scholastica, a twelfth-century conflation of Bible stories with oral history and myth, would surely not have increased Erasmus' confidence about
whether he was really making a difference in the world of learning.

The letters in this volume show indeed that Erasmus needed and demanded unstinting approval. The praise offered by a new, enthusiastic well-
wisher like the Benedictine monk Alonso Ruiz de Virués (Epp 1838, 1839)
was not to be tolerated, because it carried what its author considered to be
constructive and helpful criticism. But Erasmus had to manage more carefully similar suggestions from important Catholic patrons like Pope Clement
VII and Duke George of Saxony, who constantly urged that he devote more
time to refuting the religious reformers. Thus, in regard to Martin Luther,
he tells Duke George that he had 'never found anything so troublesome as
replying to such a prolix recital of abuse and bombast, the reading of which
itself required a strong stomach' (Ep 1924:15–16). In other letters he likewise confesses openly his disagreement and dislike of Luther (Epp 1853,
1901) and of Johannes Oecolampadius (Ep 1893). Any hesitation that Erasmus may have had in earlier years about remaining in the Catholic church
is no longer visible in these letters of 1527. Prior to his first book against
Luther he had already broken with reformist leaders like Ulrich von Hutten,
Wolfgang Capito, Huldrych Zwingli, Conradus Pellicanus, and Otto Brunfels. He remained on civil terms with the former Dominican Martin Bucer,
now the pastor of a reformed church in Strasbourg, but Ep 1901 to Bucer
contains incisive criticism of the reformers in general and a remarkable profession of Erasmus' fidelity to the established church (lines 24–37). In Ep
1887 he urges an anonymous monk to remain in his way of life, confiding
to him, 'I am sorely grieved that I once preached freedom of the spirit in
my books' (lines 13–14).

Still, such criticism of the Reformation movement did not diminish Erasmus' combat against Catholic traditionalists. Apart from his book
against the Spanish 'monks,' which he dedicated to the grand inquisitor
Alonso Manrique de Lara, Erasmus attempts in two long letters to dissuade
the Parlement of Paris and the Paris faculty of theology from making common cause with his relentless critic Noël Béda (Epp 1902, 1905).

In the midst of so much controversy, Erasmus was nevertheless able
to produce some works not polemical in nature: translations of sermons and
minor works by the church Fathers Origen and John Chrysostom, an edition of St Ambrose, and one volume (the epistles – see Ep 1895A) of the ten-
volume *Opera omnia* of Saint Augustine to which Froben was devoting two
(and sometimes three or four) of his presses (Ep 1890). In the preface to the
four-volume edition of Ambrose (Ep 1855) Erasmus sums up his predilection for this kind of work: 'It seems to me a more noble enterprise to restore

the works of ancient authors that have sunk into oblivion through the ravages of time or the recklessness of scribes than to hammer out new volumes'
(lines 16–19).

Those sentiments notwithstanding, Erasmus did not refrain from ham-
mering out new volumes of his own. In addition to the polemical and patristic books already mentioned, we find an allusion to his preparation of
the *Ciceronianus*, an attack on those humanists who 'consider it to be more
disgraceful not to be called a Ciceronian than to be called a heretic' (Ep
1875:166–8). Moreover, in Epp 1881 and 1921 he writes of making progress
with his long-awaited treatise on preaching, which would not, however, be
published until 1535.

Erasmus continues during this period to complain about his health,
notably a debilitating toothache and the old complaint of kidney stones and
other urinary disorders. His exchange of letters with Theophrastus Paracelsus (Epp 1808–9) affords some insight into the latter condition. The late
Charles B. Schmitt thought that Ep 1808 should be seen as Paracelsus' reply to Erasmus' Ep 1809, but in the absence of conclusive proof we have
maintained here the order in which Allen placed them.

Worry about money loomed large in Erasmus' early letters but rarely
comes up in those of 1527. His finances must have been more secure –
largely, no doubt, because of the Polish nobleman Jan (II) Łaski's purchase
of Erasmus' library, while leaving him the use of it as long as he lived. In
our volume, however, we see that Erasmus nevertheless maintains his correspondence with the Antwerp banker Erasmus Schets, on whom he relied
to manage the collection and transfer of annuities and pensions owed to
him from various sources. Any worries about the eventual disposition of
his goods seems to have been set at rest for the time being by the will that
he had drawn up in January 1527 (CWE 12 538–50).

We have limited the introductions of these letters to essential facts
about the correspondents, their importance to Erasmus, and the significance
of the letter concerned. While we generally continue the practice in previous volumes of referring the reader to earlier letters and annotation on
them, we often refer the reader to *Contemporaries of Erasmus: A Biographical
Register of the Renaissance and Reformation* ed Peter Bietenholz and Thomas
Deutscher (CEBR). There the reader will find comprehensive biographical
sketches, cross-references to the correspondence, and references to additional literature. In the introductions and in the annotations we have called
attention to some scholarship that has appeared since the publication of Allen
and of CEBR.

Several of Erasmus' correspondents inscribed a cross at the beginning
or the end of their letters – a not uncommon practice used over the centuries

as a prayerful declaration of one's faith in the crucified Christ. Past volumes of the CWE have not reproduced that symbol; but an editorial decision has now been made to include it, because it is an integral part of the original manuscript and was a clear manifestation of the writer's piety.

As with all previous volumes of the correspondence, the translations and annotations in CWE 13 rely heavily on the fine Latin edition of Erasmus' letters to which P.S. Allen (assisted by his wife H.M. Allen) devoted most of his adult life. Although we have often updated or expanded his notes to the text, we have only rarely needed to correct them. As always, the University of Toronto Press likewise acknowledges the pioneering work of the Allens and is grateful to the Oxford University Press for permission to use its edition as a basis for textual translation and annotation.

The translator of these letters, Charles Fantazzi, provided most of the classical references that Allen had not identified, as well as several notes on linguistic matters. Alexander Dalzell and Sr Mechtilde O'Mara CSJ likewise gave invaluable help with some of the classical and linguistic problems. James Estes, former teacher and now colleague and friend, has been a careful reader, pointing out a number of connections between these letters and earlier ones, and helping me refine syntax and prose. I am grateful to John H. Munro for annotating the matters of money and coinage found in these letters. Help with particular annotations has been acknowledged in those specific places. The book was copyedited by Mary Baldwin, whose thorough readings have greatly enhanced its accuracy and clarity. It was typeset by Lynn Browne and Philippa Matheson.

In the longer course of things I owe to my family in Texas, my confrères in the Congregation of Saint Basil, and colleagues at the Pontifical Institute of Mediaeval Studies the moral and material support that I have needed to bring this work to completion.

JKF CSB

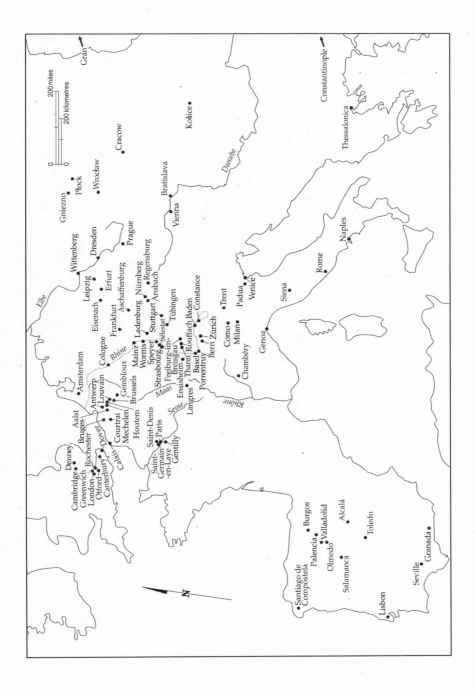

200 miles

200 kilometres

Gran

Constantinople

Thessalonica

Košice •

Cracow •

Gniezno • Płock •

Wrocław •

Bratislava •

Elbe

Wittenberg •

Dresden •

Prague •

Vienna •

Danube

Naples

Leipzig •

Erfurt •

Regensburg

Eisenach •

Aschaffenburg

Nürnberg •

Rome •

Frankfurt •

Ladenburg Ansbach

Siena •

Mainz • Stuttgart •

Sélestat Tübingen •

Trent •

Padua •

Constance

Venice •

Worms •

Speyer •

Como •

Milan •

Rhine

Strasbourg Baden

Thann Rouffach

Amsterdam •

Freiburg-im- Basel

Bern Zürich •

Genoa •

Cologne

Breisgau

Chambéry •

Antwerp Louvain Gembloux

Ensisheim

Brussels

Porrentruy

Maas

Langres •

Bruges Aalst

Courtrai Mechelen

Rhône

Denney •

Houtem

Cambridge • Rochester

Saint-Denis

Greenwich Otford

Dover

Paris •

London •

Canterbury Calais

Saint-

Gentilly

Germain-

en-Laye

Santiago de •

Compostela

Burgos •

Palencia •

Alcalá •

Valladolid •

Olmedo •

Toledo •

Salamanca •

Granada •

Seville •

Lisbon •

N

THE CORRESPONDENCE OF ERASMUS
LETTERS 1802 TO 1925

1802 / From Maximilianus Transsilvanus   Houtem, 28 March 1527

The autograph of this letter (Ep 63 in Förstemann-Günther) was in the ill-fated
Burscher Collection at the University Library in Leipzig (on which see Ep 1254
introduction).

Allen concluded – without convincing justification – that Maximilianus was
the natural son of Matthäus Lang, bishop of Gurk, who was his early patron.
He became secretary and councillor to Emperor Maximilian I, who included
him in imperial embassies to England (1511) and Italy (1512). He followed
Charles v to Flanders and Germany in 1519, and in 1521 it fell to him to read
out the titles of Luther's books at the Diet of Worms. In 1522, his report of
an interview with the survivors of Magellan's circumnavigation of the world
aroused great interest. As secretary to Charles v, he was helpful to Erasmus in
the matter of his pension. He maintained residences in Brussels, at Bouchout
near Brussels, and at Houtem (which Allen calls Hantem), south of Ghent. His
acquaintance with Erasmus dated from 1521.

✝

Even though a long time has elapsed since I last wrote to you,[1] I would not
have you think on that account that I have ever forsaken your memory or
would ever wilfully shirk any duty owed to your distinguished self. But I
have for some time put off the task of writing, partly for want of someone to
whom I could safely entrust a letter, partly because my occupations detained   5
me, and in some measure too for lack of news. It will devolve upon your
great kindness to grant me pardon if at times inadvertence is the cause of
my silence.

I sent to you in recent days a letter from the emperor.[2] I had received
it in duplicate copy;[3] but, since your detractors were spreading the news   10
hither and yon that it was not a letter from the emperor but a forgery, I
kept one copy and opened it and in your name sent it to a supporter of
yours in Louvain through the intermediacy of Gilles de Busleyden,[4] a man

* * * * *

1802
1 Probably the letter answered by Ep 1645
2 Ep 1731. This and later statements suggest that letters addressed to Erasmus
   were often sent to Transsilvanus for forwarding to Erasmus.
3 The sending of important letters in duplicate, using different couriers and
   routes, was a caution Erasmus says he learned from cardinals (Ep 1674:96).
   For other instances see the introductions to Epp 729 and 794 and Ep 1645:1–2.
4 The eldest of the four Busleyden brothers, he was an influential admirer of
   Erasmus and a patron of the Collegium Trilingue founded at Louvain by his
   late brother Jérôme.

of great prominence and a tireless defender of your honour. In the same post
I received another letter from the high chancellor of the emperor addressed   15
to the chancellor and theologians of Louvain, full of your praises.[5] I shall
send you a copy of it shortly. I send you as well letters that the chancellor
of the emperor himself and our friend Valdés have written to you.[6]

I have nothing else to write to you. I am in the country, as usual. I am
not at court unless summoned, which nonetheless occurs more often than   20
I would wish. And I am not at all concerned with what the theologians of
Louvain are plotting. If the rest of mankind were to give as much attention
as I do to their calumnies, there would be no one to deem them worthy of a
response, no more indeed than I would heed the barking of a toothless dog.

Farewell, and hold me dear. From my country house at Houtem, 28   25
March 1527

Your friend, Maximilianus Transsilvanus, as much devoted to you as
to himself

†

To the most celebrated and acclaimed Master Erasmus of Rotterdam,
at Basel or wherever he may be   30

1803 / From Leonard Cox   Cracow, 28 March 1527

Autograph throughout, the manuscript of this letter (Ep 64 in Förstemann-
Günther) was in the Burscher Collection at the University Library in Leipzig
(on which see Ep 1254 introduction). Erasmus will answer it with Ep 1824.

* * * * *

5 Ep 1784A from Mercurino Gattinara, a letter probably written for him by Alfonso de Valdés, the emperor's Latin secretary, who recast in it many of the
  arguments suggested to Gattinara by Erasmus' Ep 1747. It was probably addressed to the vice-chancellor Nicolas Coppin. The only extant draft of Ep
  1784A exists in the hand of Valdés, who likewise wrote in his own name to
  the chancellor and faculty of theology of Louvain in the same cause. For its
  text see Caballero Valdés Ep 8 321–2. For Alfonso de Valdés, the brother of the
  more famous Juan de Valdés, see Ep 1807 introduction and ER IV 212. Allen
  Ep 1784A introduction prints an excerpt from Transsilvanus' letter to Alfonso
  de Valdés reporting that Gattinara's letter to the theologians of Louvain had
  met with greater success than had earlier letters from Emperor Charles V and
  from his aunt Margaret of Austria, regent in the Netherlands for her nephew.
  For the full text of Transsilvanus' letter see Caballero Valdés Ep 21 344–6.
6 The letter of Gattinara is Ep 1785; that of Valdés is not extant. Transsilvanus
  and Valdés were in frequent contact: for the texts of seven extant letters exchanged between them, with Latin originals and Spanish translations, see Caballero Valdés Epp 6 316–19, 10 323–6, 17 335–40, 21 344–6, 34 364–71, 38 379–
  80, 58 432–7.

Earlier letters from Cox, as well as another written in the spring of 1527, have not survived.

Leonard Cox, from Thame in Oxfordshire, studied in Tübingen, where he knew Philippus Melanchthon, and in Cracow, where he was named poet laureate in 1518. He lectured on Livy and Quintilian and was schoolmaster successively in at least three Polish and Hungarian schools. He would later teach in England at Reading and then at Caerleon in Wales. His *Arte or Crafte of Rhetoryke*, the first rhetorical treatise in English, drew heavily on Melanchthon's *Institutiones rhetoricae* (see the edition by Frederic Ives Carpenter [Chicago 1899]). It was published first in English and reprinted in Latin in Cracow. For more recent comment on it see Jacqueline Glomski 'Careerism at Cracow: The Dedicatory Letters of Rudolf Agricola Junior, Valentin Eck, and Leonard Cox (1510–1530)' in *Self-Presentation and Social Identification: The Rhetoric and Pragmatics of Letter Writing in Early Modern Times* ed Toon Van Houdt et al (Louvain 2002), 165–82. After the execution of his patron Thomas Cromwell in 1540, Cox received an annuity from the king, perhaps in view of his English translations of Erasmian treatises and paraphrases. He died in 1549.

Manifold greetings. I did not expect a return with such huge interest from you. I thought it would be more than ample reward if you agreed to read my unlettered letter with forbearance. Indeed I would never have sent it to you except that our friend the Palatine had constrained me to do so.[1] Not that I took on this task unwillingly, but I was well aware that it is not for every man to sail to Corinth;[2] that is to say, it is granted to the very few – those whom kindly Jupiter holds dear, as the poet said[3] – to write letters worthy of Erasmus. I would have preferred to remain secluded within my customary obscurity rather than venture forth into public donning the lion's skin,[4] perhaps to arouse laughter in some, but, what is worse, to provoke your annoyance by my absurdities. But what was I to do? The order came from one to whom no one here ever refuses anything, and it was given in good faith, although far exceeding my abilities. Then, as one who teaches good letters in the employ of the state, how could I decline this charge?

* * * * *

1803
1 Cox's letter is not extant. On Krzysztof Szydłowiecki (Ep 1593), a Polish nobleman and advisor to King Sigismund I, see Ep 1820 introduction.
2 Horace *Epistles* 1.17.36; cf *Adagia* I iv 1.
3 Virgil *Aeneid* 6.129–30
4 Cox renders this in Greek: καὶ τὴν λεοντὴν ἐνδυόμενος; cf *Adagia* I iii 66. Hercules habitually wore the skin of the Nemean lion he had killed.

Therefore I wrote but (if you will allow me to turn the saying to this use) 15
like a sow to Minerva,[5] or at any rate like a man with less than average
learning to the most learned man of our age. I hoped for nothing more
than that you would take my rustic simplicity in good part. Yet, far from
disdaining my rustic, incoherent style you asked in your letter to Jan Łaski,[6]
a man of great distinction in every respect and now one of my patrons, 20
that greetings be given to Cox in your name. What is this, I pray you, but
repaying bronze with gold?[7] Certainly, as far as I am concerned, I should
rather be mentioned once by Erasmus than be proclaimed in the volumes of
all others put together, however elaborate they might be. You may interpret
this as you like; but, so may Christ show me his favour, I regard this act as 25
a very great kindness. Wherefore, as I previously rendered thanks to you
in another's name,[8] so now I must in turn render my own debt of gratitude.
But once again neither will your kindness allow me to tally up my real debt
to you – since there is nothing you credit less than praise of yourself – nor
does my lack of talent and learning allow me to redeem the entry under my 30
name in your ledger of sums paid out. Therefore I shall imitate Sallust on
this point, who preferred to say nothing about Carthage rather than describe
it in words that failed to do justice to its greatness.[9] Neither do I wish, for
lack of ability, to detract from your illustrious praise. I am therefore obliged
to make this one avowal: that I am so indebted to you for your kindness 35
that, even were my capital to increase, I do not think I could ever square
my accounts. And I shall make every effort that no future age may prove
unmindful of such singular generosity.

But enough on this subject. Concerning events here I think you have
been abundantly informed of them through the letters of others; and I have 40
no doubt that it has become well known there that the Tartars have been
overwhelmed by Duke Constantine, the leader of the Lithuanian army.[10]

* * * * *

5 *Adagia* I i 40 and I i 41
6 For Jan (II) Łaski, a Polish nobleman and ecclesiastic, see the introduction to
Ep 1821. The letter here mentioned is not extant but is clearly contemporary
with Epp 1751–4.
7 Cox resorts again to the Greek. See *Adagia* I ii 1, referring to the exchange of
armour between Glaucus and Diomedes (*Iliad* 6.234–6).
8 Cox had perhaps been employed by Szydłowiecki (line 4 above) to write Erasmus a letter of thanks for the dedication of the *Lingua*.
9 *Bellum Iugurthinum* 19
10 The Tartars (Tatars), a remnant of the thirteenth-century invasion of the Mon-
gols, settled in parts of Russia, from where they often tried to invade eastern
Europe. Konstanty Ostrozhsky, *voivode* of Troki (near Vilna) since 1522, led a

But if this news has not reached you yet, I send you herewith a complete
account of it in German written by your devoted friend Justus Decius.[11]
You are undoubtedly aware of his adverse state of health during this past   45
summer and all through the year; but now, thank heavens, he is recovering
more and more with each passing day. I think he will write to you if his
pressing activities will allow him to do so.[12]

The parish priest of Košice has recently relinquished of his own accord
the provostship of Eger,[13] which yields a thousand gold coins a year, as well   50
as the archbishopric of Tarnov, from which he received three hundred gold
coins each year.[14] He would have given up his pastoral charge too if the
people had not dissuaded him with earnest entreaties. He had made up
his mind to free himself of every responsibility and come to see you. He
will still do so, I think, if ever he has the opportunity. He was with us at   55
Shrovetide, as they say,[15] and enjoined upon me the duty of giving greetings
to Erasmus in his name.

* * * * *

Polish-Lithuanian army that defeated an invasion of Tartars at the Olszanica
River on 27 January 1527.

11 *Sendbrieff von der grossen Schlacht* (Cracow: Hieronim Wietor 1527; repr
Nürnberg 1527). Decius was royal secretary and economic advisor to King
Sigismund I of Poland. In the difficult times after the battle of Mohács, he
served as a diplomatic intermediary between the king and the Hapsburgs,
whom he much admired. Erasmus had dedicated to Decius the short *Precatio
dominica* in 1523. Decius had also published a more comprehensive narrative
of Sigismund's reign, *De Sigismundi regis temporibus liber* (Cracow: Hieronim
Wietor, December 1521). Alsatian by birth, Decius had studied commerce and
mining. After a long career in banking, he became secretary to King Sigismund, who granted him letters of nobility and used him for diplomatic embassies. Decius became a correspondent and supporter of Erasmus and other
humanists in eastern Europe. See *Christophe Scheurl's Briefbuch* ed F. von Soden
and J.K.F. Knaake (Potsdam 1867–72; repr Aalen 1962) 235; CEBR I 380–2.

12 Ep 1958

13 Johann Henckel of Levoča, a chaplain to Mary of Austria, queen of Hungary
and admirer of Erasmus, resigned his commendatory benefices in order to
escape the political turmoil in Hungary following the battle of Mohács (29
August 1526), in which King Louis II of Hungary lost his life; cf Ep 1810 n14.

14 The coins were probably ducats or florins (Venetian or Hungarian). If so, a
sum of 1,000 ducats would have been worth £333.333 *groot* Flemish, or 2,275
livres tournois, or £233.333 sterling. If, however, they were Rhenish florins, this
sum would have been worth only £245.833 *groot* Flemish, or £1,500 *tournois*,
or £166.667 sterling.

15 Cox's *in carnisprivio*, translated by Niermeyer *Mediae Latinitatis lexicon minus* as
'Shrovetide,' is defined by the *Shorter Oxford English Dictionary* as 'the period
comprising Quinquagesima Sunday and the following two days, "Shrove"
Monday and Tuesday,' that is, the three days before Ash Wednesday. But

My Lord Jan Łaski, setting out from here with the archbishop,[16] who
never wishes to be separated from him, left his servant Anianus behind in
my care.[17] Need I recount his abilities, his moral purity, and earnestness   60
far beyond his years, all of which are well known to you? He is very much
like his master, especially in the love he bears you. We pass no day without
frequent mention of Erasmus. Often we spend the morning with you, my
dear Erasmus, and at the noonday meal we dine with you; after lunch we
are often with you as we take our walk, we are together with you at supper,   65
and we prolong the night in your most pleasant company. You are always
with us, and we, however little we deserve it, are never parted from you –
so much so that, just as it is told of St Ambrose that he was in two places
at the same time,[18] so it is with you and us. For you are ofttimes occupied
in Basel and in Cracow at the same time; and we, while in the middle of   70
Poland, often spend the time together with Erasmus in Basel.

The day before I wrote this to you, the Lord Bishop Andrzej Krzycki, a man endowed with every virtue, was chosen to replace the deceased
bishop of Płock.[19] Aside from its great wealth this bishopric seems to me
also to be abundantly blessed in the three men, among the most learned of   75
the realm, who have successively held the see: first Erazm Ciołek, whom

* * * * *

Adriano Cappelli *Cronologia, cronografia e calendario perpetuo dal principio dell'era
cristiana ai giorni nostri* (Milan 1930; repr 1960) 110 says that the words *carnis-
privium, carnislevamen,* and *privicarnium* sometimes indicate the first days of
Lent but other times Septuagesima Sunday (which is two weeks earlier). He
further specifies that the term *Carnis privium novum* indicates Ash Wednesday,
and that an older usage of it describes the first Sunday of Lent.

16 Jan (I) Łaski, archbishop of Gniezno. For Jan (II), his nephew, see Ep 1821
   introduction.
17 Anianus Burgonius, or Aignan Bourgoin, of Orléans, whom Łaski took as a
   servant. After stopping with him for six months in Basel, where they both
   made Erasmus' acquaintance, Łaski dispatched him to Rome and then took
   him to the court at Cracow, where he entrusted him as student to Leonard
   Cox. See Epp 1604 n1, 1824 n6; CEBR I 222–3.
18 See Gregory of Tours *Libri IV de virtutibus sancti Martini* 1.5 in *Monumenta Germaniae Historica* Series Scriptores rerum Merovingicarum (Hannover 1885) I
   591 no 5.
19 Andrzej Krzycki, since 1522 bishop of Przemyśl, was named bishop of Płock
   on 27 March, just three days after the death of Bishop Rafał Leszczński, and
   took possession in September 1527. A consummate diplomat and servant of his
   king, he opposed the Reformation and tried to attract Melanchthon to Poland
   in order to separate him from Luther. He also made generous offers to attract
   Erasmus to Poland. Krzycki's own literary talents produced a wide range of
   poems and comedies. He died in 1537, two years after being raised to the
   archbishopric of Gniezno.

Beroaldo celebrated not undeservedly in several of his works, and who showed himself during his lifetime a staunch patron of good letters;[20] then Rafał Leszczński, exceptionally gifted in his knowledge of many languages;[21] and now our friend Krzycki. Whenever I mention his name, I imagine to my-   80
self that I am speaking of an absolute paragon of every virtue. He too, as no other, is most devoted to you; and on the feast of the Annunciation, when I was dining at his home, he pledged that he would write to you.[22] His nephew, his sister's son, is staying with me.[23] He has had good success in the study of letters. I am giving him lessons in your De copia together with   85
other private pupils of mine. I began to lecture on this work here five years ago, and when I was later summoned to Hungary I lectured on it twice there to a sizeable group of students. I may add that our charge is so attached to you that he fully intends to come to see you some day (may God grant life enough to each of you) and finally speak face to face with the one whom   90
he admires so intensely from afar. This would be a simple matter for him, seeing that he holds three lucrative prebends. If you would encourage the young man with a few words to persevere in the path he has chosen and embrace learning with all diligence, you would be performing a very great service to the excellent prelate. And although you do not much care for such   95
things, you will not – to close with a Greek phrase – 'write in vain.'[24] His name is Andrzej Zebrzydowski.

Farewell, pillar of learning. At Cracow from Jerusalem College,[25] 28 March, in the year since the birth of our Lord 1527

Yours, Leonard Cox
                                                                               100
I omitted one thing. What is the meaning of the phrase in the first book of the Copia: synere ac melle fluere videtur 'it seems to flow with sweetness and

* * * * *

20 Ciołek, called Vitellius, an accomplished rhetorician and diplomat, was bishop of Płock from 1503 until his death in Rome in 1522 (CEBR I 304–5). Filippo Beroaldo the Elder (1453–1505) dedicated to him his Opusculum de terremotu et pestilentia (Bologna: Benedictus Hectoris 1505).
21 Leszczński entered the ranks of the church late in life after a successful career as courtier and diplomat. He died on 23 March 1527 (CEBR II 327).
22 This letter, written some time after 25 March, is not extant. It answered Ep 1753 and was answered by Erasmus' Ep 1822.
23 Andrzej Zebrzydowski (see line 97 below), on whom see Ep 1826 introduction.
24 δωρεάν; cf Gal 2:21. The Vulgate translates it as gratis, Erasmus as frustra. Erasmus obliged Cox's request with Ep 1826
25 A college for a hundred students founded in 1454 from the legacy of Cardinal Sbigneus de Olesnica, bishop of Cracow; see Codex diplomaticus uniuersitatis Cracouiensis (Cracow 1870–1900) II 156–9.

honey'? I do not understand it at all. I read *cinnare* in Pliny; but all copies
of your *Copia*, Schürer's edition and others, and even the one printed by
Froben, have *synere*.[26] If you would be kind enough to resolve this difficulty   105
for me, you will render a great service to me and all others here interested in
higher learning. Once again farewell, and may you enjoy long-lasting good
fortune.

To the renowned Master Erasmus of Rotterdam, father and incompa-
rable glory of all men of learning. In Basel   110

1804 / To Thomas More   Basel, 30 March 1527

This letter answers More's Ep 1770, written a week before Christmas 1526,
which reached Erasmus only c 1 March 1527. Here Erasmus describes in confidence and at length how he sees himself caught between three conflicting
groups: the conservative, traditionalist Catholics, who consider him a supporter of Luther; his Catholic friends, who want him to attack Luther; and the
reformers, who are disappointed by his refusal to join them. With More he
candidly discusses theological positions that he had not yet dared divulge to
the public. In CWE 76 lxxix–lxxiv Charles Trinkaus comments on the significance of this letter for revealing Erasmus' mood as he composes book 2 of
Hyperaspistes, and quotes copiously from his own translation of it.

Allen was the first to publish this letter, using the rough draft in Erasmus'
hand (f 249 in a collection of Erasmus' autograph writings, Royal Library,
Copenhagen MS GKS 95 Fol, on which see Allen III Appendix 13 630–4). The
manuscript is slightly emended, probably by Erasmus' own servant-copyist.
Allen had to reconstitute many places in the manuscript where water has
severely damaged the sides of the leaves.

Biographies of, and literature about, Thomas More are legion. For a study of
his long relationship with Erasmus see J.B. Trapp *Erasmus, Colet and More: The
Early Tudor Humanists and Their Books* (London 1991); see also CEBR II 456–9.

* * * * *

26 *De copia* I 31 CWE 24 353; cf Pliny *Naturalis historia* 8.41.101. On this query
and Erasmus' response in Ep 1824:31–47 see ASD I-6 81:252n. In the 1526 edition Erasmus had changed the doubtful reading *synere*, drawn from Aulus
Gellius 15. 20.8, about which Cox inquires, to read instead *saccaro*, from *Naturalis historia* 12.17.32. Between its first edition (Basel: Nicolaus Brylingerus
1511) and 1527 over a dozen presses had issued thirty-four reprints of
De copia; there were five by the Strasbourg printer Matthias Schürer between 1513 and 1519. See Ferdinand van der Haeghen *Bibliotheca Erasmi-
ana: Répertoire des oeuvres d'Erasme* (Ghent 1893; repr Nieuwkoop 1972) part 1
65–6.

Thomas More
Hans Holbein the Younger, coloured chalks on white paper, 1526/7
Collection of her Majesty the Queen, Windsor Castle

Best greetings. Both you and Tunstall are exerting every effort to have me take up my pen against Luther.[1] What am I to do in the face of two friends, to satisfy either of whom I could be prevailed upon to do anything, whatever the outcome? Still, I should prefer that this task be undertaken at the bidding of reason rather than emotion. You are both convinced that it would have great influence if I were to make a full-scale attack upon Luther. But I am all but certain that I would only stir up a hornets' nest.[2] That was exactly what I expected when I published the *Diatribe*.[3] Cuthbert makes amazingly light of this faction's power. If it could be weakened by words, I too would apply all my energies to overthrow it. But, to speak freely among ourselves, the situation is not like that at all; and I fear that in a short time this smouldering fire will break out into a worldwide conflagration. That is where the insolence of monks and the intransigence of theologians are leading us.

In England, since the fortunes of state depend on the will of one man, this pestilence is more easily contained. In other countries that is not the case. One can only confide one's thoughts on this subject to a letter. What could be more restrained than the *Diatribe*? And yet it would not have been permitted to print it except that shortly afterwards the factions here in Basel conceived an intense hatred for Luther because of their different views concerning the Eucharist. No sooner was the *Diatribe* finished than Oecolampadius secretly procured some pages from the printer and was preparing a response.[4] When I learned of it, I took the opportunity to meet with him.

* * * * *

1804
1 That is, to fulfil his promise to produce the second book of his *Hyperaspistes* against Luther. For his part, More had already written two versions of a *Responsio ad Lutherum*, the first (which he quickly suppressed) under the pseudonym Baravellus, and a second, expanded version under the name Guillelmus Rosseus. Both were produced in London in 1523 by Richard Pynson. See *The Complete Works of St. Thomas More* v ed John M. Headley (New Haven and London 1969), especially part 2 832–40. Tunstall's letter, mentioned more specifically in Ep 1815:41–3, is not extant. Bishop of London since 1522, he was one of Erasmus' most trusted and intimate friends. Erasmus had already resisted his entreaties to write against Luther (Ep 1367), but the *De libero arbitrio* (1524) was largely the result of Tunstall's urging.
2 Cf *Adagia* I i 60.
3 *De libero arbitrio* διατριβή *sive collatio* (CWE 76)
4 Johannes Hussgen of Weinsberg in the Palatinate adopted the humanistic name Oecolampadius by building on the sixteenth-century variant of his name, 'Husschin,' or 'Hausschein,' which means 'House-glow.' The corresponding Greek roots would be οικο- [oiko-] 'house' and λαμπαδ- [lampad-] 'light' – achieving the sense of adding a 'Schein' or lustre to his 'house' and family name. He

He showed me what he had written. By force of many arguments I persuaded him to leave this task to others, for this reason above all: that if we
were to inveigh against each other we would create an uproar in a city al-   25
ready torn apart by various factions. He discussed this decision with certain
magistrates, who concurred with it. On their advice, therefore, he took no
action.[5] At the time, I enjoyed favour with both sides; and even now I am
not regarded with disfavour, except in the eyes of a few mean-spirited individuals. What is more, you should know that it is safer for me to offend   30
a great king than one of these magistrates.

   As things now stand, and considering my state of health, it would be
impossible for me to live in safety elsewhere, unless I were to attach myself
to kings or other princes or to wealthy cities. I have had many invitations.[6]
But such is my nature that I think death is easier to bear than servitude.   35
Besides, my health is such that I would not dare give myself three days to
live if I were constrained to adopt an unfamiliar mode of life. Moreover, I
am invited by certain parties whose intentions are unknown to me.[7] I cannot
be the leader of any human faction. And time presses upon me to gather
up my belongings and depart hence.[8] What use is it for me to conceal what   40
you know all too well, that there are a great number of recruits who are
superior to me in this kind of contest? And even if I had the ability, I have
neither the courage nor the training. There is nothing that I more greatly
abhor and for which I am less trained than such wrestling arenas. I pass
over the fact that the whole controversy is more truly one of words than   45
of substance, and not very conducive to piety, in my estimation, if one gets

* * * * *

learned Hebrew and Greek at the urging of both Reuchlin and Melanchthon,
and Johann Froben put him to work at his press in Basel. There he became
friendly with Wolfgang Capito and with Erasmus, whose *Novum instrumentum*
profited from Oecolampadius' knowledge of Greek. Then, after several years
as cathedral preacher in Augsburg and in quiet retreat from theological debate,
he joined the Lutheran cause. Returning to Basel, he at first avoided polemic;
but his subsequent agreement with Zwingli on the solely symbolic or spiritual
presence of Christ in the Eucharist, expressed in his *Genuina expositio* (1525),
caused a definitive break with both Luther and Erasmus which, as we learn
here, Erasmus had tried to prevent by urging Oecolampadius not to publish.
5 See Ep 1519 n20.
6 See Epp 809:146–55, 1408:11–13, 1431:11–12, 1442:12–15, 1629:20–1, 1652:116–
   32, 1683:1–2, 1697:103–23.
7 Probably reformers like Wolfgang Faber Capito and Martin Bucer, whom Erasmus will later attack more directly in his *Epistola contra pseudevangelicos* and
   Epistola ad fratres Inferioris Germaniae
8 A foreboding of his death more than of his eventual move from Basel

mired in it more deeply than he ought. And you see how many people have treated this subject to show off their own ingenuity, and continue to do so even now.[9]

But your love for me will not put up with the insolence of certain individuals who are elated to think that I have nothing to respond to Luther. I am preoccupied by other greater problems, so it is easy for me to hold these trivial matters in contempt. If it is important to have made an answer, the *Diatribe* and the *Hyperaspistes* have already demolished whatever argument he can introduce.[10] He has but two bastions of defence: that the Law has no efficacy except to have us know or, rather, recognize sin, and that through the sin of Adam the mass of mankind has been so corrupted that not even the Holy Spirit can produce anything in it except evil. If he is dislodged from these two positions, he will fall. But with what weapons will you throw a person to the ground if he accepts nothing but the Sacred Scriptures and interprets them according to his own rules? Let us suppose for a moment that man to man I am his equal; but what will I avail alone against so many? The only one here is Baer,[11] but he has long since grown unaccustomed to the wrestling floor of the Sorbonne; besides that, he is busy and fearful of everything, so that he would be of no help, even though there is much solace to be had in the pleasant company of an exceptional friend. If only I could count as one whole person. At the moment I scarcely amount to half a man.

* * * * *

9 Jacobus Latomus, Luigi Marliano, Silvester Prierias, Johannes Cochlaeus, Jacob of Hoogstraten, Johann Maier of Eck, Josse Clichtove, John Fisher, King Henry VIII, and Thomas More himself had all published rebuttals of Luther.

10 *De libero arbitrio* διατριβή *sive collatio* appeared in September 1524 (Basel: Froben; several printings in other cities followed quickly). Luther's reponse, *De servo arbitrio*, appeared more than a year later (Wittenberg: Hans Lufft 31 December 1525). Its brutal treatment of Erasmus as a secret atheist who had no authentic religious faith shocked Erasmus and provoked the sharp rejoinder in his hastily composed first book of *Hyperaspistes*, which was published in early March 1526; see Ep 1667 introduction. *Hyperaspistes 2* was published in late summer 1527; see Ep 1853 introduction. In both the *Diatribe* and *Hyperaspistes* Erasmus aimed to refute two anthropological positions of Luther that he could not abide: the total depravity of human nature after the fall of Adam, and the notion that whatever we do, whether good or bad, is a matter of absolute necessity. But he failed to move Luther from his understanding of the Scriptures. On the controversy see the introduction by Charles Trinkaus in CWE 76.

11 Ludwig Baer, Paris-trained theologian and dean of the faculty of theology at Basel (Farge BR 22–6 no 22)

Consider how little time this poor health of mine leaves to me. Almost
half of that is immediately taken up by the letters that speed their way here   70
from every corner of the world, to say nothing of books, some sent to me
personally, others published.[12] It would be no easy matter to calculate how
much labour was expended on this fourth edition of the New Testament,
on the revision of the *Adages*, and on my translations of Chrysostom and
Athanasius,[13] nor how much tedium I had to endure in refuting Béda's ob-   75
tuse calumnies,[14] as well as others that the Parisian theologians are secretly

* * * * *

12 For other references to the number of letters and parcels Erasmus sent
   and received, some from high-ranking persons, see Epp 786:6–10, 873:4–6,
   1745:11–13, 1874:49–72, 1875:13–15, 1891:3, 73–8, 1893:39–40, 1909:74–6, 1910:3–
   6, 1922:15–19.
13 The fourth edition of the New Testament appeared in this same month, March
   1527. On the revised *Adagia*, see Ep 1659; the next edition was in September
   1528. On the Chrysostom, see Ep 1805 n86; on Athanasius, Ep 1790.
14 Noël Béda, the syndic, or director, of the Paris faculty of theology, was convinced that there was a dangerous connection between the works of humanists,
   especially Erasmus and Lefèvre d'Etaples, and Luther and his followers. Erasmus and Béda exchanged eleven letters between April 1525 and November
   1527 (Epp 1571, 1579, 1581, 1596, 1609, 1610, 1620, 1642, 1679, 1685, 1906), in
   each of which both correspondents showed increasing hostility; see CEBR I 116–
   18. His *Annotationum in Jacobum Fabrum Stapulensem libri duo, et in Desiderium
   Erasmum Roterodamum liber unus* (Paris: Josse Bade 28 May 1526; Renouard *Imprimeurs* II 227–8 no 549) contained specific criticisms directed against Erasmus' Paraphrases on the Gospels and Epistles. In addition to his letters to
   Béda, to the faculty of theology (Epp 1664, 1723, 1902), to the Parlement of
   Paris (Epp 1721, 1905) and to King Francis I (Ep 1722), Erasmus answered
   Béda's charges with four tracts and books: *Divinationes Erasmi ad notata Bedae*
   (LB IX 405–514), written in 1525 but probably published first only in March
   1527; *Elenchus in Bedae censuras* (LB IX 496–515), written in 1526 and sent, perhaps only in manuscript, to the Parlement of Paris and to the Paris faculty
   of theology in February 1526; *Prologus supputationis errorum in censuris Bedae*
   (Basel, August 1526; LB IX 441–50), a hasty reply to Béda's *Annotationes*; and
   Supputatio errorum in censuris Bedae (Basel, March 1527; LB IX 516–702). This last
   was Erasmus' lengthy (470 pages long) and most considered reply to the *Annotationes*. In March 1527 Johann Froben published an omnibus volume containing all four works (*Divinationes* and *Elenchus* appearing perhaps for the first
   time in print, *Prologus supputationis* and *Supputatio* in reprint) entitled *Supputationes errorum in censuris Natalis Bedae*. Two years later, in reply to Béda's *Apologia adversus clandestinos Lutheranos* (Paris: Josse Bade, 1529) Erasmus wrote a
   fifth work against Béda, *Notatiunculae quaedam extemporales ad naenias Bedaicas*
   (Basel 1529; LB IX 701–20), in which he calls Béda 'the most stupid of bipeds'
   and 'a hot-headed monster that is also impotent, stupid, doting, and out of
   his mind.' For an extended analysis of these works and of the polemic between Erasmus and Béda see Rummel *Catholic Critics* II 38–43 and CWE 82

concocting.[15] And these books would have been published if Froben had
not been hindered by lack of time. A good bit of time was devoted also to
revising the *Paraphrases* and Seneca; and, in the latter case, I was dealt with
in a perfidious manner by that stupid imbecile Nesen, a humiliation that I   80
must redress before I die.[16]

Now suppose that neither time nor strength were lacking to me. If I
treat the subject from the point of view of the monks and theologians, who
attribute too much to man's merits because it is to their advantage to hold
this opinion, clearly I speak against my conscience and knowingly obscure   85
the glory of Christ. But if I govern my pen in such a way as to attribute
some power to free will but greater efficacy to grace, I offend both sides,
which was my experience with the *Diatribe*. If I follow Paul and Augustine,[17] very little is left to free will. Augustine, in fact, in the two books he
wrote in his old age against Valentinus,[18] does indeed affirm the existence   90

* * * * *

Introduction. The final chapter in their polemic opened with the appearance
of *Determinatio facultatis theologiae in schola Parisiensi super quam plurimis asser-*
tionibus D. Erasmi Roterodami (Paris: Josse Bade, July 1531; 2nd rev ed September 1532; cf Renouard *Imprimeurs* II 266 no 672, 297 no 774). It contained 176
propositions which the faculty, still under Béda's direction, considered offensive, dangerous, or, in some cases, heretical. Erasmus responded to it with
Declarationes ad censuras Lutetiae vulgatas sub nomine facultatis theologiae Parisien-
sis (Basel: Hieronymus Froben and Nicolaus Episcopius [February] 1532); see
CWE 82.

15 The Paris theologians had censured Erasmus' *Colloquies* in May 1526; see Ep
    1723. A more general condemnation, alleging thirty-two categories in which
    Erasmus had erred, would be voted on 16 December 1527 but not published
    until July 1531 (Farge *Orthodoxy* 194–6).

16 For the dates of original and revised editions of the Paraphrases on the Gospels
    see Ep 1672 n25. Erasmus was perhaps already revising the Paraphrases on
    the Epistles, which would appear in 1532. On the edition of Seneca, see Ep
    325. Wilhelm Nesen, who drowned in a boat accident near Wittenberg in 1524,
    was the frequent target of Erasmus' reproaches for his negligence in seeing
    Seneca's *Lucubrationes* through the press; cf Epp 1479:99–102. Melanchthon's
    attempts to exculpate his dead friend (Ep 1981) would go unheeded by Eras-
    mus. The new edition did not appear until March 1529.

17 The Epistles to the Romans and to the Galatians contain St Paul's strongest
    views on the primacy of faith as salvific for Christians. In attacking the soteri-
    ology of Pelagius, who attributed much importance to the free actions of hu-
    man beings, Augustine strongly diminished the role of human free will and
    merit in salvation.

18 Augustine *De gratia et libero arbitrio ad Valentinum abbatem et cum illo monachos*
    Adrumetinos, written c 426/7 (PL 44 881–912 / FCNT 59 245–308). This treatise
    should not be confused with Augustine's earlier and more important work,
    De libero arbitrio (PL 32 1221–1303 / FCNT 59 65–241).

of free will; but he makes such a case for the power of grace that I do not see what is left to free will. He admits that works performed before the action of grace are dead; he attributes to grace our ability to repent, our will to do good, the good we have done, our perseverance in doing good. He admits that grace works all these things in us. Then where is merit? Confronted by this dilemma Augustine had recourse to saying that God imputes his good works to us as merits and crowns his own gifts in us. Is that not a clever defence of free will? For myself, I should not be averse to the opinion according to which we can of our own natural powers and without particular grace acquire congruent grace, as they say, except that Paul opposed this view.[19] For that matter not even the schoolmen accept this opinion.

Now let us weigh the dangers. There is the fear that with the removal of free will some might abandon their zeal for good works. So much for Scylla; but more forbidding is Charybdis directly opposite:[20] attributing to our own strength what is owed wholly to divine munificence. If the subject pertained to human affairs I might justly indulge my wit at this point. But in matters that treat of piety it is not prudent to play the rhetorician. I have to make good a promise made concerning the *Hyperaspistes*.[21] I would have done so long ago if the Parisian Furies had not set upon me unexpectedly as I was hard at work on it.[22] In fact I had finished a good part of the second section in a single spurt of inspiration; and if more free time had been at my disposal the whole work would have been published. But I thought it best to confront these Furies first – not that I relish constantly contending with them or fancy that so many foes conspiring together can be held in check by my writings. And I thought it important for the world to know what coals that brood was producing, when we were expecting a rich treasure.[23] Tunstall thinks that they will be favourably disposed if I leave them alone and join battle with the Lutherans. But he is greatly mistaken. I know their mysteries, I know their character. And there will be no end to their madness unless they are brought to submission by the authority of

95

100

105

110

115

120

* * * * *

19 For example, 2 Cor 3:5, Gal 2:16, Eph 2:8. For Erasmus' attempts to reconcile God's action on the soul by grace with 'a very small share to free will' see Charles Trinkaus' introduction to CWE 76, especially xciv–civ.
20 *Adagia* I v 4
21 To complete the second book of this work; see Ep 1853.
22 Notably Pierre Cousturier and Noël Béda, with both of whom Erasmus had already traded polemical tracts
23 *Adagia* I ix 30: 'The treasure consisted of coals,' said of disappointed hopes

princes[24] or unless the younger generation throws the sexagenarians off the bridge, as the saying goes.[25] Lastly, supposing I were to disregard my conscience altogether and satisfy their wishes by writing, what praise would I receive? They will say that I have come to my senses and made amends 125 by recanting. On the contrary, I am prepared to continue to be thought a heretic, if I ever was one. And, although I should prefer the previous state of things, whatever its defects, to this present confusion, yet the world had to be awakened from the torpid ceremonials over which it had fallen asleep. 130

They complain that I have raised questions which the Lutherans seize for their own advantage. But they find more to pillage from the Sacred Scriptures. I do nothing but make observations. Nowhere have I introduced new rites or brought in new constitutions. 'This smacks of something,' 'this can provide an occasion,' 'this seems to have a certain tendency.' If one pays 135 any attention to these protests there will be no end to it. I must so govern my pen that, when ere long I must stand before Christ's tribunal, I shall not be driven to recant. Why should I now compromise myself for the sake of the world, whose advantages can never make me happy? In a pious cause in which the victory would fall to Christ, I should be willing even to die. 140 At present I see swarms of harpies ready to rob Christ of his victory;[26] I am not willing to serve under their banners. Indeed, many things have led me to believe that God is the director of this turbulent drama. He has set loose upon us for our just deserts these beetles, dog-flies, and locusts.[27] He will likewise grant a happy outcome if we change our lives and throw ourselves 145 upon the mercy of the Lord.

But to return to our argument: in this deadly tumult, in which you can scarcely please anyone, I had decided to devote whatever time I had to revising my works, translating the Greek commentators, and completing the long-awaited *On the Art of Preaching*.[28] But meanwhile I am untrue to my promise 150 concerning the *Hyperaspistes*. I am accused of making vain promises, people

* * * * *

24 Hence Erasmus' Ep 1722 to King Francis I, urging him to intervene against the Paris theologians
25 *Adagia* I v 37
26 These spirit-wind creatures, sometimes depicted as birds with women's faces, snatched away their prey, leaving only defilement in its place.
27 *bruchos, cynomyas et locustas*; cf Exod 10:12–15, Lev 11:22, Ps 105 (Vulg 104):31, 34.
28 For earlier references to Erasmus' plans to produce his *Ecclesiastes, sive de ratione concionandi* see Epp 1332:40–3 and 1581:742–4. The work finally appeared in 1535 (Basel: Hieronymus Froben and Nicolaus Episcopius).

call me faint-hearted or incompetent: faint-hearted for lacking the courage,[29] incompetent for not having the ability. There is no way to avoid their criticism. And should I respond, no matter how successfully, they will make more heinous charges. You try to allay my fears, saying that if they were 155 going to make any threats they would already have done so.[30] Well, I must inform you that they have already taken some steps. That madman Otto has published two editions of his rubbish; and he would not have stopped there had I not held him back by invoking the magistrates of Strasbourg.[31] A bookseller from Worms by the name of Schöffer has sent a pamphlet here 160 written in German containing defamatory illustrations.[32] Leo Jud,[33] who first

* * * * *

29 See Allen Ep 1459:80n / Ep 1477B n21.

30 See Ep 1770:43–69.

31 Otto Brunfels, a humanist scholar and former Carthusian monk, yearned to reform education by replacing medieval textbooks with classical authors. Under the influence of Ulrich von Hutten he became an enthusiastic convert to Lutheran theology. He accepted direction of a Latin school in Strasbourg, but never entered the inner circle of Reformers there. He published a biting criticism of Erasmus' *Spongia* against Hutten; see Ep 1405, Brunfels' preface to *Pro Vlricho Hutteno defuncto, ad Erasmi Roterodami Spongiam responsio* (Strasbourg: Johann Schott c February and c July 1523). The *Responsio* elicited vehement replies from Erasmus (Epp 1432, 1437, 1445) along with demands that the Strasbourg magistrates take action against Brunfels and his printer and protector Johann Schott (Epp 1429, 1477). Brunfels later wrote treatises on medicine and Sacred Scripture, and became professor of medicine in Basel (1532) and, later, town physician in Bern. See Epp 1405–6; CEBR I 206–7; ER I 300–1. On Johann Schott and other printer-apologists of the early German Reformation see Mark U. Edwards Jr *Printing, Propaganda, and Martin Luther* (Berkeley 1994).

32 Probably Schöffer's *Die Lutherisch Strebkatz* (Worms 1524), which carried several dozen illustrations showing Luther and his followers winning games of strength against the pope and Catholic theologians; see R.W. Scribner *For the Sake of Simple Folk: Popular Propaganda for the German Reformation* (Oxford 1981; repr 1994) 60–1. In the same year a similar pamphlet, entitled *Gesprech Büchlein, von eynem Bawern, Belial, Erasmo Roterodam* [Speyer: Jakob Schmidt] depicted Erasmus stroking a fox-brush crowned with a papal tiara – an accusation that Erasmus' refusal to break with the papacy was motivated by a hope of gain (ibidem 77). The fox-brush became for Reformation propagandists a favourite synonym for hypocrisy. Peter (II) Schöffer (c 1460–c 1542), third son of the illustrious Mainz printer Peter Schöffer, printed at Worms 1512–29 and produced a large number of Reformation books, among them the first printing of Tyndale's English Bible and a book by Otto Brunfels. He is sometimes confused with the Strasbourg printer Johann Schott (1477–c 1548), on whom see the preceding note.

33 Leo Jud had been a friend of Erasmus, and had translated several of his works. His devotion to Huldrych Zwingli and other reformers, however, caused a painful alienation from Erasmus; cf Ep 1737 introduction and CEBR II 248–50.

published a pamphlet without a title, and then published another written in
German, full of menacing statements, has added a hand-written Latin epistle more venomous than the pamphlet, thinking that I would immediately
leap into the arena. In response, I wrote to an acquaintance of his that, owing   165
to my occupations and my poor state of health, I had no time to read either
the pamphlet or the letter.[34] In these he tries to bring odium upon me for
writing a certain dialogue in which Pope Julius received some unfavourable
treatment. I would not hesitate to put a curse on my head if I ever published
anything to which I did not affix my name;[35] and if anyone would dare to   170
publish this work as a book, which in any case they do not have the nerve
to do,[36] it would create great unpopularity for me with the Roman pontiff.
This is pretty much the natural inclination of mankind. The more atrocious
the accusation, the more readily it is believed, for people cannot believe that
anyone is audacious enough to hurl such fabricated accusations against an   175
innocent person.

Now consider for a moment the rabid hatred some people have for
me. What monstrous deed could be invented that they would not believe it
straightaway, even if I were charged with infanticide or poisoning? There
is another debauchee, the most depraved of the lot by far, at whose insti-   180
gation Hutten turned his fury upon me.[37] He is withholding publication of

* * * * *

Jud's 'pamphlet without a title' is probably the anonymous pamphlet *Maynung
vom Nachtmal* (*Opinion concerning the Lord's Supper*) setting forth the Eucharistic
theology of Luther and Erasmus, to which Erasmus responded first with Ep
1708 and then more formally with *Detectio praestigiarum*; cf also Ep 1737 n1.
On Jud's *Uf Entdeckung Doctor Erasmi ... Antwurt und Entschuldigung* ([Zürich:
Christoph Froschauer] 1526), cf Ep 1737 n1, which translates German excerpts
published by Allen Ep 1804:154n. The handwritten epistle is now lost.
34 Conradus Pellicanus; see Ep 1737:1–2.
35 Jud tried to excuse his publishing the *Maynung vom Nachtmal* anonymously by
   naming Erasmus as the anonymous author of the *Julius exclusus*, on which see
   CWE 27 xxiv–v, 156–60 and Ep 502 introduction. Erasmus' disclaimer denies
   the publication – but not the authorship – of the *Julius exclusus*, of which More
   had seen a manuscript in Erasmus' hand (Ep 502:11).
36 Several editions had indeed appeared in print, among them Dirk Martens'
   Louvain edition in September 1518, which Erasmus must have seen.
37 Erasmus blamed Heinrich Eppendorf for promoting the dispute with Hutten;
   see Ep 1893:44–6 and n16. Ulrich von Hutten, long an admirer of Erasmus,
   turned violently against him shortly before his death (August 1523) in his *Expostulatio adversus Erasmum*, which drew Erasmus' bitter reply, the *Spongia adversus aspergines Hutteni*. On the quarrel see Ep 1331 n24; see also R.J. Klawitter
   The Polemics of Erasmus of Rotterdam and Ulrich von Hutten (London and Notre
   Dame, Ind 1977).

his worthless drivel for fear of the duke of Saxony, whose protégé he once was.[38] Pellicanus had begun to utter nonsense, but he was silenced;[39] the timorous Capito accomplishes everything by secret channels;[40] it was from his house that Otto emerged to publish his pamphlet.[41] I often receive spuri- 185
ous pamphlets and letters containing veiled insinuations and menacing lan- guage, which I ignore and toss into the fire. To put it briefly, the majority of the Lutheran faction is convinced that I am the only obstacle to the conver- sion of all of Germany to the gospel. But others fear that if I am provoked I will do grave harm; still others hope that, exhausted by the endless show 190
of hatred directed at me by certain monks and theologians, I will desert to their camp.

That is my position with the Lutherans. Now the other side is striv- ing with every ounce of energy to knock my books from men's hands. This could be tolerated, but the pretext they devised to camouflage the rashness 195
of their actions cannot and ought not be tolerated. From this first step they would go on to do away with good letters altogether. Of the tragic events in Spain you will learn from Maldonado's letter.[42] Bear in mind that sim- ilar or more dreadful things have occurred in Poland.[43] The campaign is

* * * * *

38 Duke George of Albertine Saxony was firmly committed to Catholic orthodoxy and to reform in the Church. He was the most determined and ablest of the princes who firmly opposed Hutten and Luther. He had at one time supported Eppendorf; cf Ep 1437:13–15.
39 Conradus Pellicanus; see Epp 1637–40, 1644.
40 Wolfgang Faber Capito (Fabricius), a doctor of theology (Freiburg-im-Breisgau 1515) and humanist scholar proficient in Hebrew and Greek, was called in 1515 to be the cathedral preacher in Basel. There he also taught in the university and collaborated in editions published by Froben and Andreas Cratander. He and Erasmus admired each other's abilities, and Erasmus even spoke of 'passing the torch' of the new learning to Capito (Ep 541:7–8). But Capito's enthusiastic support for Luther and his subsequent embrace of the reformed theologies of Oecolampadius and Bucer led to a breach with Erasmus (Ep 1374). Erasmus signed Ep 1485, his most recent letter to Capito, 'Erasmus, once your friend in Christ.' See also CEBR I 261–4 and the Introduction to *The Correspondence of Wolfgang Capito* ed and trans Erika Rummel (Toronto 2005–) I xvii–xlii.
41 Probably a reference to the supposed caricature of Erasmus published on a title-page of *Problemata Othonis Brunnfelsii* (Strasbourg: Johann Schott n d). On this see Ep 1477B n7 (Allen Ep 1459). On Brunfels see n31 above.
42 Erasmus apparently sent a copy of Ep 1742 to More. For Juan Maldonado see Ep 1805 introduction.
43 Spain and Poland regularly appear in Erasmus' lists of the many places where his opponents are active; see for example Epp 1743:38–41, 1753:40–2, 1805:117, 1823:16–17, 1864:4, 186, 1886:126, 1891:9, Allen Ep 2126:171–2.

being waged through the conspiracy of a pharisaical band. Formal decrees 200
are passed in those synods to which they flock once every year,[44] while in
the meantime they regularly scurry to and fro to all corners of the world. In
these sessions they have resolved that each of them to the best of his ability
shall so vilify the name of Erasmus in secret and in public, in speech and
in writing, that there is no one who will not shudder at the mention of it. 205
They are confident that they will succeed in this villainy, placing their trust
in countless legions of tongues, in their reputation for sanctity and, finally,
in the stupidity of the masses, of whom they have already made trial, discovering how easily they can be manipulated and how willingly they allow
themselves to be deceived by chicanery. In order to be better equipped to ac- 210
complish their purpose, whatever misfortunes may have fallen to my lot[45] –
be it some heaven-sent calamity,[46] some event in my lifetime that may serve
the cause of calumny, charges made against me by my enemies in writing,
or hearsay bandied about by some ranting fanatic – all this they commit to
memory. They have a wealth of such stuff, holding it as a prized posses- 215
sion and never missing an occasion to hawk it about. With these weapons
they promise themselves certain victory; and I provide them with ammu-
nition by fighting against Luther. Hutten retains their great gratitude; they
are more than willing to forgive him for what he wrote against them, mol-
lified by the services he rendered them in venting his fury upon Erasmus.[47] 220
With Luther himself they are much more lenient than previously after his
insolent attacks upon me.

That book put together by the combined efforts of four Dominican
rogues, which they dedicated to Lee, excited such admiration from a certain prior of the canons regular at Roode Clooster near Brussels that he had 225
it read in the refectory in place of the sacred reading.[48] But I demonstrated

* * * * *

44 Probably the general chapters of the mendicant orders. The Franciscans did
indeed convene every year, but the Dominicans met, on the average, every
three or four years. In 1526 the Franciscans denounced in chapter the very
persons and problems in Swiss cities about whom and which Erasmus himself
frequently complained. There is no reference to Erasmus in the proceedings
of this or any other Franciscan general chapter. See Lucas Wadding *Annales
Minorum* 16 (1516–1540) (Quaracchi 1933) 257–60.
45 Allen Ep 1102:6n gathers many of Erasmus' expressions about his misfortunes.
46 Erasmus uses the Greek, εἴ τις συμφορὰ θεήλατος (Euripides *Orestes* 2).
47 Cf n37 above.
48 The book appeared under the pseudonym 'Taxander.' It defended canonical
strictures about auricular confession and abstinence from meat; see Rummel
Catholic Critics II 1–3 and the introduction to Ep 1581A. Edward Lee was one

to the theologians of Louvain that in such a tiny book there were more than
seventy superb lies, not counting the scurrilous abuse – to put it mildly.[49]
There are not a few figures lurking there in Louvain who write whatever
they please against me. And they do this with impunity, thanks to the con-   230
nivance of the theologians. The chief perpetrator of all these stratagems is
that lame-footed Latomus.[50] It was at his advice and recommendation that
Lee sent his brother[51] to Paris to have his book[52] completed through the efforts of Béda. (For at that time Lee could not have written a single page on
a theological topic. And indeed in several passages the style is pure Béda.)   235
He it was who succeeded in having Adrian censure Reuchlin's books,[53] he
it was who incited Dorp against me.[54] He led both Dorp and Briart around
by the nose,[55] as one would a buffalo, sometimes with coaxing, sometimes
with threats. Blocked by an imperial decree,[56] he ceded his function to the
likes of Béda. For this ill-starred chick issued from the same nest.[57] He came   240

* * * * *

of the first critics of Erasmus' biblical annotations. See Rummel *Catholic Critics*
I 95–120 and CEBR II 311–14. For his later efforts against Erasmus see Ep 1814
n39. Roode Clooster was located in the Soignes forest south-east of Brussels;
Steven van Heetvelde was prior 1521–8.

49 See Ep 1582; *Manifesta mendacia* CWE 71 113–31, 165–71 (notes).
50 Jacobus Latomus (Jacques Masson), a master of theology at Louvain. Luther regarded him as a formidable adversary, but Erasmus usually sought to lampoon
   him; see Ep 1830:8–9.
51 Wilfred Lee (CEBR II 314–15) often acted as arbitrator between his brother
   Edward and Erasmus.
52 Edward Lee's *Annotationum libri duo* (Paris: Gilles de Gourmont c 15 February
   1520), contained 243 notes on Erasmus' first edition of the New Testament and
   25 notes on the second.
53 Reuchlin's *Augenspiegel* had been condemned at Louvain on 28 July 1513. By
   this time Adriaan Floriszoon of Utrecht, the future Pope Adrian VI, had left
   the university and was a councillor of Emperor Charles V. Ludwig Geiger
   Johann Reuchlin, sein Leben und seine Werke (Leipzig 1871) 440–1 attributes the
   20 June 1520 Roman condemnation of the *Augenspiegel* to him.
54 Maarten van Dorp had initially been scandalized by Erasmus' *Praise of Folly*
   (see Epp 304 introduction, 337, 347), but Dorp and Erasmus remained on good
   terms.
55 Cf Ep 1123:21–4 and nn10–11.
56 Allen Ep 1690:119n / CWE n11
57 Both Latomus and Béda had been disciples of Jan Standonck at the Collège
   de Montaigu in Paris, where Erasmus spent an unhappy year in 1495–6, possibly in their company. Standonck had constituted Montaigu as a 'community of poor students'; after 1504, under Béda's direction, a separate 'community of rich students,' whose fees subsidized the poor students, became
   an important feature of Montaigu. At the recommendation of Adriaan of
   Utrecht, Latomus was given direction of the new college for poor students

to us famished and dressed in rags, but he has amassed great riches and has
hopes for the mitre.[58] It is such types as this that the monks suborn so that
they will not be the only objects of unpopularity.

As for Louis de Berquin, a favourite with the king, they have thrown
him into prison for the second time because he translated some of my trea-   245
tises into French.[59] The counts of indictment, which were completely unfounded, were secretly brought to me. If he had wished to abjure them in
the form in which they were presented, he would have been acquitted, and
the books would have been consigned to the flames instead of him. Since he
responded with great skill to each charge, they began to hurl insults at me,   250
to see if in this way they could not turn him from his devotion towards me.
And if it were not for the precautions of the said Louis, those absurd denunciations would have been officially recorded and would have come under
the jurisdiction of the Parlement, which was what those demented judges
had in mind.[60] Need I say more? Seeing that they were not successful in   255

* * * * *

founded by Standonck in Louvain in April 1500; see Renaudet *Préréforme*
309.
58 The charge that Latomus coveted a bishopric is not documented; but he had
acquired the good will and patronage of Robert de Croy, bishop of Cambrai.
59 Louis de Berquin, a member of the Picard gentry, was devoted to evangelical
reform and humanism. He translated several works of Erasmus into French,
but introduced into them excerpts from Luther (via certain quotations of
Luther by Guillaume Farel). Arrested for heresy in 1523, his trial had been
removed from the jurisdictions of the Parlement of Paris and the bishop of
Paris by King Francis I, whose *grand conseil* released Berquin after extracting
from him a retractation of his errors. But in January 1526, during the king's
captivity in Spain, the Parlement had arrested him once again, and the papal
judges delegate appointed to prosecute heterodoxy had convicted him of relapse into heresy, a capital crime. Berquin's second imprisonment lasted from
mid January 1526 to 19 November 1526. After the Parlement of Paris several
times refused royal orders to release Berquin, the king sent royal officers to
free him forcibly from the Conciergerie and take him into royal protection in
the Louvre palace (Paris, Archives nationales x[1a] 1530 f 11v–12r), where he remained for an undetermined time. The indictments against Berquin included
translations of both Luther and Erasmus, with mention of several other suspect authors. See Margaret Mann (Phillips) *Erasme et les débuts de la Réforme
française (1517–1536)* (Paris 1934) 120–40. According to Francis Higman in his
edition of Guillaume Farel *Le Pater Noster et le Credo en françoys* (Geneva 1982)
19–20, the passages of Luther were all taken from the *Pater noster* of Farel, who
quoted them from Luther's *Betbüchlein* (WA 10-2 331–75). See Farge 'Berquin'
49–77; cf CEBR I 135–40.
60 Erasmus refers not to the Parlement of Paris itself, which was the supreme
court in Paris, but to the judges delegate of the pope; cf n59 above.

this attempt, they called in three monks as witnesses and pronounced him a heretic.[61] I shall soon let them know what those charges are, although I shall pretend that I do not know from whence they came. And if first the Parlement and then the king had not interposed their authority, they would have thrown the poor man into the flames.[62] I also discovered that some   260
of the opinions of the faculty were purchased at a price[63] – and, my God! what opinions! Often they do not understand what I mean. They cry out against those who pay little respect to human institutions. But there is no one in the world who makes less of both human and divine decrees than they, whenever it is to their advantage. In that regard, whatever they want is   265
holy.[64] Theologians endowed with more intelligence stay away from Paris. Of the rest, those who are of a more guileless spirit dare not drown out the voices of those who are engaged in the business, so to speak, of the faith. The general of the Carthusian order has imposed silence on Cousturier,[65] but in matters of faith he owes obedience to no one. They are plot-   270
ting something against me at this very moment, and it seems that they will

* * * * *

61 The archives of the judges delegate have not survived. The registers of the Parlement never mention any testimony of three monks against Berquin. Erasmus perhaps means the judges delegate themselves, whose number was reduced to three – two *conseillers clercs* of the Parlement and one theologian – by the death of master Guillaume Duchesne in 1525.
62 This was not possible. The judges delegate had no authority to execute, but would have to rely for this on the 'secular arm,' that is, the Parlement of Paris. Moreover, contrary to Erasmus' opinion stated here (probably derived from Berquin), the Parlement would gladly have executed Berquin for recidivism. King Francis I, urged on by pleas of his sister Margaret, acted to free him; but his arrest a third time in 1529 would lead to his conviction and execution as a relapsed heretic.
63 The source of this claim is unknown.
64 *Adagia* IV vii 16; cf Epp 1858:346–7, 1875:49–50, 1891:346–7.
65 Pierre Cousturier (Petrus Sutor), of Chêmeré-le-Roy in the county of Maine, joined the Carthusians in January 1511 shortly after taking his doctorate in theology at Paris. Although never a student or teacher at the Collège de Montaigu, he had doubtless been influenced by Jan Standonck, and maintained contact with the latter's disciple Noël Béda. His *De tralatione bibliae et novarum reprobatione interpretationum* (Paris: Pierre Vidoue for Jean Petit 1525), which rejected all new Latin versions or vernacular translations of the Bible, was approved by the Paris faculty of theology. Erasmus denounced him in at least sixty extant letters between 1525 and 1531. See Farge BR 119–21 no 123; cf Rummel *Catholic Critics* II 61–73. Erasmus had petitioned the Carthusian superior general, Willem Bibaut of Tielt, to silence Cousturier (Ep 1687), but there is no documentation in Paris records that he did so.

never make an end of it. To what lengths will the audacity of such hellish
fiends go?

You will be receiving Aleandro's pamphlet.[66] It is circulating anonymously from hand to hand among the papal secretaries. Alberto, prince   275
of Carpi, has sent me a good-sized volume bearing his name;[67] he shows
great forbearance, mitigating all his remarks with praise, but at times confusing the Luther cause with mine and violently attacking my *Paraphrases*,
the *Folly*, and good letters. I have the impression that he did not read my
works but drew his knowledge from conversations with theologians, with   280
whom he spends a great deal of time. He is a layman who wishes to pass
for a theologian, and he takes great pride in vaunting himself as an Aristotelian. There is a Dominican in Rome who has written against the *Folly* but
in such a foolish manner that he outdoes Folly herself.[68] In Rome, however,
they do not dare print anything against Erasmus.[69] What a fate is mine! I am 285
feared by the highest prelates in the world, but am spat upon, shit upon, and
pissed upon by the dregs of mankind! In Spain a theologian named Alonso,
a Benedictine monk, twice now has sent me seven *Collationes* in which he
treats me exactly as the cohort of soldiers treated Christ. At times he refers
to me as 'an oracle of divine wisdom,' 'three- and four-times Reverend Fa- 290
ther,' and even 'dearest son.' And, what is more, he champions the cause of
Erasmus among his own people at great personal peril – in other words, he
dresses me in a royal robe, puts the sceptre in my hand, bends the knee, and
greets me: 'Hail, Rabbi.' But suddenly, assuming another guise, he insults
me, strikes me, mocks me, beats me, spits upon me,[70] adds stinging enigmas. 295

* * * * *

66 This tract, known as *Racha*, was denounced by Erasmus in several letters between 1526 and 1531. Presumed by Allen to be lost, it has been identified by
Eugenio Massa as Paris, Bibliothèque nationale de France MS Lat 3461, and is
described in Rummel *Catholic Critics* II 111–13.
67 Probably a manuscript of *Ad Erasmi Roterodami expostulationem responsio accurata et paraenetica* . . . (Paris: Josse Bade 1529), reprinted anonymously by Pierre
Vidoue (Moreau *Inventaire* III 504 nos 1883, 1884). On Alberto Pio, a distinguished nobleman devoted to the church and to theology, see Rummel *Catholic
Critics* II 115–23. For the controversy with Pio see CWE 84 Introduction.
68 Possibly Lancellotto de' Politi (Ambrosius Catharinus Politus), whose polemical works in 1520–1 targeted Martin Luther but likewise cast aspersions on
the orthodoxy of Erasmus. From 1535, Politi opposed Erasmus much more
directly, seeing him as a major influence on the Protestant reformers.
69 Zúñiga, for example, did not (Rummel *Catholic Critics* I 165–6); cf Ep 1864:19–
20 and n7.
70 Cf Matt 27:27–31, Mark 15:16–20. In his *Collationes*, which were never printed,
Alonso Ruiz de Virués (1493–1545), a master of theology at Salamanca, had

Pieter Gillis
Quinten Metsys, 1520
Landesmuseum für Kunst und Kultur, Oldenburg

I have never seen anyone so impudent and offensive. Sometimes he is carried away with such fervour that he seems to lose his mind. And he thinks of himself withal as marvellously witty. He pleads the cause of monks with incredible zeal, as if I had any misgivings about monks worthy of the name. At the end of his work he invites me with grandiose praises and promises 300 that, as I have shed the lustre of my presence on the rest of Europe, I should also deign to bestow this honour upon Spain. In short, the book is such that its author must be either insane or a most cunning scoundrel or egregiously stupid or driven mad by the desire for fame. And in a subsequent book he has added some more barbs.[71] 305

Such are my consolations, as I struggle with this poor health of mine and try to catch my breath amidst the gruelling efforts of my studies. I know it will be tiresome for you even to read this, but you will not refuse, I trust, to sympathize with your friend at least to this extent. Although I am in this condition, nevertheless, even against my will, I will gratify your 310 wishes, whatever the outcome may be. I will finish the *Hyperaspistes*, and if it is not safe to publish it, I will send it to you by my own servant,[72] and that very soon, if someone can be found to accompany him. I suspect my treatise on marriage was less pleasing to the queen because I include a discussion on the relaxation of the marriage bond.[73] I had resolved not to add anything 315 on that subject. My mind dictated one thing, my pen wrote another.[74] There are those who think that the church will experience a spectacular flowering if things are restored to their previous state. I fear their hopes are in vain.

For you and for all your family I pray for every blessing. Your letter of 18 December reached me towards the beginning of March – not through the 320 emissaries who delivered the packet of Tunstall's letters but separately.[75] By what accident that came about I know not, except that nothing passes through Pieter Gillis' hands without that nuisance from Gelderland getting

* * * * *

pointed out passages that Erasmus should delete or emend to mollify his orthodox Catholic critics; see Ep 1838 introduction and n4.
71 An expanded and revised version, again not printed, that Virués sent to Erasmus (cf line 288 above). He also wrote a short defence of Erasmus (in Spanish) to the guardian of the Franciscan convent in Alcalá, which had a wide circulation, first in manuscript and later in print; see Ep 1838 nn10 and 11.
72 Perhaps Nicolaas Kan (Ep 1832 introduction)
73 It was within a few weeks of this letter that Henry VIII first took steps to seek the annulment of his marriage with Catherine of Aragon, but no connection is here implied. *Institutio christiani matrimonii* was dedicated to Catherine; see Ep 1727 introduction, and cf Ep 1816:14–15, Allen Ep 1960:68–71.
74 Erasmus uses this same phrase in another context (in Ep 1830:13).
75 See introduction and line 1 above.

wind of it and interfering. For ten years now he has been tormenting me, taking advantage of the easy-going nature of my dearest friend.[76] And I see   325 no remedy at hand.

Basel, 30 March in the year 1527

1805 / To Juan Maldonado   Basel, 30 March 1527

The manuscript of this letter is contained in a collection of letters and papers of Juan de Vergara at the Biblioteca nacional, Madrid (MS 17460 f 144), among which are included Epp 1748, 1813, and 1814. It answers Ep 1742, in which Maldonado described the mixed reception of Erasmus' works in Spain. Allen concluded that the manuscript is a copy commissioned for Vergara by the imperial Latin secretary Alfonso de Valdés, to whom the letter was alternatively directed (Ep 1839:9–14). The letter was first printed by Adolf Helfferich in *Zeitschrift für historische Theologie* N F XXIII (1859) 605–16, then by Adolfo Bonilla y San Martín *Erasmo en España* 149–62; repr *Revue hispanique* 17 (1907) 527–41.

Valdés chided Erasmus for including in the letter what he judged to be indiscreet remarks and for sending with it copies of letters from Emperor Charles v and Chancellor Mercurino Gattinara to Maldonado, a person whom Valdés did not know and did not consider trustworthy to receive such confidential remarks (Ep 1839:51–8, 85–92). Valdés thus never forwarded the letter to Maldonado and suppressed his name in this copy made for Vergara. He implored Erasmus never to publish the letter but rather to burn it at once. Erasmus took the first counsel but not the second, as he was later able to send Maldonado a copy when the latter inquired (Ep 1908:1–6) whether Erasmus had received Ep 1742. Erasmus had in the meantime heard high praise of Maldonado from his friend Conradus Goclenius (Ep 1768:26–33), who had intercepted and read

* * * * *

76 Pieter Gillis, the town clerk of Antwerp, was a close friend of Erasmus. Their correspondence dates from 1505. After editing the letters of Angelo Poliziano, the *Opuscula* of Rodolphus Agricola, and Aesop's fables in Latin, he edited Erasmus' correspondence in 1516 and 1517 and More's *Utopia* (Louvain: Dirk Martens, December 1516). He frequently acted for Erasmus in financial matters, although this relationship changed in 1525, largely for the reasons invoked here. See CEBR II 99–101. The 'nuisance from Gelderland' was Franz Birckmann, a bookseller with shops and connections in many cities of Europe. Erasmus had at first counted on him to handle his English annuity but later complained about his lack of discretion and business methods. See Epp 258:14n 1388:27–8, 1362:59–60, 1437:414, 1488:49–51, 1494:37–9, 1513:46–50, and especially 1507:14–25; cf CEBR I 149–50. Erasmus took revenge in the colloquy *Pseudocheus et Philetymus* 'The Liar and the Man of Honour.'

Ep 1742 before forwarding it to Erasmus. In Ep 1971 Erasmus therefore would assure Maldonado that the present letter had been sent, and as proof included the copy; but nothing confirms that Maldonado received it.

Juan Maldonado (c 1485–c 1554) studied at the University of Salamanca under the humanist Elio Antonio de Nebrija. No record of a theological degree is extant. An ordained priest, he served in the diocesan administration in Burgos. He was an avid reader of classical authors and wrote about contemporary affairs like the *comuneros* rebellion (1520–1) using humanistic historiographical methodology, which he urged activist bishops and statesmen to employ in their service of church and state. At the time of this letter he admired Erasmus, although he feared that Erasmus' blanket attacks on mendicant orders would give comfort to heretics. His enthusiasm cooled considerably during the inquisitorial climate after 1534, and in 1541 he wrote, 'In truth I was never so attached to Erasmus that I did not suspect that there was something venomous in his writings' (*Praxis seu de lectione Erasmi* in *Quaedam opuscula* [Madrid 1549] f viii), cited in 'Paraenesis ad literas' in *Juan Maldonado y el humanismo español en tiempos de Carlos V* ed Eugenio Asensio (Madrid 1980) 51. On Maldonado see also Ep 1742 introduction and CEBR II 370–1; Heliodoro García García *El pensamiento comunero y erasmista de Juan Maldonado* (Madrid 1893).

DESIDERIUS ERASMUS OF ROTTERDAM TO JUAN N, GREETING
You have truly painted me a vivid picture, my dear N,[1] of the tragicomedy of the pseudomonks! What more could I have seen even had I been present at the events myself? But I shall respond briefly to your letter, which gave me all the more pleasure because of its ample detail, although I am   5
overwhelmed, as you may well imagine, by the exertions of my studies, as always, and sorely tried by my poor state of health, as often. The praise that you heap upon me, while proving your sincere affection, strikes me nonetheless as excessive and has the effect of lowering my morale rather than reviving it. I feel a great burden placed upon me, which I am incapable   10
of supporting even in the least degree; and there is a danger that those who, as you write, have conceived so grandiose an opinion of me, once they have had a closer look at Erasmus, will cry out in protest that they have been deluded, having found coals instead of treasure, as in the Greek proverb.[2]

*   *   *   *   *

1805
1 Abbreviating the generic *Nomen*. San Martín 'Erasmo en España' *Revue hispanique* 17 (1907) 527 reads 'M.' Juan de Valdés suppressed Maldonado's name; see the introductions to this letter and to Ep 1742.
2 *Adagia* I ix 30

In promoting the study of languages and humane letters, I confess   15
that I am one of those who have devoted their energies diligently to that
task, even though I am eclipsed by many,[3] which I consider a great personal
glory. For the victory that I strove to achieve was that these studies would
flourish auspiciously, rising from rude beginnings to their present prestige.
It turned out no less successfully than I had hoped, and even sooner than I   20
hoped. Yet I gave my support to the pursuit of humane letters for no other
reason than that they would be the handmaid of higher disciplines, in particular theology, because I saw that it was the neglect of the humanities that
had brought about the deplorable corruption of all disciplines and the ex-
tinction and distortion of good authors, scarcely retrievable even by those   25
writers themselves. And since I realized how important it is whether you
draw living water from the source or turbid water from pools that endlessly
flow back and forth, from one place to another,[4] I urged the serious reading of the Sacred Scriptures and then of the authors whom the church has
regarded as its chief teachers and defenders. For those who are completely   30
unversed in humane letters can perhaps read the learned works of the Fathers (although I doubt whether they can do even that), but certainly they
are utterly incapable of understanding them, as they themselves reveal more
and more with each passing day. And this plan might have gone reasonably in accordance with my wishes, save that there rose up a band of men,   35
strangers to the Muses,[5] philobarbarians, who stirred up an incredible tumult over nothing at all, missing no occasion to bellow out their protests in
sermons to the people and in public lectures, in committees and in the confessional, at table, in the courts of princes and the homes of the rich, on the
road and aboard ship – in a word, where are they not to be found? they are   40
everywhere.

When the works of St Jerome appeared,[6] they hoodwinked some
people, even leading public figures, into believing that I had embellished the
simple style of Jerome with the frills of rhetoric. When my New Testament
came out,[7] like frenzied lunatics they openly provoked the unschooled mul-   45
titude to stone Erasmus, this man who was rash enough to correct the Magnificat, to emend the Lord's Prayer, to make changes in the Gospel of John.[8]

* * * * *

3 *obscuror a multis*: a favourite expression of Erasmus; cf Allen Ep 1107:8n.
4 Cf Allen Ep 1002:15n.
5 Rendered in Greek; cf *Adagia* II vi 18.
6 See Ep 396.
7 See Epp 373, 384.
8 Cf Epp 948:99–119, 1126:25–8.

And yet by their inane clamours they succeeded more in betraying their own ignorance, joined with equal malice, than in damaging my reputation.

While we were giving battle to these bogeymen in a rather evenly matched contest, behold suddenly Luther rose up and set loose the curse of Eris upon the world.[9] My immediate concern in this was to ensure that the cause of the Muses not be confounded with the Luther affair, as both sides would have it.[10] Although the cause of languages and the humanities has suffered more harm from certain of its defenders than from its enemies, nevertheless some measure of success was attained in the midst of many obstacles in that several universities, with the support of their theologians, are welcoming these studies – which are not new, as they would have us believe, but rightfully restored, as it were, to their previous status[11] (if novelty gives offence, it is they who have introduced it; we bring back old-established things, we shed light on new things, we do not spread darkness) – into their curriculum after a long interval of time. May the other universities do the same. In the end, those who make the loudest protests page through the sacred books and ancient commentaries, willing or not. They even emend a phrase here or there, although with more zeal than success, sprinkling in a bit of Greek borrowed from somewhere else. From such beginnings it may be augured that some day there will be great harmony between theology and good letters.

I also made it my purpose that the study of literature, which among the Italians and especially the Romans smacked of pure paganism,[12] might begin openly to celebrate the name of Christ, in whom as our unique guide to wisdom and happiness we ought solely to glory, if we be true Christians. What semblance of a Christian spirit is there, I pray you, in one who scorns as barbarous and uncouth a language in which the names of Jesus and Peter frequently occur? who on the contrary admires as genuinely Roman one in which 'Jupiter greatest and best,' 'gods and goddesses,' 'gods of the dead,' 'to forbid the use of fire and water,' 'to devote to the gods below,' and suchlike are found? Is there any name that should sound sweeter to us than that

* * * * *

9 The goddess of strife; see Hesiod *Theogony* 225, where she is daughter of Night and mother of battles, slaughters, disputes, and lawlessness.

10 Allen Ep 1155:18n points out that Erasmus himself had linked Reuchlin to Luther in order to escape criticism, and points out others of Erasmus' inconsistencies.

11 Erasmus uses the word *postliminium*, a term from Roman law meaning the resumption of rights suspended during exile.

12 On this see n15 below.

of Jesus Christ? Has the name Romulus a more elegant ring than that of
Christ? Does the name of Camillus have a sweeter sound to discerning ears   80
than the name of Peter or Paul? Is the surname Africanus more Latin than
the title 'apostle'?[13] Now if in the rules of rhetoric they can put up with
'basis,' 'definition,' 'hyperbole,' 'build-up,' and numerous other expressions
that in themselves either mean nothing at all to speakers of Latin or have a
far different meaning from their ordinary usage,[14] can they not allow 'faith,'   85
'grace in the Lord,' and other similar words from the language of Scripture?
For it too has a language of its own.

I hear that a fairly new sect has risen up among the Italians known as
the Ciceronians.[15] I venture to say that if Cicero were living now, and he
were to speak about our religion, he would not say, 'May Almighty God   90
bring this about' but 'May Jupiter, greatest and best, bring this about'; nor
would he say, 'May the grace of Jesus Christ sustain you' but 'May the
son of Jupiter, greatest and best, prosper whatever you do.' Nor would he
say, 'Peter, make the Roman church to prosper' but 'Romulus, concede your
favour to the Senate and people of Rome.'[16] Since the chief virtue of the   95
orator is to use appropriate language, what praise do they deserve who in

* * * * *

13 Marcus Furius Camillus was called the second founder of Rome after his victory over Gallic invaders in 387/6 BC (Livy 5.49.7). Publius Cornelius Scipio
Africanus Major (236–184/3 BC), the brilliant Roman military tactician who
conquered both Spain and Carthaginian North Africa, was given the name
'Africanus' after his defeat of Hannibal at the battle of Zama in 202 BC. Erasmus implies that the 'title' apostle is equally acceptable in good Latin as the
surname Africanus.
14 *status, finis, superlatio,* and *gradatio,* technical terms of rhetoric drawn from
Cicero *De oratore* and Quintilian, had very specialized meanings.
15 Erasmus' increasingly barbed criticism of a slavish imitation of Ciceronian
style and vocabulary came to full fruition in his dialogue *Ciceronianus,* sub-
titled *The Ideal Latin Style* (Basel: Froben 1528; see CWE 28). In it he took aim
mostly at certain Italian writers whose exaggerated reverence for Ciceronian
vocabulary he considered a kind of slavish neo-paganism. He also singled out
for criticism Christophe de Longueil, a recently deceased French-educated native of Brabant who had taken up residence in Italy. The book aroused opposition in both Italy and France. On Erasmus and Ciceronianism see especially Epp 1701:26–31 and n6, 1706:38–45 and n11, and 1717 n2; cf also Epp
1479:180–5, 1595:138–40, 1713:12–19, 1719:36–8, 1720:50–5 and n9, 1791:37–43,
1875:164–77, 1885:135–75.
16 A convoluted statement: Erasmus seems to posit that a Cicero redivivus would
fail to employ appropriate Christian vocabulary in a Christian society; but
he doubtless wants to posit that, unlike the sycophantic Ciceronians, Cicero
would use the idiom of his own culture in writing about Christianity.

speaking of the mysteries of our religion use such words as might be written
in the time of Virgil or Ovid?

This, I confess, has been the goal of my efforts; what influence I have
had is for others to judge. The role of the dogmatist I have always avoided,[17]   100
except for some casual admonitions that might serve to correct inveterate prejudices and perverse judgments. The world was in a deeper sleep
from the soporific of rituals than someone drugged with mandrake. Certain
monks, or rather pseudomonks, reigned over men's consciences and held
them ensnared in inextricable bonds. Not unlike them are a great many   105
theologians, since practically the whole method of scholastic teaching originated with monks;[18] thus, as someone has said, 'we change our morals to
suit our goals.'[19] For the rest, although no other class of mankind seems to
have benefitted more from my services than monks and theologians, yet I
learn by experience that I have no fiercer enemy.   110

These latest machinations of the pseudomonks are nothing new. They
were debating over this in their synods nine years ago,[20] not a little annoyed by the *Enchiridion*[21] but more so by the *Folly*.[22] They have been in

* * * * *

17 Cf Ep 1742:159 and n6 and line 358 below.
18 The earliest scholastics were neither monks nor mendicant friars (whom Erasmus frequently calls monks) but secular clerics like Peter Abelard, Peter Lombard, and Peter the Chanter. Erasmus probably has in mind here later scholastics who were members of mendicant orders, like Thomas Aquinas, John Duns
   Scotus, Robert Holcot, and William of Ockham.
19 Ovid *Heroides* 15.83
20 See Ep 1804 n44.
21 The *Enchiridion militis christiani*, or *Handbook of the Christian Soldier*, first appeared in 1503 as part of a collection of Erasmus' works and was reprinted
   seven times in that way. The second edition (Basel: Froben 1518) was the first
   time it was printed separately. It contained as a preface Erasmus' letter to
   the Benedictine abbot Paul Volz (Ep 858). This letter attributed more importance to the ethics of the Christian life than to its doctrine – an orientation
   highlighted by the expression 'philosophy of Christ.' Moreover, the growth
   of Erasmus' renown since 1504 put the new edition much more in the public
   eye. The notoriety of the *Enchiridion* was particularly increased by the spate of
   vernacular translations. Juan de Vergara (Ep 1814:129–34) told Erasmus that it
   was the Spanish translation of the *Enchiridion* that roused the theologians in
   Spain so much against him. On this see CWE 66, especially the general introduction by John W. O'Malley (xxxix–xliv) and Charles Fantazzi's introduction
   to his translation (1–7).
22 Erasmus' publication of the *Moriae encomium* in 1511 had occasioned criticism
   from foes and friends alike. Among the latter, Maarten van Dorp in Louvain –
   not a monk but a secular priest – protested both its tone and content in 1514 (Ep

labour for some time. What these elephantine birth-pangs will bring forth
I know not;[23] but this comedy did not have its origins in one place alone.   115
They have sprung up in almost every country at the same time: in France,
in England, in Hungary, in Poland, in your own Spain, in Brabant.[24] They
were repressed twice by the authority of the Roman pontiff[25] and once by
a threatening interdiction of the emperor,[26] which at least had the effect
of mitigating their madness. In England, thanks to the king and the cardi-   120
nal and other learned and influential friends,[27] they were not allowed to
do whatever they pleased. And in Hungary defenders of Erasmus were not
lacking, including the king and queen, whose tragedy has brought me great
sorrow.[28] In Poland Jan Łaski,[29] a baron of this realm, was ready to play
the deus ex machina. He had shared my lodgings for several months as a   125
most congenial guest. Summoned back to his native country, he was immediately charged with the administration of the archbishopric of Gniezno,
that is, in collaboration[30] with his uncle, a man endowed with all manner

* * * * *

304) and 1515 (Ep 347), but was eventually won over by Erasmus himself (Ep
337) and Thomas More ('Letter to Martin Dorp' in *The Complete Works of Saint
Thomas More* ed Louis L. Martz et al 15 vols in 21 [New Haven 1963–97] xv 1–
127). One of the 'monks' who was most critical of the *Folly* was the Dominican
friar Lancellotto de' Politi (Ambrosius Catharinus Politus); cf Ep 1804 n68. Another critic of the *Folly* was the Dominican Laurens Laurensen (Ep 1166:25–33).
23 See *Adagia* I ix 11.
24 Cf Ep 1804 n43.
25 First through the mediation of Theodoricus Hezius with Pope Adrian vi (cf
Epp 1324, 1338) and then by Albert Pigge, papal chamberlain (Ep 1589).
26 Erasmus conceals his role in obtaining the imperial intervention; cf Epp
1554:37–50, 1643:15–17, 1690:30–3 and n11, 1700:2–3.
27 Henry viii and Wolsey; cf Ep 1062:140–1.
28 Louis ii, king of Hungary and Bohemia (1 July 1506–29 August 1526), had received a humanistic education and attracted several humanists to his court.
His queen, Mary of Austria (17 September 1505–18 October 1558), was a sister
of Charles v and Ferdinand i; her marriage to Louis had established the Hapsburg claim to Hungary and Bohemia. After Louis' death on the field of battle
during the defeat of the Hungarian forces by Turkish invaders at Mohács on
29 August 1526 (the 'tragedy' to which Erasmus refers) Mary became regent
for her brother – first in Hungary and, from 1531 to 1558, in the Netherlands.
29 On Łaski see Ep 1821 introduction. For *deus ex machina* see *Adagia* I i 68, and
cf Ep 1875 n13.
30 Erasmus uses the Greek σύνεργος; Jan (ii) Łaski was provost of the archdiocese
of which his uncle was the archbishop. Jan (i) Łaski, archbishop of Gniezno

Mary of Austria
Netherlands School? c 1550
Rijksmuseum-Stichting, Amsterdam

of virtue and accomplishments. But returning to Jan, I have never before
experienced a more able, acute, open, and friendly spirit. He has an elder   130
brother of lofty mind, Hieronim Łaski,[31] a palatine, and a younger brother,
a lad of great promise, Stanisław Łaski.[32] Now upon learning that, beyond
every expectation, such defenders of my cause have arisen in Spain, more
powerful and sympathetic than any I can boast of, I can readily conjecture
that these events are being directed by some power of divine providence.   135

In France too there are those who are kindly disposed towards me, but
the authority of the Parlement and the conspiracy of some sophist theologians deter even the great.[33] They are quick to raise the shout 'He favours
heretics.' The leaders of this madness are the Carthusian Pierre Cousturier,[34]
hot-headed by nature but now roused to a frenzy by his thirst for glory, and   140
Béda, no less insane than he but much more stupid;[35] he is not a monk but
belongs to some intermediate breed founded by a certain Standonck. They
wear a mantle and a cowl but are not bound by vows; they eat fish and

* * * * *

and primate of Poland, maintained a coolness towards Erasmus, suspecting a
secret sympathy for Luther but especially resenting Erasmus' loyalty to the
Hapsburgs. Erasmus will attempt to win his favour with the dedication of his
edition of St Ambrose; see Ep 1855.

31 To whom Erasmus had dedicated his *Modus orandi Deum* (Ep 1502). For the
career of Hieronim Łaski, who made diplomatic contact with the Turks only a
year after Mohács, see CEBR II 294–6.

32 Having enrolled in the Knights of the Holy Sepulchre after a pilgrimage to
the Holy Land (1521), Stanisław Łaski served King Francis I from 1524 to 1528,
joining him in captivity after the battle of Pavia. He subsequently served his
brother Hieronim, but is also noted for his literary talents (CEBR II 301–2).

33 The Parlement of Paris was a system of courts, not a legislative body, but it
claimed the right to register, or put into legal effect, decisions taken by the
king. It comprised approximately 120 *conseillers* presided over by three presi-
dents, one of whom was designated as the *premier président*. In the main a conservative body, it allied closely with the University of Paris in 1516 against
the Concordat of Bologna negotiated between King Francis I and Pope Leo X,
and it retained a strong bias against royal actions taken under the provisions
of the concordat. During the captivity of Francis I the Parlement and the university cooperated in initiatives against persons like Jacques Lefèvre d'Etaples
and Louis de Berquin who favoured either a humanist approach to theology
or an evangelical reform of the church.

34 See Ep 1804 n65.

35 For the polemical exchange between Erasmus and Béda, undertaken both in
correspondence and in books, see Rummel *Catholic Critics* II 29–46, the Introduction to CWE 82, and Ep 1804 n14.

vegetables. It is the training ground and hothouse of all monks.[36] From that
band the Carthusians, Franciscans, Dominicans, Benedictines, and Bernar-   145
dines[37] recruit their troops.[38] The third is a man named Clichtove,[39] once a
friend of mine, and one not totally alien to the Muses, but they have dragged
him into their company so that they would not be without a third line of attack. Cousturier has already written two volumes against me,[40] Béda one;[41]
but so simple-minded are their efforts that I would never have wished that   150
so much disgrace would befall them as that which they have brought upon
themselves by their own writings.

* * * * *

36 Erasmus refers to the 'community of poor students' founded at the Collège de
Montaigu by Jan Standonck of Mechelen (d 5 February 1504), who hoped to
promote a reform of discipline in the church by educating priests who could
embrace a spirit of evangelical poverty. Members of this community – including Béda – had no canonical status other than that of secular priest. Standonck
was well known to Erasmus, who had lodged during the year 1495–6 at his
collège. Noël Béda succeeded Standonck as principal there. In his 1526 colloquy Ἰχθυοφαγία 'A Fish Diet' Erasmus describes a diet of rotten fish and
tainted drinking water imposed on him at the Collège de Montaigu (CWE 40
715–17). Composed thirty years after his year's lodging there, the colloquy
must be viewed as part of Erasmus' campaign to discredit Béda.
37 The Cistercians, sometimes called Bernardines after their renowned second
founder St Bernard of Clairvaux
38 No documentation exists to verify this statement which, if true, confirms Standonck's success. Montaigu did however produce more secular priests who became masters of theology than any other arts college (Farge *Orthodoxy* 72–3).
The Carthusian prior of Vauvert (near Paris) was entrusted by Montaigu's
statutes with the oversight of the college, but no connection can be established
between Montaigu and Pierre Cousturier, who studied and taught arts at the
Collège de Sainte-Barbe and theology at the Collège de Sorbonne prior to joining the Carthusians. There is a similar list of religious orders in Ep 1879:46–7;
cf also Ep 1893:38.
39 Josse Clichtove, a humanist disciple of Lefèvre d'Etaples but more lately a
staunchly conservative theologian. He had arrived in Paris in 1488, studying arts first at the Collège de Boncourt and then at Cardinal Lemoine, and
theology at the Collège de Sorbonne; see Jean-Pierre Massaut *Josse Clichtove,
l'humanisme, et la réforme du clergé* (Paris 1968). For Clichtove's polemic with
Erasmus, see CWE 83 xxxiii–l, 109–48 and Rummel *Catholic Critics* II 73–9.
40 *De tralatione Bibliae et novarum reprobatione interpretationum* (Paris: Pierre Vidoue for Jean Petit 1525) and *Adversus insanam Erasmi apologiam antapologia*
(Paris: Pierre Vidoue for Jean Petit 1526)
41 *Annotationum in Jacobum Fabrum Stapulensem libri duo, et in Desiderium Erasmum
Roterodamum liber unus* ... (Paris: Josse Bade 1526)

For my part I was fearful that through imprudence I might have blurted out something that was contrary to the approved decrees of the church. But I honestly congratulated myself when the two hundred propositions cen- 155 sured by Béda – in which (with the exception of three or four, where it was not my error but that of the copyists or the printers) he had not understood the Latin or had taken what was said in the person of Christ or the Apos- tle against the Pharisees, scribes, and pseudo-apostles and misapplied it to the monks and theologians of today – were made public.[42] He repeatedly 160 condemns opinions expressed in the Sacred Scriptures, interpreted by or- thodox commentators, at times interspersing his own words with mine to leave room for calumny, regularly distorting with supreme impudence con- scientious and morally correct statements for the purpose of calumny, and not infrequently lying with great boldness and effrontery. I replied to these 165 calumnies once,[43] giving more thought to the danger to which the weak were exposed than to my reputation, although one must be hard-hearted in- deed to neglect his own reputation. Nor is it my intention to waste any more precious hours in future on disputes of this sort.[44] Those who are of sound judgment will see that there is no soundness in their allegations. Those who 170 are corrupted by prejudice or hatred either hardly read my writings at all or, if they do, read them with their left eye, whose judgment is perverted, if indeed it has any judgment at all.

In the face of their excesses I would have been adequately protected by the patronage of the king of France, who frequently invited me to his 175 kingdom with magnificent and princely terms.[45] But I had firmly decided not to move to France unless there was an alliance of peace between the king and the emperor, a decision which I still do not regret. Before the em- peror crossed over into Spain,[46] I had sensed that there was movement afoot to put me in charge of opposition to the Lutheran party, which was grow- 180 ing in numbers. I withdrew myself from that duty, I admit. Even though

* * * * *

42 That is, in the publication of his *Annotations* against Erasmus. This same charge, which allows Erasmus to feign innocence for interpretations that he knew most readers would infer, will be repeated in a later letter to the Parlement of Paris (Ep 1905:63–79); cf also Ep 1864:126–32.
43 By this date Erasmus had already published four books or tracts against Béda; see Ep 1805 n14.
44 For Erasmus' responses to Béda see Ep 1804 n14.
45 Since 1517 French humanists had been urging King Francis I to bring Erasmus to Paris. The most recent attempt was Ep 1375 (7 July 1523), a short letter from the king concluding with fourteen words in the king's own hand.
46 In June 1522

Glapion wrote me many flattering words, I could not really trust him; the sacred garb exercised too much influence.[47] The negotiations were being handled by him, but by underhanded methods. I have never liked any faction. Yet I saw that I would be the colleague of those who wished me ill, or   185 rather who can never love anyone other than themselves; and if I did not make myself entirely subservient to their petulant emotions and implacable ferocity, they would have turned against me and shouted 'turncoat and champion of heretics.' My natural disposition is far removed from anything that is tainted with bloodshed. If the misdeeds of certain individuals call for   190 it, executioners are not wanting anywhere, so that there is no need of me. There are articles of belief on which the schools themselves disagree; there are those which do not pertain properly to the faith, those which are not sufficiently defined, those which can be argued from both sides; there are those in which, if a suitable translator intervenes, a common opinion will   195 be found and the dispute becomes merely one of words. Nowadays for any theological statement whatever you are thrown into jail, and there the legal proceedings are carried on in private. If the case is lost by default, as they say,[48] the victim is thrown into the fire. Why mention here the kind of interrogators I have known?[49] how lacking in judgment, how given over to   200 violent prejudices, how spurred on by implacable hatred!

Therefore I withdrew myself from that duty without desisting from my efforts to assure that this dissension, whatever its origins and whatever its progress, should have a fruitful outcome. Obviously the affair seems at the present moment to be going the way of Mandraboulus,[50] as they say,   205 with the fire spreading so rapidly, especially when we see now that in place of one sect four have sprung up: Lutherans, Karlstadtians, Anabaptists, and

* * * * *

47 Probably a reference to Glapion's background in the Observant Franciscans. Jean Glapion (d 1522), confessor to Charles v, abandoned his earlier irenic approach to Luther. Of the several letters exchanged between him and Erasmus, only Ep 1275 (Erasmus to Glapion) survives; cf also Allen Ep 2792:19–23.
48 An undefended case by reason of the defendant's absence; cf *Adagia* I v 80. An undefended case may also be an instance of the plea *noli contendere*.
49 No formal, personal interrogation of Erasmus ever took place. He probably refers here to the implacable criticism he incurred in Louvain, especially from certain Dominican and Carmelite friars, that was often aired in public and must have seemed to Erasmus like a public inquisition.
50 That is, day by day it gets worse. In Lucian *De mercede conductis* 'On Salaried Posts' 21 a shepherd named Mandraboulos, finding a treasure, gave to Hera first a golden ram, then a silver one, and finally one of bronze; cf *Adagia* I ii 58. Erasmus wrote the phrase in Greek.

some other prophets,[51] so that if we look to human resources there will be no
hope of ending this evil without an immense shedding of Christian blood.
Nevertheless, I do not abandon my hope, considering how wonderful is that   210
master craftsman, the ruler of human affairs, whom on the strength of multiple proofs I consider to be the director of this play.[52] On one side this affair
is being conducted by insignificant, even ignoble men, and it is being carried
on, in my opinion, in an absurd manner. There is no consensus among them,
and yet they are successful despite the vain struggles of so many monks.   215
On the other side I have observed that none have more hindered the cause
of the pope, theologians, and monks than those who imagine they are upholding it with the utmost fervour. I could illustrate what I say with many
examples, but I must finish this letter.

The world has awakened from its lethargy. The screeching of the   220
sophists has everywhere been hissed off the stage. The study of languages
and good letters is being embraced by youth, and not by youth alone. Theologians have been compelled to return to the Sacred Scriptures and the early
Doctors of the church. The pretences of the pharisees have been stripped
away, the prejudiced opinions of the multitude have been exposed to scorn.   225
But, you will say, what a great upheaval in human affairs! Who ever saw a
change for the better in the state of the world without great turmoil? Who
ever saw a grave and chronic illness disappear without the organism being
first shaken by harsh and effective medicine? Meanwhile renegade monks
hither and yon take virgins vowed to God as their wives; many priests con-   230
duct themselves as though they were laymen; the people do not bow to the
will of their bishops but insult them to their faces and rebel against their
princes; fasting is ignored, abstention from certain foods is ridiculed, and
many gratify their gullet and their belly.[53] Among these same individuals
the liberal arts are neglected and powerless, and morals that are anything   235
but evangelical thrive and flourish. But can it be that the Lord has sent these

* * * * *

51 Perhaps the 'Zwickau prophets,' who appeared in Wittenberg in December
   1521. Their claims to special revelation were rejected by both Karlstadt and
   Luther; see Ep 1258 n13. On the Anabaptists cf Epp 1369:40–9, 1901 n9, Allen
   Epp 1689:62n, 1780:12n.
52 Erasmus probably intends God, architect of the universe and of human affairs,
   not the emperor.
53 Erasmus makes similar accusations at Epp 1822:23, 1834:10, 1873:16, 1875:54
   and 140, 1924:24–5; cf also Ep 1858:4 and n2. Because of their tradition of begging for food, Erasmus sometimes calls the mendicant friars, whose theologians were among his most violent critics, *ventres*; see line 373 below, Epp
   1864:11, 1903:30, and cf *Adagia* II viii 78.

beetles and locusts upon us as our just deserts so that warned by these evils we may be converted to the Lord?[54] In my view it seems that we have all but suffered the fate with which Moses in Deuteronomy threatens the people who neglected his law: 'The Lord will bring a nation against you from afar, 240 as swift as an eagle in flight, a nation whose language you understand not, a nation of stern countenance, who will show no respect for the old or pity for the young, and will devour the offspring of your cattle, etc.'[55] From the far-off confines of Saxony this people has poured out and spread through all the world with incredible speed. Their leaders are versed in Greek, He- 245 brew, and Chaldean letters, yet are so without shame that they do not cede to bishops or academics, to princes or magistrates, to emperors or the supreme pontiff. As far as respecting my grey hairs is concerned, sufficient proof, aside from the many infamous pamphlets written against me, is the *Servum arbitrium* of Luther,[56] in which he has outdone himself in acrimony, having 250 already surpassed all others in his other books. The rest of this prophecy has been fulfilled by the peasant rebellion.[57] What follows, 'You shall be besieged within your gates,'[58] has already come to pass. This would have been the end for this city had not the wisdom of the magistrates shown itself vigorously alert.[59] We priests did not dare set foot outside our doors. 255

Although these are clear signs of God's indignation at our crimes, yet no one turns to a more virtuous way of life, but everyone in his own interests turns public misfortune to private gain. I am afraid that certain princes have it in mind to increase their own power through the confiscation of the property of priests and monks. Then there are among us a number of bish- 260 ops who are anything but bishops. They are busily consolidating their tyrannic rule. Among the monks and theologians some seek out honours, others riches, others glory, others vengeance. The people are led on by the hope of freedom to be allowed to do whatever they please. As a consequence, what-

* * * * *

54 Cf Ep 1804:144.
55 Deut 28:49–51
56 Luther's mordant answer to Erasmus' more irenic *De libero arbitrio* (Ep 1419). See the preface to Erasmus' reply (Ep 1667). For a general appreciation of this controversy see the CWE 76 Introduction.
57 The peasant uprisings began in the Black Forest and Upper Swabia in May 1524 and quickly spread into Franconia, Alsace, the Rhine Palatinate, and northward to the Thuringian Forest and Saxony. It ended with a surrender of peasant forces at Freiburg-im-Breisgau in May 1525; see OER III 234–7 and Ep 1917:56.
58 Deut 28:52
59 See Ep 1585:31–4.

ever the fall of the dice, it seems certain that the victory will not go to Christ   265
but to men. And I do not see what we will profit from a general council if
its participants are the actors we see strutting in this play. Violence up to
now has only made things worse,

> As the ilex hewn by the woodsman's axe
> Draws strength and vigour from the very steel.   270
> ...
> It grows even stronger than the Hydra,
> Its hacked-off heads resprouting, to Hercules' despair.[60]

Certainly much blood would have to be shed if we intended to kill all those
whom this fatal pestilence has infected. What hope remains to us, then, what
counsel? that all of us, without exception, great, small, or in between, ac-   275
knowledging our guilt should humble ourselves beneath the mighty hand
of God, admitting to our injustice and imploring his mercy. He, always open
to our prayers, will immediately turn these disorders, storms, and tempests
of human affairs into a hoped-for tranquillity.

You exhort me to write something that testifies to my favourable opin-   280
ion of good monks, so that I may appease those monks who cry out against
me not from the heart but driven to it by the outrageous conduct of others,
for fear that their silence be interpreted as a sign of approval.[61] But how often has what you advise been done in my writings! On this subject there is
no need to dissemble. I sincerely love and revere monks in whom the image   285
of true monasticism is reflected, and no other way of life would be more at-
tractive to me even now, except that this health of mine is so fragile and troublesome that I would be bound to become a nuisance to anyone with whom I
lived. A change of garb, another kind of cooking, a different type of wine set
before me, a change of location, having to sit longer than I am accustomed,   290
or a more severe climate thrusts me into this present state and puts my life in
danger. And so, although I am invited by monarchs, bishops, and cities, and
under enviable conditions, still, in order to be a burden to as few persons as
possible, I live by myself, allotting but one or two hours of the afternoon on
fixed days to conversations with friends. After supper the weakness of my   295
stomach can barely tolerate conversation, so I have my servant read to me.[62]

* * * * *

60 Horace *Odes* 4.4.57–62
61 Ep 1742:193–7
62 For examples of this see Epp 1552:5–6 and Allen 5n, 1616:23–4, 1759:60–1,
   1790:71–3, 1833:19–20.

As a matter of fact I have very strong ties of friendship with those monasteries where religious discipline is most strictly observed. I could demonstrate this point with countless letters, with which my files are full.[63] There is a monastery of Carthusians here, in which there is not one man   300 with whom I do not share mutual esteem.[64] There is a convent of Franciscans who count me as one of their patrons.[65] The same was true at Louvain and wherever else I lived.[66]

It would be out of place to mention my generosity even if I could make a sizeable donation; and yet from my scant resources I can say that I   305 am not lacking in the desire to do good. This will not be denied by those to whom I am more intimately known. And although I am not unaware of what many of them are plotting against me and with what virulence they vent their fury against my reputation, I have never been unjust to any order nor have I imputed to good men what evil men have devised. Luther in a re-   310 cently published prologue vowed that he would expose the secret scandals of priests and monks.[67] In a letter written to Duke John of Saxony I immediately warned him to restrain that man's audacity.[68] So much for my hatred of monks! Nor do I ever make any careless remarks about their disgraceful

* * * * *

63 For Erasmus' preservation of his letters, see Epp 1197, 1874:69–70, 1909:74–6, Allen Epp 1927:24–5, 1940:12.

64 A certain Georgius Carpentarius of Brugg, a Carthusian of Basel, translated Erasmus' *Hyperaspistes* into German (see the introductions to Epp 1667 and 1708). For Erasmus' respect for Carthusians generally, see Ep 1196:457–72.

65 Not identified

66 Amandus of Zierikzee (d 1524/1534), the Observant Franciscan guardian of the Louvain convent, lectured in Louvain's faculty of theology. He knew Greek, Hebrew, and Syriac, and wrote commentaries on the Bible that were later published by his fellow Franciscan Frans Titelmans. Maarten van Dorp assured Erasmus of Amandus' admiration (Ep 1044:40–2). For other, less specific references to Louvain Franciscans favourable to Erasmus and humanistic studies see Epp 1174:17 and 1189:9–10.

67 Perhaps Luther's *Das Bapstum mit seynen gliedern gemalet und beschriben* (Wittenberg: [Josef Klug, c 1 January 1526]), in which the hierarchy and religious orders are held up to ridicule, one by one, in illustrations and verse; see WA 19 1–43.

68 See Ep 1670 introduction and lines 23–50, in which Erasmus complains about Luther's *De servo arbitrio* but does not mention his *Das Bapstum*. In 1525 Duke John had succeeded his brother Frederick III 'the Wise,' whose protection of Luther Erasmus had at first encouraged both in writing (Ep 939) and in a personal interview at Cologne on 5 November 1520 (see Ep 1155 introduction). Duke John showed Erasmus' letter to Luther and Melanchthon but never sent Erasmus a reply.

behaviour which is, alas! too well publicized already. But certain admoni-   315
tions I did make, against my will, which seemed to me to be necessary for
the protection of the young,[69] for the good of simple folk, and for the reputation of the monks themselves. For they will not more readily regain the
world's favour in any other way than the one by which they merited it in
the first place.   320
     What is it, therefore, that rouses many of them against me? To speak
frankly, it is first of all crass stupidity. What some petty rabbi said in his cups
is seized on by one and all as an oracle sent from heaven, while globetrotting
couriers carry it promptly to every corner of the earth. Others among them
who have charge of temporal concerns and seek out their own advantage at   325
the price of others resent me for no other reason than that they blame my
writings for the fewer young men of means who fall into their net,[70] the
fewer matrons who entrust their fortunes to them, and the smaller number
of those who wish to be buried in the Franciscan habit.[71] It is against such
men that the monks should have raised their outcries with greater zeal than   330
against me. But just as I never pushed anyone by urging them into that form
of life, so will no one step forward to say that he was in any way turned
away from the mode of life he had chosen. There will be many who can testify that both by counsel and exhortation I encouraged those who were wa-
vering.[72] And yet all the while I was well aware of what spirits, what minds,   335
what native talents were buried alive in those caverns. The theologians have
nothing to reproach in me except that I denounce sophistic theology – not
without reason, though, as they see it, without moderation. Otherwise there
has always been and always will be the closest friendship between the best
theologians and myself.   340

          * * * * *

69 Allen Ep 1183:122n gives a number of examples; cf CWE Epp 1697 n12,
   1747:105–12.
70 Cf Ep 447:345–6, 460, where Erasmus uses the images of bait and net to describe how he was persuaded to enter the Augustinian priory of Steyn as a
   postulant.
71 Cf Epp 1886:75–7, 1891:248–9. For other comments on this custom see Ep
   447:559–60; the 1526 colloquy Funus 'The Funeral' (see CWE 40 774, 775); the
   1531 colloquy Exequiae seraphicae 'The Seraphic Funeral,' a satire of the obse-
   quies of his critic Alberto Pio (see CWE 40 1000–1, 1006, and cf n18); Allen Ep
   2700:73–8; and De praeparatione ad mortem (Basel: Hieronymus Froben, December 1533), CWE 70 420.
72 For Erasmus' advice in this regard to Maarten Lips see Epp 901:21–8, 1070
   9–12; to Paul Volz Ep 1075:8–11; to an unknown monk Ep 1887:10–47. But he
   clearly interceded for dispensation from vows for another unknown religious
   in Ep 1363.

If I had as great a desire for revenge as they for doing harm, they would long ago have experienced what manner of expert they had challenged. But I shall not retreat from my plan of action. I shall conquer the malice of the wicked by good deeds. If the present age will not acknowledge my services, posterity will render a more impartial judgment. And if it too 345 will not notice or recognize them, then Christ, the judge of this marathon contest, the one for whom we run, for whom we struggle, for whom we toil, will not defraud anyone of his reward. What they dread in the security of their fortresses, that some of my toilsome tomes might breach their walls, has kept them busy now for many years in Brabant and in France, but in se- 350 cret. With the same goal in mind they exploit the confession of the young. In this tactic I find their prudence lacking on two counts: first, how could they believe that young people would be silent about what is confided to them there? Second, what do they expect? that they will immediately be regarded as gods for rendering my name odious? There are other things that 355 they must correct if they wish to lessen the hatred in which they are held by the world. I can easily surmise the vile language they use to censure me,[73] for which you substitute the milder term 'dogmatist.'[74] Obviously it is not sufficient for them that I govern my life according to necessary and unimpeachable principles, in accordance with the advice of the most pru- 360 dent and upright men, with the approbation of the sovereign pontiff and my own ordinary,[75] at peace with superiors, inferiors, and equals who might have an interest in such matters, with the approval of God and my own conscience; no, I must render an account of all my plans to each and every one of them. 365

The Roman pontiffs have imposed silence on Zúñiga so many times now![76] Adrian VI gave proof of his sentiments towards me in two briefs

* * * * *

73 Allen (344n) suggests this is a reference to Alonso Ruiz de Virués, whom at this time Erasmus mistakenly believed to be a critic. Virués' Ep 1786, written on 23 February 1527, had perhaps not yet reached Erasmus.

74 In Ep 1742:159–60 Maldonato told Erasmus of Spanish enemies who spoke of him as '"that dogmatist Erasmus" (to use the milder term),' that is, milder than 'heretic.'

75 Christoph von Utenheim, bishop of Basel, with whom Erasmus was on friendly terms. He died exactly two weeks before Erasmus wrote this letter.

76 Diego López Zúñiga (Stunica) attacked Erasmus' New Testament scholarship in 1520–4. For Paolo Bombace's report of Pope Leo x's reaction, see Ep 1213:35–41; cf also Ep 1431:13–14. In a letter of 4 May 1522 to Juan de Vergara, Zúñiga had hopes that the new pope, Adrian VI, would condemn Erasmus, adding that 'it was Erasmus and Erasmus alone who armed and equipped and trained

written with exceeding devotion.[77] From the present pope I have not sought anything in vain, either in my own name or in another's behalf. Twice, of his own accord, he has sent me an honorary gift.[78] I am sending you a copy 370 of the most recent letter of the emperor to me.[79] So many kings, princes, · bishops, men in high places, scholars, so many young men of great promise have been won over by my works, and yet these gluttons[80] do not realize that they are stirring up trouble for themselves. I have always written reverently about the early monastic founders, and – as Christ is my witness! – 375 I never thought otherwise than what I wrote. I refer to Benedict, Dominic, and Francis, whom I have always considered as pious men and dear to God, no matter how their posterity lives up to them.

I recognize, my excellent friend, how much I owe to all of Spain and in particular to your compatriots of Burgos, and, to each by name, the arch- 380 bishop of Toledo[81] and his archdeacon,[82] then the archbishop of Seville[83] and the other illustrious and learned men, to whom I would give thanks one by one both in my name and in the name of religion and the world of studies if my works had as much efficacy as you so graciously attribute to them. For me, in any case, it is a great pleasure to see that sincere piety and the pur- 385 suit of humane learning are flourishing in Spain, a land renowned in the past for its celebrated geniuses, with a success hardly paralleled elsewhere. I have no serious disputes with any Spaniard. I have become reconciled with

* * * * *

Luther with these blasphemous notions of his, turning him against the true religion' (CWE 8 345 Ep 4:9–11). On this controversy see Rummel *Catholic Critics* I 145–77 and *passim*.
77 Epp 1324 and 1338, in both of which he encouraged Erasmus to write against the new heresies
78 Clement VII, cousin of Pope Leo X, assumed the office of pope on 19 November 1523. On 3 April 1524 (Ep 1443B), Clement sent Erasmus a gift of 200 florins in return for the dedication of his *Paraphrase on Acts* (Ep 1414 and CWE 50). Another gift of the same amount was sent later, along with 'all sorts of promises' (Ep 1796:22).
79 Ep 1731
80 *ventres*. See n53 above.
81 Alonso de Fonseca, archbishop of Toledo since 1523; see Epp 1813, 1874.
82 Francisco de Mendoza y Bobadilla, only eighteen years old at this time, later became a patron of the Jesuits in Rome and a leading Spanish humanist. As bishop of Burgos he strove to reform his diocese according to the decrees of the Council of Trent (CEBR II 431–2).
83 Alonso Manrique de Lara, archbishop of Seville and inquisitor-general in Spain since 1523; see Epp 1864, 1879, 1888.

Carranza;[84] with Zúñiga a truce is in force,[85] and there is good hope that
peace will be established shortly. I am presently translating some sermons   390
of John Chrysostom not previously translated. I was thinking of dedicating
them to the most reverend archbishop of Toledo, but I decided that I should
first ask the opinion of my friends in this matter. In the meantime I have
dedicated them to the king of Portugal, at the urging of my friends,[86] as
well as for other reasons. I have other commentaries of Chrysostom that no   395
one has previously translated.[87] I shall proceed according to your advice, if
you will see fit to communicate your wishes to me.
    Farewell.
    Given at Basel, 30 March in the year 1527. You will note another's hand,
since, being in such great haste, I was afraid you would be tormented by   400
my horrible scrawl. I enclose a copy of letters from the emperor,[88] the chancellor,[89] and Cardinal Campeggi;[90] likewise some passages in the *Paraphrases*

* * * * *

84 Sancho Carranza de Miranda. Like Alonso Ruiz de Virués, he had at first irritated Erasmus by his attempts to convince him to present certain points of his
   scriptural exegesis and interpretation more moderately, but Juan de Vergara
   had been able to reconcile the two. See Rummel *Catholic Critics* I 154, 156–61,
   168–9; see also Ep 1814:527–33.
85 See n76 above.
86 Especially Erasmus' Antwerp financial agent Erasmus Schets; see the introduction to Ep 1800, the dedicatory letter to John III, who ruled from 1521 to
   1557. St John Chrysostom (c 347–407), a Doctor of the church, was the bishop of
   Constantinople. His insistence on literal interpretation of the Sacred Scriptures
   establishes him as one of their greatest expositors, and his eloquent homiletic
   style earned him the name 'golden-mouthed.'
87 Some of which he dedicated to Jean, cardinal of Lorraine (Ep 1841) and the
   others to Nicolas Wary, principal of the Collegium Trilingue in Louvain (Ep
   1856).
88 See Ep 1731 from Charles v.
89 Mercurino Gattinara (CEBR II 76–80), imperial chancellor to Charles v, who had
   tried to silence Erasmus' Louvain opponents, presents in Ep 1757 his vision
   of Christendom as fragmented into three parties – the Romanists, the Erasmians, and the Lutherans – and concludes that only the Erasmians could establish a true reform of its current ills. Gattinara's description of the papal
   party 'with its ears blocked and its mental vision blinded, [which] sticks to the
   pope whether his judgments and decrees are good or bad' (lines 12–13) caused
   Valdés to criticize Erasmus for sending a copy of Ep 1757 to Maldonado (see
   the introduction). Erasmus had not yet received the chancellor's Ep 1785.
90 Lorenzo Campeggi, a senior diplomat in papal service. The letter is not extant;
   but see Ep 1806:37.

Jean de Carondelet as St Donatian
Jan Gossaert, also known as Mabuse or Maubuse
Collection Musée des Beaux-Arts de Tournai

that I noticed had been omitted, most of them through the carelessness of copyists and printers.[91]

1806 / To Jean (II) de Carondelet   Basel, 30 March 1527

Although this letter was included in the *Opus epistolarum* (1529), the posthumous *Opera* (1538) was the first edition to assign it this date, probably from the similarity of its contents to Epp 1805 and 1807.

Jean (II) de Carondelet (1469–1545) was not only archbishop of Palermo from 1519 (an appointment contested by Tommaso de Vio [Cajetanus], who refused to resign that position, previously given to him) but also one of the highest officials in the imperial council of the Netherlands of Charles v. He was the provost of the collegiate church of St Donatian in Bruges, where he is buried. A little-known likeness by Jan Gossaert (*dit* Mabuse or Maubuse), now in the Musée des Beaux-Arts in Tournai, portrays him as St Donatian, wearing cope and mitre and holding the saint's legendary attribute, a cartwheel with burning candles (see 48 illustration); the image is reminiscent of Jan Van Eyck's portrait of the saint (1436), which graced the church during Carondelet's time. Erasmus had dedicated to him his edition of St Hilary (Basel: Froben 1523), and both the edition and the dedicatory letter (Ep 1334) contained propositions that his opponents considered heretical. On Carondelet see CEBR I 272–3.

ERASMUS OF ROTTERDAM TO JEAN DE CARONDELET,
ARCHBISHOP OF PALERMO, GREETING

Reverend Lord Bishop, I have already expressed my thanks for the support you have shown me, and I am indeed greatly in your debt. It is not my own cause that I plead today,[1] since I consider it hopeless, but rather I commend to you the cause of learning. As I discern in the letters of many, a Carmelite in Mechelen named Paschasius rants publicly from the pulpit against the study of languages and good letters,[2] and specifically against the Collegium Trilingue established in Louvain by Jérôme de Busleyden, a man

* * * * *

91 It is not clear to which titles and editions of the *Paraphrases* these remarks apply. See Ep 1807A introduction.

1806
1 Probably the payment of his pension, which was now long in arrears (Epp 1434, 1708)
2 Jan van Paesschen, a Carmelite friar and doctor of theology, took the place of his recently deceased confrère Nicolaas Baechem in publicly attacking Erasmus in Louvain (Ep 1788:28–30); cf CEBR III 39–40.

worthy to be remembered for all ages.[3] Let such busybodies do what they 10
are supposed to do, which is to combat heresy;[4] but to wage war upon these
studies, without which all other disciplines are speechless, crippled, and
blind, is far from the mind of either the pope or the emperor. 'But Philippus
Melanchthon,' they say, 'and several others who know Greek and Hebrew
have rallied to the side of the condemned faction.' That is not the fault of 15
learning but of men; besides, Luther counts more supporters by far among
those who know neither Greek nor Latin. And the great majority of those
trained in these studies are opposed to Luther. In Louvain, I assure you,
there is not one of this category of men who is not totally unsympathetic to
the Lutheran cause. 20

This matter may seem inconsequential to you. But there is a danger
that, if the monks are allowed to do whatever they please with impunity,
this business may break out into a greater turmoil than anyone could imagine. The humanities enjoy great favour everywhere, and their usefulness is
universally acknowledged; they have powerful patrons. Therefore, let those 25
fanatics be content with their victory and not involve the humanities in an
alien cause. If the teaching of languages must be banned because a certain
few of those trained in them have supported a condemned sect, then for the
same reason the teaching of theology must be suppressed because many
theologians have championed this faction, and their number grows from 30
day to day; and monasticism must be suppressed because a great number of monks have taken the side of Luther. The easiest and the best tactic
would be to repress the first onslaughts of these fanatics. If you would not
be averse to doing this, you would have all the devotees of higher learning
in your debt. 35

* * * * *

3 Erasmus had met Busleyden c 1501 in Orléans, where the latter was a student of law. After further studies in Padua, Busleyden began a career in
the imperial service and acquired several ecclesiastical benefices. In 1517,
two days before leaving in the emperor's cortège for Spain (where he
died that same year) he made his will, which provided for the establish-
ment of the Collegium Trilingue. Founded to promote the study of Greek,
Hebrew, and Latin, it was opposed by some traditionalists in the university who favoured scholasticism. Erasmus frequently intervened in its behalf; see de Vocht CTL passim; de Vocht *Jérôme de Busleyden, Founder of the
Louvain Collegium Trilingue: His Life and Writings* (Turnhout 1950); CEBR I
235–7.
4 Since 1523 Jan van Paesschen had belonged to a committee of theologians investigating heresy under the aegis of the inquisitor Frans van der Hulst. He
left a manuscript record – now lost – of his activities; see de Vocht CTL II 341 n5.

I send you copies of the last letter sent to me by the emperor and also those of Chancellor Mercurino and Cardinal Campeggi.[5] 'For what purpose?' you will say. So that in your wisdom you will understand that my fidelity and zeal in the cause of piety has the approbation of the highest leaders of both powers, and so that you will not be in the least influenced by the utterly shameless calumnies of certain individuals. And I am confident that one day the integrity with which I conducted myself in this universal upheaval will become more evident. May the Lord watch over Your Honour.

From Basel, 30 March in the year 1527

1806A / To Nicolas Wary   Basel, 30 March 1527

> Allen numbered this letter 1806A because its existence came to light only after his volume VII was at press. The printer thus tipped it in as pages 24a and 24b. It is held as MS 121 A 27 by the Royal Library, The Hague, which acquired it in September 1927 in an exchange with the Jesuit Fathers of Maastricht. Autograph throughout, it has stains and serious fraying on its right side, where the ink – seriously faded – has been only partially restored by chemical intervention. Allen therefore had to resort to editorial speculation in several places.
>
> Nicolas Wary, of Marville (formerly in Luxembourg, now in the French department of Meurthe-et-Moselle), was present at the founding of the Collegium Trilingue in 1517. He became its second president in 1526, and was on familiar terms with Erasmus. His delegation to Rome in June 1522 to defend the university's privileges in nominating scholars to benefices almost failed when Pope Adrian VI died, but Erasmus intervened successfully on his behalf (Epp 1481, 1509). Wary died on 2 October 1529. See CEBR III 432.

Best greetings. I hear that you are seeking to appoint a new professor of Greek.[1] I hope it will turn out for the best. A certain Spartanus wrote to me in Greek from Rome, and he composed the letter impromptu in the presence of my friend Hovius, who said that he also knew Latin.[2] He says that

* * * * *

5 On these letters of support see Ep 1805 nn88–90.

1806A
1 The incumbent Rutgerus Rescius, who had held the chair in Greek since 1 September 1518, had recently married and moved out of the college. This made it impossible for him to fulfil the terms of his contract, which provided for supervision of student life as well as teaching.
2 Johannes Hovius, a former secretary and copyist for Erasmus (Ep 1762:4 and n2). The 'certain Spartanus' has not been identified.

he would be content with a modest remuneration; still, it is dangerous to   5
hire strangers. He might possibly bring with him personal traits that could
undermine the whole cause of letters. If you do not have anyone who is
clearly superior to Rutgerus, I think you would act more wisely if for the
time being you pretended not to take notice of his young wife.[3] It is easier to find another than to find a better.[4] Rutgerus is already well known   10
and well liked by the students. And the situation of the college is still precarious. Novelty often brings unexpected ills in its train. So, unless you are
motivated by more grave reasons than the matter of the wife, I think nothing should be changed right away. But if there are other things that incline
you to this decision, I pray that what you decide will be favourable to good   15
learning and to the college.

At the same time Rescius must be advised to make up for the disadvantage of taking a wife by his assiduity in teaching,[5] which I am certain
he will do. Moreover, were I not aware that you have done so up to now
with diligence and success, I should urge all of you, through irreproach-   20
able conduct and zealous teaching, to bring commendation to every branch
of learning. That is the only way the Zoiluses,[6] these carping critics who
envy excellence rather than emulate it, can be driven to hang themselves.
For you understand that you are acting out an important role in full view
of the whole world, and this is what you are doing in very fact. In a drama   25
like this you must not give way to sleep, since it is being played out not
only before spectators of our own age but also before those of the future.

* * * * *

3 On the problem of Rescius' marriage see Ep 1768 n10. Erasmus, who defended
   marriage even for clerics in major orders, would have considered the rule of
   celibacy for teachers unreasonable. At the same time, he understood the position of the college and urged Rescius to be ever more diligent in his duties (Ep
   1882:44–52). Wary followed Erasmus' advice and retained Rescius. Five years
   later, however, when Rescius took on other duties extraneous to the college to
   increase his income, Erasmus would judge that the Collegium Trilingue had
   erred in permitting Rescius to marry and to live outside its precincts (Allen
   Ep 2644:26–7).
4 This line reproduces the sentiments of Conradus Goclenius on the affair (Ep
   1768:68).
5 In line 9 above Erasmus referred to Rescius' wife as *uxorcula* 'the little wife.'
   Here, where we would expect the term *uxor*, he calls her *Eva*, perhaps recalling
   that, just as in Genesis Eve was both a 'helpmate' to Adam and the source of
   his fall, so Rescius' taking a wife was both an advantage to him and a potential
   cause of losing his job; see Ep 1882:3–26.
6 The original Zoilus was a sophist who had the audacity to attack Homer. His
   name therefore became synonymous with any harsh critic; cf *Adagia* II v 8.

When the disciplines of higher learning will blossom forth, corrected and refined, among theologians, lawyers, doctors, philosophers, mathematicians, and grammarians; when the courts of princes will be more richly adorned   30
with men distinguished for their eloquence and learning; when Chrysostom, Athanasius, Basil, and others of this company will begin to speak in their own tongue to the Latin world, then your names will be celebrated by the applause of learned men as the leaders and founders of a most splendid achievement. Wherefore it behoves you all the more to bring about a unity   35
of purpose in the attention given to teaching and to sanctity of life, without which mighty ventures crumble[7] and with which the humblest enterprises prosper. Diversity of tongues matters not to those of like mind. The confusion of tongues put an end to the tower of Babel,[8] while the church was built up by those speaking various languages, but with the same spirit.   40

Be assured that your upright manner of life endears you to me more than scarcely any other. Give my greetings to that Hebrew scholar with the gloomy face but cheerful heart – how like a Greek in all things save for that beard flowing to his waist.[9] Were each of you to take a wife, the college would expand more quickly! I pray for its abundant success. Please convey   45
my fond greetings to our common protector, the lord Gilles de Busleyden.[10]
Given at Basel, 30 March in the year 1527

Erasmus of Rotterdam, in my own hand

To the most honoured Master Nicolas of Marville, president of the college of Busleyden, in Louvain   50

1807 / To Alfonso de Valdés   Basel, 31 March 1527

Alfonso, elder brother of the more famous Juan de Valdés, was the Latin secretary of Charles v from c 1522 to his death from the plague in 1532 in Vienna. His letters are therefore a first-hand source for political and religious matters in Spain. By 1526 he was also the 'imperial secretary' to Chancellor Mercurino Gattinara. He became Erasmus' most enthusiastic supporter at court, but urged him to use moderation when dealing with members of religious orders. He is said to have promoted the moderate tone of the Augsburg Confession (1530), and he arranged for its reading in the presence of Em-

* * * * *

7 Sallust *Bellum Iugurthinum* 10.6
8 Gen 11:1–9
9 Probably Jan van Campen, professor of Hebrew at the Collegium Trilingue since 1521
10 The brother of the college's founder; see Ep 1802 n4 above.

peror Charles v; see *Bibliotheca Wiffeniana: Spanish Reformers of Two Centuries from 1520* ed Edward Boehmer, 3 vols (Strasbourg and London 1874–1904; repr New York 1963) 63–7. As a loyal imperialist he defended the sack of Rome (Ep 1839 n22). He wrote treatises, Erasmian in their style, to criticize ecclesiastical abuses. See further CEBR III 366–8; ER VI 206.

This letter, first published in the *Opus epistolarum* (1529), will be answered by Ep 1839. For the texts of eighty-five letters of his correspondence see Caballero *Valdés* 287–483.

ERASMUS OF ROTTERDAM TO ALFONSO DE VALDÉS, GREETING
I received, albeit with some delay, a very friendly letter from his Majesty the emperor together with several other dispatches, including one no less courteous from Mercurino Gattinara, whose wise and trustworthy advice I have determined to follow.[1] As to your salutary devotion and zeal towards   5
me, my excellent young man,[2] they are well known to me and confirmed by many clear proofs; and if my powers were equal to my intentions you would perceive that you have by no means conferred so many services upon an ungrateful person. This is all I can write at the present moment. To all my patrons I earnestly beseech you to express thanks on my behalf. Farewell.   10
Given at Basel, 31 March in the year 1527

1807A / To the Pious Reader   Basel, March 1527

This short letter appears on the first of four unnumbered pages in the omnibus volume *Supputationes in censuris Natalis Bedae,* dated by its colophon: 'Basileae, apud Joan. Frob. an. MDXXVII men. martio.' This rare volume, conserved in the Centre for Reformation and Renaissance Studies, Victoria University, Toronto, contains four different books or tracts written against Noël Béda's censures of Erasmus' works (see Ep 1804 n14). Unlike Erasmus' other letters 'to the pious reader,' this one (like Ep 1895A) appears neither in Allen nor in LB. It thus appears here for the first time in a modern edition.

The letter is a short introduction to three pages of errata and corrections to an unspecified printing (or printings) of some of Erasmus' *Paraphrases* on the New Testament. For the paraphrase on Matthew's Gospel Erasmus acknowl-

* * * * *

1807
1 Cf Epp 1731 from Charles v and Ep 1757 from Gattinara. Valdés criticized Erasmus for sending copies of these two letters to Maldonado; see Ep 1805 introduction.
2 Valdés was about twenty-seven years old.

edges twenty-two misprints or corrections; on Mark only one; on Luke eight; and on the Gospel of John only one. One single correction is listed for each of the *Paraphrases* on Romans, first Corinthians, and Philippians.

At the time of writing this letter, Erasmus had just completed *Supputatio errorum in censuris Bedae* (LB IX 415–702), his longest, most detailed response to Noël Béda's *Annotationes*, which consisted largely of criticism of his *Paraphrases*. It can therefore be presumed that Béda was the enemy foremost in Erasmus' thoughts as he composed this letter and the list of errors and corrections to the *Paraphrases* that accompany it.

ERASMUS OF ROTTERDAM TO THE PIOUS READER, GREETING
The good service that my friends should have rendered has been rendered to some degree by my enemies, whose hostile prejudice has made my *Paraphrases* more acceptable even to myself. For when I see that in their malicious passion to find fault no other errors could be detected, I feel that my involve- 5
ment in this labour has turned out to be quite successful. And I think that I responded adequately to their false accusations, except in the case of those who refuse to be satisfied, after the example of the asp, which wisely blocks its ears to the voice of the snake-charmer. But whatever lapses of the printers or the copiers or of my own pen have occurred I shall make note of here 10
so that it will be easier for anyone who so wishes to emend his own copy.

1808 / From Theophrastus Paracelsus [Basel, c March 1527]

Allen dated this letter and Ep 1809 to March 1527 on the basis of similar medical complaints voiced by Erasmus in Epp 1804 and 1805 and especially on Paracelsus' cure of Johann Froben early in 1527 (Ep 1809:22–4). Charles B. Schmitt (CEBR III 50) believed that Allen mistakenly reversed their order: that the present letter should be seen as Paracelsus' response to Erasmus' Ep 1809. The difference may well depend on whether Erasmus' phrase – 'As to the third matter, I do not understand it; but your analysis seems plausible' (Ep 1809:11–13) – should be seen to precede, or to respond to, Paracelsus' phrase, 'The third element – I speak as plainly as I can' (Ep 1808:13).

Theophrastus Philippus Aureolus Bombastus (c 1493–1541), sometimes called Theophrastus von Hohenheim, was the son of a physician at Einsiedeln in Switzerland. His assumed name 'Paracelsus' perhaps derives from his notion of surpassing (*para*) the second-century Roman medical author Celsus, whom Paracelsus preferred to Hippocrates, Galen, and later authorities. Reports that he had practised medicine in Venice, in Scandinavia, and in the Middle East are probably without foundation. He narrowly avoided prosecution in Salzburg for supporting the Peasants' War of 1525, and he showed

FAMOSO·DOCTOR PARESELSVS

Paracelsus
Attributed to Quinten Metsys
Musée du Louvre, Paris
Cliché des Musées Nationaux, Paris

sympathy for certain heterodox theological opinions. He met Erasmus in the winter and spring of 1526–7 when he came to Basel to treat Johann Froben. Appointed town physician there, he broke academic conventions by giving lectures in the Swiss-German dialect rather than in Latin. He rejected Hippocrates' and Galen's view of disease as a disorder of the humoral balance, and instead proposed the theory that the human body is composed of mineral and chemical principles, and that its ailments must be treated with chemical therapeutic remedies. See Walter Pagel *Paracelsus: An Introduction to Philosophical Medicine in the Era of the Renaissance* 2nd ed (Basel 1982). The most authoritative edition of his works is *Sämtliche Werke* part 1: *Medizinische, naturwissenschaftliche und philosophische Schriften* ed Kurt Goldammer 14 vols (Berlin 1922–33; 2nd ed with index volume Einsiedeln 1960). German translations of this letter and the next are provided in *Paracelsus: Sämtliche Werke* ed Bernhard Aschner, 4 vols (Jena 1926–32; repr Bischofswiesen 1993) I 936–7.

This letter was first published in Paracelsus' *Collectanea* (Basel 1568–9), but with many misreadings, corrected by Allen, of the manuscript (Wrocław, University Library MS Rehdiger 254 151).

The things which my sapient muse and my study of salts have divulged to me cry out clearly from within me.[1] I am the undisputed master of diagnoses of this kind. The region of the liver has no need of drugs; nor do the other two symptoms require laxatives. Rather, the remedy is a mysterious but potent elixir, consisting of a specific fortifier and abstergents (that is, consolidants) 5 made of honey. It is a concoction that makes up for deficiencies of the liver.

Second. As far as treatments for fattiness of the kidneys are concerned, I have kingly remedies of proven efficacy. I know that your delicate physique

* * * * *

1808

1 Eduard Schubert and Karl Sudhoff believe Paracelsus uses the Latin *sagax musa* and the puzzling term *Alstoos* as personifications of deities relating to his scientific theories about salts. They interpret *Alstoos* as a bold derivation from the Greek *als* (salt) meaning *Salzkünderin* or *salzkundige Muse*, that is, a muse which has knowledge about salts; *Paracelsus-Forschungen. Eine historischkritische Untersuchung. Zweites Heft. Handschriftliche Documente zur Lebensgeschichte Theophrasts von Hohenheim* (Frankfurt-am-Main: Reitz and Koehler 1889) 108. During this period of his life Paracelsus considered salt as a third principle beside sulphur and mercury, and in this letter he elaborates about the treatment of stones or salts coagulating in the kidneys and urinary tract. (I am grateful to Dr Urs Leo Gantenbein, director of the Paracelsus-Projekt, Medizinhistorisches Institut der Universität Zürich, for help with this note.)

cannot tolerate the colocynths of Mesue[2] or anything of a cathartic nature – not even a minimum dosage of a purgative. I know that I am quite proficient and skilled in my art, and understand what is efficacious to ensure for your frail body a long, tranquil, and healthy life. You need not resort to enemas.

The third ailment – I speak as plainly as I can – results from some morbid matter or other, either an ulcerated putrefaction, a congenital presence of phlegm, or something contracted by accident; perhaps a sediment in the urine or tartar in the vas deferens or a mucinous substance from sperm residue; or perhaps a viscous nutrient humour, a dissolved, oil-like fattiness, or something of that sort, occurring through the action of salt, which has coagulating powers, just as in flint or, rather, in beryl. The origin of your ailment is akin to this, but it is not congenital, according to my observations. Whatever opinion I have given about the marble-like particulate deposits in the kidneys themselves I have diagnosed under the heading of coagulated substances.

If, most estimable Erasmus, this specific diagnosis is to your Excellency's liking, I shall see that you have both doctor and medicine. Farewell.

Theophrastus

To the renowned patron of theologians, Master Erasmus of Rotterdam, most learned of all men and dearest friend

1809 / To Theophrastus Paracelsus   [Basel, c March 1527]

According to Allen, this letter answers Ep 1808; but Charles B. Schmitt (CEBR III 50) proposed that the order of the two letters should be reversed. This one was published for the first time in a posthumous edition of Paracelsus' *De gradibus* (Mulhouse: Petrus Fabricius 1562). Allen used a copy contained in a sixteenth-century manuscript collection of Paracelsus' papers now conserved in the Österreichische Nationalbibliothek, Vienna. For the dating of the letters see the introduction to Ep 1808.

ERASMUS OF ROTTERDAM TO MASTER THEOPHRASTUS OF
EINSIEDELN, ETC, GIFTED MASTER OF THE ART OF MEDICINE,
GREETING

It would not be inappropriate in addressing a doctor, through whom God secures for us the health of the body, to wish for him the everlasting health

* * * * *

2 Perhaps Johannes ibn Mesue, whose work *De consolatione medicinarum simplicium solutivarum* had been printed several times. The name could likewise apply to Yuhanna Ibn Massawayh, a ninth-century author of the tracts *Antidotarium* and *Methodus medicamenta purgantia*.

of the soul. I am utterly astonished how you could know me so well after seeing me but once. That your enigmatic pronouncements give an accurate diagnosis I recognize not from the art of medicine, which I have never learned,
but from my own poor senses. For some time now I have felt pain in the
region of the liver, but I could not imagine what was the source of the trou-   10
ble. The fat in my kidneys I noticed from my urine several years ago. As
to the third matter,[1] I do not quite understand it; but your analysis seems
plausible.

As I told you, for several days I have had no time to get sick, to be
treated, or to die – so overwhelmed am I by the burden of my studies. Nev-   15
ertheless if there is anything that can alleviate my malady short of destroying this frail body of mine, I beg you to communicate it to me. And if you
would be so kind as to explain in greater detail what you jotted down in
so few words with such succinctness, and would prescribe other remedies
which I may take when I have the time, I cannot promise you compensation   20
equal to your skill and your solicitude, but a grateful heart I surely promise.

You have called back Froben, my other half, from the world below.[2] If
you can also restore me to health, in each of us singly you will have restored
us both. May it be our good fortune that you remain in Basel!

I am afraid you may not be able to decipher these words written on   25
the spur of the moment. Farewell.

Erasmus of Rotterdam, in his own hand

1810 / From Jan Antonin   Cracow, 1 April 1527

This letter (Ep 65 in Förstemann-Günther), which lacks the address sheet, is
autograph throughout. It was in the Burscher Collection in Leipzig (on which
see Ep 1254 introduction). Of the many letters Antonin wrote to Erasmus only
this one and Epp 1660 and 3137 are extant.

Jan Antonin of Košice, a city in present-day Slovakia, had served as Erasmus' physician in Basel in 1523–4, and Erasmus claimed that no one else had
been able to relieve his pain so well (Epp 1512, 1564). He became physician
to Polish bishops and to King Sigismund I, and promoted Erasmus and humanistic studies in Cracow; see Ep 1602 introduction and CEBR I 63–4.

* * * * *

1809
1 See Ep 1808:13–19.
2 Johann Froben, Erasmus' printer of choice, made a brief recovery from the
   illness for which Paracelsus treated him in 1526 and was able to travel to the
   Frankfurt book fair (Ep 1875:26), but he died after a seizure and fall in October
   1527 (Ep 1900:113–16).

I greatly treasure, as I ought, the book of Galen and the letters your Excellency has sent to me,[1] for in my view these riches far surpass those bestowed on Callicrates.[2] With greater reason, then, would I aspire to your majestic style, Erasmus, greatest ornament to all the world and most dear to me personally, so that I might fittingly express how magnificent is this gift which your Excellency has lavished upon me. Do not think that this dedication was any less gratifying to me, coming after so many other most honorific references, by which you have drawn me from the shadows into the full light of day.[3] May Christ grant that my shortcomings never give you cause for embarrassment.[4] I for my part have ardently striven as far as I could to live up to your commendations of me. Indeed because of you my efforts up to now give me confidence that a solid foundation has been laid for an upright and honourable life among men who by word, affection, and acts of kindness hold me in high esteem – thanks be to God and to you. And the future looked bright for me in Hungary until it suffered this transformation[5] of which, I think, our friend Ursinus and Piso have painted you a fair picture, so that I need not repeat it.[6]

* * * * *

1810
1 Erasmus dedicated to Antonin his translation of three treatises from the Aldine Greek edition of Galen (Basel: Johann Froben, May 1526). See Ep 1698 introduction. Of letters sent previously to Antonin only Ep 1698 survives.
2 Alexander the Great entrusted to Callicrates the treasures he found at Susa (Quintus Curtius *History of Alexander* 5.2.17). The phrase 'bestowed on Callicrates' is rendered in Greek.
3 Erasmus had praised Antonin to Johann Botzheim in Ep 1341A:1820–32 and to Alexius Thurzo in Ep 1572:35–48. Both letters had been circulated in epistolary collections. Epp 1512 (to Rudbert von Mosham) and 1564 (to Heinrich Stromer), which likewise contain praise of Antonin, had not yet appeared in print.
4 Horace *Epistles* 1.18.77
5 Expressed in Greek. Antonin must refer to the disastrous defeat of the Hungarian army by the Ottoman forces of Suleiman I at Mohács on 29 August 1526. In it 16,000 Christian soldiers – nearly 80 per cent of the Hungarian army – fell in battle, among them King Louis II himself, two archbishops, five bishops, twenty-eight magnates, and five hundred noblemen. Antonin's personal fortune changed in that his friend Ursinus' appointment as historian of Ferdinand of Hapsburg left him politically opposed to Antonin, who supported Ferdinand's rival King John Zápolyai as successor to the Hungarian throne.
6 Caspar Ursinus Velius, a Silesian-born poet and jurist, and Erasmus had exchanged letters since 1517, when Ursinus composed a poem in Erasmus' honour. After visiting Erasmus in Basel in 1521, he moved on to Freiburg, where he studied under Udalricus Zasius (Epp 1252, 1266). In 1522 he described his journey down the Danube to Vienna in a verse letter to Erasmus (Ep 1280A).

Suleiman the Magnificent
Albrecht Dürer, silverpoint drawing, dated 1526
Musée Bonnat, Bayonne

But concerning the present situation in Hungary you will learn of it
from Krzycki and your good patron Jan Łaski,[7] unless you should wish also
to hear what my Josephus writes to me from the court of King John (whose   20
image is on the coinage):[8] that he is a king so blessed with fortune and
endowed with such admirable wisdom as to be able to hold the threats of
Ferdinand in open contempt. There is hope that our palatine in Cracow will

* * * * *

Another letter to Erasmus, mentioned in Ep 1825:5–6, is not extant. On Ursinus Velius see Ep 1280A introduction, Ep 11825 n1, and CEBR III 356–7; his
recent change of fortune is mentioned in the preceding note. For a later letter
from him see Ep 1917.
No letter of Jacobus Piso to Erasmus is extant for this period. Piso, whose
house in Buda had become a centre of humanistic influence, had been a friend
and correspondent of Erasmus since 1509. The death at Mohács of King Louis
II, who had been Piso's pupil, the loss of his house at Buda, and the increasing threat of Turkish hegemony cast him into a deep depression and affected
his health. In March 1527 he died at Wrocław (Ep 1917:79–80), shortly before
Antonin wrote this letter. See CEBR III 94–5.
7 Andrzej Krzycki was bishop of Przemyśl and provost of St Florian at Cracow.
  On him see Ep 1822 introduction. On Łaski see Ep 1821 introduction.
8 Josephus Tectander, Antonin's brother-in-law, had visited Basel with Antonin
  in 1524 and was with him in Hungary in the spring of 1527 (CEBR III 313–14).
  John Zápolyai of Transylvania was elected king of Hungary by the nobles of
  the land in October 1526 after the defeat and death of King Louis II at Mohács.
  Their choice was not recognized by the Hapsburgs, whose dynastic arrange-
  ments with the late King Louis II had left Hungary to Prince Ferdinand. The
  latter invaded Hungary shortly after the time of this letter, driving Zápolyai to
  seek the protection of the Turks, who restored him to the throne. King John's
  image appeared in fact only on the coronation *dreifacher Goldgulden* (November
  1526), which bears the image of a crowned and bearded Zápolyai, encircled
  by the inscription IOANNES.I.REX.UNGARIE. Its reverse portrays the 'Zápolyan
  wolf' in the foreground with a patriarchal cross and the Hungarian shield in
  the background, all encircled by the inscription DEXTERA.DEI.FACIT.VIRTVTEM;
  cf Ladislaus Réthy *Corpus nummorum Hungariae* (Budapest 1899; repr Graz
  1958) 124 no 320 and Table XLV. The *Catalogus numorum Hungariae ac Transilva-
  niae instituti nationalis szécjéyiani* (Pécs 1807) III 129 describes it as 'very rare.'
  All of the thirty-three later issues of coins struck by Zápolyai from 1527 to
  1540 portray the Virgin and child Jesus on the obverse and either St Ladislaus
  or the Hungarian shield on the reverse; see Artur Pohl *Ungarishe Goldgulden
  des Mittelalters (1325–1540)* (Graz 1974) Tables 55–9, and his *Münzzeichen und
  Meisterzeichen* (Graz and Budapest 1982). The uniface thaler suggested by P.S.
  Allen, following William C. Hazlitt in *Coinage of the European Continent* (London 1893; repr 1974) 345, was struck not by Zápolyai but by his successor
  John Sigismund. The annotator is grateful to Allen G. Berman, numismatist,
  for help with this note.

The dreifacher Goldgulden (November 1526)
Obverse: image of John Zápolyai
Reverse: image of Zápolyan wolf, a patriarchal cross, and the Hungarian shield
Kunsthistorisches Museum, Vienna

allay the fervour of those princes who are stirring up war, and we are confident that through his influence an accord will finally be reached between   25
Ferdinand and the king of Hungary. He has already been sent to Prague to
confer with Ferdinand, and he will leave no stone unturned in order to arrive at agreement with all diplomacy.[9] For unless Ferdinand will yield to
the best course of action, Moravia will surely be in dire straits together with
Austria, having to face this summer a heat wave that may prove quite un-   30
pleasant: the Turks themselves – a curse upon them! For us there is also the
multiform image of death[10] represented by the Tartars; and yet, wretched
creatures that we are, we sleep on a cargo of salt.[11]

I read the letter of the merchant to the Carthusian. I had myself a good
laugh at that witty remark about the tanner who said that Noël Béda himself   35
should be flayed alive, so as to procure the hide of an ass big enough to cover
not one but many volumes. If only Christian princes would listen to the sane
advice of that thrice-greatest merchant! then we would all come to our senses
at the same time.[12] I am eager to know to what extent Thurzo has shown
you his gratitude;[13] he will soon be returning here to his old haunts, as you   40

* * * * *

9 Krzysztof Szydłowiecki (see Ep 1593) stressed to Ferdinand the joint threat
   from the Tartars and the Turks. Two days before this letter was written, the
   embassy had already failed to produce the desired results. Ep 1917:23–5 suggests that Szydłowiecki's direction and handling of it gave offence in Hungary.
10 Virgil *Aeneid* 2.369. The subsequent mention of the Tartars evokes their peren-
   nial menace to Christian eastern Europe. Just two months before this letter
   was written their invasion of Lithuania had been repulsed (Ep 1803 n10).
11 A cargo of salt is easily spoiled by bilge water; see *Adagia* I vii 81. Antonin
   implies that, despite the dangerous times in which we live, we continue our
   idle and careless manner.
12 Erasmus often received and sometimes passed on in letters to others similar *fabulae* or *loquaces nugae.* Cf Ep 1773:6–13 for the story about Béda and
   Duke George of Saxony's reaction; on Béda see Ep 1804 n14. The Carthusian
   lampooned in the story is probably Pierre Cousturier, the French theologian
   whom, of all his critics, Erasmus held most in contempt; on him see Ep 1804
   n65. The lampoon in question here has not been identified, and the meaning of
   'thrice-greatest' (*ter maximi*) for the merchant is not clear. In Ep 1773:1 Hieronymus Emser applied the same expression, translated there as 'thrice-mighty,'
   to Erasmus himself.
13 That is, in return for Erasmus' dedication to him of a Greek edition, with
   facing Latin translation, of two treatises by Plutarch (Epp 1572, 1602). Erasmus apparently never received the gift in return from Thurzo that Antonin
   hopes for here; cf Epp 1660, 1825, 1916. Alexius (Elek) Thurzo had become
   enormously wealthy through a long career in mining and financial service to
   King Louis II of Hungary and his wife Queen Mary of Austria, whom Thurzo

might surmise. Henckel has deserted his mistress; when she invited him
to Bratislava he failed to go – this so as not to arouse the wrath of King
John. The latter has shown great affection for my friend Henckel since his
earliest childhood, and now he is even offering him a bishopric, which this
fellow in his total lack of ambition seems to disregard. But you will learn   45
of this more fully in his letter.[14] It was our solemn resolve to pay a visit to
your Excellency this month. Henckel had arrived from Košice, and we were
preparing for our departure. But on the second day after his arrival he was
suddenly summoned back by a letter sent from the city of Košice, stating
that the king did not approve of his departure at that time, since the affairs   50
of state were not yet put in order, and many similar inanities.

Your Excellency will learn the remaining details from Severinus,[15]
bearer of this letter, a young man born for study, who spent the greater
part of the winter at my house. I did not think that I should commit everything to paper. There is one thing that I beg of your Excellency repeatedly   55
in the name of Christ: that you would dedicate your divine talent to translating into Latin the best and more useful of the remaining books of Galen,
if you have not the time to give your attention to all of them. You should see
how I have nearly worn out through constant use the pages of the book you
sent me as a gift. It is not so much Galen's book as it is yours, for it is, as I   60
recorded right on the title page, 'more precious than any precious gold';[16]
and together with your letters it forms the most valued part of my trea-
sured possessions. I have bought myself another copy, and it too undergoes
daily wear and tear, to my great profit.

* * * * *

helped to flee from Buda after the battle of Mohács. He was a loyal supporter
of the Hapsburgs and worked for the cause of Ferdinand as king of Hungary.
See CEBR III 322–3.

14 The letter is not extant. Johann Henckel of Levoča became court chaplain to
Queen Mary, wife of King Louis II of Hungary. After the battle of Mohács, he
left her entourage but refused a bishopric offered by the new anti-Hapsburg
King John Zápolyai. In 1528, Henckel rejoined her service and became her
confessor. See Epp 1672 introduction, 1803:49–57, 1810:41–51, 1825:24–6, Allen
Ep 2011:27–30, and CEBR II 175–6. In Erasmus' time Bratislava, the capital of
current-day Slovakia, was in Hungary and was known as Pozsony. Situated on
the Danube near the Austrian frontier, it became the capital of the Hapsburg
part of Hungary after the Turks captured Buda (1541). The Germans call it
Pressburg.

15 Severinus Olpeius, a messenger. Upon returning to Poland, he carried letters from Erasmus and Bonifacius Amerbach (cf Epp 1915:49–50, 1916:10–11),
which do not survive.

16 Apparently inscribed by Antonin in his own hand

Concerning Cratander's edition of Hippocrates,[17] good God! how clear-   65
ly it reveals the callow mind of Calvo who so badly translated such a good
doctor.[18] The truth is that all of them, except for those by Brenta, Cop, and
Leoniceno, are so insipid.[19] They have no life; they would, however, if you
were to translate them.

Enough on this subject. I have been summoned to serve as King John's   70
doctor. I should not like to bargain my safety together with my freedom, and
I am debating seriously not so much what would be more expedient as what
would be more salutary. Therefore I seek counsel from your Excellency with
all possible earnestness. Your Excellency would be able to give the sanest
advice; no one will know of it but me, and I shall do all in my power to   75
show my gratitude. May Christ preserve you and render efficacious for us
all the salutary things you write. My little wife commends herself sincerely
to your Excellency,[20] and I devote myself entirely to you, my master and
father, after God my guiding principle, worthy of all honour and respect.

* * * * *

17 *Hippocratis Coi medicorum ... principis, opera: quibus maxima ex parte annorum
   circiter duo millia Latina caruit lingua: Graeci vero & Arabes, & prisci nostri medici
   ... nunc tandem per M. Fabium Rhavennatem, Gulielmum Copum Basiliensem,
   Nicolaum Leonicenum, & Andreas Brentium, viros doctissimos Latinitate donata, ac
   iamprimum in lucem aedita* (Basel: Andreas Cratander, August 1526). It proved
   to be more reputable than Antonin credits it here.
18 Marco Fabio Calvo of Ravenna was the first to translate into Latin the complete works of Hippocrates of Cos (b 460 BC): *Hippocratis octoginta volumina,
   quibus maxima ex parte ... Graeci vero, Arabes, et prisci nostri medici, plurimis tamen
   utilibus praetermissis, scripta sua illustrarunt* (Rome: Francesco Calvo 1525). Johann von Vlatten had sent this work to Erasmus in the hope that it would benefit his health (Ep 1912:1–8). Antonin's low opinion of Calvo was not shared
   by most; see *Dizionario biografico degli Italiani* 43 (Rome 1993) 723–7. In his reply
   to Antonin (Ep 1825) Erasmus will confuse Marco Fabio Calvo, the translator,
   with Francesco Giulio Calvo, the printer; they were apparently not related. In
   May 1526 the Aldine press published the Greek *editio princeps* of sixty texts
   attributed to Hippocrates. Founded on poor manuscripts, this Aldine edition
   had little lasting value (Antoine Renouard *Annales de l'imprimerie des Alde, ou
   histoire des trois Manuce et de leurs éditions* 3rd ed (Paris 1834; repr 1953) 102.
19 The translations of Hippocrates into Latin by Andrea Brenta of Padua (d 1484)
   predate this letter by almost fifty years, but a Paris edition appeared from the
   press of Henri (1) Estienne on 20 April 1518 (Moreau *Inventaire* II 477 no 1874).
   Guillaume Cop's translations of Hippocrates appeared in Paris from the press
   of Henri (1) Estienne c 1512 and were reissued in 1516 (Moreau *Inventaire* II 137
   no 359, 380 no 1400). Some authors speak of Niccolò Leoniceno's translations at
   the Aldine press beginning in 1514; these do not appear in Antoine Renouard
   Annales de l'imprimerie des Alde 3rd ed (Paris 1834; repr 1953) 102.
20 Anna Zimmermann, daughter of a Cracow goldsmith, Jan Zimmermann

Cracow, 1 April 1527   80
Ever obliged to your Excellency, Jan Antonin, doctor

I commend to your Excellency Martin Dobergast,[21] a man of unblem-
ished life, preacher in Cracow, admirer of your works, and great herald of
your fame, a man of great learning and moral rectitude beyond reproach,
whose acquaintance I made but recently.   85

There are many others who beseech me to recommend them to you,
but I hold them suspect, and rightly so. They pretend to be great trumpeters
of your praises, but this is mere trumpery; for, when they ought to speak
in your behalf, they can barely mutter three words.

Krzycki, the most reverend bishop of Płock, a great friend of your Ex-   90
cellency, has asked me to enclose in my letter to your Excellency his book
On the Sufferings of the Church.[22]

1811 / From Henricus Caduceator   Frankfurt, 18 April 1527

The autograph manuscript of this letter is in the Rehdiger Collection (MS 254
41) of the University Library in Wrocław. Erasmus answered it with Ep 1833.
It was first edited in Enthoven Ep 50.

Apart from his matriculation at the University of Erfurt, Henricus Caduceator of Aschaffenburg is known solely by means of this letter and by
a brief correspondence with Fridericus Nausea; see CEBR I 238. This letter contains seven Greek phrases, doubtless added to inform Erasmus of the writer's
ability in that language, but we have noted only two of them here. Caduceator
posted the letter from Frankfurt, where he travelled to attend the book fair,
but he lived and worked in Mainz.

Greetings. It is not without good reason, most distinguished and most eminent of men, that I, the vilest of creatures, should importune you, such a
great and noble man, with a letter of mine and should burden you with
these trifling and foolish matters, when undoubtedly more pressing duties

* * * * *

21 Martin Dobergast, German-speaking preacher in Cracow, delivered a series
   of sermons in 1524 against Lutheranism. In 1526, he published Pope Leo x's
   bull *Exsurge Domine* (1521) threatening Luther with excommunication, as well
   as the edict of King Sigismund I against the Lutheran movement.
22 *De afflictione ecclesiae, commentarius in Psalmum XXI* (Cracow: Hieronim Wietor,
   January 1527; Rome 1527), which took issue with Luther's *Operatio in Psalmum
   XXI* (1523). It shows a deep concern about the future of Christianity and a
   desire to atone for the author's earlier anticlerical satires. On Krzycki see Ep
   1822 introduction.

demand that you be free from occupying yourself with my concerns. But in   5
virtue of your great kindness, most kind Erasmus, you will show forbearance to your herald[1] in his first mission. I have never written to you, nor
did I have the courage to do so, although the opportunity presented itself to
me, especially some time ago at Erfurt when I was still preparing myself for
public life under the tutelage of my excellent instructor Eobanus Hessus.[2] 10
Nor should I venture to write now, fearing that I might disturb the tranquillity of the worthiest of men, save that necessity, a formidable weapon,
so urgently forced it upon me. You must not imagine that I am writing to
you for a frivolous reason or to gain your attention or your friendship, for
I already enjoy a certain intimacy and familiarity with you through the fre- 15
quent and devoted reading of your works. I am not so light-headed as to
distract great scholars with foolish letters (for from my childhood I have
always regarded them with the utmost awe and reverence, although I am
the most unlearned of men and a complete stranger to the Muses).

But, not to detain or keep you in suspense any longer, give ear to my   20
complaints, I beg you. I shall explain them briefly one by one. The situation is as follows. From my infancy and the earliest years of my life I have
been afflicted with a grievous defect of vision, to such a degree that, unless I bring papers, books, and any smaller items squarely up to my eyes,
my ability to see them falls off sharply, and I can scarcely distinguish any- 25
thing at all. Indeed if the objects towards which my gaze is directed are
even slightly remote, my sight immediately becomes dull and blurred; and
the further removed the object, the weaker it becomes. Truly, my learned
Erasmus, this condition so afflicts my spirit that I have more than once become weary of this present life, and with Virgil's Dido I pray for death   30
and 'tire to gaze upon the vault of heaven.'[3] For what joy can there be in
life for one who is bereft of sight or not much different from a blind man,
since this faculty is such a great boon to wretched mortal men? And when
I see that nature has bestowed this power on all other living things in full

* * * * *

1811
1 Caduceator here translates into Greek his Latin name, which means 'herald
  bearing a staff.'
2 Helius Eobanus Hessus, whose poetic works were greatly esteemed by German humanists, admired Erasmus' principles concerning the reform of education and religion. Appointed to the University of Erfurt, he became strongly
  committed to the reforms of Martin Luther but continued a friendly correspondence with Erasmus (Epp 874, 982, 1498, 2446, 2495). See Carl Krause *Helius Eobanus Hessus, sein Leben und seine Werke* (Gotha 1870; repr Nieuwkoop
  1963); cf CEBR I 434–6.
3 *Aeneid* 4.451

measure, as it were, but hardly a meagre ounce to Caduceator, should I 35
not mourn, dear Erasmus? should I not weep even tears of blood, O noble sir, if it were possible? Should I not justly accuse nature, which created
me without fault or defect in all other endowments of mind and body, for
having left me maimed and mutilated, at least as far as this one precious
faculty is concerned? It is something surely more to be pitied – yes, to be 40
pitied more than to be mentioned: how I was afflicted with sorrow and
mental anguish that often caused me to weep over the injuries and insults
cast my way by insolent and disdainful rogues. Not content with hurling
a single jibe at me, they have called me one-eyed, squint-eyed, blind, myopic; as blind as Hypsea or as a sloughed skin or as Tiresias or as blind as 45
a mole,[4] and whatever other clever witticisms they could fling at a poor,
hapless wretch. 'He lives on darnel'; 'the blind leading the blind'; 'as dim-
sighted as the cave-dwellers'; 'he's got sties in his eyes as big as pumpkins';
'as blear-eyed as a saucepan,'[5] and dozens more along the same lines. I can
usually put up with such raillery, but sometimes I can scarce hold back my 50
tears.

Therefore, most excellent Lord and Master Erasmus, whose years and
grey hair earn you respect, I beg you, by all that you hold holy, by your
very body and soul, I beseech and implore you again and again to deign
to write to me in some detail, explaining whether any medical remedies 55
exist to counter this affliction of the eyes. For my part I know for certain,
having learned it many years ago from a servant of Wolfgang Fabricius
Capito,[6] how you easily surpass all those who practice the art of medicine
there in Basel;[7] indeed you are leagues ahead of them. And how, I ask of

* * * * *

4 Cf *Adagia* I iii 58: *Hypsea caecior*, quoting Horace *Satires* 1.2.91; *Adagia* I iii 57:
  Tiresia caecior, quoting Juvenal 13.249; *Adagia* I iii 55: *Talpa caecior*.
5 Cf *Adagia* II i 29: *Lolio victitant*, quoting Plautus *Miles gloriosus* 321; *Adagia* I
  viii 40: *Caecus caeco dux* (rendered here in Greek), where Erasmus mentions
  its use in the Gospels (Matt 15:14, Luke 6:39); *Adagia* II i 75: *Saturniae lemae*,
  quoting Aristophanes *Plutus* 581; *Adagia* II i 76: *Cucurbitas lippis* (written here
  in Greek), quoting Aristophanes *Clouds* 327; *Adagia* II i 77: *Ollas lippire*.
6 Probably Hartmann von Hallwyl (1503–73), who read the Greek Fathers with
  Capito in Basel and then accompanied him in 1520–1, probably as amanuensis, to Mainz, where he could easily have encountered Caduceator. Hallwyl
  later served the city of Bern, and administered the territory of Aargau for
  Bern from 1563 (CEBR II 159–60). The only other known servant or secretary of
  Capito was Jakob Truchsess von Rheinfelden (CEBR III 348), but his chances of
  having met Caduceator are less probable. These two identifications have been
  suggested by Erika Rummel. For Capito see Ep 1804 n40.
7 Caduceator's attribution of medical science to Erasmus arose perhaps from
  an early composition of Erasmus, *Encomium medicinae* (CWE 29 31–50 / LB I

you, can the cause and remedy for this malady be unknown to you who 60
are familiar with Hippocrates,[8] Galen,[9] Averroës,[10] Celsus[11] and all other
leading writers who profess the art of medicine in their own native tongue?
In fine, most excellent Lord Erasmus, I beg and beseech you, even by the
name of our Saviour Jesus Christ, to make every effort that either through
you or through others learned in medicine I might be restored to full sight; 65
write me in full detail your sound and trustworthy advice. No one will
ever be able to brand me with the charge of ingratitude for such a great
kindness of yours towards me. My undying gratitude will live on after your
death, should fortune grant me a longer life, among all those to whom the
account of your benefaction will be told. Moreover, for no other reason do 70
I long to regain my vision unimpaired than that I might devote my fuller
and unhindered attention to the study of sacred letters and Holy Scripture.
For I seem to have been inclined by nature towards that study, and your
Enchiridion, Methodus, Paraclesis, and *Paraphrases,*[12] and in general all your

* * * * *

537A–544E / ASD I-4 164–86), which first appeared in Dirk Martens' printing of *Declamationes aliquot* (Louvain: 30 March 1518; repr Basel: Froben 1518).
In his reply (Ep 1833) Erasmus concluded that Caduceator thought he was a
physician.
8 The authentic works of Hippocrates (fl fifth century BC) are lost. Many of the
spurious ones differ radically from one copy to the other. For the editions and
translations done in the early sixteenth century see Ep 1810 nn17–19.
9 Galen of Pergamum (AD 129–?199), who rose to become court physician in
Rome during the reign of Marcus Aurelius, had the reputation for excellent
diagnosis and prognosis and for rejecting specialization in favour of general practice. His observations on anatomy were founded on dissection, while
his pathology propagated the doctrine of the four humours. In pharmacology
and dietetic he codified the work of predecessors. Combined with his strong
monotheism, these accomplishments made him the leading medical authority
during the Middle Ages.
10 Averroës (Ibn Rushd; 1126–98) of Córdoba was an important commentator
on Aristotle who influenced the work of early scholastic philosophers, but he
had no reputation in medicine. One may conjecture therefore that Caduceator
intends here Averroës' predecessor Avicenna (Ibn Sīnā; 980–1037), who was
known in Europe as the 'prince of physicians' because he made important
discoveries in both preventive medicine and pathology. His *Quānūm,* a grand
synthesis of the teachings of Hippocrates, Galen, and Dioscorides, was printed
in Latin nearly thirty times.
11 Aulus Cornelius Celsus, a Roman layman writing for laymen during the first
half of the first century. His only works to survive are those that reconstruct
Hellenistic medicine. His Latin became the model of Renaissance writing on
medicine and earned him the name 'Cicero of the doctors.'
12 Caduceator gives the last three titles in Greek. The *Methodus* was the introduction to the 1516 *Novum instrumentum,* which Erasmus amplified considerably as

works of piety, have inspired me with the desire to dedicate myself wholly   75
to this pursuit.

Now, if you wish to know more about me, I shall inform you that I
am from Aschaffenburg, a charming little town in the diocese of Mainz. I
lived for about eight years in Erfurt to complete my education, and there I
was promoted to the baccalaureate, as it is called. At present I am living in   80
Mainz at the home of a worthy nobleman, a steward of Mainz. The name
of this gallant gentleman is Philipp von Schwalbach,[13] whose five well-bred
children I have tutored for almost a year now in the liberal arts.

I had decided to set out for Basel to see you during the fifteen-day
period after the middle of Lent,[14] in order to plead my cause in person, but   85
I was prevented from doing so by a violent fever, accompanied by chills,
which confined me to my bed. I have written this to you at the height of the
Frankfurt fair, with the result that I do not have the leisure to reread it. In
truth, most generous man that you are, up to now I have regarded you as by
far the dearest and best of teachers; hereafter, when you will have carried   90
out my request (as is my fond expectation), what place shall you occupy in
my heart but that of a blessed parent? Be of good health, most excellent of
men and paragon of teachers.[15]

At Frankfurt, on the day in which the solemnity of the Lord's Supper
is celebrated throughout the Christian world,[16] in the year 1527 after the   95
birth of Christ

Forgive my excessive loquacity, excellent sir, my unfinished style (for
it was not possible for me to write anything with careful discernment amidst
the din of the fair), and finally for writing on both sides of the paper.

Henricus Caduceator of Aschaffenburg, tutor to the assistant steward   100
of Mainz

To the universally honoured and most consummate of theologians,
Erasmus of Rotterdam, his most revered teacher

* * * * *

Ratio seu Methodus compendio perveniendi ad veram theologiam (sometimes shortened as *Ratio verae theologiae*) for the second edition, the *Novum Testamentum*
(Basel: Froben, March 1519). He published the *Ratio verae theologiae* separately
the previous year (Louvain: Dirk Martens, November 1518). The *Paraclesis* was
part of the introductory matter of the *Novum Testamentum* of 1519. After that
it was printed separately. Erasmus published paraphrases on every part of the
New Testament except the Apocalypse.

13 Schwalbach was assistant steward of the cathedral chapter of Mainz (line 100
   below; CEBR III 234–5).
14 The forty days of Lent in 1527 ranged from 6 March to 20 April.
15 'Be of good health ... teachers' is rendered in Greek.
16 Maundy Thursday ('Holy Thursday'), which fell in 1527 on 18 April

1812 / From Guillaume Budé   Paris, 22 April 1527

This letter first appeared in the *Opus epistolarum* (1529). Written in Latin but replete with Greek phrases and sentences, it responds to Erasmus' Ep 1794, and will be answered by his Ep 1840.

Guillaume Budé (1468–1540) was the leading humanist in France. After preliminary studies in Paris he went to Orléans, where he studied civil law. He learned Greek under Georgius Hermonymus and Janus Lascaris but was to a great extent autodidact. A number of municipal, judicial, and royal offices provided him with the resources and leisure to pursue the philological studies that were his real passion. The correspondence of nearly fifty letters exchanged between him and Erasmus began in 1516 (Ep 403:1–2). For an overview of the letters see *La correspondance d'Erasme et de Guillaume Budé* ed Marie-Madeleine de la Garanderie (Paris 1967) 9–47. For an appreciation of Budé's work see Jean-François Maillard et al *La France des humanistes: Hellénistes I* (Turnhout 1999) 41–97.

BUDÉ TO ERASMUS, GREETING

Look here! First of all, I wish that you and others with you would make less of my Greek and Latin commentaries. To begin with, whatever their worth, they are concerned almost exclusively with Greek, so it is right that your appreciation of them be diminished at least by half.[1] Secondly, Toussain, who is overly zealous for my reputation, on his own initiative and perhaps also because of a foolhardy promise of mine, wished you to give greater importance to something of only mediocre worth.[2] I leave it to you, therefore, to judge how much you should subtract from his praise, taking

* * * * *

1812
1 The crowning work of Budé's unflagging philological research would appear two years later as *Commentarii linguae graecae* (Paris: Josse Bade, September 1529). This edition contained about 5,000 articles on Greek matters and 700 on Latin ones. Robert Estienne's 1537 edition (repr 1548) raised these totals to about 7,000 Greek and 1,500 Latin articles. The references about Greek matters were composed in Latin. The book became a rich source for later lexicographers. See Guillaume Budé *Correspondance I Les lettres grecques* ed and trans Guy Lavoie and Roland Galibois (Sherbrooke 1977); see also M.-M. de la Garanderie *Christianisme et lettres profanes* 2nd ed (Paris 1995) 81–2, 203, and passim.
2 Jacques Toussain was a protégé of Budé. In 1528 he would come to Budé's defence by circulating epigrams attacking Erasmus for calling Josse Bade a better Latin stylist than Budé in his *Ciceronianus* (ASD I-2 672:5–673:1 / CWE 28 420–1). Erasmus' attempt to appease Budé in a second edition was of no avail, and Budé never wrote to him again. For Toussain see also Ep 1842 introduction.

5

into account his excessive enthusiasm as well as the epistolary convention of 10
enlarging on someone else's promises. You must prune back Toussain's generous commendation in accordance with what you know my limited powers
are capable of accomplishing. Lastly, I had hoped in the beginning that this
enterprise would win approval and bring new vigour to my sagging and
ageing reputation, especially in view of the enthusiasm engendered in our 15
age for the study of Greek; but now I lack confidence that it can satisfy the
expectations of the young, which are overblown and exaggerated, as I hear.
So much so that for eight months now I have been reluctant to disturb the
pile of notes now covered with dust, even though I had begun the work
with diligence and verve. Would that, without fear of disgrace, I could con- 20
sider it as a lost cause! I assure you there is nothing I would more willingly
abandon at some crossroads and in full public view for someone else to retrieve and use to his own advantage than this bundle of nuisance that I have
unwisely put together. The love I had for the work has grown cold after but
a brief interval, and the feeling of excitement that took away the sense of 25
toil has vanished.

The result is that a good part of the work lies there in first draft: a great
mass of material that had suggested itself to me during the course of composition, nothing but a pile of unorganized data that I had never planned to
include for fear of adding too much to my task of annotation. At any rate, 30
the way things have turned out, I do not think it was of great relevance,
at least as the work was originally conceived. From the beginning, the con-
tinuity of the writing was interrupted and then broken off completely by
my departure for the court.[3] Then, after my return,[4] a few minor works and
some very pleasant reading distracted my thoughts from that concern.[5] Nev- 35
ertheless, I shall have to face up to it one of these days, if I can somehow

* * * * *

3 Perhaps in May 1520, when Budé accompanied King Francis I to the parley
  with Henry VIII at the 'Field of Cloth of Gold' near Calais; he later followed
  the court to Amboise, Blois, Romorantin, Dijon, Autun, Troyes, and Reims.
  In 1522, in September 1523, and from October to December 1524 he was in
  attendance at the court in Lyon.
4 Budé's attendance at court was interrupted after King Francis I's defeat and
  captivity at Pavia (24 February 1525) and after a break in relations with Chancellor Antoine Duprat.
5 Not his earlier *De contemptu rerum fortuitarum* (Josse Bade 1520, 1521), his *Epistolae* (Josse Bade 1520, 1522), or the French *Summaire ou epitome du livre De asse*
  (Galliot Du Pré and Pierre Vidoue 1522). Perhaps Budé considered revisions
  of his *Annotationes in Pandectas* (Josse Bade 1526, 1527) and of *De Asse* (Josse
  Bade 1527) to be 'minor works.'

shake off this laziness and inertia. But even if I wished I could never be like you, capable of instantly rekindling enthusiasm of mind and spirit to carry out one task after another of this kind. In addition, I cannot neglect domestic cares,[6] and I must also devote a good deal of time to public affairs each   40
day.[7] Therefore cease burdening me, not with your expectation for the work to appear, for in that you will not be disappointed, but with this excessive publicity you give it.

You write that certain people suspect that I have some misgivings about you. Perhaps they have some reason to think so, but they are nevertheless   45
mistaken in their opinion. The truth is that on numerous occasions in the company of close friends I made no secret of the fact that I could not help being somewhat annoyed with you because, given the least opportunity, you take pleasure in making fun of the French character, which you describe as being slow-witted, sluggish, superficial, and obtuse. Although it is well   50
known that you have done this on many occasions, I am ready to pardon you and to condone your saucy wit and inclination to facetiousness if you did not give the impression of doing this deliberately, intentionally, and almost overtly. It is extraordinary to see how pleased you were in your commentary on the Epistle to the Galatians, how it delighted you, how you relished   55
hearing the saint's criticism of the Galatians;[8] nowhere else, making due allowance, do you seem to have reaped more profit from your labours than in the expounding of that passage. Of course[9] you manage to paraphrase it in such a way that you revel in applying what the Apostle said about the

* * * * *

6 Budé had twelve children, at least eight of whom survived infancy. In addition to his house on the rue Saint-Martin in Paris he maintained two country homes at Marly and at Saint-Maur.
7 From August 1522 to the time of his death, Budé was *maître des Requêtes* in the royal household, a position which sometimes demanded attendance in sessions of the Parlement of Paris. He also served for several years as provost of the merchants of Paris, and he held for life the appointment as royal librarian.
8 For the passage that annoyed Budé see Erasmus' 'Argument of the Epistle of Paul to the Galatians' CWE 42 94. Composed when Erasmus was translating the Epistles in 1505–6 (see Ep 384 introduction), the 'arguments' for each epistle were printed separately in 1518 (Ep 894) and taken up again in the second edition of the New Testament (1519); this one was finally prefixed to the *Paraphrase on Galatians*.
9 Except for the first few words, Budé writes this sentence and the next in Greek. His accusation is that, since the Galatians of central Asia Minor were thought to be related ethnically to the Gauls of France, Erasmus was attacking Frenchmen when he belittled the Galatians. In Ep 1840:25–50 Erasmus will deny this charge.

Galatians of his time and Jerome's various commentaries on this text to the   60
Celts of the present day.[10] I suppose this can be attributed to your irrepress-
ible love of raillery; but many allege, although I certainly am not of their
number, that you attack the Celtic race openly and with deliberate design,
and gladly give voice to your antagonism and thinly veiled hatred towards
the French whenever the occasion presents itself. And then there is in Hilary   65
that famous accusation concerning the Gauls that you wished to immortal-
ize in your works to save it from oblivion,[11] out of pure nobility and love
of the truth,[12] I am sure. You would never have done so, in my opinion, if
you did not consider the Gauls so dull that they would not sufficiently understand your innuendoes. Otherwise, surely, it would not have occurred to   70
you to offend and attack us; you do not have the time to spare from the demands of serious writing, nor enough respite from your involvement with
other nations. As far as I am concerned, whatever grievances I have voiced
on this score are more of a public than a private nature, since I have learned
quite well how to put up with your Socratic irony and carping criticism;[13]   75
despite all this you found me no less favourably disposed towards you, even
if at times you thought otherwise.

To return to the subject, I have made no attempt to conceal my feelings
about you in this matter so that you would not think me to be indifferent to
patriotic sentiments. But aside from that I categorically deny that I ever said   80
anything improper or spiteful about you, unless, as it sometimes happens,
something fell from my lips, contrary to my true feelings, that could be

* * * * *

10 'The Galatians are Greeks, but they are descended from the Gauls and, according to St Jerome, "they resembled their forebears in dullness of wit" ... Paul,
   in a scolding voice, calls them ἀνόητοι "foolish"' (CWE 42 94). Erasmus paraphrases Jerome's commentary on Galatians; cf PL 26 (1884) 380C. Budé uses the
   generic designation Κέλτας 'Celts' for the principal inhabitants of pre-Roman
   Gaul. Although many Celts withdrew into Brittany or crossed to the British
   Isles, most remained to intermarry with the Franks and other tribes who invaded from Germany. The Romans called them all *Galli* 'Gauls.' Budé obviously associates the Franks, and hence the French people of his day, with the
   Celts. See also line 153, where he calls himself a 'Frank Celt.'
11 Jerome cites a treatise of Hilary of Poitiers (apparently lost). Erasmus had
   written, 'Hilary, himself a Gaul, also says in his book of hymns that the Gauls
   are "slow to learn"' (CWE 42 94). Jerome had used the word *indociles*.
12 'pure ... truth' is expressed in Greek
13 Literally 'satirical Momus.' Momus – more a literary than a mythological figure – was the personification of carping criticism. He was invoked especially
   by Lucian, one of Erasmus' favourite authors, to satirize Stoic theology and
   otherwise make fun of the gods. See Hesiod *Theogony* 214; cf *Adagia* I v 74.

ambiguously interpreted, particularly by those who think that the embers
of hidden rivalry lie deep down in our hearts ready to burst into flames at
the first breath of rumour. If I thought it proper to mention here the words   85
of praise I have always reserved for you and your writings, without any
artificial verbal embellishment (owed to your merits and in the service of
truth rather than of friendship, lest you think that I wish to claim credit for
this with you), I would either charge you with ingratitude for continuing to
ignore them or I would demonstrate to you that it is a spiteful rumour that   90
has reported to you only one side of the story.

And what about the two Greek letters I wrote to you two years ago,
in which I attempted to offer you a position and uproot you from where
you are?[14] in what sense, pray, did you interpret them? as a demonstration
of good will, or not? The duty of writing to you I took upon myself, in case   95
you do not know it, rather than being commissioned to do so by the king.[15]
You are aware, I suppose, that you behaved shamelessly in this matter[16] and
afterwards acted with such mistrust that I came to know of your desires and
intentions through others, not through your letters.[17] And while you confided your secrets to others, you dealt with me as if I were a rival. And what   100
is more, if I had wished to produce here as evidence all that dissembling
of yours,[18] I would have wrung from you the confession of your severing
of our friendship, to put it mildly, after I had given so many pledges of
my good will, which was neither feigned nor calculating. Was it the act of a

* * * * *

14 Epp 1439 and 1446, written 11 April and 8 May 1524. The letters continued
   Budé's attempts, begun in 1517, to attract Erasmus to Paris in hopes of emu-
   lating there the new Collegium Trilingue in Louvain (Ep 1434:18–21). As compensation Erasmus was promised £1,000 per annum, the income from the treasurership of Tours (Epp 1434 n12, 1439:30–5), but he would 'live in peace in
   a city which is well known and well situated,' that is, in Paris. Cf Ep 1840:60
   and nn16–18. Several phrases in Bude's discussion of this matter are written
   in Greek.
15 A strong indication that Budé, not the king, kept alive the project for endowing
   royal lecturers. On this see Farge *Parti conservateur* 36–8.
16 'you behaved shamelessly' is written in Greek.
17 See Ep 1484 to François Du Moulin, in which Erasmus pleads poor health, lack
   of resources, and fear of war; but see also the belated explanation to Budé that
   'something unpleasant was brewing' in France (Ep 1601:12–14) – perhaps the
   war with the Hapsburgs but also perhaps the growing opposition there to
   humanism.
18 This complete phrase is rendered in Greek. Budé's point is that this was a
   unilateral and unprovoked break. For Erasmus' response to this charge see Ep
   1840:64–81.

rival to select you for a position superior, or at least equal, to my own? Who   105
would not be apprehensive for himself in such a situation? who other than
a friend with a clear conscience could confidently estimate the other's feelings?[19] But you obviously either considered me a friend of doubtful loyalty
or at least one too inclined to unbosom himself incautiously, to whom you
were afraid to confide things that were close to your heart at the time.   110

But that is enough complaining, even if it was justifiable and spoken
with all sincerity. Still, I think your tacit complaint called for a direct answer.
I should like you to be aware, however, that I have exercised great restraint
in my words. For if I thought that I should attend to rumours, I believe
you are well aware they travel in both directions and are no less eloquent   115
here than there. In my case things are just as they were formerly, that is,
as far as my attitude of mind is concerned. I shall place myself equally at
your disposal hereafter, as is proper, for whatever need you may have of
my services; provided, of course, that you, on your part, show the same
courtesies to me. I say this in answer to what you wrote about eliminating   120
suspicion, which I am prepared to do as much as you, whenever you wish.[20]

Concerning the chorus of Ciceronians I am so much in agreement with
you that I am prepared to append my name, should there be need of it. The
extravagance of its chorusmaster,[21] whom you said I knew, has brought hatred upon this group of men and made them obnoxious to everyone. This   125
personage has acquired the nickname 'Fanfarone'[22] in Italy and is, I hear,
celebrated everywhere, especially in virtue of a recent canticle and Parnassian ode in which he, the sole protagonist, sang to himself as the son of
Philokalia,[23] performing alternating strophes in the guise of various heroic

* * * * *

19 Allen's critical apparatus for line 102 shows that *non* in the phrase *non ex suo
ipse animo* does not appear in Budé's edition of his own correspondence; see
Budaei epistolarum libri v (Paris: Josse Bade, February 1531). Following Budé's
modern editor, we conclude that insertion of the word *non* was an error in
Erasmus' 1529 *Opus epistolarum* and have not translated it here; cf M.-M. de la
Garanderie *La correspondance d'Erasme et de Guillaume Budé* (Paris 1967) 256n.
20 Most of Budé's rejoinder to Erasmus' appeal (Ep 1794:16–24) is rendered in
Greek.
21 Erasmus had meant to refer to Girolamo Aleandro, but Budé wrongly understood him to mean Pietro Alcionio (CEBR I 26–7). On this see Ep 1794:46 and
n13.
22 *philalazonis* (Allen lines 120–1). Budé coins a Latin compound word by joining
the Greek root *phil* 'love' and the noun *alazón* 'braggart.' In his response (Ep
1840:82–4) Erasmus fails to understand Budé's allusion.
23 *philocalia* 'love of beauty'; the personification here renders the whole passage
difficult to interpret. The 'Parnassian ode' is not known.

figures. In the eulogy at the end, he deleted the names of French and Ger- 130
man writers from the lists of those meriting distinction – as if this were his
prerogative.[24] He contrived to appear so exactly like Cicero that he even surpassed and left far behind him the father of Latin eloquence, at least in the
art of self-commendation, as I mentioned recently in my *Annotations*.[25] Mar- 135
cus Tullius did indeed sing his own praises, thereby exasperating the senate, the courtroom, and his closest friends, even if the praises he proclaimed
were real and deserved. More impudent by far, this charlatan has vaunted
his own totally unmerited praises. What is truly astonishing is that he got
away with it in the eyes of influential people, whose names he did not blush
to employ for the production of this absurd and intolerable performance.   140

I would have mourned Longueil, once our countryman, more grievous-
ly had he not ceased by his own choice to be one of us, that is, a Frenchman.[26]

Farewell from Paris on the day after our festival of Liberalia, or birth-
day of our immortality,[27] the day on which we worship God in the fruits
of the fields and recognize our Lord by his fruits, if we ourselves are good   145
fruit.[28] I received your letter of 23 March on Good Friday,[29] a day solem-
nized by the ritual burial of our Saviour in grateful and pious commemo-
ration of the salvation he won for us in his memorable Passion. I received

* * * * *

24 Already in his *Medicus legatus de exilio* (Venice: Aldine Press, November 1522),
a dialogue in Ciceronian style, Alcionio had criticized French and German
humanists for sprinkling their Latin too freely with Greek words (f b5).

25 *Altera aeditio annotationum in Pandectas* (Paris: Josse Bade, July 1526) f 29; cf *Omnia opera Gulielmi Budaei* (Basel: Nicolaus Episcopius 1557; repr Farnborough
1969) III 334–5.

26 Christophe de Longueil (c 1488–1522), the natural son of a Norman bishop
and a Flemish mother, renounced an early predilection for things French and
chose to make his career as a writer in Italy in the pursuit of perfect Ciceronian
Latinity (CEBR II 342–5). For this he became a prominent target in Erasmus'
Ciceronianus. See CWE 28 Introduction; cf Ep 1805 n15.

27 Liberalia, the Roman festival in honour of Liber, or Bacchus, was observed on
17 March, but Budé, in the manner of the Ciceronians is referring to the Christian feast of Easter Sunday, which celebrates Christ's liberation of believers
from eternal death. In 1527 it occurred on 21 April. This kind of substitution
of 'pagan' vocabulary for Christian events or feasts was one of the traits that
Erasmus criticized in his *Ciceronianus* (1528).

28 Budé's triple usage of *frux* 'fruit' here may evoke the impending celebration
of the 'Major Rogation,' which was always observed on April 25 and was associated with intercession for a good harvest. It was a Christianized observance of the pagan 'Robigalia,' which took the form of processions through
the fields of grain.

29 Ep 1794; in 1527 Good Friday occurred on 19 April.

it late at night, returning home from a château in the suburbs where court
was being held.[30]   150

Farewell once more. And do not think that I have written anything in
this letter in a mood of pique. I assure you on my life that there is not the
slightest bit of animosity in it. But I am a Frank Celt,[31] if ever there was one,
who does not conceal anything if there is no need for it.

1813 / From Alonso de Fonseca   Valladolid, 24 April 1527

The manuscript of this letter is in the Biblioteca nacional, Madrid (MS 17460,
f 159); see Ep 1805 introduction. The letter replies to Ep 1748, and will be
answered by Ep 1874. It was first published in the *Opus epistolarum* (1529).

Alonso de Fonseca (c 1475–1534), archbishop of Toledo since 1523, was the
son of the archbishop of the same name who had been a patron of Antonio de
Nebrija. He was an active supporter of Erasmus and of humanism in general;
cf Ep 1748 introduction and CEBR II 42–3. In Ep 1875:21–4, Erasmus expresses
a fulsome admiration of Fonseca's literary style.

ALONSO DE FONSECA, ARCHBISHOP OF TOLEDO, PRIMATE OF
SPAIN, ETC, TO DESIDERIUS ERASMUS OF ROTTERDAM,
THEOLOGIAN, GREETING

Things are exactly as your friends reported them to you, most learned Erasmus. I promote your cause with all my heart, and I have given evidence of   5
it up to now whenever I could and would continue to do so in future even
if no expression of gratitude had arrived from you. With all the more reason, I feel that your brief note written in your own hand,[1] has been reward

* * * * *

30 The château of Saint-Germain-en-Laye, to the west of Paris, where the court
   sat from 12 November 1526 to 16 April 1527. On the day after Budé wrote his
   letter, the king moved his court to the château of Vincennes, located on the
   eastern edge of present-day Paris, where it remained until at least 27 May.
   See *Catalogue des actes de François Ier* (Paris 1905) VIII 453.
31 ἐλευθεροκελτῶν, a compound joining the adjective 'free' or 'frank' and the noun
   'Celt,' which was perhaps meant to evoke the French vernacular intonation
   of *fran-çais*. When Budé later printed this letter himself, he abandoned this
   complicated usage and substituted for it a Greek word meaning 'outspoken';
   see *Budaei epistolarum libri v* (Paris: Josse Bade, February 1531) and cf *Omnia
   opera Gulielmi Budaei* (Basel: Nicolaus Episcopius 1557) I 383.

   1813
1 Ep 1748

enough for all the efforts I have expended in your behalf. Prior to this I
seemed to be defending the cause of good letters without regard to persons;   10
but now, at your bidding, I am obliged to take on your private case as well.
For some time now, as you write, a tumult has been stirred up here concerning your books; but that was only child's play compared to the way everything has been turned upside down now by this dread Fury.[2] She seems
sent on a mission from hell, undertaking to throw all of Christendom into.   15
disorder through division of opinion. Up to now she had somehow allowed
our part of the world to be at peace, that is, until she found men willing
to assist her by making public accusations against you, and in so doing she
has disturbed our tranquillity. But God will be with us; we hope he will so
thwart their baleful designs that a period of greater calm will follow after   20
the storm. There seems to be some sure promise of this in the attitude of
the emperor and the consensus of good men in your defence.

Give proof then of that fortitude and moderation of which your sublime and truly heroic talents are the guarantee, so that your ever unconquered and lofty spirit, relying on firm faith and trust in Christ, may not   25
allow the injustice of men to diminish its mildness and integrity. It is shameful that you are constantly exposed to danger as a result of your studies,
from which you should have derived the greatest of praise for your talent
and the just reward of your labours. Yet it has long been the fate of sublime
virtue to be faced with adversaries at every turn; and, since its dwelling   30
place and proper dignity is far away in heaven, it is treated here like an
exile and a stranger. But that is no reason for you to be cast down or to disappoint men's expectations of you. Rather must you devote yourself with
still greater energy to your holy and laborious task, lest as one who has
borne aloft with such acclaim the banner of pious and Christian studies you   35
should seem to desert the cause through weakness of spirit.

You will learn more fully in a letter from Juan de Vergara of the course
of events here.[3] Whatever he writes to you in my name you may consider as
written by me. We will fulfil our promises, and more than fulfil them. But
it is not now a matter of promising our enthusiastic support and authority   40
for the future, since it is no longer only a question of the matter itself but
also of our steadfastness of purpose, so that we may not seem to fail you in
any way.

Farewell. Valladolid, 24 April 1527

* * * * *

2 That is, the onset of heresy and dissent in the church throughout Europe
3 Vergara was secretary to Fonseca; see Ep 1814.

1814 / From Juan de Vergara   Valladolid, 24 April 1527

The manuscript of this letter exists in two copies made by the same scribe, probably for Vergara, and bound together in MS 17460 (f 153, f 162) of the Biblioteca nacional in Madrid. It was first published by Marcelino Menéndez y Pelayo *Heterodoxos españoles* 3 vols (Madrid 1880–1) II 719–29.

Juan de Vergara was made a fellow of San Ildefonso College at Alcalá by its founder, Cardinal Francisco Jiménez de Cisneros. There he translated several works of Aristotle from Greek and helped prepare the interlinear translation of the Greek text of Proverbs, Wisdom, Ecclesiastes, and Job for the Complutensian Polyglot Bible (1514–17). As secretary to three successive cardinal-archbishops of Toledo (at this time Alonso II de Fonseca) and perhaps on occasion chaplain to Emperor Charles V, he played an important role in helping promote Erasmian ideas in Spain between 1522 and 1529. During the subsequent backlash against Erasmus, Vergara's connections spared him at first. But his half-brother Bernardino Tovar was among its first victims in 1530. Vergara used every means possible to secure Tovar's release, but in June 1533 he himself would be arrested on charges of defending heretics, subverting the inquisition, and suborning its members. In his trial he denied the charges and refused to repudiate Erasmus. In the end he was forced to make a public abjuration and to withdraw from public life. See Lu Ann Homza *Religious Authority in the Spanish Renaissance* (Baltimore and London 2000); cf CEBR III 384–7.

In the first part of this letter Vergara replies to Erasmus' Ep 1684 but more directly to a longer letter (or perhaps a longer version, not extant, of which Ep 1684 is only a fragment) in which Erasmus mistakenly treated the Benedictine monk and scholar Alonso Ruiz de Virués as one of his Spanish enemies. Vergara is intent here on convincing Erasmus that Virués was a friend and strong advocate of Erasmus who had merely been suggesting ways for Erasmus to avoid stirring up enemies in Spain (see Ep 1684 introduction).

More importantly, Vergara here apprises Erasmus of recent developments in this regard. So much public censure of Erasmus was abroad that the inquisitor Alonso Manrique de Lara had ordered the critics to submit their opinions in writing. When these proved on 28 March 1527 to be badly ordered and repetitious, Manrique ordered those critics to compile a single list of alleged heresies for official consideration by theologians in proceedings preliminary to a formal inquisition. Although this assembly in Valladolid would not convene until 27 June 1527, Vergara managed to obtain the gist of the charges to be laid against Erasmus and relates them here (cf also the letters and excerpts detailing the growing anti-Erasmianism in Spain translated in CWE 12 519–35). In the end, the assembly in Valladolid was able to address only four of the

twenty charges before an outbreak of plague induced Manrique to prorogue
it on 13 August.

For the charges against Erasmus at Valladolid see Miguel Avilés Fernández
*Erasmo y la Inquisición (El libelo de Valladolid y la Apología de Erasmo contra los
frailes españoles)* (Madrid 1980). For the theologians' responses see Beltrán de
Heredia *Cartulario* VI. For the most recent account of the assembly, an interpretation of its debates, and a revisionist assessment of the Erasmian controversy
in Spain, see Lu Ann Homza 'Erasmus as Hero, or Heretic? Spanish Humanism and the Valladolid Assembly of 1527' *Renaissance Quarterly* 50/1 (1997)
78–118; cf Erika Rummel 'Erasmus and the Valladolid Articles: Intrigue, Innuendo, and Strategic Defense' in *Erasmus of Rotterdam: The Man and the Scholar*
ed J. Sperna Weiland and W.Th.M. Frijhoff (Leiden 1988) 69–78.

†

JUAN DE VERGARA, THEOLOGIAN, TO HIS FRIEND DESIDERIUS
ERASMUS OF ROTTERDAM, SINCERE GREETING
I owe great thanks to this Alonso of Olmedo,[1] whom I knew neither by
sight nor by name when your letter reached me.[2] Gladly would I render
him a good service, should the occasion present itself, for having rewarded   5
me with such a long and excellent letter from my Erasmus, of a kind that
I should never have hoped to extort even by torture from a man who is
the model of courtesy but engrossed in more serious matters. Indeed, apart
from the very brief note you sent me from Basel some years ago, I had
received no letter from you since I took leave of you.[3] But neither have I   10
written you in the meantime, having been called away by some unknown
fate from the midst of my tranquil studies to these tumultuous occupations

* * * * *

1814
1 On Alonso Ruiz de Virués and his *Collationes* see Ep 1838 introduction and n4;
   cf n2 below.
2 Ep 1684, a fragment of what was apparently a very long letter (see lines 30–4
   below). For a full description of what the letter probably contained, including
   Erasmus' reaction to the criticisms of Virués, see the introduction. For Vergara's subsequent identification of Virués, see lines 61–73 below and cf the
   letter of Vergara to Virués in CWE 12 522–6 Ep 2.
3 Probably Ep 1312, dated 2 September 1522. At the end of July 1520 Erasmus
   and Vergara had conferred in Bruges about Diego López Zúñiga's criticisms
   of Erasmus' annotations on the New Testament. Vergara, having disappointed
   Erasmus by forgetting to bring Zúñiga's book with him, consequently took
   great pains to allay Zúñiga's suspicions of Erasmus. See the five letters exchanged between Vergara and Zúñiga in CWE 8 335–46, especially Vergara's
   description of his meetings with Erasmus in Ep 1:15–71 (pages 337–8).

of life at court.[4] It is already the fourth year that public and private affairs there pull me in various directions, as the Bacchae did Pentheus,[5] so that it is altogether impossible to remember literary pursuits or those engaged in them. And if at times it is possible, I am so ashamed and humiliated at this turn of affairs[6] that I think it more prudent to avoid all familiarity with you and men of your talents, even by letter.

In the meantime, however, I learned that you had included in letters to your friends thoughtful greetings to me, that is, Guillermo Vergara. I interpret your calling me Guillermo instead of Juan as a particularly good omen, since I hear that this name has always betokened good luck in your friendships.[7] But although I have not written to you, my dear Erasmus, I have certainly often written about you and constantly spoken about you and have not ceased to be the herald of your praises before princes, men of learning, and men of all ranks; what is more, whenever the occasion arose, and this occurred more often than I would like, I have shown myself to be an energetic defender of your dignity and reputation.[8]

But to return to your letter. While it afforded me great pleasure, coming from you, I can hardly express my consternation at your mention of that pamphlet of Alonso of Olmedo written, you say, at my instigation.[9] The fact is that I had never to that day read a single page of such a work, nor had I ever laid eyes on the author or heard tell of him; nor for that matter am I one who would instigate others to write something so exhortatory[10] to you. For I do not have such a low opinion of my own abilities or such a mistaken

* * * * *

4 In fact, Vergara himself had declined the chair of rhetoric at Alcalá, preferring to remain near the centre of ecclesiastical power (CEBR III 385).
5 Pentheus, king of Thebes, was torn to pieces by the frenzied Bacchae for having beheld their orgies in honour of Dionysus, whose divinity Pentheus denied (Euripides *Bacchae* 1114).
6 Rendered in Greek, τῆς ἀλλαγῆς
7 See Ep 534:33–51, where Erasmus tells Guillaume Budé of eleven other supporters in his 'tribe of Williams,' and Ep 957:138–144, where he adds Guillaume de Croy to his 'list of Williams.' Erasmus had made the same mistake about Vergara's first name before; see Ep 1431:34 and n24.
8 Notably in his correspondence and dealings with Diego López Zúñiga; see n3 above.
9 Probably one of the series of seven manuscript *Collationes ad Erasmum* (see Ep 1838 introduction and n4); or perhaps Virués' letter to the guardian of the Franciscan convent at Alcalá, written in defence of Erasmus, which was circulated widely and eventually printed in Spanish and in Latin, a copy of which Juan Luis Vives sent to Erasmus (cf Epp 1838:45–52 and nn10–11, 1847:142–3).
10 Rendered in Greek, προτρεπτικῶς

understanding of your good nature that, if I had thought it of great importance to draw your attention to some matter, I would not have availed myself of my own resources rather than relying on borrowed or, as it must
surely seem, hired assistance. Thus it was that for some time I debated with
myself whether that letter had been intended for me or, as it sometimes hap-   40
pens, there had been some error in the address. I would have been totally
convinced of that opinion had not the last words of the letter made it clear
that it was addressed to me. As a result, after racking my brains to no avail,
without having any recollection of such a person, I began to make diligent
inquiry among my learned friends at the imperial court and even to ask   45
everyone I met whether they knew a certain Alonso of Olmedo, a monk of
some learning, as I could divine from your letter. There was no one who
knew a man of that name. Thereupon, somewhat annoyed that I was spending so much time invoking the name of my Osiris,[11] I decided to try writing
to absent friends. Meanwhile, as is the case when one is upset about some-   50
thing, passing from one suspicion to another, I was boiling with rage. 'Ah!'
I said to myself, 'such are the morals of the age! such the cunning of malicious men! Since they see that my devotion to Erasmus is too zealous for
their own comfort and convenience, they have found a method to set me at
odds with him, and to that end are preparing the way to implicate me in an   55
odious suspicion. They insinuate that I secretly set Momuses on him to practice their deceptions upon his writings,[12] but in a flattering and solicitous
manner, because such services usually terminate in cruel tragedies.'
      While I was in this state of uncertainty, a letter finally arrived for me
in Granada, where I was at the time,[13] from my brother Bernardino Tovar   60
in Alcalá,[14] from whom I had sought counsel by letter in this matter. He informed me that this Alonso was a Benedictine monk, usually stationed at

            * * * * *

11 In the Isis myth, the god of darkness Seth killed his brother Osiris, a god of
   the underworld, and scattered his dismembered body all over Egypt. Isis had
   to search for the mangled remains.
12 See Ep 1812 n13.
13 Following his marriage to Isabel of Portugal, Charles v took the court to
   Granada in Andalucia; then, from January to October 1527, the court sat in
   Valladolid in Castile.
14 Bernardino Tovar was the half-brother of Juan de Vergara. Until 1524 he had
   been a devoted disciple of Francisca Hernández, the director of the *alumbrados*,
   who would later, after her arrest, turn informant against Vergara. Tovar left
   her to join the followers of María Cazalla, who exercised some influence over
   a group of Erasmian clerics in Alcalá. There Tovar transformed his home into
   a centre of evangelical humanism; see CEBR III 338–9.

Burgos, a city of some four days' journey from Alcalá, famous among your
Belgian compatriots for its commercial activities. He is an upright man, a
theologian of some distinction, and moreover a devoted follower of yours. 65
He has given public lectures on your *Enchiridion* in his city and has often
spoken favourably of you in his homilies to the people, and on that account
incurred a considerable amount of resentment and found himself involved
in serious disorders and public disturbance. Since this Alonso was burning
with desire to be admitted to your friendship, my brother persuaded him 70
not to hesitate to write to you, taking the opportunity from literary interests and the present state of social upheaval; he assured him as well that
a learned man such as he would readily win favour with you. But as for
criticizing your writings, nothing of the sort had occurred to my brother,
and he had not yet himself had the chance to see the book in question. 75
He said that only the prologue and epilogue had been made available to
him a short time previously, and he sent me that part of the book. When
I noticed in that epilogue that my greetings were conveyed to you by a
man unknown to me, and read his ambiguous words about my advice to
him,[15] I decided to voice my complaint about this affair to the author him- 80
self, enclosing also a copy of your letter to me.[16] Finally, I received a letter
from him and another written to you,[17] in which he gently makes light of
the matter. I decided to send those letters to you together with my letter
to him.

In the interim I discover through conversations and letters of many 85
acquaintances that he is so enthusiastic in his devotion to you as to arouse
animosity. He has exerted strenuous efforts in your behalf against certain
'Erasmus-floggers' who in recent days have been criticizing your writings.
Finally, without a shadow of pretence, in all disputes having to do with
your honour and teachings he has given an example of exceptional loyalty 90
and devotion in your regard and it is clear that he will continue to do so.
This knowledge brought great pleasure to me both on your account and also
because it freed me from a false suspicion. For I had begun to take pity on
you, fearing that as a result of the elm switches of the man from Olmedo
you would suddenly turn from Erasmus into the 'elm-consumer' in the play 95

* * * * *

15 See Ep 1684:1–2.
16 Vergara's letter to Virués is in CWE 12 522–6. Erasmus' letter to Virués is Ep
   1684, but probably in its original longer version.
17 For Vives' letter to Vergara see CWE 12 529–33 Ep 4; his letter to Erasmus is
   not extant. Erasmus' reply, also not extant, may be dated c 31 March 1527; see
   Epp 1838, 1839.

of Plautus.[18] And what irked me most of all was that I was portrayed as the commander of the cruel lictor, the one by whose authority he untied the fasces to flog you.[19] But, as things now stand, far from your having to fear some hostile action from him, it is he on the contrary who must fear harm from your enemies. But if by chance there are some phrases in the book (which for the moment, at least, I think has been suppressed) which give you offence as being too outspoken or unpleasant, it is right that you should pardon him in consideration of all the good he has done for you. In his desire, as I believe, that you and your works be praised without reserve he took it upon himself to give you a friendly admonition. But, fired with enthusiasm for the work he had begun and carried along by the headlong rush of his pen, he could not help giving utterance in places to words that were somewhat harsh, which you in your great wisdom and moderation should nonetheless take in good part. You will perform an action worthy of yourself if you would write a kind and courteous letter to this earnest and learned man who is so devoted to your cause. This would be the best way to ensure that he will not think his efforts in celebrating your works were misplaced and that he will display even greater enthusiasm in defending them, should the need arise.

We have gone on too long about this matter; now learn what is happening here. War – an implacable war – has now been openly declared on you, Erasmus, by our monks. They had long since given veiled intimations of their hatred, murmuring in hidden corners that Erasmus was suspected of Lutheran impiety. Then in popular assemblies they began to assail your writings, nibbling away at them indirectly, while some more daring individuals attacked you head-on. Since they made little headway with popular opinion, some of them brazenly took public powers into their own hands. Usurping for themselves the right of public censure, they removed your books from the printing shops and banned them from the country in some kind of modern-day ostracism.[20] But these excesses, if not remedied, seemed

100
105
110
115
120
125

* * * * *

18 Plautus *Persa* 278B. Vergara attempts a triple pun in the Latin: *ulmeis Ulmetani ... ulmitriba*, the last word a macaronic coinage, half-Latin, half-Greek, used by Plautus to describe a slave who, by being flogged so often with elm switches, 'consumes' or 'uses up' elm trees.
19 The lictor was the Roman officer who accompanied chief magistrates in public appearances and who bore as a symbol of office the fasces, a bundle of rods tied together, to one of which the blade of an axe was attached.
20 A generation earlier, Spaniards were accustomed to expulsions of Jews and Moors, but the banning of books was a more recent phenomenon. It was provided for under Spanish civil law by the Pragmatic Sanction of 8 July 1502,

at least to have been mitigated, partly by the authority of the magistrates, who by virtue of their power restrained the insurgents with stern severity, partly through the support of good men and devotees of your cause.

But lo! in the meantime, when we thought passions had been calmed, your *Enchiridion* suddenly leaped on to the stage speaking in the Span-   130
ish tongue and ushered in a turbulent sequel to our drama.[21] Immediately shouts issued forth from the pulpits, the squares, the churches, the basilicas (for there was no place where these bellowers were not posted), proclaiming Erasmus a heretic, a blasphemer, impious, and sacrilegious. Need I say more? Of a sudden there arose from the translation of your book into the   135
vulgar tongue more foes than from Cadmus' sowing of the dragon's teeth.[22] But it was confined to that that type of person; for among all the rest no book of yours has ever won you a richer yield of friends anywhere. Therefore every day new rumours of disturbances caused by the publication of

* * * * *

decreed by the monarchs Ferdinand and Isabella, and under canon law by the constitution *Inter sollicitudines* of the Fifth Lateran Council (1515); see *Concilio-rum oecumenicorum decreta* ed Giuseppe Alberigo et al (Freiburg im Breisgau 1962) 608–9, trans Norman Tanner *Decrees of the Ecumenical Councils* (London and Washington DC 1990) I 632–3. The interdiction of specific Lutheran books in Spain had been put in place by the inquisitors Adrian of Utrecht, the future pope, in 1521, and Alonso Manrique de Lara in May 1523. See *Index de l'inquisition espagnole* ed J.-M. De Bujanda (Sherbrooke 1984) 45.

21 First published in 1503 (Louvain: Dirk Martens), the *Enchiridion militis chris-tiani* became considerably more famous in the elegant corrected reprint, which contained a long dedicatory letter to Abbot Paul Volz (Ep 858), that Froben published in 1518; cf Ep 1805 n21. It was reprinted in Latin forty times within a decade, with a total of about seventy editions by 1600. There were many vernacular translations: first into Czech (1519), then into German (1520), Dutch (1523), Low German (1525), Spanish (1526), English (1527), French (1529), and Italian (1529). As Vergara notes, the Spanish translation by Alonso Fernández de Madrid, archdeacon of Alcor, aroused both the enthusiasm and the ire of many; cf Epp 1792:16–17, 1836:50–62, 1904:13–24. It was completed by early 1525. No copies of the first edition (Alcalá: Miguel de Eguía 1526?) are extant. A second edition appeared from the same press probably in September 1526, with a dedicatory epistle to Alonso Manrique de Lara that repeats Erasmus' boldest remarks about reading the Scriptures in the vernacular. It would be reprinted twelve times before 1567.

22 Cadmus was the mythical son of King Agenor of Tyre, who sent Cadmus to rescue his abducted sister Europa. After slaying a dragon to gain access to water, and following Athena's guidance, Cadmus sowed the dragon's teeth, from which armed men arose, whom he killed by setting them to fight one another.

your book were reported to the magistrates in charge of investigating mat-   140
ters of impiety. Since their unremitting efforts to crush these uprisings were
of little avail – and indeed when one disorder was suppressed another more
serious one arose – they decided to pronounce judgment on the whole affair
once and for all.

Towards the beginning of March, therefore, a full assembly to deal   145
with this matter was held under the leadership of Don Alonso Manrique,
archbishop of Seville, a man of the highest principles, distinguished both by
birth and by the splendour of his own virtue. By authority of the assembly
fathers, monks of high repute from several religious orders were summoned
there. Word has it that they were severely reprimanded; that, although they   150
had been prohibited more than once by public edict from making seditious
public attacks upon Erasmus charging him with heresy, they continued in
their unbridled licence of speech, never ceasing to lash out daily from public
platforms and to lay indiscriminate charges of impiety against a learned
man, recipient of the most solemn and honorific eulogies of the Holy See.   155
Such intense feelings did they display that by now no one is inclined to
believe them to be motivated by a zeal for piety but rather to be goaded
on by hatred and resentment. Accordingly the members of the assembly by
virtue of their authority have urged and indeed ordered them to refrain
henceforth from their attacks and to moderate their sharp tongues and mad   160
proclivity to slander. If there were anything erroneous or pernicious in the
writings of Erasmus it was not for them to make judgment on such matters;
if there were anything that seemed to be of that nature, they were to make
careful note of it and report it to that assembly, which would see to it that
the best interests of the state were consulted.   165

It is said that the monks responded to these admonitions at great length
in accordance with the gravity of the affair. They said that for too long they
had turned a blind eye to the grave errors and blasphemies of Erasmus;
that they had been afraid that such a presumptuous and headstrong individual, in secret collusion with Luther, if provoked to anger by severe criti-   170
cism, would throw off any last vestige of shame and begin openly to profess
Lutheranism and reveal at last the sickness of his mind, ill-concealed until
then. Yet seeing that his temerity and madness had progressed to the point
that there seemed to be much less danger in driving him into the enemy
camp than in retaining a treacherous and destructive ally, they had decided,   175
in their zeal for the orthodox church, to undertake its defence publicly in
this moment of crisis. They said they could not permit Christian souls to be
seduced impiously by diabolical deceptions and enticements without publicly pointing out to them the snares and pitfalls against which they should
guard themselves. When they were held back from that course of action by   180

edicts obtained through the influence of their opponents, they complied at
first. But then, as the evil gained strength, divine authority prevailed over
human. They took it upon themselves to urge and beseech the authorities in
their turn to assume the governance of the Christian people as their office
obliged them and to bring immediate aid to them in this extreme peril. The   185
evil was growing in force day after day as new works of this heretic continued to appear, which by their illusory pleasantness of speech beguiled
the ignorant multitude and led simple souls, unable to recognize the poison
hidden beneath the honey, into abominable heresies. Again and again they
urged the authorities to consider the perilous situation in which the church 190
of Christ in other parts of Christendom found herself, and not to allow such
a deadly contagion to establish itself here as well. They should take timely
precautions lest the virulence of the disease require still more severe remedies which, if applied, the people might spit out. At the present moment this
creeping epidemic could be cut off with a minimum of effort if the books of 195
Erasmus were condemned for impiety in a public pronouncement and banished from Spain. In order that this might proceed properly and correctly,
the theological responsibility should be delegated to respected and learned
theologians (of whom there was an abundance in their own convents), who
would subject them to a careful, painstaking examination. In the meantime, 200
however, so that the evil would not progress any further, the reading of
those books should be officially forbidden, and they should all be collected
from every quarter and kept in custody until the results of the investigation
were made public, as they said had been done in Paris.[23]

When these and similar statements, delivered perhaps with more so- 205
lemnity and rhetorical flourish, were ended and some of the monks, 'un-
skilled in speech but unable to be still,'[24] began to behave in a rather unruly
and boisterous manner, the fathers imposed silence on them and issued the
following judgment on the matter. As far as they were concerned, to that day
no charge whatever of impiety against Erasmus had been established, and a 210
great number of learned men of orthodox beliefs were on his side. In addi-

* * * * *

23 The Parlement of Paris had enacted several measures of censorship beginning
   in 1521, and normally ratified decisions of the Paris faculty of theology about
   books, including those censuring works of Erasmus, especially those translated into the vernacular. See Farge *Procès-verbaux* (Paris 1990) 96, 97 nos 94A,
   95A, and passim. But, since the formal censures against Erasmus were not
   officially promulgated until 1531, they were not rigorously implemented in
   Paris.
24 Rendered in Greek; see Aulus Gellius *Attic Nights* 1.15.15, a fragment of the
   Greek comic writer Epicharmus.

tion, two popes, Leo[25] and Adrian,[26] had commended his teachings in very honourable terms in official briefs. The *Enchiridion*, which the monks had branded with impiety, had been issued to the public after being submitted to official examination. This seemed to the authorities more than sufficient reason that Erasmus' writings be tolerated until more certain evidence to the contrary could be brought forward. If, however, there was something in his books that gave offence, the monks should take note of it calmly without causing any disturbance and bring it to the attention of that body.[27] The fathers in their turn would make judicial investigation into the matter and would devote their efforts to ensure that no harm would befall the church of Spain. In the meanwhile they decreed and ordained that the monks conduct themselves with great moderation in this affair and that each of them enjoin this upon his subordinates; they were not to blurt out anything irresponsibly against Erasmus or burden readers of his books with religious scruples. The dispute should be carried on not in an atmosphere of hatred

* * * * *

25 Erasmus dedicated his first edition of the New Testament to Pope Leo x (Ep 384) and received in return the pope's dispensation from impediments arising from his illegitimate birth (Epp 518, 519). But for some time, and especially as he prepared the second edition, Erasmus had wished for some formal expression of the pope's approval of his New Testament. This he received through the offices of the papal legate Antonio Pucci (Ep 860), cardinals Raffaele Riario and Domenico Grimani (cf Epp 360:33, 865:22), and his friend Paolo Bombace, who actually wrote the papal brief that Leo x signed (Ep 864; cf Ep 865). In August 1519, however, Erasmus appealed to Leo for a more general endorsement of his work and that of other humanist scholars and for a pronouncement against their critics (Ep 1007:118–27), and he renewed this appeal in September 1520 (Ep 1143). He received an answer from Leo (Ep 1180, written by Jacopo Sadoleto and dated 15 January 1521), which, while commending his work, also called upon Erasmus to enter the lists against Luther and his followers with formal rebuttal of their heresies. Leo's last intervention on behalf of Erasmus was a warning in 1520 to Diego López Zúñiga not to publish his book *Blasphemiae et impietates Erasmi*; but, after Leo's death, Zúñiga renewed his attacks (Rummel *Catholic Critics* I 166–73).
26 See Ep 1324 (1 December 1522), a papal brief composed by Theodoricus Hezius for the signature of Pope Adrian vi. While praising Erasmus' works it also expressed an 'urgent request' that he write more actively against Luther. See also Ep 1324A, a parallel draft written by Girolamo Aleandro but neither signed nor sent by the pope. Its praise for Erasmus is more guarded and its desire for anti-Lutheran polemic more pointed. On these two letters, see Ep 1324 introduction. Still another papal brief (Ep 1338, dated 23 January 1523), was likewise laudatory in tone but even more urgently called on Erasmus to write a formal refutation of the new heresies.
27 That is, those who had originally approved it for publication

and verbal abuse but for pious ends. Whoever behaved otherwise was to be
considered as having acted against the interests of the state.

When it seemed that the monks wished to oppose their own authority
to this resolution, they were dismissed. But without delay they began to pro-   230
claim in all the convents roundabout that all the most subtle minds should
prepare to scrutinize the books of Erasmus and note down all errors, since
a pronouncement upon them was imminent. In the meantime they spread
the rumour among the people that they were going to burn all the books
of Erasmus very soon. They also secretly stationed some of their own fol-   235
lowers in the bookshops who, pretending to be occupied with something
else, were to frighten off those interested in buying your books by citing
the charge of heresy. Inside the convents there was an incredible monkish
fervour, an amazing assiduity to pore over your works. They split up the
task, each one taking the portion that had been assigned to him, and bus-   240
ied themselves in mutual rivalry to 'fish out' heresies, and not gather pearls
from dung, as Virgil did with Ennius,[28] but dung from pearls. The work
went ahead at a great heat, so much so that if people came for confession,
since it was the Lenten season, or for any other reason, they gave the excuse
that they were occupied in crushing a certain heretic.   245

Finally on 28 March,[29] behold! our monks emerged from their hid-
ing places stuffed to the gills with heresies. A crowded assembly gathered
on that day, presided over by the eminent archbishop of Seville,[30] assisted
by two close advisers of the emperor, men of great wisdom and authority.
The cohort of monks was ushered in. After being seated, they were first   250
reminded by the archbishop of the seriousness of the matter under discussion and of the freedom from prejudice required in such deliberations. They
were then asked to produce their findings. Thereupon first a Dominican friar
read from written notes the errors he had collected.[31] Then a Franciscan

* * * * *

28 See *Vita Donati aucti* in *Vitae Vergilianae* ed Giorgio Brugnoli and Fabius Stok
(Rome 1997) 7. The passage reads 'gold,' not 'pearls.'
29 Not 5 April, as some have translated *quintum Kalendas Aprilis*. A letter from
Alfonso de Valdés to Maximilianus Transsilvanus, written 1 August 1527, describes this session in some detail and with slight variations from this account
by Vergara; see Caballero *Valdés* Ep 17 335–40.
30 Alonso Manrique de Lara, grand inquisitor in Spain; his two assistants were
probably Luis Coronel and Juan de Quintana, both graduates in theology at
Paris.
31 The persons Vergara describes here were not necessarily present later at the
formal session on 27 June, for which Antonio Paz y Meliá and Manuel Serrano
y Sanz 'Actas originales de las congregaciones celebradas en Valladolid en 1527

added his.[32] After him a Benedictine (the brother of Alonso of Olmedo) in   255
a solemn and lengthy speech testified that his congregation was far from
bringing false accusations against a man of such eminent learning who had
rendered such great services to the cause of Christian piety. He spoke at
length with great moderation and dignity of the benefits and soundness of
your teachings, of the untiring efforts of your enemies scattered through ev-   260
ery region to bring charges against you, to which you have given satisfactory
answer in *apologiae* and defences, and of your rightful indignation towards
the crass vulgarity of some monks.[33] His speech was received with general
acclaim, as could be determined by the nods of approval, facial expressions,
and gestures of each hearer, with the result that you began little by little to   265
grow in favour in the eyes of that assembly. Next came an Augustinian;[34]
he in turn without the aid of any notes spoke of you in the most honorific
terms. At the end a representative of the Trinitarians (an order not very well
known in your country, I think, but very numerous here) brought in some

* * * * *

para examinar de Erasmo' *Revista de archivos, bibliotecas y museos* 6 (1902) 60–
73 list twenty-nine theologians, while Beltrán de Heredia *Cartulario* VI 23–4
lists thirty-three. Two Dominicans appear in each list, with only Fray Juan de
Salamanca in both. The first list names a Fray Gil as a *Predicator* (normally used
to indicate a Dominican), while the *Cartulario* names the Dominican Francisco
de Vitoria, regent at Salamanca (115–17).

32 Probably Francisco Castillo (CEBR I 281), whose redaction of these notes was
assisted by Francisco de Meneses (CEBR II 433); see Beltrán de Heredia *Cartulario* VI 23, 46–7, 79–82. Castillo, who knew both Latin and Greek, was admired
by the humanist Nicolaus Clenardus; but his interventions were firmly anti-
Erasmian. Luis de Carvajal affirmed that Castillo – not Edward Lee, as Erasmus claimed – played a major role in drawing up the list of alleged errors; on
this see n39 below. But the Franciscan could be Gil López de Béjar, who consistently supported Erasmian positions, and whom Beltrán de Heredia *Cartulario*
VI 79 identifies as a Franciscan.

33 Jerónimo Ruiz de Virués of Olmedo, a monk of San Juan at Burgos, had studied (as did his brother Alonso) at San Vicente, the Benedictine *studium* at the
University of Salamanca. Like Alonso he supported Erasmus and humanistic
studies generally. Unlike Alonso, however, he did not participate in the assembly proper at Valladolid, possibly because he had been called in the meantime
to a post at court by Empress Isabella of Portugal (CEBR III 401).

34 Allen 243n identifies him as Dionisio Vázquez, of Toledo, a master of theology
and court preacher for Charles V; on him see CEBR III 381–2. Beltrán de Heredia *Cartulario* VI 12 affirms his involvement and describes him as an expert in
the three languages, but does not list him with those convened at the assembly proper in June (ibidem 23–4). A certain Bernardino Vázquez de Oropesa
(identified as an Augustinian), master of theology at Salamanca and a noted
preacher, did intervene in June against Erasmus (ibidem 111–13).

articles.[35] After the monks had drawn out the debate for the entire day, the   270
senators, observing that many of the comments presented were substantially the same, decreed that all the communications should be condensed
into a single report, in order to avoid repetition, and brought back to them.
With that the senate was adjourned for the day, while your adversaries were
much less jubilant than before.   275

A few days later the fathers sent the composite version to be read and
examined by a group of theologians, some from Alcalá, others from Salamanca,[36] the majority of them (as I hope) fair-minded but some of them suspect. Their meeting has been fixed for Ascension Day,[37] when they will treat
of this matter and render a judgment, not with the authority of judges but   280
of official investigators. In other words, after examining the charges and
eliminating all calumnies they will permit only those points to be noted
that may reasonably be disputed and may present some ambiguity either in
your meaning or in the concept itself. Then they will send their observations
either to you or to the pope or both.[38] You will be given the opportunity to   285
speak in defence of your writings, and the whole affair will be resolved not

* * * * *

35 The Order of the Most Holy Trinity, which followed an austere form of the Au-
    gustinian Rule, had as its chief work the redemption and ransom of hostages.
    The Trinitarian mentioned here may be Benet Safont of Barcelona, the order's
    superior general since 1520 (CEBR III 188), because a postscript to Pedro Juan
    Olivar's letter to Erasmus (Ep 1791:78–80) adds, 'The general of the Order for
    the Redemption of Captives, an honest and scholarly man who wields consid-
    erable influence, is a great supporter of yours.' Neither Safont nor any other
    Trinitarian, however, appeared at the actual inquisition later in the summer.
36 The list of those who finally spoke on the articles at Valladolid appears to
    be drawn from a larger pool of theologians than the one described here. It
    included six graduates of the Paris faculty of theology – only one of whom
    (Pedro de Lerma) had a connection with Alcalá and one other (Francisco de
    Vitoria) with Salamanca. The others were Antonio de Alcaraz, who taught at
    Valladolid, the Portuguese Diogo de Gouveia, who still resided frequently in
    Paris, and Luis Coronel and Juan de Quintana, both Spaniards in the service
    of Emperor Charles v.
37 In 1527 the movable feast of the Ascension fell on 30 May. This date for the
    opening of the formal inquisitorial assembly is confirmed by Manrique's letter
    of 14 April convening the meeting for 'el dia de Pascua de Ascensión' (Allen
    Ep 1791:255n and introduction); and in Epp 1836:38–9 and 1847:75–6 Juan Luis
    Vives reports Virués saying it was postponed until the day after the Ascension.
    In the end it did not convene until 27 June, and was prorogued on 13 August.
38 The procedures outlined here by Vergara are consistent with normal practice
    of the inquisition; see Lu Ann Homza 'Erasmus as Hero, or Heretic? Spanish
    Humanism and the Valladolid Assembly of 1527' Renaissance Quarterly 50/1
    (1997) 83.

hastily and not without due consideration (as the monks hoped) but with
full deliberation and counsel.

I hear that I shall not be one of those judges; I have been rejected
by the other side as one too prejudiced in your favour. I accept this will-   290
ingly because I see that I will have a freer role to play as advocate if that
of judge is denied me. Besides, by nature I am averse to that type of assembly in which, while the case is decided more by the weight of numbers than by the authority of the opinions, the ill will engendered afterwards by an unjust decision is attributed to all equally. However things   295
may turn out, you can be assured that my loyalty to you will take prece-
dence over even the most pressing of my other duties. For your part, you
must not take it as an insult if your writings are subjected to public scrutiny
in this way. No better plan, believe me, could have been devised to put a
curb on the tongues of your enemies, who were insisting daily with incred-   300
ible contentiousness that your books be consigned to the flames. No more
convenient way could be contrived to silence once and for all the audacity of these slanderers, which we had attempted so often to control in vain.
Even if a legitimate form of judicial procedure does not exist among our
provincial judges concerning your person, they do nevertheless have juris-   305
diction to allow or to prohibit your books in Spain. I should think then that
you will readily allow your defence to be taken up rather than see them destroyed without your having been informed, as they say has been attempted
elsewhere.

I understand that the monks' dossier is being procured for you through   310
the agency of your friends, and even in duplicate copy. There is the suspicion that it was concocted for the·most part in the workshop of Lee.[39] It

* * * * *

39 Edward Lee, the English cleric with whom Erasmus had fought a running
   battle from 1517 to 1522 over criticisms of his *Annotations* on the New Testament, was from 1525 to 1530 the ambassador of King Henry VIII to Spain. It
   would not be surprising that Lee would attempt to gain sympathy in Spain
   for his opposition to Erasmus. According to Luis de Carvajal, however, the list
   of Erasmus' alleged heresies was drawn up not by Lee but by the Franciscans
   Francisco de Castillo and Francisco de Meneses; see Carvajal's *Apologia* (Salamanca 1528) f 24v; Bataillon *Erasme* (1991) 236 n1; and cf n32 above. There is
   no evidence that Lee was composing a new book against Erasmus, but Erika
   Rummel has shown that there was a serious (albeit unsuccessful) intention by
   Girolamo Ghinucci, the apostolic nuncio to England who was in Spain with
   Lee, to print in Spain a new edition of Lee's first book against Erasmus *totum
   et integrum*; see 'New Perspectives on the Controversy between Erasmus and
   Lee' *Nederlands Archief voor Kerkgeschiedenis / Dutch Review of Church History*
   74/2 (1994) 230. The ensuing rumour of a new book from Lee was to exercise

is up to you to decide whether an answer should be made to it immediately or whether we should wait for the judgment of the theologians
upon it. Whichever tactic you decide, you will act with your customary 315
prudence if you conduct yourself in this defence with the utmost moderation. For in that way you will better support your cause and you will
confirm very effectively the reputation you enjoy as a man of Christian
piety and a model of gentleness and forbearance. You know the austerity of our way of life; we have the bad reputation abroad of affecting an 320
excessive sternness.[40] Thus be assured that your defence will find great
favour among us if it is at once very controlled and very dignified. Otherwise I warn you beforehand that you will turn what we consider an excellent cause into a disastrous one, nor will you serve the best interests of
your reputation. Everyone here entertains very optimistic hopes concern- 325
ing the outcome of this second investigation. For you will find the judges
to be most fair-minded, and the archbishop of Seville and the respected
assembly of the fathers of the inquisition to be men of virtue and wisdom. We know that they will exercise great care in safeguarding your honour and the public peace. In addition to recognizing that you are an or- 330
thodox believer and a man of piety, they know that your adversaries are
borne precipitously along by envy and hatred, rather than by good judgment, to compass your destruction. The papal declarations by which you
have been honoured carry great weight, and for that reason the judges
will not allow any decision or resolution concerning the entire affair to 335
be made without consulting the Roman pontiff. Furthermore, the emperor
truly and sincerely supports your reputation. Words of the greatest commendation from our generous prince have been heard regarding your cause.
You have the support of princes and all men of worth. If the judges were
to admit advocacy of your cause by an external party, there would have 340
been no lack of those who would plead your case with great zeal and fidelity. Far from extinguishing men's enthusiasm (as it was strongly feared),
the initiation of these proceedings against you has lent it more ardour. So
from this moment on you may be of good cheer, Erasmus. The great excitement stirred up here concerning you will add, I hope, further lustre 345
to your name. Merely see to it (I repeat it once more) that no insults that
men hurl at you may dislodge you from your Christian moderation and

* * * * *

Erasmus' pen frequently at this time (see for example Epp 1735 n7, 1744 n19,
1747:79–82, 1893:22, 1902:85–7, 101–4, 1903:1–2, 1906:29); cf Rummel *Catholic
Critics* II 84–6.
40 Vergara apparently intends here the Spanish temperament in general.

integrity.[41] Let nothing be more important to you than true piety, as is the case, for in that way the most reliable resources, both human and divine, will be at your disposal.   350

Now let me advise you to take every precaution to remain in the good graces of the sovereign pontiff and to persist in your efforts to maintain favour with him and the sacred college[42] and (given the prestige and favour you enjoy in Rome, this should prove an easy task) to obtain approval from the Holy See of all your works mentioned in the *Catalogus*[43]   355 with lavish praise of them and of your teachings. There is no better method to weaken the obstinacy of your enemies than by making them understand that they cannot attack your reputation without offending papal authority. As for the more general situation, I have not come to any satisfactory conclusion about what would be most beneficial to you and therefore to   360 the cause of Christian piety. Would it be advisable, by some honourable means, if not to gain the alliance of these men scattered throughout the world (for how could that be possible in such a diversity of interests?), at least to pacify them and render them more reasonable, or must there always exist a state of open conflict? For my part, when I consider the solid de-   365 fences at your disposal to withstand the violence of your adversaries – the favour of princes, the support of good men, and, in particular, your outstanding learning and invincible eloquence – then full of good hope I take heart and impatiently urge you into the fray. On the other hand, when I remember that you and your supporters undertake an unending combat   370 against countless hosts who renew and replenish their forces each day, each year, and each century, and who, when you are gone, will seize every opportunity, whether through popular favour, the indifference of princes, or the turbulence of the times, to make insidious attacks upon your memory, then, believe me! fear creeps over me for those priceless legacies, your writ-   375 ings, and I would want every provision made for them, no matter what, provided it be honourable. For just as it is not enough for a wealthy father of a family merely to provide for his own and his family's interests during his lifetime but he must also consolidate his patrimony in such a way that his children and descendants will retain their honoured place   380

* * * * *

41 Archbishop Alonso de Fonseca, probably prompted by Vergara, gave Erasmus the same warning against precipitous and excessive rebuttal (Ep 1813:23–6).
42 That is, the college of cardinals in Rome
43 Ep 1341A / Allen I 1–46 to Johann von Botzheim. This *Catalogus lucubrationum* was published separately by Froben (Basel 1523; rev ed 1524).

in the future, so it behoves you as the father not of children of the flesh but of the spirit – namely, your books, the most freeborn of offspring – to ensure that nothing untoward befall them after your death, or at least that they are not doomed to live out their existence in constant fear and danger.   385

And in this matter my fears, which perhaps are unfounded, as I hope to be the case, are motivated by my immense and, I might almost say, immoderate love of the memory you will leave behind you. Yet when we perceive that, while you are still alive and conscious and, moreover, supported by powerful protectors and friends, there is nonetheless no end to the an-   390
noyances you must suffer on every side, what can we presage for the future, pray, when your enemies will have to deal with a mere spectre? Other men in the past have published books crammed with new and unheard-of doctrines for the time in which they lived. But since the authors of those books had implanted themselves in one of these orders, it was easy for them   395
to leave disciples behind them sworn in allegiance to their name, who in daily devotion to their leaders hold firm against the phalanxes of their adversaries and, having once joined battle, never desist from the fight. Hence all these buttresses, shields, defences, elucidations, and a thousand other weapons of that kind. Trusting in this arsenal, men of the same fraternal   400
sect (for the others are quick to desert their post) contend in battle sometimes over the most trivial opinion as if it were the very essence of our religion. They drag out the contest to the point that, while never ceasing from their wrangling, neither side will ever yield to the other; yet neither faction would ever dare to accuse the other of heresy. But should one un-   405
dertake a war against a whole nation of these confederates, he would not be able to maintain indefinitely a band of volunteer conspirators of the kind they have constantly on armed alert. How could he withstand the attack of the enemy and be a match for their violence, without in the end adorning their long triumphal procession as a proscribed enemy of the church?   410
especially since the controversy does not concern itself with second intentions and objective concepts but with one's daily bread,[44] a matter in which those relentless stimuli of the stomach add an invincible ferocity to men's behaviour.

* * * * *

44 Vergara contrasts 'weapons' of disputation cultivated by mendicant scholars adept in the scholastic method with the friars' practice of begging, both important components of the life of the mendicant orders. Vergara develops this at length in the following paragraph.

What can be the reason why the Benedictines, the Bernardines, the Cis-   415
tercians,[45] and the Hieronymites[46] are less hostile towards you, save that they
are self-sufficient and do not depend altogether on the liberality of others?
They seem to have prepared themselves for the time of need in the manner of the snail, which always expects the dew but retreats into its shell and
lives off its own juices if it does not fall. But for those who, like mice, as the   420
character in the comedy boasts, always eat someone else's food,[47] once their
power of persuasion over the multitude, on which their table depends, is
taken away, what is left to them but that their family die of hunger? Before
they experience this in earnest, they are already beginning to snarl like dogs
devouring their scraps, each fearful for his own morsel. Naturally, I am well   425
aware that your objectives have nothing to do with their dinner plates; but
as they see the enthusiasm of the populace gradually turning away from
them, which is probably owed to other factors, they hold you solely responsible. Their rage is nurtured by certain unscrupulous, licentious individuals
who peruse your books without deriving the least benefit from them but if   430
they light upon any outspoken remark directed against the monks commit
it to memory. Then, witty and clever charlatans that they are, they use it in a
jocose manner in situations where it will be most offensive, at the same time
citing the author so as to rouse great hostility against him. Then, as they attempt to defend him in a bungling and obstinate manner, they expose him   435
to still greater hatred. Although you can hardly accept responsibility for the
conduct of these hypocrites, those whom they dupe, stung with indignation,
attribute to you alone the humiliation they have received and rise immediately to the attack in a hostile and combative spirit, so that by now the name
of Erasmus is thoroughly accursed and ill-omened in their eyes.   440

* * * * *

45 The Benedictines were the most widespread monastic order in western Europe, each monastery remaining autonomous but all observing the Rule of St
Benedict of Nursia (c 480–c 550). Unlike the mendicant orders, who begged
for their daily bread, the Benedictine Rule provided that the monks work
to produce their own food. 'Bernardines' and 'Cistercians' are two names
for the same order, whose second founder in the twelfth century was St
Bernard of Clairvaux. Vergara could not intend here the Cistercian nuns
who were known as Bernardines, nor could he intend the Cistercian branch
that was reformed only in 1577 and came to be called 'Bernardines' at that
time.
46 Originally a grouping of hermits who, first in Italy and then almost exclusively
in Spain and Portugal, developed from the mid-fourteenth century a somewhat more coenobitical rule of life. They enjoyed the patronage of royalty and
the favour of several popes.
47 Plautus *Persa* 58

Just recently a man of great learning and stern morals was participating in a solemn religious procession when he noticed two orders of monks squabbling to have the first place, disturbing the public order. In outrage he said to them, 'Be quiet, be quiet! May the evil Erasmus get you!' They became quiet immediately, not daring to utter a word: to such an extent has   445
Erasmus become for them the same as a bugbear[48] for little boys.

Irritated daily both by serious attacks and by banter, mindful of the words of the slave in Plautus that the worker is a slave but his tongue is free,[49] they never cease to avenge their injuries with slanders and insults, whether in princely assemblies, among the common rabble, or in the com-   450
pany of housewives – in a word, with everybody, even in the secrecy of the confessional. They slander your reputation sometimes by innuendo and trickery, at other times with brazen effrontery. Since such a powerful enemy, sworn to your destruction and driven on by hatred, cannot be put down by force, you should consider whether it is wise to provoke them. For while   455
their frenzy may be contained for the present, as is my hope, I strongly fear that there is little likelihood of its being permanently suppressed. Would to God that my fears are proven wrong!

You must not think, on the other hand, that as I recount these things I am swayed by fear or uncertainty in proffering my advice. My devotion to   460
you is too well known for that suspicion to fall upon me. You have among us a great number of men outstanding in learning and rank who are sincerely devoted to you; but to this day there has been no one to surpass me in loyalty and allegiance towards you. I have never failed to seize any occasion either to praise your name and protect your reputation or to win over to   465
your cause and bring together from all sides honest men of good will. In these disputes my patronage of your cause has made my devotion to you so evident that among your adversaries I have earned the reputation of a zealot rather than an impartial judge. It is for that reason that I thought I could permit myself to lay bare my feelings to you at some length, but with   470
the understanding that I shall always cede to your authority; and whatever I see to be your wish I shall hope that it is for the best and that all will turn out well.

The Most Reverend Don Alonso de Fonseca, archbishop of Toledo, my patron, who is known for discovering and supporting men of genius, is ex-   475
traordinarily partial to your good name, and has approached the emperor

* * * * *

48 Rendered in Greek but wrongly spelled by Vergara. See Lucian *Philopseudes* 2.
49 Plautus *Persa* 280

more than once on your behalf.[50] He considers himself much in my debt because it was through my recommendation that he came to read your books. I in turn am much obliged to you because owing to that circumstance I can enjoy an intimate familiarity with my distinguished patron. For whenever he has the slightest respite from his weighty occupations he spends it in the reading of your books with me as his reader.[51]

He is now responding to your brief letter.[52] But he told me to write to you in his name that if ever you would like to come here either for the purpose of settling this present dispute or to travel to Spain to visit this famous country or to pay your respects to the emperor, he would give you four hundred gold ducats a year, and would make it his business to see that your imperial pension be paid in full. And should you decide to remain for a while at the academy of Alcalá (a city which is under his jurisdiction) he will add a very handsome residence and ample provisions for your household.[53] As far as a benefice is concerned,[54] we have no intention of offering you one, like inviting Cato to the Floralia,[55] since from your earliest youth you have shrunk from such ambitions. Nonetheless, you would soon enjoy the benevolence of the most powerful and most bounteous pontiff second

* * * * *

50 See Ep 1813 introduction.
51 Erasmus received this same service from his pupils and servants; see Ep 1805 n62.
52 See Ep 1813, Fonseca's response to Ep 1748.
53 The University of Alcalá had been founded only recently (1508–9) by Cardinal Francisco Jiménez de Cisneros. Its arts curriculum was modelled only partly on that of the University of Paris, adding an emphasis on philology, with two years of Greek mandatory for all students. In theology, students were obliged to learn the three principal scholastic approaches of Thomas Aquinas, Duns Scotus, and William of Ockham, but they were also exposed to the Scripture-oriented philology that produced the six-volume Complutensian Polyglot Bible (Alcalá, January 1514–June 1517). See Antonio Alvar Ezquerra *La Universidad de Alcalá a principios del siglo XVI* (Alcalá 1996) and 'Le modèle universitaire d'Alcalá de Henares' in *Les origines du Collège de France (1500–1560)* ed Marc Fumaroli and Marianne Lion-Viollet (Paris 1998) 209–56, especially 232–4, 240–6. See also Rummel *Jiménez* 125–136 Appendix 1 'The Constitution of San Ildefonso College,' a translation of brief excerpts from Ramón González Navarro *Universidad Complutense, Constituciones originales cisnerianas* (Alcalá 1984) 180–347.
54 That is, an ecclesiastical endowment which technically carried with it the obligation to perform pastoral duties. Church reformers criticized clerics who accepted such benefices without assuring the pastoral services.
55 Valerius Maximus 2.10.8. The stern, old-fashioned Cato would be out of place at the feast of the Floralia, noted for its licentiousness.

only to the pontiff of Rome. Moreover the favour of the prelates of Toledo   495
seems to be yours by right of heredity. The Reverend Cardinal Francisco
Jiménez,[56] founder of the Alcalá academy, a man of the highest rank and of
equal nobility of spirit, thought the world of you and anxiously desired to
enjoy your company. Then our friend Croy,[57] a young man of the highest
character and of great promise, looked to you as his mentor or, rather, as his   500
father. And now Alonso, a man of no lesser endowments, yields to neither
of them in this rivalry. Born to high estate, endowed with outstanding gifts
of nature, he is moreover naturally inclined to the study of good authors.
You will see straightaway that his attachment to you is born not of blind
enthusiasm but of mature reflection. He is presently building two colleges   505
for students, one at Compostela, where he had long exercised his episcopal
office,[58] and the other at Salamanca, his birthplace.[59] In both colleges the liberal and traditional disciplines are pursued, but especially the study of the
humanities. We hope that the Alcalá academy will also some day be made
illustrious with distinctions of no lesser kind.[60]   510

* * * * *

56 Francisco Jiménez (or Ximénez) de Cisneros (1436–1517) abandoned his early
    penchant for seeking ecclesiastical preferment to become a Franciscan friar,
    but his talents brought him administrative responsibilities in the order. In
    1492 he became confessor to Queen Isabella of Castile and later archbishop of
    Toledo and primate of Spain. He was the instigator and patron of the Com-
    plutensian Polyglot Bible and founder of the University of Alcalá; see Rummel
    Jiménez; cf CEBR II 235–7 and n53 above.
57 Guillaume (II) de Croy (1498–1521), was made abbot of St Bavo in Ghent, arch-
    bishop of Toledo, and cardinal primate of Spain, all in 1517, his nineteenth year.
    Erasmus had met him twice, in 1519 and 1520, before his untimely death near
    Worms in 1521 as a result of a fall from his horse.
58 On Alonso de Fonseca see Epp 1813, 1875. The college at Santiago de Com-
    postela receives no mention in Hastings Rashdall *The Universities of Europe in
    the Middle Ages* 2nd ed F.M. Powicke and R.B. Emden, 3 vols (Oxford 1936); but
    Blazius Ortiz *Summi templi Toletani descriptio* (Toledo: Juan Ayala 1549) f 135,
    describes it as 'Collegium aliud literarium priuilegio etiam studii generalis.'
59 The Colegio de Santiago at Salamanca, also known as the Colegio del Arzo-
    bispo Fonseca, was founded in 1521–2. Its impressive buildings were not com-
    pleted until long after Fonseca's death. Judged as one of the four 'greater col-
    leges' at the University of Salamanca, it later became known as the 'College
    of the Noble Irish,' a seminary for training Irish priests (Rashdall [n58 above]
    90 n2) and, at a still later date, a Jesuit residence. See Julián Alvarez Villar
    La Universidad de Salamanca (Salamanca 1990) 167–79. According to CWE II 42
    Fonseca was born not in Salamanca but in Santiago de Compostela, where his
    father was archbishop before him.
60 This is slight praise indeed for the University of Alcalá (see n53 above).

So then, should your age or the state of your health make it impossible to accept the offer made by this most generous prelate, nevertheless let your goodness of heart give suitable importance to it, coming as it does from such a noble spirit. And would that some saint would instil the thought of this pilgrimage in your mind, Erasmus! You would bring happiness to me, you would bring happiness to our country, and you would crush the conspiracy of these barbarians and haters of the beautiful,[61] whom you could beat off and utterly destroy with no trouble at all. But I see that the matter is too serious for my exhortation to make much difference in persuading you one way or another. You have, therefore – returning once again to your own cause – the unlimited favour of my prince; what is more, you have many influential men on your side. Mercurino Gattinara, the imperial chancellor, who is also most favourable to your cause, set out not so long ago on a trip to Italy, but has not yet left Spanish territory.[62] Rumour has it that he has abandoned his intended journey and will return here. Alfonso de Valdés, the emperor's secretary, is one of your keenest defenders.[63] To Luis Coronel, a man of great learning and influence, you owe much.[64] I hope Sancho Carranza will be present at the meeting of the theologians on the feast of the Ascension; I count him in the first rank of your defenders. He has taken great care to make up for that first little resentment, and misses no occasion to sing your praises, so that even if there has been a leak in your friendship you must admit that the roof has been repaired.[65] Guy Morillon misses no opportunity to be of service to you as an attentive and loyal friend.[66] And

* * * * *

61 Given in Greek
62 Gattinara had been the grand chancellor of Spain since 15 October 1518; Erasmus already had ample proof of his good opinion; see CEBR II 76–80.
63 See Ep 1807 introduction.
64 Luis Núñez Coronel was a graduate in arts at Salamanca, doctor of theology of the University of Paris (1514), and a preacher and confessor in the court of Charles v. He served in inquisitions in Brussels, Ghent, Bruges, and Antwerp in 1521–2, and accompanied Charles v on his visit to England in 1522; later he was a secretary to the inquisitor Alonso Manrique de Lara. He wrote a defence of Erasmus' Enchiridion that has not survived (cf Ep 1581:856–7) and remained an admirer. He gave a balanced appraisal of the articles proposed for the Valladolid assembly; see Beltrán de Heredia Cartulario VI 59–62, Farge BR 114–16 no 117, CEBR I 342–3.
65 See Ep 1805 n84. Carranza did intervene in Erasmus' favour at the Valladolid assembly, as Vergara hopes here (Beltrán de Heredia Cartulario VI 43–4). On the date see n37 above.
66 Previously secretary to the imperial chancellor, Morillon was at this time one of the secretaries of Emperor Charles v. A humanist scholar in his own right,

even among the monks you will find some well-born individuals who will
put piety above factionalism. Among those who show their favour openly,   535
you can place Alonso of Olmedo in the first rank.[67] There are others as well,
not few in number, who would demonstrate their devotion to you were they
not afraid of being punished by their confrères as deserters. Almost everyone at Alcalá has sympathetic and friendly feelings towards you, saving one
here or there too long imbued with stale doctrine, from whose skulls you   540
would never eradicate those ingrained prejudices.[68] On the whole they love
good letters and combine them with the higher disciplines. You would have
a hard time finding anywhere else a group of scholars less willing to defend
the sorry state of public education.

Moreover the new academy, instituted in the light of our own age and   545
free of the tyranny of the old-school dispensers of bad learning (which frequently prevails elsewhere), easily distinguishes what are the best studies
and gives them a very honourable place alongside the more common and traditional disciplines. My brother Francisco Vergara, an exceptionally learned
young man, formerly my pupil in the rudiments of Greek, now better than   550
his teacher, as the proverb goes,[69] teaches Greek literature there with great
acclaim.[70] I have enclosed a Greek letter of his written some time ago.[71] If
you would think it worthy of a response, both of us would be very pleased.
Bernardino Tovar,[72] his elder brother, works together with us; he is a learned
and more especially a pious man, who rivals me in his affection for you.   555
He applies himself to the reading of your books and takes up their defence
with such determination that he seems to have been specially cut out for
this mission. Thus you have a triumvirate proclaiming your praise – created,
one could say, for this very task – joined to you no less by the bonds of love
than they are to each other by those of blood. If their support is not of much 560
help to you, at least their intentions are not to be despised. Farewell.

Valladolid, 24 April 1527

* * * * *

he dealt with Erasmus concerning payment of his Courtrai pension; see CEBR
II 461–2.
67 See n1 above.
68 *veteres avias* (Persius 5.92)
69 *Adagia* III v 23, rendered here in Greek; cf Epp 962:34, 1146:23.
70 Francisco de Vergara was first a student and then, from 1522, a professor of
   Greek at Alcalá. He had studied with Demetrius of Crete and Hernán Núñez
   de Toledo, better known as *Comendador griego* or *El Pinciano*, in the college of
   San Ildefonso at Alcalá. See Ep 1876 introduction; cf CEBR III 383–4.
71 Not extant; Erasmus acknowledged its receipt and sent a copy to the Collegium
   Trilingue in Louvain (Ep 1876:13–15).
72 See n14 above.

1815 / To Mercurino Arborio di Gattinara   Basel, 29 April 1527

This letter, which answers Epp 1785 (but not 1790A), repeats a number of items already communicated to Gattinara in Ep 1747. It was first published in the *Opus epistolarum* (1529). The original manuscript, written and addressed by a secretary but bearing corrections, signature, and subscription in Erasmus' own hand, is in the Biblioteca nacional, Madrid MS Est 18 gr 1 5 f 7.

Gattinara (1465–1530), a native of Savoyard Piedmont and an expert in Roman law, enjoyed the entire confidence of Emperor Charles V, whose election he had managed. He believed Erasmus to be the most promising counterforce to incipient confessional division. As imperial chancellor, he successfully intervened against Erasmus' Louvain enemies by writing to them a stern letter (Ep 1747) that followed closely Erasmus' own instructions and warned them against continuing to ignore the imperial edict ordering them to cease their attacks on Erasmus. See CEBR II 76–80; ER III 21.

Sincerest greetings. Permit me to respond in a few words to your second letter,[1] noble sir. Whatever good fortune has come my way, I should wish to share it with you, since your integrity and singular piety have surely merited continued success. We have been favoured with more than one fortunate occurrence. Death has snatched from the earth the two persons expressly named in the emperor's decree:[2] Vincent died of tympanites, an excruciating condition;[3] and Nicolaas Baechem,[4] who had become insuffer-   5

* * * * *

1815
1 Ep 1785, which apparently arrived before Erasmus had answered Ep 1757. In the second letter, Gattinara considers providential the deaths of Erasmus' Louvain enemies Vincentius Theoderici and Nicolaas Baechem.
2 See Ep 1643:17; but the imperial letter itself is not extant.
3 Vincentius Theoderici, a Dominican master of theology at Louvain, who was convinced that Erasmus' works were giving aid to the Lutheran cause. Erasmus' long and satirical letter to him (Ep 1196) and his letter to the Louvain faculty of theology (Ep 1217), both published by Erasmus in 1521, had only made the rift between them deeper (CEBR III 317–18). On the manner of his death see Ep 1765:26–8 and n7.
4 Nicolaas Baechem, or Egmondanus, a Carmelite friar, was Erasmus' most vociferous critic in Louvain as well as a censor and inquisitor in the Low Countries. He particularly denounced Erasmus' scriptural exegesis. Erasmus in turn satirized Baechem repeatedly in letters and works, and eventually had him silenced by two popes and by the imperial regent in the Netherlands (CEBR I 81–3). There is no record of correspondence between them, but Erasmus' own letters are replete with negative remarks about him (eg Epp 878:15–

able to all alike, choked to death in a fit of vomiting while walking up
and down, just after dismissing the maid who was usually present to attend him, saying that he wished to finish praying the hours,[5] as they are   10
called. Then, too, Noël Béda, who wrote that frenzied and libellous book
against me,[6] was thrown into prison together with some others by the king
of France.[7] This shows clearly that, unless rulers use their authority to keep
the insensible and defiant arrogance of certain individuals in check, they
will stir up a new storm for us just when the present one is about to sub-   15
side. There is no mystery about what for centuries now has aroused and

* * * * *

16, 948:141–9, 1166:20–4, 1196:598–675, 1225:36–63). In Ep 1162 to Thomas
More Erasmus devotes the entire letter to a description of Baechem's confrontation with Erasmus in the presence of the rector of the University of
Louvain.
5 Obeying the injunction of Jesus to 'pray at all times' (Luke 18:1; cf Eph
6:18), many early Christians prayed at specified hours every day. A number of different rites or approaches evolved in different areas over the centuries. St Benedict (sixth century) adapted for his monks the rite used in the
basilicas of Rome. He mandated communal prayer (usually chanted) at eight
(later seven) specified times each day: vigils or nocturnes, later called matins,
in the middle of the night; lauds at daybreak; terce, sext, and none at the
third, sixth, and ninth hours of daylight; vespers in the evening; and compline before retiring; see Jonathan Black 'The Divine Office and Private Devotion in the Latin West' in *The Liturgy of the Medieval Church* ed Thomas J.
Heffernan (Kalamazoo 2001) 45–71. This practice and rite, known as the Divine Office, gradually became common throughout the West. While monks
continued to chant these canonical 'hours' in choir, secular priests and dea-
cons and members of mendicant orders (like the Carmelite Nicolaas Baechem)
were obliged to pray them in private, using a manual known as the breviary. The Divine Office consisted primarily of the 150 psalms, arranged so
that the whole psalter was prayed each week. Antiphons, lessons drawn from
Scripture, canticles, lives of saints, and orations were added over the years.
It was not uncommon for pious nobles or other wealthy persons to own and
use their personal 'Book of Hours.' Contemporary post-Vatican ii terminology
for the Divine Office, the 'Liturgy of the Hours,' has revived Erasmus' usage
here.
6 Béda's *Annotationes* against Lefèvre d'Etaples and Erasmus (Paris: Josse Bade,
28 May 1526); see Ep 1804 n14.
7 A false rumour that Erasmus later corrected by substituting *cohiberi coepit* 'has
begun to be restrained' when he published this letter in the *Opus epistolarum*
(1529). In Ep 1875:91–4 Erasmus speaks of an overnight detention at the royal
court; but this also was a false rumour. Only later, in 1533, would Béda be
exiled (and in 1535 imprisoned) for his consistent opposition to royal policies
that he considered favourable to the spread of heresy.

fomented discord among great princes.[8] I am astonished if they themselves
do not recognize it; and if, though fully aware of it, they feign ignorance, I
wonder all the more. But to these events divine providence will bring about
a happy outcome.   20

I have long experienced, most honoured sir, your unwavering and sincere attachment to me; and yet with greater proofs each day you reveal your
commitment to the cause of higher learning and Christian piety, for the advancement and preservation of which, if in no other way, I shall surely maintain a sincere and stalwart spirit until my last breath. A copy of the letter   25
you sent to Louvain[9] has not yet reached me. From letters of my friends,
however, I am kept informed of what you have to say. But these scoundrels
flout everything, suborning those around them and resorting to a thousand stratagems. The whole business is being managed by the wiles of two
people.[10] With Baechem dead there has appeared in Louvain a Franciscan   30
who in his public lectures repeatedly casts slurs upon my name.[11] This sort
of person fears no one; at the first sign of danger they shift their position
and retreat to safer ground; and, although they succeed only in drawing
worse hatred upon themselves, still they keep on as if driven mad by the
Furies. But Christ in his great goodness will turn even all these woes to a   35
good end.

What opportunities Spain holds for Lee I know not.[12] This one thing I
do know, that he will incur the disfavour of his king, the cardinal of York,[13]
and countless other bishops, noblemen, and scholars of England. And assuredly it would have added to the glory of that land had the world not   40
learned that it harbours such a venomous talent. I have included in this letter an excerpt from a letter of Cuthbert Tunstall,[14] whom Lee succeeded as
ambassador, so that you would more readily believe my words. The law

* * * * *

8 Erasmus' presumption that Gattinara would comprehend this statement leaves
   other readers, and perhaps Gattinara himself, to ponder his meaning.
9 Ep 1784A
10 Probably Nicolas Coppin of Mons and Jacobus Latomus of Cambron, who,
   after the deaths of Theoderici and Baechem, became Erasmus' most vocal critics in the University of Louvain
11 Frans Titelmans of Hasselt, a student of Jacobus Latomus, who exchanged letters with Erasmus and published works critical of Erasmus' exegesis; cf Epp
   1823 introduction, 1837A, and CEBR III 326–7.
12 See Ep 1814 n39.
13 Thomas Wolsey
14 See Ep 1804 n1.

that restricts reckless publishing I heartily approve.[15] But at the same time
care must be taken that an excellent law does not turn into a deplorable   45
precedent, as has begun to be the case in Paris.[16] Some conspiring parties
were freely venting their fury in calumnies and lies against whomever they
pleased.[17] If you tried to answer, they forbade you to print it. Thus you
first of all, together with the archbishops of Toledo and Seville,[18] must be
on your guard, using great vigilance and prudence, lest such things happen   50
in Spain as well.

I was hoping to broach more subjects with you, knowing that in your
great kindness and despite your many occupations you are so receptive to
our intrusive letters that you even urge me to write more frequently. But
I have returned to the gladiatorial arena.[19] My *Hyperaspistes* and *Diatribe* I   55
think you have seen. In the *Hyperaspistes*, which, since I was running out
of time, I finished in a great hurry in a matter of days, I had promised the
remaining part of the argument.[20] The truth is I would have preferred to
dedicate my energies to other subjects; but Luther, in published pamphlets,
boasts that I make no answer – as if indeed I have not already answered   60
him – and the Lutherans are elated. Therefore at the urging of my friends I
have set myself to fulfil my promise. Farewell, great patron, together with
your excellent prince. At Basel, on the day before the last day of April in
the year 1527

* * * * *

15 For censorship in Spain see Ep 1814 n20. Erasmus complained to the magistrates of Strasbourg (Epp 1429 and 1477) and to the town council of Basel (Ep
   1477A) about pamphlets he considered libellous, and gave reasons why such
   works should be suppressed; but he stopped short of actually asking them to
   prohibit publishing and selling or to destroy such works.
16 On 21 March 1521 the Parlement of Paris issued in the king's name a decree
   authorizing the faculty of theology to examine, approve, or prohibit all books
   dealing with religion. It actively enforced the faculty's decisions against Erasmus' books. See Farge *Parti conservateur* 32–5; cf 47–52, 53–7; and James K. Farge
   'Early Censorship of Printed Books in Paris: New Perspectives and Insights'
   in *Le contrôle des idées à la Renaissance* ed J.M. De Bujanda (Geneva 1996) 75–91.
17 Erasmus probably shifts his attention here from Paris back to Spain, where a
   number of theologians were seeking to censure his books.
18 Alonso de Fonseca (see Ep 1748 introduction) and Alonso Manrique de Lara,
   grand inquisitor (see Ep 1846 introduction).
19 *Adagia* I iii 76. Erasmus frequently compares himself to a gladiator (see, for
   example, Epp 1825:32–3, 1875:125–6, 1885:124).
20 For Erasmus' response to Luther in *De libero arbitrio* and *Hyperaspistes* see Ep
   1804 n10.

Your Excellency's most devoted client,
Erasmus of Rotterdam
Signed in my own hand
To the most illustrious Mercurino Gattinara, grand chancellor of the
invincible Emperor Charles. In Spain

1816 / From William Blount, Lord Mountjoy   [Greenwich?] 1 May [1527]

William Blount was one of the students whom Erasmus tutored in Paris c
1498–9. His invitation to Erasmus to accompany him back to England provided
Erasmus with his first encounters with Thomas More, John Colet, and other
humanists, and with Prince Henry. Mountjoy was now head of the household
of Queen Catherine of Aragon. On the vicissitudes of his correspondence with
Erasmus see Ep 1740 n3.

The manuscript of this letter (Ep 66 in Förstemann-Günther), written and
addressed by a secretary but signed by Mountjoy, was in the University Library in Leipzig. Internal reference to the queen (lines 13–17) confirms the
year date as 1527.

Greetings, my dearest Erasmus. I was delighted to receive your last letter
and even more delighted to read it.[1] It is not so, as you write, that you
overwhelm me with the frequency of your letters, since I received only
two this year.[2] And yet if you had sent me several packets of them, you
could have done nothing more gratifying for your Mountjoy, since in the
reading of them he becomes more learned, as is his fondest ambition, and
seems almost to converse with Erasmus, whose absence causes him such
great sadness. I am quite astonished that you are so disturbed by my silence, for if you were truly aware of the feelings Mountjoy entertains for
you, you would know that the sincerity of his devotion has no need to be
confirmed by any words, spoken or written. As to the fact that I let Kan[3]
get away without a letter from me I can only blame my own carelessness.
He set sail from Dover before my letter was ready. But be well assured that
our glorious queen is favourably impressed with your *Institution of Christian*

* * * * *

1816
1 The letter is not extant; it was probably contemporary with Ep 1804 to
   More.
2 Neither is extant.
3 Nicolaas Kan of Amsterdam, who was now in Erasmus' service as secretary
   and courier; see Ep 1832 introduction.

Marriage.[4] She is most grateful to you for this devoted act of yours, and you   15
will learn amply of her good will towards you from the servant to whom I
myself have made it known in some detail.[5]

Your servant whom you sent to me I welcomed with great pleasure,
since I found him to be both a learned, modest, and sensible young man,
and one very dear to you.[6] But there is one thing of which I must complain: 20
you recommended him to me in such terms as if Mountjoy would require
multiple petitions to do something in an Erasmian cause. Believe me, no one
sent by you can be other than most welcome, even if he be the most humble
of men. I am sorry that Franz Birckmann has behaved so unfairly to you;
on the other hand I am happy that I have been forewarned of his character,   25
and have not had extensive dealings with him.[7]

As for your making your way here, no one can give you better counsel than yourself, for you best know your state of health and the degree of
strength necessary to undertake such a journey. If you think yourself to be
sufficiently strong and robust, then we have good reason to encourage you   30
in your intent, first because you have so many old friends here – not just
ordinary friends, but staunch and true ones, who bear you great affection.
Next because there is no country anywhere in these times that is more tranquil and at peace, where you can more freely devote yourself to your scholarly pursuits, especially to publish very useful works against the iniquitous   35
founders of new heresies, a task you cannot perform in the places where
you now reside without great personal danger and distraction. Added to
this is a consideration that should particularly influence you, that here you
will find our prince to be one of your most fervent followers. He has invited

* * * * *

4 For this text see CWE 69 203–438. It was Lord Mountjoy, acting in Queen Catherine's name, who had originally asked Erasmus to write a book about marriage
   (Ep 1624:68–72). Thomas More, however, first mentioned the queen's receiving it (Ep 1770:21–3), and Erasmus expressed surprise to More at not having
   heard directly from Mountjoy or the queen about the book, a presentation
   copy of which Kan had carried to her. But when he wrote, 'My mind dictated
   one thing, my pen wrote another' Erasmus seems to have anticipated a certain coolness on the part of the queen for some of the opinions he expressed
   in it; cf Ep 1804:316.
5 Probably Nicolaas Kan (n3 above), to whom Mountjoy had failed to give a
   letter but to whom he may well have spoken about this matter
6 Nicolaas Kan (nn3 and 5 above)
7 Birckmann was a bookseller with offices in many cities whom Erasmus, after
   years of financial dealings of different kinds, no longer trusted. See Epp 1804
   n76.

you by his own letter,[8] as I have learned, not merely allowing you freedom,   40
greater than any you could desire, to pursue your career but also offering
very lavish conditions. I do not think these should be rejected, my dearest
Erasmus, for in my opinion you will thus be enabled to look to your reputation, your tranquillity and, what is most important by far, to advance
vigorously the cause of Christ and his church for the salvation of your soul.   45

Finally, at the end of your letter[9] you write, 'if you have any concern
for me' and 'if you will deign to speak to my servant.' The first statement is
to no purpose, if your feelings are as you described them at the beginning
of your letter: 'For I cannot in any way be led to have doubts about your
unfailing good will towards me.' As for the second statement, your servant   50
can be my witness; unless I am mistaken he cannot complain that I was ever
querulous or the slightest bit disdainful in conversing with him. Of a certainty no one has held himself or his possessions more dear than I have held
you and your interests. If you feel otherwise, you would be very much in
error, as you would abundantly experience if ever the services of Mountjoy   55
could in any way be of use to Erasmus.

Farewell, from the British court, 1 May 1527.

Very truly yours, William Mountjoy

To the renowned theologian Desiderius Erasmus of Rotterdam, his
dearest of friends. In Basel   60

1817 / From Germain de Brie   Paris, 10 May 1527

This original letter (Ep 66 in Förstemann-Günther) was written in the hand
of a secretary, but Brie made several corrections and inscribed the heading,
the address, and the Greek phrases in his own hand. It was in the ill-fated
Burscher Collection in the University Library at Leipzig (see Ep 1254 introduction). The letter answers one from Erasmus that is not extant but contemporaneous with Epp 1794 and 1795, which accompanied the presentation copy
to Brie of Erasmus' translations of John Chrysostom (Ep 1800), a volume that
included Brie's translation of Chrysostom's treatise on the priesthood.

* * * * *

8 Because the invitation from Henry VIII would not be written until mid-Septem-
  ber 1527 (Ep 1878), Henry de Vocht (*Englische Studien* 40 [1909] 386–8) suggested the year-date of the present letter should be corrected to 1528. But
  Mountjoy's reference to the royal letter is based on hearsay, not first-hand
  information, and allows the present date to stand.
9 Not extant; cf n1 above.

Germain de Brie (c 1490–1538), a native of Auxerre, studied Greek with
Janus Lascaris in Venice and with Marcus Musurus in Padua. He had been
familiar with Erasmus since their meeting in Venice in 1508, and they had
already exchanged several letters (Epp 212, 569, 620, 1045, 1117, 1184, 1185,
1233, 1733), some of which concerned Erasmus' settling a feud between Brie
and Thomas More that had broken out when More disparaged one of Brie's
poems. With benefit of several ecclesiastical prebends Brie was able to live in
Paris as a leisured scholar. For his works see Jean-François Maillard et al *La
France des humanistes: Hellénistes I* (Turnhout 1999) 11–40. On his role in French
scholarship see Marie-Madeleine de la Garanderie *Christianisme et lettres profanes: Essai sur l'humanisme français (1515–1535) et sur la pensée de Guillaume Budé*
rev ed (Paris 1995) 133–60.

GERMAIN DE BRIE TO ERASMUS OF ROTTERDAM

While I was in the country your long-awaited and greatly desired letter was
brought to me.[1] Shortly afterwards, upon my return to Paris, the man to
whom you had entrusted its delivery came to present me with a book as a
gift from you. A most agreeable gift in itself, it was made all the more so   5
because there, among the learned and elegant products of your long vigils
(a good part of which I have already examined), you allotted a place of honour and distinction to the fruit of my labours – whatever it may be worth:
namely, my translation *On the Priesthood*.[2] You placed it, in fact, immediately
after your version of Chrysostom's *Third Homily on the Acts of the Apostles*, to-   10
wards the end of which Chrysostom takes the opportunity to discuss the role
of the priest, treating the subject in such a way that either that whole passage
depends on his lengthy treatment of the same theme in the work I translated or this latter work is heavily dependent on the passage in that third

* * * * *

1817
1 Brie was probably at his country home in Gentilly, located south-east of Paris
  near Créteil in the Val-de-Marne. The letter is not extant.
2 Brie's Latin translation of Chrysostom's treatise, the Greek text of which Erasmus had edited for the first time (Basel: Froben 1525), fills pages 212–304 of
  Erasmus' Latin edition *Chrysostomi lucubrationes* (Basel: Froben, March 1527).
  Brie's translation appeared first in Paris (Josse Bade, 5 August 1526; see Moreau
  Inventaire III 302 no 1039) before its republication in Basel. With several later
  reprintings it would remain authoritative until the thirteen-volume Greek-
  Latin folio edition by the Maurist Benedictine Bernard de Montfaucon (Paris
  1718–38; repr Venice 1734–41). See Jean Chrysostome *Sur le sacerdoce* ed Anne-
  Marie Malinguey SC 273 (Paris 1980) 42.

homily.[3] You could not have effected a more cohesive arrangement. In ad-   15
dition to the gratitude I owe you for including my work among your own
polished writings, I am further indebted to you for your letter to the king of
Portugal. If I may express my genuine feelings, in reading it I was deeply
touched by your recommendation of me, 'brief, but exceeding sweet.'[4] For,
like Hector in the play of Naevius,[5] it is gratifying to be praised by one who   20
is himself praised; to which I may add – as it befell me through your kindness – in the presence of one who is praised and who is at the same time a
king of great distinction. It is an old proverb that says: 'All mortals enjoy
being praised.'[6]

Regarding your exhortation that I seek immortality for my name (which   25
you demonstrate is most readily attainable to me through the translation of
Chrysostom's writings), this is indeed very kind and friendly of you. Far
from being envious of Brie, you call upon him to join in your own success;
you invite him to share the immortality you already enjoy, even transfer-
ring and conceding to him a small part of those means by which he may   30
arrive there without too much difficulty. Would it were possible, most kind
Erasmus, now that your exhortation has added no little stimulus to my ambitions and given me the courage to attempt other more important projects
of the same order, seeing that my efforts do not lack the support and approval of the chief arbiter in this field of learning; if only, I say, it will not be   35
too arduous a task for you to have your friend Froben print Chrysostom's
Greek commentaries on the Epistle to the Galatians or the two Epistles to
the Corinthians, which you say you have in hand.[7] For if I had either of

* * * * *

3 We have fifty-five extant homilies on the Acts of the Apostles composed seriatim by John Chrysostom. The concluding section of the third homily, which
concerns Acts 1:12, warns priests against seeking preferment, especially the
office of bishop, which carries a multitude of burdens. See PG 60 40–2 / NPNF
1st series 11 22–5.

4 *Iliad* 3.214; Brie writes this phrase in Greek. See Ep 1800, the dedication of
Chrysostomi lucubrationes to King John III, lines 102–9, where Erasmus praises
Brie's translation, comparing his eloquence to that of Chrysostom himself.

5 See Naevius *The Departure of Hector* fragment 2 in *Remains of Old Latin* ed E.H.
Warmington (Cambridge, Mass 1936) II 118; cf Cicero *Tusculan Disputations*
4.31.67, *Ad familiares* 5.12, 15.6.

6 Menander *Sententiae* ed Siegfried Jaekel (Leipzig 1964) 753. Brie quotes the
phrase in Greek.

7 Probably a reference to the Greek manuscript bought at Padua, perhaps by
Reginald Pole, and made available to Erasmus, who doubted its attribution to
Chrysostom (Ep 1675:10–11) but eventually published several of its homilies.
For its provenance and Erasmus' attitude towards it see Allen Ep 1623:9n. For

these two commentaries at my disposal, I would gladly devote my energies
to translating one of them while you worked on the other, and would not   40
account it a disgrace or dishonour to be outdone by you. It would be sufficient glory to my name to be thought to be your rival, to follow in your
footsteps, to be and to be regarded as coming after you 'next, though far
behind.'[8] And you write that you have also delivered the Life of Babylas to
Froben to be printed in Greek.[9] As soon as I can procure a copy I will set   45
to work on a Latin translation; especially since I hear (and I am certain the
report is true, if you say so) that Oecolampadius' version contains many
faults.[10] In any case he was always suspect to me in whatever translations he
undertook because of his deficiencies in both languages, if you will permit
me to speak frankly. And that is not to mention what your letter points out   50
and about which Lupset had cautioned me long before I read your letter,[11]
namely, that learned men have discovered many distortions in Oecolampadius' versions in which he has perverted the meaning to fit beliefs rejected

* * * * *

the commentary on Galatians see Ep 1841, the dedication of Erasmus' Latin
translation. Though not unanimous about its authenticity, later editors have
included this commentary with Chrysostom's works. In Oeuvres de Saint Jean
Chrysostome (Arras 1888) x 571 M. Jeannin wrote, 'Chrysostom did not take the
care with this commentary that he took with the others.' At this time Erasmus
thought Lefèvre d'Etaples and Gérard Roussel had already translated Chrysostom's commentaries on 1 and 2 Corinthians or that they were in the process of doing so; see Ep 1795:1–16. The commentaries are in the form of a
series of homilies on the pericopes taken seriatim: forty-four homilies for 1
Corinthians and thirty for 2 Corinthians. See Oeuvres de Saint Jean Chrysostome
IX 297–610, X 1–185.
8 Virgil Aeneid 5.320
9 See Ep 1856, the preface to Erasmus' Greek text of St John Chrysostom's De
Babyla martyre (Basel: Johann Froben, August 1527).
10 Brie's Latin translation, Liber contra gentiles, Babylae Antiocheni episcopi ... vitam
continens ... Contra Ioannis Oecolampadii translationem appeared c March 1528
in the Paris press of Simon de Colines (Moreau Inventaire III 420 no 1528).
This also contained Brie's Insignium Ioannis Oecolampadii erratorum ... elenchus,
that is, a list of the errors in Oecolampadius' 1523 translation. Oecolampadius' translation De sancto Babyla had appeared in his Psegmata quaedam (Basel:
Andreas Cratander, March 1523).
11 That is, the letter (not extant) mentioned in line 1. Thomas Lupset, a former
pupil of John Colet, had met Erasmus in 1499. He edited Thomas Linacre's
translations of Galen and was a former regent in Oxford, but was lately resident in Padua in the retinue of Reginald Pole. In 1525 he assisted in the Aldine
Greek edition of Galen. He probably met Brie in Paris when travelling with
Pole from Italy in October 1526; see Ep 1761:1–11.

by good men. Lupset closely shares my enthusiasm now in the pursuit of
learning. His good nature and charm of conversation have been of such ad-   55
vantage to me that he has offered me a splendid opportunity to contract a
friendship with his patron Reginald Pole, of whom your letter makes mention. When you wrote that letter, you were hoping that Pole had already
árrived here. He is still living with his kinsmen in England, but is to arrive
here shortly.[12] I am all the more desirous of being admitted into his friend-   60
ship because I hear that he has brought with him a rich collection of Greek
manuscripts from Venice.

   With regard to More, what else, I pray, can I write to you than what I
have declared over and over again in my published writings – that I in no
way shun his friendship, even if he has gravely offended me without my   65
deserving it,[13] especially since you act as mediator and special envoy[14] between us, with whose wishes obviously I cannot honourably disagree? Such
is my devotion and so great is my affection for you that whatever you consider the right thing to do and whatever you wish seem to me to be right
and just. Therefore in restoring the friendship between More and myself   70
'do as you wish and as your heart desires.'[15] I shall follow without hesitation
wherever you will lead. Besides, I feel inclined of my own will to renew

* * * * *

12 Although inclined by temperament to seek peaceful resolution to conflict, Reginald Pole (1500–58) later broke with his royal cousin over his repudiation of
   Catherine of Aragon and his break with Rome, directing his *De unitate* (Rome
   1539) to Henry himself. Pole's mother and brother having both been arrested
   and executed in England, he remained in Italy and served three popes as
   legate. He was a member of the Roman commission which drafted the *Consilium de emendanda ecclesia* (1536) calling for extensive reform of the church, and
   was made a cardinal in that year by Pope Paul III, who later named him as one
   of the three legates to open the Council of Trent. In 1549 he narrowly missed
   election as pope. He was ordained a priest in 1556, when he became archbishop of Canterbury under Queen Mary, whose stringent policies he tried to
   mitigate. He died in the plague of 1558 on the same day as the queen. See
   Thomas F. Mayer *Reginald Pole: Prince and Prophet* (Cambridge and New York
   2000). See also Ep 1627 introduction; CEBR III 103–5; ER V 105–6. Pole's presence in Paris is not documented until 1529, when he was a reluctant member of
   the ambassadorial group seeking the university's approval of the annulment
   of Henry VIII's marriage to Catherine of Aragon.
13 For the quarrel between More and Brie, which grew out of More's criticism
   of Brie's anti-English sentiments, see Epp 620, 1045, and 1087.
14 Brie uses the term *pater patratus*, a Roman term for a senator appointed as
   'father' of a deputation sent to a foreign power to ratify a contract which, in
   civil law, only a father could carry out; cf Cicero *De oratore* 1.181; Livy 1.24.4.
15 *Iliad* 4.37 and cf 22.185; the phrase is rendered in Greek.

my friendship with More, especially at this time when I see the wonderful
agreement that exists between our King Francis and King Henry of England. In these favourable circumstances the idea of visiting that island of-   75
ten suggests itself to me; and in such a visit, unless some untoward chance
should prevent me, I have resolved to pay a visit directly to More (who, I
hear, enjoys rare and even unrivalled favour with both the king and the cardinal),[16] to give him my greetings and join hands with him in a generous
spirit, as the Muses clearly invite me. I am far from thinking that I shall find   80
More alienated from me. Indeed I have every confidence that in my visit
to Britain I shall find in this devotee and host of the Muses and Graces a
faithful intermediary and obliging friend in every need, unless perchance
he should wish to belie and even adulterate the portrayal of his character as
many have described it to me. He will not do that, I am sure, especially after   85
learning from your letters not only how I have forgotten about that unfortunate quarrel which once rose up between us through some adverse fate but
also how on my part I extend to him my open arms, since every trace of that
discord has disappeared, and that I am prepared with all my strength to
enter into, fashion, and consolidate a mutual understanding and friendship   90
with him in a lifelong accord, for which I augur every good fortune.

But enough on this subject. To respond last of all to what you touched
on in the first part of your letter, the labours you have endured in subdu-
ing so many monsters. You have no reason for chagrin or regret, since you
brought no less ignominy on your enemies than glory upon yourself, though   95
there be no glory greater than yours. And certainly I do not think that it
was through any displeasure of Minerva, guardian of men of talent, towards
you; rather, her bounty and kindness have thus far exposed you to so many
glorious battles, which we have seen you bring to such a successful conclusion. For she knows and wishes to give concrete proof to those whose cause   100
she sustains that such is the nature of praiseworthy and honourable things,
that the more you try to crush and oppress them, the more they rise up and
increase in strength, while the efforts of evil men are turned to the opposite
effect. Thus, as you have always done, bend all your efforts to the service
of literary studies, branding the enemies of such learning with an indelible   105
mark of ignominy and procuring lasting, unending glory for yourself, with
Apollo always at your side. Farewell, and continue to love me as you do.

Paris, 10 May 1527

To the most eloquent Master Erasmus of Rotterdam

* * * * *

16 Thomas Wolsey

1818 / To Lazarus a Parentibus   Basel, 11 May 1527

This letter, autograph throughout, was in the possession of Dr Carl Geibel
of Leipzig when Allen transcribed it. The year-date can be determined from
mention of the new, fourth edition of the New Testament.

The addressee, a citizen and resident of Genoa, is known only from this letter. One can presume, however, that he was the unnamed merchant of Genoa
who in September 1525 had carried Ep 1613 from Juan Luis Vives at Bruges
to Erasmus at Basel (CEBR III 51).

Sincere greetings, Lazarus, truest of friends. I replied to your earlier letter
but not to the last one because there was no one who could deliver it for me.[1]
Crato, who brings this to you, is a very good-natured young man who once
boarded with me.[2] He plans to do business in your part of the world; please
consider him as having my recommendation. I wish it were convenient for   5
you to have business transactions in Basel so that I could at last enjoy your
company more near at hand!

You promised that you would send me a work written against me.[3]
The world is full of writers of this sort; nevertheless, I would be pleased if
you would send me some excerpts so that I may get the flavour of it. The   10
New Testament with annotations has been published again for the fourth
time in a handsome edition.[4] I pray that my friend Lazarus will be blessed
with every happiness and prosperity.

At Basel, 11 May in the year 1527

Your friend, Erasmus of Rotterdam (written in my own hand, as you   15
will recognize)

To the most distinguished gentleman, Lazarus a Parentibus, citizen of
Genoa. In Genoa

* * * * *

1818
1 Neither the most recent letter from Lazarus nor Erasmus' reply to the first one
   is extant.
2 Crato Stalburg of Frankfurt, a former member of Erasmus' household, now
   engaged in commerce (Ep 1673 n3)
3 Allen speculated that it might be a work of the Dominican Lancellotto de'
   Politi (Ambrosius Catharinus). His polemical works against Erasmus were
   published much later; but Parentibus might have had access to a manuscript
   copy, since Erasmus asks only for some excerpts.
4 Erasmus' earlier editions appeared in 1516, 1519, and 1523. He had already undertaken this fourth edition, the first to make use of the Complutensian Polyglot Bible, in July 1524. Froben began the printing in mid-1526 and finished it
   in March 1527. The Froben press would issue the fifth and last edition in 1535.

1819 / To Sigismund I   Basel, 15 May 1527

This letter, which constitutes a short treatise on kingship and on war and peace, first appeared in a volume now rare, *Desiderii Erasmi Roterodami Epistola ad inclytum Sigismundum regem Poloniae* (Cracow: Matthias Scharffenberg 1527). Edited by Stanislaus Hosius, who dedicated it to Bishop Piotr Tomicki of Cracow, it contains some phrases that Erasmus had obviously not intended for publication and that he either omitted or changed when he later published it in the *Opus epistolarum.* Jan (II) Łaski had urged Erasmus to write to Sigismund (Ep 1674:21–2), a fact about which Erasmus apprised his Polish correspondents (Epp 1820:10–11, 1821:16, 1915–16, 1918).

Sigismund, born in Cracow in 1467, reigned in Poland from 1506 to 1548. His extremely complex reign is masterfully summarized in CEBR III 249–51.

TO THE MOST SERENE KING OF POLAND, SIGISMUND, FIRST
OF THAT NAME, FROM ERASMUS OF ROTTERDAM, GREETING
As I took my pen in hand, King Sigismund, eminent glory of the princes of our age, many things came suddenly to mind to deter me from writing. In the first place it seemed hardly proper that I, an insignificant creature, un- 5
known, unbidden, with hardly any motive for writing, should address myself to such an august personage. And, as Pliny relates from ancient chronicles that it went badly for Tullus Hostilius when he called upon Jupiter,[1] so it has not always proved free from risk to address the greatest monarchs of the earth, whom it behoves us to approach not only at the proper mo- 10
ment but also with a sense of religious awe. Furthermore it seemed almost an act of impiety to address an unnecessary letter to a prince engaged in so many serious matters of state, especially in the restoration of concord among kings. But all these hesitancies were quickly dispelled by the thought of the singular goodness of your nature, which, in my eyes at least, contributes 15
no less to your grandeur than does the majesty of your throne, and by my own fervent devotion to you and my particular admiration for your merits, which was engendered in me not only by the clarion trump of fame[2] but also through the conversations and letters of that most distinguished gentleman Jan Łaski.[3] While he was with us, never was there a moment when the name 20

* * * * *

1819
1 Cf *Naturalis historia* 28.2.4, where it is related that Tullus Hostilius – traditionally believed to be the third king of Rome – was struck by lightning because he performed a rite incorrectly.
2 Juvenal 14.152
3 For Jan (II) Łaski, cf Ep 1821 introduction.

of King Sigismund was not on his lips; and his letters to me resound with
the praises of Sigismund.[4] Finally, I was induced to write through weariness
of these violent storms that shake the world, and through an overwhelming desire for peace, which torments me with agonizing expectation, having
learned too well the truth of Homer's depiction of Ate as fleet-footed and   25
keen-eyed and of the Litae as myopic and limping.[5] Gladly and eagerly the
old man Simeon took leave of this life after he had seen Christ the Lord.[6]
I think that I too should leave this world with untroubled spirit if through
the benevolence of God and the deliberations of princes this public turmoil
could be abated.   30

To this dutiful and heaven-sent task I hear that your Majesty is setting
his hand with great wisdom and an equal measure of zeal, and this has
emboldened me all the more to urge on one already in full flight, as they
say;[7] not that your zeal – infused, I believe, with the divine spirit – has
any need of the promptings of men. It often happens that God in the most   35
desperate situations brings forth, as if by a clever stage device, someone
endowed with extraordinary virtue to restore tranquillity to a situation of
total chaos. So it was that when the Romans were reduced to buying back
their freedom with gold, suddenly Camillus rose up.[8] When their fortunes
again seemed destined for utter hopelessness, Scipio Africanus came on the   40
scene.[9] In the same way, when the Hebrews were subjected to unendurable
and prolonged servitude in Egypt, Moses appeared;[10] and, when Susannah's
life was in danger, as if out of nowhere Daniel appeared, vindicator of her
innocence and confounder of the malicious charge made against her.[11] May
God in his almighty power and goodness grant fulfilment to my prayers!   45
May he vouchsafe that this good hope be not in vain! For my spirit is stirred

* * * * *

4 None are extant.
5 One of the daughters of Zeus (*Iliad* 19.90), Ate is the personification of reckless
  folly and moral blindness, in whose behaviour neither right and wrong nor
  advantageous and ruinous conduct can be differentiated. The Litae, goddesses
  of entreaty, move slowly in answering prayers (*Iliad* 9.502–12); cf Ep 1707:25–6.
6 Luke 2:29–32, a passage recited daily at the end of Compline, the night prayer
  of the Divine Office
7 *Adagia* I ii 46
8 Marcus Furius Camillus, the saviour and second founder of Rome after the
  Gallic invasion in 387–6 BC (Livy 5.49.7)
9 Publius Cornelius Scipio v (236–184/3 BC), whose many victories in Africa
  and finally over Hannibal in 202 earned him the name 'Africanus'
10 To lead the Hebrews from slavery in Egypt into the promised land of Palestine
   (Exodus 2–40)
11 Daniel 13

by some portent beyond all ken that God at long last, turning his anger into compassion, has appointed you, most holy king, to quell the storms of unrest by your piety, your wisdom, and your authority.

What strengthens this hope in me is the fact that in no other man have I   50
perceived endowments requisite for the accomplishment of such a mission. Not to mention the powers of kingship or to rehearse the many arduous exploits carried out with such great success as if by divine assistance, to which has recently been added the brilliant victory over the Scythians,[12] three things above all others seem required of one who is to bring order to   55
the present turbulent state of human affairs. These qualities are piety, a lofty spirit, and wisdom. The term piety comprises two aspects: love of country and zeal for religion. In each of these you have merited singular praise; for in securing, maintaining, increasing, enhancing, and consolidating the interests of your kingdom you have exercised such vigilance, zeal, and care   60
that beyond all consideration of age you have shrunk from no toil that might have discouraged even a young man.[13] In former times the title of Father of their country was conferred on those who had rendered exceptional services to the state, and there was something in that title more noble than the name of king or emperor. The honour of this title is owed to you for many reasons,   65
and it is much more gloriously imprinted in men's minds than if it were inscribed on monuments or statues. Furthermore, your equal devotion and care for the Christian religion is manifest in the integrity of your whole life, to which must be added the sanctuaries erected, enriched, and adorned with great munificence. Last of all is the subjection and reform of Prussia, which   70
had begun to be corrupted by heresy.[14]

To such a spirit the present discord among princes cannot but engender strong displeasure. Were they to engage in armed conflict among themselves it would be not merely a civil war but sheer fratricide. Plato considers a civil war to be one that Greeks wage against Greeks.[15] But a Christian   75

* * * * *

12 A reference to the recent victory of his combined Polish-Lithuanian army over the Tartars on 27 January 1527
13 Born in 1467, Sigismund I was sixty years old at this time – exactly contemporaneous with Erasmus.
14 In April 1525 Sigismund pragmatically recognized his nephew Albert Hohenzollern, former master of the Teutonic knights, as the secular, hereditary prince in Prussia. He made no moves to prevent Albert, who was acting on Luther's advice, from introducing a Lutheran reformation of the church into Prussia – a policy that traditionalists would judge to be contradictory to Erasmus' statement here.
15 *Republic* 470

has closer ties to another Christian than citizen with citizen or brother with brother. In our day the struggle of monarchs among themselves has paved the way for the Turks to invade first Rhodes and more recently Hungary.[16] Their cruelty has achieved inordinate success, and they will penetrate even closer to us unless with common cause we join forces to block their path. 80 What man of Christian feelings would not be tormented at such a sight? And all this is more dreadful still because, while princes wrangle among themselves, the Christian religion falls into utter ruin, totally disrupting the social order and throwing the commonweal into such confusion that those who ought to obey demand instead the right to give orders to those more 85 powerful than they. But the line of demarcation is not clear. Each party, while having something positive to recommend it, also has within its ranks those who seem to be fighting under the banners of the church but who are prepared to appropriate to themselves the victory due to Christ, unless the authority of the greatest leaders check their senseless strife and keep 90 them from plunder. Only in that case can it come about that from this bitter medicine that torments the world a more healthy condition will result; and the victory will belong not to men but to Christ, the prince of the church, to whom all glory is due. Perhaps he has permitted these tempests to fall upon the world so that those who have become drunk with the abundance of this 95 world's goods might be awakened to the sobriety of a Christian conscience. The emperor Charles is said to be of this mind, as I have learned from the letters of those closest to him.[17] Of these matters I think it neither safe nor prudent to commit any further thoughts to paper, since in your exceptional wisdom you will know my meaning. 100

So much for the subject of piety. As for your loftiness of spirit, it shines out not so much in boldly waging war or in extending your kingdom's frontiers as in despising those things that only a man of truly lofty character despises. A person shows himself superior to the extent that he can forego something when the welfare of the state demands it. One who is incited to 105 make war through wrath or craving for revenge is inferior to his own passions. One who is lured into the fray through ambition is inferior by the very fact that he yields to ambition. But he who puts the public good before all these things is a man of truly sublime and lofty spirit. In the many necessary wars you waged with no less success than courage against the Wal- 110 lachians, the Tartars, the Muscovites, and the Prussians, you clearly mani-

* * * * *

16 Rhodes fell in December 1522; see Ep 1362 n25. On the battle of Mohács see Ep 1810 nn5 and 8; cf Ep 1754 n12.
17 See for example Ep 1757:29–30.

fested a kingly nobility of spirit.[18] But proof of an even more exalted spirit
was your preference to sign a truce with the Muscovites, whom you had
so often subdued in battle, rather than bring that rich province under your
control by force of arms, although it would have cost little effort and you   115
were urged to it by the leading men of your country. Later when some of
them, out of loathing for the name 'schismatic,'[19] considered it impossible
to enter into an alliance of peace, you did not hesitate to prolong the truce.
It matters not to you how the masses interpret your action. More important
in your eyes is the general tranquillity of your kingdom and the sparing   120
of Christian blood than the armed occupation of vast lands or the opinion
of the crowd. For as that famous writer elegantly expressed it, 'It belongs
to kings' – that is, to those of truly lofty spirit – 'to be ill spoken of in the
cause of right.'[20] You did not refuse to make a truce with the Turks; you
would even be willing to enter into a treaty with the Scythians if they, who   125
are more like wild beasts than men, would cease making savage raids upon
your borders. To repel these wild and ruthless barbarians from swooping
down on the fortunes and the necks of your subjects is more an act of piety
than of war. But if it be war, it is a war so inevitable that it could not be
avoided without committing a grave crime. What is more, although in your   130
frequent battles against the Prussians the fortunes of war smiled favourably
upon you, through love of peace you preferred to concede to the duke of
Prussia a portion of his territory rather than subjugate it all to your rule,
which you could easily have done.[21]

   That same greatness of spirit revealed itself when the princes of Ger-   135
many had sent ten thousand infantrymen and a cavalry of two thousand
to aid the duke in his battle against you Poles; but you did not allow your
greatly superior forces (sixty thousand mounted men) to engage them in
battle. Instead you charged a mere eight hundred with the task of inter-
cepting the advance of the German troops or cutting off their supply lines.   140
You did this knowing that feeling the pangs of hunger they would return
home, thus avoiding the spilling of blood. I need not mention how after the

* * * * *

18 Leonard Cox had sent Erasmus an account of the Polish victory over the
   Tartars: Justus Decius' *Sendbrieff von der grossen Schlacht* (Cracow: Hieronim
   Wietor 1527). The book was reprinted in Nürnberg the same year; see Ep
   1803:11.
19 Muscovy and neighbouring lands refused recognition of primacy to the pope,
   according it instead to the patriarch of Moscow.
20 Plutarch *Alexander* 41.1, a text cited also in Ep 1578:37–8
21 See n14 above.

expulsion of King Christian from his throne you firmly refused the crowns
of Norway and Sweden, which were freely offered to you, lest by the opportunity thus offered you provide your people with a pretext for war.[22]   14?
These are not old events that I relate. But there is a more current example:
at the recent death of the king of Bohemia and Hungary,[23] who was your
nephew on your brother's side, although the succession seemed to belong to
you even by right of kinship, you were so without ambition that you sent
ambassadors to advise them to choose a king who they considered would be   15(
of greatest benefit to their country, since you were content with your lot. Not
stopping at this, as soon as you saw that a climate of hostilities was devel-
oping between Ferdinand and John, the king of Hungary,[24] you sent your
respected and princely chancellor Krzysztof Szydłowiecki, the castellan and
governor of Cracow, whom you regard as the wisest and most honourable   15?
of your subjects,[25] thus assuring that war would not be ventured upon until
every effort had been made to prevent it.

These actions betoken a truly sublime spirit, elevated high above ordinary human concerns. And yet from these same examples I think one may
perceive your remarkable wisdom, which both age and long experience have   16(
brought to perfection in you. War is sweet to those who have not known
it,[26] but one whose vision can pierce the darkness and discern things from
afar prefers an unjust peace to a just war. If leaders would follow your example by renouncing their private ambitions and, as if from a high vantage
point, fix their gaze on piety, that is, on the glory of Christ and the salvation   16?

* * * * *

22 Christian II, known as 'the Cruel,' became king of Denmark and Norway in
   1513 and reconquered Sweden in 1520 with a brutal massacre of its nobility.
   Revolutions in Sweden in 1521, led by Gustavus Vasa, and in Denmark in
   1523 sent him into exile in the Netherlands. His unsuccessful attempt to seize
   Norway in 1531–2 resulted in captivity, which lasted until his death in 1559.
   The Danish Rigsraad elected Christian's uncle Duke Frederick of Schleswig-
   Holstein as king of Norway, and Gustavus Vasa became king in Sweden.
23 Louis II, killed at Mohács in 1526
24 See Ep 1810 n8. Erasmus' use of the title 'king' to describe John Zápolyai, the
   brother of Sigismund's first wife, was no doubt acceptable to Sigismund, but it
   gave offence to King Ferdinand of Hapsburg, who claimed the title for himself
   (Ep 1917:20–2, Allen Epp 2030:52–4 and 2032:8–15). When he published this
   letter for wider consumption (Opus epistolarum 1529) Erasmus changed 'John,
   the king of Hungary' to read 'John, who has usurped the title of king.'
25 See Ep 1820 introduction. For a different view of him see Ep 1917:23–5.
26 Erasmus developed one of his longest and most important adages on this
   phrase, Dulce bellum inexpertis, drawn from Pindar (Adagia IV i 1). In it he
   develops his views on war and peace.

of the Christian people; and if they would place the general peace of the world before any personal interests, which frequently prove vain, or if not, are bought at too great a price; then, united in mutual understanding, they would rule more successfully and more gloriously and would easily rid the Christians of the Turkish menace and resolve by suitable means this deadly   170
discord within the church. I fear that at present there are those who for lack of piety would attempt to turn this public misfortune to their own private advantage; or who, devoid of any loftiness of spirit, are incapable of relinquishing any of their prerogatives for the love of universal peace; or who through inexperience prefer war to peace. Yet war should never be under-   175
taken unless in seeking to avoid it one risks the sin of impiety. If only the princes, inspired by unfeigned Christian sentiments, would act in this way, then Christ himself would lend them his aid, would further their plans and alliances, and give to their affairs a happier issue than they themselves could ever dare hope.   180

Now, however, just as wars are for the most part brought on by wrath or ambition or some other private emotion rather than by any regard for piety or the state, so do we see weak and short-lived treaties and, worse still, treaties that too often provide the seedbed for war. What is more to be desired than hoped for – although I consider it of utmost importance for   185
the safeguarding of friendships among princes and peace among nations – is that princes be persuaded to renounce far-flung possessions. How many disasters did those repeated assaults upon Milan bring upon the French?[27] Would any kingdom be more flourishing than France if France had not tried to conquer Naples, Lombardy, and Insubria?[28] Just as certain ships are too   190
big to be steered, so it is extremely difficult to govern successfully an empire that stretches far and wide; and it is even more difficult if the parts of that empire are separated by great distances. In our times the desire to add to one's possessions has no limit, so much so that for some it seems to have

* * * * *

27 Since 1494 the French kings Charles VIII, Louis XII, and Francis I had waged intermittent wars in Italy. The most recent culminated in the battle of Pavia (24 February 1525), in which many of France's great fighting barons were killed and Francis I was taken captive into Spain. Francis had been successful in his earlier Italian campaign (Marignano 1515), a victory that had won him important concessions from the papacy by means of the Concordat of Bologna.
28 Western Lombardy (northern Italy), on the south slope of the Alps. The name is taken from the Celtic tribe (Insubrae) which settled between the Ticino and the Adda rivers. It was also known as Gallia Cisalpina. After several clashes with Rome c 232–194 BC, the Insubrae disappeared as a separate nation and gained full Roman citizenship in 49 BC.

Sigismund I and Bona Sforza
National Museum, Cracow
Princes Czartoryski Foundation

become a matter of course – as with those whose ambition it is to heap one   195
ecclesiastical benefice upon another. Whatever profit they have been able
to scrape together from less important positions they consume in obtaining something greater; and the revenues of several of them together are ab-
sorbed by the single dignity of bishop, while the proceeds of that office then
go towards the purchase of the title of archbishop. And finally, how many   200
profits of high-ranking prelacies and abbacies has the glory of the name of
cardinal devoured! It is the sign of a mean spirit not to be able to suffer
someone greater than oneself.

In fine, he is a great and lofty spirit who neither disdains his inferiors nor envies his superiors, who makes it his aim not to extend his rule so   205
far and wide (which for that matter fortune sometimes accords even to the
wicked) but to administer to the best of his ability that which fate has assigned to him. But since now the succession to kingdoms passes from one to
another partly through wedlock and partly through kinship, it is, as I said,
easier to desire than to hope for what I deem best. It would be a breach   210
of piety and it is not my intention to detract in any way from the authority of him whom Christ has wished to preside over his universal church.
Nevertheless, to speak frankly, he too would discharge his duties more successfully and great leaders would engage less readily in such internecine
wars if, persuaded in his own mind, he would never enter into treaties with   215
any monarch but would show himself equally a father to all. And now from
such treaties so often concluded, rescinded, restored, and abandoned how
many occasions have we not seen and still see for the stirring up and fomenting of wars! Why seek examples in the annals of history when, during these past twenty years, we have witnessed so many with our own   220
eyes?

But I have too long abused your indulgence, invincible king; I leap the
bounds, as they say.[29] So I shall conclude, making this ardent prayer: that
God take pity on us and that he grant to your most godly efforts an outcome
worthy of your piety, your loftiness of spirit, and your wisdom; and may   225
he grant long life and happiness to your Queen Bona,[30] wedded to the best
of kings, for the good of your kingdom and of all Christendom.

Given at Basel on the Ides of May, in the year of our Lord 1527

* * * * *

29 *Adagia* I x 93
30 Bona Sforza, daughter of the duke of Milan, Giangaleazzo Sforza, and Isabel
   of Aragon, became the second wife of King Sigismund in 1518. Well educated
   and skilled in politics, she exercised considerable influence on the reign of her
   husband (CEBR I 165–6).

1820 / To Krzysztof Szydłowiecki   Basel, 16 May 1527

Szydłowiecki (1467–1532), a Polish nobleman, was a lifelong friend and close
adviser to King Sigismund I of Poland, who named him grand chancellor of
the realm in March 1515 and prefect-general and *voivode* of Cracow in August
of that year. In 1527 he was delegated to try to effect a reconciliation between
Ferdinand of Hapsburg, who claimed succession to the throne of Hungary,
and John Zápolyai, recently elected king of Hungary by the nobility. As a
reward for faithful service he was appointed castellan of Cracow. A wealthy
man, Szydłowiecki was a lavish patron of authors and artists, and received
a number of book dedications, among them the *Lingua* of Erasmus. See Epp
1593, 1752; cf CEBR III 304–5.

This letter first appeared in *Opus epistolarum* (1529).

ERASMUS OF ROTTERDAM TO THE ILLUSTRIOUS KRZYSZTOF
SZYDŁOWIECKI, ETC, CHANCELLOR OF THE KINGDOM OF POLAND,
GREETING

Letters travel rather slowly between us, honoured sir, although yours arrived quite quickly: it was dated the first of March and it reached me before   5
the ides of May. I presume that you begin the new year at Easter.[1]

In the Gospel the Lord proclaims the peacemakers blessed;[2] and since
you are now engaged in that task in obedience to your excellent king, I pray
that your efforts will have good success and that through your wisdom you
will render many persons blessed. On this subject I have written at some   10
length to the glorious king of Poland, Sigismund,[3] as I was called upon to
do so on more than one occasion in the letters of the honourable young man
Jan Łaski.[4] He demanded it of me with such solicitude that I think there
must have been good reason for his eagerness. Most leaders of our time
are young men: all the more do I pray that God will long preserve Sigis-   15
mund for us free of harm, for his piety, greatness of mind, and remarkable

* * * * *

1820

1 Erasmus concludes that, like many places in Europe, Poland dated the new
  year from Easter, which occurred in 1527 on 21 April. Szydłowiecki's letter
  therefore bore the year-date 1 March 1526. It reached Erasmus before 15 May
  (the ides fell on the eighth day after nones in the Roman calendar, thus 15
  March, May, July, and October but 13 of all other months). The letter is not
  extant, but probably answered Erasmus' Ep 1752.
2 Matt 5:9
3 Ep 1819
4 Eg Ep 1674:21–2; on Łaski see Ep 1821 introduction.

wisdom, together with his vast experience, will be of much profit through his salutary advice both to the interests of princes and the tranquillity of the state.

Your gifts are a clear indication of your generous spirit,[5] but in the reck-   20
oning of your services to me they occupy but the last line. That my friend Antonin is dear to you gives me great pleasure;[6] I have never encountered a more good-natured disposition, except for Jan Łaski, the provost of Gniezno; one could hardly imagine a more amiable person. I count his friendship too among my chief blessings. This letter is written in my own hand, but I am   25
afraid you may not be able to read it. I am still feeling weak from a violent attack of diarrhoea. May the Lord preserve you free of harm.

Given at Basel, 16 May in the year 1527

1821 / To Jan (II) Łaski   Basel, 17 May 1527

Jan (II) Łaski (1499–1560) was the nephew of Jan (I) Łaski, archbishop of Gniezno and primate of Poland. The younger Łaski had accompanied his uncle to Rome, where he continued the studies that he had begun in Vienna, Bologna, and Padua. In 1524, while carrying out an embassy to Paris, where he stayed more than a year, Łaski had visited Erasmus in Basel both going and returning, and in the second instance stayed six months in Erasmus' house. Erasmus had very much enjoyed Łaski's extended visit; he was a generous guest, and the two became friends (Epp 1622, 1674). Before his departure, Łaski contracted to purchase Erasmus' library, granting Erasmus the use of it during his lifetime. In November 1526 Łaski was promoted by his uncle to the lucrative provostship of Gniezno, and he had expectations of succeeding his uncle as archbishop and primate. The Łaski family, however, committed itself to the claim of John Zápolyai to the kingship of Hungary, a stance that alienated them from Emperor Charles v and would lead to their political and financial ruin. At first a strong critic of Luther and an advocate of reform within the Catholic church, Łaski after 1540 would defect from the church and find his theological home in adherence to Calvinism and to Zwinglian Eucharistic views. See CEBR II 297-301.

This letter first appeared in *Opus epistolarum* (1529).

* * * * *

5 Erasmus had received from Szydłowiecki an hourglass containing gold dust and a gold fork and spoon in return for the dedication of his *Lingua*, which Szydłowiecki had reprinted in Poland (Cracow: Hieronim Wietor 1526). Erasmus had previously thanked the chancellor for the gifts (Ep 1752).
6 On Jan Antonin, who served Erasmus as physician in Basel for a time, see Epp 1602, 1810 introductions.

ERASMUS OF ROTTERDAM TO THE HONOURABLE JAN ŁASKI,
PROVOST OF GNIEZNO, GREETING

That my missive was faithfully delivered to you gives me great cause for
joy.[1] I was concerned about it, seeing that there is such incredible bad faith
among men nowadays, while everywhere men are disputing about matters   5
of faith. I was also a bit apprehensive that something might have befallen
you and yours otherwise than I would have wished.

   The *Enchiridion* has been translated into the vulgar tongue and printed
in Spain, arousing great turmoil among the monks.[2] But this reaction met
head-on with powerful patrons of Erasmus, among whom was the emperor   10
himself, whose letter, if I am not mistaken, I sent to you from the last fair.[3]
I took care that your letter be taken immediately to Beatus Rhenanus, for
he is living in Sélestat, driven away from here by fear of the plague and by
his aversion for constant contention.[4] Doubtless you have already received
both his book and that of Glareanus.[5] Glareanus gives public lectures on   15

* * * * *

1821
1 Like the letter from Łaski which this one answers, it is not extant. It was probably contemporaneous with Epp 1751–4 addressed to other persons in Poland.
2 The translation by Alonso Fernández was printed by Miguel de Eguía (Alcalá
   1526 and January 1527). Cf Ep 1814:130–1 and n21.
3 Ep 1731, sent via the booksellers going to the spring Frankfurt book fair in
   March; but no letters of Erasmus to Poland at that time are extant.
4 Łaski's letter is not extant; Beatus Rhenanus' reply (BRE 372 Ep 263) was likewise written on 17 May. Beatus had left Basel in June 1526, undoubtedly to
   avoid 'constant contention,' since he departed two months before the plague
   struck in October and November 1526 (see Ep 1777:3–6 and n1); he stayed
   in Sélestat until at least September 1527. He would quit Basel definitively in
   September 1528 because of his distaste for the Reformation there, remaining in
   Sélestat until his death – with a brief sojourn in Augsburg in 1530 for the imperial diet; see Robert Walker *Beatus Rhenanus, citoyen de Sélestat, ami d'Erasme:
   Anthologie de sa correspondance* (Strasbourg 1986) 31.
   Beatus Rhenanus had been educated in Paris under Lefèvre d'Etaples, Fausto
   Andrelini, and Georgius Hermonymus. For sixteen years he was an editor and
   corrector at the Froben press, where from 1521 he was in close relationship
   with Erasmus. He played a major role in Froben's 1525 *Naturalis historia* of
   Pliny the Elder, for which Erasmus was the editor of record. He was also an
   influential and respected scholar in his own right, dividing his time between
   Basel, Strasbourg, and his native Sélestat. His published works include editions
   of patristic authors and works of German history. He oversaw the posthumous
   edition of Erasmus' works in 1540. See John F. D'Amico *Theory and Practice
   in Renaissance Textual Criticism: Beatus Rhenanus between Conjecture and History*
   (Berkeley 1988); cf Ep 327 introduction, CEBR I 104–9, and ER I 193–4.
5 The two works were dedicated to Łaski at Erasmus' suggestion. The first,
   Beatus Rhenanus' edition *In C. Plinium* (Basel: Johann Froben, March 1526),

his. I wrote to the king,[6] since you entreated me so many times to do so; but I have enclosed an exact copy, so that you may suppress anything in the original as you think best. It is difficult to write to kings. Still, I do not want you to be unaware of the fact that I have mentioned this matter in a letter to Krzysztof, the chancellor of Cracow.[7]   20

Some of my enemies have perished. In Louvain the Carmelite Baechem suffocated from an attack of vomiting, when just a little before that he had delivered a public tirade against Jan de Neve, recounting how he had been seized by paralysis and had breathed his last within six hours.[8] Dead too is the Dominican Vincent, against whom there exists a letter of mine with   25 the title 'To my most obstinate opponent.'[9] Rosemondt is dead also, a better man than the types usually found among theologians,[10] and our friend Dorp died before him.[11] In Cologne Jacob of Hoogstraten, the chorus leader of this tragedy, passed away. It is said, however, that in dying he revealed in a few brief words that his conscience was not clear.[12] For all of these I pray   30

* * * * *

consisted mainly of textual corrections, about one-third of them applying to the preface of Pliny's *Naturalis historia* (Basel: Johann Froben, March 1525) and the rest to books 7, 8, 10, and 14 of the same work. The latter edition had appeared under Erasmus' name even though Beatus had composed most of the notes. See Allen Ep 1544 introduction; BRE Ep 252. The second book dedicated to Łaski was authored by the Swiss humanist Henricus Glareanus. His *De geographia* was a mathematical-physical description of Asia, Africa, and Europe. See Epp 440 introduction, 604, and CEBR II 105–8.

6 That is, King Sigismund I of Poland (Ep 1819)

7 Ep 1820:10–14

8 Erasmus sees ironic justice in the unexpected and unattended death of Baechem, who supposedly had preached a sermon on sudden death in which he used Neve as a precautionary example. See Ep 1765:55–7 and n9. Neve, Erasmus' host and genuine friend at the Collège of the Lily in Louvain from 1517 to 1521, had tried without success to settle disputes between Erasmus and the conservative theologians there; see Ep 298 introduction and CEBR III 15. On Baechem see Ep 1815 n4. He died on 23 or 24 August 1526 – nine months before Erasmus wrote this letter.

9 Ep 1196, a lengthy letter in which Erasmus spells out his grievances against Theoderici; cf Ep 1815 n3. He died on 4 August 1526.

10 Godschalk Rosemondt (Epp 1153 introduction), who had tried to reconcile Erasmus and his opponents and for whom Erasmus had a sincere respect. He died 7 December 1526. See Ep 1768:46–56; CEBR III 171–2.

11 Maarten van Dorp, whose early criticism of Erasmus' *Praise of Folly* contained no malice and whom Erasmus respected as a colleague. He died in May 1525, two years before Erasmus wrote this letter. See CEBR I 398–404.

12 That is, about his attitude to Erasmus and humanistic studies generally. Jacob of Hoogstraten (c 1460–21 January 1527), a Netherlander and Dominican theologian at Cologne, was the inquisitor of the archdioceses of Cologne, Mainz,

the Lord's mercy. Jacques Lefèvre has been called back to France on very honourable terms – for he had left it through fear[13] – and he is very dear to the king. And the one whom Béda had destined for the holocaust is a good man, as I hear,[14] and especially dear to the king. The king was not willing to use force to rescue him from danger, but he did not allow the trial to be   35 held until he returned to Paris.[15] There is an example for you; and, unless

* * * * *

and Trier. He supported Johann Pfefferkorn's attack on Johann Reuchlin and on Hebrew books (Epp 615, 636). When he led the movements by the universities of Cologne and Louvain to censure Luther, he also circulated Erasmus' friendly letter to Luther (Ep 980) and challenged Erasmus' views on divorce. Because this caused a break between Erasmus and the Louvain University officials, Erasmus frequently linked his name with other Louvain opponents like Nicolaas Baechem (Egmondanus) and Vincentius Theoderici, although he never broke with Hoogstraten in the same way. See CEBR II 200–2.

13 *hinc ... revocatus est.* Jacques Lefèvre d'Etaples (CEBR II 315–18) had actually quit Switzerland a year earlier. He had fled Paris in October 1525 during the repression of heresy by the Parlement of Paris, arriving in Strasbourg under the pseudonym Antonius Peregrinus. No documentation exists to show that he visited Erasmus; however the printing of his book *Commentarii in epistolas catholicas* in Basel (Andreas Cratander July 1527) suggests that he had contact with Cratander there. It would be surprising if he did not pay a visit to Erasmus as well. Although Erasmus had openly quarrelled with Lefèvre on certain scriptural interpretations, he appreciated his contributions to a new, humanist approach to Scripture, and he appealed to Rome on his behalf in 1525 (Ep 1650A:17–18 and n4).

14 Louis de Berquin had been charged with heresy in 1523 but released after a general abjuration. His second arrest by order of the Parlement of Paris, acting upon a request of the archbishop of Amiens, occurred on 8 January 1526. See Ep 1804 nn59–62. Burning at the stake was the normal sentence for relapsed heretics, that is, those who returned to their errors after first repenting of them. Berquin would suffer this penalty on 19 April 1529 at the hands of the Parlement of Paris, acting as 'secular arm' of the papal judges delegate. For Noël Béda, see Ep 1804 n14. Although Béda was a consistent enemy of Berquin, the registers of the Parlement (Paris, Archives nationales x^{1a} 1529 passim) demonstrate that any judgment about Berquin's heresy belonged not to the Parlement but to the judges delegate, the tribunal constituted in 1525 by agreement between the regent Louise of Savoy and Pope Clement VII to try cases of heresy in France and reconstituted in 1529 by King Francis I.

15 The translation requires the insertion of *non* in the second clause of this sentence, an emendation demanded by the facts of the case. Nevertheless, Erasmus' report is not accurate. Berquin's trial did indeed take place, against the express wishes of King Francis I, during his absence. The judges delegate found Berquin guilty of relapse into heresy and delivered him over to the secular arm (the Parlement of Paris) for capital punishment. He remained in the Conciergerie du Palais for nearly a year, during which time the Parlement

it is displayed more frequently, those who operate under cover of darkness will make attacks on princes under the pretext of defending the faith.[16] If only the king had been equally successful in all other things as well![17]

The principal reason for their deciding to immolate this friend of the king in his absence was that he was making ready to publish a French translation of my *Paraphrases* and several other books.[18] This is the reasoning of certain pseudomonks: 'If Erasmus begins to talk to the multitude, he will lay bare our lies, by which we have made him unpopular up to now with gossipy old women and the unlettered. The facts of the case will be a refutation of our falsity, revealing that he is other than we depicted him.' I therefore think there is nothing more expedient for uncovering their malice or for proving my innocence than that my writings, especially my works on

* * * * *

refused several times to obey royal orders to release him. After Francis returned to the Paris area, he sent royal agents on 19 November 1526 to remove Berquin from prison and placed him in house arrest in the Louvre, from where he was released several weeks later. This was however only a reprieve. Berquin was arrested again in 1529, and on 15 April 1529 a newly constituted panel of eleven judges delegate appointed by Francis I and confirmed by Pope Clement VII found him guilty of recidivism. He was burned at the stake the next day. Francis had interceded twice for Berquin, in 1523 and 1526, probably at the behest of his sister Margaret of Navarre, but he did not do so in 1529. For further details about his execution see Farge 'Berquin' 70–2.

16 An example, that is, of concrete action taken by a prince in the defence of the humanities
17 An allusion to his defeat at Pavia and subsequent captivity in Spain; but see Erasmus' criticism of Francis' penchant for war in his letter to King Sigismund I of Poland (Ep 1819:187–90).
18 On 1 March 1526 Nicolas Le Clerc, the theologian member of the tribunal of judges delegate, brought for the inspection and judgment of the faculty of theology 'several books of Luther and Erasmus along with other writings which were found in the possession of Louis de Berquin, now a prisoner in the palace.' In deliberations of the theologians on 2 and 7 March and in the final censures of Berquin's translations on 12 March (Farge *Procès-verbaux* 127–8 no 142C, 129–30 no 143A, 144A), no reference to specific titles of Erasmus' works can be found. On 1 May, however, the faculty began a more intensive examination of Erasmus' books, with special mention made of the *Colloquies* (ibidem 134–5 no 149D, 136–7 no 151B, 152A). Noël Béda's renewed attention to Erasmus' *Paraphrases* came on 26 May 1526, when he announced that he was making annotations on these works (ibidem 137 no 152B). These notes ultimately appeared in his *Annotationes* (Paris: Josse Bade, 28 May 1526), composed to refute certain writings of Lefèvre d'Etaples and Erasmus that he considered heretical or dangerous.

living an upright life, should be in the hands of the public. Nothing escapes
the notice of these pharisees, and for that reason they band together in a   50
great conspiracy to make sure this does not come about. But almost all of
their attempts, as we see, turn out differently than intended. And your talents deserve to be employed on better subjects, even if there is no one in
my opinion who could perform this service more successfully.[19]

　　Proof of your extraordinary good will towards me is the fact that, dis-   55
regarding all manifestations of envy, you wish all to know how much regard
you have for me; and you do not reject the title of disciple, provided that you
are regarded as one who for the sake of Erasmus would not hesitate to suffer anything or refuse to do anything. But as for me, my dear Jan, I should
be guilty of extreme impudence if I were to allow a young man destined for   60
a glorious career and already superior to me in certain branches of learning
to be thought to be my disciple. On the other hand I should be a singularly
ungrateful creature if I were to allow such a devoted, faithful, and sincere
patron to be consigned to the darkness of oblivion. It is important above all
that such a rare example of good will be transmitted to posterity, especially   65
in these times when there are no bonds among friends save those forged
by conspiracy. If only there were such inspiration in my writings that they
could adequately portray your merits! For this purpose I wish I could have
temporary access to Cicero's felicity of style.[20] Certainly a subject worthy of
acclaim in itself will be chosen,[21] to which I will add a little further care in   70
the refinement of style to ensure its acceptance by posterity. What prevented
me from doing this before now, to speak frankly, was a certain misgiving,
from which I am happy to have been liberated by your letter.[22]

　　Glareanus upholds the cause of learning here single-handed. He gives
courses on your book to a crowded audience.[23] Others in spite of their learn-   75
ing barely have six students, and that not regularly; he has sixty, and the
number grows day by day. I think this is due to your special talent,[24] for

*　*　*　*　*

19　From this one could conclude that, in letters no longer extant, Łaski had pro-
　　posed to translate some of Erasmus' works into Polish.
20　Criticism of Erasmus' style was not unknown: see eg Epp 1720:52–5, 1791:40–
　　68.
21　Erasmus' promise here will be fulfilled in his dedication of the edition of St
　　Ambrose to Łaski's uncle (Ep 1855).
22　Probably Łaski's letter to Bonifacius Amerbach, 30 March 1527, to which Amer-
　　bach replied on 19 May (AK III Epp 1186, 1191). Neither letter reveals the nature
　　of Erasmus' 'misgiving.'
23　That is, on the book he dedicated to Łaski; cf lines 14–15 and n5 above.
24　Erasmus' meaning is not evident.

it is totally contrary to the usual practice of this academy. You would give
the man great gratification if you were to send him some young boys who
might possibly go elsewhere to learn their letters. Since he resides in the 80
college he must act as a pedagogue for a few years.

I am surprised that there is no mention in your letter of Hieronim
Łaski.[25] All the same do give my fond greetings to both your brothers. I am
glad to know that Stanisław is also there with you, returned from France.[26]
Take good care of your health. Given at Basel, 17 May in the year 1527   85

1822 / To Andrzej Krzycki   Basel, 17 May 1527

This letter first appeared in the *Opus epistolarum* (1529). It answers a letter,
not extant, of Krzycki written c 25 March 1526 (cf Ep 1803:83), and will be
answered by another, also not extant, mentioned in Ep 1895:21–3.

Andrzej Krzycki (1482–1537), a nephew of Piotr Tomicki and former secretary to King Sigismund I and Queen Bona, became bishop of Płock in 1527. Although a strong opponent of Luther and the Reformation, he helped to negotiate the secularization of the state of the Teutonic Knights in Prussia, defending it on political grounds in a letter to the papal nuncio. He also defended
King Sigismund against charges of favouring Luther. He backed the election
of John Zápolyai in Hungary and became a leading proponent of peace with
the Turks. Later, as archbishop of Gniezno, he worked for reform within the
church. He was a creative poet and writer devoted to the cause of humanism. See CEBR II 275–8 and cf Epp 1803 n19, 1810 n7. For an appraisal of Erasmus' opinion of Krzycki, see Claude Backvis 'La fortune d'Erasme en Pologne'
Colloquium Erasmianum (Mons 1968) 180–5.

ERASMUS OF ROTTERDAM TO ANDRZEJ KRZYCKI, BISHOP OF PŁOCK,
GREETING
Most honourable prelate, I have merely sampled your book[1] rather than
given it a thorough reading, but I have no doubt that it will please me as

* * * * *

25 The Latin reads *Hieroslaus*, which translates more properly 'Jarosłav,' the name
   of the father of the three Łaski brothers, but Erasmus certainly intends here
   Hieronim, the brother of Jan II and Stanisław, whom he habitually invokes in
   letters to Jan. The three brothers had been house guests of Erasmus in 1524.
26 Stanisław Łaski had attached himself to the service of Francis I, with whom he
   was taken captive at Pavia. Ransomed, he later returned to France and then to
   Madrid to help in the negotiations to free the French king.

1822
 1 The *De afflictione ecclesiae, commentarius in Psalmum XXI*; see Ep 1810 n22.

a whole when I have read it from beginning to end. I perceive a vigorous   5
defender of the church. Still, I do not think that your wisdom has need of a
mentor; otherwise I would advise or even entreat you so to do battle with
the enemies of public order that the glory of victory be given not to men but
to Christ. For just as when a fire engulfs a whole city many bent on pillage
turn public woe into private gain, so in this dread tumult of the world you   10
undoubtedly know that many want to seize for themselves the victory due
to Christ alone. I should hope that some sort of cure will result from this
bitter medicine, which perhaps God has prescribed to correct our vices and
which has so convulsed the whole body of the church. In the present circumstances what advantage will there be for us if those who preside over the   15
church, of whom not a few show themselves to be almost more worldly than
the world itself, are more blasphemous than they were before; if princes,
especially petty rulers, are better equipped through their plunder of church
possessions to pursue their lives of debauchery and gambling; if the monks,
whose tyranny the world has long been suffering, are hereafter rendered   20
more arrogant by their victory? Not that I do not think some among them to
be pious, prudent, and learned men; but among these same ranks we see too
many who serve their belly, not Jesus Christ;[2] and while each shows strong
partiality for his own order, the order of Christ is neglected.

In exchanging unpleasant surroundings[3] for those not a whit more   25
agreeable, your fate, I think, is like that related in the proverb, 'You meted
out evil and you received it in return.'[4] You delude yourself about being
free. Once you have taken the bit of the court in your mouth, you must endure the rider.[5] Yet it serves the common weal if learned men are drawn to
positions of public authority. Sweet is the leisure of the scholarly life; but   30
man is not born so much for himself as for his country.[6]

From Łaski you have a miserable portrait of me,[7] which would afford more pleasure to those who wish ill to Erasmus than to you, unless
perchance the painter has appealed to your own sentiments about me. He
made off with this portrait stealthily without my knowledge. Would that   35

* * * * *

2 Cf Ep 1805 n53.
3 Erasmus gives the Greek, ἀλμυρὸν γειτόνημα (Plato *Laws* 705A).
4 *Adagia* II ii 83, which translates the proverb as 'I got as bad as I gave.' This
   alludes to Krzycki's appointment to the see of Płock, a desirable living which,
   however, committed him to political duties to King Sigismund and Queen
   Bona.
5 *Adagia* I iv 14
6 *Adagia* IV vi 81
7 Nothing is known about this portrait, which Łaski took with him when he left
   Basel in October 1525.

the image expressed in my writings might receive your approval and that of those close to you.

This answers your letter which, as you put it, you committed to the wind.[8] Hardly any other letter has arrived more quickly. I wish for your reverend Excellency abiding happiness in the Lord.

40

Given at Basel, 17 May in the year 1527

1823 / To Frans Titelmans   Basel, 18 May 1527

Born in Hasselt (Limburg) in 1502, Frans Titelmans enrolled in the University of Louvain in the *Collège du Porc* founded by Jan Standonck to inculcate in students scholastic learning and ascetic discipline aimed at reform in the church. He was *primus in artibus* among all the graduates of Louvain's four arts colleges. His approach to theological studies was strongly influenced by Jacobus Latomus, one of Erasmus' Louvain critics. Titelmans joined the Franciscan order. Hearing of Titelmans' criticisms of him, Erasmus first complained to Chancellor Mercurino Gattinara (Ep 1815:30). The present letter, answered by Titelmans with Ep 1837A, stirred up rather than diminished the controversy, which grew more heated in 1529–30. He died on 12 September 1537 in Anticoli di Campagna, Italy, where he had joined the Roman province of the Capuchin order in 1535. His brother Pieter published four of his commentaries on Scripture posthumously. The *oeuvre* of Titelmans comprised sixteen books, which appeared in 100 separate printings and vernacular translations. The fullest biography of Titelmans is in Benjamin De Troeyer *Bio-bibliographia franciscana neerlandica saeculi XVI* (Nieuwkoop 1969–70) I 87–100; for his bibliography see ibidem II 278–365; cf Stephan Meier-Oeser *Biographisch-bibliographisches Kirchenlexikon* (1997) 12 190–2; cf DTC 15 part 1 1144–6. For this letter and his controversy with Erasmus in general see Paolo Sartori 'La controversia neotestamentaria tra Frans Titelmans ed Erasmo da Rotterdam (1527–1530 ca): Linee di sviluppo e contenuti' *Humanistica Lovaniensia* 52 (2003) 77–135; Rummel *Catholic Critics* II 15–22.

The first publication of this letter in the *Opus epistolarum* was based on a rough draft that Erasmus had retained. After Allen's publication of it in 1928, Henry de Vocht discovered a manuscript copy of the actual text received by Titelmans, along with Titelmans' reply (Ep 1837A). Although de Vocht's copy contains textual variations, none of them alter the substance of the letter published by Allen.

* * * * *

8 *vento commiseras*; cf 1885:207.

ERASMUS OF ROTTERDAM TO FRANS OF HASSELT, FRANCISCAN,
GREETING

Honoured brother in Christ, I hear that in your public lectures you repeatedly
make adverse comments about me. If this be true, I admonish you to remember what becomes the dignity of your order.[1] You are aware that neither the   5
pope nor the emperor approves of such hostile criticism, as each of them has
sufficiently declared,[2] even in writing. You know that it serves no good purpose in the present state of affairs, in which I expose my life to so many perils
in the interests of the faith. I am the enemy of no religious order. In fact, your
congregation has always enjoyed my unique favour, since it has remained   10
less corrupt than others.[3] If in my works I admonish in certain ways, I do it
for all of you, not against you, since neither do you approve of such things.
If you Franciscans wish to regain your former popularity in the world, you
must do so in the same way you first earned it; you earned it by purity of life,
not by conspiracies or malicious attacks. Look at the disorders your confrères   15
have created in Spain![4] What have they achieved? They have exacerbated
everyone's hatred for them. The same thing has happened in Poland and
Hungary.[5] As far as I am concerned, even though I cannot harm you personally, I could inflict more harm on your order than you think, if I did not have
my eyes firmly fixed on Christ. No, I shall never be provoked to that extent.   20
All the more reason, then, that it ill behoves you to give me cause to do so.

Some time ago through stealth and intrigue you removed my books
from libraries,[6] leaving on the shelves the virulent calumnies of others. I

* * * * *

1823
1 Erasmus may be alluding to the original name given by St Francis to his brothers, the 'Friars Minor,' a name that evoked both the material poverty and the
  spirit of humility that Francis wished his followers to practice.
2 Probably alluding to Albert Pigge's letter to the theologians of Louvain (Ep
  1589:5–8) affirming Pope Clement VII's high regard for Erasmus. For the sentiments of Emperor Charles V see Epp 1690 n11, 1735:31.
3 Eg Epp 1174 n5, 1805:301–3 and n66, 1891:24–5
4 A reference to the squabbles and public debates about to culminate in the
  formal examination of Erasmus' works at Valladolid. See Ep 1814 introduction
  and n32.
5 No mention of this survives in letters received from Poland and Hungary;
  but the same statement occurs in Epp 1743:38–40, 1804:199, 1886:126 Allen
  2126:171–2.
6 Titelmans ignores this charge in his answering letter (Ep 1837A); but Allen
  (18n) implies that Titelmans would later do so in his *Epistola apologetica pro
  opere Collationum suarum ad Erasmum* (Antwerp: Willem Vorsterman 1530), a
  work we have not seen.

took no notice, and I consider it of slight importance. If you serve the cause
of piety with sincerity, the Lord will further your efforts; but if you deal in   25
subterfuges and cunning conspiracies, it will all, believe me, rebound upon
your own head. The Lord be with you.

At Basel, 18 May in the year 1527

1824 / To Leonard Cox   Basel, 21 May 1527

This letter, an answer to Ep 1803, first appeared in the *Opus epistolarum.* For
Cox see Ep 1803 introduction.

ERASMUS OF ROTTERDAM TO THE ENGLISHMAN LEONARD COX,
GREETING

If only, my dear Cox, it required as little effort to answer everyone's letters
as to return affection to all those who wish us well! But the labours dedicated
to study require all one's time and more, so much so that there is no time to   5
get sick or to care for this feeble little body – not to mention the possibility
of answering everyone's letters. Your recent letter[1] was pleasant in every respect except two. One was that your lavish praise is more of an onus than an
honour, even if this slight annoyance is mitigated by your unaffected good
will, which I know for certain to be the cause of your lapse. The other was   10
the news of the poor health of our dear Justus, a man for whom I should
wish all prosperity as he deserves. He had written me previously about his
fractured shoulder-bone.[2] Whether he has suffered any further harm I know
not; this courier has brought me no further news from him.

I cannot sufficiently express my astonishment at the decision of the   15
pastor of Košice;[3] I think good fortune is to be grasped, either to do good
for many or to avoid the derision of the malicious. Even if those in high
positions cannot correct everything they see being done by the people or
by the princes, they can nevertheless prevent much evil. If he calls on me,
he will find here no treasure but only coals.[4] I am well acquainted with the   20

* * * * *

1824
1 Ep 1803, to which this letter closely responds
2 Ep 1803:45–7; on Justus Decius see n11 there. Decius, who had fallen from a
   galloping horse, breaking a bone in his arm, wrote a few lines in the letter
   sent to Erasmus by the physician Jan Antonin on 21 January 1526; see (Ep
   1660:59–64).
3 Johann Henckel; see Ep 1803 n13.
4 *Adagia* I ix 30

Alexander Stewart (c 1493–1513)
Jacques Le Boucq of Valenciennes (fl c 1559)
Recueil de portraits, Bibliothèque municipale d'Arras,
Photo Giraudon (reproduced with permission)

talents of Jan Łaski,[5] and each day I experience them anew. I should consider myself fortunate if I had only him as a friend. I am happy to know that our friend Anianus is staying with you. You have good material here, which you have the skill to mould; give him my greetings.[6] I answered the letter from Krzycki, now invested with his new title of bishop of Płock.[7] This church 25 must be dear to God to have had in succession three bishops of such calibre, while other churches can scarcely claim the good fortune of having had one such prelate over a number of years.

The *Copia* was reissued six months ago, enhanced by me in a number of ways; I shall send this edition to you if it does not overload my packet. 30 Concerning the word *synere* about which you enquire,[8] the solution is as follows. About twenty years ago in Siena when I was charged with the education of Alexander, archbishop of St Andrews, brother of the present king of Scotland,[9] I came upon a very old edition of Aulus Gellius – the first, if I am not mistaken. There both in Greek and in Latin the reading *synere* 35 was given.[10] Although the translations that begin with the phrase 'that is' do not belong to Aulus Gellius, nevertheless they are of such a nature that I think he would have rendered it no better himself. Now also in the Aldine edition[11] I see the two letters reversed, *sirenon* in place of *synere*, and

* * * * *

5 Jan (II) Łaski; see Ep 1821 introduction.
6 Anianus Burgonius, a young French servant to Łaski, was staying with Cox during Łaski's absence (Ep 1803 n17). Erasmus alludes to Anianus Burgonius' penchant for poetry, which Cox was encouraging. In his edition of the Roman poet Statius, Cox published notes that Burgonius had written in Cox's honour (*Statii Papini . . . sylvae cum scholis* (Cracow: Matthias Scharffenberg 1527).
7 See Ep 1822 introduction.
8 The new edition appeared about a year earlier, in May 1526. For Cox's query, see Ep 1803:101–2 and n26.
9 Alexander Stewart, an illegitimate son of King James IV of Scotland, whom Erasmus tutored in Italy in 1508–9. He presented Erasmus with a gold signet ring bearing the effigy of the god Terminus (on which see Ep 1907 n19).
10 Aulus Gellius 15.20.8. The *editio princeps* of Aulus Gellius' *Noctes Atticae*, edited by Johannes Andreas de Buxis, appeared in 1469 in Rome from the press of the German printers Konrad Sweynheym and Arnold Pannartz. They reprinted the work in 1472. Later editions have *saccaro* 'sugar,' which fits with the other word in the phrase, *melitos* 'honey.' The confusion arose probably through the gloss on the Greek word Σειρήνων 'Sirens.' The original Latin gloss in Gellius was *Sirenibus*, corrupted subsequently to *sineribus* or *syneribus*, which gave no sense – hence the anomalous *synere*.
11 Venice 1515. See Antoine Renouard *Annales de l'imprimerie des Alde* 3rd ed (Paris 1834; repr 1953) 73 no 9. A counterfeit bearing the Aldine mark and the date 1512 was printed in Lyon (ibidem 312 no 41).

the meter remains intact; but whether it is the authentic reading I know not. 40
I had the impression that *synar* was a noun similar to *piper*. I have found
nothing in the authors up to this point that satisfies me. Pliny does not describe the nature of *cinaris*, except to say that by browsing on it the deer
heals itself when it has eaten toxic herbs.[12] Hesychius refers to *cynar*, which
others call *cynosbaton*.[13] But this also is irrelevant. Accordingly it seems best 45
to me to delete the word, which is what I think has been done in the latest
edition.[14]

I shall write to your friend Zebrzydowski, if I am given the least opportunity.[15]

Given at Basel, 21 May in the year 1527   50

1825 / To Jan Antonin   [Basel, c 21 May] 1527

An answer to Antonin's Ep 1810, this letter was first published in the *Opus
epistolarum* (1529).

ERASMUS OF ROTTERDAM TO THE PHYSICIAN ANTONIN,
GREETING

How you surpass your own self in kindness when you exaggerate my humble services to you while neglecting to mention your own far greater services to me! Ursinus has already described to me in detail a part of his 5
tragicomedy or, shall I say, comic tragedy,[1] reserving the best part of the
story for Johannes Fabri, with whom I have not yet had the opportunity to

* * * * *

12 *Naturalis historia* 8.27.101
13 Hesychius was a fifth-century Alexandrian lexicographer. The edition of *Hesy-
   chii Dictionarium* that Erasmus cites (Venice: Aldo Manuzio, August 1514) was
   based on a single fifteenth-century manuscript in the possession of Giovanni
   Giacomo Bardelloni of Mantua. *Cynar* (the correct Greek is κινάρα or κυνάρα) is
   the Greek for artichoke, and κυνόσβατον is often equated with κάππαρις 'caper.'
14 In fact Erasmus did not delete the word in the 1526 edition. He substituted
   for it the word *saccaro* (ASD I-6 81:252 and note).
15 See Ep 1803:92–7; Erasmus would write Ep 1826 to Zebrzydowski this same
   day.

1825
1 This letter from Caspar Ursinus Velius (on whom see Ep 1810 n6) is not extant. The reference to tragedy and comedy perhaps alludes to Velius' appointment, just after the battle of Mohács, as historian of King Ferdinand – a promotion that left him on the opposite political side from his friend Antonin,
   who supported Ferdinand's rival for the throne, John Zápolyai.

converse.[2] Nor have I been able in the meantime to find out whither he has betaken himself. It seemed he could not make up his mind.[3]

That matters in Hungary are so troubled distresses me, especially for your sake, for whom I wish, as you deserve, that all be favourable and serene. Since you ask my counsel, as long as that business of the princes is still unsettled,[4] I should not come out strongly for either one; and, of a certainty, I should give offence to no one.

They write me here that Béda with a band of pseudomonks is actively at work.[5] He would have hauled a certain person I know to the stake had not the Parlement and the king intervened.[6] His crime was to have translated some of my works into French – so convinced are they that it is an act of high treason against them if Erasmus speaks in the vulgar tongue. For the moment, they blabber whatever they like to women, whom they have driven out of their minds, and to ordinary people. But if the people were to read my works, they would see through their incredible shamelessness.

From Thurzo (you refer to Alexius, I suppose) I have heard nothing either good or ill, but I still think that he is satisfied with my efforts.[7] From Henckel I had no letter from the present messenger and nothing at the last fair. His refusal of the episcopate must have been motivated by good reason;[8] yet, as mortal affairs stand at present, it is preferable to be a swineherd

* * * * *

2 Trained as a lawyer, Johannes Fabri of Leutkirch had been promoted as an auxiliary bishop of Constance. His attempts to deal moderately with Luther, Zwingli, and other reformers brought their contempt and spurred him to urge suppression of their heresies by Ferdinand of Hapsburg, of whom he was a councillor. He continued to admire Erasmus, and was in Basel at this time. See CEBR II 5–8.

3 Fabri was on the point of leaving Basel to travel to Spain, France, Flanders, and England to recruit help in the Hapsburg wars against the Turks.

4 The struggle over the crown of Hungary between Ferdinand of Hapsburg and John Zápolyai

5 See Ep 1804 n14. Antonin had mentioned him in Ep 1810:35.

6 Louis de Berquin had been imprisoned from 18 January to 19 November 1526, and afterwards was detained in the Louvre; see Ep 1821 n15. Béda in fact had no jurisdiction over Berquin, whose case fell in the first instance under the jurisdiction of the tribunal of papal judges delegate appointed jointly by the pope and the queen regent and, in second instance, of the Parlement of Paris acting as secular arm. Erasmus correctly recounts that King Francis I came to Berquin's rescue; but he is unaware that the Parlement of Paris was Berquin's determined enemy.

7 See Ep 1810:39–40 and n13.

8 Offered by King John Zápolyai, the new anti-Hapsburg king in Hungary; cf Ep 1810 n14.

than a swine.[9] I ask you, what serious business could have persuaded you to get ready to set out here on such a long journey? Was it to see Erasmus dying? I die daily,[10] my dear Antonin. 30

In the matter of Galen, even if I were perfectly capable of fulfilling your wish,[11] I have not the time. I am being drawn back into the gladiatorial arena.[12] If Hippocrates is poorly translated, you must not blame it on Calvo, for he is nothing more than a printer, and an unlearned one at that.[13] For Martin Dobergast I pray for every blessing.[14] If I can do anything for 35 him, I shall undertake it ungrudgingly. One must not trust false friends, but nonetheless Cicero tells us they must be utilized in such a way as to cause least harm.[15] And there is much truth also in what Ovid wrote:

Oft too one who dissimulates
Begins to love in earnest.[16] 40

I received the little book of Andrzei Krzycki – or, I should say, the bishop of Płock, to use his new title – together with a letter of his, however brief.[17] For your excellent wife[18] I wish every possible happiness. The plague has carried off several of our doctors, among them Silberberg.[19]
Farewell. 1527 45

* * * * *

9 Not in *Adagia*, nor have we found it in lexicons of proverbs. It is antithetical to the parable of the prodigal son (Luke 15:11–32) who, working as a swineherd, realized that the swine ate better than he did.
10 1 Cor 15:31
11 Erasmus had already dedicated to Antonin some translations of Galen. In Ep 1810:54–6 Antonin asked Erasmus to translate more of that same author.
12 A reference to the many requests and demands that he complete the second part of his *Hyperaspistes* against Luther. Cf Ep 1815:55, where Erasmus used the same phrase. On his responses to Luther, see Ep 1804 n10.
13 Erasmus confuses Marco Fabio Calvo of Ravenna, the translator of the work, and Francesco Giulio Calvo, the Roman printer; on the latter see *Dizionario dei tipografi e degli editori italiani: Il Cinquecento* ed Marco Menato et al (Milan 1997–) I 234–7. Antonin had complained of the edition produced by Andreas Cratander (Basel, August 1526). See Ep 1810:65–7; cf Ep 1912 n1.
14 Ep 1810 n21
15 *Ad Atticum* 1.18.1
16 *Ars amatoria* 1.615
17 The letter is not extant; see Ep 1822 introduction. On his book, see Ep 1810 n22.
18 Anna Zimmermann, daughter of Cracow goldsmith Jan Zimmermann
19 Johann Silberberg, Basel physician, whose death Beatus Rhenanus reported on 5 November 1526 (AK III Ep 1154). On this outbreak of the plague, see Ep 1777:5–6 (11 January 1527), although Bonifacius Amerbach reported it to be slacking off as early as November 1526 (AK III Ep 1157:39–40).

1826 / To Andrzej Zebrzydowski   Basel, 21 May 1527

Erasmus wrote this letter to please Leonard Cox who was tutoring Zebrzydowski in Cracow (Epp 1803:92–7, 1824:48). The boy was the son of the sister of Andrzej Kryzcki (Epp 1803 n19, 1822) and the great-nephew of Piotr
Tomicki, bishop of Cracow and vice-chancellor in Poland. Zebrzydowski was
to make an extended visit to Erasmus in the spring of 1528, perhaps as a result
of this letter, which was first published in the *Opus epistolarum*. Zebrzydowski
eventually became bishop of Cracow (CEBR III 473–4).

ERASMUS OF ROTTERDAM TO ANDRZEJ ZEBRZYDOWSKI, GREETING
This letter is owed, first, to the exceptional friendship sealed by an exchange
of letters which has existed for some time between me and the most honourable prelate Andrzej Krzycki and, second, to your outstanding qualities
worthy of such an uncle, which have been vividly portrayed for me in the   5
letters of Leonard Cox, mentor of your adolescent years. Thus I have presumed to send you greetings and to spur you on to the love of the highest
disciplines of learning, if that be appropriate to one already in hot pursuit,
as they say, and if what Cox writes is true, in whom I have the greatest confidence: 'No need to spur the running horse.'[1] But that you may always sur-   10
pass yourself in enthusiasm on this fairest of courses, dearest Zebrzydowski,
you have a great many merits which must surely quicken your spirit. First
of all your own prolific talents promise nothing but the most remarkable
distinction for you; then your teacher Cox, like a good artisan working with
good material, adds even further to this expectation. I may also add that   15
fortune, which when unfavourable hinders the noblest efforts of many, in
your case is a generous and timely servant to your talent. But the greatest deterrent to your becoming sluggish is the shining example you have in
your own family, in whom as in a mirror you see reflected a faultless image
of virtue and learning. Andrzej must show himself the equal of Andrzej,   20
nephew of uncle. This your lineage demands and requires of you, this your
fatherland expects. Carry on, then, my Zebrzydowski; set yourself to press
on with untiring zeal towards the palm of victory in this meritorious cause.
Your efforts will have the help of God, who has lavished on you so many
advantages of nature and fortune, so that by your industry you may put   25
to worthy use the rich endowments that have fallen to your lot. Remember
that the best part of life is also the most fleeting: once it has slipped by it
will nevermore return.

* * * * *

1826
1 Ovid *Ars amatoria* 2.732; *Adagia* I ii 46 and I ii 47

For the present it is not possible to write further. Farewell.

Given at Basel, 21 May in the year 1527   30

1827 / To Nicolaus Vesuvius   Basel, 23 May 1527

The year date of this letter, first published in the *Opus epistolarum* (1529), can be confirmed by the reference to Erasmus' translation from Origen (line 2). Its recipient remained unknown to Allen, probably because the 1529 editorial salutation is to a medical doctor. This attribution is not likely, since Erasmus' reference to 'the doctors' (line 10) implies that the addressee was not a member of that profession (the remedy he sent to Erasmus notwithstanding). The addressee was in the service of a French bishop – most likely Michel Boudet of Langres – because Erasmus sends greetings to Boudet's vicar-general Claude Félix (line 16) and probably to Boudet himself (line 23) but fails to do the same to Nicolaus Vesuvius, Boudet's chaplain and a correspondent of Erasmus. The recipient should therefore be identified as Vesuvius himself, and this letter should be seen as a reply to Ep 1784 from Vesuvius, since it deals with themes of that letter and because Erasmus twice employs the term *malicia* (Allen lines 14 and 18), which echoes Vesuvius' *malivolentia* (Allen line 11). Although Ep 1784 does not mention the medical remedy that Erasmus here rejects out of hand, it could well have been entrusted to the courier Anton Bletz, whom Erasmus knew personally and had employed to carry letters to and from Vesuvius (see Epp 1784 n1, 1894:1–2; cf CEBR I 153–4).

Apart from Vesuvius' correspondence with Erasmus little else is known of him (CEBR III 389–90).

ERASMUS OF ROTTERDAM TO A CERTAIN MEDICAL DOCTOR,[1]
GREETING

I have not yet spoken to the man who delivered your letter. When he came I was totally engrossed in translating a fragment of Origen on St Matthew that I came across.[2] When he returned, I was suffering from an unbear-   5
able toothache that had suddenly taken hold of me, so that I could not

* * * * *

1827
1 A mistaken attribution, probably of the 1529 editor; see the introduction.
2 See Ep 1844. The *Fragmentum commentariorum Origenis in evangelium secundum Matthaeum* was printed by Froben in July 1527 and reprinted by Josse Bade (Paris, 23 February 1530). See *Origenes Matthäuserklärung* GCS *Origenes Werke* 10 ed Erich Klostermann (Leipzig 1935); cf the Greek *editio princeps* ed Daniel Huet (Paris 1668), who refers frequently to Erasmus' translation. PG 5 835–1800 uses the 1759 Paris Maurist edition. On the manuscript used by Erasmus see Ep 1844 n17. See also SC 162 ed Robert Girol (Paris 1970).

talk without aggravating the pain with each breath I took. In the midst
of summer weather we have suffered winter here. For the remedy you
pointed out to me I am extremely grateful, even if in my case the problem was not traces of sand but stones; that is why the doctors call it lithi-   10
asis.[3] But this malady has turned into something else, which produces a
continuous malaise, although the pain is more tolerable. Had this not occurred, Erasmus would by now have been delivered from these tumultuous
times.

Gervasius was with us, a truly open-minded theologian whose conver-   15
sation brought me great solace.[4] I wish every felicity for Claude Félix.[5] In
response to your very warm words of consolation concerning men's envy,
or rather malice,[6] rest assured that I am distressed not so much for my own
sake as for the good name of the Christian religion, which has such doctors
and champions of the faith. Christ will see to my welfare and to that of my   20
studies. Would that no one other than Béda and Cousturier were infected
with this malice![7]

Please give my warm greetings to your venerable prelate.[8] Farewell.
23 May 1527

1828 / To William Warham   Basel, [c 26 May] 1527

This letter was first published in the *Opus epistolarum* (1529). Its date can be
confirmed by the departure for England of the courier Nicolaas Kan (Ep 1832).

William Warham, archbishop of Canterbury since 1503 and chancellor of
England from 1504 to 1515, was a patron and benefactor of Erasmus since

* * * * *

3 The closest English equivalent to Erasmus' λίθωσιν [lithosin]
4 Gervasius Wain of Memmingen, a doctor of theology of Paris in 1522, was
  loyal to Erasmus and other humanists. He later served as King Francis I's
  ambassador to a number of German princes (Farge BR 431–5 no 471). See other
  allusions to his visit to Erasmus in Epp 1884 and 1840 n20.
5 Claude Félix was a doctor of theology of Paris (1508). He was canon of Langres
  and vicar-general of Bishop Michel Boudet (see Farge BR 162 no 179; CEBR II
  16).
6 *malicia*, used again in line 22 below; see the introduction.
7 On Noël Béda and Pierre Cousturier, against whom the accusations are made,
  see Ep 1804 nn14 and 65.
8 Surely Michel Boudet, bishop of Langres since 1511. He was a friend of Guillaume Budé and other French humanists. Erasmus had exchanged letters with
  him (Epp 1612 and 1618) and sent him a presentation copy of the first book of
  Hyperaspistes (Ep 1678). For Boudet see the introduction to this letter and CEBR
  I 178–9.

1506 (Epp 188, 208). He steadfastly recommended a policy of peace to Henry
VIII, and strongly opposed reformation theology in the 1520s. Like Thomas
More and Bishop John Fisher, Warham opposed the attempts to declare null
the king's marriage and the ecclesiastical policies that led to the schism with
Rome. See CEBR III 427–31.

TO WILLIAM WARHAM, ARCHBISHOP OF CANTERBURY, FROM
ERASMUS OF ROTTERDAM, GREETING

Most distinguished prelate and most liberal Maecenas of my studies, that
old conspiracy against me of monks and pseudotheologians has finally burst
out into the open.[1] Their aim is to wrest my books from men's grasp; but,
believe me, they will not succeed. They have set themselves to this task
in many places simultaneously, and with singleness of purpose; but everywhere they have encountered powerful leaders to stand in the way of their
mad designs. I am in possession of practically all their censures of my books
and can truly rejoice that this is all that can be adduced by such men, who
with malevolent animosity distort everything in spreading their false accusations.[2] If you have time to read their charges,[3] you will see what lies and
deceptions they bring against me. In this general confusion that old master
of histrionics plays the brave hero, like Androclides forgetful of his mission;[4] and this despite his knowledge that I am well regarded by the archbishop of Toledo[5] as well as several other bishops, by many high-standing
men at court, and by the emperor himself.

* * * * *

1828
1 Erasmus has in mind the coming inquisitorial proceedings at Valladolid, the
 recent books from the Paris theologians Noël Béda and Pierre Cousturier, and
 the continuing opposition of theologians in Louvain.
2 Pedro Juan Olivar, a humanist in the entourage of Chancellor Mercurino Gattinara, had sent Erasmus the twenty-one articles of censure that would serve
 as the basis for the inquisitorial assembly in Valladolid (Ep 1791). Erasmus had
 not been able to procure the censures of the Paris faculty of theology, which
 were held *in camera* until their publication in July 1531.
3 Erasmus must have enclosed a copy of the twenty-one Spanish articles with
 this letter.
4 Cf Ep 1831:16. The reference is to Edward Lee, Erasmus' old enemy, who
 was on a diplomatic mission to Spain for King Henry VIII; see Ep 1814 n39.
 Androclides stands for the mean and contemptible man. See *Adagia* II ii 91: 'In
 civil war even Androclides is a general.'
5 Alonso de Fonseca (Ep 1813). It was important that Erasmus be able to assure
 Warham, the primate of England, that he had the support of the primate of
 Spain and many other bishops.

Let us concede that some things in my books might have been said
with more circumspection; but in no case do they exhibit impiety. What
kind of example is it to launch an assault on one man by means of a ma-   20
licious conspiracy spread through the whole world, with frenzied outcries
and angry pamphlets? This is not to defend the faith, which is the pretence under which they advertise themselves, but to stir up new troubles
when there is already more than enough general turmoil. I have roused a
good number of people to the study of good letters; I have even encour-   25
aged and assisted the studies of theologians through many of my works.
If they contain some human error, the matter could have been entrusted
to some honest and learned men, who in their good judgment might correct those things that truly give offence. Truth to tell, they are not offended by errors; it is something else that galls them. As the study of   ·30
languages and humane letters flourishes everywhere, they see their prestige dwindle in the eyes of all – and no wonder, since for so many years
now they have waged a violent war against higher learning. If they had
been willing to engage in these studies rather than denigrate the reputation of others, they would have given more lustre to their own. Now   35
they are tormented by jealousy. In all the nations of the world the pages
of Erasmus' works, whatever their worth, are frayed from constant turning, while the books of men like Cousturier and Béda are laughed at by
schoolboys.[6]

There is yet another sore point. In my books at times I admonish the-   40
ologians to abandon sophistic debates and draw near to the biblical sources,
to read over the holy Doctors of the church; and I indicate certain passages
in which they have fallen into error through ignorance of languages and
antiquity. Similarly I remind monks also of the true nature of religion. They
have no stomach for such things. They preferred to keep intact the old cabal 45
of monks and theologians; but this was of little use to the Christian people.
My books have planted no seed of heresy or schism. It is instead these detractors who with hue and cry give rise to all these troubles. But within
a few years you will see a turnabout on the stage of human history, and
men will welcome with open arms that moderation which I have contin-   50
ually pursued in my writings. In England they protest loudly against my
Colloquies,[7] although hardly any other book is more conducive to ridding

* * * * *

6 Pierre Cousturier and Noël Béda; see Ep 1804 nn65 and 14.
7 This is a milder claim than Erasmus' complaint to Cardinal Wolsey that the
  Colloquies had been banned in England (Ep 1697:26–7), for which there is no
  evidence. However, just as in Louvain and Paris, many English persons, in-

men's minds of stupid prejudices. It will be left to the wisdom of princes
to quell these confused tumults through their authority; if not, they will develop into a more serious disaster than the one incited up to now by the   55
Lutherans.

Princes have good grounds for doing this. There is enough turmoil in
the church without our seeking out new cause for disturbance; and we have
more than enough trouble with those who openly profess and defend in
writing the teachings of Luther without picking a quarrel with those who   60
fight on our side against Luther. Besides, since the emperor has it in mind to
breathe new life into certain established usages in the church, which cannot
be accomplished without a great assemblage of princes, it is best to put off
any consideration of such matters until that time.[8] For the present moment
we must strive for peace with all our powers, and subjects of discord must   65
be set aside. Finally, even if I may have written otherwise than I ought, it
does no good to correct men's failings by clamours, calumnies, conspiracies,
and mad pamphlets of this sort. For in such a way the Lutheran affair was
enkindled from tiny beginnings into this conflagration, which now rages far
and wide throughout the world.   70

If on these grounds princes will crush the attacks of these madmen,
their turbulence will soon cease. But if they are lenient towards their uncontrolled hatreds, things will come to such a pass that when the princes
wish to restrain them, they will not be able to do so. These fatal upheavals
that rock the world seem to have arisen not without divine consent, and in   75
incredible fashion have reached their present state. The ways of God are inscrutable. What men strive for we see from their ambitions; God's designs
are unknown to us. He knows how to turn the malice and stupidity of mortal
men to his glory and to the salvation of the just. It will therefore always be
my concern to approach him with a sincere conscience; of the final outcome   80
let him be the judge.

If your Highness wishes to know more of what is happening here it
may be learned in the letter I sent to Bedyll, your secretary.[9] I charged Pieter

* * * * *

cluding friends of Erasmus like Cuthbert Tunstall, were disturbed by certain
passages that they found dangerous (Allen Ep 2226:56–62). As well, Tunstall,
Wolsey, and Thomas More had taken action to prevent importation of Lutheran
books into England from Germany (Ep 1697 n8).
8 This statement puts Erasmus firmly in the conciliarist camp, that is, with those
who believed that ecclesiastical reform need not await initiative from the pope
or bishops but could be effected by a council convened by secular authorities.
9 Not extant. Thomas Bedyll, Warham's secretary since 1516, annually sent to
Erasmus the pension awarded him by Warham. Contrary to Warham's own

Gillis to send you the latest volumes of St Jerome in a beautifully bound
edition;[10] whether he did so I know not.   85
     Basel, in the year 1527

1829 / To Tielmannus Gravius   Basel, 29 May 1527

This note, the initial letter in an exchange with Gravius that lasted until Erasmus' death, was first published in the *Opus epistolarum*. Unable to confirm the
date and year assigned there by the editors, Allen placed it here because its
form is similar to that of Epp 1830–2.
     Tielmannus Gravius, a layman and the father of eight children, held various
positions at the Cologne cathedral chapter and in the service of Archbishop
Hermann von Wied. A friend and patron of Cologne humanists and printers,
he possessed a fine library. He rendered several personal services to Erasmus,
who would dedicate to him in 1529 an edition of Lactantius (CEBR II 125–6).

ERASMUS OF ROTTERDAM TO TIELMANNUS GRAVIUS, GREETING
Challenged to a contest of friendship by a gift of iron, I respond with a gift of
paper, not returning bronze for gold,[1] but still rendering inferior compensation for what I received. But so far is it from my mind to decline this humble
gift that I deduce from it the high opinion you sincerely entertain of my char-   5
acter. In general even those who send expensive gifts invent long excuses
for sending something inferior to one's worth. Therefore the modesty of
your little gift has increased its value in my eyes, and I declare myself much
bound by your good will, to which I wish this brief letter to bear witness as
a legal written agreement for all and sundry. I wish you the best of health.   10
     Given at Basel on the eve of the Ascension 1527

* * * * *

policies, Bedyll later became active in the English annulment of Henry VIII's
marriage to Catherine of Aragon and in the suppression of monasteries.
10 The last nine volumes of the revised second edition; see Ep 1740:16–17 and
   nn4–5. Gillis, the city clerk of Antwerp, who had performed a similar service for Erasmus in 1516 (Epp 477:3–7, 491:2–4), was a trusted friend. For a
   while he served as Erasmus' financial agent in the Low Countries, but in 1525
   Erasmus named Erasmus Schets to act in this capacity; cf Ep 1804 n76.

1829
1 *Adagia* I ii 1, drawn from *Iliad* 6.234–6, where Diomedes, recognizing in single
   combat with Glaucus that an ancient bond of friendship exists between their
   families, immediately exchanges armour with him, gold for bronze, as a pledge
   of their friendship. Gravius' 'gift of iron' has not been identified.

1830 / To Juan Luis Vives   Basel, 29 May 1527

This letter answers Vives' Ep 1792 and would in turn be answered by Vives' Ep 1847. It was first published in the *Opus epistolarum* (1529). Erasmus' correspondence with Vives began in March 1519 (Ep 927).

Juan Luis Vives (1492–1540) left his native Spain in 1509, never to return, and studied at the Collège de Montaigu in Paris. Not satisfied with the scholastic curriculum there, he moved in 1512 to Bruges, which became his permanent home. He tutored privately (Guillaume de Croy was his student [Ep 628:70]), lectured publicly in Louvain, and made trips to Paris, Louvain, and England. His *In pseudodialecticos* (1520), a diatribe against the scholastic method, and his extensive commentary on Augustine's *City of God* (commissioned by Erasmus, who thought the end result too long) won him the attention of humanists. Wolsey gave him a position at Corpus Christi College, Oxford. He gained the patronage of Queen Catherine of Aragon, and composed his *De institutione feminae christianae* (1524) for her daughter Mary. Vives published copiously for the rest of his life. In time his relationship with Erasmus grew less close as the two took different positions on a number of political and theological issues. See CEBR III 409–13; ER VI 281–3.

ERASMUS OF ROTTERDAM TO LUIS VIVES, GREETING

I see that you have become an amphibious animal,[1] unless you prefer the name of Mercury, 'beloved of the gods above and those beneath.'[2] Concerning my silence you are correct in the many reasons you infer; you should have added one further reason: that sometimes letters do not reach their 5 destination.

With regard to the *Colloquies*,[3] I am quite astonished that arguments should be lacking to such a great advocate even in the worst of causes. These days such things are debated even by children; and old Club-Foot

* * * * *

1830
1 'Amphibious animal' is rendered in Greek. When Vives questioned him about its meaning (Ep 1847:50–1) he clarified it in Ep 1889:10–12. See also Ep 1518:50 and n14.
2 Horace *Odes* 1.10.19–20
3 Vives had accused Erasmus of impropriety in his treatment of unspecified subjects in the *Colloquies*, singling out *De votis temere susceptis* 'Rash Vows,' *Confabulatio pia* 'The Whole Duty of Youth,' and Ἰχθυοφαγία 'A Fish Diet' (CWE 39 35–43 and 88–108, CWE 40 675–762); see Ep 1732:33–45. Other friends of Erasmus likewise had reservations about some of his *Colloquies*; see Ep 1828 n7.

seems to have written his works for children, so puerile are they.[4] But in   10
the end children grow up; so, for those who have now reached adulthood,
more serious topics were suitable. But, to be frank, I lost my free will: in
that work my mind dictated one thing but my pen wrote another.[5]

Your writings have my enthusiastic approval, especially what you have
written about marriage.[6] But you aspire to extemporaneity, which in your   15
case is certainly more successful than the most minute care exercised by a
great many writers. If, however, you would be willing to restrain your enthusiasm and adapt yourself more to the opinion of the reader, for whom
the play is being performed, you would have expressed certain things more
gently. On the topic of marriage you seemed too hard on wives; I imagine   20
you are more gentle with your own.[7] And you write too much about scabies.[8] That you take delight in making mention of your own relatives is
something you have in common with Cicero and it is undoubtedly a sign of
filial devotion;[9] but men, being envious by nature, more willingly tolerate
praise of persons unrelated to them.   25

* * * * *

4 ὁ χωλός. Erasmus is referring to his Louvain opponent Jacobus Latomus, who
  was a cripple (cf Ep 1256:26). His estimation here of Latomus differs radically from that of Martin Luther, who considered Latomus to be a formidable
  opponent (CEBR II 304–6).

5 Erasmus uses the same expression regarding things he wrote in his *Institution
  of Christian Marriage* in Ep 1804:316; cf Ep 1816 n4.

6 In *De institutione feminae christianae* (Antwerp: Michaël Hillen for Franz Birckmann 1524), written to advise Catherine of Aragon on the instruction of
  Princess Mary, Vives writes with great affection about his parents and the
  state of matrimony in general. For the critical edition with facing English
  translation see *De institutione feminae christianae* ed Charles Fantazzi and Constant Matheeussen (Leiden 1998); cf also *The Education of a Christian Woman: A
  Sixteenth-century Manual* ed and trans Charles Fantazzi (Chicago 2000).

7 See Ep 1455:2, where Vives announces to Erasmus his marriage to his kins-
  woman Margarita Valdaura.

8 In Ep 1847:48 Vives seems to think that it was the word *scabies* itself, not his
  description of the disease, that Erasmus found objectionable, and he thus cites
  there Jerome's using it to justify his own use of the word. But Erasmus was
  probably objecting to the graphic details into which Vives enters in describing the symptoms of his father-in-law. Although in that passage Vives calls
  the disease *morbus gallicus* 'the French disease,' one cannot conclude that the
  scabies of Vives' father-in-law was a syphilitic condition.

9 In his *De institutione* Vives has great praise for his own parents, who were
  Jewish *conversos* and victims of the Inquisition, and for his mother-in-law
  Clara Cervent, who ministered heroically to her husband, Bernardo Valdaura,
  a prosperous wool-merchant (and possibly a gem dealer) in Bruges. Vives
  was frequently a guest at their home in his early years in that city. See Juan

Such is my opinion, but it is one on which you in turn are free to have
an opinion of your own; you should at least appreciate my compliance with
your wish, as it was you who asked it of me. Do write back whatever you
wish by the present courier.

Farewell. At Basel on the eve of the Ascension 1527   30

1831 / To William Warham   Basel, 29 May 1527

Erasmus sent this letter and Ep 1832 with an unnamed traveller to England,
described as 'eloquent,' 'bursting with clever stories,' and 'very dependable'
(Epp 1832:3, 6; 1833:75–6), hoping he would overtake his own servant Nicolaas
Kan, who had already set out for England carrying Ep 1828, so that the present
letter could be delivered to Warham with that one.

TO WILLIAM WARHAM, ARCHBISHOP OF CANTERBURY, FROM
ERASMUS OF ROTTERDAM, GREETING
I fear I may overwhelm your reverend Lordship with my letters and couriers;[1] but something unexpected has happened which required that Nicolaas Kan, my most faithful and devoted servant, be dispatched to England   5
on this matter, although it cost me considerable inconvenience.[2] I wrote you
lately and sent you a copy of Jerome decorated in gold;[3] if these volumes
have safely reached you, I shall be immensely happy. Too often have I experienced the extent of human perfidy in such matters.

Here everything seems to point towards revolution, and I fear bloody   10
uprisings, so extensively do these factions send out their roots; you must
see it to believe it. I have had the ill fortune of growing old in these times.
From the church I cannot withdraw. And the opposing party has a following
with whom I would not wish to be allied. The rampaging monks,[4] to their

* * * * *

Luis Vives *De institutione feminae christianae* ed Charles Fantazzi and Constant
Matheeussen (Leiden 1998) 43–7; CEBR III 365–6 (Margarita Valdaura). He also
speaks of his own mother in his annotations on Augustine's *De civitate Dei*
(Basel: Johann Froben 1522) 381 XII 20.

1831
1 See the introduction. As well, this was Nicolaas Kan's second trip to England
   within two months on Erasmus' behalf.
2 See Ep 1832 introduction and lines 24–5, where Erasmus describes him as
   'more of a friend than a servant.'
3 See Ep 1828:84 and n10.
4 Erasmus uses this term generally for his theological critics, though many of
   them were neither monks nor mendicant friars.

own detriment, make this melodrama worse. And your compatriot in Spain 15
is hard at work pursuing his schemes, forgetful of his mission,[5] although
perfectly aware that I am in the good favour of the emperor and the leading
churchmen of Spain. Evil mind, evil heart.[6]

In Rome everything is in turmoil,[7] and letters cannot get through. Some
think an alliance will be formed between the emperor and the pope. As long 20
as princes allow the pope to make and unmake treaties first with one, then
with another,[8] I fear the world will never be at peace. The pope should be a
father dealing justly with all. But the ambition and hatred of princes either
do not see this or, if they do, they obey their passions rather than reason.

I fear I shall not be able to reside here for long;[9] but these things are 25
in the hands of Christ. Other news, if you have time, you will learn from
my servant Kan, whom you will find to be not at all lacking in judgment or
reliability.[10] May the Lord preserve you unharmed.

Basel. The eve of the Ascension in the year 1527

1832 / To Nicolaas Kan   Basel, 29 May 1527

Nicolaas Kan of Amsterdam was a graduate of the Collegium Trilingue in Louvain. He obviously knew Greek, as this letter contains a dozen Greek words or
phrases. Kan, in Erasmus' service since the spring of 1527 at least, was a faithful copyist, servant, messenger, and friend; Erasmus would cast him as an in-
terlocutor in the colloquy *Cyclops, sive evangeliophorus* 'Cyclops, or the Gospel
Bearer' (1529). After helping Erasmus move to Freiburg in April 1529, he took
holy orders in Amsterdam, served as parish priest and chaplain to a house of
nuns, and made plans to join the Jesuits (CEBR II 252–3).

This letter first appeared in the *Opus epistolarum* (1529).

* * * * *

5 Edward Lee; see Ep 1828 n4.
6 Terence *Andria* 164
7 The sack of Rome, sparked by failure to pay the marauding imperial troops,
  had begun on 6 May of this year and lasted about two months; see ER V 354–6.
8 Pope Clement VII had joined France and Venice in the League of Cognac
  against Emperor Charles V. Earlier in the century, Pope Julius II had allied
  against France, but the French defeat of papal forces at Marignano (1515) had
  resulted in Pope Leo X joining France in an alliance against the Empire. Charles
  V had enjoyed a relatively free hand in Italy after the defeat of the French army
  at Pavia (February 1525).
9 In light of the preceding descriptions, Erasmus may be sounding out Warham's
  reaction to his moving from Basel to England.
10 See n2 above.

ERASMUS OF ROTTERDAM TO NICOLAAS KAN, GREETING

What good fortune belongs to astrologers, my dearest Nicolaas, who from their knowledge of the stars can choose days and hours favourable to them! If you had left here two days later, you would have had an eloquent travelling companion, who for your journey on foot would have been 'as good as a carriage.'[1] For he is bursting with clever stories; and, as you know, the greatest part of toil is our imagining of it. I sent him off without delay, and he is certain that he will overtake you within three days. He knows your pace, I think, to be that of one who makes haste slowly.[2]

For many reasons, my dear Kan, I should wish that you return here as soon as possible. You know how difficult it is for me to be without your assistance, especially in the copying out of Greek. But since you will be facing the dangers of the sea and sailors no more good-tempered than the sea, and sometimes too will have to make your way through regions notorious for their brigands, I have fixed no prescribed day for your return. All the same, your loyalty, proven to me on numerous other occasions, gives me confidence that you will not linger anywhere unless forced to it by necessity. I prefer that you return late but safe and sound, rather than that through excessive speed either you should be in danger or my affairs should not be properly carried out. As the proverb says, flee in such a way that you do not lose sight of home.[3] I have given you letters for a rather restricted number of friends,[4] and they are exceedingly brief, since there is hardly any aspect of my affairs that is unfamiliar to you and since I rely in no small measure on your prudence. For, as you know, I have always considered you more of a friend than a servant; you will not disappoint my confidence in you, I am certain.

I would prefer that you not incur the expense of setting out on a journey to revisit Holland. What could possibly attract you there except for some drinking parties, which suit neither your character nor your health? It is something to be able to see Britain, celebrated in the writings of all men of learning; and for your good manners and practical understanding it will be of great profit to have met so many learned men and so many important personages in England. Take heed, however, that their exceptional kindness does not render you careless or disrespectful; and however deferential they

* * * * *

1832
1 Publilius Syrus *Sententiae* 17; cf Ep 1264 n1.
2 *Adagia* II i 1
3 Terence *Phormio* 768; cf *Adagia* I v 3.
4 Among letters to England only Ep 1828 to Warham is extant.

may be you must always be mindful of your modesty. Great men of that   35
sort do not always entertain in their mind the sentiments they display on
their countenance. As formerly with the gods, so now with men of high rank
one must speak with a religious awe.

In accepting gifts – for that nation is as generous as Brabant is niggardly – remember the ancient proverb: 'not everything, not everywhere,   40
and not from everybody.'[5] If on their own initiative wealthy and sincere
friends offer you something, accept it – but with a demonstration of your
gratitude. If less fortunate or somewhat aloof friends offer you something,
make excuses for not accepting – but in a polite way. It requires more skill
to refuse a favour than to accept it in the proper manner. Yet there are those   45
who, though they could hardly be considered friends, become open enemies
if you reject their gifts. For they understand it to mean either that the poor-
ness of the gift is regarded with contempt or that they are disliked. You must
show respect for their good intentions, but with convincing words. Far be it
from you to exhibit a vulgar spirit, avid for petty rewards of this kind. But,   50
unless my opinion of you is entirely erroneous, you would have acted in
this upright manner even without my admonition. Otherwise I would rather
have you take ten times the amount I give you.

There is no reason for you to fear the Straits of Dover,[6] you a marine animal[7] and virtually born of the waves, if the impression I formed   55
long ago of your native Amsterdam was correct.[8] It is, to be sure, a bother-
some and expensive crossing; but, as it is short, it is not too notorious for
shipwrecks. And if you do suffer some discomfort, 'one day its recollection
will be sweet.'[9] But once you have crossed the sea, another peril will await
you, perhaps graver still. You know the proverb about the Dutch horse-   60
man.[10] But take heart; horses are very clever. They know the road and have

* * * * *

5 *Adagia* II iv 16, quoting the jurist Ulpian. Erasmus renders the proverb in
   Greek.
6 Erasmus uses the continental expression 'Straits of Calais.' Although he tries
   to reassure Kan, Erasmus himself strongly disliked making this crossing of
   the Channel; see Epp 756:35, 961:8.
7 The term 'marine animal' is rendered in Greek.
8 Erasmus' former convent of Steyn was located almost midway between his
   native Rotterdam and Amsterdam. He may also have visited that city, noted
   for its canals, in the spring of 1501, when he travelled to Dordrecht, which
   lies west of Amsterdam (Ep 153 introduction).
9 Virgil *Aeneid* 1.203
10 Erasmus humorously translates the vernacular saying, 'Een Hollander te
   peerdt' ('a Hollander on horseback') into Greek to tease his young assistant

no need of spurs. Just slacken the reins and they will not stop their gallop until they have brought you to your destination like any other burden. You will get on well with the inhabitants. if you imitate the polyp.[11] Bare your head, extend your hand, give way, smile at everyone, but without trusting anyone you do not know. Above all make sure that you do not scorn or condemn anything about their country. Those people are extremely patriotic,[12] and not without reason, for it is an outstanding country; though in admiring things pertaining to our native land we are all chauvinists. There are some ill-mannered people who immediately condemn anything that seems unusual to them – just as, for the most part, we do not like music to which we have not become accustomed.

To a large extent I reminded you of these things as you were taking leave; and if I had not done so I still anticipated that you would fulfil your duty in a manner befitting your good sense. All the same, since this very dependable person happened along and I had some free time, I thought I should drive it home again, lest it be forgotten. It does no harm at times to remind the mindful.[13] I pray you will return to us, your mission accomplished, in good cheer and with all speed, and that you will return to your Muses and by your alertness make good this little expense.

Farewell, and, if by chance you come upon a reliable courier on the way, give me a brief report of anything that will be important for me to know.

Given at Basel, in the year 1527, on the eve of the Ascension of our Lord

1833 / To Henricus Caduceator   Basel, 10 June 1527

This letter, which answers Ep 1811, was first published in the *Opus epistolarum*. This is the only epistolary exchange between Erasmus and Caduceator, for whom see Ep 1811 introduction.

* * * * *

about his riding abilities. Hollanders, being more accustomed to seafaring, were not thought to be good horsemen, but their ancestors the Batavians (Erasmus uses this adjective) were known as excellent horsemen. See Ari Wesseling 'Dutch Proverbs and Expressions in Erasmus' Adages, Colloquies and Letters' *Renaissance Quarterly* 55 (2002) 130–6.
11 That is, one must attempt to adapt oneself to every contingency of life; *Adagia* I i 93
12 Erasmus uses the Greek, φιλόπατρις.
13 *Adagia* I ii 12

ERASMUS OF ROTTERDAM TO HENRICUS CADUCEATOR OF
ASCHAFFENBURG, GREETING

If I were a doctor I would be so for myself first of all, since the cruel malady
of the stone gives me no respite. Since we read that many very learned men
were completely blind, I am quite surprised that you support with so little 5
self-control a slighter disadvantage, your inability to discern objects save
close at hand.[1] If it is a real defect, I have found it in a great many men of
superior intellect, although they were afflicted with it in varying degrees.
Alexander, son of King James of Scotland, whom I think you know from the
Adages,[2] suffered so severely from this malady that, unless he brought the 10
book up to his nose, he could not see a thing. Therefore if it is a congenital
defect, do not counter it with drugs but make use of those glass seeing-
devices adapted for this purpose, by means of which those who are nearly
blind can see things even at a distance.[3] They are not all suited to all eyes.
You must choose suitable ones from many types. But if the defect came 15
about by mere chance, it can be alleviated by various remedies with which
surgeons are familiar. But the most important thing is to avoid anything that
may harm the eyes, such as studying after supper by lamplight. It would be
useful to become accustomed, when possible, to study with the ears rather
than with the eyes.[4] That is all I can answer to your letter at the present 20
moment. Farewell.

Basel, the day after Pentecost in the year 1527

* * * * *

1833
1 Apart from the obvious example of the poet Homer, Erasmus may have in
  mind, among others, Didymus the Blind, whose treatise on the Holy Spirit
  St Jerome had translated and Erasmus himself had edited (CWE Ep 1855 n29).
  He refrains from citing Jerome's letter about 'heathen philosophers [who] tore
  out their eyes to direct all their thinking towards a purity of mind' (Ep 76 to
  Abigaus, a blind presbyter in Spain, in NPNF 2nd series 6 157; cf PL 22 [1854]
  689 / CSEL 55 35:23).
2 Adagia II v 1, where, in many early editions he is mistakenly named William;
  Erasmus was his tutor in Italy (Epp 216 introduction and 604 n4) and had
  recently mentioned him (Ep 1824:33) to Leonard Cox.
3 The thirteenth-century Franciscan friar Roger Bacon (d 1294) was aware of the
  properties of lenses to provide better vision; see his treatise 'Optical science'
  in The Opus majus of Roger Bacon trans Robert Belle Burke, 2 vols (Philadelphia 1928) II 574, 582. In 1306 Giordano of Pisa claimed that, twenty years
  earlier, he had met the man who first made eyeglasses. Tommaso da Mod-
  ena painted a portrait of Hugh of Provence wearing spectacles in 1352, and
  Petrarch acquired his first pair c 1360.
4 Erasmus sometimes had others read to him and recommended the practice to
  several of his correspondents; see Ep 1805 n62.

1834 / To Fridericus Nausea   Basel, 10 June 1527

After taking a doctorate in law at Pavia, Nausea served Cardinal Lorenzo Campeggi, papal legate in Germany and Hungary. Named as cathedral preacher at Frankfurt in 1525, he was prevented from exercising this office when the city opted for the Reformation, and therefore accepted a similar position in Mainz. He remained strongly Catholic; but, profiting from Erasmus' works, he adopted an irenic approach in relations with Protestants. He had visited Erasmus in 1526, receiving from him the ring mentioned here (line 3).

This letter first appeared in the *Epistolae miscellaneae ad Nauseam* (Basel: Johannes Oporinus 1550). Like the letter which prompted this one, none of the letters from Nausea to Erasmus have survived.

ERASMUS OF ROTTERDAM TO THE MOST HONOURABLE PREACHER
FRIDERICUS NAUSEA, GREETING

I had long forgotten about the ring I gave you, but Fridericus had not slipped from my mind. Truly you are worthy of very great presents, since you give exaggerated importance to such small ones; you judge rightly in measuring   5
the worth of the little gift by the sentiments of both parties. It is my wish that you acquit yourself with great success in the holiest of charges,[1] never diverting your eyes from Christ, so that the entire victory will fall to him. It is not of great importance that Luther be crushed if the victory is usurped by certain pharisees who serve their gullet and their belly, not Jesus Christ.[2]   10

From Rome dire rumours are reported;[3] whether they be true or false, I see no hope of peace among rulers. But Christ will turn everything to a good end, and let us hope it will be soon! I have written this so that you would not say I did not write in return. There was no time for more. Farewell, dearest Nausea.   15
Basel, on the day after Pentecost in the year 1527

1835 / To Germain de Brie   Basel, 10 June 1527

This letter to the Parisian humanist Germain de Brie answers Ep 1817. It was first published by Erasmus in the *Opus epistolarum*.

* * * * *

1834
1 That is, preaching
2 That is, traditionalist Catholic theologians, especially members of the mendicant orders, who were among the most vociferous of Erasmus' critics. Cf Ep 1805 n53.
3 The sack of Rome began on 6 May; cf Ep 1831 n7.

ERASMUS OF ROTTERDAM TO GERMAIN DE BRIE, GREETING

It gives me immense pleasure to know that my services have proved to be
of such great use to you.[1] This was my fervent wish, although not without
some apprehension. I am delighted that it turned out well. I have finished
my commentary on the Epistle to the Galatians.[2] I shall add a fragment of   5
Origen,[3] but shall not be able to do any more for the coming book fair[4] because no small amount of time is dedicated to finishing the *Hyperaspistes*.[5] I
gave my word, and my friends demand it of me with great insistence, since
they cannot put up with the insolent insults of my adversaries. Some attention must also be given to Ambrose, which now will be published with   10
a complete and corrected text.[6] Babylas will be visiting you, but he speaks
Greek. He wishes to learn Latin from you. Oecolampadius knows Greek
well enough, but he is less experienced in the Roman tongue; his errors are
due more to lack of care than to want of knowledge.[7] The work that Lupset
described to you was actually done by some other presumptuous individ-   15
uals – at least with regard to that incomplete work bearing the title *Commentary on Matthew*. I am quite certain that it is not by him.[8] I shall debunk

* * * * *

1835
1 In Ep 1817:17–18, Brie expressed his gratitude for Erasmus' recommendation
 to the king of Portugal (Ep 1800) and for including his translation of John
 Chrysostom in Erasmus' recent edition.
2 That is, his translation of Chrysostom's commentary on that Epistle; see Ep 1841.
3 That is, a fragment of a commentary of Origen on the Gospel of Matthew; see
 Epp 1827 n2, 1844.
4 The Frankfurt book fair, which attracted printers and booksellers from many
 parts of Europe
5 That is, *Hyperaspistes* 2 (Basel: Froben 1527), Erasmus' more considered reply
 to Luther's *De servo arbitrio*, following upon the first, hasty retort in book 1. It
 was ready for the autumn book fair in Frankfurt; see Ep 1804 n10.
6 Froben published Erasmus' four-volume edition of Ambrose in August 1527;
 see Ep 1855.
7 Froben published Erasmus' Greek edition of John Chrysostom's *De Babyla
 martyre* in August 1527; see Ep 1856. Brie planned to translate it, and these
 comments reply to Brie's criticisms of Oecolampadius' translation; see Ep
 1817:46–8 and n10.
8 Cf Ep 1817:50–4. Erasmus rejects the opinion of the English humanist Thomas
 Lupset that Oecolampadius was responsible for a defective Latin translation of
 Origen's commentary on Matthew – the very treatise on which Erasmus himself was currently working. Instead he attributes it here to members of Oecolampadius' circle, since it was then in the hands of the Basel printer Andreas
 Cratander; but the latter never brought it out, probably because of Erasmus'
 own pending edition. A short time later, however, Erasmus would recognize

this wretched undertaking but without attribution, lest they treat with like fidelity the many other authors they are publishing. The same people have published Prudentius,[9] and now they are turning their hand to Cicero.[10]   20

You shall have me as an admirer, not a rival. Even if scholarship were not lacking to me, I lack the time to equal your achievements in the translation of Greek; and there are none to examine my work, to alert me when I go astray. I am surprised to find no mention of Lascaris in your last letter. If he is in good health, I will promptly lay aside my anxieties.[11] That is all I   25 could write for the present; on another occasion we shall converse at greater length. Farewell.

Given at Basel, on the day after Pentecost in the year 1527

1836 / From Juan Luis Vives   Bruges, 13 June 1527

The autograph of this letter, written by a secretary but bearing traces of Vives' own hand, is in the Rehdiger collection (MS 254 161) of the University Library in Wrocław. Erasmus Schets forwarded it to Erasmus (see Ep 1847:67), who would answer it with Ep 1889. It first appeared in LB III-2 1719–20 / *Appendix epistolarum* 340.

For Vives see Ep 1830 introduction.

VIVES TO DESIDERIUS ERASMUS, HIS TEACHER, GREETING

You write to me very seldom;[1] but when I consider the magnitude and variety of cares that press upon your advancing years and precarious health, not only do I pardon you from the bottom of my heart but indeed I commend

* * * * *

the antiquity of the defective version, which contains interpolations and omissions but no particular dogmatic position, and would attribute it to Rufinus of Aquileia (c 345–410), whose free translations Erasmus, like St Jerome, generally held suspect; see Ep 1844:73 and n13.
9 Cratander's edition of Prudentius appeared in March 1527, with notes by Johann Sichard, a distinguished legal scholar and editor of at least twenty volumes of Latin literature and jurisprudence.
10 With the assistance of Michael Bentinus (CEBR I 124–5), Cratander produced a three-volume edition of Cicero in 1528.
11 Concerns probably expressed in Erasmus' letter (not extant) to Brie of c 24 March 1527. Lascaris is mentioned in Epp 1733:98–9 (from Brie), 1794:7–10 (to Brie), and 1842:5–6 (from Toussain).

1836
1 Vives had not yet received Erasmus' Ep 1830, written six weeks earlier on 29 May.

you for writing less often to those very persons you know to be your most   5
devoted friends. The omission of such conventional rules about letter writing will not prevent them from acknowledging your fondness for them,
which they infer from their own warm feelings towards you. For that reason I feel a true sense of gratitude that you include me among your special friends. In all sincerity, I interpret your silence in no other way. There-   10
fore you may answer my letter whenever it may suit you, whenever you
wish.² I ask only this of you, that in the letters you write to Goclenius or to
Pieter Gillis you enjoin them both to keep me informed with a few words
about your health and state of affairs and whatever else they deem fitting
to confide to me from what you write to them.³   15

From Spain a Benedictine by the name of Virués has written to me,⁴
a person I had never heard of before now; but, as I have discovered from
hearsay and from speaking with others, he is a learned and pious man and is
as strongly attached to you as anyone could be. He sent me the proceedings
of one day's session convened by the inquisitor of the faith.⁵ I have enclosed   20
for you his letter and these same proceedings, which I have had my secretaries put into Latin. I have also added a letter that Maldonado⁶ wrote in
Latin to a certain Osorio⁷ concerning an encounter of Virués with Vitoria.⁸

* * * * *

2 Erasmus will answer it in October (Ep 1889).
3 Erasmus will write to Conradus Goclenius, his closest friend in Louvain, on
  15 October 1527 (Ep 1890). No letters from Erasmus to Gillis (on whom see
  Epp 1804 n76, 1828 n10) are extant for this year.
4 Alonso Ruiz de Virués; see Ep 1838 introduction. His letter to Vives was probably of about the same date as Ep 1791, with which Pedro Juan Olivar sent documentation to Erasmus similar to what Vives describes here. Although Virués'
  letter to Vives is not extant, we do have a letter from Virués to Juan de Vergara
  and another from Vergara to Vives; see CWE 12 529–34.
5 The assembly of theologians at Valladolid, convened by Alonso Manrique de
  Lara, archbishop of Seville and inquisitor-general, to examine points of criticism levelled against Erasmus, did not formally convene until 27 June 1527.
  Thus the charges mentioned here are probably those preliminary ones that Juan
  de Vergara says were aired on 28 March (Ep 1814 introduction and lines 246–
  75) and which the inquisitor instructed their authors to refine and resubmit
  for formal examination later.
6 On Juan Maldonado, theologian and priest who worked for the diocese of
  Burgos, see Ep 1805 introduction; his letter is not extant.
7 Don Diego Osorio of Burgos, *corregidor* of Córdoba, a patron of Maldonado
  (CEBR III 36)
8 The identity of the person named here remains problematic. Vives believes
  him to be the blood brother of the illustrious theologian Francisco de Vitoria
  (Ep 1909) and, like him, a Dominican friar. Allen (21n), relying on what Erasmus says in Epp 1902:93 and 1909:46, calls him Pedro and accepts him as the

You will learn all you need to know from the letters themselves. This Vitoria has a blood brother, but entirely unlike him, Francisco de Vitoria,[9] like-   25
wise a Dominican, a Paris theologian, a man of great renown and authority among his people, who has defended your cause on more than one occasion before a crowded assembly of theologians in Paris.[10] He is very well trained

* * * * *

Dominican brother of Francisco de Vitoria – yet he hesitates in this because the extant original documents show that the 'el Maestro Vitoria' (without the name Pedro) of the Colegio de Cardinal had a more positive appreciation for Erasmus' work than did the person Vives describes here; see 'Actas originales de las congregaciones celebradas en Valladolid en 1527 para examinar las doc- trinas de Erasmo' ed Antonio Paz y Miliá and Manuel Serrano y Sanz *Revista de archivos, bibliotecas y museos* 6 (1902) 72, where the name Pedro was given to this master. In publishing the complete text of the intervention of 'Maestro Vi- toria' at Valladolid, Beltrán de Heredia *Cartulario* VI 118–20 (without documen- tary evidence) likewise assigns him the name Pedro but does not call him a Dominican. L.G.A. Getino *El maestro Fr. Francisco de Vitoria: Su vida, su doctrina e influencia* (Madrid 1930) 93 argues that the Dominican brother of Francisco was named Diego, not Pedro. Marcel Bataillon *Erasme* (1991) I 262 n5 suggests that the 'Doctor Vitoria' and 'Maestro Vitoria' in the inquisition documents was indeed named Pedro de Vitoria (d 1540) but that he was a secular priest and theologian, not the Dominican brother of Francisco, because a friar could neither have taught at the Colegio de Cardinal nor later become rector of the university, as this person did. Further complexity arises from Ep 1908, where, because Erasmus believed Vives' account, Allen states the unnamed Domini- can of great learning who had spoken against Erasmus at Valladolid was Pe- dro de Vitoria, brother of Francisco, whereas Bataillon rightly concluded that this critic of Erasmus was Francisco de Vitoria himself.

9 The background and education of this eminent Dominican theologian are thor- oughly studied in Ricardo García Villoslada SJ *La Universidad de París durante los estudios de Francisco de Vitoria OP (1507–1522)* (Rome 1938). During his twenty- year tenure at Salamanca, where he replaced Peter Lombard's *Sentences*, the traditional text for theological studies, with Thomas Aquinas' *Summa theologiae*, Vitoria would influence the Spanish theological scene for a century or more. His innovative criticism of the theory and practice of war and colonization had practical results in the 'New Laws for the Indies' (1542) which sought to moderate exploitation of the native peoples in America. According to Batail- lon *Erasme* (1991) II 95, Francisco de Vitoria was caught between the 'humanis- tic' influence of Tommaso de Vio (Cajetanus) and a more traditionalist view of Erasmus not as a heretic but as a 'dangerous author' and 'helper of heretics.' See the sketch on Vitoria in Farge BR 424–31 no 470; cf CEBR III 405–7.

10 This statement was probably the reason for Erasmus' later letter to Vitoria (Ep 1909), but there is no documentary evidence – and little likelihood – that it is true. After taking his doctorate on 27 June 1522, Vitoria remained in Paris as regent in the Dominican convent during the year 1522–3, then quit Paris definitively to teach in Valladolid for the academic year 1523–4. If he were

in the type of nonsense[11] they engage in, but he is also well grounded in
the humanities, which he has pursued with great success since childhood. 30
He admires and reveres you; but, while being a man of acute intelligence,
he is also of a tranquil and even somewhat indulgent nature. Otherwise he
would have prevented his brother from carrying on in such an unseemly
manner; and many points concerning these questions could have been settled in Spain by him through the authority and reputation for great learning 35
that he enjoys among his colleagues and with the majority of the populace.[12]

I have no doubt that this same Francisco de Vitoria was present at the
session of which Virués writes, which was to take place on the day after
the feast of the Ascension,[13] for he is a professor at Salamanca in what they
call the *prima* chair,[14] a very lucrative post. I have even fewer doubts that 40
Luis Coronel[15] and Lerma,[16] abbot of Alcalá, were appointed to this com-

* * * * *

still in Paris on 16 June 1523, he would have been eligible, as a regent doctor of theology, to speak in the faculty's deliberations, which began on that
date, about the orthodoxy of Louis de Berquin and Lefèvre d'Etaples, in which
certain works of Erasmus were likewise considered. But Vitoria's name never
appears in the faculty proceedings, whereas his Flemish Dominican confrère
Pieter Fabri of Nijmegen spoke openly in a faculty meeting that year about
linguistic problems in the Latin Vulgate, and he supported new versions and
translations of the Bible like those of Erasmus (Clerval *Procès-verbaux* 379–80).
Had Vitoria likewise defended Erasmus 'on more than one occasion,' as Vives
says here, some record of those interventions would have survived.

11 Rendered in Greek

12 Vives' opinion notwithstanding, Francisco de Vitoria's testimony at Valladolid
(dated 6 July 1527, a month after this letter was written) convicts Erasmus on
most of the nineteen propositions under consideration there: some he terms
heretical, others scandalous, temerarious, or offensive; most are to be either
retracted or amended (Beltrán de Heredia *Cartulario* vi 115–17). Like many of
the Spanish theologians, Vitoria was likewise concerned about the negative
satirical impact of the *Colloquies* and thought they should be suppressed.

13 According to Juan de Vergara (Ep 1814) the assembly took place on Ascension
day itself, 30 May. But Vives, writing the words here in the margin in his
own hand and repeating the same precision in Ep 1847:46, probably follows
Virués' report of the date.

14 The *prima* chair was indeed prestigious, but it derived its name merely from
the fact that the one who held it gave the first lecture of the day during the
ordinary term. Vitoria occupied it from 1526 until his death in 1546.

15 On Luis Núñez Coronel see Ep 1814 n64. His judgment about propositions
drawn from Erasmus' works and presented to the commission was much more
positive than that of Francisco de Vitoria.

16 Pedro de Lerma, promoted as doctor of theology of the University of Paris
in 1504, was named the first chancellor of the University of Alcalá in 1508.
Although his judgment on Erasmus was quite positive, he nevertheless shared

mission and perhaps Vergara[17] as well. These men give me excellent hope
that your cause, that is, the cause of letters and piety, will emerge victorious,
for they are men of great integrity, particularly favourable to the cause of
good learning and for that reason staunch friends of yours. They will exer-   45
cise great influence in whatever direction they turn their sympathies. What
power will the others have compared to them? Even if all the others were
placed on one side of the scales, they will outweigh them. All that is needed
is that they agree to defend your cause, as I am certain they will.

I think that all this tumult has arisen from the translation of your *En-*   50
chiridion, for if it achieves wide circulation, as I hear it has,[18] it will detract
considerably from the inveterate tyranny[19] of the friars. And perhaps that
has already begun to happen, since evidently the minds of many have been
inspired by that reading to the knowledge of noble and beautiful things that
have long been hidden from them. Moreover, a great many were beginning   55
to tire of the ignoble slavery to which some men have subjected the poor
common people – a slavery which, though hard to bear in all parts of Christendom, in our nation is such that it would not be tolerated even by slaves
or beasts of burden. The friars, convinced that to be thrown down from the
pinnacle of authority, wealth, power, and countless fortunes by the read-   60
ing of one little book was something not to be endured, launched an attack
upon its author. But the sickness has become grave through avarice and ambition, and has been strengthened by the passage of time. And since the
medicine is strong, as it must be, the illness now reveals its virulence; and,
as doctors say, the disease and nature are fighting it out. Never have I had   65
greater hope that Spain might come to know and understand you. From similar disturbances and controversies glorious things have always struggled
free to greater magnificence and splendour. Such was the case with literature in France and Germany. And I hope that Christ one day at last will be
aroused to take pity on his miserable flock, so that it will not always wan-   70
der blindly and ignorant of the way, exposed to a thousand perils by those
to whom it has entrusted itself for guidance. Christ[20] provided an excellent

* * * * *

the opinion of many others that certain passages in the *Colloquies* should be
excised (Beltrán de Heredia *Cartulario* VI 76–9). In 1536 he was censured as an
Erasmian and, after an absence of thirty years, returned to Paris, where he
assumed, by statutory seniority, the position of dean of the faculty of theology.
See Farge BR 268–9 no 295; CEBR II 325.
17 Contrary to Vives' hopes here, Juan de Vergara (Ep 1814 introduction); was
not appointed to the commission.
18 See Ep 1814 n21.
19 This expression is rendered in Greek.
20 This sentence and the next are rendered entirely in Greek.

opportunity to accomplish this in our own day through the victories of the
emperor and the imprisonment of the pope.[21] My advice is that you write to
the archbishop of Seville, the grand inquisitor, about your own affairs and   75
to the emperor concerning the general affairs of the state.[22] But of these and
similar matters you will be the better judge.

I beg you that, if my *City of God* is to be issued again, as I have learned
from Franz, on whom I can safely rely,[23] you inform me of it so that I can
change a few passages in my commentary; I shall also add other things,   80
though these are few.[24] I returned from Britain at the end of May and, Christ
willing, intend to return there before the first of October.[25]

Farewell, my beloved teacher.

Bruges, 13 June 1527

                                                                    JLV   85

1837 / From Maarten Lips   Louvain, 17 June 1527

This letter (Ep 69 in Förstemann-Günther) was in the Burscher Collection in
the University Library at Leipzig (on which see Ep 1254 introduction). Autograph throughout, it lacked only the address-sheet. Erasmus' reply is perhaps
the letter mentioned in Ep 1899:105.

Like Erasmus, Maarten Lips was an Augustinian canon regular. Their
friendship dated from 1516, and Lips copied (probably in his own hand) two

* * * * *

21 That is, during the sack of Rome, which began on 6 May 1527. Vives' countryman Alfonso de Valdés first saw it as a 'calamity,' and only later wrote about
   it as a victory for the empire (Ep 1839 n15). Vives regarded the defeat of the
   pope as a victory for Spain and the empire and, as a member of the church,
   may likewise have been pleased to see the political and military ambitions of
   the papacy thwarted.
22 Erasmus complied with this advice with Ep 1864 to Manrique de Lara (cf n5
   above) and Ep 1873 to Emperor Charles v.
23 Franz Birckmann, bookseller and agent, about whom Erasmus had opinions
   completely different from those expressed here by Vives
24 Vives' first edition of Augustine's *De civitate Dei* (Basel: Johann Froben,
   September 1522) was the first printed edition to include critical notes about the
   manuscript tradition. In fact, however, the new printing of the *City of God* appeared almost as an afterthought in the ten-volume 1528–9 Froben *Opera omnia* of Augustine. It carried only the plain text without Vives' scholarly introduction and notes, which had distinguished the 1522 edition. But the complete
   edition with all the notes was to reappear shortly thereafter (Paris: Claude
   Chevallon 1531) and would be reprinted several times in later decades.
25 On 18 March Vives had announced his intention of returning to England in
   the near future (Ep 1792:32).

collections of letters by Erasmus and his friends (see Ep 750 introduction). At
the time of this letter Lips was installed as chaplain to a nunnery at Lens-Saint-
Rémy in the French-speaking province of Liège, where he had been moved
because of his unpopular defence of Erasmus in the Louvain convent. As librarian there, he had pored over the manuscripts of Augustine preserved in
Flemish convents, and had discovered twenty-two unknown letters and some
sermons of Augustine that he sent to Erasmus. He continued this work at Lens,
and was Erasmus' principal collaborator on the Augustine edition being prepared for publication at this time, although he received little recognition for
it. See further CEBR II 333–4.

Greetings. I cannot tell you how cheered I was by your letter,[1] in which
you indicated that what I sent to Goclenius around the feast of St Martin in the year 1526 is in safe keeping. I thought it had been lost, since
you did not write that you had received it.[2] My anxiety was all the greater
because I devoted more effort than usual to those pages because of my   5
change of abode.[3] So, then, in order to make sure that you will not receive this page, which contains my corrections to Augustine's book against
Fortunatus,[4] without my message, I decided to enclose it with this letter. I
accept willingly what you write concerning the publishing of the Augustine,
and the terms you prescribe are agreeable to me.[5] As long as the Augustine is   10
published, I am little concerned with the rest. But I would really like to know

* * * * *

1837
1 Not extant
2 Conradus Goclenius, Erasmus' closest friend in Louvain, through whom Lips
  kept in touch with Erasmus, was regent at the Collegium Trilingue at this time;
  cf Ep 1857 introduction. Lips had taken a long time to submit for Goclenius'
  perusal a large quantity of his notes on Augustine. Sent around 11 November
  1526, they did not arrive in time for Goclenius to forward them with his letter
  to Erasmus of 12 November (Ep 1765:1–6). Because they subsequently proved
  too bulky to send with Ep 1768 (lines 86–8), Goclenius sent Lips' letter first
  and forwarded the notes at a later time – to Lips' obvious relief here.
3 Lips had recently taken up his new position as chaplain at the Augustinian
  nunnery at Lens-Saint-Rémy.
4 Obviously an additional page to be added to the already bulky research
  that Lips had done on behalf of the Augustine edition. Fortunatus was a
  Manichaean priest at Hippo with whom Augustine had formal doctrinal debates, the transcripts of which he published as *Acta seu disputatio contra Fortu-
  natum Manichaeum* (PL 42 111–30 / CSEL 25 part 1 81–112). This work appeared
  in volume 6 of the Froben 1528–9 folio edition.
5 See Epp 1473:7–9 and n5, 1547:19–22, 35–7. Lips had been one of the first to
  encourage Erasmus to oversee a new edition of Augustine.

whether the work is going forward; perhaps I would have something to write to you that is of some relevance. How kind it is of you to encourage me to pre- serve my integrity even in my outspokenness! May Christ Jesus grant this.

My health has not been very good this year; I hope it improves in 15 the future. According to all reports Winghe (whom you call Winantius) is remaining quiet, to a certain degree, in his writing, if not in spirit.[6] The sub- prior Rochus has the same opinion of you and your writings as he always did.[7] He says they are harmful, pernicious, a scandal for the weak, and a seduction of the mind towards Lutheranism. He says that no truly pious 20 man agrees with you. He is strongly suspicious and all but declares that the letter of the grand chancellor to the university as well as the other letter were forged by you.[8] The style is yours, he says, and it is hardly possible that letters can reach here from Spain in so short a time. He gives no importance to the judgment of popes, Mercurino, the emperor, etc,[9] for he says 'They 25 have not read your [writings], and therefore they cannot judge aright.' He says that he finds out every day, as do many others, how many young people are turned away from piety by your books. You are subverting the whole institution of monasticism, he says. 'Yes,' I say, 'bad monasticism.' 'But,' he says, 'he never depicts a true monasticism or a good monk.' As far as he 30 was concerned, he would have wanted Winghe's book to be published;[10] and he said that it would stir up the feelings of all pious men more than all the books that have been written against you because he refuted your teachings, not with his own words and arguments but with the authority

* * * * *

6 Nicolaas van Winghe, an Augustinian canon regular of St Maartensdal in Louvain, wrote a book against Erasmus that was never published. His Flem- ish translation of the whole Bible was reprinted twenty times, and of the New Testament alone another thirty times (CEBR III 453–4).
7 Rochus Hyems is not otherwise known (CEBR II 221–2).
8 Mercurino Gattinara had been imperial grand chancellor since 1518. About half of his letter to the theologians of Louvain, warning them to desist from their attacks on Erasmus (Ep 1784A:26–50), was drawn from Erasmus' own letter to him (Ep 1747:127–51), resulting in accusations such as this. The 'other letter' might be Ep 1757, in which Gattinara assured Erasmus of his devotion and support. Although it was not published until 1536, Erasmus would have probably seen to its circulation by means of manuscript copies.
9 Popes Adrian VI and Clement VII had taken action to silence Erasmus' critics in Louvain; cf Ep 1805 n25 above. Charles V also supported him; see especially Ep 1731, an appreciative letter to Erasmus that was probably a response to the publication of *Hyperaspistes 1*).
10 Cf n6 above. This obviously anti-Erasmian polemic had been sent, without the permission of its author or of the prior, to Erasmus (see line 80 below) – a fact that perhaps explains its disappearance.

and utterances of the saints, and because he adopted a different manner 35
from the others. He prays for you when he says mass, but he hopes that
before long the truth, which you indirectly impugn, he says – and always
in such a way as to make good your escape – will be revealed. You pile up
excuses one on the other, and no one can pin you down; you never give way
in the least, no matter how much you are admonished. What shall I say, my 40
dear Erasmus? These and many other things he says with such confidence
and affirms with such vehemence that it seems a holy angel has given him
absolute certitude of everything. I write this to give you something to laugh
about.

Concerning the remuneration you conferred on me,[11] Goclenius and I 45
were in agreement, even if our letters did not agree. His letter mentioned
six Philippus florins,[12] mine exactly six gold coins.[13] He thus gave me the six

* * * * *

11 Compensation for Lips' work on the Augustine edition, which Erasmus would
expect to collect from Froben; see n5 above.

12 The Philippus florin (or gold florin of St Philip) was a Burgundian-Hapsburg
gold coin that Archduke Philip the Fair first issued in April 1496, containing 2.205 grams fine gold, with a value of 4s 0d or 48d *groot* Flemish. In
February 1500, he slightly reduced its gold contents to 2.193 grams fine gold,
while raising its official value to 4s 2d or 50d *groot*. Its fineness, weight, and
value were retained until August 1521, when it was replaced by the Carolus florin (that of Charles v, ruler of the Low Countries from 1506 to 1556,
and emperor from 1519), with just 1.700 grams fine gold, and a value of 3s
6d or 42d groot. In relation to the gold content of the Carolus florin, the
Philippus florin, if it continued to circulate with its full, prescribed weight,
would have been worth (2.193/1.700 × 42) 54d *groot* Flemish. Indeed, in
Ep 1848:41–2, Marcus Laurinus does confirm that the Philippus florin was
worth 27 *stuivers*, which was in turn worth 54d *groot*. Thus six of these coins
would have been worth £1 7s 0d *groot*. The *stuiver* was a silver coin also
known as the *patard* or *double gros/groot*, which thus had a value of 2d in
the Flemish pound *groot* money-of-account system. By the later fifteenth century, it had also become the 'shilling' in the equally popular florin or gulden
money-of-account system, originally based on the Rhenish gold florin: thus,
1 florin (*gulden*, or guilder) = 20s (*stuivers*) = 40d *gros/groot* of Flanders =
60d *groot* of Brabant. See CWE 1 316–17, 322–3, 327, 331, 340 (Appendix B),
347 (Appendix E); CWE 8 347–50; and CWE 12 577–91, 649 (Table 3C), 655
(Table 4C).

13 *sex aureos*. Erasmus had evidently agreed that this amount was identical to six
Philippus florins (on which see the previous note); but in Ep 1848:42 Marcus Laurinus says that the coins were Rhenish gold florins, which, according
to him, were in 1527 each worth 31 *stuivers*. This would be the equivalent of
62d *groot*; see CWE 12 650 (Table 3D), in which the value of the gold florin
(for 1521) has been estimated, by relative gold contents (with the ducat and
the Carolus florin) as having a value of 59d *groot* Flemish. Erasmus Schets,

Philippus florins, which I accepted[14] because I am lacking a few essential items as a result of my move, and also because I intended to buy the fourth edition.[15] My brother gives me little now, and that unwillingly because of the lawsuit between him and the people of St Maartensdal; my father died intestate, you see.[16]

I sent the letter addressed to Willem to him, together with my own.[17] I know he will be happy to receive it and will admire your kindness. I saw also the letter to Heemstede.[18] If you wish anything, give the command. What good are words? I belong to Erasmus; you know the mind of your Maarten, and I shall not allow myself to be corrupted (I trust in the grace of Christ) by loudmouths and troublemakers or by those virgins with whom I live. Once I attended a lecture of the Minorite Frans Titelmans, a great enemy of yours, as everybody knows.[19] He was interpreting the passage in the Apostle 'We do not boast beyond limit.' 'In Greek,' he said, 'the word is *ametra*, which means without limit or with-

50

55

60

* * * * *

however, in a letter dated 22 July 1527, indicates that the Rhenish florin was then worth just 28 *stuivers* or 56d *groot* Flemish (Ep 1849:18–19); cf Allen 30n. We may also note that gold values on the Antwerp market were rising, with some fluctuations, during the 1520s. See n12 above and CWE 12 577–83.

14 It is hard to know whether Lips, because of his straitened circumstances, settled for something less than agreed or accepted more than he had bargained for. In 1536 (Allen Ep 3119:21) Erasmus instructed his banker Erasmus Schets to pay Lips forty gulden (or florins-of-account; see n12 above).

15 That is, the fourth edition of Erasmus' *Novum Testamentum*, which appeared in March 1527 (see Ep 1818:10–12).

16 Joost Lips, a prominent citizen of Brussels, died some time prior to 9 May 1527. He and his sons were of the same family as the famous jurist Justus Lipsius (1547–1606) who bore his name. His intestate death perhaps failed to provide a bequest that had been promised to St Maartensdal, the convent in Louvain where Maarten Lips was professed and from which he had recently been moved. Maarten's brother Nicolaas was about twenty years older.

17 Willem Gheershoven, or Willem of Louvain, an Augustinian canon regular, was librarian in the convent of Groenendal at Hoeilaart (near Brussels). Through their common connection with Lips, Erasmus had been able to study two manuscripts of Augustine that Gheershoven had charge of there. Seven letters from Lips to Willem Gheershoven are extant, all dating from 1525–6 and dealing with the two manuscripts of St Augustine in the Groenendal library; cf CEBR II 92–3. The letter of Erasmus to Gheershoven mentioned here is not extant.

18 Not extant. For Jan of Heemstede, a Carthusian at Louvain, see CEBR II 171.

19 See Epp 1823 introduction and 1837A.

out measure. Similarly *immensum* in Latin means without limit or without measure.'[20]

I wrote an index of the four Gospels and the Acts of the Apostles.[21] Conradus urged me on somewhat in this,[22] but I don't know if he will be pleased. I laboured over it in several places because of the fact that I had to put 'of' at the beginning of each entry.[23] Let me give you a sample: 'Of the royal and at the same time priestly genealogy of Christ'; 'Of Joseph, husband of the Virgin Mary, who considered an honourable separation from his espoused wife'; 'Of the angel who freed that same person from his anxiety of mind, and foretold the name of the son to be born of Mary,' etc. Perhaps you will say 'Why are you so prolix?' It would have been sufficient to say: 'Of the genealogy of Christ'; 'Of Joseph, the spouse of Mary'; 'Of the angel who appeared to him in his sleep,' etc. And that would have been much easier for me. But I strove, as best I could, to sum up the passage in the Gospel to which I referred in the index in such a way that the index itself would have a little substance. To proceed into the Epistles seems to me to be an almost unbearable labour. If you wish, I will send it to you.

The subprior says that the one who passed Winghe's book on to you should be condemned for theft, as Augustine has it in the Rule.[24]

* * * * *

20 2 Cor 10:13, 15. As reported by Lips, Titelmans translated the Latin *in immensum* (Greek ἄμετρα) to mean 'infinitely'; but the meaning here is 'beyond [Paul's] limits,' that is, going beyond what God had appointed him to do.
21 Presumably based on Erasmus' fourth edition of the *New Testament*, perhaps with a view to incorporating it in future editions
22 Goclenius; see n2 above.
23 Lips is faced with the dilemma between a grammatically correct arrangement – beginning each entry with 'of' (Latin *de*) – and a more useful index that would omit the preposition in order to list alphabetically the subject of each entry.
24 Lips, unlike Erasmus, does not appear to question St Augustine's authorship of the Rule bearing his name. Nine different forms of the Augustinian Rule are known, only one of which is attributable to St Augustine himself. Lips' convent doubtless followed a medieval elaboration of it which contains the warning *Si aliquis rem sibi collatam celaverit, furti iudicio condemnetur* (no 8 PL 32 1382). This late version of the Rule differed greatly from Augustine's own fourth-century Rule. See the critical edition in Luc Verheijen *La Règle de saint Augustin I: Tradition manuscrite* (Paris 1967) 417–37 and *Nouvelle approche de la Règle de saint Augustin* in *Vie monastique* 8 (Bégrolles-en-Mauges 1980). The only reference to books in Augustine's own Rule is 'Books will be available every day at the appointed hour, and not at any other time'; see *The Rule of Saint Augustine: Masculine and Feminine Versions* intro and comm Tarsicius J. Van Bavel osa, trans Raymond Canning osa (London 1984; repr Kalamazoo, Mich 1996) 21, 35. On Winghe's book see n10 above.

In the monastery of Gembloux there is a manuscript of Jerome on
the Apocalypse. Those who have seen it say that its style is very close to
Jerome's.[25]

Farewell, my dear Erasmus. Give greetings to Froben and all his fam-   8
ily. Written in haste in Goclenius' room, on the seventeenth day of June in
the year 1527

Yours most sincerely,
Maarten Lips of Brussels

1837A / From Frans Titelmans   [Louvain, 1527]

This undated letter answers Ep 1823, in which Erasmus accused Titelmans of
'conspiracies' and 'malicious attacks' – accusations that Titelmans here denies,
while defending the authority of the Vulgate Bible and his right to criticize
Erasmus' departure from it. It exists only in a contemporary copy, made by a
certain Thibault of Leiden, a Franciscan friar who describes himself as a close
friend of Titelmans, and is conserved in the Premonstratensian abbey of Aver-
bode in Vlaams-Brabant (Archives IV, MS 22 f 190). Because Allen learned of
its existence too late to include it in his volume VII, he published it in volume
VIII, where it is the third of four newly discovered letters that follow page
xliv. He numbered it to accompany Ep 1837, where Titelmans is mentioned
(line 60).

For Titelmans and his dispute with Erasmus see Ep 1823 introduction and
the references there. On his defence of the Latin Bible and his attitude towards philological criticism see Jerry H. Bentley *Humanists and Holy Writ: New
Testament Scholarship in the Renaissance* (Princeton 1983) 199–212.

TO MASTER ERASMUS OF ROTTERDAM, RESPECTED PRIEST AND
THEOLOGIAN, IN CHRIST
It often happens that vague and uncertain rumours provide the seedbed for
many grave conflicts, which are dissipated by truth once they are brought

* * * * *

25 The manuscript has not been identified. Lips' comment on the style would
   preclude its being merely Jerome's translation of that book (see PL 29 [1865]
   894–914); but no commentary or homily on it by Jerome is known. Erasmus
   had used the monastic library at the Benedictine monastery of Saints Peter
   and Exupéry at Gembloux in Flanders, which was particularly rich in patristic
   manuscripts, but could not recall its name when writing the preface to the Augustine edition in 1529 (Allen Ep 1547:9n). The monastery ceased to function
   c 1800.

Frans Titelmans

Johann Löffler, engraving in Charles d'Aremberg OFM Cap

Flores seraphici, siue Icones . . . virorum . . . illustrium, qui ab anno 1524 ad 1588
in Ordine Fratrum Minorum S. Francisci, Capucinorum nuncupatorum floruerunt
(Cologne: Constantine Munich 1640) page 87. Titelmans is pictured holding a book
'against Jacques Lefèvre d'Etaples and Desiderius Erasmus of Rotterdam.'
Joseph Pope Rare Book Room, Pontifical Institute of Mediaeval Studies, Toronto

forth into the light. It is all too clear from the letter you sent me,[1] dear 5
master, that false rumours have led you to believe that I was stirring up
unpopularity for your name and provoking slander against your reputation
through malicious detraction. Therefore, let me give you a brief and true
account of what has been reported to you.

When I saw that the old translation of the New Testament[2] was the 10
object of universal scorn, to such an extent that even those with only a smat-
tering of learning hardly deemed it worthy of their attention, I was deeply
saddened, as was only right, that age had tarnished its authority and that,
haphazardly and without discretion, new and unexamined ideas that had
the approval neither of custom nor of good judgment were being accepted 15
by almost everyone. With each new edition more scorn was heaped upon
the old translation. Therefore I turned my attention to the careful examination of the editions of the modern interpreters and compared your translations and those of Jacques Lefèvre from the Greek with the original Greek
texts and the old translation.[3] As I reflected upon this within myself I found 20
that throughout the text the authority of the old translation was being undermined, and I perceived clearly that your investigations and annotations
were responsible for this depreciation. I saw that many things were scruti-
nized, annotated, censured, and altered by you with great severity or rather,
I should say, with undue liberty. I began to question the wisdom of this and 25
whether you had acted rightly, and concluded that in most cases you had
merely devised captious criticism and that there was hardly anything in
your allegations against this authority that could not be refuted by anyone
with even a modest knowledge of the Scriptures and of languages.

I decided therefore that after finishing an interpretation of one of Paul's 30
Epistles,[4] returning to the commentary of St Thomas on the old translation as
to the true source,[5] I would refute with suitable arguments, according to the

* * * * *

1837A
1 Ep 1823
2 That is, the Vulgate edition in use in the schools and in liturgical texts at that
  time
3 From its first edition in 1516 Erasmus' New Testament offered his own Latin
  translation from the Greek – an innovation he justified in many places, notably
  in the preface to his edition of St Jerome (Basel 1515). On Lefèvre see n6 below.
4 The *Collationes quinque super epistolam ad Romanos* (Antwerp: Willem Vorsterman, May 1529), which pits its author Titelmans in debate against Erasmus,
  Valla, and Lefèvre d'Etaples.
5 Thomas Aquinas *Expositio et lectura super epistolas Pauli apostoli* had been printed
  frequently in the decade of the 1520s. For its place in the complete works

powers that God has given me, all that you – I mean Lorenzo Valla, the first
to have meddled with the sacred text, Jacques Lefèvre, who succeeded him,
and you, the last to enter the fray – have criticized, impugned, and rashly   35
modified in the old translation, thereby diminishing its authority.[6] I gladly
expose my own name to public disfavour as long as I can provide some service (I dare not say protection) to the holy truth and to venerable antiquity.
This is what gave rise to the rumours, spread by those who had not heard
in what way I was treating this matter, that there were teachings among   40
the Friars Minor directed against Erasmus, Lefèvre, and Valla – indeed that
there were specific accusations made against 'Erasmus and the others.'

So it is that, giving credence to these rumours, you write that I de-
fame your reputation in my lectures. I confess with all modesty, reverence,
and respect that I have mentioned your name whenever I refuted any of   45
your criticisms, but nothing was done for the purpose of arousing hostility
against you. I do not refrain from using the name of Jerome or Ambrose
when I reject what they have changed or censured. I do not therefore mount
conspiracies against your name, nor do we resort to calumny, but simply
give modest responses. Furthermore, I believe that just as Jerome is not of- 50
fended if I refute with all modesty things that he seems to have criticized
in the old translation,[7] so I do not expect that you will take offence if I dare

* * * * *

of Aquinas see G. Emery OP 'Brief Catalogue of the Works of Saint Thomas
Aquinas' in Jean-Pierre Torrell *Saint Thomas Aquinas* I: *The Person and His Works*
trans Robert Royal (Washington, DC 1996) 340.

6 It was Erasmus himself who had discovered and published a manuscript of
  Valla's *Adnotationes in latinam Novi Testamenti interpretationem* (Paris: Josse Bade
  1505). Titelmans is correct in seeing this as a principal source of the humanists' programme to correct the Vulgate Bible. After publication of his *Quin-
  cuplex Psalterium* (Paris: Henri Estienne 1509), Jacques Lefèvre d'Etaples undertook research and commentary on the Pauline Epistles (1512), the Gospels
  (1522), and the Catholic Epistles (1524). In the late 1520s Lefèvre was working
  to finish the French translation of the whole New Testament; but, caught in the
  backlash of conservative French reaction against the reform movement after
  1523, he worked exclusively from the Vulgate edition and gave up all use of
  Erasmus' emendations and annotations on it. See Pierre Aquilon 'Paris et la
  Bible française 1516–1586' in *Censures: de la Bible aux larmes d'Eros* (Paris 1987)
  17–18. Erasmus' *Novum instrumentum* was published in 1516 (cf n3 above).
7 Here Titelmans obviously means the so-called *Vetus Latina*, which predated
  Jerome's translation. Jerome himself was generally held by traditionalists like
  Titelmans to have formulated the Vulgate version referred to in line 10 as the
  'old translation.' Unlike Titelmans, Erasmus and other humanists held that St Jerome's translation had been irretrievably corrupted in the manuscript tradition.

to answer the objections and criticisms that you make against the translation
of the old interpreter (whose authority both with me and the church is not
to be disdained).[8]   55

As far as I am concerned, whatever I do, I do for God's sake and in
the sincerity and simplicity of my heart, seeking only to defend truth and
antiquity, with him who searches our inmost thoughts as my witness. Do not
think that anything you have heard about was done in secret or in private.
I have always taught in a place where all assemble together; and if you   60
yourself were to come there and I should see you in person you would
hear the same things that are heard by those who draw nigh to my humble
person. I have said nothing in secret. You may therefore be assured that no
conspiracies are being formed against you, for the public defence of truth
cannot be called conspiracy or detraction.   65

You believe it to be your duty not to pass over in silence any lapses
of the ancient translators; all through the text you scrutinize, examine, and
sometimes pass harsh judgment on the opinions of the ancient interpreters.
You do not spare the names of Jerome, Ambrose, Augustine, Hilary, or others if they have said or written anything that meets with your disapproval   70
– not to mention for the moment those sarcastic witticisms you reserve for
their successors Thomas, Nicholas of Lyra, and Hugh of Saint-Cher,[9] whom
I do not think should be disparaged in any way or made fun of. Therefore,
if you can indiscriminately belittle and ridicule the names of those whom
we believe to reign with Christ in eternal beatitude, I beg that you allow   75
me to refute in modest responses what I see is written without sufficient
knowledge or wrongly criticized in others by modern authors still alive in
the flesh. Surely it is not the mark of a generous spirit to deny to others what

* * * * *

8 That is, St Jerome
9 Although Thomas Aquinas is known more widely for his *Summa theologiae* and
  Summa contra gentiles, he wrote commentaries on Job, the Psalms, the Song of
  Songs, the prophets Isaiah and Jeremiah, on the four Gospels, and on the Epistles of St Paul. Perhaps because of Aquinas' devotion to Sacred Scripture, Erasmus was less critical of him than of other scholastic authors.
  The *Postillae perpetuae super totam Bibliam* of Nicholas of Lyra, the fourteenth-
  century Norman Franciscan exegete known as the 'clear and useful doctor,'
  still exist in hundreds of manuscripts and was reproduced in numerous early
  printed editions, both alone and in editions of the *Glossa ordinaria*.
  Hugh of Saint-Cher was a thirteenth-century Dominican theologian, exegete,
  and cardinal of the church. Under his direction the Dominicans produced
  three landmark aids to study: the *Postillae* (commentaries on all the books
  of the Bible), *Correctoria* (variant readings of the Latin Vulgate), and the first
  alphabetical concordance to the whole Bible.

you have permitted yourself and, after passing severe judgment on everything and everyone, sparing no one, not to be willing that anyone should   80
so much as touch on anything of yours even in a modest way. You owe
more respect to those who are united with Christ in blessed peace than we
owe to you, who still dwell among us in this miserable flesh for as long as
it may please God. What I have done for love of God and of the truth I
shall with God's help continue to do for as long as it shall seem useful to   85
me; not in scurrilous abuse or fanatical harangues but with reasonable arguments and modest responses according to your own wise counsel, most
worthy of all acceptance.[10] Whatever I have said or will say in the presence
of my hearers God will perhaps grant you to see with your own eyes, so
that you may perceive with what intention I have undertaken and pursued   90
this task. I hope before God that the desire of my heart will be manifest,
my dearest Desiderius, and that God will recompense me according to my
works.

    If you have Christ before your eyes, there is nothing you should fear;
no one's tongue or pen will be able to harm you if you look to Christ with   95
all your heart. For the truth has its own light and triumphs felicitously in all
things. May the God of truth strengthen it in you so that you may always
write and do what is worthy of Christ, who is God blessed for all ages.

    Farewell, and give us your love, as we also love you. Grace be with
you.   100
    Friar Frans of Hasselt

1838 / From Alonso Ruiz de Virués   Valladolid, [19 June] 1527

Alonso Ruiz de Virués (1493–1545) was a Benedictine monk professed at the
monastery of San Juan in Burgos and a master of theology of the University
of Salamanca. He was an admirer and staunch defender of Erasmus and had
read publicly from the *Enchiridion*. Nevertheless, in a series of seven manuscript *Collationes ad Erasmum*, he urged Erasmus to tone down certain passages
and tried to suggest ways in which Erasmus could express himself more ireni-
cally in order to avoid criticism. In Ep 1684 to Juan de Vergara, Erasmus expresses irritation at Virués' advice, believing him to be part of the group of
hostile Spanish critics who wanted to censure his works, and in Epp 1781:14–
15 to Erasmus Schets and especially 1804:287–305 to Thomas More Erasmus
describes Virués as a troublemaker and detractor. In Ep 1786 Virués expressed

* * * * *

10 Cf 1 Tim 1:15.

support and even enthusiasm for Erasmus' work, as he had earlier done in
a letter to Juan de Vergara (CWE 12 529–33), but also encouraged Erasmus to
publish an apologia that would mollify his Spanish critics. The present letter
and Epp 1836 from Juan Luis Vives and 1839 from Alfonso de Valdés effected
a reconciliation (Ep 1875). On Virués see Epp 1684 introduction, 1786; CEBR III
400–1; see also Rummel *Catholic Critics* II 86–8.

Autograph throughout, this letter (Ep 68 in Förstemann-Günther, wrongly
dated 20 May 1527), was in the Burscher Collection at the University Library
in Leipzig (on which see Ep 1254 introduction).

†

TO THE MOST DISTINGUISHED MASTER DESIDERIUS ERASMUS OF
ROTTERDAM FROM BROTHER ALONSO VIRUÉS, ETC

Cordial greetings. On 17 May,[1] while I was conversing together with that
excellent gentleman Alfonso de Valdés, a courier brought us a packet of
letters among which there was a letter of yours addressed to me,[2] a young   5
theologian, as you say, from an old man who has now discharged his duties
in the service of theology.[3] Yet a youthful ardour was not lacking in the
letter, of a sort that might be more likely to irritate rather than appease or
instruct the mind of a young man. In it you mention several times that you
received my little book,[4] which is so impudent, you say, that it would rouse   1
the spirits of old Entellus.[5] But at the same time you make no mention of a

* * * * *

1838
1 We translate Allen's *Decimosexto Kalendas Iunii*, which is also in Förstemann-
  Günther; but Allen recognized the discrepancy between this and Ep 1839:1,
  where Alfonso de Valdés clearly specifies that the packet of letters arrived on
  the feast of the Holy Trinity, a movable feast, always on the octave of Pentecost Sunday, which occurred in 1527 on 16 June – *xvi kalendas Iulii* (not *Iunii*).
  Since Allen and Förstemann-Günther both read *Iunii* in the manuscript (now
  destroyed) one must conclude that Virués mistakenly wrote *Iunii* for *Iulii* – an
  error he repeats at line 73.
2 Not extant; it was written c 31 March (cf Ep 1839:8). On Valdés see Ep 1807
  introduction.
3 Erasmus had probably drawn this image from a letter of St Jerome to St Augustine; see Ep 68:4–6 CSEL 34 242 / FCNT 12 319.
4 Virués' *Collationes* remained for the most part in manuscript, but he published
  the section in defence of monasticism in his *Philippicae disputationes viginti adversus Lutherana dogmata* (Antwerp: Joannes Gymnicus 1541) chapter 20.
5 A boxer, past his prime, who accepts the challenge of Dares, a younger man,
  in a contest that was part of the commemorative games in honour of Aeneas'
  father Anchises (Virgil *Aeneid* 5.387–423). This allusion too was drawn from
  Jerome (see n3 above).

letter sent to you for a third time, which could have appeased the fury of Ajax.[6] You can in no wise deny that you received it, because at the end of your letter you respond to what I wrote in it concerning the publication of the little book. I said in response to your letter to Juan de Vergara[7] that I had entrusted the book to one or two friends to be read privately; but you maintain that this is improbable, because when it first arrived in Brabant it was not sealed with my signet, as if I forcibly removed the seal en route so that it would be read by all who wished to do so.

At the beginning of your letter you say that you are unable to conjecture what my attitude is towards you. It may well be that you cannot divine my attitude from what you have sampled sporadically, as you say, from my book. But do you put so little faith in the letters of your friends that even from what you have learned before you wrote this letter you cannot conjecture what my attitude is towards you? And yet either I am in error or you could have I shall not say conjectured but perceived this clearly from my book and from the second letter enclosed with the book.[8] Up to now so many men of profound learning have written against you that at times it seems that what we read in *Genesis* concerning Ishmael can be applied to you: 'His hand against all and the hand of all against him, and he will pitch his tents in the face of all his kinsmen.'[9] Yet none of them wrote you a letter of admonition in secret; on the contrary, as soon as they completed their works, with no regard for your reputation, they made every effort to make public what they thought they had written for the common good. But in my case you could have been persuaded of the sincerity of my friendship even on this account, that whatever I found displeasing in your works (and it was not for this purpose that I read them, as God is my witness) I did not immediately publicize but rather reported to you openly and without pretence. I merely drew your attention to what gave offence to me and to others, while at the same time giving reasons for this resentment; and I did this more to practise my pen than to acquire a name for myself, as you suppose. I ask more than once in my little commentaries to be taught by

* * * * *

6 Ajax, son of Telamon, in reprisal for not having been awarded the armour of Achilles, planned a night attack on the Greek camp; but Athena drove him mad, and he killed himself (Ovid *Metamorphoses* 13.395). The letter is not extant.

7 Ep 1684

8 Ep 1786

9 Gen 16:12. Books by Catholic authors against Erasmus had by this time been composed, among others, by Edward Lee, Diego López Zúñiga, Alberto Pio, Jacques Masson, Noël Béda, and Pierre Cousturier. The best overview of these polemics is Rummel *Catholic Critics*.

you, not to be praised; if that were my goal, I would have had no trouble publishing them.

I wrote a rather long letter some time ago to the guardian (that is   45
the title they use) of the Franciscans at Alcalá, in which I advised him
in a friendly manner (as I often do with others in writing or by word
of mouth) not to fulminate against your name as he had already begun
to do with great gusto.[10] It was deemed worthy of publication by your
friends in order to further your favour and popularity. More than a thou-   50
sand copies were made by hand, and in the end a printed edition light-
ened the labours of the scribes.[11] Do you think your enemies would have
been lacking in like zeal to publish my commentaries if I had wished them
to be divulged? But it was not for that purpose that I wrote them; it was,
rather, that by affording you the opportunity of answering your calumni-   55
ators I might also reap the personal benefit of acquiring some learning. I
recalled that Augustine had once written Jerome with this intention.[12] But
intolerant of my *Collationes* you look upon me as the Roman cohort that
mocked Christ, clothing him in purple, placing a diadem upon his head
and saluting him as king.[13] My intention in writing was similar to that of   60
the church Fathers, whose zeal for learning and piety you have attempted
to revive, to refer humbly to themselves and in pious and lofty terms to
others![14]

* * * * *

10 Written in Spanish, it has been published by Adolfo Bonilla y San Martín
   Luis Vives y la filosofía del renacimiento; obras filosóficas (Madrid 1903 693–8; repr
   Madrid 1929 III 123–8), and again in 'Erasmo en España' *Revue hispanique*
   17 (1907) 437–43. Juan Luis Vives translated it into Latin and sent a copy to
   Erasmus (Ep 1847:142–3). Neither Virués nor his modern editor reveals the
   identity of the Franciscan guardian ('warden' in British usage), or prior, of
   Alcalá.
11 No copies of this 1527 printing are known to be extant; but the letter also
   appeared along with Epp 1873 and 1920 as an appendix to the 1528 volume
   of nine of Erasmus' *Colloquies* (np nd) translated by Virués and Luís Mexía
   (Allen Ep 1838:45n).
12 Augustine wrote Jerome in this vein regarding two particular issues: he feared
   that Jerome's new Latin translation of the Scriptures, based on Hebrew texts
   as well as the Greek Septuagint, would divide Latin Christians from Greek
   ones because their Scriptures would no longer be the same; and he criticized
   Jerome for dismissing Paul's reproof of St Peter's dissimulation (Gal 2:14) as
   a polite but sinless lie (Epp 28, 40, 71; cf n3 above). See also Ep 1841 n12.
13 Matt 27:27–31; Mark 15:16–20. Cf Ep 1804:293–5.
14 For example, Jerome referred to the younger Augustine as 'your Worthiness,'
   'your Prudence,' and even 'your Beatitude,' while Augustine calls Jerome 'your
   Charity' and 'your Holiness.'

But there again is the barbed vehemence of youth and the bite of innuendo of which you complain in your letter. Therefore since I know not   65
how to speak, it will be better to keep silence. I would not even have written this except to let you know that I had received your letter. Concerning
events here at the court of Charles you will be informed in a letter from my
lord Alfonso Valdés,[15] which with good cause will give you more pleasure.
Farewell, and see that that tranquil spirit, which you miss in me, will never   70
be lacking to you – or, rather, may this be brought about by Christ, greatest
and best, who instilled it into the hearts of the apostles. Given at Valladolid,
on 20 May[16] in the year 1527.

Your most devoted, whether you wish it or not, Alonso Virués

†

To the most illustrious Master Desiderius Erasmus of Rotterdam, cel-   75
ebrated interpreter of the Sacred Scriptures, residing in the famous city of
Basel

1839 / From Alfonso de Valdés   Valladolid, 20 June 1527

First published by Förstemann-Günther as Ep 70, this autograph letter was
in the ill-fated Burscher Collection at the University Library in Leipzig (on
which see Ep 1254 introduction). An answer to Ep 1807, it should be read
in the context of Ep 1838; Erasmus' reply of 28 August (see Ep 1907:1–3)
is not extant. For Valdés, a priest educated in the humanist tradition and
working at this time as Latin secretary of Emperor Charles v, see Ep 1807
introduction.

Cordial greetings. On the feast day of the Holy Trinity I was in the company
of the eminent theologian Alonso de Virués of Olmedo,[1] and we were talking about our Erasmus and the calumnies of the monks against him and how
we could more effectively defend you from them. That excellent man (as you
are aware), when I called upon him to undertake this task, promised that,   5
more than a simple defender, he would be a fierce champion of your cause
and would be prepared even to risk his life for you. Lo! at that untimely
moment your letters, which you had sent on 31 March, were delivered to

* * * * *

15 Ep 1839
16 Actually 19 June: see n1 above.

1839
 1 This moveable feast occurred in 1527 on 16 June; cf Ep 1838 n1. On Virués see
    Ep 1838 introduction.

us, and they very nearly alienated a good and devoted friend. One letter
was addressed 'To the most distinguished master Juan Maldonado or to Al-   10
fonso de Valdés, etc.'[2] As I pondered diligently who the first distinguished
man might be, Alonso said, 'It could perhaps be a certain bachelor of theology who is now in Burgos; he showed me a letter he had written to Erasmus
a year ago.'[3]

But enough of Maldonado, and let us return to your letters. For the   15
letter to me, very brief though it was, I am most grateful.[4] It gave me great
pleasure in that I learned from it that you were in good health, for it was
written in your hand. Then when we read together the letter[5] you had sent
to my – or, I should say, your – friend Alonso, in which you treat a man who
has done so much for you with such mordancy and acrimony as I have never   20
seen you use against anyone before, you would have seen your Valdés, my
dear Erasmus, constantly changing colour and almost fainting away. Then
Alonso said, 'This is the thanks my friend Erasmus, whom I have so often
praised, gives me in return for all my services to him?' And I, my dear
Erasmus, must frankly admit that I could not think of anything to reply. I   25
was afraid, and not without reason, that with that one letter you had not
only lost an earnest and learned man but had also pushed him into the
enemy camp. But, that you may understand the man's piety, his wisdom,
his loyalty, and his devotion to you, when he saw me practically beside
myself with apprehension, he said, 'Be of good cheer. For even if there are   30
many things in this letter that could give me good reason to turn away from
Erasmus, nevertheless I shall not allow this incivility of his to deter me from
the duty I have embarked upon, especially since I assumed this role not so
much for the sake of Erasmus as for the sake of Christ and of religion. I wish
to have the satisfaction of knowing that I am the only one to have surpassed   35
Erasmus, usually such a model of kindness and moderation, by my example
of restraint. I shall pardon this offence, if not for the sake of Erasmus then
for the sake of Christ, under whose banner we all fight, and I shall lend

* * * * *

2 Ep 1805; see the introduction.
3 Ep 1742, in which Juan Maldonado described not only the popular reception in
  Spain of those of Erasmus' works that had been translated but also the growing sentiment among conservative theologians and monks to censure them.
  Erasmus answered it with Ep 1805. On Maldonado see the introduction there.
4 Ep 1807. Valdés can scarcely conceal his irritation that Maldonado, whom he
  considers to be an unknown tyro, should be favoured with such a long and significant letter (Ep 1805), whereas Valdés, Erasmus' 'oracle' in Spain (as Virués
  called him), received only a short paragraph; cf line 49 below.
5 Not extant: surely suppressed by Virués and Valdés (see line 80 below)

my services in the cause of Erasmus just as I promised. Erasmus will then
understand that in the young monk Christian charity is not so torpid as he   40
thinks.'

He reiterated these and many other similar sentiments, and I in my
turn praised him for his friendly disposition and his truly Christian intentions. At the same time I asked him not to make a copy of that letter for
anyone. That was a necessary precaution, of course, to safeguard your hon-   45
our and reputation; for, if it had been made public, it would have done more
harm to you here than the calumnies of all the monks put together. And he,
such is his moral integrity, gave me the letter on the spot. After settling this
matter, when I saw that huge letter to Maldonado, fearing that you might
have also written something about this affair to him, I decided to open it,   50
confident that this would not cause him displeasure. As I opened it I saw
first of all the copy of the letters sent to you both by the emperor and by the
chancellor.[6] I said to myself: 'What could have prompted Erasmus to write
such a letter to a mere novice, someone practically unknown, a letter that
would bring him more disgrace than honour? and that he should send him   55
a copy of a letter of the chancellor, in which that eminent old man wrote
in a rather unguarded manner about the Roman pontiff,[7] as one would to
a friend, thinking that it would go no further?' When I came to the end of
the letter, where you again spoke ill of your Alonso, I was very glad that I
thought to open it. And for that reason I decided I should keep the letter,   60
and contented myself with giving your greetings to your friend Maldonado,
to whom you wished to reserve such an honour.

Sustained by the good will I bear you, Erasmus, there are many things
in this business about which I must admonish you. First, that you should
wish to treat so harshly a man who is most dedicated to you, to such an   65
extent that I was frequently compelled to find lacking that Christian moderation and charity you so often proclaim, even if, as it seems, this is to be
attributed to the ill humour engendered by the reading of other people's
books. I could scarcely be led to believe that anything else could have induced you to act in this way. It is therefore expedient, my dear Erasmus,   70
to write as soon as possible to your Alonso in a friendly and polite manner, telling him that you are grateful to him for his services (you owe that
to him on many counts), and that you have not yet had the time to read his

* * * * *

6 Epp 1731 and 1757
7 Gattinara wrote that one sort of Christian, closing his eyes and even his mind,
   'sticks to the pope whether his judgments and decrees are good or bad' (Ep
   1757:12–13).

book of *Collationes*,[8] but that, when you have the opportunity, you will read it thoroughly and respond to it point by point. With that letter he will curb the tongues of his confrères, who have begun to ridicule him because you, whom he defends and for whom he lays himself open to criticism, have not even deigned to write him a letter. What must especially be avoided is that your very elaborate letter to your friend Maldonado be made public. What is more, I beg and beseech you that you consign it to the flames straightaway, for it would be a great disgrace to you if it were published.[9] Concerning the publishing of Alonso's little book you need not concern yourself, since that has never entered his mind.[10] He is a man totally removed from this ambition, and he guarded the book with such secrecy that he did not make it available even to me. In addition, I shall not shrink from advising you against writing so casually to strangers on any topic whatever and circulating indiscriminately copies of letters from your friends hither and yon. It would certainly arouse unpopularity for the chancellor if this letter of his were made public,[11] and it would not advance you in his good graces. Yet he is a man who esteems you so highly that he has no equal among mortals in his good will and devotion towards you. But on this subject I have said more than enough. One thing, however, I ask of you, my dear Erasmus, that if something was said in this letter without due circumspection that might give you offence, that you pardon it in a friendly spirit, seeing that I write this to you for no other motive than that I am the most zealous guardian of your honour and reputation.

But let us come finally to the matter that concerns you, of which I wrote to you at some length in recent days and Vergara at even greater length.[12] Since that time nothing has been done except that, after the theologians were assembled on the following Saturday, it was decided to begin the proceedings. The monks were there, Franciscans and Dominicans, of course, once the greatest of enemies,[13] but now, conspiring together for your destruction, the best of friends in the world; and, armed with more elaborate machinations,

* * * * *

8 See Ep 1838 introduction and n4.
9 Erasmus never published the letter, but he did not destroy it. He later sent a copy to Maldonado (Ep 1908 n10), although there is no evidence that the latter received it. Valdés himself had a copy made for Juan de Vergara (Ep 1805 introduction).
10 See Ep 1838 n4.
11 Ep 1757; see n7 above.
12 Valdés' letter is not extant. Vergara recounted in detail the preparations for the inquisition at Valladolid into Erasmus' orthodoxy in Ep 1814.
13 Founded within a few years of each other early in the thirteenth century, the two largest mendicant orders were traditional rivals.

they are making dire threats against us. But, believe me, they will get the
worst of this, if you will only appease your Virués with a single letter. I   105
would also wish that you write another letter to the whole Benedictine order, in which you would express your gratitude for their devotion and service to you, praise their order, and ask them to continue their support as
they have begun.[14] In this way you will render a useful service to yourself
and a very great favour to me, because of my fondness for you. I write noth-   110
ing to you about the sack of Rome; yet I should like to hear from you what
you think we should do in the face of this great and unexpected calamity
that has fallen upon us, and what you foresee for the future.[15]

   Farewell.

   Given at Valladolid, 20 June 1527   115

   Postscript. The Marquis of Villena,[16] who wields great influence among
Spanish princes because of his noble rank, wisdom, prestige, austerity, and
piety, is an enthusiastic partisan of yours. He wrote to me recently wishing
to know how he could demonstrate to all his favourable disposition towards
you. I gave him advice, which perhaps was not without some utility. He not   120
only promised that he would put it into practice but also wrote that he was
sorry that because of his poor health, resulting from old age, the mother of
all ills, he could not be present at this assembly to defend his Erasmus to
the best of his abilities against the calumnies of the monks.[17] With advocates
such as these, my dear Erasmus, you cannot help but win.   125

   Sincerely yours, Alfonso de Valdés

   * * * * *

14 Virués was a Benedictine monk. Such a letter, however, would have little
   chance of influencing his order as a whole, since each Benedictine monastery
   was autonomous under its own abbot, governed only by the sixth-century Rule
   of St Benedict.
15 As an imperial functionary Valdés would later write to depict the sack of Rome
   as a judgment of God on abuses in papal Rome. Circulated first in manuscript,
   his *Diálogo* was then printed several times, the first in 1529: *Diálogo: en que
   particularmente se tratan: las cosas acaecidas en Roma: el año de* MDXXVII *a gloria
   de Dios y bien universal de la República cristiana* (np [1529]), probably in Italy.
   There is a modern edition by José S. Montesino (Madrid 1928). A first English
   translation appeared in London (Abel Jiffro for Roger Ward 1590); a modern
   one by John E. Longhurst and Raymond R. MacCurdy, *Alfonso de Valdés and the
   Sack of Rome: Dialogue of Lactantio and an Archdeacon* (Albuquerque 1958). See
   Edward Boehmer *Bibliotheca Wiffeniana, Spanish Reformers of Two Centuries from
   1520* 3 vols (Strasbourg and London 1874–1904; repr New York 1963) I 101–5.
16 Diego López Pacheco, duke of Escalona and titular grand master of the Order
   of Santiago (CEBR II 346–8)
17 The marquis was particularly devoted to, and a patron of, the Observant
   Franciscans.

1840 / To Guillaume Budé   [Basel], 22 June 1527

This letter answers Budé's Ep 1812. It first appeared in the *Opus epistolarum* (1529).

ERASMUS OF ROTTERDAM TO GUILLAUME BUDÉ, GREETING

As to your promise regarding the *Observations on the Greek Language*, even if we must reduce our hopes by half we nonetheless eagerly await its publication.[1] I do not wish to conceal from you the fact that a commentary on the same subject has arrived here.[2] I have not yet had the opportunity to   5
see it. Bentinus[3] has a copy, and he claims that it is a work of considerable erudition; he has withheld the name of the author, while maintaining, however, that it is not Budé. You had better make sure that no one has pillaged your bookshelves; that suspicion came immediately to mind. A new dispute has arisen concerning the little book on weights and measures by Leonardo   10
Porzio from Vicenza, I believe, which is so similar to your *De asse* that no one doubts that the one is borrowed from the other.[4]

* * * * *

1840
1 See Ep 1812:2–4 and n1.
2 Probably the *Mega, kai pany ophelimon lexicon ... Magnum ac perutile Dictionarium quodquidem Varinus Phavorinus ... ex multis variisque auctoribus in ordinem collegit* (Rome: Zacharias Kallierges [1523]; repr 1525). It is a compilation (1,090 folio pages) made by the humanist Benedictine monk Guarino Favorinus Camers, a pupil of Demetrius Chalcondyles, Janus Lascaris, and Angelo Poliziano. He was a teacher of Giovanni de' Medici, who as Pope Leo x became his patron. See Mario Emilio Cosenza *Biographical and Bibliographical Dictionary of the Italian Humanists and of the World of Classical Scholarship in Italy, 1300–1800* 2nd ed (G.K. Hall 1962) v 227 nos 868–9. In a 1538 Basel reprint Robert Winter described it as 'totius linguae Graecae commentarius' (Allen Ep 1840:3n).
3 A Flemish cleric with whose work as a corrector in Froben's press Erasmus had long been displeased and whom Erasmus distrusted generally. After returning for several years to Flanders and France, Michael Bentinus worked again in Basel for the printers Valentinus Curio and Andreas Cratander, where he established relations with Guillaume Farel, Johannes Oecolampadius, and other reformers, including the Anabaptist Hans Denck. He died five months after this letter was written, a victim of the plague (CEBR I 123–4).
4 Leonardus de Portis *De sestertio, pecuniis, ponderibus et mensuris antiquis libri duo* (Venice: Georgius de Rusconibus n d) appeared c 1500 in an edition by Giambattista Egnazio. It was the earliest printed work on the ancient measures of length, weight, and value, and was reprinted by Froben. In 1517 (Ep 648:57–60) Erasmus referred to Egnazio's reliance on Portis for numismatic matters when editing *De caesaribus libri* III (Venice: Aldine Press, July 1516),

You write that you were offended that I made reference to the French people in less than flattering terms.[5] Nothing ever came to me as such a complete surprise. As far as my attitude towards all countries is concerned, I am an unmarked rule, as they say.[6] On the other hand, if there is any nation to which I feel more favourably inclined, it is France. Indeed I have incurred criticism on this account more than once both in my own country and in England, especially at the time when you were on bad terms with Julius, while the English were lending the supreme pontiff their support.[7] Read the *Panegyric* in which I celebrate the return of Prince Philip from Spain.[8] And yet these sentiments seem to be something instinctive, not a matter of reasoned judgment. The truth is that no nation has been so niggardly with me as the French, if you do not take into account the generous good will of my friends.

If in my preface to the Epistle to the Galatians I disparage the Gallic race, it is evident that it was not my purpose to do so, since I treat the question with greater brevity and restraint than Jerome.[9] And my reporting of his words served to illustrate the peculiar character of this Epistle. Moreover, the word ἀνόητοι, usually translated as *insensati*, I have rendered with a milder word.[10] I surely did not expect that this would offend any Frenchman, much less you, who have been trained in philosophy from your earliest

* * * * *

but hinted that he may have plagiarized Guillaume Budé's *De asse* (Paris: Josse Bade 1516). Here, ten years later, Erasmus keeps his insinuation ambiguous, subtly leaving Budé himself open to that charge. In *Adagia* v ii 16 (1533), Erasmus states that Janus Lascaris was called in to adjudicate this matter.

5 Ep 1812:46–77
6 *Adagia* i v 88
7 In 1512 France was at war with the Holy League led by Pope Julius ii. By 'my own country' Erasmus means the Netherlands.
8 The *Panegyricus ad Philippum Austriae ducem* (Antwerp: Dirk Martens, February 1504), in which Erasmus described the reception that France accorded to Philip the Handsome, father of Charles v, at Paris, Blois, Tours, and Bayonne (CWE 27 21–3). The occasion was Philip's progress from Flanders into Spain, not his return from there, as Erasmus here implies, which is mentioned only briefly in passing (CWE 27 26).
9 In the Argument that prefaces the Paraphrase on Galatians (CWE 42 94–6), the Galatians, who were ethnically linked to the Gauls, are deemed to be fickle and foolish, because after their conversion by St Paul they followed 'pseudo apostles' who convinced them to retain Mosaic law and to incorporate Jewish ceremonials into the practice of their Christian faith. Erasmus cites Jerome; cf PL 26 (1884) 310C.
10 Instead of the Vulgate *insensati* (Gal 3:1) Erasmus' annotation uses *stulti* (*O stulti Galatae*) and *rudes parumque cordati*; cf LB VI 812B / Reeve *Annotations* 575.

years and should be free of such vulgar sentiments. And even if some harsh
comment was made about present-day Frenchmen, what nation exists that is
not the butt of some proverb? Pindar and Plutarch seem even to have been
amused by the saying concerning the Boeotian sow,[11] although both of them   35
were Boeotians. Almost sixteen hundred years have gone by now, if I am not
mistaken, since the Gauls migrated into Asia Minor and formed Galatia,[12]
and it is not certain from what part of Gaul they came. If some slant is made
against the Gauls of that time, would it be interpreted as pertaining to all of
Gaul in all of its territorial extension? Is it not true that it is common among   40
Frenchmen even today to ridicule Normans, people from Maine, Bretons,
and Picards?[13] Or do you think perchance that the modern inhabitants of
Rome are the descendants of the ancient Romans? I am more inclined to believe that they are Goths or Vandals – such a flood of invasions blurred all
distinctions. And is someone to believe that what was said against the Gauls   45
of yore pertains to the Gauls of the present century? If that does not satisfy
you, I should at least have you believe on my word of honour that nothing
was further from my mind than wishing to cast aspersions upon the French
nation. I leave the rest to your interpretation; but I was greatly astonished
that you could really be angry in such a trivial matter. I admit that at times I   50
can be ironic and something of a Momus;[14] but this time, at least, I was not.

You remind me of your friendly offices towards me, especially your
efforts to tear me away from here, to which I respond,

I never shall deny, Budé,
The countless favours done me,   55
Nor shall I soon forget so true a friend.[15]

* * * * *

11 *Adagia* i x 6
12 The Gauls and the Galatians were separate tribes, probably linked ethnically,
   of the Celtic nation that, prior to the Roman invasions, had spanned Europe
   from Asia Minor to the British Isles. In former times Galatia was thought to
   have been on the south shore of the Black Sea, but most scholars now believe
   it lay squarely in the centre of Asia Minor.
13 In Ep 62:5 Erasmus himself had employed a derogatory comment about Normans. In his *Supputatio* against Noël Béda (LB IX 539B–C) he invokes conventional prejudice against Normans and people from the province of Maine (the
   home province of his critic Pierre Cousturier), and he mocks Béda's *lingua
   Picardica* (LB IX 531A).
14 Cf Ep 1812:75 and n13.
15 Cf Virgil *Aeneid* 4.333–5, which Erasmus adapts: he substitutes Budé for *regina*
   'queen' (that is, Dido) and *amico* 'friend' for *Elissae* (another name for Dido);

Still, it was never my intention to emigrate to France. If that had been the case, I should have accepted the conditions that Etienne Poncher offered to me personally on more than one occasion, which were more advantageous to me than if the king had given me that post of treasurer.[16] Whether you 60 had solicited for yourself the office of writing to me I am unaware.[17] This at any rate is certain: that I had been informed of the king's intention before you wrote a single word to me.[18]

* * * * *

and he alters the gender of the participle to adjust the grammar accordingly – all without destroying the hexameter rhythm.

16 Poncher's first offer came c 12 February 1517. Poncher had evidently offered to add 400 *écus d'or au soleil*, then worth exactly 725 *livres* 4 *sols tournois*, or £123.333 *groot* Flemish, or £85 sterling, to the benefice of 1,000 *livres tournois* that Francis I had already guaranteed – thus increasing the total emolument by almost 75 percent. In 1517, that sum was worth the equivalent of 2,550 days wages for a London mason (8d sterling per day), 3,400 days wages for an Oxford mason (6d per day), and 2,960 days wages for an Antwerp mason (at 10d *groot* Flemish per day). For the chronology of the 1517 invitation, see n18 below.

The 1524 invitation to Erasmus offered him the treasurership of Tours worth 1,000 *livres tournois* (Ep 1434:23–5) – the same position and sum offered in 1517 but without Poncher's personal offer to increase it by 725 *livres*.

Note that in 1527 the value of 400 *écus d'or au soleil* had risen to 800 *livres*, that is, the value of the *écu* had been raised to 40s or 2 *livres tournois*. Unfortunately, in CWE 12 650 (Table 3D), a computer error doubled the true value of the *écu*, after 1519, from the actual value of 480d (40s) to 960d (80s), and thus from the true value of 2 *livres* to 4 *livres tournois*.

17 In 1517 Guillaume Petit had suggested to the king that Budé invite Erasmus. The initiative in 1524 is less clear; but in 1529 Budé clearly took the strongest initiative in the actions which led, in 1530, to the appointment of the first regius professors, that is, the forerunners of the Collège royal, later known as the Collège de France (Farge *Parti conservateur* 36–9).

18 This is technically incorrect, but Erasmus correctly recalls having the offer first from Bishop Etienne Poncher. The chronology of the invitation is the following: On 3 February 1517 Guillaume Petit, confessor to King Francis I, mentioned the name of Erasmus to the king and suggested Budé as an intermediary in inviting him. Petit spoke to Budé on 4 February, and Budé wrote to Erasmus on 5 February (Ep 522), mentioning Petit's role first (lines 40–58) and then informing him that Bishop Etienne Poncher, who was on a diplomatic mission to Brussels, would approach Erasmus personally on the subject (lines 124–9). On 6 February, the king's physician Guillaume Cop wrote to Erasmus (Ep 523) to confirm the invitation. Before either of those letters reached Erasmus, Poncher made the offer in person; but on 14 February, Erasmus wrote (Ep 529) from Antwerp to Poncher to decline, suggesting instead the Swiss humanist Henricus Glareanus. He wrote to Budé on the following day, but had

The dissemblance[19] you speak of puzzles me. If there were such, it did
no harm to anyone. I made no attempt to disguise my feelings, but no one   65
believed me. Changing countries was not in my best interests, although to
be sought after by such a great king was a singular honour. Finally, I should
not wish to take advantage of Budé's intercession in such lowly matters, no
matter how important they may appear to the crowd. I am not so fickle that
because of a little gossip I should alter my sentiments towards such a friend   70
as you; I am acquainted with the vanity of some of our colleagues, the envy
of others, who cannot abide that people should be on good terms with each
other. There is one whom, were I to name him, you yourself would acknowledge to be loyal and sincere.[20] He heard you during a banquet at court, in
the hearing of many, give a clear intimation of your ill feeling towards me.   75
You found me lacking in constancy in the preservation of friendships. But
those were not the words of an enemy but of a friend giving voice to his
complaint. And yet this much praise, if there is any praise I can claim, I shall
justly lay claim to for myself: that there is scarcely a man who having once
vowed himself to a friendship clings to it more tenaciously, a trait that has   80
often cost me dearly.[21]

The riddle about the braggadocio[22] escapes me, unless, as I suspect,
some book has come from Italy heralding some swaggering soldier of fortune. Nothing of that sort has reached us here. There did arrive, however, a
little book written by a Neapolitan named Sannazaro, bearing the glowing   85

* * * * *

not yet seen Budé's Ep 522, and makes no mention of the offer or of the interview with Poncher. On 21 February, Erasmus wrote a letter of fulsome praise
to the king (Ep 533), but referred to the invitation in an offhanded manner
and pleaded his unworthiness. On the same day, having now received Budé's
Ep 522, he wrote to Budé (Ep 534), again declining the king's offer and specifically mentioning that it had been made by Poncher prior to the arrival of
Budé's letter (lines 13–15).
19 ἀκκισμόν; see Ep 1812:101.
20 Allen suggests Gervasius Wain (CEBR III 422–3), a German-born doctor of theology of Paris (1522) who had visited Erasmus earlier in the spring and whom
Erasmus called 'open-minded' (Ep 1827:15). But at that time Wain was not yet
in attendance at court, as Erasmus says here. An alternate source of this report is Jacques Toussain, who was an admirer of both Erasmus and of Budé
and whose most recent letter at that time (see Ep 1794:1) is not extant.
21 Cf Ep 1572:92–5. Erasmus refers to disappointment in friends in, for example,
Epp 1244:41–2, 1479:87–9, 1523:216–21.
22 *philalazonia*; see Ep 1812 nn21–2. The misunderstanding about the identity of
this person continues.

recommendations of two pontiffs and, more enthusiastically, that of Cardinal Egidio of Viterbo.[23] In it I did recognize a pretentious style.[24] Georg Sauermann, a young man of remarkable talent, was preparing to publish some work or other.[25] Alberto of Carpi, the leader of this fraternity, expunged whatever had been added in praise of Erasmus.[26] I do not impute this to Alberto, but to that fellow who does not allow anyone, be he god or mortal, to be praised outside of himself.[27] Alberto, I hear, makes much of him.

Concerning Longueil, I am astonished that he was able to forsake your friendship. But he won sufficiently great praise for himself – he died a Ciceronian.[28] And yet few read this Ciceronian's lucubrations,[29] while there is no one who does not read my Batavian rubbish.[30]

* * * * *

23 Jacopo Sannazaro of Naples wrote an epic poem about the virginal birth of Christ, *De partu virginis* (Naples, May 1526), based on a sermon of Cardinal Egidio Antonini, better known as Giles of Viterbo. Erasmus is referring to the second edition (Rome: Francesco Calvo, December 1526), which contained briefs from Leo x and Clement vii along with an undated letter from Giles. See the critical edition by Charles Fantazzi and Alessandro Perosa (Florence 1988) and a modern English translation by Michael C.J. Putnam in *Latin Poetry* I I Tatti Renaissance Library 38 (Cambridge, Mass 2009) 1–93. Giles of Viterbo, an Augustinian friar, became a reformist general of his order in 1507, cardinal in 1517, and bishop of Viterbo in 1523. Knowledgeable in Hebrew and Greek as well as Arabic, he was admired in humanist circles, and was one of the most formidable preachers of his day. He led a troop of two thousand men to relieve Clement vii during the sack of Rome; see CEBR I 64–5; F.X. Martin OSA *Friar, Reformer, and Renaissance Scholar: Life and Work of Giles of Viterbo, 1469–1532* ed John E. Rotelle (Villanova, Pa 1992).

24 *phrasim philalazonos*. For Erasmus' more extended estimate of Sannazaro's style, see *Ciceronianus* ASD I-2 700–1 / CWE 28 437–8.

25 See Allen Epp 1342:323n, 1479:130n; a year later (Allen Ep 2008:23–4), Erasmus regrets not having remembered to mention Sauermann in the *Ciceronianus*; cf CEBR III 197–8.

26 Alberto Pio, prince of Carpi, was one of Erasmus' most determined critics; see CWE 84 Introduction; Rummel *Catholic Critics* II 115–23.

27 No doubt Girolamo Aleandro who was a close friend of Alberto Pio; see Rummel *Catholic Critics* II 108–13.

28 See Ep 1812:141–2, where Budé complains that Christophe de Longueil's devotion to Ciceronian language had led him to renounce his northern origins.

29 Longueil's posthumous *Opera*, edited by Reginald Pole, were first published in Florence by Giunta (1524) and reprinted by Josse Bade (Paris 1526). They consisted of a few orations and a correspondence comprising 150 letters.

30 An allusion to the fact that Longueil tried to hide his Brabantine descent, while Erasmus openly acknowledged his own Netherlandish roots.

What I wrote about eliminating all suspicion was meant most of all for the sake of our common studies.[31] If you do so, I shall be most gratified; but if something hinders you in this you may disregard it without any infringement of our friendship.   100

I could barely write this, since I am suffering from a terrible toothache.[32]

Keep well.

22 June in the year 1527

1841 / To Jean de Guise, cardinal of Lorraine   Basel, 29 June 1527

This preface to Erasmus' translation of St John Chrysostom's *Commentary on Galatians* first appeared in Froben's 1527 edition.

Cardinal Jean de Guise-Lorraine (1498–1550), the second son of Duke René II of Lorraine, was one of the most trusted advisors of King Francis I. Having accumulated an array of bishoprics, archbishoprics, and abbacies, he became the patron of a number of humanists and had joined in the efforts of Guillaume Budé and others to bring Erasmus to France in 1524. He should not be confused with his nephew Charles, likewise known as the cardinal of Lorraine, who became a powerful force in the early wars of religion, nor with his grand-nephew Louis, cardinal of Guise, who was assassinated in 1588 along with Duke Henri de Guise-Lorraine. Erasmus here solicits his support in the increasingly serious matter of the examination of his works in Paris, a topic he will later pursue more directly with the cardinal in Ep 1911.

TO THE REVEREND LORD JEAN, CARDINAL OF LORRAINE,
FROM ERASMUS OF ROTTERDAM, GREETING

How fortunate we are that not everything is at the mercy of this evil fate or wicked genius which now embroils human affairs in deadly discord on every side. It is still possible for men of good will to be united in fellow-   5
ship; it is possible to converse together in writings that pass to and fro. Thus, by the path that lies open to me, I present myself, invited by your

* * * * *

31 Rendered here in Greek; cf Ep 1812:120–1. In Ep 1794:16–24 Erasmus had written that he would like any suspicion that Budé harboured unfriendly feelings towards him to be dispelled completely (*suspicionem penitus abolitam*). Budé's response used the Greek phrase Erasmus echoes here.
32 Cf Ep 1827:6.

most friendly letter;[1] and, to make my arrival more pleasant, I bring with
me a most agreeable and eloquent companion, John Chrysostom, who will
expound to you the Epistle of Paul to the Galatians, discoursing in Latin   10
with precision and elegance. In this way, one might say, the Galatians too
will resume their civic rights and return to their land of Gaul.[2] Claudius
Cantiuncula repeatedly urged me to embark upon this venture and well
nigh drove me to it.[3] Is there anything at all that he could not easily persuade anyone to do? He is a man endowed with such talent, with such un-   15
common knowledge of philosophy and both branches of the law, so well
equipped too in the practical knowledge of literature. Add to all this a natural eloquence over and above the speaking ability imparted by the rhetoricians, so that he might justly be called, if not the only (for that might invite
envy), certainly a very rare example and adornment of your land of Lor-   20
raine, and with good reason especially endeared to you, a shrewd judge of
such qualities. Since therefore I had long been inclined and favourably disposed to the project, he easily convinced me in the end, delivering me the
letter from your reverend Lordship – very brief, to be sure, but brimming
with kindness.[4]   25

I had heard that you were a personage of very high rank by your noble
ancestry but greater still in personal distinction and that, in addition to this,
when you were in the flower of youth, in the midst of the occupations and
pleasures of the court, you carried around in your hands the Gospels and
the Epistles of St Paul, and frequently feasted your eyes and mind upon   30
them, which was for me the unmistakable sign of a pious mind. For he who
cherishes the Sacred Scriptures cannot be much or for long corrupted by the
vices of this world. This piety of yours thus invited me to dedicate specifically to you something from the treasury of the sacred writings, but I was

* * * * *

1841
1 Not extant
2 For Erasmus' contention with Guillaume Budé about the Gauls and the Galatians see Epp 1812:50–70, 1840:25–50.
3 Claude Chansonnette had been a distinguished professor of civil law, rector
   of the University of Basel, and syndic of the town council, but quit Basel in
   1524 to avoid the tensions of the growing Reformation movement there. He
   was chancellor to Cardinal Jean de Guise-Lorraine in 1527, and served the
   Guise family in several capacities before moving east to serve the Hapsburgs.
   He and Erasmus shared sincere mutual admiration and friendship. See Epp
   852:85n, 1616, and CEBR I 259–61.
4 See line 8 above; the letter is not extant.

put off by the grandeur of your high position. With this scruple removed   35
by your letter, I made ready my little gift.

To commend it to you in a few words, this is the first time this work
has ever been translated, so that, if for no other reason, it may be acceptable to you on the score of novelty. Next there is scarcely any other Epistle in which the ardour and solicitude of Pauline charity towards the dis-   40
ciples whom he had begotten in Christ is more apparent. From this example bishops could be reminded what affection they should bear towards the
flock entrusted to them. You have here as well an interpreter very much
akin to the Apostle, evincing on every page a maternal affection for his
people, and as clear and conscientious in his teaching as a nurse caring for   45
her child.[5] Paul pointed out the distinction between a tutor and a father:
'For though you have countless guides in Christ, you do not have many fathers. For I became your father in Christ Jesus through the gospel.'[6] The
same Apostle here shows himself a mother, bringing forth the Galatians
a second time, until Christ be formed in them.[7] Again he showed himself   50
a nurse to the Thessalonians, and not merely any nurse, but the nurse of
her own son.[8] These three persons can be seen in this bishop: father by
his priestly authority, mother in his zeal to bring forth and care for his
offspring, nurse by his nourishing the souls of his children with the pre-
masticated food of the doctrine of salvation.[9] Of the Mosaic priest it is writ-   55
ten in Exodus 28: 'and its sound shall be heard when he goes into the holy
place before the Lord, and when he comes out, lest he die.'[10] And so he
wore golden bells on his vestment. But for our bishop, in place of bells,
a golden tongue never ceases to ring the sounds of Sacred Scripture into
the people's ears – teaching, affirming, exhorting, consoling. For, accord-   60
ing to the teaching of the gospel, the priest always abides in the sanctuary,
going in and going out to find pasture for his sheep. And it is a sign of
mortal danger should the ringing cease. For by this ringing the sheep of
Christ are nourished. Here then is revealed a twofold example of the good
shepherd.   65

* * * * *

5 That is, St John Chrysostom, who was the bishop of Constantinople
6 1 Cor 4:15
7 Gal 4:19: 'My little children, with whom I am again in travail until Christ be
   formed in you!'
8 1 Thess 2:7: 'But we were gentle among you, like a nurse taking care of her
   children.'
9 Cf *Puerpera* 'The New Mother' CWE 39 605:25–6; *Adagia* III v 30, IV viii 93.
10 Exod 28:35

Finally there occur in this Epistle certain passages that have led many strongly to suspect a lack of agreement between Paul and other leaders of the apostles, especially Peter.[11] From the same source the well-known debate arose between Augustine and Jerome on the subject of falsehood. The discussion became very heated even to the exchange of insults, and did not end until Augustine gave in.[12] Nevertheless, if one weighs the matter more carefully, neither sufficiently understood the other, since Jerome speaks of dissimulation of action while Augustine treats the question of falsity of speech. I am astonished that Augustine so treated Peter, the prince of the apostles

70

* * * * *

11 St Paul refers to Peter, James, and John as 'columns' and 'leaders' of the nascent church (Gal 2:9). His disagreement with Peter was about obliging Christian converts to observe Mosaic laws like circumcision, diet, and eating with Gentiles. Peter had previously renounced this 'Judaizing' approach; but later, fearful of offending Jewish converts or potential converts, he agreed to condone it. Paul strongly opposed Peter for this change and accused him of 'dissimulation' (Gal 2:11–14).

12 Like Tertullian, Cyprian, Cyril of Alexandria, and others St Augustine believed that St Peter lied when, through fear of scandalizing the Judaizing Christians, he failed to tell them that he had eaten meals with non-circumcised Gentile converts. St Jerome, however, shared the view of Origen and St John Chrysostom that Peter's dissimulation was a providential opportunity for St Paul to proclaim the freedom of all converts from the Jewish Law; see *Commentariorum in Galatas libri tres* PL 26 (1884) 363–9 / *Opera D. Hieronimi* ed Erasmus (Basel: Hieronymus Froben and Nicolaus Episcopius 1537) IX 166–70; see also Jerome's Ep 75 to Augustine CSEL 34 part 2 280–324 / FCNT 12 342–67. Augustine believed that Jerome's interpretation of St Peter's dissimulation put the infallibility of Sacred Scripture at risk: see *Expositio ad Galatas* PL 32 583–656 / CSEL 84 69–73, and cf Epp 28, 40, 82 CSEL 34 part 1 103–13, 34 part 2 69–81, 351–87 / FCNT 12 93–9, 172–9, 390–420. See also Ralph Hennings *Die Briefwechsel zwischen Augustinus und Hieronymus und ihr Streit um die Kanon des Alten Testaments und die Auslegung von Gal. 2:11–14* (Leiden 1994). There is no evidence that Augustine ever 'gave in.' In the last of the letters exchanged between him and St Jerome, Augustine still held strongly to his position that the credibility of the Bible demands that we regard St Peter's dissimulation as an 'officious lie' CSEL 34 part 2 351–75 / FCNT 12 Ep 82 393–9. Writing his commentary on Isaiah ten years later, Jerome reaffirmed his own view PL 24 (1844) 513B, 24 (1865) 532B. In AD 415, after reading a book of Jerome against the Pelagians, Augustine told the Roman nobleman Oceanus that Jerome had finally yielded CSEL 44 698 / FCNT 30 Ep 180 119–20, but he was probably reading too much of his own position into Jerome's text. On this view see Paul Auvray, 'Saint Jérôme et saint Augustin: la controverse au sujet de l'incident d'Antioche' *Recherches de science religieuse* 29 (1939) 608–10.

and first proclaimer of the faith,[13] that at one time he accuses him of superstitious dissimulation, at another of the misguided ambition to impose
the burden of the Law on the shoulders of the Gentiles; at one time of perverse dissimulation, at another of perversity;[14] and, far from lessening this
sin, he compares it to his threefold denial of Christ.[15] Although the great
Doctor of the church insists on this in several places, he does not mitigate
his accusation in the *Retractations*,[16] although he glosses over other rather insignificant matters. Following the example of Augustine,[17] the articles of the
Paris theologians attribute an error in faith to Peter.[18]

     From this surprise another ensues. Although we may accept with equa-
nimity these statements directed against the one to whom Christ delivered
the keys of the kingdom of heaven and whom he wished to be prince of his

* * * * *

13 Matt 16:18–19; Acts 2:14–42
14 See n12 above.
15 In several of his sermons and in his *Expositio ad Galatas* (CSEL 84 70–1) St Augustine sees Christ's threefold question – 'Simon, son of John, do you love
   me?' (John 15:17) – as reparation for Simon Peter's threefold denial of Christ
   (Matt 27:69–75; cf Mark 14:66–72, Luke 22:54–61).
16 In AD 427 or 428 Augustine wrote to Quodvultdeus, 'I am revising all my
   works and, if there is anything in them which displeases me or could offend
   others, I have been making clear, partly by correcting and partly by defending,
   what can and ought to be read. I have finished two volumes of *Retractations*
   after having gone over all my writings' (Ep 224 CSEL 57 451–2 / FCNT 32 118).
   See *Retractationum libri duo* (PL 32 583–656 / CSEL 36).
17 But Augustine regarded Peter's dissimulation and his threefold denial of
   Christ as sins of fear, not as an error in faith, just as he considered Peter's
   drawing his sword against the servant of the high priest (John 18:20) as a sin
   of disobedience, not apostasy. In numerous places Augustine writes that Peter's repentance for these sins made him a model for faithful Christians and
   the most appropriate disciple to lead the church – affirmations that he could
   not make about him if he was guilty of errors in faith.
18 The Paris faculty of theology never accused St Peter of an error in faith.
   One can therefore only speculate about what Erasmus may have in mind.
   He cannot be looking at anything in the faculty's final rulings about him,
   since they were not drawn up until December 1527 and were kept secret until 1531. Those rulings do mention St Peter's disobedience in drawing his sword (John 18:10; see Argentré *Collectio judiciorum* II-1 56), but
   both that and his threefold denial of Jesus constituted human weakness,
   not lack of faith. Noël Béda's *Annotationes*, which were approved by the
   whole faculty on 16 May 1526 (Farge *Procès-verbaux* 137 no 152B and n41),
   do treat of St Peter (the Paris edition on f 207v, the Cologne one on f
   264r–v), but nowhere in them does Béda conclude that St Peter erred in
   faith.

entire church,[19] and our ears are not offended when we hear that an error
in faith and a perverse spirit is attributed by eminent men to the supreme
teacher of the faith even after he received the Spirit from on high and
performed miracles,[20] yet today some cry schism, scandal, blasphemy, and   90
heresy if someone says that Jerome was a learned and pious man but nevertheless still a man; or if someone says that Jerome held virginity so much in
awe that he came close to deriding marriage, since everyone is aware of the
words concerning marriage that he uttered in moments of vehemence.[21] But
Chrysostom here treats this material with such skilfulness that he shows not   95
only that there were no feelings of rancour between Peter and Paul but indeed that concord and good will existed between them, that there was no
disagreement concerning the faith, and that the whole quarrel concerning
falsehood is superfluous. He explains that nothing came between them in
this matter except charity suited to the occasion as a concession to the invin-   100
cible ignorance of the Jews,[22] and except for a pious dissimulation adopted
in an effort to be of help. In my opinion this interpretation is more worthy
of those great princes of the gospel and more acceptable to the ears of pious
men.

But concerning these questions you will be able to judge better when   105
you have read through the volume, which you will easily accomplish with-

* * * * *

19 Matt 16:18–19
20 That is, after Peter's reception of the Holy Spirit at Pentecost and the miracles
   that he performed in the first days of his preaching about Jesus (Acts 2–3). The
   term 'offensive to pious ears' was one of sixty-nine designations of disapproval
   or censure employed in ecclesiastical censures; see Bruno Neveu *L'erreur et son
   juge: remarques sur les censures doctrinales à l'époque moderne* (Naples 1993) 326.
21 In his *Life of Jerome* Erasmus makes a similar statement: 'he had extolled virginity to the point of incurring odium' (CWE 61 48). There again he did not
   provide a specific example. Jerome's most comprehensive treatment of virginity and marriage was his *Adversus Jovinianum libri duo* (PL 23 [1883] 216–354).
   In book 1 Jerome responded to Jovinian's statement that 'a virgin is no better as such than a wife in the sight of God' with lengthy commentary on St
   Paul (chapters 4–13), from other books of Scripture (chapters 14–39), and from
   examples in non-Christian societies. See NPNF 2nd series 6 346–86. Erasmus
   wrote on virginity in *A Comparison of the Virgin and the Martyr* (Basel: Froben,
   September 1524; LB V 589–600 / CWE 69 159–82), where he cited both Scripture
   and patristic authors. His most thorough treatment of marriage was his *Institutio christiani matrimonii* (Basel: Johann Froben, August 1526 / LB V 615–724 /
   CWE 69 204–436).
22 Erasmus uses the canonical term *invincibili . . . imbecillitati*, which implies ignorance of the law but not moral culpability.

out boredom. For without being long it is clear and eloquent, unless I have
detracted something from it by a poor translation. I pray, moreover, that
the Lord will inspire in you more and more a sincere love of his gospel,
for which I see no less danger from those who attempt to seize for them-   11
selves the victory due to Christ than from those who under the banners of
the enemy rend asunder the concord of the church. It is a calamitous victory that frees a city from one tyrant only to deliver it to many others more
oppressive than he.[23] If they have set their sights on anything other than
Christ, there will be no joyful victory. But I nourish very high hopes in my   11
heart that Christ will bring a happy end to all these disturbances, if only we
deserve it. Farewell.

Basel, 19 June in the year 1527

1842 / From Jacques Toussain   Paris, 29 June [1527]

> The autograph of this letter is preserved in the Rehdiger Collection (MS 254
> 154) of the University Library at Wrocław. It was first published in Enthoven
> Ep 52.
>
> Jacques Toussain, a Greek scholar and protégé of Guillaume Budé, first cor-
> responded with Erasmus in 1518 (Ep 810). He taught privately and was oc-
> casionally employed as secretary to jurists and bishops. His defence of Guil-
> laume Budé, whom he felt had been slighted in Erasmus' *Ciceronianus* (Basel:
> Froben 1528), angered Erasmus, but Germain de Brie was able to heal the
> breach; cf Epp 2021, 2046. Budé secured for Toussain one of the four origi-
> nal royal professorships in Paris – precursors to the future Collège royal and,
> later, the Collège de France. See Epp 1713, 1794; CEBR III 336–7.

Marcus Mamucetus,[1] the bearer of this letter, is a young man of excellent
character, as proven to me here over a period of many months. He is, moreover, most devoted to you and most eager to acquire learning either from
you or from one of your disciples. That is the object of his visit. In my
company he approached Lascaris, Budé, and Brie to obtain letters for you.[2]   5

* * * * *

23 Luke 11:24–6

1842
1 Or Mamuretus, otherwise unknown
2 Janus Lascaris, of Constantinople, had taught Greek to Guillaume Budé and
  Germain de Brie in the early years of the century. He returned to Paris in 1526,
  where he saw his *Epigrammata* (n5 below) through the press; but he returned

Lascaris and Budé send you their greetings, but both of them, pleading pressing personal affairs, said they could not write. And not without good reason, to be sure; the one is constantly plagued by the gout,[3] and the other is occupied at the court of the king, who is residing here.[4] Besides, neither had any special reason to write. Since Brie was away from the city, I have   10 provided the young man with this letter for you, so that he would not arrive in your presence without a letter and without introduction.

Badius, who also sends you his greetings, is printing the *Greek and Latin Epigrams* of Janus Lascaris.[5] In order to meet and consult with the same Lascaris more freely I have suspended my public lectures. This was not hard   15 for me to do, since up to now they were free of charge,[6] although meanwhile some of my students are continuing the work all the same. If learning had its rewards here, nowhere would good letters flourish more. Neither outstanding talents nor splendid enterprises are lacking; what is lacking is a favourable and benign generosity towards professors. For an entire year   20 now I have rolled this stone to no avail,[7] and in the end I thought the simplest course of action would be to withdraw from this post. I have decided to stay with Lascaris for a few months; as to what action I should take or where I should live after that I have no clear idea.[8] I cannot bear the thought

* * * * *

to Italy towards the end of 1527 after failing to persuade Francis I to endow royal professors in Paris (CEBR II 292–4). On Budé see Ep 1812 introduction. Erasmus had recently published Brie's Latin translation of John Chrysostom on the priesthood (Basel: Froben, March 1527); see Ep 1817 introduction.

3 Cf Ep 1794:9–10.

4 The court was in Paris 1–19 June, and then moved to Saint-Denis (just north of Paris) until 5 July. Budé was *maître des requêtes* of the royal household; but, his relations with Chancellor Antoine Duprat being strained at this time, his activity at court was curtailed.

5 *Epigrammata*, edited by Toussain, appeared from the press of Josse Bade on 1 July 1527 (Moreau *Inventaire* III 353 no 1251). Bade printed the first edition of the *Moriae encomium* in 1511 and reprinted other editions of them. For his complete *oeuvre* see Philippe Renouard *Bibliographie des impressions et des oeuvres de Josse Badius Ascensius, imprimeur et humaniste* (Paris 1908; repr New York 1963); cf his *Imprimeurs* II 6–297.

6 Toussain had no contractual position at the university. At that time the colleges, not the faculty of arts, engaged professors. Those not under contract sometimes taught without payment.

7 An allusion to the mythical Sisyphus (*Odyssey* 11.593), whose torment in Hades consisted in eternally rolling a massive stone up a hill, only to see it always roll down again.

8 Toussain found interim patronage in the service of Lodovico Canossa, bishop of Bayeux, before finally being appointed in late 1529 as a royal lecturer in

of returning against my own will to the same stone or rather to my hapless   2⬦
treadmill. Last year our king of his own initiative promised Budé that he
would grant me some sort of stipend to teach Greek here.[9] But I have no
one among all those surrounding the throne to refresh his memory of me,
since at the present moment Budé and all those who enjoy the king's favour
for their literary accomplishments are totally involved with promoting the   3⬦
cause of Lascaris,[10] leaving no room or at least very little room for anyone
else.

If I could readily pursue what I have recently engaged upon[11] with a
certain vigour, as I flatter myself in thinking, our idle talkers[12] would lose
much of their prestige and authority. For you can surmise how much their   3⬦
hauteur has been diminished by the fact that those who are their declared
enemies not only retain their former dignity but, laden with honours, they
advance day by day to ever higher and more honourable positions. But if the
study of Greek also had its rightful place here, I have no doubt that these rabid, abominable sophists would become the object of extreme unpopularity   4⬦
and would condemn themselves to self-imposed exile. To bring this to pass
as quickly as possible it will devolve upon you, in your singular good will
towards me, to assist me, as soon as you have the time, with a brief testimo-
nial letter to one of your followers either here or at court. For my part, out
of my respect or, rather, religious devotion to you, I will do battle against   4⬦
your adversaries with all my strength, standing by you with courage and
conviction.

Farewell from Paris, the city of light,[13] 29 June.

* * * * *

Paris; see Henri Omont 'Le premier professeur de langue grecque au Collège
de France, Jacques Toussain' *Revue des études grecques* (1903) 417–19.
9 Royal stipends to lecturers and colleges both in Paris and in provincial cities
were not uncommon; but the claims of humanists to royal patronage in a com-
petitive situation were often exaggerated. Francis i had failed to provide the
special patronage for Greek and Latin studies sought by Budé and others since
1517, and even when a start was made in 1530 their actual remuneration was
disappointing for a number of years (Farge *Parti conservateur* 36–8).
10 See nn2 and 5 above.
11 Perhaps his revised edition of Budé's *De contemptu rerum fortuitarum libri tres
cum brevi expositione* (Paris: Josse Bade, 2 April 1528); or perhaps the *Lexicon
graecolatinum*, a joint project finally published in 1552 (Paris: Charlotte Guillard
and Guillaume Merlin)
12 'idle talkers' is rendered in Greek.
13 Using *Lucetia* instead of the normal *Lutetia*, Toussain follows Janus Lascaris
Epigrammata f c 2v, which suggests a derivation from the Greek adjective
λευκός, 'bright' or 'brilliant' – probably a pun on the Latin *lux, lucis* 'light.' Cf

Your friend Toussain

To Erasmus of Rotterdam, peerless authority in both languages and   50
celebrated theologian

1843 / From Jacobus Ceratinus   Louvain, 1 July [1527]

Jacobus Ceratinus (Jacob Teyng of Hoorn) could claim acquaintance from 1517
not only with Erasmus (Ep 22) but also with Henricus Glareanus and Guillaume Budé, and may have worked briefly for Froben in Basel c 1519. He
had possibly been Erasmus' choice for the chair in Greek at the Collegium
Trilingue, a position taken instead by Rutgerus Rescius. A year later he applied for the chair in Latin at the college, but Conradus Goclenius received
the appointment. At Erasmus' behest (Ep 1460) he published with Froben in
1524 a new edition of Johannes Craston's Greek and Latin lexicon, which had
first been published in Milan in 1478. In 1525 Erasmus recommended him for
the Greek chair in Leipzig; but Duke George of Saxony dismissed him, causing Erasmus to think (mistakenly) that Ceratinus was a Lutheran sympathizer.
Shortly before writing this letter Ceratinus had been ordained a priest, a fact
that served to dispel Erasmus' suspicions that he favoured the Reformation
movement. In October 1528 Erasmus will recommend him once again to the
University of Cologne (CEBR I 288–9).

This letter was the preface to Ceratinus' short treatise *De sono literarum, prae-
sertim Graecarum* on the phonetic value of the letters of the alphabet. It first
appeared in 1527 (Antwerp: Johannes Grapheus).

TO DESIDERIUS ERASMUS OF ROTTERDAM FROM JACOBUS
CERATINUS

Among the many and varied gifts with which God has equipped man and
distinguished him from other living things, the power of speech is not to be
placed among those of least importance. We may clearly recognize the extent   5
of its vigour and sweetness if we consider how far the naked sound of the
human voice surpasses all music, whether produced by wind instruments,
strings, or any other means. The distinction will become all the more plain
to us if we reflect that all those sounds, however much they soothe the ear
with their charms, are but a pale image of the sound emitted by the pure   10

* * * * *

the form *Leucotecia* used by Johann Maier of Eck in a letter to Joachim Va-
dianus (March 1517); *Vadianische Briefsammlung der Stadtbibliothek St Gallen* ed
Emil Arbenz and H. Wartmann, 7 vols (St Gall 1890–1908) I 183 (106) no 91,
185 (109) no 92.

voice. The closer they succeed in imitating it the more perfect they seem to
our natural sensibility. Indeed without any added support the voice has the
power to rouse, depress, excite, or revive the spirit, fill it now with joy, now
with sadness, again with hope, still again with fear, and in general affect us
in as many ways as nature has endowed us with feelings.   15

First of all, what can the voice not attain when, in addition to mere
sound, it flows freely with a certain grouping of letters and words marked
off, as it were, by joints and members bound together by sinews? Then, supposing that the sound be not devoid of sense,[1] what is not effected by the
supervenience of meaning, which is the life of speech? For one may say that 20
words constitute the body and meaning the soul. From this comes that infinitely harmonious song, which is said to have moved wild beasts, trees,
rivers, and solid rock,[2] to have soothed them by its delights when it first began to hold sway. From this comes persuasion, more suitably expressed by
the Greek word Πειθώ, justly named by Euripides 'the queen of the world.'[3] 25

The moderator of this divine gift of speech is pronunciation;[4] and this
has its own sounds, which are determined by the letters of the alphabet. Let
us see, then, whether through a systematic investigation we can discover
a method of understanding the nature and the force of each letter and the
special technique of modulating the voice. Such a study is both necessary   30
for perceiving the nature of speech, which would otherwise lie hidden, and
very pleasant for us to know. For as the doctor cannot know the structure
of the human body and its members without anatomy, as it is called, so
you will not have certain knowledge of the nature of speech unless you
dissect it piecemeal, examining each single part, then breaking it down into 35
its primary elements.

And as to you, most amiable[5] Erasmus, it behoves you to take it in
good part if at this time I seem to use for my own ends the good omen of
your lovable name – especially as I do not do so, as is so often the case,
to cajole patronage for my book from a patron whom it does not deserve.   40
Nor do I seek to win new favours for myself, since your previous good will

* * * * *

1843
1 Virgil *Aeneid* 10.640
2 Ceratinus evokes the powers of music attributed to the mythic Orpheus.
3 *Hecuba* 816
4 Erasmus would produce, in March 1528, his own treatise on pronunciation;
  see Ep 1949.
5 Ceratinus gives the Greek, ἐρασμιώτατε [*erasmiotate*], using the play of words
  on the name Erasmus and the word-family of ἔρως [*eros*].

towards me has been even more than I deserve; nor even less do I seek out some service, since you have so often treated me with more kindness than my wishes would have allowed. And, taken altogether, your benefactions towards me are greater than I can ever deserve. But I offer this work on 45 the letters of the alphabet to you, prince of letters, in that spirit in which antiquity, superstitious but not ungrateful, offered the first fruits of the harvest to Ceres and Bacchus.[6] It was not that they thought they had need of them; rather it was in veneration of them as the authors and donors of those blessings. Farewell.

Louvain, 1 July

50

1844 / To Nikolaus von Diesbach   Basel, 6 July 1527

This preface to Erasmus' Latin translation, *Fragmentum commentariorum Origenis in evangelium secundum Matthaeum* (Basel: Froben 1527) was, in later editions, either shortened and readdressed to the 'pious reader' or omitted altogether.

Nikolaus von Diesbach had gained Erasmus' favour with regular gifts of the Burgundian wine that Erasmus believed to be a preventive cure for kidney stones (Epp 1342:504–9, 1353:284–99). He was dean of the cathedral chapter of Basel when Pope Leo x named him coadjutor bishop with the right of succession to Bishop Christoph von Utenheim. Despite Utenheim's dislike of him, Diesbach had administered the diocese and its lands well, struggling hard in a losing battle over the encroachment on the bishop's secular powers by the city council. On 21 February 1527 he had resigned his office after negotiating a financial settlement with the council (CEBR I 391).

TO THE REVEREND LORD NIKOLAUS VON DIESBACH, DEAN OF THE CHURCH OF BASEL, FROM ERASMUS OF ROTTERDAM, GREETING
So vast is the production of new books these days, honoured sir, that there is danger that this profusion may become an obstacle to learning the truth, especially since there is so much disagreement among them[1] that it all but calls 5

* * * * *

6 Ceres was the goddess of grain crops, Bacchus the god of wine.

1844
1 Erasmus expresses discontent not only with the many books that attacked his views but also with what he saw as his critics' lack of a sense of history. It is this latter aspect that he professes to address with his editions of the Fathers of the church (lines 14–39 below) and to justify by this letter. He will make the same complaint about new books in another dedicatory letter, Ep 1855:15–16.

to mind those battle lines sprung from the serpent's teeth which, the poets tell us, destroyed each other in hand-to-hand combat as soon as they emerged.[2] For just as the mime says, 'By too much discussion the truth is lost,'[3] so will excessive loquacity sooner obscure the truth than illuminate it.

But of this let each have his own opinion. For my part I certainly prefer to spend my time restoring the ancient writers, from the reading of whom we at least derive the profit of arriving at a truer understanding of Chrysostom, Jerome, and others like them of more recent times, recognizing the various sources from which they drew. In the same way no one adequately understands the poets and those who seasoned their writings, as it were, with the sayings of poets without being steeped in the poetry of Homer. One can have a more certain and more lively understanding of the commentaries of Thomas by reading the authors from whom he borrowed.[4] Among the early interpreters of Scripture pride of place is given to the Greek writer Origen[5] and the Latin writer Tertullian;[6] it is not certain which was the more learned, but certainly Origen was by far the more celebrated. Both suffered from the pre-eminence of their learning; or rather we suffered from our uncouthness in not knowing how to make good use of blessings placed at our disposal. We judge Origen according to the morals, usages, and beliefs of our times. If you wish to see the absurdity of this, reverse the scene and pretend that Origen lived in the present age, and that people like Scotus, Ockham, Thomas, Capreolus, Egidius, Gregory and the rest of that crowd lived in Origen's age;[7] then recall from that age to

* * * * *

2 Ovid *Metamorphoses* 3.1–140
3 Publilius Syrus in Aulus Gellius 17.14
4 The *Summa theologiae* of Thomas Aquinas (d 1274), an Italian-born Dominican, is generally considered to be the most successful exposition of the scholastic method of theology. Erasmus considered him the least offensive of all the scholastic doctors; see line 29 below; cf Rummel *Annotations* 77–81 and *passim*.
5 On Origen (c 185–c 254), prolific exegete, theologian, and spiritual writer in Alexandria, see André Godin *Erasme lecteur d'Origène* (Geneva 1986).
6 Tertullian (c 160–c 225), a North-African convert to Christianity before AD 195, wrote numerous apologetic, theological, polemical, and ascetical works in Latin, as well as a few in Greek. The rigorist strain in his thought and the opposition that it evoked in Carthage led him into the heightened eschatological expectations and ecstatic prophecy that marked the sectarian doctrine of Montanism.
7 In addition to Thomas Aquinas (n4 above), Erasmus singles out five of the 'crowd' of scholastics. John Duns Scotus (d 1308), a Franciscan, was known as 'Doctor subtilis.' His neologisms represented, for Erasmus, the nadir of scholastic theology; cf Allen Ep 337:316n. Medieval writers referred to William

this any one of them – let us say Thomas (who of this number falls less
below the standard of the ancients, except that Augustine, whom he fol-   30
lows in most respects, was bold enough to disagree with all the ancient
writers, both Greek and Latin).[8] Who would allow him to make the dogmas of the church conform to the precepts of Aristotle and Averroës?[9] But
now the church has passed through its infancy, its coming of age, its maturity, and perhaps its old age as well; and further, although there is such   35
a great variety of epochs and countries, yet some examine all writings by
the standards of the present age, thus showing themselves at one and the
same time ungrateful towards those worthy of their gratitude and hurtful
to themselves.

 There are many things that it would be the height of impiety to call into   40
question today, while in an earlier age inquiry into those same matters constituted religious fidelity. Origen supplied material for almost all the Greek
writers, investigating every single point, affirming nothing that was not expressly stated in Scripture and often repeating his favourite word, 'never.'
Yet he has had no other reward for such services than the greatest hatred,[10]   45

* * * * *

of Ockham (d 1349), an English-born Franciscan, as the 'Venerabilis inceptor.'
His philosophy has traditionally been known as Nominalism. Recent historians see him as the instigator of the *via moderna*. Johannes Capreolus, a Dominican (d 1444), was the leading late-medieval scholastic commentator on Thomas
Aquinas. Egidio Colonna (Giles of Rome, d 1316), a follower of Aquinas, was
known as 'Doctor fundatissimus.' Gregory of Rimini (d 1358), an Augustinian
canon, was a follower of Ockham.
 8 Aquinas habitually refers to Augustine as 'the theologian.' In his youth Augustine had been greatly impressed by Ciceronian style, but in book 3 of
the *Confessions* he sketches his reasons for preferring Christian literature. He
rarely quoted pagan writings prior to 397, when he began the *Confessions*, and
almost never afterwards. A more systematic elaboration of the same view is
found in *De doctrina christiana* books 2 and 3, where he deals with the classical
philosophical problem of ambiguity. His definitive farewell to Greek and Latin
philosophy is found in Ep 118 to Dioscorus (CSEL 34 665–98 / FCNT 18 262–94).
 9 Aquinas held great respect for Aristotle, whom he called 'the Philosopher.'
He employed many of Aristotle's works, rejecting only those aspects of his
thought that contradicted Christian dogma, for example, the eternity of the
world. Aquinas called Averroës (Ibn Rushd; d 1198), a Spanish-Arab philosopher, 'the Commentator' for his interpretation of Aristotle. He was disgraced
and exiled for accepting Aristotelian thought, which contradicted Muslim
dogma.
10 Some of Origen's teachings were condemned posthumously at the Second
Council of Constantinople (5 May–2 June 553). Erasmus may refer here to the
seven-year-long court suit brought by Noël Béda against Jacques Merlin, a

which would not be the case if we were willing to judge each person according to his own age. To my mind, in addition to admirable zeal in knowing thoroughly and commenting on Sacred Scripture, in which Origen has no rival, he possesses the peculiar quality of leaving in the mind of the gifted and well-trained reader various incentives and diverse material for medita- 50 tion, making him unequalled for the formation of the church preacher. Some writers, lighting upon a commonplace, dwell on it to the point of nausea, while he touches on one passage and immediately turns off in another direction. This he does particularly in the tomes that he destined for the private reading of learned men, where he included some rather abstruse matters 55 that would not be appropriate for general consumption. Origen intimates in more than one place that this was his intention.

To this class of writing belongs this work that we have on Matthew, as is evident not only in the titles found in the Greek manuscripts but also by the subject matter itself, whatever the reason for its having been divided 60 up into homilies by some unknown person. For you never see here the ending traditional to homilies, which always conclude with a doxology.[11] And of these commentaries, mutilated as we have them, ten volumes are missing, as is indicated by the titles in the Greek manuscript from which I have drawn the eleventh and part of the twelfth.[12] If only we could have restored 65 the whole work, eminently worthy of being read! I have inserted one or two pages of the original alongside the translated portion that has come down to us, for two reasons: first to demonstrate that what I give is a part of the work that we possess in truncated form, and second, so that the reader may be able to judge from this small sample how much freedom the translator, 70 whoever he was, permitted himself. Although I admit this to be uncertain, since there is no inscription, yet reasonable conjecture may conclude that it was Rufinus, who was not sufficiently skilled either in Greek or in Latin, even though we find him more lacking in fidelity than in learning.[13] For there is no author that he has touched whom he has not mutilated and cor- 75 rupted, whereas the chief commendation of a translator, as of a historian, is fidelity. He admits this to a certain degree in his prefaces, but he reveals more than he admits.

* * * * *

Paris theologian who published an *Apologia* for Origen; see Farge *Parti conservateur* 81–94.
11 Rendered in Greek
12 See n17 below.
13 Rufinus of Aquileia (c 345–410) translated a great part of Origen's works; see DTC 14 153–60; cf Ep 1835 n8. Erasmus shares St Jerome's negative view of Rufinus.

This addition to these splendid commentaries, therefore, whatever its
worth, I have deemed fitting to dedicate to you, Nikolaus, since you are so   80
avid for riches of this sort. I hope you will take in good part this outward
symbol of a grateful and mindful heart for your many services towards me.
You will elicit no less praise for your kindness if you accept a humble gift
with cheerful countenance than you have done hitherto by bestowing great
gifts without hesitation. You seem to have retired with this particularly in   85
mind, that amidst these baneful disturbances in human affairs you might
delight the mind in the quiet reading of sacred tomes, since it is impossible
to exercise the role of bishop, the storm being too much for the skill of
the helmsman. It is a sublime thing to perform diligently the function of a
bishop, if it is possible; but it is not the mark of a lesser spirit to relinquish   90
of one's own accord the high office of bishop rather than administer it. With
good reason St Jerome approves this maxim: 'It is nobler to have merited the
fullness of the priesthood than to have obtained it.'[14] But it is rarer still to
relinquish unbidden, with an equitable and willing spirit, the high position
which one has long occupied.[15] That spirit alone is suitable for exercising the   95
priesthood which refuses high rank if it can no longer be of service. If only
your church could have suffered no loss of its rituals just as you suffered
no diminution of honour after laying aside the trappings of your episcopal
office.[16]

   But I am keeping you too long from conversing with Origen; one more   100
word and I shall desist. The Greek manuscript was supplied to me by the
library of Ladenburg through the efforts of a man no less famous for his
precise knowledge of the law as for the nobility of his family and one who
has had great success in his studies, Wolfgang von Affenstein, vicar for
external affairs of the bishop of Worms.[17] It was not fitting that this fact be   105

* * * * *

14 Jerome's maxim 'minus est tenere sacerdotium quam mereri' (Ep 48 [49].4 CSEL
   54 349:9–10 / NPNF 2nd series 6 80) is remembered by Erasmus as 'pulchrius
   est summum sacerdotium promeruisse quam obtinuisse.'
15 Erasmus puts a more irenic interpretation on Diesbach's negotiations about
   his retirement than had actually prevailed.
16 Religious dissent, especially over the Eucharist and preaching, was already
   rampant in Basel. The city council tried to remain neutral in this respect, but
   used the unrest to take control of the local church. A month before Erasmus
   wrote this letter, it had abolished religious festivals and, in some churches,
   the mass itself (ER I 125–7). In 1529, when Catholic liturgy was completely set
   aside, Erasmus felt constrained to leave the city.
17 See Ep 1774 introduction. In one capacity or another Affenstein attended
   almost every major imperial diet and colloquy of his day; cf CEBR I 10–12.
   Ladenburg, the castle of Johann von Dalberg, an earlier bishop of Worms, is
   located on the Neckar below Heidelberg. PG 13 835 nn5–6 notwithstanding,

passed over in silence, for two reasons: first, that the reader might know to whom he owed a portion of this benefaction, and second, if anyone should wish to test the fidelity of the translator, he would know where to seek the exemplar.

Given at Basel, 6 July, in the year 1527   11

1845 / From Johannes a Mera   [?]

The manuscript of this letter and poem, autograph throughout, is in the Rehdiger Collection (MS 254 102) of the University Library in Wrocław. It was first published in Enthoven Ep 156. Allen, who professed to have 'no clue' as to date, place, or author, put it here to take the place left vacant when he redated Ep 2005, originally placed here as Ep 1845, to the year 1528.

We can speculate that the author was from Artois or Hainault, a region Beatus Rhenanus in 1543 called *tractatus Armoricarum inferior* (BRE 368). The Latin name a Mera (van der Meer, Meeren, etc in the vernacular) is common enough; but this author may in fact be the highly respected Bergen op Zoom burgher of that name whose home Erasmus (in 1532) recalled visiting 'about forty years ago' (Allen Ep 2700:124–30). See CEBR II 433.

TO THE MOST ILLUSTRIOUS HERO AND PRINCE OF THE MUSES,
DESIDERIUS ERASMUS OF ROTTERDAM, CELEBRATED LUMINARY
AND DEFENDER OF ANCIENT ELOQUENCE AND OF ALL GOOD
DISCIPLINES OF LEARNING, AN EPIGRAM OF JOHANNES A MERA

Hail, prince unvanquished of the Muses nine,   5
Hail, chiefest glory of the German race.
I'll not essay to sing a hero's praise
Or hymn his deeds, more fit for Homer's lyre.
Nor shall I try to add to Phoebus' light;
So great a task ill suits my feeble strength.   10
One thing I pray, take pity on my fate,
And give safe haven to my sinking craft.
For if your goodness fails me in my need,

* * * * *

the fourteenth-century paper manuscript Erasmus borrowed from there is the same one known as 'Holmiensis' to its 1668 Paris editor Daniel Huet. It is now Cambridge (Trinity College MS 194B 8 10); see *Origenes Matthäuserklärung* GCS *Origenes Werke* 10 ed Erich Klostermann (Leipzig 1935) vii–viii; cf Origène *Commentaire sur l'évangile selon Matthieu* SC 162 (Paris 1970) I 124. Cf Ep 1827 n2.

Tantalean hunger will consume my strength.
If you should ask the reason for my plight,   15
Or why my Muse lies idle in neglect,
A Zoïlus adept in Circe's art
Has dealt me poison dipped in Hydra's gore.
From that time on recurring lassitude
Has sapped my strength with its devouring tooth.   20
Pity my need, I pray; relieve my plight;
Counter my weakness with some healing drug.

A QUATRAIN OF THE SAME AUTHOR TO THE SAME MAN

The beech tree strikes the clouds with lofty crown,
Its spreading branches far and wide are sent;   25
Erasmus' lustrous fame outsoars the clouds,
And reaches to the radiant firmament.

ENVOI

As Jove in Heav'n, on earth Erasmus shines,
The first in glory of the wise divines.   30

I would have written several letters to you describing my more than tragic calamity, most learned Erasmus, but I was discouraged from this initiative both by the poverty of my talents and for fear of appearing utterly shameless in having the audacity to distract the Muses of so great a man, reserved for more abstruse and sacred studies, with my worthless rubbish.[1]   35

Swayed by these sentiments I have not wished to plead with you any further lest I appear to lack confidence in your generosity, which surpasses that of Gillus.[2] What need is there to make further appeal when you know and carry deep in your heart that passage of Lactantius Firmianus, book 6, chapter 18, where he writes: 'Therefore (to return to our previous discus-   40 sion), since the truth has been revealed by God to us alone and wisdom sent down from above, let us do what God, our enlightener, bids us; let us come to each other's aid and endure the labours of this life with mutual assistance.'[3]

* * * * *

1845
1 Literally 'Sicilian trash' (*Adagia* II iv 10)
2 Gillus, a native of Taranto, restored the Persian captives to Darius (Herodotus 3.138).
3 *Divinae institutiones* 6.18.2–3

Grace, peace, and eternal salvation be ours from God, greatest and best 45
Father, through Jesus Christ, who is our only true salvation. Amen.

1846 / From Clement VII to Alonso Manrique de Lara   Rome, 16 July 1527

This papal brief survives in two seventeenth-century copies (one at the Vatican
Archives and the other at the Vatican Library). It was first published by Allen.
At the urging of Juan de Vergara (Ep 1814:354–5) Erasmus had no doubt applied for something like this through friends at Rome. Although dated shortly
after Clement's deliverance from the sack of Rome, it was not dispatched by
the Spanish secretary until 1 August.

Clement VII (Giulio de' Medici), an illegitimate son of Giuliano de' Medici,
who was assassinated in the Pazzi conspiracy (1478), was brought up by
Lorenzo de' Medici and became attached to Lorenzo's son Giovanni, who,
in his first consistory as Pope Leo x, created Giulio a cardinal. After successful military and diplomatic achievements, he was elected pope in November
1523. In earlier responses to Erasmus' appeals, he silenced the Spanish theologian Diego López Zúñiga (Epp 1431–3, 1488) and the Louvain Carmelite
Nicolaas Baechem (Epp 1467, 1589, 1589A). He also invited Erasmus to Rome
(Epp 1408, 1417, 1418, 1422).

Alonso Manrique de Lara, an early advocate of the Hapsburg presence in
Spain, became archbishop of Seville and inquisitor-general in Spain in 1523.
As an adamant opponent of Lutherans and of the *alumbrados* (Christians claiming to have a mystical connection to God), he adopted coercive measures to
secure effective christianization of the *moriscos*, or converts from Islam, in Va-
lencia. He was one of the chief protectors of Erasmus in Spain, and the 1526
Spanish translation of Erasmus' *Enchiridion* was dedicated to him. He warned
superiors of religious orders against public attacks on Erasmus and, when
they submitted written accusations, convened the assembly of theologians at
Valladolid (27 June–13 August 1527) to examine Erasmus' orthodoxy. Its ad-
journment (for reasons of plague) without either censuring or approving Erasmus' works was considered a victory for Erasmians; but Manrique's fall from
favour in the imperial court between 1529 to 1533 and again in 1534 ended
his ability to ensure the safety of Erasmians in Spain. See CEBR II 373–5.

CLEMENT VII, POPE, TO THE VENERABLE BROTHER, THE
ARCHBISHOP OF SEVILLE, GRAND INQUISITOR INTO
HERETICAL DEPRAVITY
Venerable brother, greeting and apostolic blessing. Recently we have heard
with no little anguish of mind that some, in preaching the word of God 5
publicly in your land of Spain, affirm that the books of our beloved son

Erasmus, in which he strives to refute the writings of the heresiarch, Martin Luther, are not to be read. They give as their reason that, although the sovereign pontiff Leo x, our predecessor of happy memory, officially forbade anyone to read or have in his possession the writings of the said Martin, it happens that in the books of Erasmus statements first published by the same Martin are cited verbatim. We, therefore, having verified that Erasmus, famed for his learning and eloquence, has written many things deserving of the highest praise and continues to earn praise for his condemnation of the said Martin, and recognizing that men's judgments are often varied and diverse, have entrusted the following task to you as grand inquisitor in those lands, upon whom this duty chiefly devolves. It is our wish that, calling together four of the most learned authorities in sacred writings to be found in your regions, God-fearing men free of ambition and any suspicion of bias, you examine, appraise, and investigate with all zeal and trustworthiness the books of Erasmus in question; and those that you find by common consent to be approved you declare to be worthy of being read; but if you find some that do not reflect the gospel teachings and orthodox belief or depart from them, you declare that they should not be read. We lay these matters upon your conscience and theirs.

Yet since no one is so circumspect that he does not fall into error at one time or another,[1] and since some books of the Abbot Joachim were approved and others not,[2] and even St Augustine, illustrious Doctor of the church of God, retracted many of his teachings while still alive,[3] so then do you enjoin these preachers to say nothing henceforth that is not to the honour of Erasmus, a man of eloquence, learning, and untiring zeal. For honour and praise should be awarded to those who by virtue and industry have devoted themselves to the service of the human race.

Given at Rome in the Castel Sant'Angelo, July 1527, in the fourth year of our pontificate

Evangelista[4]

* * * * *

1846
1 Cf Ep 1864:104–7 and n16.
2 Several works of the Cistercian abbot Joachim of Flora (or Fiore, d c 1202) had been condemned by church councils, but others were published in the sixteenth century. Clement VII has a surprisingly benign view of him.
3 For Augustine *Retractationes* see Ep 1841 n16.
4 Evangelista Tarasconio of Parma (documented 1518–29), secretary to Popes Leo x and Clement VII, had drafted the former's letter approving Erasmus' New Testament in 1518 (Ep 864). He was the author of a four-volume manuscript *Commentarii calamitatum Italiae*, which he dedicated to Clement VII (CEBR III 309).

1847 / From Juan Luis Vives   Bruges, 20 July 1527

This letter, a response to Erasmus' Ep 1830, was first printed in Vives' *Opera* (Basel 1555).

VIVES TO ERASMUS

At long last a brief letter from you which, since it was so long awaited and desired, was all the more appreciated.[1] It gave me even greater pleasure because that recommendation or, I should say, lesson in style set you before my eyes in a double guise, as the learned teacher and the affectionate father.   5

Concerning the *Colloquies*, everything is fine. As far as I am concerned, the whole matter was fully settled long ago by your own doing,[2] I might say, which for me and many others carries greater weight and importance than the many carefully reasoned arguments of others. From the first I thought I should be governed by Cicero's words to Pompey: 'If I can-   10
not understand your objectives, I do not on that account think that you have acted without good reason.'[3] But what do I have to do with Lato-mus, and why do you mention him?[4] We have not lost our free will, as you maintained.[5]

You cannot imagine how much support I find in your suggestions and   15
how grateful I am to you for them, and I entreat you again and again to continue your advice whenever you see anything else of mine. I think there is no greater good fortune either in this kind of writing or in any other aspect of life than to have a friendly and prudent counsellor. Would that you did this more often!   20

But to make you cognizant of my reasons and motivations, you should know that I was worn out by the Augustine when I came to write that work, but I had determined at all costs to send something to the queen.[6] Conse-quently there was no time to polish the style, if indeed I could have pol-ished it, however much I tried. Then I took into account those for whom I   25

* * * * *

1847
1 Ep 1830. In Ep 1836:1–12, Vives had resorted to a rather strained *captatio bene-volentiae* to mask his disappointment at Erasmus' failure to write.
2 With his *De utilitate Colloquiorum*; see CWE 40 1095–1117, and cf Ep 1704:24–45.
3 *Ad Atticum* 8.11D.5
4 Jacobus Latomus; cf Ep 1830:9–10 and n4. This sentence is written in Greek.
5 See Ep 1830:12.
6 Vives' *Institutio foeminae christianae* (Antwerp: Michael Hillen 1524) was dedi-cated to Catherine of Aragon, queen of England. His commentary on the *City of God* was published two years earlier (Basel: Johann Froben 1522).

was writing, namely women, and especially the one to whom I was dedicating it. I thus adopted a plainer style so that it would be understood by the one for whom I was composing the work and whose approbation I sought. But Horace says correctly and shrewdly, 'Three guests have I': there is no style either so good that it does not displease someone or so bad that it does not please someone.[7] A good number of people have expressed their enthusiastic approval of the simple and unaffected style of that work;[8] at least that is what they said. But as for me, and it could not be otherwise, I should prefer that Erasmus give his approval, as an athlete would wish that of Hercules, rather than have the unanimous approval of the crowd. In future, therefore, I shall follow your advice.

I send you a little book of mine,[9] in which there are some things that are written with somewhat more care. Do write me your opinion of it when you have the time and leisure to do so. Now that I have transgressed the bounds of modesty, I may be allowed to be well and truly shameless. You say that I treat women rather harshly.[10] Do you, the man who brought Jerome back to us, say this? What is more ungovernable than a woman? If you relax the reins even a little, there will be no limit or restraint. But Cato will stand up for me and the *Lex Oppia* in the same speech.[11] I did not mention those things by way of example or hyperbole but because I think that is the way they should live; and doubtless they will if they keep in mind two things: that they are Christians and that each of them forms one person with her husband. On scabies, how much more can be found in Jerome and with much more explicitness![12] – if I understand correctly what you mean by *scabies*,

* * * * *

7 Cf Horace *Epistles* 2.2.61, where he states that if you invite as few as three guests you can be sure that someone will not like the menu (or will disagree with the conversation). Erasmus used a more extended quotation of this in an early letter to Guillaume Budé (Ep 480:80–1).

8 Cf Allen Ep 1306:12n.

9 Probably the *De Europae dissidiis* (Bruges: Hubert de Croock, December 1526), which contained a number of sections, each of which was dedicated to a different ruler or notable person.

10 Erasmus (Ep 1830:20) had accused Vives of being hard on wives (*uxores*), not on women in general.

11 The *Lex Oppia*, a sumptuary law especially regarding women's dress, was enacted in 215 BC. It was repealed in 195 BC, despite the protests of the Elder Cato; see Livy 34. 1–8.

12 Jerome uses the word *scabies* and its declined forms eight times in his works – all of them in commentaries on Scripture. Vives is justifying to Erasmus his use of the word itself, not his graphic description of his father-in-law's condition. See Ep 1830 n8.

for I do not quite follow you on this point or in your reference to the 'am- 50
phibious animal.'[13] You say that I take delight in mentioning my family, but
who does not? Does not Seneca? and Quintilian? and Caecilius?[14]

Tacitus even dedicated a sizeable volume to the life of his father-in-
law.[15] I mention my family three times in all, I think: my mother twice and
my mother-in-law once.[16] But I do not refer to her as my mother-in-law, 55
nor was she yet at that time. In her case I was motivated by truth, and in
my estimation it was a story worthy of being recorded, no less than many
other stories that have been handed down to history by other writers. In the
case of my mother I am justified by filial piety; and I related her story with
restraint, fearing to excite envy and keeping in mind that by nature men are 60
more willing to hear blame than praise. The association with Cicero drew
a smile of pleasure from me; I was immediately reminded also of the line
of Martial, 'That I write verse without the Muses or Apollo.'[17] Thus I have
two points of comparison.

So much for your letter. Now about affairs in Spain that concern you. 65
I recently sent you what Alonso Virués wrote me from there.[18] I think you
received it, for I entrusted the material to Erasmus Schets, who customarily delivers many other messages to you, as I am told.[19] If you did not
receive it, I would have to retell a long tale. The sum of it is as follows:
your name was reported by the mendicant friars to the grand inquisitor, 70
the archbishop of Seville;[20] the matter was deliberated and investigated during Lent. Nothing more was done there than hear the accusations made by
the friars against you. Orations were pronounced in your defence by two

* * * * *

13 Rendered in Greek; see Ep 1830:1.
14 Caius Plinius Caecilius Secundus, that is, Pliny the Younger
15 *De vita et moribus Iulii Agricolae* (AD 98), written in praise of his life and his
   administration in Britain
16 Vives' mother had died in 1509. A year after Vives wrote this letter, inquisitors
   in Spain ruled against the sincerity of her conversion and ordered her body
   exhumed and burnt. His mother-in-law was the wife of Vives' host in Bruges,
   Bernardo Valdaura. Cf Ep 1830 n9.
17 *Epigrams* 2.89.3, where he addresses a writer: 'The fact that you write poetry
   without inspiration may be turned to a compliment, for this is something you
   have in common with Cicero!'
18 With Ep 1836; but Virués letter to Vives is not extant.
19 A merchant and banker in Antwerp and frequent correspondent of Erasmus,
   he became Erasmus' faithful financial agent and friend.
20 Alonso Manrique de Lara; see Ep 1846 introduction.

Benedictines,[21] another by an Augustinian friar named Dionisio,[22] and there
was a semi-defence given by a Friar Minor by the name of Castillo.[23] So the   75
hearings were postponed until the day after the Ascension. For this session
the most learned and impartial theologians in all of Spain were appointed,
among them Virués,[24] a true Erasmian. I think Coronel, Lerma, and Dionisio were to be there,[25] men greatly devoted to your cause, that is, the cause
of true piety and learning. Bishops sent by the emperor will also be present.   80
    All of this I have explained to you in great detail. Afterwards I re-
ceived letters from Vergara, De Schepper, and Virués.[26] I have undertaken
to describe to you in this letter what pertains to you in theirs. Schepper had
this to say: 'Here the monks have declared war on Erasmus with intense animosity. They are expending every effort and exercising every vigilance to   85
ensure that the reading of all of Erasmus' books will be forbidden in Spain.
In the meantime several of us scholars are opposing them and plying the
chancellor with prayers that he assume the defence of this most learned and
excellent man; and indeed he does, but that function belongs to others. Pre-
siding over the inquisition (as it is called) is the most reverend archbishop of   90
Seville, a good man, assuredly, and he quelled their fury for a time; but he
cannot satisfy everyone, and their rage is something to behold! It has been
several days since they ceased to have public reading in the convents so that
each one could cobble together something against Erasmus. They have produced some articles that they call heretical or schismatic. Coronel is keeping   95

* * * * *

21 See Ep 1814 n33. That letter mentions only one Benedictine speaking in favour
   of Erasmus; see n24 below.
22 Dionisio Vázquez, of Toledo; see Ep 1814 n34. Contrary to Vives' report (lines
   78–9), Dionisio Vázquez was not among the thirty-three theologians and bishops who spoke at the Valladolid conference listed in Beltrán de Heredia *Cartulario* VI 23–4.
23 Francisco Castillo OFM (Ep 1814 n32). Vives' view contradicts that of Luis de
   Carvajal, who reported that Castillo had drawn up the nineteen allegedly
   heretical propositions from Erasmus' writings that stirred up the situation in
   Spain.
24 Alonso, not his brother Jerónimo; see Epp 1684 introduction, 1838, 1839.
25 On Luis Núñez Coronel, secretary to Alonso Manrique de Lara, see Epp 1814
   n64, 1836 n15; on Pedro de Lerma, chancellor of the University of Alcalá, cf
   Ep 1836 n16; on Dionisio, see n22 above.
26 For this letter from Juan de Vergara see CWE 12 533–4 and lines 102–13 below.
   Cornelis De Schepper of Nieuwpoort, an experienced diplomat, was now councillor and secretary of Charles V and confidant of Chancellor Mercurino di Gattinara (CEBR III 218–20). Neither his letter nor that of Virués is extant.

a close watch on things; the bishop of the Canary Islands is present along
with several others.[27] In the meantime we are distressed at how little we can
do in this sad state of affairs, for grave danger would immediately threaten
those bold enough to take action. But why do I tell this to you, a Spaniard,
who are well acquainted with such tyranny. I do not wish therefore to detain   100
you any longer; for Louis, lord of Praet,[28] will give you a full account.'

While De Schepper's letter is from the month of February, Vergara's
letter is more recent, dated 12 April.[29] He writes to this effect: 'Recently our
monks have launched a conspiracy against Erasmus – not all of them, of
course, but the majority. The less a monastic order depends on begging, the   105
less hostile it is to him. The case has been referred to the commission. So
far at least, the results have been most favourable to Erasmus. My prince
has undertaken to do his utmost to protect him.[30] The emperor is openly
favourable; the commissioners themselves are also on his side, as are all
good men. Since his enemies see they will gain nothing from this contro-   110
versy except general unpopularity, they are now beginning to lose interest,
and in my opinion would gladly undo what has been done if this could be
accomplished to the general satisfaction of everyone.'

Virués enclosed all these letters in the packet sent to me to be forwarded to you, so that you would understand that he is not one to be sus-   115
pected of not devoting himself to you in good faith, or of defending your
cause with the purpose of acting in collusion with your opponents. All those
who arrive from Spain report that he has exposed himself to terrible quarrels with the friars for your sake, and there is no one who has embraced or
defended your doctrine with more openness and sincerity. In addition, he is   120
a preacher of the first rank, as they say, and a man of great moral integrity
and blameless life, a man most worthy of your personal acquaintance and

* * * * *

27 Luis Núñez Cabeza de Vaca of Jaén (c 1465–12 December 1550), had tutored
   the future Charles v and later became a member of his imperial council. He
   served as vice-president of the inquisitorial assembly at Valladolid. Bishop
   of the Canaries since October 1523, he was transferred to Salamanca in 1530
   and to Palencia in 1536 (CEBR III 20–1). The approximation of his episcopal title here with the name of Luis Coronel has led some authors mistakenly to
   identify the two.
28 Louis of Flanders (Lodewijk van Praat or Praet), was a descendant of the counts
   of Flanders. A seasoned diplomat in the service of Charles v, he was a friend
   and patron of many scholars. Erasmus would send him greetings in 1528 (Ep
   1966) and praise him in a dedicatory preface (Ep 2093); cf CEBR II 41–2.
29 See n26 above.
30 Vergara was secretary to Alonso de Fonseca, archbishop of Toledo.

friendship and, as our friend[31] is given to remark, of being entered into the calendar of your friends – the most select and qualified ones, I mean – and there given a place of honour. He is moved to pay you homage and de-   125 fend and extol you with all his skill for no other reason or advantage than that he considers your doctrine to be derived from the true and pure fount of Christian piety. Do not disregard, I beseech you, such advocates of that noblest of causes that you have undertaken.

Very recently a letter arrived from Alvaro, the agent who used to   130 send you your pension from England.[32] He has married a woman from Burgos. He writes that according to popular hopes and opinions there will be a pronouncement made within a fortnight in your favour and against the friars,[33] and that those who favour your teaching have formally re- quested the inquisitor to inquire into the works of Thomas Aquinas and   135 Scotus.[34] They wish that their opinion be submitted to examination to see if they contain anything contrary to Sacred Scripture or the ancient writ- ers of our religion. They demand that a formal decision be given in the matter and that anything judged as heretical be condemned. If I learn more certain and precise details about this from others, I shall let you   140 know.

Together with this Alvaro sent me a letter of Virués written in Spanish to a certain Friar Minor of great authority and renown in Spain.[35] That letter is being circulated throughout Spain and read with universal approval; it is very elegantly written in our language. I have translated it into Latin merely   145 that you may understand it.

Best greetings, my teacher and father
Bruges, the feast of St Margaret, 1527

* * * * *

31 Allen Ep 1847:119n suggests Guillaume Budé, who uses the expression 'cal- endar of friends' in his letters to Vives.
32 Alvaro de Castro and his brother Luis were Spanish merchants living in Lon- don. As a business associate of Erasmus Schets Alvaro collected Erasmus' Eng- lish annuity and sent it to Schets. He also provided hospitality for Vives in England. See CEBR I 281–2.
33 'and against the friars' is rendered in Greek.
34 Three weeks later (14 August 1527), in a letter to Juan de Vergara, Vives ex- pressed his horror at this movement of certain Spanish Erasmians to submit Thomas Aquinas and Duns Scotus to the Inquisition at the same time and in the same manner as Erasmus. See CWE 12 534–5 and n1; see also Bataillon *Erasme* (1991) I 284.
35 The letter sent by Alvaro (n32 above), written by Alonso Ruiz de Virués to the guardian of the convent of Alcalá, is not extant; see Ep 1838 nn10–11.

1848 / From Marcus Laurinus   Bruges, 20 July 1527

Autograph throughout, this letter (Ep 71 in Förstemann-Günther) was in the
Burscher Collection in the University Library at Leipzig (on which see Ep 1254
introduction). Erasmus' reply is Ep 1871.

Erasmus claimed Marcus Laurinus (CEBR II 307–8) as an acquaintance since
childhood (Ep 1512). He was dean of the chapter of St Donatian of Bruges since
1519. Although not a scholar himself, his home was a meeting place for numerous humanists, politicians, diplomats, and other dignitaries. His lack of diligence in attending to Erasmus' Courtrai benefice, however, induced Erasmus
to transfer this duty to the Antwerp banker Erasmus Schets.

Best of greetings. Your letter,[1] testifying to your affection for me, afforded
me great pleasure, most learned Erasmus. Would that you could feel free
to come back to us![2] At Bruges you would find Marcus' home, table, and
whatever the Lord has lavished upon him shared in common with Erasmus.
I should wish to see the day when it will once more be granted that we live   5
in the same house. I know not if that can be hoped for. Flanders will not be
so fortunate as to be revisited by Erasmus. Certain it is that many people
miss you. You have become more popular than usual with our monks; their
tongues have taken a turn for the better. Only in Louvain are there some who
murmur, but they would be silenced by your presence. Those who wished   10
ill to Erasmus, powerless even when alive, are dead.[3] Do what seems to be
in your best interests. You cannot satisfy everyone's desires.

The money I received from Jan de Hondt I gave partly to Erasmus
Schets and partly to your servant.[4] Since there were many annuities that
had come due, it amounted to quite a bit of money. Notes in the hand   15
of Jan de Hondt give an account of every piece of gold and silver, which
shows how faithfully all the money was set aside. Your friend Lieven is in

* * * * *

1848
1 Not extant
2 In 1523 Erasmus had discussed at great length with Laurinus his thoughts
  about moving (Ep 1342:293–649).
3 Although the Carmelite Nicolaas Baechem (Egmondanus) was now dead, both
  Jacobus Latomus and Frans Titelmans were still living in Louvain.
4 On this transaction see Ep 1849 from Schets. Erasmus drew an annuity from a
  Courtrai benefice settled on de Hondt, a Flemish cleric, by Pierre Barbier; see
  Ep 1862 introduction. On Nicolaas Kan of Amsterdam, Erasmus' messenger,
  see Ep 1832 introduction.

Paris.[5] I am sure you will have a letter from him. I thank you for remembering him in your will.[6] He desires that you remain alive for a long time; of that I am certain. According to news received from Bruges, Master Gian   20
Matteo, the former datary, died in Rome.[7] The pope has been restored to his see in Rome; he has resumed the management and control of spiritual concerns but has been deprived of the secular powers that he exercised there in Caesar's name. You will have more complete and more accurate information, since you are closer to Rome.
                                                                              25
My brother, the lord of Watervliet, sends his greetings.[8] He said to me today that if you would entrust to him in writing the care of the payment of the imperial pension, he will be completely at your service. And your trust in him will not be in vain. He enjoys great favour with the treasurer, whose daughter he married.[9] The treasurer is well disposed towards you also: there   30
is no one at court who speaks of you with more loyalty. Shortly, the court will be in Bruges. I will 'angle' for whatever news I can find. If there is any hope, you will hear from me. In the meantime write a nice long letter to my brother. He is enchanted by your letters and is your strongest champion. In debate he is invincible; he fears no one and is very free with his tongue. Your   35
interests could not be handled more promptly by anyone else. Farewell. The two widows, my sisters,[10] are possessed with great longing to see you and wish you good health. Bruges, 20 July 1527.

                    * * * * *

   5 Lieven Algoet, originally recommended to Erasmus by Laurinus in 1519, had
     regularly served Erasmus as a courier until 1525. He went to Paris to study
     medicine but returned to the Netherlands, apparently without a licence to
     practise.
   6 Erasmus did not in fact list Algoet in his first will, 27 January 1527 (CWE 12
     538–50); but in 1535 he instructed Erasmus Schets to give Algoet a large sum
     of money to help him in his serious financial difficulties (Allen Epp 3028:1–7,
     3042:3–9).
   7 A false rumour. Gian Matteo Giberti, bishop of Verona since 1524 and a re-
     cent patron of Lieven Algoet, was captured and held hostage during the sack
     of Rome; as one of the instigators of the anti-imperial League of Cognac, he
     had been threatened with execution. After escaping, he retired to his dio-
     cese, wrote commentaries on Scripture and edited patristic texts, and became
     a model for Catholic reform. He died in 1543 (CEBR II 94–6).
   8 Matthias Laurinus, Marcus' elder brother, was lord of Watervliet and several
     times treasurer and burgomaster of the free district of Bruges (CEBR II 308–9).
   9 Jean Ruffault of Lille (1471–1546) had been imperial general treasurer since
     1515. His daughter Françoise married Matthias Laurinus.
  10 Mentioned, but not named, in Epp 1342 and 1458

Master Jan de Hondt did not give me the note for the Rhenish florins. He merely referred to them in a letter, since the sum of money was prac- 40 tically unchanged. There are forty-one gold florins and one Philippus (the value of the Rhenish florin was thirty-one stuivers, the value of the Philippus 27 stuivers) and one groot.[11] To that was added three groots, making the sum of sixty-five florins.[12]

Your Lordship's most dutiful servant, Marcus Laurinus, priest.   45

To the most learned master, master Erasmus of Rotterdam, most eminent professor of sacred theology, in Basel

1849 / From Erasmus Schets   Antwerp, 22 July 1527

Autograph throughout, the original manuscript of this letter is in the Öffentliche Bibliothek of the University of Basel, MS Scheti Epistolae 12.

Erasmus Schets was a prominent Antwerp merchant and banker who also dealt in metals and supplied guns and munitions to the Netherlandish government. He admired Erasmus openly, and volunteered his financial services. Erasmus accepted immediately and gave Schets his complete trust and friendship. More than seventy letters between them, dating from 1525 until Erasmus' death in 1536, are extant. See CEBR III 220–1.

†

I wrote to you a while ago about how much trouble I had before I was able to extract from the lord dean of St Donatian's the money he had received in your name from Jan de Hondt for the Courtrai pension.[1] He had received four pensions in all, and up to now he has paid me only one of them. Your

* * * * *

11 On Rhenish gold florins, sometimes called florins of the Four Imperial Electors, which had become the chief medium of exchange in the eastern Low Countries as well as in the Rhineland and southern Germany, on the gold florin of St Philip (Philippus florin), struck from 1496, and for an explanation of the term *stuiver* and the value of the Rhenish florin in *stuivers*, see Ep 1837 nn12–13. The *groot* or *gros* of Flanders and of Brabant was the silver coin that constituted the base or 'link money' of the Flemish and Brabantine money-of-account known as the *pond groot* or *livre gros*. After the Burgundian monetary reform of 1433–5 the relationship between the two was fixed at the ratio of 1 *pond groot* Flemish = 1.5 *pond groot* Brabant. See CWE 1 322–3, 328, 347 (Appendix E); CWE 12 566–91, 655–6 (Table 4C).
12 This reckoning is the same as that of Erasmus Schets in Ep 1849:7–22; cf n8.

1849
1 See Epp 1783 from Schets and 1848 from Marcus Laurinus.

servant went to see him in Bruges. Induced by a sense of shame, I believe, he   5
gave him the remaining three pensions,[2] but in debased currency, resulting
in a considerable financial loss to you. These pensions should have been
worth two hundred sixty florins at the current exchange, but since they were
withheld instead of being paid out, as a result of the reduction in value that
took place there some time ago, the settlement came to two hundred twenty-   10
nine florins and four stuivers.[3] This loss is owed to the delay of Laurinus,
who held on to your money for such a long time. If he had transferred the
funds to you earlier, you would not have suffered such a loss. Henceforth
write to Jan de Hondt not to deliver your pension money to anyone except
the one whom I shall designate,[4] and I shall see to it that the money reaches   15
you more quickly and still intact.

Furthermore, this same servant of yours received from the above-
mentioned Jan de Hondt a fifth pension of sixty-five florins in non-debased
currency.[5] I received this entire amount from your servant, the bearer of
this letter, as well as the remaining amounts included in the receipt I gave   20
him. I shall set this sum aside for the Frankfurt fair and I shall deliver it to
Froben or to his son,[6] for I think that is what you wish.

The book dedicated to the king of Portugal and sent to him as a gift
was richly embellished and delivered to him personally.[7] You have amply

* * * * *

2 Laurinus makes no mention in Ep 1848 of giving Nikolaas Kan these three
  pensions.
3 This sum is in terms of the Burgundian-Hapsburg florin money-of-account
  (see Ep 1837 n12), in which the *stuiver* represents the shilling. This sum would
  have been worth 229.2 × 40d = 9168d = £38 4s 0d *groot* Flemish (equal to 833.45
  days wages for an Antwerp master mason, now at 11d *groot* Flemish per day).
4 Erasmus complied with this instruction; see Ep 1862.
5 If these are Rhenish florins – by far the most likely assumption – and if Erasmus
  Schets was then correct in providing an exchange rate of 56d per florin (see
  n8 below), this sum would have been worth £15 3s 4d (£15.1667) *groot* Flemish (331 days wages for an Antwerp master mason, now at 11d *groot* Flemish
  per day); or, with the prevailing exchange rates in England (40d) and France
  (£1.500), £10 16s 8d (£10.8333) sterling (325 days wages for a London master
  mason, still at 8d sterling per day); and 97 *livres* 10 *sols tournois* (£97.500). See
  CWE 12 650 (Table 3D), which indicates that the value of the Rhenish florin had
  risen from 56d *groot* Flemish in 1520 to 59d *groot* after 1526. Note also that this
  is the same value mentioned by Laurinus (Ep 1848:44).
6 Hieronymus Froben, the elder of Johann Froben's two sons
7 Translations from St John Chrysostom, made from a manuscript recently acquired by Erasmus (cf Epp 1705, 1769, 1801) and printed as *Chrysostomi lucubrationes* (Basel: Froben, March 1527), carried a dedicatory letter to King John
  III of Portugal (Ep 1800).

praised the excellence of that king. I hope your efforts have not been in vain.   25
When I come upon some news from this quarter, you will be kept informed.

Farewell, Master Erasmus.

From Antwerp, 22 July 1527

Your most devoted friend Erasmus Schets

I gave your servant Nicolaas Kan fifteen gold florins, which are worth   30
twenty-one florins at the current rate of exchange,[8] to purchase some linen
for your needs and also for his journey. He himself will give you an account
of the money.

†

To the eminent and most learned professor of sacred letters, Master
Erasmus of Rotterdam, at Basel   35

1850 / From Frans van Cranevelt   Mechelen, 26 July 1527

> Autograph throughout, this letter (Ep 72 in Förstemann-Günther) was in the
> Burscher Collection of the University Library of Leipzig (on which see Ep 1254
> introduction).
>
>   On Frans van Cranevelt, see Epp 1145 introduction, 1546; cf Henry de
> Vocht *Literae virorum eruditorum ad Franciscum Craneveldium, 1522–1528* (Lou-
> vain 1928) xxxiii–lxx.

CRANEVELT TO ERASMUS OF ROTTERDAM

When I received a letter from More through your servant,[1] I could not refrain
from writing you a few words, since it was through your instrumentality
that I have been blessed with such a great friend. I hear that he has arrived in
Calais with the cardinal to make a visit to France.[2] May God in his goodness   5

* * * * *

8 If, at the current rate of exchange, 15 gold Rhenish florins were worth 21
  florins in the Burgundian-Hapsburg florin money-of-account, then the gold
  florins were worth 21 × 40 = 840d *groot* Flemish; and thus each gold florin was
  worth 840/15 = 56d *groot* or 28 *stuivers*. See Epp 1837 nn12–13 and 1848 n11;
  cf Allen Ep 1849:30n, CWE 12 650 (Table 3D), CWE 1 347 (Appendix E).

1850
1 More's letter was dated 14 July from Calais; see Elizabeth Frances Rogers *The
  Correspondence of Sir Thomas More* (Princeton 1947) Ep 155, and Henry de Vocht
  Litterae ad Craneveldium Ep 242. The introduction to the latter contains a long
  digression on the vicissitudes of Erasmus' relations with Nicolaas Kan. Kan
  had recently returned from England; see Epp 1832, 1849.
2 Wolsey landed at Calais on 11 July. He would meet King Francis I at Amiens
  on 4 August.

and omnipotence grant that this embassy bring honour to More and prove
salutary to our country. Some suspect that we will get the worst of it in the
end and that Flanders is destined to become a common battleground. But
let such a suspicion be far from our minds concerning a king who has such
close family ties with the emperor.[3] And God forbid that the royal marriage   10
should now be made null and void after so many years of legal wedlock, and
that whom God has joined together man should put asunder.[4] But these times
seem to be so full of tragedies! On every side occasions for violent outbreaks
arise, so that if these days are not shortened 'no flesh would survive.'[5]

    I heard from Albert Pigge about what has been perpetrated in Rome   15
by the soldiery.[6] I consoled him as best I could in these misfortunes. He
has come to learn for himself in these vicissitudes of fortune the wisdom of
those Greek senarii[7] that have passed into proverb:

> Learning is man's fairest gift;
> Wisdom far surpasses wealth.[8]   20

I do not doubt but that much of what is reported these days brings profound
displeasure to you and all men of worth. But all this is the consequence of
war once it has begun. The words spoken by Caesar in Lucan are not far
from the truth in this respect:

> To deny the armed his due   25
> Is to surrender all.[9]

In a brief moment the glory of such a great city and of such a great pontiff[10]
has sunk low, to the great joy of the Turks, as one might imagine. The path to

* * * * *

3 Henry VIII's queen consort, Catherine of Aragon, was the aunt of Emperor
  Charles V.
4 Matt 19:6, Mark 10:9. Foremost on Wolsey's agenda in meeting Francis I was
  support for Henry VIII's desire to have his marriage with Catherine annulled.
  Wolsey and Henry will attempt to show that Henry had not been joined in a
  valid marriage to Catherine. See Guy Bedouelle Le 'divorce' du roi Henri VIII:
  Etudes et documents (Geneva 1987).
5 Matt 24:22, rendered in Greek
6 For the sack of Rome see Ep 1831 n7. On Pigge, a Dutch theologian who served
  both Adrian VI and Clement VII as chamberlain, see CEBR III 84–5.
7 Verse consisting of six feet, each of which is either an iambus or some foot
  which the law of the verse permits to be substituted; an iambic trimeter
8 Menander Sententiae 275, 482
9 Bellum civile 1.348–9
10 Clement VII

an even greater victory is open to them after these events,[11] unless Christian
princes finally lay aside their animosities and rivalries and begin to live up   30
to their name; but these things are in the hands of God.[12] Farewell and love
me, as you do. Robbyns is in good health save that he suffers from gout,
which keeps him from his promenade.[13]

    Again farewell. Mechelen, 26 July in the year 1527[14]

    Your most devoted Frans   35

    To the illustrious and most learned Master Erasmus of Rotterdam, the-
ologian, at Basel

1851 / From Jan Becker of Borsele   Louvain, 28 July 1527

The autograph of this letter was in the Burscher Collection in the University
Library in Leipzig (on which see Ep 1254 introduction). It was first printed as
Ep 73 in Förstemann-Günther who, reading *quintus idus augustus* where Allen
read *quintus k[a]l[enda]s augustus*, dated it 9 August 1527; it is answered by Ep
1860.

    Becker and Erasmus had become friends at Louvain in 1502–3. A correspon-
dence between them is extant from 1514 (cf Ep 291 introduction, where he is
mistakenly said to be a kinsman of Anna van Borssele). He refused the post
of first Latin instructor at the Collegium Trilingue, preferring to tutor students privately. He encouraged Erasmus to produce a manual on preaching
and to arrange his published letters chronologically; see Epp 932, 952, 1321,
1787; CEBR I 115–16.

Fond greetings. Your letter brought me great delight, most learned master, even though it was brief – as it had to be, considering the pressures
of your occupations in matters of great concern. It at least gave me the as-
surance that you were in good health and that you were still mindful of
your humble friend of former days despite his continued silence of three   5
years, which should have merited your just rebuke, as I would be the first to

* * * * *

11 Just a year earlier, Turkish forces had defeated Hungarian and imperial forces
    at Mohács.
12 'but . . . God' is rendered in Greek.
13 Jan Robbyns, a Flemish cleric, was influential in the affairs of the Collegium
    Trilingue in Louvain. Erasmus wrote him three times about professorial ap-
    pointments there (Epp 805, 1046, 1435). One of Robbyns' replies is extant, Ep
    1457. See CEBR III 165–6.
14 The year-date is rendered in Greek.

confess, rather than such a friendly and cajoling letter.[1] But that you should
suspect that my friendship, or rather my love and devotion for you, had
cooled, because of an incident you learned of in a letter from Dorp concerning someone who babbled on against you for a full hour in his pres-   10
ence in an attempt to win me away from your cause – such a thought leaves
me greatly troubled.[2] Surely you could not believe that I, your humble follower and disciple, could be so induced and prevailed upon by the passing
detractions of an insignificant babbler that I would cease to love, honour,
and respect you who are so deserving of my gratitude – and not of mine   15
alone but of that of humane learning, to which I am and have always been
devoted, and of the Christian faith and of all those engaged in the study
of the Sacred Scriptures, among whom I wish to be numbered. If I were
thus to forsake Erasmus, who has, I repeat, such a claim to the gratitude
of all mankind that there is no one by whom he should not be cherished,   20
then I should be the most ungrateful man alive. Not even if the most vehement and impassioned orations of Demosthenes and Cicero were brought
together and combined into one would I retreat even one step from my love
for you. What would be less worthy of a man than that I should not bear the
strongest love for one whose kindnesses I have enjoyed for twenty years   25
without interruption, offered at great sacrifice and in the face of the envy
of detractors, freely and with no reward but thanks? Be assured, therefore,
my dear Erasmus, that at no time would I allow myself to desist from my
love for you.

But enough of this display of words that are more a crude outpouring   30
of emotion than a model of polished style. In any case I am grateful that
you promise to do what I advised, namely to arrange your letters, which are
so numerous and treat of so many different subjects, in the order in which
you wrote them.[3] I also beg of you (to continue in my impudence now that
I have begun) that you do not postpone your promise as you did in the case   35

* * * * *

1851
1 Erasmus' letter is not extant but surely answered Ep 1787.
2 The letter from Dorp is not extant, and this incident remains obscure. Maarten
  van Dorp was Becker's closest neighbour (Ep 1321:22). For another mention of
  this letter, see Ep 1860:1–2.
3 See Ep 1787 n1. Although Erasmus accepted the idea, the task proved too
  burdensome in view of his migration to Freiburg. Thus, in reworking *Epistolae
  ad diversos* (Basel: Froben 1521) to produce the *Opus epistolarum* (Basel: Froben
  1529), he had to content himself with adding year-dates to many of the early
  letters and with minimal revisions of the texts. See Allen I 596 and the preface
  to the *Opus epistolarum* (Ep 2203).

of the *Concionandi ratio*, which you promised eight years ago but which, to my knowledge, you still have not produced.[4]

I am now living in Louvain, as you know, and shall remain here, in all likelihood, for the next two years, with the elder son of the lord of Beveren.[5] When you have time I ask that you remember your Borsele, if at all possible, 40 when you write to your numerous friends here or to me, which I dare not ask of you with any insistence.

Farewell, most respected of teachers.

Louvain, 28 July 1527

Jan of Borsele, your most devoted and humble client   4[5]

To Erasmus of Rotterdam, peerless high priest of sacred and profane learning, most respected of teachers. In Basel

1852 / From Claude-Louis Alardet   Chambéry, 3 August [1527]

The Alardet family had strong connections with the diocese of Geneva and the duchy of Savoy. Amblard Alardet was secretary to Duke Charles II of Savoy and was a colleague of Joachim Zasius (CEBR III 468). His brother Claude-Louis, unable after 1536 to hold his benefices in the reformed city of Geneva, served in the duke's household in a number of capacities, including tutoring the duke's son (the future Duke Emmanuel Philibert), conspiring against the French, and participating in a plan to assassinate Calvin that failed to gain the approval of the duke. He became bishop of Lausanne in 1560, but was forced to reside in Chambéry until his death in 1565.

The manuscript preserved in the Rehdiger Collection (MS 254 3) in the University Library, Wrocław, is an original autograph throughout. It was first published in LB III-2 1720–2 *Appendix epistolarum* no 341. It will be answered indirectly by Erasmus' Ep 1886 to Duke Charles and directly by Ep 1892.

I do not think I need take the trouble, most learned Erasmus, to absolve myself from the suspicion of ambition or to make excuses for my temerity in daring to disturb you with my trivia – I, one brought up amidst rocks and

* * * * *

4 *Ecclesiastes sive de ratione concionandi*, Erasmus' treatise on preaching, finally appeared in 1535; cf Ep 1804 n28.
5 Maximilian II of Burgundy, the pupil of Jan Becker, was the second of the four sons of Adolph of Burgundy; upon the death of his elder brother late this same year, he had become his father's heir. See Ep 1859 introduction. On Adolph of Burgundy, lord of Flushing, Veere, and Beveren, see Ep 1859 n1.

ridges, an insignificant creature with less than average learning, addressing
himself to Erasmus, a god among mortal men. While I am aware that con-   5
siderable renown redounds to all those to whom you have not begrudged
even the briefest of notes, you must not think that I was so attracted by
this easy road to fame that I should put pen to paper under the influence
of some ill-considered ambition rather than in the cause of fraternal charity. If that were the case I should deservedly be thought to have exceeded   10
the bounds of modesty. I write to you, therefore, not to find favour with the
public some day because as a young man two years past his fifteenth year
I wrote thrice to Erasmus, glorious hero, whose fame transcends the highest heaven.[1] (What else would that be but to betray my imprudence com-
pounded by impudence?) Instead I give assistance to my brother, Amblard   15
Alardet, who serves as secretary of the illustrious Charles, duke of Savoy.[2]
Since the affairs of the court scarcely leave him time to scratch his ears, as
they say,[3] I could not refuse him the tiny favour of a day's work. I am bidden to depict for you in his true colours a certain cowled preacher called
Gachi.[4] This will not be new to you, since my brother has already given you   20
an ample description of his unbearable loquacity in a previous letter, but
my portrayal will be much more accurate, since no one knows him better
than I. Thus I shall describe the man to you with such frankness that the
facts themselves will leave no room for falsehood.

Jean Gachi is one of those professors of that most holy religious or-   25
der whom the ignorant throng call by the falsest of names sacred theologians and masters. According to his rule of life he is a sandalled Franciscan,[5]
but he is also very experienced in the ways of the world. He is a man of
great physical stature and of very comely appearance; as for his spirit, he is
quite pretentious, because through his fluency in the vernacular tongue he   30

* * * * *

1852
1 Virgil *Aeneid* 1.379
2 Apart from his position as secretary to Duke Charles II, little is known of
  Amblard. He apparently wrote a letter to Erasmus that is not extant (line 21
  below); cf CEBR I 21.
3 *Adagia* II iii 15
4 Jean Gachi, a respected Franciscan who had already written against Luther
  and now began to inveigh against Erasmus in his sermons; see Ep 1891
  introduction.
5 That is, a member of the Observant, or reformed branch, not the Conven-
  tual Franciscans. The branch known as 'Discalced' was organized only in the
  seventeenth century.

has easily won for himself the favour of the motley crowd in popular sermons. His knowledge of literature is so scant that he knows nothing beyond
the tricks of sophistry and his baggage of theological quibbles. But when
he delivers his harangues in the churches, great God immortal! what arguments, what subtleties, what syllogisms does he not marshall to attack the
writings of Erasmus! With how many counts of impiety does he charge you!
how many insipid remarks, idiotic lies, and venomous calumnies (and slander is a powerful weapon) he hurls against you when you are not present
to defend yourself!

'But,' you will ask, 'whom can I rely on there to avenge the wrongs
done to me?' The response is simple. My brother, Amblard Alardet, was the
first to descend into the arena to defend your cause staunchly against such a
dull-witted theologian, as might be expected from one whose chief concern
it has been to proclaim your praises, Erasmus, to glorify you alone, to extol
aloud and acclaim with full voice in public and in private your genius, your
learning, your eloquence in the Greek and Latin tongues. Subsequently, I
expended my ungrudging efforts, whatever their worth, in the cause and
engaged the savage beast in combat to demonstrate my feelings for you to
those who profess interest in humane letters. But I had little success in my
duel with this madman who could vie with twenty hand-picked women in
garrulity. Therefore we thought we should resort immediately to the sheet
anchor[6] and forewarn Erasmus to restrain this scandalmonger and persistent blabberer with a pointed and lengthy letter to show him that he is not
dealing with some toothless coward. Or in a letter you might bring the man
to the attention of our illustrious prince and of the assembly of Chambéry[7]
in such a way that Gachi will finally understand that he had no right to permit himself the conduct he has pursued up to now, and so that he will cease
being a nuisance to the cause of higher learning.

These are the reports that the two Alardets din into your ears, most
learned Erasmus, so that you may not be unaware that this rocky land of
Savoy, bristling with rough crags, also nourishes men who with sincere and
undying respect revere and honour Erasmus and defend your good name
with as much good judgment as dedicated commitment. Farewell.

Chambéry, 3 August 1527

Unreservedly yours, Louis Alardet

To the eminent theologian Erasmus of Rotterdam. In Basel

* * * * *

6 *Adagia* i i 24. Sailors called the biggest and most effective anchor the 'sheet
  anchor,' in Latin *sacra anchora*.
7 The capital city of the duchy of Savoy

1853 / To the Reader   [Basel, c August 1527]

This is the preface to Erasmus' *Hyperaspistes liber secundus adversus librum Martini Lutheri cui titulum fecit Servum arbitrium* (Basel: Johann Froben, c August 1527). It is the second book of his answer to Luther's *The Enslaved Will*, in which Luther had replied to Erasmus' *De libero arbitrio* διατριβή *sive collatio* (*A Discussion of Free Will*). In the prefatory letter to *Hyperaspistes 1* (Ep 1667, dated February 26 1526), Erasmus had promised to complete his refutation 'in a more carefully thought out form' when he could find the leisure to do so. He had begun work on it in April 1527 (Ep 1815:55–62), and its publication was doubtless timed to be ready for the autumn Frankfurt fair. Copies of *Hyperaspistes 2* were dispatched to princes, patrons, and friends early in September (Epp 1869, 1873, 1875, 1881). The earliest reaction to it reached Erasmus from Christophorus Pistorius, an otherwise unknown German tutor (Ep 1881). Philippus Melanchthon wrote to Georgius Spalatinus that the book was *argutissimus* – a superlative that could mean either shrewd or garrulous (*Corpus Reformatorum* [Halle 1826; repr Hildesheim and New York 1974] 1 896]). In a letter to Michaël Stifel of 8 October 1527, Luther wrote of it and its author: 'The viper Erasmus has brought forth two *Hyperaspistes* or, I should say, two viperous and superviperous hyperasps against me' (WA-Br IV 263).

ERASMUS OF ROTTERDAM TO THE PIOUS READER, GREETING
For my part I had resolved to grant myself a respite after that first skirmish of the *Hyperaspistes*,[1] however improvised it may have been, not so much through aversion for a disagreeable task – although I frankly admit that my temperament recoils from these quarrelsome disputes as from the   5
very gates of hell – as because I do not see what advantage could come from it. What use is it to battle with a man who has no regard at all for Doctors of the church who from the time of the apostles themselves have been commended for their learning and sanctity,[2] a man who does not respect the

* * * * *

1853
1 That is, *Hyperaspistes 1*. On the controversy with Luther see also Ep 1804 n10. For the English translation of *Hyperaspistes 2*, see *The Second Book of a Warrior Shielding a Discussion of Free Will against Martin Luther's Book The Enslaved Will* (CWE 77).
2 In *De servo arbitrio* Luther showed particular disdain for two of Erasmus' favourite patristic authors, Origen and St Jerome. They 'filled the world with such trifles,' he wrote, and added that 'hardly any of the ecclesiastical writers have handled the Divine Scripture more ineptly and absurdly than Origen and Jerome' (WA 18 735:1–2, 703:26–8 / trans Philip S. Watson *Library of*

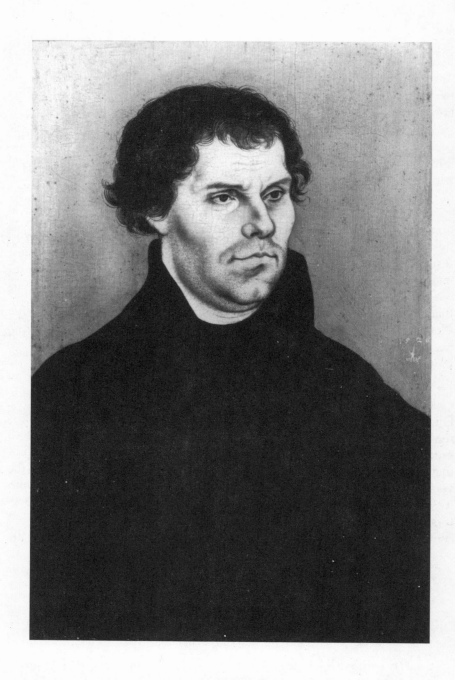

Martin Luther
Lucas Cranach the Elder, 1526
National Museum, Stockholm

decrees of even the most ancient councils and the consensus of the Christian   10
people? who accepts nothing except the testimony of infallible Scripture,
but reserves for himself the right to interpret it at his own discretion, while
the opinions of others are but fluttering shadows?[3] who, whenever it suits
him, produces new words for things, new definitions, new distinctions, new
paradoxes, creating such noisy commotion on all sides and confusing the   15
issue with such verbosity that he wears out anyone who attempts to refute
him. And yet he thinks he is waging a marvellous fight, staging frequent
triumphal celebrations and dinning into our ears boisterous hymns, paeans
of victory and praise, with almost every sentence he utters.

To this we must add the hypercritical, not to say malicious, observa-   20
tions and persistent suspicions of certain individuals. Since in the *Discussion* I purposely refrained from abuse so that, with the clouds of emotion
dispelled, the truth of my arguments would shine forth more clearly, some
men concluded that I was in collusion with Luther. Others claim that I did
not make full use of my intellectual powers; they infer this from the fact   25
that, although in some places I press the attack with great vigour, at other
times I seem somewhat lackadaisical and timorous, deliberately drawing in
my claws and sparing my opponent. Unjustified as that suspicion is, much
more absurd is the suspicion of those who persist in saying that we acted
in collusion, even now after Luther's frenzied attack upon me and after   30
my foray in the *Hyperaspistes* – rather outspoken, I think, even if less abu-
sive (in which category I gladly allow myself to be bested). Immortal God!

* * * * *

Christian Classics 17 [London 1969] 264, 224). Although Saint Jerome, as Erasmus indicates here, enjoyed the esteem of Christian writers through the ages
and was considered one of the four great Doctors of the Latin church, the same
was not true of the pioneer exegete and theologian Origen (d 254). Because
a number of his theological conclusions had been condemned at the Second
Council of Constantinople (AD 553), he was seldom cited and little known in
the medieval western tradition until Giovanni Pico della Mirandola championed his work in the fifteenth century. The Paris theologian Jacques Merlin
published some of the works in Latin and wrote an apology for him (Paris:
Josse Bade 1512) – for which he was later pursued by Erasmus' Paris critic
Noël Béda during several years of litigation in the Parlement of Paris (Farge
Parti conservateur 79–94). Erasmus readily overlooked Origen's errors in order to profit from his insights into Christian exegesis and theology; see André
Godin *Erasme lecteur d'Origène* (Geneva 1982).
3 A sarcastic reference to Luther. At *Odyssey* 10.434–5 Circe tells Ulysses that he
    must go down to Hades to consult the shade of the seer Teiresias, who alone
    among the dead retains his wisdom while the rest are but fluttering shadows.
    Cf *Adagia* II iii 53.

what do they call a fight if such a bloody encounter is nothing more than collusion?

Other reasons had also persuaded me that it would be better to deal   35
with subjects that were more profitable and more appropriate for our times. But, since my friends legitimately demand that I be true to my promise,[4] and since those who favour Luther or bear ill will towards me vaunt that I have abandoned the cause and conceded the victory to my opponent, and especially since Luther himself – as if no response at all had been given –   40
celebrates his triumph with a show of vainglory in that German pamphlet, provoking me scornfully[5] – or, I should say, flaunting[6] his battle cry 'Defiance' in everyone's face[7] – I return to the fray. As far as Luther is concerned I know full well that I shall have no other effect than to have him proclaim his teachings with still greater insolence, even adding further absurdities.   45
But I do this partly to fulfil the obligation under which I placed myself to the reader, as if bound by a public oath, and partly to give support to vacillating spirits and offer a remedy to those susceptible of a cure. I pray that, either through me or anyone else, he whose cause we believe we are upholding will deign to bring this about. I shall not detain you with further   50
prefatory words, excellent reader, from learning the facts with a more open mind. Farewell.

1854 / To Margaret of Navarre   Basel, 13 August 1527

Erasmus may have written this letter at the request of friends of Louis de Berquin, as he had done once before (Ep 1759:61–3). Margaret of Navarre needed no encouragement to protect Berquin and had already interceded on his behalf on several occasions. But, although royal agents had freed Berquin

* * * * *

4 For example Duke George of Saxony (Ep 1776:51–5) and Thomas More (Ep 1804:2–3)
5 *Adagia* III vi 45. The phrase *minimo me provocat* in Horace *Satires* 1.4.14 means to challenge to a contest contemptuously. The reference is probably to Justus Jonas' German translation of Luther's *De servo arbitrio: Das der freie Wille nichts sey, Antwort D. Martini Lutheri an Erasmum Roterodamum* (Wittenberg: Hans Lufft 1526); but Luther's *Auff des Königs zu Engelland Lesterschrift Titel Martin Luthers Antwort* (Wittenberg: [Michael Lotter] 1527) not only responded to Henry VIII but also attacked Erasmus, Cochlaeus, and other critics (WA 23 17–37, especially 27, 33, 36).
6 *oppedens*; cf Horace *Satires* 1.9.70.
7 Luther repeatedly uses the German *Trotz* in his *Antwort* (see n5 above). In *Hyperaspistes* 2 Erasmus calls such usage *indecora* 'unseemly' (LB X 1482B / CWE 77 632).

from prison in November 1526, the capital sentence against him as a lapsed heretic had never been revoked; and, although Berquin believed himself to be safe, a new trial in 1529 would result in his conviction and hasty execution on 17 April 1529.

Margaret of Angoulême (1492–1549), the sister of King Francis I and widow, since 1525, of Duke Charles of Anjou, became the wife of Henri d'Albret, king of Navarre, on 3 January 1527. Encouraged in her evangelical piety by Bishop Guillaume (II) Briçonnet, she was committed to the kind of reform in the church that Briçonnet and Jacques Lefèvre d'Etaples had tried to accomplish in the diocese of Meaux; see Michel Veissière *L'évêque Guillaume Briçonnet (1470–1534)* (Provins 1986). Although Margaret answered neither this letter nor the earlier one (Ep 1615) that Erasmus had addressed to her, the prevailing conclusion that she remained cool and aloof to Erasmus' ideas about religion (Pierre Jourda *Marguerite d'Angoulême* [Paris 1930]) has been challenged by Margaret Mann Phillips 'Marguerite de Navarre et Erasme: une reconsidération' *Hommage à Marcel Bataillon, Revue de littérature comparée* 52 (1978) 194–201.

ERASMUS OF ROTTERDAM TO MARGARET, QUEEN OF NAVARRE, GREETING

I am assailed by what might more truly be called the reproaches than the exhortations of certain individuals, O queen more glorious for holiness of life than for lineage or diadem, that in the midst of the affairs that well nigh 5 overwhelm me I do not address a letter to your Majesty. Yet no opportunity for writing presents itself, and I do not think your occupations allow you the leisure to read letters that serve no purpose. Indeed, I had no reply save for a simple word of greeting to a letter I sent you previously at their instigation.[1] They say that you recently entrusted a letter addressed to me 10 to a certain Polish man whom death intercepted on the way.[2] Whether this be true I do not know.

I should like to see prosperity in earthly affairs correspond to the piety of certain individuals. But he who moderates all things for the good of those he loves knows what is expedient for us. And when he sees fit, he will sud- 15 denly turn everything to a happy issue. When human counsel most despairs, then will the inscrutable wisdom of God especially show itself. He who truly

* * * * *

1854
1 Ep 1615, dated 28 September 1525. Margaret's greeting, perhaps transmitted in a letter from a third party, is not extant.
2 In Ep 1615:57 Erasmus had referred by name to the young Polish baron Jan (II) Łaski, but he cannot intend him here.

fixes the anchor of his hope upon him will never meet with anything that is not genuinely prosperous. We must therefore commit these things to God.[3]

To you, gracious queen, it is more fitting to give thanks than to provide   20
encouragement to continue, as you do, to protect good letters and men sincerely devoted to Christ against the perverse wickedness of certain persons.[4] The former are already much in debt, certainly, to your brother, the Most Christian King, and to that most pious and wise lady, your mother.[5] For all of them I pray to Jesus our Lord for much happiness. If there is anything   25
you wish me to undertake for you, I shall not shrink from the task.

Given at Basel, 13 August in the year 1527

1855 / To Jan (I) Łaski   Basel, 13 August 1527

This is the dedicatory preface to Erasmus' four-volume edition of St Ambrose, published by Froben in August 1527, which had been preceded by the 1492 Amerbach edition. As early as 1523, Erasmus was discussing textual problems in various manuscripts of Ambrose (Ep 1334:103–5), but his more concentrated work on it dates from 1525 when Jan (II) Łaski, who was residing in Basel with Erasmus, suggested the dedication to his uncle (lines 44–6). By April 1526, however, Erasmus deplored the edition's lack of progress, the blame for which he laid not on himself but on the Froben press. When it finally came out, Erasmus was not satisfied with it and spoke right away about the need for a new edition (Allen Ep 2033: 55–6n), but he made no changes when Claude Chevallon reprinted it (Paris 1529), contenting himself that year with publishing two additional works of Ambrose.

* * * * *

3 Erasmus had evoked this theme of abandonment to divine will in his earlier letter to Margaret (Ep 1615:44–51), seeking then to console her about the smashing defeat of the French army at Pavia (24 February 1525) and the captivity by imperial forces of her brother King Francis I.
4 Erasmus intends here his and Berquin's Parisian critics on the faculty of theology of Paris, notably its syndic Noël Béda. Margaret was the principal protector of several men devoted to evangelical piety and reform, notably Jacques Lefèvre d'Etaples, Guillaume Briçonnet, Clément Marot, Gérard Roussel, Michel d'Arande, and Pierre Caroli. Erasmus is probably referring to Louis de Berquin, whom Margaret had succeeded in freeing from detention for heresy in late 1526 or early 1527. On this see Farge 'Berquin' 67. On the circle of evangelicals around Margaret see Jonathan A. Reid *King's Sister – Queen of Dissent: Marguerite of Navarre (1492–1549) and her Evangelical Network* 2 vols (Leiden 2009).
5 Louise of Savoy, who was regent in France during Francis I's captivity (25 February 1525–March 1526).

The dedicatee, Archbishop Jan (I) Łaski (1455–1531), rose rapidly in both church and state preferment, serving as royal chancellor from 1503 to 1510 and continuing throughout his life to influence royal policy. He was the first to publish a collection of Polish statutes (Cracow: Jan Haller 1506), and undertook important diplomatic missions for two successive kings of Poland. Łaski never acknowledged this dedication from Erasmus, except in a message sent through (and possibly fabricated by) his nephew (Allen Ep 1954:20–4). The archbishop was no friend of the Hapsburgs, with whom he associated Erasmus, and moreover mistrusted Erasmus' position on the Lutheran movement. See CEBR II 296–7; cf Claude Backvis 'La fortune d'Erasme en Pologne' *Colloquium Erasmianum* (Mons 1968) 178 n11 and 180 n14.

TO THE RIGHT REVEREND JAN ŁASKI, ARCHBISHOP OF GNIEZNO
AND PRIMATE OF ALL POLAND, FROM ERASMUS OF ROTTERDAM,
GREETING

Men of ancient times, most honoured prelate, dedicated that which they wished to be venerated for all time by all people to some divinity or other, so that religious scruples, at least, would deter the insolence of mankind from wrongdoing. This example gradually passed from sacred groves and temples to the realm of studies, with the result that whenever a new work was being prepared for publication it would be consecrated to some celebrated and influential name. It has become such an accepted custom over the centuries that even a preface by itself would be sufficient to satisfy those who require a strict account. Yet this usage can appear foolish when certain writers dedicate to men of noble rank works that are not their own, and indeed to which they have added nothing by their own effort except to render them more corrupt than they were. Apart from this, since nowadays we are inundated by piles[1] of new books, as it is written in Old Comedy, it seems to me a more noble enterprise to restore the works of ancient authors that have sunk into oblivion through the ravages of time or the recklessness of scribes than to hammer out new volumes.[2] This is all the more true when

* * * * *

1855
1 γάργαρα; see *Adagia* IV vi 24, where Erasmus derives this word from the *Suda*, where it is defined as a heap or copious supply of anything. He refers to the scholia of Aristophanes, by which he probably means the scholion on the coinage ψαμμακοσιογάργαρα in *Acharnians* 3; *Prolegomena de comoedia* ed N.G. Wilson (Groningen 1969–). The word also occurs in Aristomenes, fragment 1; *Poetae comici graeci* ed Rudolf Kassel and Colin Austin (Berlin 1983–) II 563.
2 See Ep 1844:1–9, where Erasmus makes a similar complaint, and n1.

we reflect that, since what the author of Ecclesiastes truly said of his own
time – 'There is nothing new under the sun' and 'Of making many books
there is no end'[3] – can be said with even more truth of the present age.

Among the ancient Doctors of the church I think there is hardly anyone more worthy of being newly edited than St Ambrose.[4] I should like it to
be known that this is said with all sincerity and without wishing to give offence to anyone. Jerome may be more expert in the knowledge of languages
and the Sacred Scriptures;[5] Hilary may be possessed of a more polished
style;[6] Augustine may be more adroit in the resolving of knotty questions,
and others may excel in various other gifts.[7] But whom can you cite who
treats the Sacred Scriptures with equal sincerity, who avoids suspect beliefs
more prudently, who so conducts himself in all circumstances as a Christian
bishop, who expresses such paternal sentiments, who was so adept at combining the supreme authority of a prelate with the utmost gentleness? In all
circumstances you can sense that he is moved by what he says, and there is
a modest and pious joy and a pleasing civility in his words. There is one
whom with good reason they call the 'mellifluous doctor.'[8] But from Ambrose, as his very name indicates, truly exudes a heavenly ambrosia; and
he is worthy of the name he bears, which means 'immortal,' not only in
the eyes of Christ but also in those of men. As for the efforts I exerted in

* * * * *

3 Eccles 1:9 and 12:12
4 St Ambrose (c 339–97), born in Trier, was the son of a Roman prefect in Gaul.
  He practised law in Rome, and was appointed governor of Aemilia-Liguria,
  with headquarters in Milan. Elected bishop of Milan in 374 (see nn12–14
  below) he influenced St Augustine's conversion to Christianity and, in an epic
  face-off with Emperor Theodosius I (see lines 113–14, 142–84 below), zealously
  defended the church against encroachment by the civil power. His letters, sermons, treatises on the sacraments and ethics, and his knowledge of Greek,
  which resulted in the introduction of some Eastern theology into the West,
  won for him the accolade as one of the four great Doctors of the Latin church
  along with saints Jerome, Augustine, and Pope Gregory the Great.
5 Erasmus' veneration for St Jerome (c 342–420) is well known. In publishing
  Jerome's complete works Erasmus also wrote his biography: *Hieronymi Stridonensis vita* (Basel: Froben 1516); see the English translation in CWE 61 15–62.
6 Hilary of Poitiers (c 315–67) was bishop of Poitiers c 353 and engaged in extensive polemic against Arianism. Erasmus published the *editio princeps* (Basel:
  Froben 1523) which he dedicated to Jean de Carondelet (Ep 1334).
7 St Augustine of Hippo (354–430) was the most influential theologian in the
  Western tradition. His works had first been published in nine volumes by Johann Amerbach (Basel 1506). Erasmus' own edition, on which he was working
  at this time, appeared in ten volumes (Basel: Froben 1528–9).
8 St Bernard of Clairvaux (1090–1153)

the restoration of his text, collating the ancient manuscripts, emending cor-   40
rupt passages, restoring lacunae, removing interpolations, replacing Greek
words that either were missing entirely or were added in forms that had no
meaning, I leave it to your good sense to imagine.

That I should wish to publish under the auspices of your name such an
illustrious Doctor of the church as if he were reborn is owed principally to   45
Jan Łaski, who recalls his uncle no less in nobility of character than in name.
The young scion expresses the person of his forebear to such a degree that
you would think you have been reborn in him. Whenever he depicted your
image for me in words, I recognized in the narrator the exact representation
of the portrait. As he depicted his uncle he unwittingly depicted himself.   50
Although he was my guest for but a few months,[9] I count this not among
the least of my blessings. Would that I might be permitted without being
accused of adulation to proclaim the God-given gifts that I loved and respected in him! This much I must avow, that I, an old man, was made better
by my association with a young man; sobriety, restraint, humility, control of   55
the tongue, modesty, chastity, uprightness, virtues that a young man should
have learned from an old man, I, an old man, learned from a young man.
O nation born to piety! It is Poland's greatest fortune that it has been allotted such a king[10] and such an archbishop, whose signal piety strives with
equal fervour to calm the tumult of wars and dissidence and to redeem the   60
lapsed morals of the Christian people. And although your venerable years
have reached such a point that you might deservedly ask to be relieved of
your duties, nevertheless for the good of the church and your country you
are a young man.

At this point an ancient proverb comes to mind: 'How oft does God   65
join like to like.'[11] Accordingly it seemed most appropriate to me that Ambrose should set out on his journey as prelate to prelate, a man of distinguished ancestry to a noble lord, a pious man to a paragon of piety, a learned
man to an eminent patron of learning, a man of chaste life and eloquent defender of virginity to an incomparable exemplar of chastity, and finally a   70
peacemaker to a bishop keenly devoted to the cause of public peace and
tranquillity, for which role you would say Ambrose had been divinely ordained. His eloquent tongue produced this effect when he held the consular
office in Liguria; he quelled uprisings and restored concord with as much
solicitude as ability and success. This he brought about not solely in those   75

* * * * *

9 Cf CWE 1622 introduction and n3.
10 Sigismund I, king of Poland from 1506 to 1548; see Ep 1819 introduction.
11 Rendered in Greek; cf Homer *Odyssey* 17.218 and *Adagia* I ii 22.

regions where he exercised public office; indeed, whenever there were signs
of rebellion elsewhere Ambrose was summoned to calm the storm like an
experienced and accomplished helmsman. And, not to prolong the preface
by citing too many examples, at the death of Auxentius, who had favoured
the Arians, when the bishops were meeting to elect a new prelate and their   80
assemblies were seething with contention among the diverse factions – some
advocating a bishop of the Arian party, others one from the side of the orthodox, with the result that the situation was about to explode – Theodosius,
the most pious of the emperors, delegated Ambrose to resolve the deadly
impasse.[12] In his role of official envoy he entered the basilica and with his   85
incomparable eloquence urged them to come to an accord; and suddenly all
the partisan spirits of the people, divergent only a few moments ago, turned
to him alone, and with one voice and one accord they demanded Ambrose as
their bishop.[13] He demurred with many excuses, pleading the secular nature
of his office, his lack of skill in religious matters, and the fact that he was not   90
yet reborn in the sacred font, whereas Paul forbids even the newly baptized
to take the helm of the church.[14] But this time his eloquence was of no avail.
The more strenuously he refused, the more the enthusiasm of the people
was fanned. To be brief, the emperor, perceiving that divine influence was
at work, gave his approval to the unwavering determination of the people.   95
Resisting in vain, from being consular prefect Ambrose was adorned as a
bishop; instead of the lictor's rods he took up the staff, becoming leader of
the Lord's flock before he was admitted into his flock. The fatal discord was
ended and peace restored to the church.

This blessing bestowed on the church of the Insubrians,[15] which gives   10
us such cause to rejoice, we have long desired for the universal church:
namely, that someone like Ambrose would rise up who, with equal authority, would restore to tranquillity this tragic turmoil of the world, more

* * * * *

12 Auxentius (d 373/4) had continued as bishop of Milan despite his condemnation as an Arian heretic at the Councils of Rimini (359) and Paris (360) and
at the synod of Rome (372), and notwithstanding attacks on him by saints Hilary of Poitiers and Athanasius. Theodosius I ('the Great') was Roman emperor
from 379 to 395, and could not have played the role described here in an event
that took place in 374. As emperor he remained first in Constantinople before
residing in Milan from 387 to 391, when he returned to the East.
13 For this account see Paulinus of Milan *Vita sancti Ambrosii* (PL 14 [1882] 31A),
who ascribes to a child in the crowd the initial cry calling for the election of
Ambrose.
14 1 Tim 3:6; Ambrose was a catechumen but not yet baptized.
15 On Insubria see Ep 1819 n28. Milan was its capital.

destructive than any age has witnessed. If only from the ranks of popes, theologians, or monks someone might arise as Ambrose emerged from the class   105
of catechumens and the secular authority. Integrity of life has great influence, firmness joined with gentleness has great authority, prudence coupled
with eloquence is of great efficacy. But the present evil is not simple; this
pestilence, which has not only split the church into so many varying opinions but also sets the minds of princes at variance with implacable discord,   110
needs a man sent from heaven, whose authority will be respected by the
people and whose firmness of purpose will prevail against the lofty ambition of princes. In no victory gained by force of arms did Theodosius win so
much praise as in allowing himself to be vanquished by Ambrose.[16] It turned
out badly for Babylas that he barred the emperor from the temple because   115
he was defiled by a sacrilegious murder – or rather he won glorious success
because he affirmed his priestly authority by his death.[17] But Ambrose won
greater success because by defending his authority with great steadfastness
he gained the emperor himself to the cause of Christ and gave a splendid
example to rulers of the dignity of bishops, if only they be truly what they   120
should be. I do not doubt that we would have more leaders like Theodosius
if we had bishops like Ambrose, and we would have them, I think, if the
morals of the people did not alienate the favour of divine goodness.

　　To make my point more clear let us consider first the facts and then the
personages involved. In Thessalonica a certain member of the emperor's ret-   125
inue had been killed in a public tumult. Concealing his anger, the emperor
invited the populace to circus games: then suddenly soldiers surrounded
the unarmed multitude and let loose their violence upon the guilty and the
innocent alike. Punishment was meted out not to those who deserved it but
to appease hostile rage. Such an action might appear just in our age. How   130
often in war are those slaughtered whose safety had been promised as a
condition of surrender? How often when a town is taken is savagery vented
with greater ferocity upon the innocent than upon the guilty? and hatred
for the crime excuses the barbarity.

　　So much for the circumstances. Now consider that Ambrose was the   135
bishop of one city that in those days, I believe, was smaller and less populated

* * * * *

16 In 390 Ambrose refused Theodosius entry into the cathedral of Milan until he
   showed himself sufficiently penitent for a massacre he had ordered at Thessalonica, an event which Erasmus explains in more detail in lines 125–65. See
   also n20.
17 Erasmus was at this time about to publish St John Chrysostom's sermon on
   the martyrdom of St Babylas. See Ep 1856 introduction and n5.

than it is now, and he had no other weapons than those that befit a bishop: eloquence of speech, prayers, and holiness of life. On the other hand consider the power of the emperors at that time. If you were to compare present-day imperial sovereignty to it – I mean that which the title of Caesar confers on those elected (for Charles even without the title is the greatest of princes) – you would say it was something of no great importance. And yet such a bishop drove such an emperor from the portal of the church for having exercised the right of retribution too drastically, reproaching him for his inhuman cruelty and informing him that he was removed from the fellowship of the Christian flock. The emperor returned to his palace, acknowledging that it was entirely just that the pinnacle of human power should yield to the laws of Christ. There after six months of grief and tears, he dispatched his court prefect Rufinus to obtain his release from the bond of anathema,[18] so that he might at least take part in the celebration of Christmas, which was drawing nigh. Rufinus' efforts were in vain. The emperor himself, betraying not anger but sorrow, sought out Ambrose – not in his church, for he did not wish to be expelled a second time, but in a place that the Greeks call an audience chamber. For it happened that the bishop was sitting there at the disposition of all who wished to consult with him. He listened patiently to the emperor's complaints but did not absolve him until, in addition to the solemn atonement usually required of penitents, he promised to decree a law against the severity of imperial edicts. Then and there a law was proclaimed that, should any edict of the emperor order someone put to death, the execution should be delayed for thirty days.[19] During that interval it could be determined whether there was latitude for Christian clemency or whether severity was required. Then, laying aside his kingly crown, he

* * * * *

18 Probably Flavius Rufinus, praetorian prefect under Theodosius I and under Arcadius. He regularly resorted to intrigue and persecution and was murdered in 395 on the order of Gainas, a friend of his rival Stilicho.
19 A ten-day stay of execution for persons sentenced to death by the Roman Senate was already in effect from the reign of Tiberius, but Theodosius enlarged its scope to include persons condemned by an emperor and extended the delay to thirty days; see R.M. Errington 'The Praetorian Prefectures of Virius Nicomachus Flavianus' *Historia* 41 (1992) 439–61. It was incorporated into the Theodosian Code 9.40.13; see *The Theodosian Code and Novels and the Sirmondian Constitutions* trans and comm Clyde Pharr (Princeton 1952) 257, where it is dated 18 August 382 and 390 – the second of which is probably an emendation to bring it into accord with the ecclesiastical historians mentioned above. For its place in Justinian's Code (Codex 9.47.20), see the *Corpus iuris civilis* ed Theodore Mommsen, Paul Krueger, and Rudolf Schoell, 3 vols (Berlin 1880–2; repr 1967) II 393.

divested himself of the role of emperor and took on that of a penitent; pros-
trating himself on the ground and drenching the earth with abundant tears
he implored with suppliant voice the mercy of the Lord.   165

   Who would not think that for an emperor this would be more than
enough? But wait a moment to hear a further illustration of the unshakeable
firmness of the bishop and the unfeigned piety of the emperor. After he had
brought his gift to the altar in the usual way, while returning to his place
he stopped in the sanctuary. Seeing this, Ambrose had a deacon inquire of 170
him why he was remaining there. When he responded, 'So that I may assist at the sacred mysteries,' Ambrose sent the deacon back to advise him
to recognize his place, for he was standing in an area reserved for priests.
'Purple,' he said, 'makes an emperor but not a priest.' What would you expect? that the emperor, at the limits of his patience, burst out at last into 175
a rage? Not at all; rather he excused himself, saying that he had not taken
his place there in contempt of the holy place; rather, because it was the custom in Constantinople for the emperor to assist at mass in the sanctuary, he
thought that the same practice existed in Milan. After calmly pronouncing
these words, he went back to his prescribed place. Not content with that,   180
when he returned to Constantinople, even when he was invited to take his
place in the sanctuary as he was accustomed during the celebration of the
sacred mysteries, he refused to do so, adding that he knew of no one except
Ambrose who knew how to conduct himself truly as a bishop.[20]

   How customs have degenerated in our age! Now if any prince what-   185
ever deigns to approach a church, they build him a tabernacle higher than
the altar; and not only do leading men of the court take their place in the
sanctuary but even common tradesmen, whom Cicero is loath to include in
the ranks of honest citizens,[21] do so as well, ousting deans and high-ranking
churchmen from their seats. How much less pomp was afforded to Theo-   190
dosius by his sceptre and crown than that which is given these individuals
because of a little money accrued from some sordid and not always legitimate income! With similar steadfastness he resisted the Empress Justina,

* * * * *

20 The events around Ambrose's rebuke and Theodosius' public penance have
   been variously narrated by all four extant ecclesiastical historians who cover
   the period: Rufinus, Socrates, Theodoret, and Sozomenus. In a revisionist
   study Neil B. McLynn presents these events as a diplomatic solution proposed by Ambrose, who 'turned the catastrophe into a public relations triumph for the emperor'; see *Ambrose of Milan: Church and Court in a Christian
   Capital* (Berkeley 1994) 323–30.
21 *De officiis* 1.42.150–1

who threatened him with exile if he did not accept the Arians. Not in the least frightened, he said, 'I will not betray to the wolves the flock commit- ted to me. Kill me here and now, if it suits you.'[22] But no one can play the role of Ambrose unless he is prepared to die for the sake of religion. In- deed it would be difficult for anyone truly to play the role of the priest if he would gladly be anything else but a priest. It is more of an onus than an honour to pursue this career; with the prestige comes a loss of freedom; and it often happens that, while they wish to be both, they are neither princes nor priests.

But I shall desist, lest I seem to be composing a biography of Am- brose. I was led into this digression by the pitiful calamities of these times. Now I return to my purpose. The exceptional integrity of this man, joined with an unshaken constancy and equal mildness of manner, enabled him to defy kingly majesty and not succumb to the unscrupulousness of wicked men, while still retaining the favour and esteem even of those who were either unfriendly or at most only partially sympathetic. Similarly the writ- ings of no other man drew such acclaim or were less the object of envy than his. Certain writers attained notoriety late in life, others engaged in a long struggle with rivals, while the labours of many others perished altogether. That none of these fates befell Ambrose I attribute mainly to the fact that there is an unfailing moderation in all his writings. This quality is never un- mindful of Christian forbearance in the exposure of vice (you would say that he is sorry, not angry), nor does it degenerate into an appearance of complacence or ostentation. Everywhere you will recognize the Roman or, I should say, the Christian heart. There were those who turned the name of Cyprian into Caprian.[23] Not even in death could Origen avoid the hy- dra of envy.[24] Jerome carried on bitter disputes with his rivals until his last

* * * * *

22 Justina, the wife of Emperor Valentinian I and the mother of Valentinian II, was an ardent Arian Christian. As bishop of Milan St Ambrose resisted her attempt to convert the basilica of San Vittore into a church for Arian worship, comparing her to Jezabel and to Herodias; see Ep 76 to his sister Marcellina CSEL 82 108–25 / FCNT 26 365–75.
23 That is, 'Goat-boy'; see Lactantius *Divinae institutiones* 5.1.27 CSEL 19 403; cf Ep 1000:153–5 and n29. The reference could be to Cyprian of Carthage or to Cyprian of Antioch, a converted magician.
24 Comparing heresy to a hydra, the fabled many-headed monster that grew two new heads for every one its foe managed to cut off, was frequent in the Fathers of the church and became commonplace in the Reformation era even before Johannes Cochlaeus' *Septiceps Lutherus* (Leipzig: Valentinus Schumann 1529). Erasmus implies that envy, not heresy, caused the enemies of Origen (c 185–

day.²⁵ Tertullian would have perished twice, first through the corruption of his text and next through neglect, had not Beatus Rhenanus recently brought him back to light.²⁶ The same thing almost happened to Irenaeus,²⁷ who was undeserving of such a fate.

Ambrose is never cited by anyone except with honour, not even by   225
heretics; his name inspired such authority while he was still alive as others scarcely attain in death. Perhaps another writer praised virginity more elo-quently, but his sweet-sounding oratory attracted virgins to Milan from the most remote parts of the earth, such as Mauritania, who desired to be hon-oured there with the sacred veil. Perhaps another was a more vigorous de-   230
bater, but he drew into his net that great cetacean, Augustine.²⁸ Only Jerome, although he cites Ambrose in several places with preambles of praise, seems occasionally not to entertain a very favourable opinion of him. For exam-ple, in the preface to the book of Didymus on the Holy Spirit, which Jerome translated, he criticizes the books of a certain writer on the Holy Spirit as   235
a bad Latin version of a good Greek text, saying that it has no force of ar-gument but only the appearance of style tinted here and there with eclec-tic colours.²⁹ Again in his preface to his homilies on St Luke, according to

* * * * *

c 254) to attack him – most prominently Epiphanius, whose *Panarion* (375–7) made Origen into a heresiarch. On Origen and Erasmus' view of him see Ep 1853 n2.
25 In the *Hieronymi vita* (CWE 61 44–6, 49–50) Erasmus enlarges on Jerome's iras-cible nature.
26 Tertullian (c 160–c 225), who converted to Christianity in Carthage at the age of about 35, wrote works of apologetics, theology, and polemic both in Latin and Greek. A perfectionist strain in him led him to embrace Montanism, a rigorist heresy with tendencies to sectarianism. His brilliant rhetorical style appealed to humanist authors. As with Origen some were quick to condemn him, while others appreciated both his insights and style. On Beatus Rhenanus see Ep 1821 n4. He published twenty-two works of Tertullian in July 1521 (see Ep 1232 1), and a new Froben edition appeared in March 1528.
27 St Irenaeus (c 130–c 200) brought Greek thought and pastoral action to the West. He was bishop of Lyon and probably died a martyr's death. Erasmus dedicated to Bernhard von Cles his *editio princeps* of Irenaeus' *Adversus haereses* (Basel: Froben, August 1526); see Ep 1738.
28 In his autobiographical *Confessions* (PL 32 659–866 / CSEL 33 / FCNT 21) St Augustine refers eleven times to Ambrose's influence on him.
29 The 'certain writer' is Ambrose, whose *De spiritu sancto* was heavily indebted to a work on the same subject by Didymus of Alexandria (c 313–98), called 'the Blind.' Jerome judged Ambrose's work very harshly in the preface to his own translation of Didymus *De spiritu sancto*; Erasmus' phrases 'a bad Latin version of a good Greek text' (cf Terence *Eunuchus* Prologue 8) and 'eclectic

the account of Rufinus (since the work is lost), Jerome criticizes Ambrose's
commentaries on Luke, saying that he plays on words, employs uninspired
maxims, and dresses himself up in Greek plumage.[30] But whether he truly
wrote this against Ambrose, as his enemy Rufinus charges, or against someone else, he at least refrained from naming him, which in itself is a proof of
the esteem in which he held him. In Jerome's catalogue of authors he neither
praises nor blames Ambrose 'lest anyone reproach me,' as he explains, 'with
either adulation or candour.'[31] But he does not list his writings, as he generally does for others. From this it might be conjectured that, although there
were certain things in the books of Ambrose that did not please Jerome, he
preferred to pass them over in silence rather than make them public because
of the remarkable prestige Ambrose enjoyed. Yet this fact does not detract
in any way from the reputation of the sacred Doctor; Jerome too was a man,
and nothing human is happy in all respects;[32] and not all tastes are equal.

It must be confessed, but not in reproach, that the greater part of
Ambrose's writings were drawn from Greek commentaries, especially Origen, but in such a way that he excerpted what was sound while disguis-
ing what was incompatible with orthodox Catholic teaching, or contro-
versial, without adducing errors or betraying authors. In the one case it
would have been impudent, in the other odious. This aspect of Ambrose's
writings is borne out also by St Jerome in his letter to Pammachius and
Oceanus: 'Recently St Ambrose made a compilation of [Origen's] *Hexam-
eron* so that it was more in accord with the opinions of Hippolytus and
Basil.'[33] He wrote again to Pammachius and Marcella that he had a copy
of Ambrose, practically all of whose books were full of phrasings from

* * * * *

colours' echo Jerome; see PL 23 (1883) 108A. For Jerome's approach to translation, with specific application to theological vocabulary for the Trinity, see
Didymus the Blind *Traité du Saint-Esprit* ed Louis Doutreleau SJ, SC 386 96–
100.

Didymus was entrusted by St Athanasius with the direction of the catecheti-
cal school at Alexandria, where he was the teacher of Gregory of Nazianzus,
Jerome, and Rufinus. He is listed in Jerome's *De viris illustribus* 109; cf *On Illustrious Men* FCNT 100 142. He is cited by Ambrose, Augustine, Faustus of
Riez, and later medieval theologians. Erasmus published Jerome's translation
of Didymus *De Spiritu Sancto* in his *Opera divi Hieronymi* (Basel: Johann Froben
1517; repr Hieronymus Froben and Nicolaus Episcopius 1537) VIII 397.

30 We have Jerome's commentary on Luke but not his homilies; see Rufinus of
Aquileia *Apologia adversus Hieronimum* 2.25 PL 21 601 / CCSL 20 101 / NPNF
2nd series 3 469, criticizing Ambrose's *Expositio evangelii secundum Lucam*.

31 Jerome *De viris illustribus* 124; cf FCNT 100 158.

32 Horace *Odes* 2.16.27–8

33 Ep 84.7 CSEL 55 130:8–10 / NPNF 2nd series 6 179

Origen.[34] Yet no one ascribes it as a fault to Cicero that in his philosophical discussions he followed the Greeks, not as a translator but as an imitator. 265 That Ambrose suppressed the names of the Greeks was no crow's theft,[35] since most of them suffered disrepute among the Latins for their unorthodox dogmas; and as a prudent pastor he excluded any material that might constitute a stumbling block or give rise to discord.

Moreover, Ambrose's style is neither flaccid nor lowly, a criticism that 270 Jerome seems to make of his books on the Holy Spirit.[36] Ambrose has Augustine on his side in this, who said that for a topic that is lofty but subtle the more unassuming style is fitting for one who seeks to teach rather than eulogize.[37] At the same time it has its sting when the context calls for it; but it is more like a subtle pleasantness than the intensity[38] and almost 275 tragic emotion into which Jerome and Hilary sometimes break out. And in general almost all of his discourse is comprised of various kinds of terse phrases, almost like a mosaic, the style in which Seneca delighted to an excess. Ambrose is no less compact than he, but he is smoother. Despite the strictures of Fabius, who wishes that a speech be embellished with occa- 280 sional highlights, as it were, not like a mosaic of colourful phrases,[39] Ambrose frequently enhances by means of a sententious maxim the division, proof, transition, and conclusion or clausula of an argument. Sometimes the entire structure of the argument, major and minor premise, proof, confirmation, and elaboration, consists of nothing but maxims, with the addition 285 of finishing touches here and there. There is hardly any other writer who makes such frequent and insistent use of the type of wise sayings called apophthegms, in which a subtle meaning, which is understood though not expressed, is hidden and gives more delight because it is obscurely phrased. Moreover, the variety precludes any satiety or tedium that might be engen- 290 dered by this terse style, a quality so felicitous with him that you would say it is natural rather than affected, because he had imbibed this way of speaking from childhood. Sometimes by repeating the same idea in various

* * * * *

34 Not the lengthy *Apologia adversus Rufinum* nor the *Epistola adversus Rufinum* but the brief *Apologia adversus libros Rufini missa ad Pammachium et Marcellam* 1.2 PL 23 (1883) 415–514 / CCSL 79 1–115
35 Cf Horace *Epistles* 1.3.19, where he refers to the fable of the crow who stole the peacock's feathers – a fable commonly used by Erasmus in writing about plagiarism.
36 In the preface to his translation of Didymus *De Spiritu Sancto*; see n29 above.
37 *De doctrina christiana* 4.21 CCSL 32 131 / *Augustine* ... *21st Century* I-11 212
38 Rendered in Greek, δείνωσιν; on the rhetorical meaning of this term see Ep 1688 n2.
39 Cf Quintilian *Institutio oratoria* 2.4.27–8.

ways he implants in the mind that which he does not wish to slip away.
At other times he achieves a very pleasing quality through the brevity of a   295
few well-placed words. His language never becomes tiresome or obscure by
long-winded digressions and endless sentences – a trait that Jerome found
annoying in Augustine.[40] Rather, his style proceeds in regular phrases and
clauses, with a good musical combination of sounds and appealing rhythms,
harmonious and well ordered.   300

It would be tempting to cite some examples of all these qualities from
his books, but this would be not only very long but also out of place here.
Augustine gave evidence of this sort of eloquence in his *De doctrina christiana*. In brief, it would be useless to describe these matters to those ignorant
of rhetoric, while it would require no effort for the expert to take note of   30
them, especially if he were to read his books *De virginibus* and *De viduis*.[41]
For here in a subject matter likely to win applause he unfurls or, I should
say, puts on display the embellishments of rhetoric. Therefore, if we have
not provided a completely restored text of Ambrose, it is certainly a much
less corrupt one. It remains only for Rome, the city that gave birth to Am-   31
brose, to show favour to this enterprise. May it find favour in Liguria, which
merited his governorship, and in Insubria, which called him to the priesthood;[42] and may every corner of the Christian world show favour to this
remarkable doctor of Christian piety.

Accordingly, most holy prelate, if your Grace will give kind approval   3
to my study, whatever its worth, it will spur on others, who can contribute
more than I, to like endeavours. Farewell.

Given at Basel, 13 August in the year 1527

1856 / To Nicolas Wary   Basel, 14 August 1527

This preface to Erasmus' edition of the Greek text of St John Chrysostom *De
Babyla martyre / On the Martyr Babylas* (Basel: Froben, August 1527; cf PG 1
527–72), is described on the title-page as *Epistola Erasmi de modestia profitendi*

* * * * *

40 In Ep 112.15 addressed to Augustine (Ep 75 in Augustine's letters), Jerome
   cautions Augustine that 'a long-drawn-out argument frequently becomes un-
   intelligible ...' (CSEL 55 385:4–5 / FCNT 12 359). See Erasmus' earlier reference
   to this criticism in Epp 112:15, 1000:65–7.
41 *De virginibus ad Marcellinam sororem suam libri tres* PL 16 (1880) 197–244 and *De
   viduis liber unus* PL 16 (1880) 247–78
42 Liguria, shaped like an arc along the Tyrrhenian Sea, had Genoa as its capital.
   On Insubria see Ep 1819 n28.

linguas / An Epistle of Erasmus on the Discipline of Teaching Languages. Germain de Brie included it in his Latin translation of the Greek text (Paris: Simon de Colines 1528). The letter recapitulates Erasmus' fervent belief that any educational programme for students should feature elegant texts by good Christian authors like John Chrysostom, and that their teachers should be acquainted with the elegant language of good pagan authors as well. At the same time, the letter served to criticize modern authors who 'find their satisfaction only in what is totally alien to Christ' (line 25) – a premonition of Erasmus' forthcoming treatise *Ciceronianus* (CWE 28).

For Nicolas Wary, second president of the Collegium Trilingue (1526–9) in Louvain, see Ep 1806A introduction. For the college, founded in 1517, see Félix Nève *Mémoire historique et littéraire sur le Collège des Trois-Langues à l'Université de Louvain* (Brussels 1856) and de Vocht CTL.

ERASMUS OF ROTTERDAM TO NICOLAS WARY, PRESIDENT OF
THE COLLEGE OF BUSLEYDEN IN LOUVAIN, GREETING
With good cause, most learned Nicolas, you might well apply to me the proverb 'bring water to the sea,'[1] since I bring but a tiny drop, as it were, to the font of languages, except that the Gospel tells us to give to him who 5 has so that he may the more abound.[2] It seemed to me, however, that this slim volume of Chrysostom was worthy of being the subject of a course at your college on several counts: it so skilfully combines a wealth of piety with an admirable eloquence that in my opinion no other example could be more fittingly proposed for young students in their practice of treating var- 10 ious themes.[3] What is there in Aphthonius, Lysias, or Libanius that might compare with this subject – I do not say in piety, which is its particular merit, but in elegance of diction, shrewdness of reasoning or, in a word, abundance of expression?[4] What could be more useful at that age than that

* * * * *

1856
1 Rendered in Greek; cf *Adagia* I vii 57.
2 Matt 13:12, 25:29
3 See the introduction.
4 Aphthonius, a third-century rhetorician, wrote four books *De metris*, which later found their way into the *Ars grammatica* of Marius Victorinus. Lysias (c 459–c 380 BC) was imprisoned in 404 BC for his advocacy of democracy. After gaining his freedom he composed over 200 forensic speeches for others to deliver, since as a foreigner he was not permitted to speak in the courts. His orations exhibited a mastery of idiom, simplicity, and precision. Libanius was a master of rhetoric in fourth-century Antioch; his pupils probably included John Chrysostom, Basil the Great, Gregory of Nazianzus, and Ammianus Marcellinus.

they should from the first imbibe both language and eloquence from authors   15
whose speech reflects the spirit of Christ no less than that of Demosthenes?

The subject is simple. Babylas, bishop of Antioch, was put to death by
the emperor for having attempted to keep him from entering the sanctuary
of the church, since he was defiled by an impious slaying.[5] The bishop was
buried outside the city and at a much later time was transferred into the   20
city. This theme, which is neither complicated nor intrinsically impressive
or remarkable, is wondrously depicted with the colours of rhetoric and enriched with the resources of genius by this artist, who truly merits the name
of golden.[6] I am acquainted with many individuals specializing in this type
of literature who find their satisfaction only in what is totally alien to Christ;   25
and yet it is my opinion that pagan authors should be read by teachers for
their elegance of speech rather than explicated to the young. I have always
greatly admired your aim in commending the knowledge of languages for
learned and unlearned alike for this reason as well. 'What reason?' you will
ask. That parents will welcome their children home from your famous col-   30
lege not only more skilled in languages but also more pious and with better
morals (since even the best things arouse hostility by their novelty, the common crowd often attributes morals to studies, even though this is not where
they come from).

By the same token I can scarcely say how much I also admire your   35
teachers, who make sure that they do not provide any opportunities for
calumny to those who profess hatred for languages.[7] What is more free of
corruption or better disciplined than their way of life? You could say they
are teachers of religion, not of languages. They do not censure any other
profession, as we see done by some, to the great detriment of the study of   40
letters, since skill in languages has not been revived to do away with former
disciplines of learning but so that they may be learned more correctly and

* * * * *

5 Babylas became bishop of Antioch c 240. According to St John Chrysostom, he
   was imprisoned for barring an emperor (probably Philip the Arabian, AD 244–
   9) from a church because of a crime for which he had not repented. (Babylas' martyrdom actually occurred during the Decian persecution in 250–1.)
   Erasmus had compared this incident to St Ambrose's similar rebuke of Emperor Theodosius I in his letter to King Francis I in December 1523 (see Ep
   1400:276–84 and n38); cf Ep 1855:115–17.
6 Chrysostom means 'golden-mouthed.'
7 Erasmus uses Greek to refer to this latter group. Conradus Goclenius was
   among the teachers for whom Erasmus professes admiration; see Ep 1857
   introduction.

with more facility. We do not learn languages merely to speak them but to understand more accurately the works of great literature. I have known for some time how important the knowledge of languages is to that end, but recently I have begun to verify it even further. Experience itself has taught me something I would never have believed: that these calumnies by which certain sinister individuals have thrown everything into turmoil were caused in great part by an ignorance of Latin and Greek. That will immediately become evident to anyone who reads what I have written to Noël Béda.[8]

Therefore, since you confer such immense usefulness on all types of study, use prudence and care to impart your services properly and tactfully. Too often a kindness is wasted through the fault of the giver because he knows not how to give. Although it would be more than fair – as in a game of ball so in doing good deeds – that the interests of both giver and receiver should be mutually served, nevertheless it behoves both teachers and parents to tolerate the indifference and ingratitude of those whom they educate until age and experience teach them how great a gift they have received. The end result will be that those who now sneer at these studies will afterwards give them their enthusiastic applause. Those who render the greatest disservice to education are those who, to the hostility engendered by novelty and insolent behaviour, add the suspicion of impiety as well: Germany has its fair share of such examples. Since through your exceptional vigilance you have kept clear so far of all such troubles, your college flourishes more than others through God's favour, and it will flourish all the more if you continue in the direction in which you have begun. I have no doubt that a grateful awareness of this splendid fruit of his labours reaches the saintly spirit of Jérôme de Busleyden, who, I am certain, was inspired by divine providence to endow our country with this superb gift.[9] Your precautions, too, have had a role in this. Give my personal greetings to your excellent professors and to the whole chorus of those who love languages.[10]

Given at Basel, 14 August in the year 1527

* * * * *

8 The syndic of the Paris faculty of theology and Erasmus' chief opponent there (Ep 1804 n14; cf Farge BR 31–6 no 34). Béda did not in fact oppose learning Greek; he objected rather to the humanists' application of philological approaches to Sacred Scripture and to their claim that no one could be a proficient theologian without knowledge of Greek and Hebrew.
9 He was the founder, through his legacy executed in 1517, of the Collegium Trilingue; see Ep 1806 n3.
10 'those who love languages' is rendered in Greek to balance the expression 'those who profess hatred for languages' in line 37 above.

1857 / From Conradus Goclenius Louvain, 18 August [1527]

This letter, autograph throughout, is in the Öffentliche Bibliothek of the University of Basel, MS Goclenii Epistolae 12. It was published for the first time by Allen. Erasmus responded to it with Ep 1890.

Conradus Goclenius was Erasmus' closest friend and collaborator in Louvain in matters both academic and personal. He had held the chair in Latin at the Collegium Trilingue since 1519 (de Vocht CTL I 484–7), and received Erasmus' support against his rivals and detractors (Epp 1050, 1051). In 1524 Erasmus committed to Goclenius his autobiography, *Compendium vitae* (Ep 1437:233–420), and each made provision for the other in his will. Goclenius was able to return to Erasmus a manuscript of Augustine's *De Trinitate* that he had left with Maarten van Dorp (Epp 1547, 1890, 1899). The funeral monument of Goclenius in Louvain bears the inscription *alter Erasmus* (CEBR II 109–11).

Cordial greetings. You have put Frans van der Dilft so much in your debt over the past years by your kindness and good services that the customs and company of men all seem mean compared to Erasmus.[1] Therefore no one could deter him from returning to you so that he could thoroughly satiate himself with your divine learning, of which he had a taste long ago that he 5 has never had cause to regret. Thus it is that he is now devoured by an even greater thirst, which is more difficult to control after first tasting of the lotus.[2] As he was about to take leave of us he asked that I recommend him to you, but, since I considered it entirely unnecessary, I refrained from doing so. In the first place, his merits alone will be sufficient recommendation to you; 10 and, secondly, those who are fired by the love of humane studies are sure to win your affection as well as your fervent support. Since Dilft is pursuing this course so vigorously, he should now find favour with you that matches the energy he has displayed in his studies. Certainly the leading scholars here will feel his loss immensely because of the fame of his learning, his 15

* * * * *

1857
1 A wealthy former student of Goclenius, Dilft had stayed with Erasmus and performed frequent services for him while attending the University of Basel in 1524–5. Erasmus dedicated to Dilft his translation of Plutarch's *De vitiosa verecundia* (Basel: Froben 1526). He stayed once again with Erasmus from late 1527 until February 1528, often carrying letters to and from the Low Countries, and served him in Freiburg. He later served Alonso de Fonseca, then became secretary to the imperial privy council and, in December 1544, succeeded Eustache Chapuys as Charles V's ambassador to England (CWE I 392–3).
2 *Adagia* II vii 62

sincerity of heart, and his marvellous way of getting along with everyone. Ever since his return here he has frequented only the most serious scholars among us, so that in the opinion of all, although but a young man, he shows a seriousness that would do honour to one of far greater years. But his friends find consolation in the certain hope that after a short time he will return from   20 his association with Erasmus more learned than ever, more well disciplined, more judicious and, finally, a better man by far than when he left us. We are inspired in this hope especially because of Dilft's extraordinary love of humane learning and of virtue, and are confident that you will lend your generous assistance to a most devoted friend in his efforts to perfect himself.   25

I believe you have received the letter I sent through your servant Nicolaas Kan.[3] Since his departure nothing has occurred here that I think worthy of your attention; for anything else you will have full knowledge of it from Dilft. Farewell.

At Louvain, 18 August   30
Yours, with all his heart, Conradus Goclenius
To Master Erasmus of Rotterdam, indefatigable restorer of the liberal arts and of religion. In Basel

1858 / To Robert Aldridge   Basel, 23 August 1527

A major, considered defence of Erasmus' theology of the Holy Spirit, this letter first appeared, like Ep 1856, with the Greek text of St John Chrysostom's *De Babyla martyre* (Basel: Froben, August 1527). On the title-page there it is described as *Epistola ... in tyrologum quendam impudentissimum calumniatorem*. It was ostensibly aimed at an unnamed English critic, but it had wider relevance, since Erasmus' theology of the Holy Spirit was on the agenda of his Spanish detractors at the Valladolid Conference. Unlike Ep 1856, this letter was reprinted in the *Opus epistolarum* (1529) and in the first posthumous *Opera omnia* (1538–40).

For Robert Aldridge see Ep 1656 introduction. Attaching his name to this letter was probably recognition for his laborious copying and collating Cambridge manuscripts for Erasmus' revised edition of Seneca (1526), even though his work proved in the end to be of no use to Erasmus (Ep 1797). In Ep 1766:1–2 Aldrich describes himself as a former pupil of Erasmus.

* * * * *

3 Not extant. It probably contained the news of Goclenius' good fortune, to which the first part of Ep 1890 responds. On Kan, copyist and trusted courier of Erasmus at this time; see Ep 1832 introduction.

ERASMUS OF ROTTERDAM TO ROBERT ALDRIDGE, DISTINGUISHED
FOR HIS LEARNING AND EXEMPLARY LIFE, GREETING

It has been made known to me by men not at all unreliable but entirely worthy of credence[1] that a certain man in London, more of a cheese expert[2]
than a theologian, in my opinion, who from one of the most celebrated pul-   5
pits, popularly known as St Paul's Cross,[3] has with inflammatory audacity
heaped abuse on the name of Erasmus, accusing him of impiety and falsehood. He singles out for attack my translation of a passage in the Gospel
of John, chapter 7, of which the usual church reading is: 'For the Spirit had
not yet been given, because Jesus had not yet been glorified.'[4] I have trans-   10
lated what the Greek text, omitting the participle,[5] has: 'For there was not as
yet the Holy Spirit because Jesus had not yet been glorified.' By so doing,
he says, I have exposed the Catholic faith to the utmost peril, encouraging
everyone to believe once again that the Spirit is a creature who did not exist from eternity but began to exist in time. This is what that babbling idiot   15
droned on about with supreme impudence and equal stupidity before men
of learning, leading citizens of the city and a crowded assembly of towns-
people. I have no doubt that you were present also, since, as the saying goes,
you usually do not like to miss such a choice repast.[6]

I would, of course, gladly attribute the enormity of such an outrage to   20
error or ignorance, except that this type of excuse is not appropriate, first for

* * * * *

1858
1 The phrase 'but entirely worthy of credence' is rendered in Greek.
2 Erasmus coined the word *tyrologus* 'cheese expert' (or 'cheese connoisseur'),
  an obvious pun on *theologus*. He often accuses his theologian critics among
  the mendicant orders of gluttony because of their orders' provisions for daily
  begging. Cf Ep 1805 n53.
3 A gathering place in St Paul's churchyard, where the English Franciscan Henry
  Standish had likewise preached against Erasmus in 1519 (Ep 1126:21–48 and
  n6)
4 John 7:39. Erasmus' first Latin version of the New Testament, printed parallel
  to the Greek text, dated from 1516 (the *Novum instrumentum*). Later editions
  appeared in 1519, 1522, 1527, and 1535. His *Paraphrase on John* appeared in
  February 1523.
5 In his Latin version Erasmus omits *datus* 'given' (the reading of the Vulgate),
  causing this critic to accuse him of questioning the existence of the Holy Spirit
  from all eternity. But in his *Paraphrase on John* Erasmus follows the Vulgate text
  in reading 'for the Spirit was not yet given,' while in the *Annotations* he explains the textual difference between this reading and his Greek manuscripts.
  See CWE 46 101 and n49 and lines 54–64 below.
6 *Adagia* II i 37

a theologian, next for a preacher, and lastly for that pulpit which no one ever ascends without prior notice and without having rehearsed what would suit an audience there. Before mounting that platform he should at least have examined what I had written on this subject in the *Annotations.*[7] There I point out that all the.Greek manuscripts are unanimous in the reading that I translated, and I explain the orthodox meaning, lest anyone fall into error.

But suppose – which is neither true nor plausible – that the word 'given' was deliberately removed from the Greek texts, since no exemplar contains it. Did he want me to add something of my own that was not present in the Greek texts when I professed to translate from the Greek? If the word had been removed, certainly it would have been removed by the Arians.[8] But the fact is that we find this reading in the books of those who opposed the Arians very strenuously, namely Chrysostom and Theophylact.[9] And if such a corruption had been introduced by the Arians, orthodox writers would not have passed over such an impious falsification in silence, since in other cases they are careful to record any corruptions that they may have discovered. Furthermore, what Arian ever produced this passage to defend his belief? And if someone did produce it, would he not have been immediately hissed off the stage? For this passage is self-explanatory. Just before it one reads: 'This he said of the Spirit, which those who believed in him were to receive'; and immediately afterwards it continues, 'For there was not as yet the Spirit, because Jesus had not yet been glorified.'[10] You see that the Evangelist is not speaking here of the nature of the Spirit but of the gift and

* * * * *

7 See the annotation on John 7:39 (*nondum erat spiritus datus*) LB VI 371–2 / Reeve *Annotations* 244 and n5 above.
8 The followers of Arius (fourth century) professed that Jesus Christ had his beginning in time and was therefore not God but a mere creature of God. They did not hold the same about the Holy Spirit.
9 One of the greatest Doctors of the Eastern church, John Chrysostom (d 407) was bishop of Constantinople in the fourth century. He was known principally for the eloquence of his sermons, scriptural exegesis, and his attempts at reforming the morals of the city.
Theophylact, an eleventh-century Byzantine exegete and bishop in Bulgaria, produced commentaries on several books of the Old Testament and on all the New Testament except the Apocalypse (PG 123–6). His works are models of fidelity to the biblical text and reflect the practical morality of John Chrysostom. Erasmus, who had recently edited his Pauline commentaries, which had formerly been ascribed to Athanasius, knew that Theophylact 'belonged to a later age' but did not know how late he actually lived and wrote (Ep 1790:12–32).
10 In this second rendition of his own version (cf John 7:39), Erasmus omits the qualifier 'Holy'; but see line 115 below.

power of the Spirit. To say 'There was not as yet the Spirit' is no different   45
from saying 'It was not yet day.' Now there is never a time when it is not
day; nevertheless we understand that it is not day in such-and-such a place.
What could be more common than this figure of speech, to say that there
is no sun when it is obscured by clouds and is not visible to us? It is like
saying there is no water when it has not risen to such a level that a river be-   50
comes navigable. So the Evangelist speaks of the disciples: 'There was not
as yet the Spirit' – that is, they had not yet received that overflowing gift of
the Spirit of which the prophet speaks.[11]

All this is made clear in the *Annotations*, where it is explained that it
is of very little relevance for the meaning whether 'given' is added or not   55
added. Not satisfied with that single explanation, it points out with solid
proofs that Augustine also followed the Greek text. The words of Augustine
I quote there are as follows: 'But what is the meaning of the words "The
Spirit was not yet given, because Jesus had not yet been glorified?" The
meaning is clear. It does not mean that the Spirit of God did not exist, for he   60
was with God, but he was not yet present in those who believed in Jesus.'[12]
Is it not sufficiently evident from these words that Augustine did not read
'given' but that it was added by a copyist? Even if I had not drawn attention
to this, if this preacher had the slightest trace of Christian conscience, he
should have examined the available passage before giving vent to such gross   65
calumny against his brother and infecting with deadly poison the minds of
so many thousands of persons whom he would not be able to cure in the
future even if he wished to do so.

There you have the illustrious and completely orthodox[13] author Augustine! What if we find the same reading in Jerome, whose words are cited   70
in the *Glossa ordinaria*: 'It does not mean the Holy Spirit was not existing at
that moment, for the Saviour said, "If it is by the Spirit of God that I cast
out demons";[14] rather the Spirit who was in the Lord dwelt in the apostles,
although as yet unknown to them.' Here[15] Jerome does not repeat the word
'given'; and if he had repeated it, it would not give rise to discussion. For the   75

* * * * *

11 Joel 2:28–9, quoted in John 7:39
12 The passage was added in the 1522 edition. For the citation from Augustine,
   see PL 35 1644 / CCSL 36 302 / FCNT 88 45.
13 Erasmus uses the Greek, ὀρθοδοξότατον.
14 Matt 12:28; cf *Biblia latina cum Glossa ordinaria* 4 vols (Strasbourg: Adolph Rusch
   1480–1; repr Turnhout 1992) IV 243, a gloss on John 7:39
15 Erasmus perhaps refers back to the original citation from Jerome, not to the
   passage from Matthew; or he may refer to the way Jerome translated the passage from Matthew in his Vulgate translation.

fact that the Spirit was not given to the disciples by a visible sign, that God breathed the Spirit into them after the resurrection and sent him in tongues of fire after the ascension, is a matter beyond dispute. But since Jerome said, 'He was not,' namely in the disciples, there was danger of believing that the disciples seemed to have been without the Holy Spirit until the resurrection 80 of Christ. He avoids this absurdity by interpreting 'not given' in the sense of that which was not 'openly and abundantly poured out.' And a little further on in the same *Glossa* he says: 'Therefore the Spirit was not yet in the apostles, nor did spiritual graces flow from their breast, because the Lord had not yet been glorified.' And here again the word 'given' is not added.[16] 85

There, in addition to all the Greek witnesses of the text, you have two leading Latin Doctors of the church. And, to be sure, when I was making these assertions, I had not yet come upon a Latin exemplar that was in agreement with the Latin writers cited and the Greek text. But recently I came upon two codices from the cathedral library of Constance,[17] in one of 90 which the Greek reading was intact and in the other a copyist in a more recent hand had added 'given' in the space between the lines. I am certain one could find the genuine reading hundreds of times, if he were to look through old manuscripts. And that would not have been difficult for me to do, but I did not expect that someone would suddenly arise who would use 95 this passage to calumniate me.

I had added in the *Annotations* the further proof that the Greek text of this part of the discourse does not include the article: it says simply 'Spirit'; and in our texts the word 'holy' does not appear, which I point out was added by copyists in the Greek texts,[18] just as the participle 'given' was 100

* * * * *

16 In Ep 120.9 to Hedybia, a resident of Gaul not known to him personally, St Jerome treats this question: 'How can it be that, according to John, the Lord breathes the Holy Spirit into the apostles, when, according to Luke, he says that he will send [the Spirit] after his ascension [to the Father]?' (PL 22 [1854] 993–7 / CSEL 55 492–500). In Erasmus' edition of Jerome this letter is followed by *scholia* on each of the twelve questions treated in the letter, where Erasmus repeats, as here, 'For the Spirit was not yet given' (Basel: Hieronymus Froben 1536 III 154–6).
The *Glossa ordinaria*, the standard medieval commentary on the Bible, has often been ascribed to Rhabanus Maurus (ninth century) but was essentially compiled in the twelfth century at the school of Laon. It was drawn largely from patristic commentaries and arranged in the form of both interlinear and marginal glosses.
17 Erasmus had last visited Constance in 1522, but was sometimes lent manuscripts from there by Johann Botzheim. See Allen Ep 1761:10n.
18 That is, in the *Annotations*; see n7 above. Cf also lines 203–20 below.

added in our texts. This was done so that it would be clear that it was not a question of the nature of the Spirit but of his gift or grace, and not of any gift whatever but of that abundant diffusion which was not found even in the prophets. Neither can they say that the Greek manuscripts are corrupt here, since these same words, as I mentioned, are read in the books of or-   10
thodox writers. Furthermore, should anyone have the effrontery to say that those books also are corrupt, this is refuted by the commentary, which in-dicates what reading they had before them. Theophylact says, among other things: 'Because at that time the operation of the Spirit did not exist but was to be given, because the Holy Spirit was not there, that is, he did not dwell   11
among the Jews, nor did he reveal himself by his operations'; and a little further on: 'The power of the Spirit was present also in the prophets, and in the apostles before the crucifixion, but not as it was after the ascension, more bountiful and widespread, so that it might be compared to streams of water. Thus the Evangelist said rightly that the Holy Spirit was not yet   11
present, that is, not yet so generously poured forth.'[19] These words clearly indicate what text he read. And there is no cause to wonder if here and there in his commentary he says 'the Spirit given' since that is what the Evange-list meant. In any case the text does not have 'given,' and in his commen-tary he cites the passage without the word 'given.' I did not have the Greek   12
text of Chrysostom, and in his commentary the translator consistently added 'given'; he did this not only in this passage but he inserts the Latin text of the Scriptures throughout. But what is the point of quoting the words of Chrysostom, since Theophylact drew his whole commentary on this passage from this source?   12

Moreover, if the Scriptures had been corrupted by the Arians, Chry-sostom would surely not have concealed it, since he never neglected the op-portunity to refute their beliefs. But, after all, what reason was there for an Arian to think that this passage should be tampered with? Was it to make it appear that the Holy Spirit was only created after the death of Christ? No   13
heretic was ever so insane. There were some who at the height of their blas-phemies against God said that the Son was begotten by the Father and that the Holy Spirit was the minister of this creation, but they admitted that both were created before any other creature. Nor did the Arians deny that the prophets foretold the future by the inspiration of the Holy Spirit. Yet they   13
would have had to deny this, if they believed that the Holy Spirit was cre-ated after the death of Christ. Therefore no heretic could avail himself of

* * * * *

19 *Enarratio in evangelium Ioannis* PG 123 1311, 1312; cf n9 above.

this passage for the confirmation of his belief. If this could have been done, there would have been no lack of those who would attempt it, since they stop at nothing to assure victory for their impious cause.   140

What is the terrible crisis, then, that was at issue here? Nothing could come of it except that some scholars would have deduced that the participle 'given' was not expressed in Greek, but was understood. I have left the official reading of the church intact, and no manuscript bears trace of my erasure. And if there was anything involved here that was worthy of dis-   145
cussion, this play was not suited to such an audience.[20] What importance can be attributed to the fact that Latin copyists added the participle 'given'? Did they deprive the Arians of a foothold? We have shown that this passage could not be used in defence of their beliefs. But while they were intent on avoiding this matter, which presented no danger, they fell into another   150
real and more serious peril. What is that? The undermining of the authority of the whole Old Testament. How did they do that? Because it would not have proceeded from the inspiration of the Holy Spirit. How could it, if the Spirit was not given to anyone before the death of Christ? How much better, therefore, would it have been to leave the genuine reading as it was in the   155
Greek sources and in the Latin rivulets flowing from them, rather than on private authority – not to say temerity – to add a word which could provide occasion for such a dangerous interpretation.

Further, so that you can grasp the truth of what I say, the danger my adversaries bandy about gave no cause for fear to any of the ancient Fa-   160
thers, because there was none. But all of them – Chrysostom, Theophylact, and Augustine – were uneasy about the very matter I raise, as is quite clear in their commentaries.[21] The Manichaeans would have had less occasion to belittle the authority of the Old Testament if we had read, 'For the Spirit was not yet present,' understanding 'in the disciples' – I mean the abun-   165
dant Spirit, which flowed like a river, according to the testimony of Joel[22] – rather than reading 'He had not yet been given.' If for the sake of clarity the translator had added the participle, they would have grounds for making allegations if I in turn had transmitted a new reading to the church. But as it is, they shamelessly calumniate me, although I left the Vulgate read-   170
ing untouched and in good faith undertook to translate the Greek reading

* * * * *

20 That is, to be preached to the unlearned people at St Paul's Cross
21 For Theophylact's commentary see n19 above. St Augustine wrote no separate work specifically on the Holy Spirit but treats the topic in his *De Trinitate*, especially in book 15 (CCSL 50A 501–35 / FCNT 18 491–525).
22 See n11 above.

of the New Testament, whether it be correct or not. Can it be that they will express their displeasure also towards those who have recently translated the Greek Old Testament into Latin because they chose to follow the Greek copies, which differed widely in many instances from our traditional Latin readings?[23] But when it becomes clear that this was done through the presumption of the copyists, not with official authority, and not by the translator, the calumny is all the more insolent. If this had originated with the translator, or if the participle had been added by the consent of the church, then surely Augustine and Jerome would have this reading, and the ancient manuscripts would all be in agreement. Would that we could accuse the presumption of the copyists in this one instance alone! The liberty they took with the sacred writings is all too well known. So, let no one raise the objection that in Jerome's translation of Didymus or in the Latin versions of Chrysostom the word 'given' is often added,[24] since we see that it was the consistent practice of translators and scribes to insert the Vulgate reading, which often clashed with the reading used by the commentators, who objected that they did not fit the context, as if the harp were playing one tune and the singer singing another.

Suppose I had translated the version of Theodotion into Latin,[25] would they charge me with falsification if there were many variants from the church version? or would they accuse me of bad faith because I did not render into Latin what he translated into Greek, although the church does not recognize this author but does recognize those whom I followed?

Lastly, why did they single out this one passage for attack when there are innumerable cases in which the manuscripts of the Orthodox Greeks differ from ours? Rather, I should say that my purpose in expending my efforts

* * * * *

23 Probably an allusion to the Complutensian Polyglot Bible, undertaken under the aegis of Cardinal Francisco Jiménez de Cisneros by biblical scholars at the university in Alcalá. Printed partially in 1514, it was completed by 1517 but was put into circulation only in 1522. The first four volumes contain the Old Testament with the Hebrew, Latin Vulgate, and Greek Septuagint (with interlinear Latin) texts in parallel columns. For the Pentateuch alone it has the Chaldaic paraphrase, printed in Hebrew characters with a Latin translation beside it, added at the foot of the page. Volume 5 contains the New Testament with the Greek text and the Latin Vulgate in parallel columns. A sixth volume contains glossaries, indexes, and other scholarly apparatus.
24 For Didymus see Ep 1855 n29.
25 Theodotion translated the Old Testament into Greek in the second century. His translation was placed following the Septuagint in Origen's *Hexapla*. See also Ep 1800 n42.

on this point was precisely so that scholars might discover the true reading from the lack of agreement among the manuscripts, or perhaps might
understand more clearly what was written. Besides, why should one who   200
has subtracted a word be blamed more than one who has added one? Both
were condemned with equal severity by the Holy Spirit, so that we should
neither add nor subtract anything.[26] Why is it, therefore, that those who criticize the subtraction of the participle 'given' say nothing about the addition
of the adjective 'holy'?[27] Moreover, my reason for thinking that the word   205
'holy' was added by the Greek copyists is that in the preceding passage,
'This, however, he said of the Spirit,' in the Greek manuscripts the article
is added – 'of *the* Spirit' – so that it could not but be understood to mean
the Holy Spirit even if you did not add the epithet 'holy.'[28] And yet, while
the word 'holy' occurs twice in the Greek manuscripts, the Latin texts unan-   210
imously omit the word in both places. And indeed it was more appropriate
not to add it. Why? Because here it is not a question, strictly speaking, of
the nature or the holiness of the Spirit, to distinguish the Holy Spirit from
an unholy spirit, but of the manner of the bestowal of the Spirit. At the same
time, so that no one might take it to mean some other spirit rather than the   215
one and only Spirit of God, the Evangelist added the article in the first passage and did not add it in the second,[29] although he is speaking of the same
Spirit, in order to show more clearly the manner of the giving of the Spirit.
To express this meaning, the article, far from clarifying the meaning, would
have made it more obscure. Those who have a good knowledge of Greek   220
will readily understand this if they analyse this passage carefully.

　　There is the matter in a nutshell, my dear Robert Aldridge. Now consider for a moment the enormity of this preacher's stupidity. Would that
this were the only reason for my accusation! First of all, what use could it
be to drag out again before that motley crowd the fact that there were once   225
some impious men who held that the Holy Spirit did not exist from all eternity? That error was laid to rest a thousand years ago; why, even the schools
of theology would consider it a useless matter of discussion. Much less did
it suit an illiterate crowd, drawn from various nations, among whom there

* * * * *

26 Rev 22:18–19
27 Cf lines 99–114 above.
28 Erasmus wrote περὶ τοῦ Πνεύματος. By 'the preceding passage' he means the
　　first part of John 7:39, which has not been the subject of discussion up to now;
　　Erasmus omitted the participle 'given' in the second part of the verse.
29 Erasmus writes οὔπω γὰρ ἦν Πνεῦμα (without the article) in the second part of
　　7:39.

may be some who do not think very highly of God himself. But what was   230
even more stupid on his part was his failure to understand that this passage
was of no use to the impious beliefs of the Arians, since they never supported their teachings with this passage, nor could they have done so; nor
is he aware that while he stood in fear of a vain shadow he fell into a real
ditch.   235

What, therefore, are we to think came over him that he could display
his stupidity in this way to all men of learning? He thought that the celebrity
of that place called for something new and off the beaten track. For such
seems to be the goal of those who have been given permission to speak from
that pulpit, especially those fresh out of school who are puffed up with the   240
conceit of learning. It seems to me that he probably never read the passage
but was hoodwinked by some fellow tippler into thinking that with this bit
of calumny he could acquire a reputation for great learning. If it is a crime
of falsification to give translations of the Greek that do not accord with our
accepted text, why did he attack this one passage when he could equally   245
have found fault with so many others? He could have reproached me with
less impudence for having published the New Testament translated from
Greek sources. If he yields to me on this point, I would have been more
justly accused of falsification if my translation did not represent what was
in the Greek manuscripts.   250

If he reproves me also for making the Greek text available to Latin
readers who know no Greek, in addition to the many other reasons for the
usefulness of this initiative that I have given elsewhere, I shall add that it
was made necessary by the commentaries of Chrysostom, Basil, Athanasius,
Gregory, and others, which frequently do not accord with the official read-   255
ing. And what I have done for the New Testament with the authorization
of the Roman pontiff[30] has been done in Spain for the Old Testament at
the expense and under the supervision of Francisco, the cardinal of Toledo,
with the authorization of the same pontiff.[31] They had at their disposal an
exemplar of great antiquity and proven authority from the Vatican library   260
from which they were ordered not to depart; and this approved manuscript
had the very same readings as the numerous manuscripts I had consulted

* * * * *

30 See Ep 864.
31 See n23 above. The role of Pope Leo x, principally in lending manuscripts
   to the Complutensian Bible project, is acknowledged on f +[3] and +[4] of its
   first volume. His belated brief of approbation for it appears on f +[8]v of some
   copies.

when I made this translation.[32] The choice is open to this arrant calumniator
whether he prefers to bring charges against the Roman pontiff or bring suit
against me for having translated in good faith what is contained with sur-   265
prising unanimity in all the Greek manuscripts. What is more, to prevent
any untutored reader from being shocked by the novelty of the language, I
dispelled the difficulty in the *Annotations.*

Since this is how things stand – that is, since there is perfect agreement among the Greek manuscripts, since this is the reading of Augustine   270
and Jerome, since this same reading is found in some of the oldest Latin
manuscripts – we must examine whether the church has the right to add or
subtract something from the sacred writings, even in the case of a text that
may prove advantageous for heretics. If this were ever allowed, how many
things would have had to be added, deleted, and changed! The passage 'The   275
Father is greater than I' from John[33] would have to be deleted, or one would
have to add 'according to human nature.' They would also have to delete
the passage 'That they may know thee, the only true God, and Jesus Christ,
whom thou hast sent'[34] and many other passages that the Arians seize upon
to defend their impiety. Likewise, every time there is mention of the Holy   280
Spirit in the Scriptures the name of God would have to be added, which
is never clearly joined to it in the sacred writings. Again, when the Lord
says that not even the Son of Man knows the last day,[35] one would have to
add 'according to human nature,' or something similar. In brief, here there
was obvious danger from the Arians; but there was no danger in omitting   285
the word 'given.' Since all heresies establish their beliefs on the erroneous

* * * * *

32 Allen, citing Carlo Vercellone's preface to *Vetus et Novum Testamentum ex an-*
   tiquissimo codice Vaticano ed Angelo Maius (Rome 1857) I iv–v, says that the
   manuscripts Gr 330 and 346 in the Biblioteca apostolica vaticana, lent by the
   pope to the Complutensian Bible project in 1512, were sent back to Rome on
   9 July 1519 and were reintegrated into the papal library on 23 August. Both
   date from the thirteenth or fourteenth century; see *Codices Vaticani Graeci* II ed
   Robertus Devreesse (Vatican City 1937) 1–2, 23–5. Erasmus here applies the
   approbation given to a Greek manuscript of the Old Testament to the Greek
   manuscripts of the New Testament that he employed in his own editions of
   it. Although many scholars over the centuries have tried, none of the Greek
   manuscripts used for the Polyglot New Testament can be identified today.
   See Jerry H. Bentley *Humanists and Holy Writ: New Testament Scholarship in the*
   Renaissance (Princeton 1983) 91–111.
33 John 14:28
34 John 17:3
35 Mark 13:32

interpretation of the sacred writings, what end would there be to altering the texts?

What would we gain by taking these precautions except to make of Holy Scripture a Lesbian rule[36] that may be bent to fit our opinions rather than to expose whatever deviates from the truth? And if orthodox believers appropriate this privilege to themselves, either they will be constrained to make this same concession to heretics or they will render the testimony of the Scriptures ineffectual. Accordingly, just as the church has no right to institute new sacraments, so it has even less right to compose new Scriptures. And if this right is refused the church, who then is the falsifier? he who translates faithfully what is contained in the texts of both the Eastern and the Western church, or he who changes genuine scriptural readings? There is a slight ambiguity in 'there was not yet the Spirit'; but in changing the Scriptures one runs a very serious risk. He should direct his vituperations not against me but rather against the copyists who corrupted this passage on their own authority or foolhardiness. He will say, 'The little word "given" could be added without detriment to the meaning.' On the contrary, detriment could not have been avoided, as I have already shown, and I might well have uncovered another more dangerous pitfall.

Now as there is no more atrocious crime than to corrupt canonical Scripture wilfully, it was not appropriate to blurt out indiscreetly before such a solemn audience something that had not been verified. The place itself, sacred to St Paul, is possessed of a certain majesty. Usually present are prefects of the city, whom they call mayors, learned doctors, sometimes even the bishop, in addition to a numerous and mixed crowd of people. Such circumstances should have induced the man, if he had even the slightest good sense, not to divulge his malice (to say nothing of his stupidity) to men of learning, with utter disregard for the celebrated reputation of the place, nor to infect with lethal poison the minds of the ignorant. For what serpent, what asp, what viper has a more lethal venom than a slanderous tongue, inflamed, as St James says, with the fire of hell?[37] Once it has seeped into men's minds no Psyllian can suck it out, no Marsian incantations can draw it off.[38] After inflicting its sting, the scorpion will reabsorb its own poison

* * * * *

36 A mason's rule made of lead, which could be bent to fit the curve of a moulding (Aristotle *Nicomachean Ethics* 5.10 [1137b29–32]; cf *Adagia* I v 93).
37 James 3:6
38 The Psyllians, an African people dwelling near the Gulf of Sidra, were famous as snake-charmers. The Marsi inhabited central Italy in pre-Roman times. Their

if you place it in proximity to the wound.[39] In this case that would not be possible, even if one wished to do so. From the flesh of the viper a theriac is concocted, an effective antidote against poison. But if you were to grind up all the tongues of the slanderous, they would produce no remedy. Come now, if from that venerable platform before that distinguished assembly he 325 had said that Erasmus was a wine-tippler, would not all sober-minded men have expressed scorn for his untimely insolence, even if they thought it was true? How much more so if they knew he was lying? What do you think learned men concluded who knew that such gross charges were falsely laid in such surroundings, charges which, even had they been only table talk, 330 would demand satisfaction?

But perhaps he flatters himself with the thought that he has accomplished a brilliant feat; and I suspect that those same lips that spewed forth venom and preached the gospel did on that same day consume the sacred body and blood of Christ. The very thought of this atrocious act strikes hor- 335 ror into me. Oh wretched man, if he shrinks not from approaching the holy table with such a conscience, more wretched still if he is so blinded as not to perceive his pitiful plight! We shudder, we fortify ourselves with the sign of the cross, if someone names the devil. But one who maligns his neighbour with such slanders, who poisons the consciences of his hearers and an- 340 nihilates fraternal charity, is truly a devil worse than any Satan; for, in so acting, he has the worst trait of the devil from whence he got his name.[40] What has such a tongue to do with the gospel? What has such a mouth to do with the symbol of Christian concord? What has such a breast to do with Christ, its guest? 345

Perhaps he will deny it all, taking refuge in his conscience, as do all those for whom whatever they wish is holy.[41] As if adulterers and assassins do not delude themselves about their vices! In former times those who discharged the office of sacred preaching before the people did so at their own peril. He who spoke well was applauded and acclaimed; the favour 350 of the audience was signified by the clapping of hands. On the contrary, the stamping of feet, hisses, jeers, and general tumult were in store for the

* * * * *

magicians were famous for snake-bite cures (Pliny *Naturalis historia* 7.2.13–15). Both are mentioned in *Parabolae* CWE 23 247:23–5.
39 Celsus *De medicina* 5.27.5; Pliny *Naturalis historia* 29.29.91
40 The Greek word for 'devil' is διάβολος 'the slanderer,' from the verb δαιβάλλω. The name 'Satan' is from the Hebrew, meaning 'adversary,' one who plots against another.
41 *Adagia* IV vii 16; cf Epp 1804:265–6, 1875:49–50.

preacher who did not live up to what was expected of him, for in those days the manners of the popular theatre had made their way into sacred assemblies. Nowadays people listen silently and quietly to whatever is presented to them. Therefore those who abuse the patience of a Christian assembly are all the more at fault and often deserve to be driven from the pulpit not by hissing but with rubble and rotten eggs. Certainly such men should be publicly reproved by bishops and princes as an example to others. From whom and where will the people learn piety if from such men and in such a place they learn the most wicked of vices?

If anyone is guilty of the slightest offence towards his neighbour, the Gospel bids him put his offering aside and hasten to be reconciled;[42] yet these men, conscious of the crimes they have committed, approach an altar far more sacred than that of the Old Law. These same men exact restitution of others if someone has defrauded his neighbour of the tiniest sum, and yet he who has wounded the reputation of his neighbour in such a place, before such an audience, and with such calumny draws nigh with perfect tranquillity to that mystery before which even the angels stand in awe. Did anyone of that ilk ever make an effort to requite his victim by spoken or written word even if he himself discovered – and everyone else knew – that it was a manifest calumny? They are afraid of decreasing their authority if they confess to error. But they should have had this fear when they were hastening along the road to calumny, when they were preparing to vent their malice in public. He who has given sadness to his brother in a private quarrel is bidden to become reconciled to him, and he who calls his brother 'stupid' in private is adjudged guilty before the Sanhedrin.[43] Yet this man, who before such a crowded assembly, in such a famous place, and in a sacred homily lashes out against his neighbour, making accusations of heresy and of falsifying Sacred Scripture, approaches Communion as if free of all contamination, and even after learning of his error gives no thought to removing the poison that he has infused into the ears of so many men. Can anything be more deplorable than a mind like that? What excuse can be found for it? Ignorance? Such people profess to be doctors of the gospel. And, supposing that they are completely devoid of literary learning, even unlettered folk know that they should not make pronouncements about matters they do not understand, lend credence readily to the calumniator, or recklessly repeat calumny. But these wretched men have been dragged into this deep blindness by envy, hatred, and arrogance, the boon companion of stupidity.

* * * * *

42 Matt 5:23–4
43 Matt 5:22

I thought I should write this to you, my dearest Aldridge, so that you   390
could inform me by letter who this shameless rabble-rouser is, what is his
first name, his last name, his status, and what was the day of his infamous
action. To what end, you might say? I'll tell you. I have it in mind to publish a list of various persons of this sort who have given such a conspicuous
example of their stupidity and malice, not only that the world may compre-   395
hend what monsters of wickedness lurk beneath that pathetic guise, and in
that way they can enjoy the immortal fame they covet by their misdeeds and
become an example to all, but also that, by publishing the names of each
of them individually, the odium of suspicion may not linger against anyone else.[44] In fact some of the more captious people complain in their letters   400
to me that by suppressing the names of the guilty party when I record the
deed of some theologian or monk I cast aspersions upon the whole order,
whereas if I named names those alone would be blamed whose stupidity
had merited the accusation. As matters stand, suspicion devolves upon the
undeserving as well. I do not for all that agree with their opinion, for the   405
fair-minded do not impute blame to an order if one or other of their members has committed an act unworthy of his order, while the prejudiced will
stir up their hatred against the order all the more if the names are made public. I dare say that in the past no one has abstained from attacking the vices
of clerics, priests, monks, and virgins in order to avoid inciting ill feelings   410
against an order, although here too I think a certain measure should be observed. Nevertheless, I have acceded to their wishes to this extent, that in a
brief pamphlet I will depict in their true colours some of the more obtrusive
and visible of these madmen who have gone beyond all limits. I shall give
you a foretaste of the contents so that you may have a better understanding   415
of what I mean.

In the colloquy 'On Faith,'[45] in which a true believer is set against
someone suspected of heresy, these words are spoken by the orthodox believer: 'But I have scruples about sitting down at table with you.' The man
suspected of heresy answers, 'Yet doctors do this so that they may better   420
observe what is ailing their patients or what ills they pretend to have.' The
orthodox believer: 'But I am afraid of appearing to favour heretics.' To this
the suspected heretic replies: 'On the contrary, there is nothing holier than

* * * * *

44 Erasmus wants to know if the preacher was a member of a mendicant order, as
his allusion to the distinctive garb worn by members of the mendicant orders
indicates. He carried out this plan to name his critics in Ep 2045, a letter he
himself published.
45 Cf *Inquisitio de fide* 'An Examination concerning Faith' CWE 39 419–47.

favouring heretics.' Some people have excerpted these last words to prove
that Erasmus writes heresy. But isn't that a dreadful belief, not expiable in   425
a single burning at the stake? What heretic ever dared utter such a thing,
what tyrant dared state it openly? Not even heretics teach that favour should
be given the heretic; but then they do not admit to being heretics. The same
thing is said by those who favour an unholy faction. 'Only Erasmus teaches
that this is holy, and indeed that there is nothing holier.' But these men,   430
more stupid than brute beasts, even if they took no notice of the previous
passage concerning doctors, could at least have understood what follows, as
spoken by the orthodox believer: 'How is that?' The suspected heretic answers: 'Didn't Paul desire to be made anathema for the Jews,[46] who were
more than heretics? Doesn't one who tries to make a good man of a bad   435
one, a living of a dead one, "favour" him?' To which the orthodox believer
responds: 'Of course.' Then the suspected heretic says: 'Favour me in the
same way, then. You'll have nothing to fear.'

Although these observations are clear enough to be perceived by a
blind man, and simple enough to be understood by swine, yet these crass   440
individuals cannot grasp them. And don't think that I am recounting mere
table talk. On the contrary, leaders of the two religious orders thunder such
villainies in public in their sacred sermons, they publish them in their writings, dispute them in public, and expose them for condemnation; and they
earnestly call these petty accusations to the attention of archbishops and   445
even Caesar.[47] And while they busy themselves contriving these plots with
great commotion in various countries, with utter disdain for the views of
good and learned men, they blame my writings for their being held in less
esteem by the people than in days past or less than they think they deserve.
Far be it from me to bare the sharp edge of my pen against any religious or-   450
der![48] But if it were my purpose to direct all the energies of my intellect and
of my eloquence against such infamy, even with a hundred diatribes I could
not bring so much disgrace to an order as they bring upon themselves by
their outrageous behaviour. Who would not think that I was inventing such
accusations, if they did not induce belief by their own actions? Whereas, for   455

* * * * *

46 Rom 9:3
47 Erasmus will name the Dominicans and the Franciscans specifically later in
   this letter (lines 488–9) and in Ep 1864:2; cf n44 above.
48 Erasmus usually attacked religious orders in general (as in the next sentence),
   and referred indiscriminately to mendicant friars and true monks as 'monks'
   – to the extent that some of his friends advised him to criticize individuals,
   not the orders themselves.

myself, as Christ loves me, I would not have believed such things even if
they were said of an enemy.

But in the meantime, what a low opinion they have of bishops and
princes, and of the common crowd, that they should dare disturb them
with such inanities? Do they not seem to regard the whole general public   460
as dunces, completely devoid of human intelligence? They must think that
bishops and princes are either so unjust that, merely to oblige them, they
will immediately condemn pious writings without inquiring into the cause;
or so unlearned that they do not discern their nature; or so diffident that for
fear of a handful of mendicants they would offend Christ and draw down   465
upon themselves the hatred of the whole world. Pilate resisted the demands
of the Jews for a long time,[49] although pontiffs, scribes, Pharisees, elders,
and the motley crowd were of one accord in their mad fury; will Christian
prelates, will Christian princes give in to the wickedness of a few ill-starred
individuals?
                                                                              470
There you have one charge of heresy, or even worse; here is a similar
one that they bandy about, stirring up public clamour. In *The Handbook of
the Christian Soldier*, where I demonstrate how effective the simple preaching of the apostles was through the efficacy of the Spirit, I write somewhat
as follows: 'This is the true and genuine and effective theology, which long   475
ago made proud philosophers and unconquered monarchs bow the knee to
Christ.'[50] Do you see anything here against piety? I know you do not; you
suffer from myopia, no doubt. But these lynxes saw there a detestable impiety. 'What impiety?' you will ask. 'He writes,' they say, 'that there is no true
theology anywhere except in Germany, which is a beehive of heresy.' They   480
do not understand that the word *germana* has the meaning of 'genuine'[51] and
they do not take note that when I wrote those words – which was twenty-
four years ago – there was no mention of heresy in Germany.[52] Of course,

* * * * *

49 Matt 27:24
50 See the prefatory letter to *Enchiridion militis Christiani* Ep 858:116–19 / CWE 66
   10. On Erasmus' use of the Latin *germana* see line 481 below.
51 γνήσιον; cf Phil 2:20, 4:3, 2 Tim 1:2, Titus 1:4.
52 Although the first edition of the *Enchiridion* did appear twenty-four years earlier, in 1503 (Ep 164 introduction), the offending sentence appeared for the first
   time only in August 1518 (the first time the work appeared by itself), in the
   prefatory epistle to Abbot Paul Volz (Ep 858). Luther, who had indeed acquired
   notoriety by this time, interpreted Erasmus' letter to Volz as approval of his
   pamphlet on indulgences (Ep 933:22–7), and Erasmus himself told Johann von
   Botzheim that certain Dominicans who had approved earlier printings were
   now set against it because of the prefatory letter to Volz (Ep 1341A:735–40).

that is what happens to theologians who have no knowledge of grammar! I am not making this up. These words were spoken in public sermons, and they were committed to writing and made public; I know the place, the time, and the person.[53] This will be made known at the proper time. In the meantime, I beg the reader not to have a worse opinion of some good Franciscan or Dominican because of behaviour of this kind. Those who like such behaviour cannot be good, and I know that many are displeased with it.

Listen to a third article of heresy that has been condemned by these same persons. In *The Handbook of the Christian Soldier*, warning that no one should rashly rush headlong into a type of life for which he is not suited but should first consider the nature of that state of life and what are his own spiritual and physical strengths, I write to this effect: 'Being a monk is not a state of holiness but a way of life, which may be beneficial or not according to each person's physical and mental constitution.'[54] What is there in this statement with which even a Momus could find fault?[55] But these critics saw therein a heretical aberration. Of course, I should have said, 'Whoever wishes to be saved should become a monk. For every monk is pious; and whoever is a monk cannot be impious, whereas many Christians are impious.' But in order that my words might be more open to calumny, they changed the word 'monastic life' to 'religion.' They are so ignorant that they think the word 'religion' is synonymous with 'monastic life,' so that every time religion and religious are praised in the Sacred Scriptures they think they are being celebrated. If I had said: 'Matrimony is not piety, virginity is not piety, the priesthood is not piety but a way of life that suits one person but not another,' I would have spoken piously; but it is impious to say the same thing about monasticism. Indeed, if I had said that Christianity is not piety, they would have accepted it with more equanimity, and they would admit that there are many impious Christians, but that is not to say they are not Christian; only monks do not allow their name to be touched. If Christianity is the profession of the Christian life, Christianity is not piety;

* * * * *

53 Erasmus mentions similar charges of heresy in Allen Epp 1967:170–6, 1985:10–15, and 2045. Epp 1985 and 2045 identify his accuser only as a Spanish Franciscan. Bataillon *Erasme* (1991) I 241 and n3 gives his name as Juan de San Vicente.

54 See CWE 66 127. For the larger picture of Erasmus' views expressed here and in the discussion that follows see Erika Rummel '*Monachatus non est pietas*: Interpretations and Misinterpretations of a Dictum' in *Erasmus' Vision of the Church* Sixteenth Century Essays & Studies 23 ed Hilmar M. Pabel (Kirksville, Mo 1995) 41–53.

55 See Ep 1812 n13.

otherwise whoever was baptized would be pious. But if Christianity consists of fulfilling what we profess in baptism, then Christianity is the high-   515
est degree of piety. Likewise if monasticism is the observance of the three
vows over and above ordinary Christianity, monasticism is a high form of
piety. But if it is merely the profession of those same vows, together with
those things connected with the vow of obedience – such as wool, linen,
colour, cinctures of leather or hemp, open or closed shoes, fish, eggs, veg-   520
etables – then monasticism is not piety, nor was it instituted by Christ. What
danger did I pose for the church by writing that it is a way of life not to
be undertaken haphazardly by anyone? that there might be fewer monks?
May Christ so grant it, provided they are better ones. For no type of life is
more desirable for those who sincerely love Christ. But, alas! morals have   525
sunk so low these days that no one fares more successfully in this institution than those who have no concern for piety, and that those who could not
be worldly in the world find the world there. If anyone has a partiality for
this name, the best and the only way of appeasing ill will and winning back
previous favour is to devote oneself entirely to the cultivation of true piety.   530

I shall add a fourth. In a certain very famous university one of the
leading theologians bragged that he had found a weapon with which he
could do away with Erasmus.[56] I said somewhere that Jerome failed to attain the glory of perpetual virginity,[57] and that is evident from his writings.
But this fellow produced a passage from a letter of Jerome to Eustochium   535
on the preservation of virginity. 'We do not only extol virginity but preserve
it.'[58] At this point he exulted in his victory, saying: 'What do the Philerasmi-
ans have to respond to this? Jerome himself professes that he preserves virginity; but no one preserves what he does not have.' Some fellow drinking
companions cheered him on, while the learned men present could scarcely   540
contain their guffaws. For it is manifest that Jerome is speaking there not of
his own virginity but of the chastity of sacred virgins. He says that it was not
his purpose to preach that virtue in that book, because it had been done by
many other authors, whom he then lists by name.[59] His main purpose was

* * * * *

56 In repeating this story in Allen Epp 1967:164–9 and 2045:179–90 Erasmus reveals him to be a Dominican and master of theology. He might possibly be
Erasmus' Louvain enemy Vincentius Theoderici, who died on 4 August 1526.
(Erasmus invokes his name again in anger in Epp 2054 and 2443).
57 In the *Hieronymi Stridonensis vita* CWE 61 48–9
58 Ep 22.23 CSEL 54 175 / CWE 61 168. Jerome's letter is a treatise on virginity as
a way of life and on the pitfalls and vices that assail it. For a translation and
commentary see CWE 61 155–93.
59 Ep 22.22 CSEL 54 174–5 / NPNF 2nd series 6 31 / CWE 61 168

to show in what way it must be kept from being lost. But wasn't that theolo-   545
gian, who had not yet learned what the Latin word *servare* meant, worthy
of guarding pigs? You guard or preserve when you rescue someone who
is about to perish; you are said to guard even when you watch over things
that belong to another; one keeps faith or a command when one does not
violate them; lastly, the word can mean 'to be alert,' as in Horace (but us-   550
ing an expression that is more Greek than Latin): 'Here there's a big ditch,
there a boulder, look out!'[60] Just as a painter is said to set one person against
another when he has pictured them in combat, and a writer or narrator is
said to do what he represents in words, so Jerome said that he preserved
virginity when he demonstrated how it was to be preserved.   555

I hear that another person has stirred up a great fuss out of nothing,
because instead of 'Old Testament' I wrote 'Old Instrument', which I think
can be found at most twice in my writings.[61] This causes them to fear that
henceforth the Old and New Testament will disappear from the world. They
are not aware that St Jerome uses this term several times,[62] nor do they seem   560
to have read Augustine, who teaches that it is more appropriate to say 'Instrument' than 'Testament.'[63] And that is very true whenever reference is
made not to the subject matter but to the written texts. For there would be a
testament even if no written Scripture existed. For when the Lord said, 'This
is the cup of the New Testament,'[64] no book of the New Testament had been   565
composed. Likewise the Old Testament existed before Moses wrote the Pentateuch. Furthermore, tablets and parchments on which compacts are written are called instruments. If any one doubts this let him read the *Pandects*

* * * * *

60 *Satires* 2.3.59: 'Hic fossa est ingens, hic rupes maxima, serva,' where the use of
  serva in an absolute sense, as here and often in the comic writers, is modelled
  on the middle voice of the verb φυλάττω in Greek.
61 Erasmus' 1516 New Testament bore as its title *Novum instrumentum*, a usage he
  maintained in his correspondence: see Allen Ep 396:317, translated in CWE Ep
  396:341 as 'New Covenant,' and Allen Ep 456:96, translated in CWE Ep 456:106
  as 'New Testament.'
62 *Commentarius in Ecclesiasten* 11.2 PL 23 (1883) 1157B–C / CCSL 72 345:25, 32
63 *Contra duas epistolas Pelagianorum* 3.4.12 PL 44 595. In *Anti-Pelagian Writings of
  Saint Augustine* trans Peter Holmes and Robert Wallis (Edinburgh 1876) III 308
  the passage is duly rendered 'which is more definitely called the Old Instrument than the Old Testament.' In the most recent translation of that book, *Augustine ... 21st Century* I-24 168, the point Erasmus wishes to make is missed:
  'it is more precise to call these the old books than the Old Testament.'
64 Matt 26:27 and Mark 14:24 interpose the phrase 'of my blood' between 'cup'
  and 'New Testament,' while Luke 22:20 adds 'in my blood' after 'New Testament.'

Book 22. There he will find the title 'On the Validity of Instruments.'[65] On the
other hand, whoever calls a series of volumes a testament is not to be cen-   570
sured, since it is the figure of synecdoche.[66] They do not perceive that when
they vent their rage against me on this point they vent their rage against
Jerome and Augustine, pillars of the church.

This should suffice to give you a taste. But wait! I almost forgot the
most grave charge of all. In the colloquy 'An Examination Concerning Faith'   575
there is mention of random thunderbolts that strike seas and mountains, but
without effect. Hereupon certain exalted personages, who will be named
shortly, allege that excommunication by the pope is being put to scorn,
without taking note that these words are spoken by a heretic who thinks he
has been wrongly excommunicated. The orthodox believer corrects him, re-   580
sponding to his joke about a lightning bolt from a glass jar: 'Yes, and even
this is frightening,' insinuating that even an unjust excommunication should
be dreaded by a pious man. Then in the person of the heretic the dialogue
continues: 'God alone has a thunderbolt to strike the soul'; and the orthodox believer corrects him with the question: 'What if God is in his vicar?'   585
And the heretic has nothing to answer but 'I wish he were!'[67] In this passage
even in the person of the heretic nothing is said with regard to the sentence
of excommunication that was unjustly decreed that could not also be said
by the orthodox believer.

I have a great many examples of this kind, and not a few others of a   590
less flagrant stupidity but which contain no less malice. Where then is fraternal charity, where human decency, where Christian sincerity? If such example is given by those who profess the philosophy of the Gospels, what
shall we expect from the ignorant multitude? If the salt is insipid, or rather
turned into poison, with what will the stupidity of the common people be   595

* * * * *

65 See the *Digest of Justinian* 22.4 in *Corpus iuris civilis* ed Theodore Mommsen,
   Paul Krueger, and Rudolf Schoell 3 vols (Berlin 1880–2; repr 1967) I 291–2 /
   trans Alan Watson 4 vols (Philadelphia 1985) II 649. The passage treats of contracts and proofs of contracts. The distinction is between a *testimonium* (contract) and an *instrumentum* (proof of contract). The Bible is the *instrumentum*
   of God's *testimonium* with mankind.
66 The figure of speech in which a more inclusive term (here *instrumentum*) is
   used for a less inclusive one (here *testamentum*) or vice versa; a whole for a
   part or a part for a whole.
67 Cf *Inquisitio de fide* CWE 39 421:7–422:11. 'Jove's thunderbolt' is interpreted by
   Craig R. Thompson (n3) to apply to the papal bull *Decet Romanum pontificem*
   (January 1521). It excommunicated Martin Luther for refusing to recant as
   ordered in the bull *Exsurge Domine* (June 1520).

seasoned?[68] Whence will an antidote be sought, if the doctors dispense poison? I profess and have always professed that due honour be given to theologians, and that monks have always been held in high esteem from the very beginnings of the church, and with every right. Who would not respect those who point out to us the road to eternal happiness as prescribed in the 600 Sacred Scriptures? Who would not have the greatest admiration for those who practice a purer form of Christianity amidst so many vestiges of the old paganism? But, immortal God! how far their actions are from those beguiling claims! It would be more tolerable if they injured only me, but now they take away the right to enjoy the benefits of piety that many people confess 605 to finding in my works, they infect the minds of my hearers with the deadly poison of calumny, and by their pernicious example they incite them to great wickedness. Finally, not only do they stir up the hatred of all learned and pious men but, given the present state of men's opinions, they attract considerable odium upon their order. If their shamelessness cannot be appeased 610 by my moderation and numerous defences, I shall do what the Christian law compels me to do. I shall drive this calumny away from me, and I shall confute these elders who never cease from their sinful behaviour, before the eyes of all, declaring my innocence and their more than Jewish malice;[69] and, last of all, I shall turn the hatred directed at the religious order upon 615 its perpetrators. If I could heal my wounds without harming anyone else, I should be content with that; but, since they prevent me from doing this, it is only right to lay the blame upon those who drove me to this extreme.

* * * * *

68 Erasmus plays with the question that Jesus posed to his disciples, 'If the salt loses its savour, with what will you season it?' (Mark 9:50).
69 Erasmus casts himself in the role of the prophet Daniel in 'The History of Susannah,' which, in the Septuagint and Vulgate tradition, forms chapter 13 of the Book of Daniel but, in versions following the Hebrew tradition, is one of the smaller books of the Apocrypha. Before convicting the elders who falsely accused Susannah of adultery, the young Daniel declared his own innocence of her blood (Dan 13:46 Vulg). For examples of anti-Jewish language in Erasmus' letters see Allen Ep 1006:142n. Debate about Erasmus' attitude towards the Jews continues. Some argue that his general advocacy of tolerance would preclude crass racial bias in him. They contend that his tirades, like those of St Paul (himself a Jew), reject not the Jews as persons or as a race but rather the rigorist adherence to the letter of the law that often marked Jewish religion. It was an approach to religion and ritual that he criticized in Christians as well. Others argue that Erasmus' stark language betrays an anti-Semitism that is at least symptomatic of the religious and racial prejudice of his time. For a summary of scholarship on the issue see Hilmar Pabel 'Erasmus of Rotterdam and Judaism: A Reexamination in Light of New Evidence' *Archiv für Reformationsgeschichte* 87 (1996) 9–37. See also CWE 63 xlix–lvi.

Farewell, my dear Robert, beloved in Christ. I am happy that you have found a protector similar to you in openness of character and holiness of   620
life; if only the Christian world had more prelates like him.[70]

Basel, 23 August in the year 1527

1859 / To Maximilian (II) of Burgundy   Basel, 23 August 1527

Maximilian (II) of Burgundy (1514–58) was the second son of Adolph of Burgundy and Anna van Bergen. Erasmus may have seen the boy just after his birth in 1514 (Ep 301). A short while before the composition of this letter, Maximilian became his father's heir upon the death of his elder brother. He later succeeded his father as admiral of the imperial fleet, was inducted into the Order of the Golden Fleece in 1546, and became *stadhouder* of Holland, Zeeland, and Utrecht (CEBR I 227–8).

This letter of compliment and encouragement replies to one from the young nobleman, who wrote at the urging of his tutor Jan Becker of Borsele (although Erasmus was not completely certain as to the identity of the young man; Ep 1860:8–9). When Becker reported that the letter had failed to reach Maximilian (Ep 1898), Erasmus composed a completely new letter in January 1528 (Ep 1927) to assuage the young man's disappointment. Erasmus' autograph draft of the original letter, not extant, served as the basis for its publication in the *Opus epistolarum*. Erasmus will later dedicate his *De recta pronunciatione* to Maximilian.

ERASMUS OF ROTTERDAM TO MAXIMILIAN OF BURGUNDY,
GREETING

I knew your father,[1] the illustrious prince, long ago, when he was still a young boy, my dearest Maximilian. I loved him for the remarkably mild disposition he displayed, without any trace of belligerence, and I sensed   5
that he nurtured the same feelings of partiality towards me. That mutual

* * * * *

70 Probably John Longland (1473–1547), bishop since 1521 of Lincoln, where Aldridge had recently received a benefice. A friend of Erasmus since 1509 or 1515, Longland habitually wrote Erasmus twice each year, although only Epp 1570 and 2227 have survived. He thought Erasmus too friendly towards reformed theology, but he continued to send gifts of money until Erasmus died (CEBR II 341–2).

1859
1 Adolph of Burgundy (1489/90–1540) was the son of Philip of Burgundy and Anna van Borssele. Erasmus wrote for him an *Oratio de virtute* and some prayers (Epp 93, 145, 181, 492, 1927). He later carried out important diplomatic

good will has increased through the years in each of us. For that reason
it was most gratifying to have this memory of your father's favour towards me renewed through your kind letter.[2] But I rejoice all the more
in the knowledge that with your father still living you have succeeded   10
to these feelings of affection. For your letter, which is not at all lacking in polish, breathes not only a feeling of good will towards me that
exceeds the commonplace but also a certain sentiment of devotion, like
that of a son for his father or of a pupil for his teacher. This I believe
was passed on to you from both of your parents, since I was also very   15
dear to your grandmother,[3] and it was increased by Jan of Borsele, a man
to be commended both for his moral integrity and his learning.[4] Surely
on this account you seem to me more fortunate even than some kings.
You have at your disposal wherewith you can acquire two principal blessings; piety towards God, which even of itself renders man happy, and   20
liberal learning, which will be of great use and distinction for all of life
not only to you but to your family, already famed for its noble ancestry,
and to the whole country. You will add no little lustre to your line if you
strive to be more noble through piety and good letters than through your
lineage.[5]   25

I wish that my works, which you say you enjoy, were such that the
reading of them would bring you as much profit as your talents deserve. In
any case it is my goal, although I do not know whether I have attained it, to
attract young men as much to piety as to learning. But what is lacking in my
works will be readily completed and compensated by the zeal of your most   30
learned instructor. I therefore pray to Christ that in his goodness and power
he will adorn and enrich your noble character, already full of promise in
its formative stages,[6] with all the gifts worthy of a Christian prince. In the
meantime take this letter written in my own hand as a pledge of my love,
which you can use to call me to account if I fail you in any way. When   35

*****

missions for the Hapsburg court, and in 1517 was named imperial admiral.
His fleet in 1528 would anchor in the Thames estuary and force the signing
of the treaty of Hampton Court. See CEBR I 223–4.
2 Not extant
3 Anna van Borssele, lady of Veere. She was an early patron of Erasmus (Epp
88, 145), but her largesse proved to be ephemeral (Epp 128, 129, 146). See also
CEBR I 173–4.
4 On Jan Becker of Borsele, Maximilian's tutor from 1525 to 1529, see Ep 1851
introduction.
5 Cf Ep 1854:4–5 (to Margaret of Navarre).
6 *Adagia* II i 89

you write to your father I ask that you give him my fond and courteous
greetings.

    Given at Basel, 23 August in the year 1527

1860 / To Jan Becker of Borsele   Basel, 24 August 1527

The letter, which answers Ep 1851 and will be answered by Ep 1898, first
appeared in the *Opus epistolarum* (1529). For Jan Becker, tutor to Maximilian
(II) of Burgundy, see Ep 1851 introduction.

ERASMUS OF ROTTERDAM TO JAN BECKER OF BORSELE, DEAN OF
ZANDENBURG, GREETING
I had formed the suspicion from a letter of Dorp that your affection for me
if not totally extinguished had become lukewarm;[1] and I think you know
what I am referring to. But that suspicion did not penetrate deeply into   5
my heart; and, being human, I easily pardon human feelings of this sort. I
am certainly glad that you have recovered from your illness or rather been
restored to life. I wrote to Maximilian as you wished, although I was not at
all certain whether he was the son of Adolph, prince of Veere.[2] I wish you
the best of health.   10

    Given at Basel, 24 August in the year 1527

1861 / To William Warham   Basel, 24 August 1527

This letter was first published in the *Opus epistolarum* (1529). For William Warham, see Ep 1828 introduction.

ERASMUS OF ROTTERDAM TO WILLIAM WARHAM, ARCHBISHOP OF
CANTERBURY, GREETING
My sole glory and refuge in Christ, I have clearly discerned your more than
paternal devotion towards me partly through your letter, partly through

* * * * *

1860
1 The letter is not extant; on this, see Ep 1851 n2. Maarten van Dorp was a
   Louvain theologian with whom both Erasmus and Thomas More exchanged
   important letters about Dorp's criticism of the *Praise of Folly*; see Erasmus' Epp
   304, 337, 347 and More's 'Letter to Martin Dorp' in *The Complete Works of Saint
   Thomas More* 15 vols in 21 (New Haven 1963–97) xv 1–127. Dorp became a
   supporter and friend of Erasmus. See CEBR I 398–404.
2 See Ep 1859 n1.

what you confided to my servant to be relayed to me.[1] We both have the 5
same wish, but the present situation stands in the way. There can be no
withdrawal from the battle line yet. Perhaps in a little while we will be
separated from each other by a shorter distance.[2] In the meantime I bid you
to be of good cheer. This turmoil is plainly the will of destiny.[3] My life will
fail me sooner than my courage.   10

You know who is the instigator of all this tragic fuss, which was stirred
up in Paris and is now fermenting or rather raging in Spain.[4] He is a man
born for this kind of mischief, his only claim to fame in the eyes of the
world. In Spain it is principally the mendicant orders that are acting out
this play,[5] while the bishops and chief men of learning support me, without 15
mentioning the enthusiastic favour of the court. The affair will have, as I
hope, a successful outcome. The pension money had not yet reached Pieter
Gillis at the end of July; I think he has received it by now.[6] May the Almighty
preserve your distinguished self free of all harm.

Given at Basel, 24 August in the year 1527   20

1862 / To Jan de Hondt   Basel, 25 August 1527

Written in response to Erasmus Schets' suggestion in Ep 1849, this letter was
first published in the *Opus epistolarum* (1529).

* * * * *

1861
1 The letter, probably answering Epp 1828 and 1831, which had been delivered
  by Nicolaas Kan, is not extant; cf Ep 1866:4 and Allen Ep 1926:13.
2 For Erasmus' inclination to leave Basel at this time, see Ep 1889:31–2 and Allen
  Ep 1926:15n.
3 Erasmus is probably referring to his troubles in Spain and with Edward Lee
  and Spanish theologians, not to the growing schism in Germany or to Warham's overriding concern about King Henry VIII's matrimonial problems.
4 Edward Lee was now in Spain on an embassy from England, and Erasmus saw
  him as the catalyst of the growing opposition there; see Ep 1814 n39. Erasmus
  was also convinced that Noël Béda had helped Lee to compile and publish his
  attack on Erasmus' New Testament; see Epp 1571, 1721 introductions.
5 That is, the Dominicans, Franciscans, Carmelites, and Augustinians
6 Erasmus had been drawing money from a pension in Aldington (Kent) provided by Warham since 1512; see Ep 255 introduction. Erasmus always had
  difficulties with the integral transfer of this pension. Up to now Pieter Gillis
  had been his agent in this regard; but the latter's confidence in Franz Birckmann, whom Erasmus trusted not at all, led him to transfer this and all his
  financial affairs into the hands of Erasmus Schets; see Epp 1726, 1781:5–10,
  1866. See also Epp 1804 n76, 1829 n10.

Jan de Hondt (c 1486–1571) was a Flemish cleric and graduate of Louvain who paid an annuity to Erasmus on a Courtrai benefice settled on him by Pierre Barbier. On this annuity see especially Ep 1458; on Erasmus' relations with Jan de Hondt see CEBR II 100.

ERASMUS OF ROTTERDAM TO JAN DE HONDT, CANON OF COURTRAI, GREETING

For your customary loyalty towards me I am most grateful. The fact that the money remained so long in the hands of Marcus Laurinus has resulted in a notable loss for me, for which I can blame no one except the customs of the court.[1] If it had been with Schets, he would have seen to it that I suffered no loss.

I think Pierre Barbier incurred the wrath of Mercury at his birth, since, after spending so many years at the courts of monarchs, the emperor, the Roman pontiff, and in Spain, where land and rivers flow with gold, he has returned to us naked.[2] I am happy that Nicolas Barbier managed to escape safely, not only for my own sake[3] – for you write that this concerns me as well. I pray that you may have everything that your talents deserve. Barbier owes me a good amount of money; I hope he becomes rich quickly so that he can settle his debts.

Given at Basel 25 August in the year 1527

In future, if you can do so conveniently, do not entrust money to anyone without Erasmus Schets' approval. He will see that I receive it with the least possible loss. His Latin may not be very good, but he is a man of excellent loyalty.

* * * * *

1862

1 See Epp 1848, 1849, 1871:24–5.

2 An allusion to Barbier's constant shortage of funds. Mercury was the god of good luck and commercial success. Pierre Barbier of Arras (d 1551/2) had been chaplain and secretary to the imperial Chancellor Guillaume Le Sauvage and then to Pope Adrian VI, but both died before they could arrange adequate financial provision for him. At this time he was dean of Tournai, but family and financial obligations kept him poor. While still with the chancellor he had been able to settle an annual payment on Erasmus from St Mary's church in Courtrai, but its payment had at times been late or even cancelled by Barbier's own urgent needs. See Epp 476, 496, 443, 585, 621 introduction; cf CEBR I 93–4.

3 Nicolas was a brother of Pierre Barbier. He sometimes dealt with Erasmus in Pierre's name (Epp 608, 652), and he acquired some of Pierre's prebends as a caution in the event of Pierre's death in a foreign place (CEBR I 93). We do not know the circumstances of the escape mentioned here.

Johannes Cochlaeus
Wood engraving by Tobias Stimmer
in Nicolaus Reusner *Icones sive imagines* (Strasbourg: Bernhardus Jobinus 1590)
Centre for Reformation and Renaissance Studies,
Victoria University, University of Toronto

1863 / To Johannes Cochlaeus   Basel, 25 August 1527

This is the earliest extant letter in a correspondence which began in 1525 (Ep
1577:13–16). It was first published in the *Opus epistolarum* (1529).

Johannes Cochlaeus (1479–1552), born Johann Dobnek near Nürnberg, studied arts in Cologne and law in Bologna and then took a doctorate in theology at Ferrara. A protégé of Willibald Pirckheimer, he was interested in the
new learning and published in several different fields. For a while he admired Hutten; but, after direct conversations with Luther, he became an active polemicist against the Reformation. His works emphasized the unity and
coherence of Catholic teaching, but his lack of restraint in attacking the reformers, especially Luther, on whom he blamed the Peasants' Revolt, lost
him the friendship of many former colleagues. Erasmus refused to sanction the publication of Cochlaeus' German translation of *De libero arbitrio*.
Cochlaeus worked in the service of Duke George of Saxony but withdrew
to Wrocław after the duke's death in 1539. See Remigius Bäumer *Johannes
Cochlaeus, 1479–1552: Leben im Werk und Dienst der katholischen Reform* (Münster
1980); CEBR I 321–2; OER I 369–71. Cochlaeus published 199 books between
1522 and 1550. For his bibliography see Martin Spahn *Johannes Cochläus: ein
Lebensbild aus der Zeit der Kirchenspaltung* (Berlin 1898; repr Nieuwkoop 1964)
341–72.

ERASMUS OF ROTTERDAM TO JOHANNES COCHLAEUS, GREETING
I knew that the change in the order of items in the book[1] came about by
error; and even if it had been done purposely it is a matter of such slight
importance that it would not lessen the pleasantness of our friendship, not
to say give me any offence. I am happy that Thomas More has become your   5
friend.[2] For it is fitting that if, as the proverb has it, among friends all is
common,[3] friends also should be shared with friends.

* * * * *

1863
1 Possibly Cochlaeus' edition of the letters exchanged between Henry VIII and
  Luther (Cologne: Petrus Quentell, February 1527), to which he made considerable additions, including a Latin version of Luther's *Antwort* (Ep 1773 n7) and
  a *Discussio* in which Erasmus' name figures frequently.
2 Cochlaeus dedicated to More his *Fidelis et pacifica commonitio Joan. Cochlaei,
  contra infidelem et seditiosam commonitionem Mart. Lutheri ad Germanos* (Leipzig:
  Valentine Schumannn 1531). Three letters of his correspondence with More are
  extant; see *The Correspondence of Sir Thomas More* ed Elizabeth Frances Rogers
  (Princeton 1947) Epp 164–6.
3 *Adagia* I i 1

As for your plans to set out for Denmark,[4] I pray that it will turn out
well. The journey is very long, the inhabitants are uncivilized, and winter is upon us. Besides, the emperor is organizing a general council. I have   10
a record of all the official acts that passed between the emperor, France,
Venice, and the pope, published at Alcalá by the Chancellor Mercurino.[5] If
the matter is urgent and you nourish good hopes, I shall bear your absence
with more equanimity, but I would prefer that you were not so far away.

If the bishops were fighting for the kingdom of Christ and not for   15
their own I would engage in this campaign with more enthusiasm. In the
meantime, however, the rebellious temerity of wicked men must be held in
check until God inspires the minds of princes. There will never be an end
to these uprisings unless certain things change, but these changes are of
such a nature that there is no hope of their being accepted. Therefore, I can   20
give you no advice in this situation except that you look to the interests of
Christ, not of men, and that you be more concerned with saving men than
with punishing them. I do not have time, nor is it safe, to commit more to
a letter. Farewell, my dearest brother and fellow soldier in the Lord.

Given at Basel 25 August in the year 1527   25
Give my best regards to my excellent friend Nausea.[6]

* * * * *

4 After King Frederick I had made concessions to the Reformation, the bish-
  ops of Denmark, assembled at Viborg, appealed to Johann Maier of Eck or to
  Cochlaeus to help them in disputing with the heretics; but in the end both
  Catholic apologists declined. Five days before the writing of this letter, the
  Diet of Odense passed an ordinance establishing religious freedom, permit-
  ted marriage of the clergy, and transferred the confirmation of bishops from
  Rome to the crown. See *Documents of the Continental Reformation* ed B.J. Kidd
  (Oxford 1911; repr 1967) 233–4.
5 Mercurino Gattinara, imperial chancellor. Erasmus refers to *Caroli ... quinti
  ... ad duo Clementis septimi ... Brevis responsio, in qua ab ipso pontifice appellat,
  petitque generalis christianorum omnium concilii congregationem* (Alcalá: Miguel de
  Eguía, 10 April 1527; repr Basel: Andreas Cratander nd). It contains the 23 June
  and 26 June 1526 briefs of Clement VII, the 17 and 18 September answers from
  Charles V, a 6 October letter from Charles to the college of cardinals, urging
  them to call a general council if the pope refused, and a reply by Charles (12
  February 1527) to proposals for general peace proffered by the ambassadors
  of the pope, of France, and of Venice.
6 Fridericus Nausea was a vocal opponent of the Reformation, but he counselled
  Catholic rulers and church authorities to deal with it in as conciliatory a way
  as possible. He admired Erasmus greatly, and published *Ad magnum Erasmum
  Roterodamum ... oratio* (Vienna: Johannes Singriener 1524). He visited Erasmus
  in 1526, and the two maintained a steady correspondence, most of which is
  not extant. See Ep 1577 introduction and n1; CEBR II 7–8.

1864 / To Alonso Manrique de Lara   Basel, 26 August 1527

This letter survives in two manuscripts: the autograph rough draft, which is
conserved in Copenhagen (MS GKS 95 Fol f 236), and a secretary's fair copy
(signed by Erasmus) that was actually dispatched to Manrique and is preserved today in the Real Academia de la Historia (Madrid MS Est 18 gr 1
5 f 9). It was first printed by Adolfo Bonilla y San Martín *Erasmo en España*
173–70; repr *Revue hispanique* 17 (1907) 541–8.

Alonso Manrique de Lara, as archbishop of Seville and inquisitor-general in
Spain, called the theological conference in Valladolid to investigate complaints
against Erasmus (see Ep 1846 introduction; cf Ep 1814:276–309). We can presume from Erasmus' silence here that he did not yet know that Manrique had
adjourned the inquisition on 13 August 1527.

Greeting, most reverend Archbishop. I have learned from the letters of
friends what commotions and calamities certain Dominican and Franciscan friars have stirred up in your country. There is no place where they
have not tried the same thing – in Hungary, in Poland, in England, in Brabant, in France – but nowhere has it succeeded.[1] In the French upheavals, as   5
in yours, Edward Lee has played a leading role.[2] He secretly wrote a book
against me, wishing to avenge himself for the meagre glory he came away
with in a previous encounter.[3] He pretends that he wishes to publish it in
your country; I wish he would![4] I prefer a published work, so that I may
respond to it, rather than this smoke-screen that he raises in Spain and else-   10
where, secretly lining up the monks against me. For these gluttons,[5] I am
certain, would never take on the task of reading my works and collecting
snippets from them. I don't think they know enough grammar to understand things written in Latin. And this is what Lee makes bold to do in
your land, although he knows this vexes the king of England, the cardinal,   15
the archbishop of Canterbury, the bishop of London, the bishop of Lincoln,

* * * * *

1864
1 On the 'commotions' in Spain see Epp 1791 introduction, 1814. For similar
  comments about widespread opposition see Ep 1804 n43.
2 Erasmus sees Lee as the catalyst of the troubles in Spain (Epp 1815:37–43,
  1828:13–14). The same link between Lee and Erasmus' critics in France was
  made in Ep 1861:11–14.
3 For the first book see Ep 1902 n16. For the alleged new book see Ep 1814 n39.
4 Cf Ep 1909:31–2.
5 *ventres*; see Ep 1805 n53.

Autograph letter from Erasmus to Alonso Manrique de Lara (Ep 1864:1–40)
Royal Library, Copenhagen, MS GKS 95 Fol f 236

the bishop of Rochester, Thomas More, and many other learned men[6] – in
fact, knowing full well that they strongly disapprove. Nor do the monks
care that these tactics irritate the pope, who in two separate edicts imposed
silence first on Zúñiga and then on some madmen from Louvain,[7] and that
they annoy the emperor, who did the same by a similar edict in Brabant.[8]
That he did so sincerely is attested by a letter of his to me, at the end of
which are these words: 'Yet we, for our part, shall not fail to make it clear
to everyone, by our treatment of you, how highly we esteem you for your
abilities and your truly religious spirit; in this way we hope that your detractors, who stubbornly oppose all those who are interested in good literature and genuine piety, will cease at last to yelp at your heels and learn
that the emperor stands by you as a man strong in every branch of learning
and in true piety, and that he will defend your honour and reputation as he
does his own,' etc.[9]

Of his own initiative Pope Clement has twice sent me two hundred
gold florins,[10] promising to do all that a sincere supporter can do. But this
lot who flaunt their holy obedience obey neither divine nor human laws,
neither temporal nor ecclesiastical constitutions, calling holy whatever suits
their fancy. They stop at nothing, drawing strength from the conspiracy of
so many factions and from the stupidity of the crowd. They disregard the
opinions of the few, that is to say of the best; and, as they stir up new tempests in a world already rife with discord, they fail to recognize how ill-
timed such intrigues are. If anything needed to be investigated, it could
have been done at a more opportune time, especially since I have never
gathered any factions around me, nor have I professed any condemned belief and, finally, I have always submitted all my views to the judgment of
the Catholic church.

With good reason I find them lacking in prudence in all of this. It
is flagrant impiety for them to stab me in the back as I join battle against
Luther at the behest of the pope, the emperor, and other princes, at great
personal peril, and defend to the best of my ability the cause of our common

* * * * *

6 Erasmus refers to Cardinal Thomas Wolsey, Archbishop William Warham of
   Canterbury, and the bishops of London (Cuthbert Tunstall), Lincoln (John
   Longland), and Rochester (John Fisher). On More see Ep 1804 introduction.
7 For Clement VII's directive silencing Zúñiga see Ep 1443B (Allen Ep 1438):17
   and n4; for his communication to the Louvain faculty through Albert Pigge,
   his chamberlain, see Ep 1589.
8 See Ep 1690 n11.
9 Ep 1731:7–14
10 See Epp 1443B:20–3, 1796:22 (with n5 on the currency).

church, suffering personal injuries in the process. In so doing they give greater satisfaction to the Lutheran party than if they were to publish a hundred books against them! They do not profess open support of Luther, I admit, but they render him a distinct service. Luther himself could not hope for better assistance than that which they provide: enemies of Luther in name but in reality his defenders. Proof of my far from bloodless battle with Luther is his *Servum arbitrium* and my *Hyperaspistes*, the second part of which will now appear.[11] And I am doing this in that part of Germany which is girded on all sides by cities where this pestilence reigns supreme, with new dogmas arising endlessly, so much so that the latest ones are always worse than those that went before. In this region, of course, no one up to now has dared to utter a word against Luther, and especially to put it in writing. And as I engage in this struggle these sworn enemies attack me and shower me with calumnies to which I must respond constantly. They beset me with outrageous suspicions and sometimes outright lies, as if there were a lack of doctrines open to public view for them to condemn as impious, if they have the ability or the desire to do so.

Be that as it may, most reverend Archbishop, I am very grateful for your most attentive care in repressing or at least controlling these hornets,[12] who could not be curbed in any other way, by prohibiting them from venting their rage upon me in the public forum, as they had begun to do. But I already detect what snares they will lay for your gentle nature. They will write accusations and spread them throughout the world, and make pronouncements without awaiting your decision, as they have done in these 'articles' that friends of mine sent me.[13] The preface makes frequent mention of heretics, and the judgments already decided upon proclaim 'Against the most holy Trinity of God,' 'Against the divinity and glory of Christ,' 'Against the divinity of the Holy Spirit,' etc. These are not the charges of a judicial inquiry but verdicts of judges; and in one article they added, 'Behold a new heretic.' By such tricks, although they have been forbidden to speak out in public against me (which they have done up to now to their

* * * * *

11 See Ep 1853, the preface to *Hyperaspistes* 2, and cf Ep 1804 n10.
12 Cf *Adagia* i i 60.
13 Perhaps the preliminary list of twenty-one articles sent by Pedro Juan Olivar on 13 March 1527 (Ep 1791:1). This was probably the list that the inquisitor Manrique found to be repetitious and disorganized. He ordered Erasmus' accusers to rearrange and edit it for consideration by the theologians to be assembled in Valladolid on 27 June 1527. See *Revista de archivos, bibliotecas, y museos* 6 (1902) 65–6.

heart's content), they will preach against me in a different but more pernicious manner. In the meantime they do not bear in mind what methods I   80
could use to take vengeance on them, if I did not think it more Christian
to suffer their wrongs than to retaliate against them. And yet, even with
my silence, they succeed only in arousing greater odium for themselves everywhere by these actions, as if they were not already universally hated.
They make me out to be an enemy, while good and true monks know me   85
by experience to be their greatest friend.

With what liberty at times I admonish rulers in my writings, as in
The Christian Prince and the *Panegyric to Prince Philip!*[14] With what liberty
I admonish popes and bishops![15] None of them ever became the least bit
hostile to me. Only these men, who ought to be the most tolerant of re-   90
buke, do not accept a general admonition. And yet in the meantime they
pretend not to be aware of the tales about them that circulate throughout
the world, which speak in a very different tone from that of my books, tales
that, not without feelings of embarrassment, I am often obliged to hear. It
is to these that they should respond if they wish to avoid the hatred of   95
men, which they now aggravate the more by this conduct. As far as this
present matter is concerned, I have always nurtured a dislike for any kind
of faction and have always striven to instil through my writings sentiments
that would inspire men to a more sincere piety and to remove those absurdities that had all but banished Christ from men's minds. I have never   100
made claim to great learning and for that reason have always abstained
from abstruse subject matter, in which, sometimes, there is more ostentation than piety. Not only do I suffer the criticisms of learned men but I
seek and demand them, and if I am found to be in error I gladly make
amends. To avoid all lapses is not within man's reach, and there has never   105
been anyone so learned and discreet that he has pleased everyone in every
respect.[16]

* * * * *

14 *Institutio principis christiani* was written in 1516 for Prince Charles. The *Pane-*
   gyricus was written (quite unwillingly) in 1503–4.
15 In his *Julius exclusus* Erasmus had been extremely critical of the reigning pope,
   but he never acknowledged authorship of it. He frequently complained to his
   correspondents about papal involvement in wars and worldliness at the papal
   court; but he refrained from admonishing them personally.
16 The statement that no one, even the most learned and respected of Christian teachers, can be expected to be entirely free from error is repeated at
   lines 143–4 below; cf similar statements at Epp 1828:18–19, 1879:25–6, 108–11,
   1886:53–5. Cf also Ep 1846 (from Clement VII to Alonso Manrique de Lara)
   lines 26–7.

But if we are to allow for calumnies, distortions, and suspicions, one could find much more to attack in the writings of Augustine and Jerome than in mine. Imperfections would be found also in the Epistles of St Paul, if his authority did not exclude the very idea. I shall say nothing about the charge of outright lies. All of my writings are for the most part dashed off in haste; this is a defect of my nature.[17] Many things were written when I was a young man, and it was often my specific aim to speak the truth in a playful manner, so that the truth, bitter of itself, might beguile the reader by its attractiveness; but the beguilement would be for the benefit of the one beguiled. I wrote for a world at peace; and so I admit that there are many things in my writings that could be stated in a more circumspect and guarded manner. But I judged mankind according to my own nature; I would never have believed that calumniators of this sort would appear, if it had not been verified by experience. Nothing of an impious nature can be found in my books, I believe; and if it is found I shall not allow it to go uncensored. A good part of their calumnies arises from their ignorance of the Latin and Greek tongues, and next from their unfamiliarity with figures of speech, which are not recognizable to men used to unadorned syllogisms, corollaries, and irrelevancies.[18] In addition they are mistaken concerning the person of the speaker: what is spoken in the person of a heretic in the colloquies they interpret as being spoken by Erasmus,[19] or what is spoken by an impious soldier they impute to me.[20] Nor do they make distinctions in time: what is spoken by Christ or St Paul in the *Paraphrases* according to the usage of their times they interpret according to the conditions of the present-day church. They object to things to which I have responded on numerous occasions, as if no response had ever been given. Your good judgment will easily detect that they do not read what I wrote but excerpt statements useful for purposes of slander from the calumnies of Zúñiga, Lee, and others who have attempted to criticize my writings. The commotion they caused could have been quelled, in my opinion, if they had been told: 'At the present moment there are more than enough disturbances in

*****

17 Cf Ep 1879:96, 1902:296–7.
18 This is a frequent complaint of Erasmus against the traditionalist theologians. He uses the term *impertinencia*. As if in retort, Noël Béda *Apologia adversus clandestinos lutheranos* (Paris: Josse Bade 1529) used the same term to describe some of the elements in Erasmus' Ep 1581 (Allen Ep 1864:115n).
19 On misunderstanding of *Inquisitio de fide*; see Ep 1858:417–38, 575–89.
20 Perhaps *Militis et Cartusiani* 'The Soldier and the Carthusian,' in which the soldier belittles members of religious orders.

the world, without stirring up new ones by calumny and suspicion; there
are more than enough of those who openly profess heretical beliefs without 140
twisting to the uses of calumny things said correctly or with ambiguity of
meaning. Moreover it is unfair to require of Erasmus that there be no trace
of error in his prolific output, when this was not the case with Jerome or
Cyprian or Augustine or any other of the ancient writers, as I am inclined to
believe. Lastly, since a battle is now being waged with Luther in which Eras- 145
mus is totally engaged, and since the emperor is planning a general council,
this is not the opportune moment for such disturbances.'

Since this was not done, they must be required to read through all my
works and give proof that they have read them. For this purpose I have sent
a catalogue of all my works,[21] so that they will not make extracts from the 150
calumnies of others to which I have responded, or if they do extract material from them, they can also deal with the arguments I provide for my
defence. In addition, they should not circulate their criticisms prematurely,
but should show them to the appropriate persons. Lastly, do not let them do
more harm under the guise of an inquisition than they have already done in 155
private defamations and seditious preaching or let them make pronouncements on their own authority, using offensive accusations and all sorts of
abuse, converting an investigation into a mad frenzy. When these measures are put into effect, may it please your Grace to send me the articles
of accusation. If, in responding to them, I do not satisfy your criteria, it 160
will be your duty to deliver a verdict in the interests of Christian orthodoxy; it will be my duty to show myself a true Christian. Furthermore, so
that you may be better acquainted with the issues, I send you my book of
Supputationes,[22] in which I responded to the scandalous calumnies of Noël
Béda, a Parisian theologian, a man who has drawn upon himself the ha- 165
tred and ridicule of all men, good and bad, learned as well as unlearned.
Many things will prove useful in the present situation. Soon afterwards I
will send you another book against similar calumnies.[23] Have the monks

* * * * *

21 Probably the *Catalogus omnium Erasmi lucubrationum* (Basel: Froben, April 1523;
   rev ed September 1524), originally cast as a letter to Johann von Botzheim of
   Constance (Allen I 1–46 / CWE Ep 1341A)
22 *Supputationes errorum in censuris Natalis Bedae* (Basel: Froben, March 1527). This
   was an omnibus volume containing four different books or tracts of Erasmus
   against Béda, the latest and most substantial of which was *Supputatio errorum
   in censuris Bedae*.
23 The *Apologia adversus monachos quosdam Hispanos* (Basel: Froben, c October
   1527), dedicated to Manrique (Ep 1879).

read my answers to Lee,[24] Zúñiga,[25] and Carranza.[26] Likewise in the fourth
edition of the *Annotations* I explain many points.[27]   170

It is a great annoyance, most honoured Bishop, that these sycophants
should give trouble to your Excellency, and that my old age, which would
like nothing better than to occupy itself in more useful pursuits, should be
involved with such lunatics. They have given ample evidence on many occasions of their evil intentions. But it is even more intolerable that Chris-   175
tian concord should be split asunder by wrangling of this sort when every effort should have been made to re-establish it. For as I have come
to know the character of these men, born for conspiracy and sedition, unless my sense of foreboding deceives me, nothing good will come of this
inquisition. They will make use of this term to suit their own devices   180
unless the good judgment of princes prevent this from happening. For
my part, with a simple and sincere heart I entrust the whole matter to
Christ and to your wisdom. I pray that you be granted every blessing in
Christ.

Given at Basel, 26 August 1527   185

If what my friends write is true – that certain people in Spain are devoured by a fierce hatred while others are carried away by their devotion
to my cause – I am afraid your country will be plunged into chaos. I should
certainly not wish to be the cause, even if it is not my fault. I should prefer
the storm to settle – even to my detriment, if this is the only way in which   190
calm can be restored. It seems to me that the wisest course and the one most
useful for controlling their excesses is to order them to present their articles

* * * * *

24 *Apologia qua respondet duabus invectivis Eduardi Lei* (Antwerp: Michaël Hillen
March 1520) ASD IX-4 21–70; *Responsio ad Annotationes Eduardi Lei* (Antwerp:
Michaël Hillen April 1520) ASD IX-4 71–201; and *Liber tertius quo respondet
reliquis annotationibus Eduardi Lei* (Antwerp: Michaël Hillen May 1520) ASD IX-
4 202–335. See Rummel *Catholic Critics* 1 95–120 and CWE 72 xix–xx.

25 *Apologia respondens ad ea quae Iacobus Lopis Stunica taxaverat in prima duntaxat
Novi Testamenti aeditione* (Louvain: Dirk Martens, September 1521). It was en-
larged for inclusion in the *Apologiae omnes* (Basel: Johann Froben, October
1521–February 1522). This latter is probably the edition sent by Erasmus to
Manrique. See Allen IV 622. On the quarrel with Zúñiga, see Rummel *Catholic
Critics* 1 145–50, 162–77.

26 *Apologia de tribus locis quos ... defenderat S. Caranza theologus* (Basel: Froben
1522). See Rummel *Catholic Critics* 1 150, 62–77.

27 Erasmus worked on the fourth edition from July 1524 and was still revising
the notes in the summer of 1526. It appeared from the press of Froben in
March 1527. Very few additions or changes were made thereafter; see Ep 1571
n9. On the editions see also Ep 1818 n4.

in the legitimate fashion in use among theologians, that is, first to cite my words faithfully and indicate the passage, then to submit their objections. For to heap up accusations such as these: 'Erasmus defends corrupt manu- 195 scripts,' 'he rants and raves against St Jerome,' 'he pleads and defends the cause of Arians,' 'he spurns all suggestions,' 'he amasses worthless expla- nations,' is not to write articles; it is simply verbal abuse.[28] They collect such material not from my books but from Edward Lee's book or, rather, from his table of contents. But if they are forced to conform to the conditions I 200 mention, which are perfectly fair, they will either desist or act with more moderation, and we shall have an end to this affair. It is my own fervent desire that my books be purged of all errors if they contain anything that is contrary to pious doctrine. But for other matters, since the judgments of men are so divergent, and what is excellent for one is abominable for another, I 205 do not think we should become too apprehensive.

Since such is my fate, I bear up well under all this confusion that has arisen during my lifetime. May your Excellency fare well, Most Reverend Archbishop, to whom I give and devote myself entirely.

Erasmus of Rotterdam, in his own hand 210

To the Most Reverend Father and lord in Christ, Alonso Manrique, archbishop of Seville, my most venerable Lord

1865 / To Tielmannus Gravius   Basel, 27 August 1527

This letter first appeared in the *Opus epistolarum* (1529). Dating it later than Ep 1829, which initiated this exchange of letters, but unsure of the year-date for either, Allen places it in 1527 because Jacobus Sobius of Cologne, mentioned here, died sometime before 25 January 1528. For Gravius, see Ep 1829 introduction and CEBR II 125–6.

ERASMUS OF ROTTERDAM TO TIELMANNUS GRAVIUS OF FOSSA, GREETING

Mercury must be on my side.[1] In return for a casual and brief note I received two letters, one of normal length, the other almost the size of a small

* * * * *

28 These charges appear in the first 'objection' that Erasmus answers in the *Apologia adversus monachos quosdam Hispanos* (LB IX 1029E–F). See also Luis Coronel's opinion at Valladolid in Beltrán de Heredia *Cartulario* VI 59–62.

1865
1 Cf Ep 1862 n2.

volume.[2] Both gave me great pleasure, on many counts, but chiefly because   5
of your sincere devotion to me – well, not really to me but to those gifts
that you believe exist in me but that are not mine. For what is ours? Rather,
whatever there is belongs to God.

I am grieved to learn that Helias, such a fine old man, has been taken
from us but rejoice that he has returned to his heavenly home.[3] Was there   10
ever anyone more good-natured or honest? In his last letter he wrote at the
end, 'Your Helias, a barbarian, decrepit, a living corpse,' as if foreseeing the
imminence of his death. I didn't like that expression 'living corpse,' and in
my last letter I chided him for calling the temple of the Holy Spirit a corpse,[4]
since no one is more alive than those who die in that state. He answered me   15
not with the pen but by his actual demise.

I am glad to have the portrait of your family that you painted for me,
and more pleased to know that fortune fulfils your desires, since you take
care that your children are brought up in a religious manner, destining only
one of them for a business career. Since you have eight children and you   20
give them such a religious training, it is in vain that you offer me a share in
your common fortunes – I am not such an impious fellow as to cause any
diminution whatever of resources so piously invested; I have the highest
esteem and admiration for you. It remains for us to fasten with adamantine
bonds a friendship born of a modest gift made of iron.[5] May the Lord Jesus   25
bless your affairs and all your family.

At Basel, 27 August, in the year 1527
Give my best regards to Sobius.[6]

1866 / To Erasmus Schets   Basel, 27 August 1527

This autograph letter answers Ep 1849. Published for the first time by Allen,
the original is in the British Library (MS Add 38512 f 23). For Schets see Ep
1849 introduction.

* * * * *

2 Neither reply to Ep 1829 is extant.
3 Helias Marcaeus was a regent in the faculty of arts in Cologne, guardian of
  a convent of Benedictine nuns in that city, and an avid promotor of the cult
  around the supposed relics of the seven Macchabees venerated there. Erasmus
  composed a letter for him on this subject (Ep 842). Cf CEBR II 381–2.
4 Cf 1 Cor 6:19. Neither Marcaeus' letter nor Erasmus' reply is extant.
5 Ep 1829:2
6 Jacobus Sobius, a member of the humanist circle in Cologne, who had last
  written to Erasmus in December 1526 (Ep 1775); cf CEBR III 262–3.

Greeting. Marcus Laurinus is a loyal friend but a bit slow and negligent in getting things done.[1] I shall have to stomach this loss. I wrote Jan de Hondt to disburse money only to those whom you name.

The archbishop of Canterbury[2] writes that he has entrusted ninety no-bles to a German businessman named Pieter Weldanck, a person known to   5
him, to be delivered to Pieter Gillis so that this sum of money may reach me without any loss.[3] Pieter promises to send it immediately to you when he receives it. Likewise the bishop of London writes saying that he sent forty-four gold pieces, without specifying what sort, to a certain friend.[4] My ser-vant said that they too would be delivered to Pieter Gillis. I am surprised   10

* * * * *

1866
1 For the context of this statement see Epp 1848, 1849, 1862.
2 William Warham, a patron of Erasmus since 1506
3 Weldanck was a native of Zeeland naturalized in England in 1515 (CEBR III 435–6). He failed to transfer the money Warham destined for Erasmus and along with the bookseller Franz Birckmann was mistakenly blamed for trying to keep it. On its recovery see Epp 1931, 1965, 1993, 2001.
   The noble in question was not an actual gold coin but instead a notional money-of-account based on the value of the pre-1526 gold angel-nobles; three such nobles, at 80d, had the value of a pound sterling (20s = 240d). While that pe-culiar usage of the 'noble' is not evident in this correspondence, it becomes clearly evident in a letter that Erasmus Schets sent to Erasmus on 24 June 1528, in which he refers to 'nobles of the kind of which three are equal to one pound sterling, and not of those struck in gold.' Complicating our under-standing of this transaction was Henry VIII's debasement of the silver coinage in November 1526, a monetary change that necessarily raised the value of the two gold noble coins that had been in circulation from March 1465: the gold angel-noble from 80d (6s 8d) to 90d sterling (7s 6d); and the 'ryal' or rose-noble from 120d (10s 0d) to 135d (11s 3d) sterling. In 1527, a Cambridge mas-ter mason, earning 6d per day, would have had to work for 1,200 days (5.71 years at 210 days a year) in order to earn £30 sterling. Henry VIII's debasement of November 1526 plays an important role in Erasmus' correspondence with Erasmus Schets in 1528. For the origins, gold contents, and values of these two gold nobles, see CWE 1 312, 325, 329, and 336–7 (Appendix A); CWE 12 Table 3 646–7.
4 As indicated in line 24 below, this sum of 44 gold pieces was worth £11 ster-ling. These gold coins could not therefore have been English angel-nobles, which would have been worth instead (44 × 90d) £16 10s 0d sterling. In all likelihood they were Venetian or other ducats, then supposedly worth 56d sterling each, so that 44 ducats would have been officially worth at least £10 5s 4d. But with the current rise in market values for gold, £11 sterling seems to be a reasonable estimate of their value. See Ep 1837 n13; CWE 12 571–83. Cuthbert Tunstall's letter is not extant.

that Tunstall did not give them to Luis de Castro, since I had been careful
to specify this in my letters.[5]

I am glad you like the book I dedicated to the king of Portugal.[6] If he
is as generous in his gifts as I in my praise, it will be a useful transaction.

You make no mention of the fifty crowns that some agent delivered to   15
Froben at the fair; no doubt you forgot.[7] He didn't want a receipt. Perhaps
you will write by the next fair.

My servant faithfully carried out all my instructions, although his trip
to England bore little fruit because of the cardinal's absence.[8] Keep yourself
well, together with your dear wife,[9] whom I bid you to greet in my name,   20
and all your dear ones.

Given at Basel, 27 August 1527

After I had written this I learned from letters from Pieter Gillis and
Tunstall, the bishop of London, that eleven pounds sterling were remitted
to you. Tunstall was supposed to give this money to your associate, but he   25
was not in London.[10]

* * * * *

5 See Epp 1758:5–6 with n7, 1769:11–15; cf Ep 1764:4–6. Luis de Castro, a Burgos
banker working in London, had succeeded his brother Alvaro in 1526 in the
task of transmitting to Erasmus his Aldington pension. See CEBR I 281–2. On
Erasmus' servant Nicolaas Kan see Ep 1832 introduction.
6 See Ep 1800, the dedicatory preface to King John III of Portugal of *Chrysostomi
lucubrationes* (Basel: Froben, March 1527), containing several Latin translations
of Chrysostom. Despite the efforts of Schets, the book was never formally
presented to the king.
7 Erasmus had called Schets' attention to this in Ep 1781:1–4. The English rose
crown (*coronatus*) was first struck, by Henry VIII, in August 1526. Valued at 54d
sterling, it had an inferior fineness of 22 carats (vs 23.875 carats in the angel-
noble), a weight of 3.181 g (117.333 cut to the Troy pound), and thus a fine gold
content of 2.916 g. In November 1526 Henry made a significant alteration to
this new gold coin (alone), increasing its weight to 3.456 g (108 cut to the Troy
pound) and thus its fine gold content to 3.168 g; and its value was increased
even more, to 60d or 5s 0d sterling. If we may assume that the crowns were
in this new form, this sum was worth £12 10s 0d sterling (375 days wages for
a London master mason). Its equivalent value in the Hapsburg Low Countries
was £15 16s 8d *groot* Flemish (345 days wages for an Antwerp master mason);
and in France, where the crown was valued at exactly 40s *tournois*, it would
have been worth 100 *livres tournois*.
8 For Cardinal Thomas Wolsey's absence, see Ep 1850 n2.
9 Ida van Rechtergem (d 1548), whose advice Erasmus occasionally sought and
to whom he had sent a golden ring as gift (CEBR III 220–1)
10 Cf Erasmus' reference to forty-four gold pieces, lines 8–9 and n4 above. The
letters from Gillis and Tunstall are not extant. On Luis de Castro see n5 above.

Your friend Erasmus of Rotterdam
To the most honourable merchant Erasmus Schets. In Antwerp

1867 / To Richard Sparcheford   Basel, 31 August 1527

> This letter, which will be answered by Ep 1896, first appeared in the *Opus
> epistolarum*. Erasmus had first written to Sparcheford, a chaplain in the service
> of Cuthbert Tunstall, in 1517 (Ep 644). See CEBR III 269.

ERASMUS OF ROTTERDAM TO RICHARD SPARCHEFORD, GREETING
With the help of Linacre's *Syntax*,[1] which you sent me as a gift, I will make
sure to become a good grammarian; you, for your part, must see that with
the Chrysostom[2] I send in return you become a good priest. And we will
strive with one another, my dear Richard, to see who will make more skilful   5
use of his gift, on these terms: that he who derives the more profit from the
gift received will be the more indebted to the other. Farewell in Christ, and
commend me to him in your prayers.
    Given at Basel, 31 August in the year 1527

1868 / From Georg Thomas   Eisenach, 31 August 1527

> The autograph of this letter (first published as Ep 74 in Förstemann-Günther)
> was in the Burscher Collection at the University Library in Leipzig (on which
> see Ep 1254 introduction). No response to it by Erasmus is extant.
>   Georg Thomas (Thome) of Nordhausen was unknown to Erasmus. He was
> a graduate of the University of Leipzig (1504) and was at this time a priest at
> Eisenach (CEBR III 320).

Grace and peace in Christ. Many people wonder, most learned Erasmus,
what is the reason why in the midst of this morass of sects and opinions about
the Eucharist, with everyone publicizing his own belief, you alone remain

* * * * *

1867
1 *De emendata structura latini sermonis libri sex* (London: Richard Pynson 1524; STC
   15634). This work was reprinted several times on the Continent, and is available on microfiche (London 1974). See Kristian Jensen '*De emendata structura
   Latini sermonis*: the Latin grammar of Th. Linacre' *Journal of the Warburg and
   Courtauld Institutes* 49 (1986) 106–25.
2 *Chrysostomi lucubrationes* (Basel: Froben, March 1527). See Epp 1800 508–18,
   1801.

silent. They think that you have long ago gone over to the side of those
who, contrary to the explicit word of God, seem to deny that the body and 5
blood of Christ are consumed in the bread and wine. There are two reasons
for their doubts. The first is your unusual and prolonged silence, although
you are living in a region where this miserable business is being enacted
with great uproar both in public and in private.[1] As the common saying
has it: 'Silence gives consent.'[2] In the second place they are disturbed by the 10
words that you inserted in the letter to Erard de la Marck in your *Paraphrase
to the First Epistle to the Corinthians*, where you write: 'If only [St Paul] had
told us one thing at least: the persons, the time, the vestments, the rite, the
wording customarily employed to consecrate the mystic bread and the cup
that contains the Lord's most holy blood,' etc.[3] From these words they con- 15
clude either that you are disingenuous or that you hold a different opinion
about the celebration of the Eucharist. But I refuse to believe that you ever
entertained erroneous views about the Eucharist; nor is it true now, despite
your 'silence and your simulation' – to repeat what others say – especially
in view of the fact that in a great number of your books I have found that 20
you have so often maintained that the body of Christ is in the bread and his
blood in the wine. Accordingly, most noble Erasmus, lest anyone entertain
any evil suspicions about you, I ask you as a friend that you allow yourself
to be moved by those words of our sweet Saviour: 'Whoever will confess
me before men, I shall also confess him before my Father'; and again: 'Who- 25
ever will deny me before men I shall deny him before my Father.'[4] Do not

* * * * *

1868
1 That is, in Basel and the lower Rhine region, where Johannes Oecolampadius'
   book *De genuina verborum Dei: 'hoc est corpus meum' etc. expositione* (np 1525) had
   attacked not only the traditional Catholic interpretation of the real presence of
   Christ in the Eucharist but also that of Martin Luther.
2 Seneca the Elder *Controversies* 10.2.6 reads *silentium videtur confessio* 'silence
   looks like confession.' In Justinian *Digest* 48.4, on testimony about the crime
   of treason, silence is regarded as an affirmation, not a denial (*Corpus iuris civilis*
   ed Theodore Mommsen, Paul Krueger, and Rudolf Schoell 3 vols [Berlin 1880–
   2; repr 1967] I 793–4 / trans Alan Watson 4 vols [Philadelphia 1985] IV 802–4).
   In a *vita* written c 1200 by William of Canterbury, Thomas à Becket is said
   to have called it 'a proverb of our people' (*Materials for the History of Thomas
   Becket* ed J.C. Robertson 7 vols, Rolls Series 67 [London 1875; repr Wiesbaden
   1965] I 68). The medieval jurist Bartolus (d 1357) challenged its validity in law,
   but his contemporary Baldus upheld it. At his trial in 1536, Thomas More cited
   silence as a point of law in his defence; see J.D.M. Derrett 'More's Silence and
   his Trial' *Moreana* 22 no 87/8 (1985) 25–7.
3 Ep 916:68–70
4 Matt 10:32–3

be ashamed of the gospel. Confess your faith, lest by your silence someone may be led astray. For I am of the opinion that there are a great number of people among whom the name of Erasmus is venerated, who respect
and revere with wonder and veneration your extraordinary gift of literature   30
and languages. You must take them into account. Make public what God
has inspired in you. Luther has written his opinion on this subject without
fear.[5] Do you likewise; protect and defend the truth of the gospel. Do not
be afraid, for we have not received the spirit of fear.[6] The Lord will be with
you, he who is blessed for all ages. Amen.   35

    I write these things to you, most kind Erasmus, not that you have need
of me, an unlearned man on whom you have never set eyes, as a counsellor. You are well aware of what must be done in this matter. If I am of no
use to you, I should like to think that it is enough to have given you, my
master, proof of the love I bear in my heart for you, and never show my-   40
self ungrateful for all the labours you have undergone for us in the correct
interpretation of literature. It is not that I have doubts about the Eucharist.
I am satisfied with the simple word of God joined to faith, without tropes
and hidden meanings, when Christ said: 'This is my body, this is my blood'
etc.[7] Why do certain great men express doubts, and torment the people piti- 45
fully and ensnare them with various opinions? Paul alone would suffice for
us who wish to believe sincerely and simply, he who repeatedly and constantly, no doubt under the inspiration of the Spirit, inculcates these words

          * * * * *

5 Luther dismissed the scholastic notion of transubstantiation, but he strongly
  held to the real presence of Jesus Christ in the Eucharist. Oecolampadius' book
  supporting the Zwinglian view of a merely symbolic presence raised the controversy to a new level. On 1 April 1527 Zwingli wrote to Luther 'fortiter in
  re, suaviter in modo,' sending his recently published book (Zürich: Christoph
  Froschauer 28 February 1527), *Amica exegesis, id est Expositio Eucharistiae ne-
  gotii ad Martinum Lutherum* (zw v 562–758 / trans Henry Preble and H. Wayne
  Pipin *Huldrych Zwingli, Writings* [Allison Park, Pa 1984] II 233–385). On 20
  June 1527 he followed this up with his *Daß diese Worte 'Daß ist mein Leib' etc
  ewiglich den alten Sinn haben werden etc* (zw v 795–977). Luther wrote against
  Oecolampadius and Zwingli, *Daß diese Wort Christi 'Daß ist mein Leib' noch fest
  stehen wider die Schwärmgeister*, attributing their view directly to Satan (wA 23
  38–320 / trans Robert H. Fisher *That These Words of Christ, 'This is my Body,
  etc' Still Stand Fast against the Fanatics* in *Luther's Works* ed Jaroslav Pelikan and
  Helmut T. Lehmann 55 vols [Philadelphia and St Louis 1955–86] 37 5–150). In
  1528 he would write his *Vom Abendmahl Christi, Bekenntnis* (wA 26 241–509 /
  trans Robert H. Fisher *A Confession concerning Christ's Supper* in *Luther's Works*
  37 151–372).
6 Cf 2 Tim 1:7.
7 Matt 26:26–7, Mark 14:22–4, Luke 22:19–20

into us and repeats: 'This is my body, which is broken for you,' 'This is
the cup of the New Testament in my blood.' And again: 'If anyone will eat   50
or drink unworthily, he will be guilty of the body and blood of the Lord';
again: 'Not discerning the body of the Lord.'[8]

But I shall put an end to the letter, which should not take up both
hands.[9] One thing only I ask of you, as you begin to get on in years, that
through your zeal and labour Germany may have a Cicero or Pliny's *Natural*   55
History in an accurate and polished edition, as your last testament, as they
say.[10] Farewell, most learned Erasmus. Cease not to promote the cause of
the gospel, for you will receive a hundredfold reward from the great and
almighty God in the resurrection of the just.[11] Again farewell, and I implore
you to pardon my temerity and pray for me. Give greeting to the friends   60
who are there with you, teaching Christ in truth.

Given at Eisenach in Thuringia, 31 August in the year 1527

Georg Thomas, minister of the church of Eisenach

To the most learned Erasmus of Rotterdam, residing in Basel, his master and friend, worthy of unending esteem   65

1869 / To George, duke of Saxony   Basel, 1 September 1527

This letter replies to Ep 1776, in which Duke George had expressed satisfaction with book 1 of the *Hyperaspistes* but urged haste in bringing out the second book promised there and delivered now to the duke with this letter. It
was first published in the *Opus epistolarum*.

Duke George of Albertine Saxony, having originally been intended for holy
orders, was one of the best-educated rulers in Europe. He was dedicated to
reform of education and of the church, and had initially welcomed Luther's
Ninety-five Theses and even promoted his debate with Eck at Leipzig over the
objections of the university and of the bishop; but upon hearing Luther he
became an ardent opponent. He kept abreast of the polemic on both sides, and
urged Erasmus and Catholic theologians to refute the constant stream of books
and pamphlets of Luther (see Ep 1691 introduction). Erasmus corresponded
with him more than with any other ruler: twenty-one letters by Erasmus (Epp
586, 1125, 1283, 1313, 1325, 1495, 1499, 1526, 1561, 1565, 1728, 1743, 1869, 1924,
1929, 1940, 1942, 1983, 2338, 2452, 2493) and ten by Duke George (Epp 514,

* * * * *

8 1 Cor 11:24, 25, 27, 29
9 *Adagia* I ix 16
10 Thomas is unaware of Erasmus' edition of Pliny (Basel: Froben 1525); see Ep
   1544.
11 Matt 19:29

1298, 1340, 1448, 1503, 1520, 1550, 1691, 1776, 2124) are extant. At his death in
1539, both his sons having predeceased him, Duke George's brother and legal
successor Henry, who had earlier embraced Lutheranism, took the duchy into
the reformed church. See CEBR III 205–8; ER II 166.

ERASMUS OF ROTTERDAM TO GEORGE, DUKE OF SAXONY, GREETING
Illustrious Prince, it gave me great pleasure to receive that book and even
greater pleasure to have a letter from your Highness.[1] I now send you the
second book of the *Hyperaspistes*,[2] if there is anyone who will be willing to
deliver this package. Whether I treated Luther as he deserves I leave it to   5
you to judge. This much I can say, that for a long time nothing has given me
such annoyance as reading through the vainglorious rubbish of this man. I
had to put up with this boredom if I wished to respond to him seriously. It
is no secret to me what an uproar this book will arouse; and to think that
I had this audacity in their own territory! Therefore if rulers do not lend   10
me their support, I fear I cannot hold my position, not so much because
of the Lutherans as of those who call themselves Antilutherans but are in
fact the most fanatical of Lutherans, and who are attempting to arrogate to
themselves the victory owed to Christ.[3] I wish for your Serene Highness
everlasting happiness.
                                                                                 15
     Given at Basel, 1 September, in the year 1527

1870 / To Matthias Laurinus   [Basel, c 1 September 1527]

     Allen, judging this letter to be the one mentioned in Ep 1871 to Matthias Lau-
     rinus' brother Marcus, changed the year-date 1525 that it carried in its first
     publication in the *Opus epistolarum*.
        Matthias Laurinus was Marcus' elder brother. He was lord of Watervliet and
     treasurer and burgomaster of the free district of Bruges (CEBR II 308–9).

* * * * *

1869
1 In Ep 1776 Duke George had said that he would send Erasmus Henry VIII's *Literarum, quibus invictissimus princeps, Henricus octavus, respondit, ad quandam epistolam M. Lutheri, et ipsius Lutheranae quoque epistolae exemplum* (London: Richard
  Pynson December 1526; STC 13084). On the controversy between Henry and
  Luther that began with Henry's *Assertio septem sacramentorum* (London: Richard
  Pynson 1521; STC 13078), see Ep 1773 n7.
2 See Ep 1853 introduction.
3 Probably a reference to Erasmus' conservative critics like Béda, Cousturier,
  Lee, and the Spanish theologians, and not to reformers like Zwingli, Oecolampadius, and Bucer, who had serious differences with Luther on the Eucharist.

ERASMUS OF ROTTERDAM TO MATTHIAS LAURINUS, LORD OF
WATERVLIET

From Marcus Laurinus' letter I learned to my great satisfaction that you are
in good health and that your long-standing good will towards me has not
subsided through separation in space or time.[1] Because of the wickedness of   5
certain malignant individuals, good learning is in difficult straits; and those
who have laboured strenuously for its advancement – especially me – are
pilloried by magpies, jackdaws, and crows. If there were not birds of good
omen to drown out the screeching of these ill-omened ones, the powers of
heaven would forbid their audacious designs. Therefore, my noble friend,   10
I thank you not only in my own name but in the name of literature and of
learning in general for defending a worthy cause prudently and successfully
against these babblers.

Once again certain mendicants have stirred up such tumults in Spain
that neither the emperor nor the archbishops have been able to control them.[2]   15
Their power is only in the clamour they make. All their hope is in their
maligning tongues. If Christian moderation did not restrain me, and if I
were not afraid that in rendering the wicked their just deserts I might harm
virtuous men, they would realize what a clever fellow they have taken on. I
marvel that they do not put an end to their machinations, when their efforts   20
have so often gone awry. What else do they achieve but to exacerbate the
public hatred directed at them? They wish to be feared, not loved;[3] what
could be more tyrannical than that? The tyrant who is feared by many must
also fear many, and the mendicants want to make themselves feared even
by kings. That is what the present state of human affairs has come to! Take   25
care that you maintain yourself in the best of health.

Basel [1525][4]

1871 / To Marcus Laurinus   Basel, 1 September 1527

A reply to Ep 1848, this letter first appeared in the *Opus epistolarum* (1529).

* * * * *

1870
1 Ep 1848:26–8
2 See Epp 1791, 1814, 1836, 1838, 1839, 1864.
3 An allusion to the famous line *oderint dum metuant* 'let them hate so long as
they fear,' considered to be the identifying mark of a tyrant. It is attributed to
the early Roman tragedian Accius and is quoted in Cicero *Philippics* 1.11.34,
and also in Suetonius *Caligula* 30. See *Adagia* II ix 62 and CWE 34 354.
4 On this discrepancy in the year-date see the introduction.

ERASMUS OF ROTTERDAM TO MARCUS LAURINUS, GREETING

If I were to express thanks for your services and devotion towards me, I might give the impression that something new had occurred; but the fact is, my dear Laurinus, that you never cease doing what you long ago began to do. Whether the monks in your quarter are silent I know not; in Spain, to be 5 sure, they are stirring up so many riots, new ones all the time, that neither the emperor nor the archbishops of Toledo and Seville can control them.[1] It is a libertine race that knows not how to obey laws sacred or profane, divine or human. Only the peasants were able to put them in their place here.[2] The turmoil raised by the monks has always caused me as much displeasure as 10 it has brought them failure, and I had always divined the outcome.

I wrote to your brother as you wished.[3] Concerning the imperial pension I see no hope unless I return. The matter was discussed once and for all in the council and as a result of that meeting of council answer was relayed to me in the name of Lady Margaret that both the pension and other 15 honours awaited me if I returned.[4] For that reason I do not think that your brother, however articulate and forceful a patron he is, should be bothered in this case. The emperor has twice given orders that the pension be paid to me by way of exception;[5] but his orders are better carried out when he exacts payment than when he orders it. 20

I am happy to know that your sisters are safe and sound,[6] but I wonder what their intentions are. Have they decided on perpetual widowhood? If they are to marry one day, now would be the opportune moment, unless perhaps you are planning a new college of Brigittines.[7] The debasement of

* * * * *

1871
1 On the situation in Spain, see Epp 1791, 1814, 1836, 1838, 1839, 1864. On Alonso de Fonseca, archbishop of Toledo since 1523, see Ep 1813 introduction; on Alonso Manrique de Lara, archbishop of Seville and inquisitor-general in Spain since 1523 see Ep 1864 introduction.
2 Probably a reference to the sacking of certain monasteries in the summer of 1525. See Ep 1598 n6.
3 Ep 1870
4 Margaret of Austria was regent in the Netherlands for her nephew Charles v. Erasmus mentions the pension and its stipulations many times; see Ep 1408:11–13 and n5.
5 See Epp 1380 (Charles v to Margaret of Austria), 1643:15–17 (from Mercurino Gattinara).
6 We know of two brothers but not the names or the number of his sisters.
7 St Bridget (Birgitta, Brigida) (c 1303–73) of Sweden, an aristocratic widow, the mother of eight children and a peripatetic mystic, founded a monastic double order that was governed by women but guided by men. By 1500 there

money has caused me a considerable loss. Lieven writes to me frequently.[8] 25
For you and for your sisters I pray for every happiness in the Lord.

Given at Basel, 1 September in the year 1527

1872 / To Mercurino Arborio di Gattinara   Basel, 1 September 1527

The original of this letter, in the hand of a secretary but signed by Erasmus, is
in the Biblioteca nacional, Madrid MS Est 18 gr I 5 f II. It is one of seven letters
(of which six are extant), all written on 1 or 2 September 1527 and addressed
to correspondents in Spain. Erasmus would receive acknowledgement of its
receipt from Alfonso Valdés (Ep 1907:1–3 and n1).

Sincere greetings. For your singular favour towards me, accomplished paragon of all the virtues, I feel a great sense of gratitude; would that I could
return it in some way! If you read the *Servum arbitrium* of Luther and my
Hyperaspistes, the second volume of which has just been published, you will
understand what a savage struggle rages between us.[1] What infuriates these 5
sectarians the more is that I dared to do this, and was the only one so to
dare, in their own territory. I was not unaware of the uproar I would stir up
against myself; but, relying on the support of the emperor, of yourself, and
of those like you, I have never hesitated to throw myself into the breach,
confident also that divine assistance would not be lacking in pious ventures. 10
And indeed the paroxysms of these sects are sensibly abating here. Many
people are returning to their senses. For my part I shall not be lacking in
my duty as a valiant soldier; it will be left to your wisdom to make sure that
certain turbulent individuals, who consult the interests of their bellies rather
than those of Christ, do not usurp for themselves the triumph of piety. Oth- 15
erwise I predict – and would that my prediction were false! – that once the
Lutheran revolt is quelled a more severe storm will arise, stirred up by the

* * * * *

were twenty-six Brigittine abbeys or convents scattered in England, Denmark,
Poland, German territories, Hanseatic towns, and in cities in Italy and the
Netherlands. Erasmus' specific reference to her foundations can probably be
interpreted as a stamp of preference for it over other female orders, perhaps
because their rule allowed them unlimited access to books. She was canonized
in 1391.
8 Lieven Algoet of Ghent, protégé of Laurinus and former servant to Erasmus
(CEBR I 35–6).

1872
1 On Erasmus' controversy with Luther see Ep 1804 n10.

wickedness of certain men. I cannot express in words how much I desire
that to the other outstanding successes of our invincible emperor be added
that of restoring under his auspices concord to the two states.[2] For this evil   20
requires someone divinely appointed for the task. Farewell.

Given at Basel, 1 September in the year of our Lord 1527

The servant of your Eminence, Erasmus of Rotterdam, whose mind
and hand you will discern

To the illustrious lord Mercurino Gattinara, high chancellor of his im-   25
perial Majesty. In Spain

1873 / To Charles V   Basel, 2 September 1527

Delayed in transit, this letter did not reach the emperor at Burgos until c 23
November (see Ep 1907:1–3). It was published with Charles' reply in three different Spanish translations of selected *Colloquies*, the first being *Tres Colloquios*
(n p [1528]). Their translators, Alonso Ruiz de Virués and Luis Mexía, were in
close touch with the imperial secretary Alfonso de Valdés, who himself translated this letter into Spanish (published with the Latin text in Allen VII 160).
Erasmus himself printed the letter, with small changes, in the *Opus epistolarum*
(1529).

EPISTLE OF ERASMUS TO THE EMPEROR
Just as I owe immense gratitude to your Majesty, O invincible emperor, in
my own name and in that of learning in general – for you have never refused me your kind favour and assistance – so it is my earnest desire that
your sovereign power, which vanquishes and subdues the most powerful   5
of kings, may have equal authority and efficacy in quelling the disorders
brought about by certain wicked men. For my part, trusting in the support of pontiffs and princes but especially in that of your Majesty, I have
roused up against me the whole Lutheran faction, which I wish were not as
widespread as it is, with great peril to my own life. If anyone requires proof   10
of this, Luther's *Servum arbitrium*, which he wrote against me in a spirit of
malicious antagonism, will testify to it, as well the two books of my *Hyperaspistes*, in which I respond to him.[1] Now that the Luther affair is beginning
to subside, in part through my efforts and at my own peril, certain other

* * * * *

2 That is, religion and polity

1873
1 On Erasmus' controversy with Luther see Ep 1804 n10.

individuals are springing up in your country who act under the pretence of   15
religion but serve the interests of their gullets and of tyranny.[2] I give combat not for the interests of men but for the sake of Christ. They have transformed Spain, a country blessed by fortune in so many other respects, into
a hotbed of unrest through their lawless rebellion. From such beginnings
we sometimes see grave tempests arise. Certainly this Lutheran affair took   20
rise from much slighter causes.

　　As far as I am concerned, I shall not cease until my dying breath to
defend the cause of Christian piety. It will behove your Majesty and your
piety to give your steadfast and continual support to those who sincerely
and bravely fight in defence of the church of God. I fight under the banners   25
of Christ and of your Majesty, and under them I shall die; but I shall die
with more tranquillity if I may first see peace restored to the church and to
the entire Christian people through your prudence, your wisdom, and your
good fortune. That Christ in his goodness and power will grant this boon
to us is my constant prayer; and may he preserve your Majesty and exalt   30
you to ever greater accomplishments.

　　Given at Basel, 2 September in the year of our Lord 1527

　　To the invincible monarch Charles, Catholic King, elected Emperor of
the Romans

1874 / To Alonso de Fonseca   Basel, 2 September 1527

> This letter, which answers Ep 1813, was first published in the *Opus epistolarum*
> (1529). For Fonseca see Ep 1813 introduction.

ERASMUS OF ROTTERDAM TO ALONSO, ARCHBISHOP OF TOLEDO,
GREETING
Through personal experience, reverend prelate, I have discovered the absolute truth of what the apostle Paul wrote to the Corinthians: that God, who
so often promises in the Scriptures that he will not fail those who fix the holy   5
anchor of faith in him, is true to his word and grants what he has promised.
For although he allows his own to be exercised by various tribulations, to
be purified or put to the test by divers persecutions of wicked men, yet he
so tempers the degree of affliction with the help of his grace that he does
not let them be overwhelmed by the waves of evil, but assigns a happy end-   10

*　*　*　*　*

2 The conservative Spanish theologians – many of them mendicant friars – whose
accusations of Erasmus were the cause of the recent Valladolid inquisition; for
similar expressions, see Ep 1805 n53.

ing even to the most tragic events. And in the meantime, in the very heat of the fray, in his goodness he often eases and mitigates the harshness of our trials, alternating them with some small solace, so that human frailty can bear the weight of the ordeal.[1] This is very aptly expressed in the word ὑπερενεγκεῖν, which is equivalent to saying 'to conquer by endurance.'[2] Otherwise how could this meagre little spirit, this poor body, fragile by nature and now broken by old age, sickness, and that greatest of all evils, ennui,[3] be equal to so many disorders and persecutions, if divine goodness had not sustained the flagging frailty of human nature with frequent succour?

The chief consolation in adversity is a good conscience and the hope of an eternal reward. But frequently God also grants some measure of solace through the instrumentality of pious men. Thus, eminent prelate, I ascribe to his goodness your letter,[4] full of kindness and Christian piety, from which I derived such pleasure that, although it found me near exhaustion from the fatigue of so many toils and evils, it immediately wiped away every feeling of distress and restored my vigour and enthusiasm. Furthermore, just as a personal sorrow torments me less than the public calamity of Christianity, so the general happiness of the multitude cheers me more than my own advantage, if such exists. How slight is the loss of this insignificant little man, as far as his frail body and reputation are concerned, especially when one beholds the whole universe! It is of no more importance than a gnat. Yet who among those sincerely devoted to the glory of Christ would not suffer profoundly to see that Christianity has fallen so low that those who in so many ways profess to be perfect Christians lash out with such shameless calumnies, such boldfaced lies, such malicious plots, with such defiance against those who fight the good fight for the cause of true piety. If those who

* * * * *

1874
1 Cf 1 Cor 10:13. The passage speaks of God's faithfulness to those in distress but does not employ, as Erasmus does, the symbol of the anchor, which is more often used in Christian imagery for the virtue of hope, as in Heb 6:19. See also *Adagia* I i 24.
2 Erasmus reads ὑπερενεγκεῖν in all five of his editions of the New Testament; modern editors read ὑπενεγκεῖν. In the *Annotationes* of 1519 he calls the word 'a rather forceful expression,' and explains it as 'to bear up in such strength as to accomplish and surmount the task.' In 1527 he compares it to ὑπερνικῶμεν 'we overconquer,' from Rom 8:37. See Allen Ep 1874:12n.
3 Both patristic and medieval spiritual writers thought the state of *taedium* or *acedia* (ἀκηδία) – a spiritual apathy – to be particularly heinous because it destroyed the inclination to aspire to virtue. See John Cassian *Institutiones* 10.1–6; Thomas Aquinas *Summa theologiae* II-II q 35 a 1–4.
4 Ep 1813

declare themselves dead to the world act in this way, what must we expect from the rest? The more I rejoice in the flourishing progress of studies and religion in Spain, the more bitterly I feel that this success, which I wished to be solid and lasting, is vitiated by these tumults. Indeed I seem to foresee 40 the threat (would that my presentiment deceived me!) that these skirmishes will develop into a bloody war. For we are acquainted with the wiles of Satan, who never injures the Christian religion so gravely as when he is transfigured into an angel of light,[5] and under the guise of religion vents his fury upon public concord. If only it could be ransomed at the price of my head! 45

But on the other hand I am relieved each time I reflect that there are many great men who have the interests of Christ and true religion at heart. Although your spirit, which was depicted, expressed, and represented in your letter, commended itself to me almost more than all the rest, there are many others, if not equal at least similar to your Highness, whose letters 50 regularly reach me here.[6] The first in their ranks is William Warham, archbishop of Canterbury, who is so distressed at my misfortunes and so elated at my success that he is less solicitous for his own person.[7] Whatever he has is shared in common with me, so that, should I so wish, I could make as free use of it as of the things put away in my cupboards at home.[8] This I know by 55 frequent experience, and I am chided for not availing myself of his generosity. The next in order is Cardinal Lorenzo Campeggi, the most sincere and loving friend one could imagine.[9] Third is John, bishop of Rochester, who I think is known to you from his writings.[10] Fourth is John, bishop of Lincoln,

* * * * *

5 Cf 2 Cor 11:14.
6 Cf Ep 1804 n12.
7 Warham's most recent extant letter was written in March 1517 (Ep 558), but Erasmus may have seen no reason to keep or to publish later ones. Warham regularly sent Erasmus' Aldington pension, and Erasmus addressed a number of letters and dedicated several books to him. He will write to Erasmus for the last time in March 1528 (Ep 1965).
8 Revising slightly the 1524 prefatory letter to Warham in the edition of Jerome (Ep 1451) for the Paris reprinting (Claude Chevallon 1533–4), Erasmus echoes this praise of Warham: 'he frequently offered in all sincerity a sharing of all fortunes.'
9 This Italian prelate appears in this list of English prelates because Erasmus knew him as papal legate to England, and he was now bishop of Salisbury. The latest extant letter from him is dated 2 February 1525 (Ep 1542). On Campeggi see CEBR I 253–5.
10 Four of John Fisher's letters to Erasmus are extant, the latest in 1517 (Ep 592). Fisher's published writings consisted of three treatises upholding the traditional view that three women in the entourage of Jesus – Mary, the sister

from whom I receive two affectionate letters each year.[11] And even the car-   60
dinal of York sees fit not infrequently to honour me with most courteously
written letters.[12] Then there is Cuthbert Tunstall, now bishop of London, who
is not unknown to you, I believe, since he recently discharged a diplomatic
mission to your country.[13] Of him I must say that he is more my soul than
my friend. I do not proclaim my own merits here, but rather their admirable   65
kindness. I have friends of similar distinction in France, especially Michel
Boudet, bishop of Langres.[14] From the king of France, the king of England,
Duke George, and other princes I receive so many letters that at times I
do not have the opportunity to respond.[15] In addition, my files can scarcely
contain the letters from men of learning, many of whom are of pre-eminent   70
rank. This is not to mention the letters from the emperor and from Ferdinand, now king of Hungary, filled with feelings of affection and respect.[16]

* * * * *

of Lazarus and Martha (Luke 10:38–42, John 11:10, 12:1–8), Mary Magdalene,
from whom Jesus cast out seven devils (Luke 8:2); and the courtesan who
anointed Jesus' feet at the home of the Pharisee (Luke 7:36–50) – were the
same person; his *Assertionis Lutheranae confutatio* (1523); and his *De veritate cor-*
poris (1527), a defence of the real presence against the views of Oecolampadius
(CEBR II 36–9). See *Opera omnia* (Wurzburg: Gregorius Fleischmann 1597; repr
Ridgewood, N J 1967).
11 John Longland; see Ep 1858 n70 and CEBR II 341–2.
12 Thomas Wolsey. We have thirteen letters of Erasmus to Wolsey (the latest,
   Ep 1697, dating from April 1526); but no letters from Wolsey to Erasmus are
   extant; cf CEBR III 460–2.
13 Of the five names in this list, Tunstall was the most frequent correspondent.
   Six of his letters to Erasmus are extant; the one previous to this was written in
   June 1523 (Ep 1367); the last surviving letter dates from late October 1529 (Ep
   2226). In a July 1526 letter to Pieter Gillis (Ep 1726), Tunstall mentions another
   letter, now lost, destined for Erasmus that concerned the payment of an English gift to Erasmus. See CEBR III 349–54. The mission to Emperor Charles v,
   probably occasioned by Charles' capture of King Francis I in February 1525,
   lasted from April 1525 until January 1526.
14 We have only Ep 1612, a short note from Boudet to Erasmus written on 20
   September 1525 to thank Erasmus for sending a copy of the *Lingua*. On Boudet
   see CEBR I 178–9.
15 From Francis I we have only Ep 1375, written in July 1523. Henry VIII had
   written two letters (Epp 206 and 339) prior to Erasmus' mention here and one
   later (Ep 1878) written on 18 September 1527. Duke George of Saxony (Ep
   1869 introduction) was a more frequent correspondent, with ten extant letters
   to Erasmus, the most recent dated January 1527 (Ep 1776) and the next after
   this dated 15 March 1529 (Ep 2124).
16 We have five letters from Charles v to Erasmus, the latest prior to this written on 4 August 1526 (Ep 1731) and the next after this on 13 December

All these things give me good hope that these disastrous tumults
will one day be laid to rest and that these tragedies will have a happy
dénouement.[17] Christ is the architect of all this: he knows how to raise his   75
spouse up by casting her down, make her expand by hemming her in, fortify her by assaults, vivify her through death, glorify her through ignominy.
If this happens during my lifetime, I shall depart from here the more willingly and eagerly. But if he has determined otherwise, I shall never doubt
that whatever he decides will be for the best. Therefore, since your piety ex-   80
horts me to display a constant and unbroken spirit in the midst of all these
woes – which, with the help of Christ I would have done of my own accord
– I shall in future do so with more zeal and diligence, strengthened by the
voice of so great a prelate.

The offer you extend to me through the excellent theologian Juan Ver-   85
gara is all the more gratifying since it exceeds what I deserve, and for that
I express my admiration for your unheard-of kindness.[18] Since I know it
proceeds from a sincere and benevolent kindness, I think I am no less in
your debt than if I had accepted all that was offered to me. I do not doubt
that with equal good will you will take the measure of my sentiments so   90
that whatever gratitude I could have shown you, if circumstances allowed,
you will judge to have been shown. Whatever comes to pass, if an occasion arises in which I can be of service to you, there is nothing I should
do more willingly. May the Lord Jesus preserve your Excellency from all
harm.   95

Given at Basel, 2 September, in the year 1527

1875 / To Juan de Vergara   Basel, 2 September 1527

This letter answers Ep 1814 and will be acknowledged by Vergara's Ep 2004.
It first appeared in the *Opus epistolarum* (1529). The manuscript is not extant.

* * * * *

1527 (Ep 1920). From Ferdinand of Hapsburg, younger brother of Emperor
Charles v, we have two extant letters addressed to Erasmus (Ep 1343, dated
15 February 1523, and Ep1505, dated 12 October 1524) and another written in
May 1530 (Ep 2317) to the town council of Freiburg-im-Breisgau on Erasmus'
behalf.
17 Cf Ep 1875 n13.
18 Through his secretary Juan de Vergara (Ep 1814:483–91) Fonseca had offered
generous support to Erasmus to come to Spain, whether for a visit or an
extended stay.

ERASMUS OF ROTTERDAM TO JUAN DE VERGARA, GREETING
I have finished the second book of the *Hyperaspistes*,[1] which I could not have
done without first carefully reading Luther's writings, in which there is
such a great quantity of imprecations, sneers, invective, boasting, insults,
ovations, and triumphs that I was well nigh overcome with disgust before I   5
even set pen to paper. I felt fully there the bitter word,[2] as the proverb has
it; no absinth is more bitter. I have published the complete works of Ambrose,[3] magnificently printed and in a much more accurate edition. I added
the commentaries of Chrysostom to the Epistle to the Galatians, made available in Latin through my efforts.[4] I have added to this several homilies of   10
Origen on Matthew, that part of his work of which the beginning is missing[5] – indeed scarcely half of it remains. I also published some other minor
works.[6] When these labours were over another task succeeded in their place,
that of replying to the letters of friends and enemies, which are brought here
in parcels from practically all parts of the world.[7]   15
      All but exhausted by these labours and fatigues, dearest Vergara, I was
greeted by the arrival of your letter[8] – so friendly, so elegant, so sincere,
so spirited, it dispelled all weariness of body and mind. With it was a letter from the archbishop of Toledo.[9] How fortunate you are to have such a
patron – although you are already most blessed with so many excellent tal-   20
ents. Would that our Germany had many such bishops! What brilliant style
without trace of affectation, what dignity in his observations! How the entire letter radiates a heroic majesty combined with the affability of the most
modest of prelates! I speak from the heart; it is unbecoming to use artifice
with you, a man of utter simplicity and candour. Both letters were delivered   25

* * * * *

1875
1 See Ep 1853.
2 Erasmus uses the Greek ἁλυρὸν λόγον, literally 'salt-water word,' probably an
   allusion to *Adagia* III iii 26, where two styles of language are compared to
   drinking salt water and drinking clear water.
3 Basel: Froben, August 1527; see Ep 1855.
4 Basel: Froben 1527; see Ep 1841.
5 *Fragmentum commentariorum Origenis in evangelium secundum Matthaeum* (Basel:
   Froben 1527). See Ep 1844. Erasmus uses the Greek ἀκέφαλον to describe the
   work as 'headless.'
6 See Ep 1856.
7 Cf Ep 1804:69–71 and n12.
8 Ep 1814
9 Ep 1813

as Froben was already preparing his baggage.[10] I must therefore respond selectively to some parts of your letter, and discuss other parts more freely with you and at greater length some other time.

I gather from letters of my friends that Alonso Virués is a far different man than what he seemed to be from his book.[11] Therefore, I think it bet-   30 ter to settle this whole dispute and be united in Christian friendship under more favourable auspices. You really painted a vivid portrait of the tragic drama of the mendicant despots,[12] which has now heated up from a turbu- lent first act to a still more turbulent climax; there remains the dénouement,[13] which I hope will be a happy one – not so much for my own sake as for the   35 sake of Christian piety. For I am not fighting for anybody's private interests but for the public good of the Christian flock. In no wise do I defend the tyrannical rapacity of greedy scoundrels but strive only for the triumphant reign of Christian charity in all; nor shall I cease doing so. Since, as I be- lieve, the task was undertaken with right intention, I shall persist in it with   40 a clear conscience.

What they are doing now in your country they attempted eleven years ago, without success.[14] The whole tragic business was rehearsed long ago, as you know, in all parts of the world, all of it obviously prearranged, but it

* * * * *

10 Probably Johann, since Erasmus would likely specify the Christian names of Erasmius Froben or Hieronymus Froben if he intended one of them. There is thus no sign as yet of ill health (Johann Froben would die in October after a stroke; see Ep 1900:114–21). He would have been about to leave for the Frankfurt book fair; cf Ep 1877:409.

11 On the manuscript *Collationes ad Erasmum* that Virués had sent to Erasmus see Ep 1838 introduction and n4. Ep 1839 from Alfonso de Valdés defended Virués against Erasmus' criticism, and Vergara himself had gone to great trouble in Ep 1814:85–114 to convince Erasmus of Virués' good will.

12 Ep 1814:115–275; cf Ep 1791 introduction; 'mendicant despots' is rendered in Greek.

13 The terms 'drama,' 'climax,' and 'dénouement' are rendered in Greek. Erasmus often resorts to terms from the theatre to describe his difficulties, as for exam- ple at Epp 1805:124–5, 1874:74–5, 1885:186–7, 1902:114–15, 1903:6–7, 1915:54–5. Cf *Adagia* I ii 35: *Supremum fabulae actum addere* 'To add a last act to a play,' I ii 36: *Catastrophe fabulae* 'The dénouement of the play'), and I i 68: *Deus ex impro- viso apparens* 'Unexpected appearance of a god' ('A god appearing suddenly from the machine'). Cf also 1814:130–1 (from Vergara).

14 Perhaps a reference to the attempts of Henry Standish and other Franciscans in England in 1516 to collect and publish errors in Erasmus' works (Ep 481:44– 50); or to similar moves in Louvain at that time (Ep 505:9–19) and two years later (Ep 1053:34–9)

was hissed off the stage everywhere except in your own land. I am amazed   45
that such licence is permitted this type of men that they dare to fly in the
face of the emperor, the pope and the archbishop.[15] And meanwhile they
flaunt that holy obedience, the third vow, when they are the only ones who
obey neither human nor divine laws, yet demand that whatever they wish be
regarded as holy.[16] I am speaking of wicked men, and would that my words   50
applied only to a few! They vaunt the saying of the apostles: 'One must
obey God rather than men';[17] but this is the rallying call of the Lutherans as
well. In very truth these men serve God religiously – but after the example
of those of whom St Paul writes, 'Their God is their belly.'[18]

It is not clear whether those who publish my books taught to speak   55
Spanish do so out of love or hatred; certainly they stir up great animosity
towards me.[19] For this same reason a serious tragedy arose in Paris, which
you will learn of partly from other friends, partly from a book that I am
sending you.[20] The reason why they dread these translations is easy to divine. In sermons, at banquets, in conversations, on board ship, in carriages, in   60
the shops of cobblers and weavers, in the sacred confessional they are wont
to preach that Erasmus is a much more pernicious heretic than Luther,[21] and
they have won over many of the unlearned, youths, old men, and housewives. With these resources they promised themselves certain victory; but if

* * * * *

15 See Ep 1864:18–21, 46.
16 *Adagia* IV vii 16; cf Epp 1804:265–6, 1858:49–50, 347.
17 Acts 5:29
18 Phil 3:19. Erasmus frequently ridicules the custom of the mendicant orders to
   beg for their food. Later in this letter (line 140) he refers to them as 'slaves of
   the belly.' Cf Ep 1805 n53.
19 Cf Ep 1904:10–13.
20 Allen Ep 1875:58n and 87n suggests that Erasmus sent Vergara Béda's *Annotationes* against Erasmus and Lefèvre d'Etaples (Paris: Josse Bade, 28 May 1526),
   but that matter was already more than a year old. The context here seems to
   point rather to the translations by Louis de Berquin of Erasmus' *Encomium matrimonii, Querela pacis*, various *Colloquies*, and the *Paraphrases*. Berquin's evangelical agenda led him to create tendentious translations and sometimes to mix
   in passages from books by Guillaume Farel, Martin Luther (cited from Farel's
   citations from Luther's *Betbüchlein*), and other reformers. See Margaret Mann
   (Phillips) 'Louis de Berquin, traducteur d'Erasme' *Revue du seizième siècle* 18
   (1931): 309–23. For their censure in Paris see Farge *Procès-verbaux* 96–7, nos
   94A, 95A.
21 Erasmus would later accuse two Paris theologians, Nicolas Le Clerc and the
   late Guillaume Duchesne, of this (Allen Ep 2043:1–5).

Erasmus begins to speak in the language of the people, their malicious fal-   65
sity will be revealed, and they will be recognized for what they are: hence
those tears!²²

Then as to the charge that I have acted and am acting in collusion with
Luther,²³ they lie brazenly against their own conscience, for they know that
no one is more hated by the Lutherans than Erasmus. If they continue to   70
deny it, the. *Servum arbitrium* of Luther will confute them, for he never wrote
anything more venomous. Then there are the two books of the *Hyperaspistes*,
the second of which I have just published.²⁴ In this part of Germany, at least,
no one up to now has dared to take up his pen against them; I only hope it
turns out well for me! When they see that blood has been shed on both sides 75
and that all hope of coming to an accord has been removed, when they see
that the Lutheran affair is taking a turn for the worse, partly at my personal
peril, they gather their forces and launch an attack against me as I risk my
life in the midst of the conflict. Such are the tactics of the pseudomonks.²⁵
They know full well that nothing could be more pleasing to Luther or more   80
catastrophic for the tranquillity of the church. So much for their piety. They
know, too, that these disturbances displease the Roman pontiffs, cardinals,
archbishops, countless princes and learned men, and, finally, the emperor
himself. So much for their obedience.

Their claim that my books have been condemned by an official pro-   85
nouncement in Paris or that it is forbidden to read them is a shameless
lie.²⁶ All my works are for sale in Paris; and my *Colloquies*, the book that

* * * * *

22 Terence *Andria* 126; cf *Adagia* I iii 68.
23 On this charge see Ep 1853:23–4.
24 On the controversy with Luther see Ep 1804 n10.
25 Erasmus uses the Greek, τῶν ψευδομονάχων.
26 More than a year earlier (16 May 1526), the University of Paris' faculty of
   theology formally censured the reading of Erasmus' *Colloquies* as dangerous
   for all Christians but especially for young people, who could be corrupted,
   not instructed, by them (Farge *Procès-verbaux* 136–7 no 152A). It asked the Parlement of Paris to suppress the *Colloquies* on the grounds that they might 'under the guise of eloquence lead all who read him into perverse doctrine like
   that of Luther' (Argentré *Collectio judiciorum* II-1 48–52). On the same day, the
   doctors approved Noël Béda's *Annotationes* (Paris: Josse Bade, 28 May 1526)
   written against Erasmus' Paraphrases on the Gospels and on St Paul. A more
   general censure was passed by the whole University of Paris on 16 December
   1527. Finally on 22 or 23 June 1528 the university's rector, after still another
   vote by the four faculties and four nations of the faculty of arts – with the nations of Picardy and Normandy preferring to delay so that Erasmus might be
   asked to modify his book – ordered an immediate prohibition against reading

incites their greatest hostility, were recently published there by the printer Colines.[27] But the sale of the book that Béda wrote against me has been prohibited by an edict of the king,[28] notwithstanding the fact that it has been sold secretly in defiance of the king's orders. And for that same reason when Béda visited the king's court on some business or other for his esteemed faculty, he was ordered to remain there until he made answer for what he had written.[29] After inventing many pretexts and resorting to every subterfuge, he was only dismissed on the next day, on the condition that he would present himself whenever he was summoned. From that book a learned and virtuous man,[30] much esteemed by the king, extracted twelve

90

95

* * * * *

Erasmus' *Colloquies* to be posted throughout the university; see Caesar Bulaeus (DuBoulay) *Historia Universitatis Parisiensis* 6 vols (Paris 1665–73) VI 210. The specific censures in these Paris condemnations were published only in July 1531 and again in September 1532 (Paris: Josse Bade); see Renouard *Imprimeurs* II nos 672, 774.

27 Simon de Colines published the *Colloquies* in both 1526 and 1527, copying the latest editions of Froben. This probably led to the faculty of theology's censure in 1526 and the university's condemnation in 1527. Colines used a pocket-sized format called 'in-24°' – whence Erasmus' mistaken notion that Colines had printed 24,000 copies of the work (see Allen Ep 2126:139–40). For Colines see CEBR I 330.

28 Béda's book was against both Erasmus and Jacques Lefèvre d'Etaples: *Annotationum in Jacobum Fabrum Stapulensem libri duo; et in Desiderium Erasmum Roterodamum liber unus* (Paris: Josse Bade, 28 May 1526). See Farge *Orthodoxy* 191–2. On 4 August 1526 Francis I wrote from Amboise to the Parlement (Paris, Archives nationales x¹ᵃ 1529 f 351). Without naming Béda or his book, Francis ordered an inventory of its copies and forbade further sale until his return to Paris. The king invoked the 1523 precedent reserving judgment of Lefèvre d'Etaples' orthodoxy to his *grand conseil* and a panel of bishops.

29 Following a faculty resolution Béda and the faculty's dean Guillaume Cappel were delegated to warn the king about the dangers of heresy in France. They were summoned to appear on 20 March before the king at Saint-Germain-en-Laye (Farge *Procès-verbaux* 171 no 197A). Erasmus has abandoned his earlier report (Ep 1815:11–13) that Béda had been put in prison. The present version simply mirrors similar treatment by Francis I of a delegation sent to him in October 1526 by the Parlement of Paris. It was made to follow the itinerant court for about three weeks before finally being dismissed without having seen the king (Paris, Archives nationales x¹ᵃ 1529 f 454r).

30 Louis de Berquin. Erasmus and Béda both presumed Berquin to be the author of this book, *Duodecim articuli infidelitatis magistri Natalis Bedae ex libro suarum Annotationum excerpti, reprobantur et confutantur* (n p [Paris: Josse Bade] n d [1527]); but Berquin, who never put caution ahead of truth in such matters, denied authorship of it under oath. We should now instead ascribe the book to

propositions and published them together with my answers translated into French.[31] The copy of the letter I am sending you will be ample proof of how much the king was pleased with them.[32]

The man who barely escaped being burned at the stake because he had translated certain works of mine into French is pleading his case against Béda and three monkish priors, who had pronounced a definitive sentence of heresy against an innocent man, as I am told.[33] And he would have been

* * * * *

another enemy of Béda, the Parisian theologian Jacques Merlin. This is borne out by Merlin's deposition in the Parlement of Paris in which he speaks of 'a large number of erroneous propositions, suspect in the matter of faith, drawn and excerpted from the books of Béda that the faculty and its deputies have approved for printing to the detriment of its honour and the good of all Christendom as well as Catholic truth.' See Paris, Archives nationales x^{1a} 8344 f 17r, cited in Farge *Parti conservateur* 90 and n101; cf Walter Bense Jr 'Noël Beda and the Humanist Reformation' unpublished PHD dissertation (Harvard University 1967) 422 n149.

31 Erasmus' answers to Béda are used to refute only three of the alleged heresies of Béda (numbers 9, 10, and 11). Two Latin copies of this book are known, one at the Bibliothèque Mazarine, Paris, and the other at the Bibliothèque municipale, Troyes (Moreau *Inventaire* III 326 no 1135). There is no known extant copy of a version in French.

32 Surely the letter of Francis I (c 7 July 1527), found in the archives at Simancas by Marcel Bataillon, published by Allen, and translated below preceding Ep 1902. It was addressed not to the faculty of theology – as Allen (and perhaps Erasmus) surmised – but to the whole University of Paris.

33 Louis de Berquin was arrested for the second time in January 1526. Having previously abjured heresy in 1523, he was therefore liable to punishment by death as a relapsed heretic. Released from prison on 19 November 1526, he was kept under guard at the Louvre for about six weeks. See Farge 'Berquin' 57–67. On the translations, see n20 above. Translating offensive or even heretical books was not a capital offence. The death sentence was reserved for lapsed heretics, that is, those convicted who, once having recanted, turned again to heresy. For the document of abjuration by Berquin in 1523, see *Bulletin de la Société de l'histoire du Protestantisme français* 67 (1918) 180–1. Berquin's case was in the jurisdiction of the papal tribunal known as 'judges delegate' constituted in 1525 in France by Clement VII with the consent of the regent, Louise of Savoy. The tribunal was composed of two clerical members of the Parlement of Paris and one (surviving) member of the faculty of theology. Béda is never mentioned as a member of this tribunal, but both he and the Parlement of Paris worked closely with it, the latter assuming the role of 'secular arm' (Paris, Archives nationales x^{1a} 1529 f 199v–200r, 9 April 1527); see Farge *Orthodoxy* 259–60. The tribunal was originally constituted to try the evangelical Dominican theologian Aimé Maigret, whose influential family connections allowed him to flee to Strasbourg, where he died shortly thereafter. Others tried

Louise of Savoy
From a miniature in a Book of Hours belonging to Catherine de' Medici
Bibliothèque nationale de France, Paris

burned unless the Senate, the queen-mother, and the king himself, who   1(
happened to return to France just at that moment, had not checked their
onslaught.[34] This man, I tell you, whom they had destined for sacrificial
slaughter, is now bringing proceedings before judges designated by the
king, against the guilty parties: Béda, the accomplice of this crime, the priors suborned to the deed, and finally the august faculty itself, which accord-   1:
ing to report secretly abetted the affair. From defendant turned plaintiff he
promises himself certain victory, although he has a powerful and undying
enemy, so that I am plainly afraid that in the end the man's courage will
land him in prison.[35]

I thought I should cite this as an example. Apart from this, believe me,   1:
if these rogues are permitted to harm good men as much as they please, it
won't be long before they pounce upon princes and bishops. If measures
were to be taken to settle the troubles of the church, it should be a matter of
first priority to subject the mendicant orders to their ordinaries,[36] as other

* * * * *

and convicted at this time included Jacques Pauvant and Mathieu Saunier; see
Michel Veissière *L'évêque Guillaume Briçonnet, 1470–1534* (Provins 1986) 302–4.
The 'innocent man' is presumably Berquin.

34 By 'the Senate' Erasmus means the Parlement of Paris. He has been misin-
formed about its opinion of Berquin, probably by Berquin himself. The Parlement was overwhelmingly committed to the prosecution and conviction of
Berquin and lost no time in executing him after his conviction by the judges
delegate in April 1529. Louise of Savoy was regent for her son during his absence from France. King Francis I was repatriated to France from captivity
in Spain on 17 March 1526, but he tarried another year on the journey between Bayonne and the suburbs of Paris and entered the capital officially only
on 14 April 1527. On 1 April 1526, he wrote the first of several letters to the
Parlement of Paris forbidding any sentence against Berquin before his return
(Paris, Archives nationales x[1a] 1529 f 198v–9r). From 11 July until 19 November
1526 the Parlement several times refused royal orders to release Berquin from
prison. In mid-November 1526, the king's provost in Paris forcibly removed
Berquin from the Conciergerie prison and transferred him to the Louvre. See
Farge 'Berquin' 67.

35 The details of Berquin's status between his release from prison in November
1526 and his execution in April 1529 are not clear. Erasmus is surely right
that Berquin's continued search for legal absolution eventually led to his execution. The king did change the composition of the tribunal of papal judges
delegate that had convicted Berquin in 1526, but it was this new commission
of eleven lawyers (among them Guillaume Budé) who convicted Berquin once
again of relapse into heresy and, when he appealed their sentence, ordered
his execution at the stake – a sentence carried out by the Parlement of Paris
on the same day. See Farge 'Berquin' 70–2.

36 Popes in the thirteenth century had granted the friars considerable freedom
from episcopal jurisdiction. Boniface VIII effected a compromise by his bull

clerics are, and in the future to reduce all to one class. Many people had pre-   120
dicted long ago – and would that it were false – that they would bring about
the destruction of the church. How many disturbances they have aroused
already, first by their dissensions, now by their conspiracies.

But we shall leave this for another time. Even though it would be more
beneficial to my spirit, more fitting to my age and my health, and perhaps   125
more conducive to my studies if I had a holiday from these gladiatorial combats,[37] nevertheless when I see that this is my fate I am content that these
disturbances arise during my lifetime; for if they were to arise after my
death they would do more harm both to my reputation and to studies in
general. Thus I am persuaded that these things do not happen without the   130
design and providence of the gods, as the poet said.[38] If men of authority
will show me their favour to the extent that I am not engulfed by the violence of the conspirators, I will easily take care of the rest, provided that I am
given the opportunity to reply. And I am firmly determined that my books
should contain nothing that is contrary to Christian piety. If the monks will   135
conduct themselves with befitting moderation, they will win great favour in
my eyes. But if they pursue their usual manner, as I know they have done
and will continue to do, I will put their hostility to good use and will turn
their misdeeds to the public good. I know the extent of the wickedness of
these slaves of the belly,[39] and you yourself are aware that Spaniards are   140
possessed of a vehement and ardent temperament. Therefore I hope that the
wisdom of high-ranking leaders will ensure that no discord may arise from
a clash of partisan interests, which would endanger the happy tranquillity
of your country.

We have learned from experience that the most insignificant begin-   145
nings sometimes give rise to raging tempests. This whole Lutheran tempest
has grown to its present fury from slight beginnings. The Dominicans gave
shameless endorsement to papal indulgences.[40] Luther countered with his

* * * * *

Super cathedram (1301), which his Dominican successor Benedict XI annulled (Inter cunctas) but which Pope Clement V (1305–14) reinstated in 1312 with Dudum
de sepulturis (Clementis papae V constitutiones 3.7.2; see Corpus iuris canonici ed
Aemilius Richter and Aemilius Friedberg 2 vols [Leipzig 1879–81] II 1161–4).
The friars managed frequently to ignore this ruling, and only with the Council
of Trent were they more effectively brought under episcopal jurisdiction.
37 Cf Ep 1815 n19.
38 Virgil Aeneid 5.56
39 See n18 above.
40 The Dominican Johann Tetzel's perverted preaching of indulgences in 1517 in
Mainz provoked Luther to write his Ninety-five Theses. Other friars and secular
clerics as well preached indulgences, sometimes with equal imprudence; but

theses. Silvester responded ineptly;[41] Luther put up sharp resistance.[42] Then
some monks, reaping a rich harvest from all this, harangued the people, although I protested that they should desist. For my good counsel I came off
badly. The Lutherans took a pounding, but so did languages and humane
studies, for the monks had decided to bind up everything they hated in the
same bundle. We see how far this tragedy has progressed. I have such little
liking for this type of disorder that I should prefer that serenity could be restored at the price of my head alone, if it were possible, than that I should be
the occasion of this tempest, so far am I from wishing to be the cause. I think
it preferable that the authority of the pope not get involved in this matter.
For who stands in greater fear of the monks than the Roman pontiffs? Or
who despises the pope more vehemently, when it is to their purpose, than
the monks? So far, for the most part I have had the Roman pontiffs and several cardinals on my side. But his Holiness[43] has his serpents who stop at
nothing and wield great power with the sovereign pontiff.[44]

* * * * *

some Dominicans and others (like the Paris faculty of theology) were already
critical of the practice before Luther wrote his tract. See Clerval *Procès-verbaux*
232, 237; Argentré *Collectio judiciorum* 1-2 55v, 57.
41 Silvester Prierias, Dominican censor in Rome and Master of the Sacred Palace,
first felt the contempt of humanists when he censured works of Johann Reuchlin. He was the first to respond to Luther's Ninety-five Theses, with his *In praesumptuosas Martini Lutheri conclusiones de potestate papae dialogus* (np nd [Rome:
Jacopo Mazzochio, June 1518]); he later published three other treatises against
Luther. See nos 24, 25, 27, and 28 in the list of his thirty books in Michael Tavuzzi
Prierias: The Life and Works of Silvestro Mazzolini da Prierio, 1456–1527 (Durham,
N C and London 1997). Erasmus' estimation of Prierias as a theologian was not
totally negative, but he thought that Prierias provoked Luther to more virulent positions against the papacy. On him cf Ep 1337A, CEBR III 120–1, and OER
III 341–2; note that the full title of Tavuzzi's book corrects the dates of Prierias'
birth and death wrongly given in CEBR. Cf Epp 1891:363–5, 1909:128–9 and n27.
42 *Ad dialogum Silvestri Prieriatis de potestate papae responsio* (Leipzig: Melchior Lotter the Elder 1518). See WA 1 644–86. The Dominican Ambrosius Catharinus
(Lancellotto de' Politi) replied to Luther with *Apologia pro veritate catholicae et
apostolicae fidei ac doctrinae adversus impia ac valde pestifera Martini Lutheri dogmata* (Florence: Giunta 1520), a scathing attack depicting him as the Antichrist.
Luther answered in 1521 with *Ad librum eximii Magistri Nostri Magistri Ambrosii
Catharini, defensoris Silvestri Prieriatis acerrimi, responsio* (Wittenberg: Melchior
Lotter the Younger; see WA 7 698–777). On this exchange see Patrick Preston
'Catharinus versus Luther' *History* 88 (July 2003) 361–78.
43 ὁ Ἀρχιερεύς. Allen (153n) suggests that the redundant *Pontificem* in the next
line was a printer's substitution for *Clemens*, that is, Pope Clement VII.
44 Possibly Girolamo Aleandro and Alberto Pio; see Ep 1634 introduction.

Furthermore, in Italy a pagan movement is in full swing, adhered to
by certain individuals to whom nothing is pleasing unless it be Ciceronian;   165
and they consider it more disgraceful not to be called a Ciceronian than to
be called a heretic.[45] You cannot imagine how offended they are that I do not
reproduce an exact likeness of Cicero,[46] although I am not quite certain that
any of them reproduces him. At any rate I do not affect to do so, and if I
were to affect it in the treatment of Christian subjects I would be a laughing   170
stock. I have tried to placate them more than once, and I will not refuse to
appease them again. I have almost won over the good elements among them;
all the same, some are put upon because of their simplicity; others through
fear either keep silent or raise their voices with the rest in order to avoid
suspicion. Certain malicious men will never be appeased. If to admonish   175
them about what pertains to true piety is to make war with them, I will
make war until my dying day. As to my reputation and my works, Christ
will see to them. Many works more worthy of immortality than my own
have perished. If the end of the world is nigh, as certain prophets affirm,
it is not of great importance to put up a struggle for such a brief space of   180
time. If the prophets are lying, I still think that the time is at hand when less
licence will be given to certain hypocrites than has hitherto been the case.
As for myself, come what may, my conscience is clear.

All this sounds a sour note. The rest of your letter, most learned friend,
exudes honey and sugar. With what pleasure I read that languages and hu-   185
mane studies are flourishing in Spain, once a prolific mother of great geniuses! In Germany, on the other hand, they have declined to such an extent
that no one wishes to attend the lectures of professors hired at public expense. With what joy I welcome the devotion and good will shown to me
by this prelate, possessed of every kind of distinction, and his generous and   190
obliging kindness towards one not at all deserving of it! How often have I
complimented your nation for such religious leaders, such success in studies, such a rich harvest of learned men! I for my part have no great lust for
life; yet when I reflect on these things I wish I could be young again. I have

* * * * *

45 Although Erasmus did not equate the new learning (which we today call 'humanism') with any philosophical, theological, or even anthropological position, he was worried about manifestations of pagan or non-Christian thought
   among proponents of the new learning in Italy. In Ep 1479:133–5, for example,
   he named Michael Marullus (c 1453–1500) and other Greek scholars or poets in
   Italy whose works he found too pagan, and in the *Ciceronianus* (CWE 28 416–17)
   he has Nosoponus express the same opinion. See Ep 1805:88–98 and n15.
46 See the Introduction to *Ciceronianus* in ASD I-2, xxx and the remarks of Nosoponus in CWE 28 424–5.

no doubt that he makes these promises sincerely, and would be even more
liberal than his promises.[47] But the journey is enormous and my health more
fragile than glass, and I do not see how I could be of use to you at this age and
in this state of health. In numerous letters I am invited here and there,[48] with
very flattering terms; but as fortune was once lacking to me, now I am lacking
to fortune. Moreover, I must die standing in the front line of battle; to that
end Froben is most accommodating, supplying the combatant with arms.

I read your brother's letter, written in felicitous Greek,[49] with pleasure, and I passed it on to learned men who live with me to read. I shall
send it also to Louvain to the professors at the Collegium Trilingue,[50] to
spur them on. I have no doubt that it will stir their enthusiasm. I shall take
care, however, that it not be published without the consent of the author.
I have no time to answer him right now except perhaps for a hasty greeting.[51] I see also how much I owe to Bernardino Tovar.[52] Francisco makes
witty jokes about a Geryon in Spain, with three bodies and one mind, most
unfavourable to Erasmus.[53] To hell with that ominous Geryon! I take pleasure in the omen of this second Geryon, when I see three most distinguished
brothers who with one mind cherish Erasmus.[54] Give my best regards to Tovar. I shall at least send my personal greetings to Francisco if that is all my
occupations will allow me.

These are mere selected responses to the chief points of your letter.
Nonetheless, in the midst of so many occupations I prefer to write in this
way rather than not at all. Farewell.

Basel, 2 September in the year 1527

* * * * *

47 For Alonso de Fonseca's offer of support if Erasmus would come to Spain, see
   Epp 1814:482–91, 1874:85, and n18 above.
48 Most recently to France (Ep 1805:174–8), to Poland (Ep 1652:116–17), to England (Epp 1697:103–4, 1816:24–45), and to Leipzig (Ep 1683:2–3)
49 *feliciter* ἑλληνίζουσαν. The same phrase is repeated in Ep 1876:7–8, and the same
   opinion in Ep 1885:5. Francisco de Vergara's letter, sent with Juan de Vergara's
   Ep 1814, is not extant.
50 See Ep 1856 introduction.
51 Ep 1876
52 The half-brother of Juan and Francisco; see Ep 1814 n14.
53 Geryon was a legendary three-bodied monster who tended a herd of cattle
   on the island of Erythia located far in the west. Hercules' tenth labour was
   to bring these cattle back to Eurystheus; cf Lucretius 5.28; Virgil *Aeneid* 8.202;
   Apollodorus *Bibliotheca* 2.5.10. Erasmus' 'Geryon' was Diego López Zúñiga,
   to whom he responded with his *Apologia respondens ad ea quae Jacobus Lopis
   Stunica taxaverat in prima dumtaxat Novi Testamenti aeditione* (ASD IX-2).
54 This phrase is in Greek.

1876 / To Francisco de Vergara   Basel, 2 September 1527

This letter, the 'hasty greeting' responding to the Greek letter mentioned in Ep 1875:207–8, was first published in the *Opus epistolarum* (1529). Erasmus will write to Vergara again at greater length with Ep 1885.

Francisco de Vergara, the younger brother of Juan de Vergara, was professor of Greek at the University of Alcalá since 1522. He published several books in the Greek language and translated into Latin nine sermons of St Basil the Great (Alcalá: Juan Brocar 1544). On him see CEBR III 383–4.

ERASMUS OF ROTTERDAM TO FRANCISCO DE VERGARA, GREETING

At the present moment, my dear Francisco, I scarcely had the time to return your greeting in answer to such a copious, learned, friendly, and good-humoured letter. And even if I had the time I would have been discouraged from writing by a style abounding in all the embellishments of the 5 Muses and the Graces. Who would have believed that the study of Greek had made such progress that young men could write letters in such felicitous Greek style?[1] Do you expect me, an old man, to be jealous of youth? Far from arousing jealousy in me there is hardly anything that gives me more pleasure. Those who bear feelings of paternal affection for the young 10 generation are happy to be eclipsed and vanquished by them in this way.[2] Truly this gives me a deep sense of joy.

I thought fit to send a copy of your letter to Louvain to the professors at the Collegium Trilingue,[3] which is flourishing there, as an added stimulus to them. I congratulate you, my distinguished young man; I congratulate 15 Spain, where the ancient love of learning is burgeoning again after a period of decline. I congratulate Alcalá, which under the successful auspices of two prelates, Francisco and Alonso,[4] is so flourishing in every branch of learning that with good reason we may call it most wealthy.[5] Be certain of this, my dear Francisco, that nothing could please me more than your sen- 20 timents towards me, and nothing could have given me more pleasure than

* * * * *

1876
1 The letter is not extant; see Ep 1875:202 and n49.
2 Cf Ep 1107 n1.
3 See Ep 1856 introduction.
4 Francisco Jiménez de Cisneros (see Ep 1814 n56) and Alonso de Fonseca (see Ep 1813 introduction)
5 Using the Greek πάμπλουτον (Latin *panplutum*), Erasmus plays on the Latin name for Alcalá (*Compluto*).

your letter. Spain does have its Geryon, its three-bodied monster,[6] as you jokingly remark, but it also has a most auspicious Geryon, one soul in three distinguished brothers.

That is all I could allow myself for the present. I do not wish you to think of it as an answer but merely a return greeting. Best wishes to you and to all lovers of literature.[7]

Given at Basel, 2 September in the year 1527

1877 / To Alonso Manrique de Lara   [Basel, c 2 September 1527]

This is a hastily composed and partial first draft of the *Apologia adversus monachos quosdam Hispanos*, which Erasmus would complete later this same month (Epp 1879, 1888:13, 1967). It sketches out in abbreviated form only the first quarter of that later, definitive version. Erasmus had already seen the Valladolid articles before his earlier·letter to Manrique on 26 August 1527 (Ep 1864:71–2). Now, having completed the other letters that he wanted to write to Spain (Epp 1872–6), he used the time available to compose this sketch before the imminent departure for Frankfurt of the Basel printers, who would see that the packet of letters would be carried to Spain from there (see line 409; cf Ep 1875 lines 25–6, from which Allen conjectured the month-date).

The charges against Erasmus' orthodoxy discussed at Valladolid probably resembled the articles in the version sent to him by Pedro Juan Olivar, which is no longer extant (Ep 1791 introduction). Erasmus later told Vives that the account of the first day's proceedings sent to Vives by Alonso Ruiz de Virués and forwarded to Erasmus on 13 June (Ep 1836:19–20) had reached him only about the beginning of October (*sub calendas Octobris*; Ep 1889:1–13). Erasmus confronts here the first two articles. Of the eighty doctrinal points considered he answers in this letter only twenty-five (denoted by numbers in angle brackets), and of the 100 'objections' only the five first (and most important). For the Valladolid articles, see Miguel Avilés Fernández *Erasmo y la Inquisición* (*El libelo de Valladolid y la Apología de Erasmo contra los frailes españoles*) (Madrid 1980). The opinions of the thirty-three theologians convened at Valladolid have been edited by Vicente Beltrán de Heredia *Cartulario* VI. For an analysis of the theologians' opinions see Lu Ann Homza *Religious Authority in the Spanish Renaissance* (Baltimore 2000) 49–76.

Allen was the first to publish this original document (Madrid Biblioteca nacional MS Est 18 gr 1 5 f 15), which was written out by a secretary of Erasmus and sent in duplicate (Ep 1888:14). It was however headed, corrected,

* * * * *

6 Rendered in Greek; see Ep 1875 n53.
7 Rendered in Greek

subscribed, and addressed by Erasmus himself. For Manrique de Lara see Ep 1846 introduction.

SKETCH OF A RESPONSE TO THE ARTICLES CENSURED BY THE MONKS

Whereas innumerable passages in my works profess clearly and distinctly the teachings of the church concerning the Holy Trinity – that is, equal apportionment of the divine nature in three Persons, or rather the same indi- 5 visible essence in three Persons – and whereas I genuinely detest the impiety of the Arians, it is a mark of singular impudence to charge me with the suspicion of agreeing with them.[1] No one has ever before accused me of this crime except two men who were born for slander. It is from this source that they have drawn their allegations.[2] Perhaps it would be foolish to review 10 the passages proving the truth of what I say, since all my books abound with such a clear and unfaltering profession of faith that anyone would easily discern that I speak sincerely. My mind conceals nothing other than what my tongue and quill proclaim. To this the Lord is my witness.

⟨1⟩ In my paraphrase on the first chapter of John,[3] among other things 15 I give an explanation of why the divinity of Christ was not so clearly proclaimed in the Old Testament and by the other evangelists; as John expresses it: 'It could not have been taught immediately that there were three Persons distinct in particularity, each of whom was truly God, and yet there was only one God, because of the one divine nature equally shared among the 20 three.'[4] ⟨2⟩ And a little further on: 'He (I speak of the Father) exists entire and eternal in himself, and as he himself is, so is the Son, forever coming to birth from him, everlasting from everlasting, almighty from almighty, all-good from all-good; in short, God from God, not begotten later or inferior to his begetter, eternal Word of the eternal mind.'[5] ⟨9⟩ Again a little 25 further on, speaking of the Word of God: 'He was of a nature undivided

* * * * *

1877
1 The followers of Arius, a fourth-century cleric, who taught that Jesus Christ was created by the Father in time and was therefore a creature, not God. This doctrine was condemned by the councils of Nicaea (325) and Constantinople (381).
2 That is, the Spanish enemies of Erasmus have relied on the works of Edward Lee and Diego López Zúñiga; cf line 310 below.
3 The *Paraphrase on John* was first published by Erasmus in 1523, with three new editions during Erasmus' lifetime in 1524, 1534, and 1535.
4 John 1:1 LB VII 498B; cf CWE 46 14.
5 John 1:2 LB VII 499C; cf CWE 46 16. The parenthetical 'I speak of the Father' is not in the *Paraphrase*.

from the Father in such a way that he was with the Father according to the
particularity of his own person; and he was not attached to the Father as
accident is attached to substance, but he was God from God, God in God,
God with God, because of the nature of the divinity common to both. The   30
two, equal in all things, were distinguished by nothing except the particularity of begetter and begotten, of the one who utters and of that which is
uttered.'[6] ⟨5⟩ And a little further, refuting two heresies, that of the Arians
and that of those who said that Christ's existence began when he was born
of the Virgin, I say: 'Therefore those who think that the Word of God is later   35
than him who utters it, as with us intention is prior to utterance, stray far
from the truth, as do those who count the Word of God, by which the Father created all things, among created things. But even more stupid is the
mistake of those who think that the Son and Word of God came into existence only at that moment when he was corporeally born of the Virgin.'[7] In   40
that whole chapter I speak in this way of Christ, devoutly and, if I am not
mistaken, refuting heretics who hold opinions unworthy of him.

Further, if anyone should read my *Annotations* on this chapter of the
Evangelist,[8] he will find that I scrupulously affirm the divine nature of Christ
against the heretics. ⟨25⟩ At the beginning of the Paraphrase on the Epistle   45
to the Romans one will encounter these words: . . . who was born in time of
the lineage of David according to the infirmity of the flesh, but was also revealed to be the eternal Son of the eternal God according to the Spirit which
sanctifies all things,' etc.[9] Whoever declares that the Son is eternal denies
that he is a creature: for only God is eternal. And where Paul merely calls   50
Christ the Son of God, I expound more clearly that he is the eternal Son of
the eternal God, which I surely would not have said if I agreed with the
Arians. ⟨26⟩ Again in the paraphrase of chapter nine of the Epistle to the Romans, towards the beginning: 'But Christ is a man in such a way that at the
same time he is also God, not the God peculiar to this or that nation, but   55
the God of the whole world in command of all, to whom alone all praise
is owed for all eternity. Amen.'[10] ⟨27⟩ And in the annotation where I discuss the various readings and interpretations of this passage made by the
ancient writers, among other things, I say the following: 'The fact that in

* * * * *

6 John 1:3 LB VII 500A; cf CWE 46 17.
7 The passage comes earlier, not later; cf LB VII 499E and CWE 46 16–17.
8 *Annotationes* LB VI 337A–342A / Reeve 218–232
9 Rom 1:3 LB VII 779E; cf CWE 42 15.
10 Rom 9:5; cf LB VII 806D–E and CWE 42 53. Erasmus here shortens the passage
   as it appears in the *Paraphrase*.

other passages of Paul the word 'God' is usually attributed to the Father   60
and 'Lord' to the Son is not because the word is any less appropriate for
the Son than for the Father but because it was more expedient for those
times.'[11] What could be said more openly or more plainly? ⟨28⟩ Likewise at
chapter 20 of John, towards the end, the paraphrase reads as follows: 'When
Thomas had seen and touched, recognizing both the face and the familiar   65
voice of the Lord, now on receiving full faith he cried out, "My Lord and
my God!" For just as he had been more reluctant to believe, so no one proclaimed more clearly the God and the man,' etc.[12] ⟨30⟩ And in the annotation
to this passage I assert the same thing, refuting the reasoning of Porphyry.[13]
You should read the passage. ⟨31⟩ Again, the paraphrase on Philippians 2   70
says this of Christ: 'Although he was by nature God and declared himself
God in his very deeds, etc.'[14] Since this passage is variously explained by
the ancient writers, I accept both readings because I considered both to be
orthodox.[15] ⟨32⟩ Likewise in the *Annotations*, although I point out a divergent
explanation, I give my approval to this one as well.[16] ⟨33⟩ In my annotation   75
to the Epistle to the Romans, chapter 1, commenting on the words 'From
God the Father and the Lord' etc, in order to show that in Paul's Epistles the
name of God is attributed especially to the Father, that of Lord to the Son, I
conclude: 'but in such a way that that form of expression neither takes away
lordship from the Father nor deity from the Son. For in the same way that   80
the Father is Lord, and the Son God, so the Holy Spirit is also called Lord.'[17]

* * * * *

11 See the annotation on Rom 9:5 (*qui est super omnia deus*) LB VI 610C–D; cf CWE
   56 249–50. Allen (55n) explains that this passage was added in the 1518 edition
   and retained as late as that of 1527. In the 1535 edition – perhaps because of
   this controversy – Erasmus amplified it to two folio pages and removed this
   sentence.
12 John 20:28 LB VII 645B; cf CWE 46 220.
13 See the annotation on John 20:28 (*Dominus meus et deus meus*) LB IX 417–18A, E /
   Reeve *Annotations* 267. This is explained more directly in the complete *Apologia
   ad monachos* 1.30 LB IX 1025D: 'Et ne quis haereticus diceret hoc a discipulo dictum nimio studio praeceptoris, qualis blasphemias solet evomere Porphyrius
   ...'
14 Phil 2:6 LB VII 996B; cf CWE 43 371.
15 Erasmus quotes from his paraphrase on Phil 2:6. This verse had constituted
   the crux of his disagreement with Lefèvre d'Etaples in *Apologia ad Fabrum*; see
   CWE 83 xxi.
16 LB VI 867–8; cf Reeve *Annotations* 622–3.
17 See the annotation on Rom 1:7 (*a deo patre et domino nostro Iesu Christo*) LB VI
   559E; cf CWE 56 31. The last sentence is a quotation from Didymus *De spiritu
   sancto*.

⟨45⟩ Likewise in the colloquy entitled 'An Examination [Concerning the Faith]'[18] one finds this dialogue: 'Do you believe Jesus was God and man?' The answer: 'Certainly.' Again a little further on: 'Do you believe in the Holy Spirit?' The answer: 'I believe he is true God, together with the Father and the Son.' Again further on: 'Is the Son more like the Father than the Holy Spirit is?' The answer: 'Not with respect to divinity.'[19] Are these obscure or ambiguous statements? ⟨50⟩ If you read the *Paean in Honour of the Virgin Mother*, how often is it said there 'You brought forth God,' 'You bore God,' 'Mother of God!'[20] ⟨49⟩ At the beginning of the *Prayer to Jesus, Son of the Virgin*, I speak in these terms: ... from the Father, the source of all life, to whom you are so joined by the incomprehensible bond of the Holy Spirit that neither the simplicity of the Monad confuses the distinctions of Persons, nor does particularity of the Triad separate the unity of substance.'[21]

⟨34⟩ Again, at John 14 the paraphrase reads: 'Therefore since I am the image of the Father, like to him in every way, and since you ought to have known me by now by my deeds and my words (indeed, to have seen is to know), with what brashness do you say to me "Show us the Father"? As if whoever has seen me has not also seen my Father! Not that the Father is not a separate person from me, but that between the two of us there is no difference according to a higher nature.'[22] ⟨35⟩ At John 10 the *Paraphrase* includes both interpretations, stating: 'As there is complete sharing of power between the Father and me, so there is entire agreement of will. We are completely one, equally powerful, willing and not willing the same thing.'[23] Although some interpret this passage as concerning the agreement of will – and that this was the Evangelist's intention could be proved by many arguments – nevertheless I add the uniformity of nature and equality of power, which I should not have done if I agreed with the Arians.

⟨37⟩ At chapter 16, the paraphrase reads as follows, with the Son speaking about the Holy Spirit: 'not because our power is not the same but because it is best for the salvation of the human race that the parts of the task

* * * * *

18 First printed in the March 1524 edition with the title *Inquisitio*; *de fide* was added in the March 1529 edition – almost two years after this letter.
19 LB I 729B, 731A, 731B; cf CWE 39 424:17–18, 428:6–7, 428:22–3.
20 *Paean virginis matri* (Louvain: Dirk Martens 1514); cf LB V 1228–1234 / CWE 69 20–38.
21 *Precatio ad virginis filium Jesum* (Louvain: Dirk Martens 1503, 1509) LB V 1210E–F; cf CWE 69 4–16.
22 John 14:9 LB VII 609B; cf CWE 46 170.
23 John 10:30 LB VII 585E–F; cf CWE 46 137:7–10.

be divided into periods of time.'[24] ⟨38⟩ Again in that same chapter the Son speaks about the Father and the Spirit: 'Among us there is nothing that is not common to all. All things proceed from the Father, but nothing is his that is not also mine, and nothing is the Father's or mine that is not shared with the Spirit.'[25] ⟨46⟩ Likewise in the poem in which I impart the rudiments of the faith to children, I speak of the Spirit in this way:

> In thee as well with kindred faith,
> O Spirit Godhead, I believe,
> Sacred spiration and breath of God,
> Illuminating all that is.[26]

For the sake of the metre I wrote 'Godhead' for 'God.'[27] ⟨40⟩ Further, at 1 Corinthians 6, towards the end, the paraphrase explaining the passage 'Do you not know that your members are the temple of the Holy Spirit,' etc says this: 'The body too is itself consecrated to God in such a way that it is the temple of the Holy Spirit.'[28] And a little later on: 'Do not contaminate your bodies in contempt of the Spirit, but in the purity of your bodies as in the innocence of your minds bear about in you the divinity that dwells within you and show his glory among men.'[29] Do I not here call the Holy Spirit a divinity with sufficient clarity?

⟨41⟩ In the annotation on the First Epistle of St John, chapter 5, concerning the phrase 'And these three are one,' I comment: 'First of all their conclusion is altogether true that the Father and the Son and the Holy Spirit have the same single and indivisible nature. If this were not so, the Son would not truly be born of the Father nor would the Holy Spirit truly proceed from the Father and the Son, as God from the substance of God,' etc.[30]

⟨70⟩ In the apology against Jacques d'Etaples how often do I repeat that in the one hypostasis of Christ there are two natures, divine and human![31]

* * * * *

24 John 16:8 LB VII 620D; cf CWE 46 185.
25 John 16:14–15 LB VII 622B; cf CWE 46 188.
26 *Christiani hominis institutum* LB V 1357E; cf Reedijk *Poems* no 94 / CWE 85–6 94–5, 506–7 (notes) no 49. Cf also Ep 298:35–7.
27 The Latin reads, *Carminis gratia numen pro Deo posui.*
28 1 Cor 6:19 LB VII 877F–878A; cf CWE 43 85.
29 1 Cor 6:20 LB VII 878B; cf CWE 43 85–6.
30 See the annotation on 1 John 5:7 LB VI 1081D / Reeve *Annotations* 768–71.
31 LB IX 28A–30D / ASD IX-3 108–12 / CWE 83 26–31. Still, one of the hallmarks of this work is Erasmus' emphasis on the humanity of Christ vis-à-vis Lefèvre's more 'sublime' insistence on Christ's divinity.

⟨66⟩ How often do I repeat the same thing in the *Institution of Christian Marriage*,³² which I wrote for Queen Catherine of England, and in innumer-   140
able other places! ⟨74⟩ In my response to Lee's *Annotations*, 71, these are my
words: 'Since there is no controversy between Lee and me about the matter, for I have never either written or held an opinion about the single and
simple essence of the three Persons that differs from orthodox opinion.'³³
Among the new responses to the *Annotations* of Lee, number 22, I wrote the   145
following: 'Father and Son and Holy Spirit are wise, but it is the same wisdom. All three Persons have will, but it is the same will. Three foresee, but
it is the same providence. They are three, but their essence is the same.'³⁴
What could be clearer than these words?

Since my works abound with such statements, is it not with good cause   150
that I am suspected of having impious opinions concerning the most Holy
Trinity?

1/ Now³⁵ to the first article. It is very easy to collect utterances of
this sort, but it is the duty of the examiner to report the exact words that
he wishes to appear as impious or at least to give proof of his own state-   155
ments.³⁶ Let them read my latest response to the *Annotations* of Lee, number
25, and also my annotation to this passage, especially in the fourth edition;
it would be wearisome to repeat the same thing so many times.³⁷ I testify

* * * * *

32 *Institutio christiani matrimonii* (Basel: Johann Froben, August 1526). See LB V
   621E–622D / CWE 69 229–30.
33 *Responsio ad annotationes Eduardi Lei* 71 LB IX 171D / CWE 72 175–6
34 *Responsio ad annotationes Lei novas* (answering Lee's criticisms of the second
   edition of the New Testament) 22 LB IX 272E / CWE 72 399
35 The rest of this letter consists of Erasmus' initial, provisional replies to the
   first five objections raised against him in the Valladolid articles sent to him
   by Pedro Juan Olivar. With the courier ready to leave for Spain, Erasmus had
   no time to deal in this letter with all the questions. Allen (VII 174) placed the
   number '1' at the beginning of the preceding sentence.
36 In the full published version of the *Apologia adversus monachos quosdam Hispanos* (LB IX 1030–94) Erasmus discloses the objections of his critics in full
   before replying to them. The first objection clearly questioned his belief in the
   Holy Spirit and charged that his discussion of the scriptural foundation for
   the Spirit was inadequate.
37 See *Responsio ad annotationes Lei novas* 25 LB IX 275–84 / CWE 72 403–19. At issue
   is the 'Johannine comma' or 'three witnesses' interpolation in 1 John 5:7–8 – the
   italicized section of the following translation from the Vulgate: 'And there are
   three who give testimony *in heaven, the Father, the Word, and the Holy Spirit. And
   these three are one. And there are three that give testimony on earth*: the Spirit, and
   the water, and the blood; and these three are one.' Not finding the italicized section of the passage in the Greek manuscripts he employed, Erasmus omitted it

expressly there that my opinion on the three Persons coincides with that of the church. It is not called into question whether the Father, the Son, and the   160
Holy Spirit are the same essence, but the discussion concerns which is the more correct reading at this passage, the Greek one or ours. After present-ing my arguments I indicate that the reading of the Greek texts, which do not speak of the testimony of the Father, the Word, and the Spirit, is more genuine. And they are not trifling arguments. If this passage had been in   165
the emended Greek manuscripts and had constituted an effective weapon against the Arians, Athanasius would surely have introduced it in the books in which he proves the divinity of the Son, and in those in which he proves the divinity of the Holy Spirit, which I have recently translated into Latin.[38] Chrysostom and Theophylact would have done likewise.[39] And Cyril, too,   170
in his work entitled *Thesaurus*, book 14, next-to-the-last chapter, where he is combatting the doctrines of Arianism, introduces this passage but without mentioning the Father, the Word, and the Spirit.[40] In an old manuscript of

* * * * *

in his *Novum instrumentum* (1516) and *Novum Testamentum* (1519). But, as a re-sult of the controversies with Lee and Zúñiga, he restored it in the 1522 edition and all later ones. The note on the disputed *comma Ioanneum* was considerably enlarged in Erasmus' fourth edition (February 1527), the version reproduced in LB VI 1079–82; cf Reeve *Annotations* 761–82. The Complutensian Polyglot Bible included the passage, but Luther's German Bible did not. Both the Douay-Rheims Bible and the Authorized, or King James Version, included the passage; but it has been omitted in the Revised Standard Version and other modern ver-sions, including Roman Catholic ones. See *Cambridge History of the Bible* III: *The West from the Reformation to the Present Day* ed S.L. Greenslade (Cambridge 1963) 10, 59–61; cf H.J. de Jonge 'Erasmus and the *Comma Johanneum' Ephemerides theologiae lovanienses* 56 (1980) 381–9 and Joseph M. Levine 'Erasmus and the Problem of the Johannine Comma' *The Journal of the History of Ideas* 58 (1997) 573–96. On the opinions of the Spanish theologians at Valladolid about this question see Lu Ann Homza 'Erasmus as Hero, or Heretic? Spanish Humanism and the Valladolid Assembly of 1527' *Renaissance Quarterly* 50 (1997) 78–115.
38 St Athanasius (c 296–373), bishop of Alexandria, was the most adamant oppo-nent of the Arians. Erasmus could mean any one of three or more works by Athanasius against the Arians. Erasmus added *Athanasii lucubrationes aliquot* as an annex to his *Chrysostomi lucubrationes* (Basel: Johann Froben, March 1527); see Ep 1790.
39 On Chrysostom and Theophylact see Epp 1805 n86, 1858 n9.
40 George of Trebizond made a Latin version of *Preclarum opus ... quod Thesaurus nuncupatur ... et De consubstantialitate filii et Spiritus Sancti cum Deo patre ...* of Cyril of Alexandria (d 444); it was edited by Josse Clichtove in 1514 (Paris: Wolfgang Hopyl 1514; repr Paris: Henri Estienne 1521; repr Basel: Andreas Cratander 1524). For the passage see PL 75 615.

Bede I found it added in the margin. The same thing is true of Augustine,
I think.[41] Didymus in his books on the Holy Spirit does not mention this   17
passage either.[42] Furthermore, since without question there is mention here
of the unanimity of testimony (of the three Persons), the passage cannot refute the Arians, who did not deny what this passage convincingly proves.[43]
Therefore I am not favouring the Arians if I restore a passage that has no
effect against the Arians. And what need was there for this passage, when   18
one passage – 'In the beginning was the Word and the Word was God'[44] –
suffices? One does not favour heretics by advising true believers not to use
weak arguments against them. What do they do differently in the schools?
I did not write this for the general public but for the scholastics. I would
not even have written this if the passage had not been disputed by my op-   18
ponent.[45] In the first edition the simple annotation at this passage was as
follows: 'In the Greek manuscript I find only this concerning the triple testimony: that there are three who bear witness, the Spirit and the water and
the blood!'[46] I neither give preference to the Greek reading, nor do I criticize
ours, but rather defer to the church's decision on this matter. I say this in   19
the *Annotations*: 'It is pious always to submit our opinion to the judgment of
the church as soon as we have heard a clear pronouncement from her,' etc.[47]
But Jerome is not the church,[48] and the church does not automatically demand that we hold as an article of faith what we read in manuscripts, which
are frequently corrupt. These men declare the Greek manuscripts corrupt,   19

* * * * *

41 We have not found specific treatment of this problem in St Augustine. During
the octave of Easter in AD 407 Augustine composed ten tractates on the First
Epistle of John; but the tenth ended with 1 John 5:1–3, the pericope preceding
the one in question here.
42 Didymus of Alexandria *De Spiritu Sancto* (Basel: Froben 1516); for a modern
edition see Didyme l'Aveugle *Traité du Saint-Esprit* ed Louis Doutreleau SJ, SC
386 (Paris 1992) 118, 122–32. On Didymus see Ep 1855 n29.
43 Not clear. Erasmus possibly means that Arianism was primarily a Christolog-
ical heresy, not a Trinitarian one; but he would surely recognize the implications of the one on the other.
44 John 1:1
45 Edward Lee
46 See n37 above.
47 The annotation on 1 John 5:7 (see n37 above) LB VI 1080E / Reeve *Annotations*
768–9
48 That is, when Jerome used the *comma Ioanneum* in his Latin translation of
the Bible. For Erasmus' critics, however, the received Vulgate version was not
a manuscript like any other, the product of a fallible translator and fallible
copyists, but was the inspired word of God.

whereas what is at issue here – at least in this passage – is which are more correct.

Now who ever said that to disagree is to rave against someone? Augustine teaches openly in many places that even after they have been baptized infants are damned if they have not partaken of the body and blood of the Lord, which today would be heretical if anyone should wish to defend it.[49] In this present case will it not be allowed to disagree with Jerome and give my own opinion?

Furthermore, as to my saying that Jerome is often extreme – that is, he twists the Scriptures, shows little restraint, and is often variable and inconsistent – I have demonstrated the truth of these statements in my response to Lee, and I could bring many more proofs to bear if I were put to it. Is this not frequently done by theologians, when they are in honest disagreement with even the most orthodox of Doctors of the church? I was under the pressure of Jerome's authority. But my disagreement with Jerome had to be expressed in a respectful manner. And I did not shrink from doing so. In my answer to Lee I use these words: 'And in such matters St Jerome is certainly ardent and forceful, not to say violent,' etc.[50] In the Annotations I have this to say: 'But we are under the pressure of Jerome's authority, which I, for my part, should not wish to diminish, although he repeatedly' etc.[51] But this statement, which softens my disagreement, is left out by these contriving individuals in order to make it appear that I am raving against Jerome.

2/ On this point I am at a loss to know what draws their suspicion.[52] I do not think that they suspect me of agreeing with the heretics who say that the three Persons are distinct from one another only in name, since I profess over and over again that the three Persons are distinct in their properties, not in their essence. But I do criticize the recondite inquiries of certain scholars into this subject, probing matters with the aid of human reason that even angelic understanding cannot fully fathom. Further, if someone wishes to know how intricate the discussions of some theologians are on

* * * * *

49 See *Contra duas epistolas Pelagiorum* 1.22 PL 44 570 / CSEL 60 457–8 / *Augustine … 21st Century* I-24 137–8.
50 *Responsio ad annotationes Lei novas* 25 LB IX 275C / ASD IX-4 323:171 / CWE 72 404
51 On 1 John 5:7 (see n37 above) LB VI 1079E / Reeve *Annotations* 768–9
52 Having affirmed his belief in the divinity of the Holy Spirit, Erasmus goes on to answer charges against his theology of, and belief in, the Trinity of three Persons in one God.

this point, let him read in the first book of the *Sentences*, distinction 26, what scholastic doctors have written about the relations of origin, about absolute properties, about persons really but not essentially distinct, about real and absolute relations of origin, and about relations under the category of rela-   23‹ tion or under some other category.[53] And many other more elaborate distinctions are to be found; what they have to do with piety I know not, since the opinions of those who treat of such matters are so divergent. I think what I suggest accords with piety; and yet, in order not to give the impression of condemning the investigations of the scholastics, note in how many ways I   23› soften my suggestions. First I say: 'Perhaps.' Then I do not say that these things are bad, but I point out what would be more pertinent to the subject, namely, that which is the fountainhead of all piety: 'that we become one with God'; and, not content with this, I add: 'in painstaking studies.'[54] The word *studium* in Latin sometimes has the meaning of 'partisan favour,' as in   24› 'The doubtful crowd is split into opposing camps.'[55] And we are aware that among the scholastics sects and factions have arisen from investigations of this sort.[56] Lastly I add the word 'to wrangle,' criticizing their contentious

* * * * *

53 *Libri* IV *Sententiarum* 1.26. Distinction 26 contains eight short *capitula* that deal with the topics Erasmus enumerates here. See Peter Lombard *The Sentences* I *The Mystery of the Trinity* trans Giulio Silano (Toronto 2007) 139–46. The *Sentences* served as the basis for theological learning for over four centuries; see Marcia L. Colish *Peter Lombard* 2 vols (Leiden and New York 1994). Because Peter Lombard completed the *Sentences* c 1158, the theologians cited in it are largely patristic authors like Augustine, Ambrose, John Damascene, and Hilary of Poitiers. Scholastic doctors like Aquinas, Bonaventure, Scotus, and Ockham do not therefore figure in Lombard's *Sentences*.

54 Annotation on 1 John 5:7 LB VI 1080C / Reeve *Annotations* 768–9: *Fortasse praestiterat hoc piis studiis agere, uti nos idem reddamur cum Deo, quam curiosis studiis decertare* 'Perhaps it would be preferable to accomplish this through pious studies, that we become one with God, rather than debating with each other in painstaking studies.' The use of *curiosa studia* can likewise be seen as an accusation of *curiositas*, which scholastic theologians regarded as an unjustified motive for study.

55 *studia in contraria* (Virgil *Aeneid* 2.39), a forceful criticism of the scholastic method as inherently factious. On Erasmus and scholastic theology see James K. Farge 'Erasmus, the University of Paris, and the Profession of Theology' *Erasmus of Rotterdam Society Yearbook* 19 (1999) 18–46 (especially 28–9 and 39–44); see also Charles Nauert '"The Articular Disease": Erasmus' Charges that the Theologians Have Let the Church Down' *Mediaevalia* 22 (Special Issue 1999) 9–27. Cf n75 below.

56 For example, nominalists, realists, moderate realists (and, among the latter, Thomists and Scotists). For Erasmus' views of Thomas Aquinas and Scotus see Rummel *Annotations* 77–81.

wrangling over these questions, quite clearly indicating that I do not disapprove of serious and moderate discussion even in subjects that are beyond   245
comprehension.

But at first sight what I suggest is rather hard to accept. In any case,
as far as I am concerned, I do not see how one can demonstrate the doctrine that the Arians deny except by a process of reasoning.[57] And yet from
what precedes and from what I say elsewhere my position is clear. The Ar-   250
ians did not tolerate the doctrine that the Son was *homousios* with the Father, that is, of the same essence, although they admitted that he was God.[58]
But the word *homousios* is not in the Sacred Scriptures; therefore it cannot
be proved except by reasoning. For what Augustine affirms, 'Man begets
man, therefore God the Father begets God the Son,'[59] does not prove that   255
the essence of the Father and the Son is precisely identical; indeed the comparison used proves the opposite for, although the son of a human being is
born of the substance of a human, he is nevertheless not of the same individual essence with the substance of his father. To prove the validity of my
opinion, I supply a syllogism: 'The Father begets the Son' (this is proved   260
by Sacred Scripture); 'He therefore begets of his own substance' (granted);
'But the substance of God is most uniquely unique; it is necessary therefore that the Son be of the same substance as the Father.' This is the reasoning I speak of, which is not human but is founded upon the Scriptures and
drawn from philosophy. Just as one single soul giving life to the head and   265
the feet remains the same because it is an indivisible form, so with greater
reason the essence of God communicated to the various persons remains
indivisible.

* * * * *

57 Erasmus uses *ratiocinatio*, seeming to concede that only the reasoning process
    employed in scholastic theology – an approach he normally deplored – could
    sufficiently refute the Arian heresy.
58 The Greek adjective ὁμός [*homos*] 'the same,' prefixed to the Greek noun οὐσία
    [*ousia*] 'being,' forms the compound ὁμοουσία [*homousia*], which means 'the
    same in being' or, in scholastic theological terms, 'having the same substance'
    (as the Father); see nn73 and 74 below. The Arian heresy maintained that the
    Son of God was not eternal but was created in time by the Father from noth-
    ing. For all Arians therefore Jesus was not God by nature but was a creature
    of God. In the late fourth century, some Arians chose to avoid dogmatic pre-
    cision by affirming that the Son is *similar* to the Father 'according to the Scrip-
    tures,' while other Arians – still rejecting the term *homousios* – accepted the
    term *homoiousios* as expressing both the similarity and the distinction between
    the Father and the Son (ODCC 99–100 sv 'Arianism').
59 Cf *Contra Maximinum Arianorum episcopum* 2.17.4 PL 42 784–5. The sense, not
    the words, is in Augustine; the citation is closer to Erasmus' own expression
    in the *Apologia adversus monachos* LB IX 1034D.

Now I admit that the passage 'I and the Father are one'[60] is effective
in confirming the faith of believers, for there is the greatest agreement be-   27(
tween those who are of the same essence; but to counter the Arians it does
not have the same effect. But if in Scripture, whenever two are said to be
one, it is understood that they are of the same indivisible essence, then all
pious men are one with Christ according to the same passage in John. And
from this passage, 'The Spirit, the water, and the blood,'[61] they will be of   27!
the same indivisible substance. Indeed Paul and Apollos will be of the same
indivisible substance because it is written: 'He who plants and he who wa-
ters are one.'[62] And every time we commonly say, 'These two are one,' and
likewise every time we say that many have one spirit we will understand
that they have the same indivisible substance, which is not true at all.   28(

These are my words in the *Annotations*: 'Now since there are innumerable passages that support what we must understand about the unanimity
and mutual benevolence,[63] it will serve to confirm the belief of the orthodox
Christian; but I do not see what efficacy it has in repressing the obstinacy of
heretics.' But some Doctors of the church use these passages against the Ar-   28!
ians. I grant this and I voice no objection. But the Arians respond that these
passages are to be interpreted to refer to likeness and unanimity, and their
response is not altogether absurd. And sometimes Doctors of the church in
their welter of arguments include things that will not stand up to careful
examination. For example, Augustine concludes from the passage in John   29(
'Unless you eat my flesh and drink my blood, you will not have life' that
infants must be damned if they depart this life without the Eucharist![64]

Now if someone says that it is illicit to explain the Scriptures differently than the Doctors of the church explained them, even granting that all
the Doctors explained the passage in this way and that their authority car-   29.
ries weight with us, it will not for that reason be effective against the Arians,

* * * * *

60 John 10:30
61 1 John 5:8
62 1 Cor 3:8. After Christian conversion and education at Ephesus, Apollos, a
learned Jew of Alexandria 'mighty in the Scriptures' (Acts 18:24), preached at
Corinth, where some Christians wished to set him up as a rival to St Paul (1
Cor 3:4). Martin Luther and others proposed him as the author of the Epistle
to the Hebrews.
63 That is, of the three Persons; again, Erasmus is quoting his annotation on 1
John 5:7 (see n37 above).
64 See n49 above. The passage from John is 6:54; Augustine also quotes here
Mark 16:16 on the necessity of baptism. See *Apologia adversus monachos* LB IX
1035F.

for it is they who must be refuted and not true believers, who are fully convinced of this because of both the Scriptures and the official authority of the
church. Even at the time when the impiety of the Arians was at its greatest
ferment it appears that this testimony did not exist either in any Greek or   300
Latin manuscripts or, at any rate, in very few, since Cyril has no recourse
to it in his battle with the Arians, nor do Athanasius or Hilary.[65] And if the
manuscripts were of equal worth, which is not the case, the Arians would
have contended that theirs were more correct.

There is more than one variation of this passage, as we have shown   305
in the Annotations. As to the obscurity of the passage there is no doubt.
Someone will say, 'What need was there to raise this question?' I have already said that in the first edition I did not touch on any of this but was
forced by slanderous attacks to discuss these things.[66] Only two people sank
their teeth into the passage, Lee and Zúñiga, to whose charges I responded   310
fully,[67] demonstrating that I was never in agreement with the Arians and
that there was no need of this passage to refute the Arians. But the Spanish monks have made these two into legion, although that is of little importance. In the end, in the fourth edition I wrote what is in the Latin versions,
from a sole Greek manuscript that came from England, but a recent one, al-   315
though the Greek manuscript in the Vatican has what was in mine.[68] It is
known that some Greek manuscripts were emended from the reading of the
Latin manuscripts after an accord was reached between the Eastern churches
and Rome.[69] But I have issued my New Testament so that the Latins might

* * * * *

65 For Cyril and Athanasius see nn 40 and 38 above. Hilary (c 315–67), bishop of
Poitiers, was known as the 'Athanasius of the West.' His treatise *De Trinitate*
was widely known in the Middle Ages. Erasmus was the first to edit his works
(Basel: Johann Froben 1523).
66 Cf line 186 above.
67 In *Responsio ad annotationes Lei novas* 25 (see n37 above) and the *Apologia ad
annotationes Stunicae* LB IX 351–3 / ASD IX-2 252–8
68 The English manuscript known as 'Montfortianus,' which dates from about
1520, is now at Trinity College, Dublin (MS A 4 21). The codex known as 'Vaticanus B ' (Biblioteca Apostolica Vaticana Gr 1209) had been collated for Erasmus by Paolo Bombace; see Ep 1213 nn14–16. Dating from the fourth century, it and the Codex Sinaiticus (London, BL Add 43725) are the oldest extant
Bibles. Vaticanus B contains most of the Old Testament with the Apocrypha
(excluding 1 and 2 Maccabees) and most of the New Testament. It was a gift
in 1483 from the Byzantine Emperor John VIII to Pope Eugenius IV.
69 No Greek manuscript dating from before the sixteenth century is known to
contain the *comma Ioanneum*; see ASD IX-2 12, 258–9; cf Bruce Metzger *The Text
of the New Testament* 3d ed (Oxford 1992) 101–2. The statement is problematic

know what readings were available to Origen, Irenaeus, Basil, Chrysostom, 320
Athanasius, and Cyril, whose commentaries we possess.[70] Often they would
not be intelligible to us if we did not know the text they used. But on this
matter read the annotation I wrote in the fourth edition.[71]

3/ From the numerous passages I have cited above, and from many
others that could be cited, it is abundantly clear that I hold pious opinions 325
on the subject of the equality of Persons. Therefore not even an unjust calumniator could reprehend me in this matter, except that I was incautious in
my words. But I think my words were cautious enough for the fair-minded
reader. For those who seize on every occasion to use calumny not even Christ
and the apostles have spoken cautiously enough. 330

In my book *De modo orandi* these words are found at the beginning:
'Therefore the purpose of this discussion is not to cast doubt on whether
the Holy Spirit should be invoked. I want to show, before talking about
the invocation of the saints, how scrupulous our predecessors were about
adopting anything that had not been handed down by the clear authority 335

* * * * *

on other accounts as well. Greek delegates at the Council of Florence did
recognize and sign the 6 July 1439 decree of union *Laetentur caeli* and accepted the validity of the Western church's adding the term *filioque* to the
Constantinopolitan revision of the Nicene Creed, signifying that the Holy
Spirit proceeds eternally from the Father *and the Son*; *Conciliorum oecumenicorum decreta* ed Giuseppe Alberigo et al (Freiburg-im-Breisgau 1962) 499–504.
But they did not intend the Oriental church to incur thereby an obligation
to introduce the *filioque* clause into its profession of the Creed. Nor would
this have necessitated changes in the Greek text of the Bible, since the Creed
does not appear in the Bible. And the *comma Ioanneum* – the issue which exercises Erasmus here – never surfaced at the Council of Florence or in its decrees. Thus no changes in the Bible would have been made on its account.
In any event, in 1484 the Greek church formally repudiated the Council of
Florence and its decree of union. See Joseph Gill sj *The Council of Florence*
(Cambridge 1959).
70 On Origen, a prolific exegete and theologian in Alexandria and a favourite of
Erasmus, who edited an extensive Latin translation of his works, see Ep 1844,
and cf Epp 1853 n2, 1855 n24. Irenaeus, born c 130, studied in Rome and became bishop in Lyon, where he was probably martyred c 200. He is considered
the first great Catholic theologian. Erasmus edited his *Adversus omnes haereses*
(Basel: Johann Froben 1526), a refutation of Gnosticism and an affirmation of
the canon of Scripture. St Basil (c 330–79) 'the Great,' was a prominent opponent of the Arians and author of the earliest important treatise on the Holy
Spirit. On Chrysostom, Athanasius, and Cyril see nn39, 38, and 40 above.
71 See line 158 and n37 above.

of Holy Scripture, especially in those matters that surpass human understanding.'[72] So much for that quotation. Since, therefore, I taught that the
Father and the Son are invoked in a similar manner, and later declared that
the Spirit must also be invoked, do I not profess quite clearly the equality
of the three Persons? I am there merely speaking of the scrupulous cau-   340
tion of the early Christians concerning matters of the Scriptures and the
church. I have already spoken above about my deductions, which are not
haphazard but based upon Scripture, and I consider as scriptural that which
is clearly implied in Scripture, as, for example, concerning the word *homu-*
sios.[73] And yet the ancient writers ask forgiveness for the fault of irreligious   345
loquacity when, because of the unprincipled behaviour of the heretics, they
were compelled to employ this word and in a certain sense become irreligious for religion's sake.[74] The word 'religion' in its true sense denotes veneration joined with awe and dread. This is true in the highest degree of the

* * * * *

72 They are found not at the beginning but almost at the mid-point of Erasmus'
   Modus orandi Deum (Basel: Johann Froben, October 1524); cf LB V 1115E / CWE
   70 185.
73 *Homusios* is a Latin contraction for the Greek ὁμούσιος [*homousios*] and ὁμοούσιος
   [*homoousios*]. The adjective *homoousios*, translated into Latin as *consubstantialis*
   'of one substance,' was proposed by St Athanasius as the only single term that
   safeguarded and expressed the continuous teaching of the church that οὐσία
   'being' or 'essence' was acknowledged as one and the same in Father and Son.
   Added to the Nicene Creed 325 at the First Council of Constantinople 381 to
   refute the Arian heresy, *homoousios* replaced *homoiousios*, which would reduce
   the substantial unity of the Godhead to a matter of mere likeness; see James
   Franklin Bethune-Baker *The Meaning of Homoousios in the 'Constantinopolitan'*
   Creed Texts and Studies VII-1 (Cambridge 1901) 3–4. For the Greek, Latin, and
   English texts of the Creed of Nicaea and of the First Council of Constantinople see Jaroslav Pelikan *Creeds and Confessions of Faith in the Christian Tradition*
   4 vols (New Haven 2003) I 158–9, 162–3. For a more extended treatment of the
   subject by Erasmus see the *Responsio ad Annotationes Eduardi Lei* 71 LB IX 171–2
   / ASD IX-4 156–8 / CWE 72 175–9. See also n58 above and n83 below.
74 Origen's reluctance to use *homoousios* was not because it was non-scriptural
   – he had no qualms in employing the equally non-biblical term *homoiousios*
   – but because it had earlier been used by Gnostics and by the heretic Paul
   of Samosata, a third-century bishop of Antioch who taught that the Godhead
   was a closely knit Trinity of Father, Wisdom, and Word which, until creation,
   formed a single hypostasis. Paul of Samosata was therefore a precursor of
   Nestorius, who held that from the moment of Incarnation the Word rested
   upon the human Jesus as one person upon another, and that the incarnate
   Christ differed only in degree from the prophets; see ODCC 1242 sv 'Paul of
   Samosata.'

ancient orthodox writers whenever they treat subjects concerning the divine   350
nature. In modern theologians, however, we see the excesses of garrulity.[75]

In no way then do the monks' conclusions about these two passages follow any logic, since I speak of a rational argument that has its source clearly
in the Sacred Scriptures; and what is clearly implied I consider to be openly
stated. For example, when Scripture calls the second Person the Son, even   355
if the name of the Father were nowhere mentioned, it would inevitably be
deduced that he had a father. And when John calls Christ the only-begotten
Son of God,[76] it necessarily follows that the Spirit, even though he proceeds
from the substance of the Father, is not the Son. There are indeed many
things in the mysteries of the divine nature that will be understood only   360
when that which is perfect will come and we will see him face to face and
know him as we are known.[77] Such things cannot be perceived now, nor
is it expedient for us to search into them too deeply. It is for this reason I
said that 'it is a good principle of Christian doctrine to revere everything
pertaining to divinity' etc.[78]   365

4/ Whoever reads my *Apology* answering the criticisms of Lee, articles 71 and 92,[79] will easily see that these words were distorted with malicious intent. The phrase 'The Father is the beginning of himself' is an expression of the ancient writers, not mine. The theologians accept it in the
sense of 'the Father is from no other' as Augustine undoubtedly understood   370
it.[80]

I do not find these words in the first part of my *Apology* and I have
not had the time to look into the second part.[81] These men should indicate
the location of each passage, and not excerpt three words here and there,
bringing a case against the one who has to respond. I have responded amply   375

* * * * *

75 This kind of criticism of scholastic theologians dates from Erasmus' early
   work, the *Antibarbarians*, and was developed considerably in the *Praise of Folly*
   and more specifically in the *Paraclesis* and the *Ratio seu Methodus compendio
   perveniendi ad veram theologiam*. See also n55 above.
76 John 1:14,18; 3:16,18; 1 John 4:9
77 1 Cor 13:12; 1 John 3:2
78 *Modus orandi Deum* (CWE 70 186). The rest of the phrase is 'but to affirm nothing
   except what is explicitly stated in the Scriptures.'
79 Not the *Apologia qua respondet invectivis Lei* but the *Responsio ad annotationes Lei*
   71 and 92 LB IX 171–3, 183–9 / ASD IX-4 155–8, 174–83 / CWE 72 175–9, 201–14
80 *Contra Maximinum Arianorum episcopum* 2.17.4 PL 42 784 –5. The passage is the
   same cited in n59 above.
81 Again, Erasmus must be referring to his *Responsio ad annotationes Lei*, which
   was published in two parts; see CWE 72 68.

in article 71 that the most perfect property of beginning belongs to the Father alone. If they do not permit us to speak about the divine nature except with the appropriate word, then we will have to remain silent. For the words 'homousios,'[82] 'hypostasis,'[83] 'person,' 'to be born,' and 'to beget' have entirely distinct meanings when used of divine things than they do in a human context. But if we can say that many people partake of the same light, and if the individual members of the body are rightly said to share in the soul, since the soul is single and indivisible and is entirely present in each member, why is it inappropriate to say that the Son partakes of the Father's nature, which he has in common with the Father? And if Hilary, in his book *On the Trinity* 7, said with all due piety, 'God the Father imparts his perfect nature to the Son without losing it,'[84] what forbids one from saying that the Son partakes of the divine nature? 380 385

5/ All these disputes about the divinity of the Son, which Zúñiga set in motion without any reason, arise from the foregoing considerations. I pointed out in my *Annotations* the customary practice in Sacred Scripture of frequently calling the Father 'God,' but only in two or three places openly calling the Son 'God,' adding: 'even though the word "God" is common to the three Persons to an equal extent.'[85] In substance I was in agreement with Zúñiga; the controversy turned merely upon the number of these passages. And yet in this respect he did not quite understand what I had said. I was concerned with the simple attribution of the word 'God' to the Father or to the Son; he collected passages which show that the Son is God – of which there are many, and I did not deny it. For example, in the Apostles' Creed 390 395

* * * * *

82 See n73 above.

83 Ὑπόστασις, literally 'substance,' used by both Aristotle and the Neoplatonists to designate objective reality as opposed to illusion. The Fathers at the Council of Nicaea (325) used it in the anathemas appended to the Nicene Creed to mean 'being' or 'substantial reality,' which is the sense that it carries in Heb 1:3. But it also came to mean 'individual reality' and even 'person,' a development that led to confusion between some who spoke of three 'hypostases' in the Godhead and others who meant three 'substances.' The First Council of Constantinople (381) clarified and standardized its usage and removed its theological ambiguities by defining 'three *Hypostases* in one *Ousia*' as the epitome of the orthodox doctrine of the Trinity (ODCC 786 sv 'Homoousion').

84 *De Trinitate* 7.28 PL 10 224B, cited in *Responsio ad annotationes Lei* 71; cf CWE 72 178 n606.

85 This passage in the annotation on John 1:1 in the 1516 edition was removed in 1522; cf Reeve *Annotations* 221. Erasmus defends his annotation in *Apologia ad annotationes Stunicae* LB IX 309C–311C / ASD IX-2 124–30.

only the Father is called God;[86] and Paul says several times 'from God the 400
Father' whereas he almost always calls the Son 'Lord.'[87] In this way the Son
is called God only in a few places.[88] And even if there were only one passage in which Christ is clearly called God, that would be sufficient for the
certainty of our faith. Someone will say: 'It would have been better not to
raise this question.' Perhaps, but this objection should be directed at those 405
who raised the question for no reason.

I have given a sketch of my reply, most reverend prelate. I had no
more time at present, because the articles were delivered at the very moment
when those to whom we are entrusting this message were about to set out.[89]
We will treat the rest more carefully; but these monks must be required 410
to give the specific location for every passage so that it will be easier to
respond. I wish to commend myself to your reverend Lordship; your most
humble and devoted servant,

Erasmus of Rotterdam, in my own hand
To the Most Reverend Alonso, archbishop of Seville 415

1878 / From Henry VIII   Otford, 18 September [1527]

Erasmus had reopened the question of his moving to England in his correspondence with Mountjoy (Ep 1816:33–42). Still, such a step would probably
have alienated Emperor Charles v; and Erasmus would surely have known
of Henry's matrimonial crisis. After additional probing in February 1528,
when he sent his servant Quirinus Talesius (Epp 1955, 1959, 1960, 1964) to

* * * * *

86 Although the exact formulation of the Apostles' Creed we have today can be
traced back only to the eighth century, it is quasi-identical with the baptismal
confession used in the Roman church of the second century. With the exception of the Anabaptists, all the major leaders of the Reformation accepted the
Apostles' Creed as a fundamental exposition of the Christian faith; see J.N.D.
Kelly *Early Christian Creeds* (London and New York 1950) 368–434.
87 For example Rom 1:7, 1 Cor 1:3, 2 Cor 1:2, Gal 1:3, Eph 1:2 and 6:23, Phil 1:2,
Col 1:2, 2 Thess 1:2, 1 Tim 1:2, 2 Tim 1:2, Philem 1:3
88 The clearest place is John 20:27–8, where the apostle Thomas calls Jesus 'My
Lord and my God'; cf John 1:1: 'and the Word was God'; Rom 9:5: 'Christ
who is above all, God for ever blessed;' Titus 2:13: 'our great God and Saviour
Christ Jesus.' See Raymond E. Brown 'Does the New Testament Call Jesus
God?' in *Jesus God and Man* (Milwaukee 1967; repr New York 1972) 1–38; cf
Walter Pannenberg *Jesus – God and Man* trans Lewis L. Wilkins and Duane A.
Priebe 2nd ed (Philadelphia 1977) 115–87.
89 The Basel printers, starting on their journey to the Frankfurt book fair; see the
introduction.

England, Erasmus finally declined on 1 June 1528 (Ep 1998) the king's offer made here.

This letter first appeared in *De puritate tabernaculi* (Basel: Hieronymus Froben and Nicolaus Episcopius 1536).

HENRY, KING OF ENGLAND, TO DESIDERIUS ERASMUS OF ROTTERDAM, GREETING

Your incomparable intellectual endowments have always elicited our high-est admiration joined with our favour and good will. Thus it was with the greatest displeasure that we learned from the archbishop of Canterbury that   5 certain impious men, bitter enemies of the Christian religion, are laying plots against your life with such skilful stratagems that you can scarcely find refuge from them anywhere.[1] Since we first met you, at a very tender age,[2] we have nourished an uncommon devotion towards you. But that has grown greater with each passing day by your zealous care to confer on us   10 the blessing of immortality by the honourable mention you make of us in the books you have published.[3]

We have always considered this as most certain proof of your highest regard, loyalty, and love for us. Now that your unwavering and indefati-gable determination of spirit has reached its greatest height, as you devote   15 yourself unstintingly to the propagation and glorification of the Christian faith – not to seek admiration for your own works but for the immense ben-efit and advantage of the Christian world – our love for you in turn has reached such magnitude as to exceed all bounds. Indeed, since you are un-dertaking this campaign almost single-handed, we are motivated with an   20 incalculable zeal to lend our help and protection as best we can to your pi-ous and holy endeavours. For we too have felt for some years now a warm and burning desire within us, undoubtedly inspired by the divine Spirit, to

* * * * *

1878
1 See Epp 1828 and 1831 to William Warham; Ep 1861 too may have arrived in time to be shown to the king.
2 In 1499 (Ep 104 introduction)
3 For dedications to Henry see Ep 104, sent with the poem *Prosopopoeia Britan-niae maioris*, or *Ode de laudibus Britanniae* Reedijk *Poems* no 45 / CWE 85–6 30–41, 440–54 (notes) no 4; Ep 272, for the translation of Plutarch's *De discrimine adu-latoris et amici*, first printed in *Plutarchi opuscula* (Basel: Johann Froben, August 1514); Ep 657, a letter to accompany at least two presentation copies of Erasmus' books; and Ep 1381, the dedication to Henry of the *Paraphrase on Luke* (Basel: Jo-hann Froben, 30 August 1523). The king is praised in Ep 964, addressed to him in May 1519 in hopes of obtaining a favourable offer of residence in England.

Henry VIII
Hans Holbein the Younger, c 1536
Galleria Thyssen, Lugano

restore the Christian faith and religion to their former dignity. Our fondest wish has always been to devote all our labours and efforts and whatever   25
strength is ours by the gift of Christ, to whom we owe all that we have, to
disperse and set at nought the fraudulent claims of heretics and to insure
absolute freedom to the word of God.⁴ But the unhappy conditions of our
times and the decline of good morals are such, as you are aware, that everything is falling into ever greater decay. Wherefore are we all the more dis-   30
tressed by your plight, or rather that of the Christian religion; and we are
concerned for your safety, fearing that if you are removed from the scene
the impious darkness of heresy will spread further over the world, and its
forces will advance more perilously and hold more cruel sway.

In your wisdom you will perceive immediately how we must counter   35
these evils. In our opinion there seems to be no better method and solution than that you abandon Italy and your beloved Germany altogether and
agree to take up residence here in our kingdom. If this should seem pleasing
and acceptable to you, not only will you give us the greatest pleasure but
you will receive most excellent terms, which you yourself will judge to be   40
most generous and honourable. We remember you used to say that, weary
of the sea and journeying, you had chosen Britain to be the haven for your
old age and, as it were, your life's final abode.⁵ We beseech you by all that is
holy and sacred not to change this resolve. To enjoy your pleasant company
and judicious counsel, which we are determined to follow now and always,   45
will be for us a great boon. It will also be to the best interests of your security and the tranquil pursuit of your studies. Finally, by mutual effort and
with our added resources the gospel of Christ will be far better defended. If
it is friends that may influence your decision, in addition to those who have
always been your closest friends and admirers here, we will immediately   50
win to your side the leading citizens of our kingdom, who have long been
your fervent supporters. If you are concerned for your personal liberty, we
will require of you no duties that would prevent you from living wherever
you like in our kingdom with every guarantee of freedom. In brief, in whatever you wish regarding the tranquillity of your life and scholarly pursuits,   55
you will find us completely at your disposal. Do find it in you, my excellent
Erasmus, to make favourable answer to my prayers. Farewell.

Otford, 18 September

* * * * *

4 After writing the *Assertio septem sacramentorum* (1521) against Luther, King
  Henry was granted the title 'Defender of the Faith' by Pope Leo x.
5 This had been a frequent theme in letters to English friends; see Epp 781:14–
  16, 782:16–17, 783:14–16, 784:59–67, 786:21–3, 821:6–9, 937:39–41.

1879 / To Alonso Manrique de Lara   [Basel, September 1527]

This letter is the first preface to the *Apologia adversus monachos quosdam Hispanos*, Erasmus' considered reply to the attacks made upon him by Spanish theologians at Valladolid (see Epp 1791 introduction, 1967). A preliminary but incomplete manuscript draft of the work had already been sent in haste to Manrique (Ep 1877). But after Erasmus had completed the full text (sometime before 15 October), he dispatched an 'advance copy' of it to Manrique along with this letter, which he had composed a few weeks earlier, promising that it would not circulate generally until it had received Manrique's official approval (Ep 1888). There is nothing to show that the endorsement was ever given. Erasmus therefore decided to let the book go out, covering his action with the excuse that in the confusion caused by Froben's death in late October a copy had reached Cologne, and that he was afraid of being compromised. He therefore composed a new prefatory epistle to Manrique (Ep 1967) which he placed on a preliminary sheet preceding this letter when the book was finally released for general circulation at the end of March 1528 (Ep 1980). Erasmus would later issue a second, corrected edition (Basel: Hieronymus Froben 1529).

For Alonso Manrique de Lara see Ep 1846 introduction.

TO THE MOST REVEREND FATHER AND LORD IN CHRIST ALONSO
MANRIQUE, ARCHBISHOP OF SEVILLE, INQUISITOR-GENERAL
IN SPAIN IN MATTERS PERTAINING TO THE CATHOLIC FAITH,
FROM DESIDERIUS ERASMUS OF ROTTERDAM, GREETING
The apostle Paul, according to the testimony of Luke, is happy to be able to   5
plead his cause before King Agrippa, since he was thoroughly acquainted with the Judaic customs, constitutions, and issues that were under discussion in that trial.[1] Confident, obviously, of his case, the saint desired nothing more than an intelligent judge, for the cause itself should win favour with an upright and equitable magistrate. I certainly could consider myself   10
fortunate for the same reason, most honoured prelate, since the resolution of this rowdy dispute has fallen upon a judge distinguished no less for his learning and discernment than for his uprightness of life. But I am the more distressed that your piety, taken up with so many matters of grave concern, should have to deal with calumnies of this kind. Many will doubtless count   15
it little loss that I am distracted and interrupted in my labours, in which

* * * * *

1879
1 Acts 26:2–3

I exert myself unceasingly to the best of my powers – indeed beyond my powers, both of age and of strength – for the advancement of good letters, which are already successfully flourishing among all nations, and for the restoration of the study of theology and the church Fathers.   20

The books I have written are in the public forum and can be enumerated easily enough; but to estimate how many sleepless vigils they cost me is very difficult. At present I am devoting all my energies to publish St Augustine in a complete and revised edition worthy of his greatness, a work of immense labour and expense.[2] One would scarcely believe how many monstrous errors I have detected in such an illustrious Doctor of the church,   25
the result of either the ignorance of copyists or the temerity of would-be scholars. To raise a storm of protest against someone who gives freely of his efforts for the common good, in my opinion, will be seen by all sensible men as the worst kind of ingratitude. But to stab in the back with the sharp   30
points of their tongues a fellow soldier – one who has adhered tenaciously to the Catholic side when the fortunes of the church hang in the balance as never before, engaging in hand-to-hand combat with the enemy – what name shall we give to such conduct? I leave it to others to devise a name; but in point of fact nothing could have coincided more with the wishes of   35
the one against whom these men profess to wage relentless warfare.[3]

But I should bear these evils, however great, more lightly if I were contending with Jews, as was Paul, or if the conflict were with heretics or pagans; for the victory would be a source of joy to all pious men and would harm or bring correction only to the impious. But I am compelled to contend   40
with men who profess to be pillars of the Christian religion, men who should both be paragons of virtue and be regarded as such. Of these two I strongly wish the first could truthfully be said of them, and I should not envy them the second if only they did not stand in the way. For those who are behind this, as I am given to understand, are not Jews, not heretics, not schismatics,   45
not pagans, but Trinitarians, Dominicans, Franciscans, Carmelites, Augustinians, Benedictines[4] – names that have long enjoyed popularity among all the nations of the world. And as far as I am concerned, I should prefer that they should increase in popularity rather than suffer the least diminution.

Accordingly, since it is my only recourse, I pray Christ again and again   50
that no one think that the stupidity and wickedness of a few has anything to do with the reputation of their orders. I should gladly put up with personal

* * * * *

2 It appeared in ten volumes (Basel: Hieronymus Froben 1528–9); see Ep 2157.
3 Presumably Martin Luther
4 Cf Epp 1805:145–6, 253–66, 1839:101, 1893 n13.

insult to protect their honour, if it were only a question of eloquence or native talent or learning; but no one should admit to the charge of impiety unless he was audacious enough to commit it. Indeed I should not hesitate to ask the orders themselves to consent to keep this controversy a private one. In return I should be willing to caution all those who are devoted to my cause there to moderate their enthusiastic support lest a more violent clash of interests unleash some new discord in the world. There are more than enough disorders already in existence far and near, especially when we see that sometimes from the most insignificant beginnings very grave troubles take rise, stirred up by men of no account but quelled only with great effort by the authority of princes. As far as my sentiments are concerned I should rather be thrown overboard with Jonah and ransom the public peace by the loss of my life alone than be called, if not the cause, the occasion of a deadly tempest.[5] And so I shall plead my case in such a way that, as far as possible, my adversaries shall remain unharmed and unnamed.

But should this affair seem to bring some reproach upon them, that is, if in the course of my defence the truth is laid bare, revealing them to be far from what they strive to appear, let them blame themselves, not me, whom they have driven to this necessity. If they had dealt with me by private letter, the matter could have been settled without causing pain to anyone, and they would have won much favour in my eyes. But they conduct the affair not only publicly but also in an uncivil manner. I shall not bother to complain that for a long time now certain men have defiantly vented their frenzy upon my name, in public and in private, even in their sermons,[6] contrary to the wishes of pontiffs[7] and of the emperor,[8] providing an example completely alien to the teachings and practices of Dominic and Francis,[9] whose names they use to promote themselves. How far removed from their professed purity of life is this document they have presented to your Excellency![10] First comes an exordium containing a roster of early heretics; this leads to an

* * * * *

5 Jon 1:12–15
6 Epp 1805:38, 1858:443, 485, 1875:60
7 Cf Epp 1805 nn25 and 77–8, 1891:154.
8 Eg Epp 1802:9, 1805:119, 1815:6, 1821:10
9 The founders in the early thirteenth century of the Dominican and Franciscan orders
10 That is, the first list of articles (not extant) drawn up by the monks and communicated to Erasmus by Pedro Juan Olivar with Ep 1791. This was presumably the same document already rejected on April 5 by Manrique, who demanded that Erasmus' critics draft something more orderly and less repetitious. See Ep 1814 introduction.

honorific mention of my name, as if Erasmus ever had anything to do with
heretics. Then comes that formidable list of charges; is this any different
from a formal indictment? And in-between and everywhere the poison is
spread generously.   85

But I shall not respond in like manner,[11] for I should like to win the
day no less by my moderation than by the merits of my case. I seek nothing
more from your Excellency, most honoured prelate, than that in the midst
of your numerous and pressing concerns you will not be averse to granting me a little time to become thoroughly informed about my case. For if   90
there were any impiety in my writings, I am certain that in your piety you
would never show me favour, nor would my conscience allow me to ask
any favour other than correction, in the fervent desire that all impiety be
as far removed from my writings as from my heart. I am well aware and
confess that in my many works, some of which I wrote as a young man   95
and some in a lighter vein and which I dashed off in haste rather than published – this is a defect of character – there are many things that could have
been said more learnedly perhaps or more cautiously or with more moderation.[12] But I did not foresee this age of ours so prone to calumny. In
any case no one, I believe, will find any impious content. If such could be   100
demonstrated, I would be the first juryman to use the black pebble,[13] the
first magistrate to root out the error. But with such a diversity of temper-
aments, opinions, and judgments no one can satisfy all the suspicions and
allegations, the perverse and distorted interpretations that arise on every
side; and it makes no difference to do so, for even in the writings of the   105
apostles calumny will find something to nibble away at, and no orthodox
writer to this day has been so fortunate that he does not have to be read
with some indulgence.[14] To mention only a few, in the writings of Roman
pontiffs, in Jerome, and in Augustine there are things to be found that have
a heretical meaning, pure and simple, if one were to dare profess them   110
now.[15] There are certain human failings that a sense of equity condones in

* * * * *

11 Cf *Adagia* I i 35: 'To render like for like.'
12 Cf Epp 1828:18–19, 1902:296–7.
13 A method of voting in which a white pebble signified acceptance or innocence
   and a black one rejection or guilt; see *Adagia* I v 53.
14 Cf Ep 1864 n16.
15 Erasmus disapproved of the lives and actions of a number of popes, but accusation of actual papal heresies is unusual. The most famous case of a papal
   'heresy' was the private teaching of Pope John XXII (1316–34) that those who
   have died do not enjoy the beatific vision until the final judgment – an opinion
   denounced by the University of Paris and many theologians. He retracted it

consideration of other merits. I should not myself wish to be condoned in that way.

But in these matters your judgment will serve as an oracle, excellent prelate, since your noble birth, holiness of life, goodness of nature, and sin- 115 gular learning preserve you completely free of any suspicion of ill will. But I am detaining you too long with this preface; I shall get to the point. First I shall cite faithfully the content of the document sent to me by the emperor's secretary.[16] The prologue is as follows.

1880 / From Willibald Pirckheimer   [Nürnberg, c September 1527]

This is a rough and incomplete draft of a letter that was cut short by an attack of gout. The fair copy sent to Erasmus is not extant. Although longer and containing additional subjects, it too was broken off by Pirckheimer's illness (Ep 1893:53, Allen Ep 1977:4–5). The manuscript of this first draft, in Pirckheimer's hand, is among the Pirckheimer papers conserved at the Stadtsbibliothek Nürnberg (MS PP 322B). Erasmus will answer this letter with Ep 1893.

Willibald Pirckheimer (1470–1530) was trained first in the court of a noble bishop and then received in Pavia a wide-ranging humanist education that included Greek. A former member of the council of the free city of Nürnberg, he was appointed imperial councillor in 1514, and he was a writer, editor, translator, collector of books, and patron of education and the arts in a city that

* * * * *

on his deathbed. In several places Erasmus cites Jerome's irascible nature and corruptions in the text of his writings, but we have not found in the *Hieronymi vita* or in the correspondence any passages in which he accuses Jerome of heresy. In Ep 1451:15–30 Erasmus comments on Jerome's manner of response to those who accused him of heresy. Erasmus does, however, mention twice an example of heresy in Augustine (Ep 1877 lines 198–202 and 290–2; cf nn49 and 64). In Ep 1858:69 he ironically terms Augustine 'the illustrious and completely orthodox author.' Augustine himself openly acknowledged and recanted errors in his works in his *Retractationum libri duo*.

16 This is the only time that Erasmus mentions Alfonso de Valdés having sent him the articles accusing him of heresy submitted by the Spanish theologians. They are probably different from the twenty-one articles (not extant) that Pedro Juan Olivar sent Erasmus on 13 March 1527, for in his letter Olivar writes that Valdés 'wants me to send him the articles that have been compiled against you' (Ep 1791:29–30). The articles Olivar sent antedate the ones presented by the 'monks' to Manrique on 28 March 1527, which he rejected as repetitive and disordered (Ep 1814:270–3).

respected commercial profit more than culture. His friendship with Erasmus, dating from about 1513, resulted in a frequent exchange of letters. Although the bulk of his papers were burned at his death, fifty-five letters exchanged with Erasmus are extant, and his surviving correspondence prior to 1521 comprises four published volumes (*Willibald Pirckheimers Briefwechsel* ed Emil Reicke, Dieter Wuttke, and Helga Scheible (Munich 1940–   ). He had been a more avid defender of Reuchlin than Erasmus was, and his advocacy of Luther – prompted more by the reformer's attack on church abuses than by his theological positions – lasted longer as well. Disillusioned in the end with the reform (which officially ruled in Nürnberg after 1525), he realigned himself with Rome and wrote against Oecolampadius' views of the Eucharist – a subject he broaches here. See CEBR III 90–4.

Fond greetings. Neither the tedium of inactivity, much less attacks of the gout, [1] can be dispelled by these conflicts with that hypocrite Oecolappus,[2] most excellent Erasmus; for what pleasure or delight can such things afford? But I indicated to you previously that, not wishing to appear impious or to imperil my possessions or even my life, I was forced to write against my own will.[3] Into such straits had my friendship with this man drawn me. My failure to convince you of this cannot be laid to my charge; and it is not surprising that I should fall victim to fear, when I see that a man as   5

* * * * *

1880
1 Having suffered many years from this debilitating condition, Pirckheimer composed an ironical praise of the gout, *Apologia seu podagrae laus* (Nürnberg: Friedrich Peypus 1522; trans *The Praise of the Gout* London 1617), modelling it somewhat on Lucian and on Erasmus' *Praise of Folly*.
2 A contemptuous distortion of the name 'Oecolampadius' (on which see Ep 1804 n4). For Pirckheimer's other caustic play on Oecolampadius' name see Ep 1893 n21. Like Erasmus, Pirckheimer was the subject of attack from both reformers and traditionalists. He refers here to the fallout from his two books against Oecolampadius: *De vera Christi carne et vero eius sanguine* (Nürnberg: Johann Petreius, c April 1526) and *De convitiis monachi illius qui graecolatine Caecolampadius Oecolampadius nuncupatur* (Nürnberg: Johann Petreius, January 1527).
3 Pirckheimer's letter, not extant, might have explained the threats alleged here against his life. Threats against his possessions have not been documented. It was only later, in 1529, that the Nürnberg city council tried to close down convents of women. With seven of his sisters and three of his daughters in Nürnberg nunneries, such plans might have meant loss of dowries and subsequent financial responsibilities he thought he had already discharged.

Bookplate of Willibald Pirckheimer
Albrecht Dürer, c 1500–3
Kupferstichkabinett, Berlin

courageous as you is not altogether without fear. I recently read a letter of
yours to the secretary of a certain duke,[4] in which you make no secret of   10
why you did not publish the second part of your treatise against Luther,[5]
and why you do not dare to write anything stronger against Oecolappus, not
to speak of the other faction that opposes you.[6] Therefore you will pardon
me if I too preferred the truth to a false friend and feared present danger
more than the whole Oecolappian faction.[7] Nor do I repent of what I did; I   15
prefer that he be indignant rather than that I weep.

But you would prefer that I refrain from insulting language, as if he·
had not deliberately provoked my retaliation with his endless inanities, or
as if you had never done the same yourself.[8] And yet I was more lenient
than his slanders deserved; and many have reproached me for it, I know.   20
But, unless I am mistaken, if he put me in his debt, I returned it to him in
full, even if I am accused by some of collusion. Such are the ways of our
world today!

But that you complain that your name was dragged into it and that
you were treated with contempt has caused me great wonder, illustrious   25
Erasmus. For if my pamphlet has not yet reached you, as you write, you
could not have read it.[9] But if you did not read it, you can hardly know
what is written there. One can only conclude, therefore, that you gave ear
to some flatterer, or rather calumniator, who persuaded you that your name
had been tarnished by me. For I have too high an opinion of you to think   30
that you would invent this on your own. But even if I had written as you
charge, would I have committed a crime on that account? Is there any reason not to speak about the truth, even face to face with Erasmus? But if I
ever thought such a thing, let alone wrote it, I would not reject the charge

* * * * *

4 Not extant; evidently a reply to Ep 1773 from Hieronymus Emser, secretary
  and chaplain to Duke George of Saxony
5 Pirckheimer is not aware that Erasmus had already published *Hyperaspistes 2*;
  see Ep 1853.
6 Probably the Spanish theologians. Erasmus was indeed working on his *Apologia adversus monachos quosdam Hispanos* and would complete it this same month
  (Epp 1877, 1879, 1967).
7 In attacking Oecolampadius' symbolist theology of the Eucharist Pirckheimer
  would satisfy both his Catholic critics and the Lutheran faction now in control
  in Nürnberg.
8 Pirckheimer had counselled moderation in Erasmus' polemics against Edward
  Lee (Epp 1085, 1095, 1139) and had tried to persuade Erasmus against publishing his *Spongia* against Hutten – in both of which Erasmus had been accused
  of reacting not merely *ad rem* but *ad hominem*.
9 Probably his second book against Oecolampadius; see n2 above.

of sacrilege. And why should I show contempt towards you, whom I have 35
always loved so greatly, respected, and admired not only for your extraordinary learning but also for your remarkable wisdom? Nothing ever happened between us that would cause me to hold you in low esteem. Therefore, my dear Erasmus, I can in no way conceal the fact that it has brought
me no little chagrin to have this charge falsely laid against me.   40

But permit me to say that not only in this case but on other occasions
you seem sometimes to allow yourself to give in too readily to vain suspicions and at other times to take as a personal injury what was uttered with
the utmost simplicity. This does not seem to become your years, much less
your wisdom. And when you add that you were offended that I praised you 45
together with Luther, that seems to be of the same tenor as the rest. But even
if, as you vainly imagine, I had denied that I could not hate those who have
given proof of such great talents, perhaps my words would not have been
altogether absurd. If I have ever compared you with Luther, or if I praised
him, once again I do not object to being considered a boldfaced liar. I have 50
often expressed admiration for the natural abilities of Luther. But his designs are too reckless and headstrong, and his effrontery and vulgar wit[10]
have always intensely displeased me.

1881 / From Christophorus Pistorius   Ansbach, 25 September 1527

This autograph letter (Ep 75 in Förstemann-Günther), was in the Burscher Collection at the University of Leipzig (on which see Ep 1254 introduction). It is
the earliest reaction known to book 2 of Erasmus' *Hyperaspistes*. No response
by Erasmus is extant.

Little is known with certainty of Christophorus Pistorius other than what
he reveals here; cf CEBR III 97.

CHRISTOPHORUS PISTORIUS TO DESIDERIUS ERASMUS OF
ROTTERDAM, ORTHODOX THEOLOGIAN, GREAT CHAMPION
OF THE CATHOLIC CHURCH, PROFUSE GREETINGS
I am well aware, most learned Erasmus, that your time is completely occupied, and that you are constantly at work on those projects whose study will 5
further the cause of good letters and sacred theology. So true is this that anyone who would dare disturb you importunely in this important and pious
activity should deservedly be accounted as one beyond the pale of civilized

* * * * *

10 Allen's text has a blank space after 'wit,' with no explanation – an indication
   perhaps of the rough and incomplete state of the document.

behaviour. Yet I, a man of no significance, known neither for splendour of
fortune nor excellence of learning nor any particular merit, am obliged to   10
do just that, willy-nilly. But you will pardon my intrusion since it is you
who afford me the occasion to write.

It so happened lately that, as I was reading the second book of your
Hyperaspistes,[1] there arrived at that very moment a man celebrated in this
region for his illustrious birth, a great admirer of learned men and par-   15
ticularly of Erasmus.[2] After the usual exchange of greetings he asked me
what new work I was reading. 'The *Hyperaspistes* of Erasmus of Rotterdam,' I replied. He went on to inquire what was the subject of the treatise. I answered, 'On man's free will, in what way and to what extent
man has control over himself.' After some time he asked whether you also   20
touch on the paradox of Luther, that God is the author of good and evil.[3]
Hereupon I bade him listen attentively. I read to him the arguments you
bring forward on that subject from the writings of Paul. He was amazingly
pleased with all of this. He gave unending thanks to Erasmus for having
so clearly explained this difficulty. He added that he could never believe   25
that God is so unjust, so cruel that he would require punishment of a man
for something he urged the unfortunate person to do and indeed forces
him to do.

A few days later he paid another visit to me, and informed me that
someone was setting out for Basel. He directed me to write to the most   30
learned Erasmus (this is the name by which you are known here) concerning
the prayers of the Eucharist, which are commonly referred to as the canon
of the mass. I took it upon myself to do so. The fact is, my excellent Erasmus,
in this depraved age of ours, where anybody in the house of the living God,
which is the mainstay of truth,[4] is permitted to behave, write, and live as   35
he pleases, it is no wonder that there is no lack of those who think the mass
too, especially because of those prayers, should be condemned *in toto*; and
indeed it seems almost extinct already. The arguments they adopt to pursue
their cause I leave to them, and you know them very well.

* * * * *

1881
1 See Ep 1853.
2 Perhaps George of Brandenburg-Ansbach (Franconia), co-ruler of that territory
  with his eldest brother Casimir. He arrived at this time because of Casimir's
  death on 21 September. During his regency for his nephew, Pistorius' pupil
  Albert II, George was to lead all his territories into the Protestant camp.
3 See *Hyperaspistes* 2 LB X 1400E–1408A / CWE 77 468–81.
4 Cf 1 Tim 3:15.

Among other things that strongly offend the minds of pious men here, 40
besides the paradox concerning sovereignty (God as the agent of both good
and evil in man, which, with the approval of all those who had even a parti-
cle of good judgment, you have now refuted through the Holy Scriptures),[5]
is this issue, which strongly torments many: whether the mass is a thoroughly execrable thing, as some people pretend.[6] On this subject, whose 45
judgment is more worthy to be heard than that of Erasmus? His quickness
of intellect is known to all, his divine eloquence leaves us in awe, his singular learning evokes our admiration and his spirit and judgment our ado-
ration. And that is the reason, I finally confess it to you openly, why I have
taken it upon myself to write to you. Therefore, most learned Erasmus, if 50
you do not mind stealing a tiny bit of time from your labours, deign to write
back to us your opinion about the canon of the mass. It is not without good
cause that I write to make this request of you. That you will consent to do
this I beg you through Christ, whom above all things you hold most dear.

Oh how eagerly we await your *De ratione concionandi!*[7] I can hardly say 55
what great, excellent, and sublime things we hope for from this book. You
will teach our contemporaries what true faith in Christ Jesus is, what are
the deeds that truly reconcile us to him and that he requires of us.

On the question of the Eucharist, aside from one letter and a pamphlet
entitled *Detectio prestigiarum*, I know of nothing written by you.[8] But if you 60

* * * * *

5 Pistorius refers back to the 'paradox' mentioned previously (line 21).
6 Pistorius doubtless refers to the traditional primary connection between the
liturgy of the mass and the sacrifice of Christ on the cross – a doctrine that most
reformers either rejected or regarded as secondary to the liturgical celebration
of the Lord's supper. This was obviously exercising Pistorius' patron George
of Brandenburg-Ansbach.
7 Erasmus' treatise on preaching, *Ecclesiastes sive de ratione concionandi*, finally appeared in 1535 (Basel: Froben); cf Ep 1804 n28. Within a year three additional
printings appeared in Basel and Antwerp, and three more were produced
prior to 1540.
8 Pistorius could not know that Erasmus had written at least four letters dealing
with the Eucharist; only one had appeared in print at this time. The first, Ep
1523 to Philippus Melanchthon, criticized the Eucharistic theology of Andreas
Karlstadt. In Ep 1616:22–38, responding to Claudius Cantiuncula's request to
refute Oecolampadius' *De genuina verborum Domini ... expositione liber*, Erasmus revealed to Willibald Pirckheimer that he had begun to compose 'something on the Eucharist' but refused to commit himself to its publication because he sensed it would satisfy nobody. In Ep 1637, in rejecting Conradus
Pellicanus' opinion that Erasmus shared his views, Erasmus had professed

have published further works, indicate them to me in a brief note. May
Christ in his goodness and power preserve your esteemed self unharmed
for the sake of his church. Our prince Albert, margrave of Brandenburg,[9]
my pupil, sends his greetings. Farewell.

Given at Ansbach, 25 September in the year 1527   65

To Desiderius Erasmus of Rotterdam, orthodox theologian, defender
of the church of Christ, master ever worthy of the highest respect

1882 / To Rutgerus Rescius   Basel, 7 October 1527

> This letter first appeared in the *Opus epistolarum* (1529). It answers a letter
> (not extant) from Rescius, probably contemporary with Ep 1768 from Con-
> radus Goclenius, in which the problem of Rescius' marriage was raised. The
> marriage violated the statutes of the Collegium Trilingue and had spurred its
> governors to give Rescius notice of termination. Erasmus' Ep 1806A had ob-
> viously been successful in convincing the principal, Nicolas Wary, to retain
> Rescius.
>
> Rutgerus Rescius had studied Greek c 1512 in Paris under Girolamo Alean-
> dro. After several years of tutoring students in that language, he matriculated
> in the faculty of law at the University of Louvain, while also helping Dirk
> Martens with his Greek editions. He was the first to hold the chair in Greek
> at the newly founded Collegium Trilingue in 1518, and he managed to re-
> tain it despite the problems caused by his marriage (see Epp 1768 n10, 1806A
> nn1, 3, 5).

* * * * *

his adherence to the traditional doctrine of the church. In the fourth letter, Ep
1708, written to the Swiss Confederacy assembled at Baden, Erasmus rejected
the Eucharistic theology of Zwingli and reaffirmed his adherence to the traditional theology of the real presence of Christ in the Eucharist. This last letter,
published by Thomas Murner with his book on the Baden disputation, *Die Dis-
putacion vor den XII Orten einer loblichen Eidtgenoschaft* (Lucerne: 18 May 1527),
is likely the one Pistorius had seen. See Ep 1708 introduction and n1.
Erasmus conceived *Detectio praestigiarum cuiusdam libelli germanice scripti ficto
authoris titulo, cum hac inscriptione, 'Erasmi et Lutheri opiniones de coena Domini'*
(Basel: Johann Froben, June 1526) as a preliminary rejoinder to Leo Jud's recent anonymous book, *Das hochgelerten Erasmi von Roterdam vnnd Doctor Martin
Luthers Maynung vom Nachtmal vnnsers herren Ihesu Christi*. It may be the work
in progress of which Erasmus wrote to Claudius Cantiuncula in Ep 1616. On
the *Detectio praestigiarum* see Ep 1708 introduction and n2.

9 Cf n2 above.

ERASMUS OF ROTTERDAM TO RUTGERUS RESCIUS, GREETING

The matter was of too little importance for you to trouble the governors
on that account.[1] They had made no official record of it, and the person
who suggested to you that you should not change residence presumably
had your welfare at heart in so doing; that much, at least, I have attended   5
to.[2] But the situation is not so inconsequential as you wish it to appear. The
word 'wife' is not very long, but that word brings many consequences in
its train. I shall not speak of marital affection, the upbringing of children,
the anxiety to increase one's wealth, and many other things that slacken and
reduce our attention to the duties of teaching, even though they do not stifle   10
it altogether; at any rate a wife separates you from the college community.
If others are enticed by your example to pursue financial gain, to which we
are all inclined, then the college will no longer be a college but just any
ordinary school.[3] Perhaps you took a wife without consulting the board of
governors. You will say, 'Why didn't they remove me immediately?' There   15
was no one on hand to succeed you, and wise men do not readily make
changes when a situation is tolerable.

　　This courtesy and kindness of theirs,[4] my dearest Rescius, should mo-
tivate you the more to show yourself worthy of the profession in which you
are engaged and of the judgment and expectations of men of such calibre.   20
You attract numerous students, I am told. I congratulate you on that score. We
both wish and hope that by your diligent efforts you will have an even more
crowded lecture hall. Excellent conditions are offered elsewhere.[5] But what
of the fact that you owe this not only to the governors but to the very profession that has given you distinction, has rendered your name famous and   25
renowned, and perhaps also won you a wife? It is not merely financial gain

* * * * *

1882
1　The executors of the will of Jérôme de Busleyden, having established the Col-
　legium Trilingue in Louvain (1517) according to the directions in his last will
　and testament, still retained the direction of the college; see Ep 1457.
2　By writing to Nicolas Wary (Ep 1806A). Before his marriage Rescius had lived
　at the college.
3　The exact circumstances to which Erasmus refers are not clear. Only in 1529
　would Rescius attempt to manage for profit a printing press (CEBR III 343)
　while continuing to teach for the Collegium Trilingue. To the end of his life
　Erasmus considered financial gain to be Rescius' constant temptation. In June
　1536, he wrote to Goclenius that Rescius 'looks only for gain, with serious
　consequences for the college' (Allen Ep 3130:33–7).
4　In retaining Rescius, despite the statutes of the college forbidding marriage
　of its regents
5　See line 29 and n6 below.

that must be considered, but of much more importance is a solid reputation, which brings with it many advantages, even if you do not aspire to them.

As for the lavish promises with which you are invited to France, you know what the promises of the French are like as a rule; and don't forget 30 what happened to the dog in Aesop.[6] But even supposing that the conditions are as certain as they are princely, remember that you also owe a considerable part of this advantage to your college. Therefore I beg of you, my dear Rescius, strive in turn by the skill and enthusiasm of your teaching to do honour to the literary pursuits that gave honour to you. Vie with Gocle- 35 nius,[7] vie with yourself. Whether you remain where you are or go wherever the winds of fortune take you, this has more importance for you yourself than for the cause of learning.

Your letter had something contentious about it, savouring of the law-courts.[8] If you like to dispute, I think you would do better to dispute with 40 the wicked and with the enemies of the Muses. You are dealing with men of great civility, with whom no one would enter into litigation without incurring for himself the reputation of a difficult and unreasonable person. They will not oust you from your position unless they are impelled by some grave reason. And they would be even less inclined to do so if you bring 45 distinction to your profession and to the college by excellent teaching and

* * * * *

6 *Corpus fabularum Aesopicarum* (Teubner 1959) no 136; cf *Babrius and Phaedrus* ed and trans Ben Perry, Loeb Classical Library (London 1965) no 79 'De cane et umbra.' The dog in the story has stolen a piece of meat from a butcher's shop. Thinking his own shadow to be another dog with another piece of meat, he drops his own morsel to seize the imaginary one, but loses it to a real rival. The moral drawn is that people often sacrifice a real blessing for some imaginary one. Most likely Rescius had received an offer to lecture in Paris with a stipend from the king. It was a project particularly desired by Guillaume Budé, who had approached Erasmus in the same way in 1517 and in 1524 (cf Epp 534, 1375, 1812 n14, 1840:52–63), but he had declined. No concrete steps were taken until 1529, when Budé convinced the king to appoint four *lecteurs royaux*, who began to lecture in 1530 and are the forebears of the seventeenth-century Collège royal and the nineteenth-century Collège de France. See James K. Farge 'La Faculté de théologie de Paris et les débuts du Collège de France' in *Parti conservateur* 36–9. Erasmus also made disparaging remarks about the French offer to him in 1524 (Ep 1484:7–11).
7 Conradus Goclenius, professor of Latin at the Collegium Trilingue since 1519, whom Erasmus particularly trusted and liked; cf Ep 1857 introduction.
8 This last phrase is rendered in Greek. Rescius had obviously been pondering a civil suit against the governors of the Collegium Trilingue if they dismissed him for having violated college statutes by his marriage.

uprightness of life. Nor will you desert them without good cause, given
your high moral principles. Should something occur that for good cause
would put an end to your association, our friendship and your reputation
will remain intact. But I truly hope that this will not happen. Through mu-   50
tual agreement, zeal for your profession, and courteous behaviour you will
win out successfully over any and all enemies.

These words come to you from one who loves you dearly; may you
receive them in a like spirit. Return my warm greetings to your dear wife[9]
and to your young charges engaged in the pursuit of honourable studies.   55
Farewell.

Basel, 7 October, in the year 1527

1883 / To Hans Bogbinder   Basel, 7 October 1527

Erasmus published this letter, the only one to Bogbinder that has survived, in
the *Opus epistolarum*. The son of a burgomaster of Copenhagen, Bogbinder had
known Erasmus in Louvain in 1517. His travels, undertaken both for commercial reasons and as an agent of the exiled King Christian II of Denmark, took
him from time to time through Basel, where Erasmus received him warmly.
Bogbinder often carried letters for Erasmus (CEBR I 160–1).

ERASMUS OF ROTTERDAM TO THE DANE HANS BOGBINDER,
GREETING
You see that Homer is no lying poet. If the waves and married life are
favourable to you, I have great reason to rejoice.[1] You can hardly imagine

* * * * *

9 Anna Moons of Louvain

1883
1 In *Adagia* III x 21, *Foemina nihil pestilentius* 'Nothing is more noxious than a
woman,' Erasmus comments: 'Among the poets of antiquity the race of women
often has a bad name; indeed in our times too they do their best to prove that
the poets were not complete liars.' The reference is to *Odyssey* 11.427 where,
in his visit to the underworld, Odysseus learns from Agamemnon that it was
neither the sea nor his enemies on land who caused his death but his accursed
wife Clytemnestra who, bored by his long absence at war, plotted with her
lover Aegisthus to kill her husband and his men. Homer has the shade of
Agamemnon conclude bitterly, 'There is nothing more noxious nor more vile
than a woman who devises such deeds in her heart'; but he has Agamemnon
tell Odysseus that he will not suffer such a fate from his faithful wife Penelope. Erasmus assures Bogbinder here that, like Penelope, his wife will prove
to be an exception to Homer's rule about the perfidy of women.

how much you owe your friend Dilft,[2] such is the sincere affection he has   5
evinced in upholding your good name, first by letter and then in person.
Wherefore you are all the more obliged to reciprocate his loyalty and good
will. He is living with us, cultivating familiarity with the Muses. He managed to conciliate just about everyone who felt your loss after your departure and undoubtedly would have appeased all of them if he had as   10
much resources as he had good will. He arrived here penniless, so much
so that he was virtually in need of a generous creditor himself; far be it
from me to take anything from him. So then, I await a letter from you,
with an enclosure[3] worthy of you and me, which can deliver Bogbinder,
Dilft, and Rotterdam from all anxiety. You could give us a fuller account by   15
telling us something of your life, but do so as soon as possible. I have
awaited a gift from Christian in vain;[4] in truth I did not really expect
anything.

    Here a certain Dominican has openly taken a wife, at the instigation of
the devil, as the Decretals say;[5] she is old enough to be Hecuba's sister.[6] And   20
that Augustinian suffragan – an old man takes an old bride – is a septuagenarian suitor.[7] If you had not hurried away from here in such great haste,
there could have been some hope even for me, with you as the matchmaker.
But we shall exchange further pleasantries on another occasion.

    Farewell, and do write.   25

    Basel, 7 October in the year 1527

    * * * * *

2 On Frans van der Dilft see Ep 1857 n1.
3 Erasmus uses the Greek οὐ κενάς 'not empty'; he must have expected Dilft to
  bring money from Bogbinder to pay Dilft's expenses for room and board.
4 On King Christian II, in whose service Bogbinder was engaged, see Ep 1819
  n22.
5 Allen cites the *Decretales Gregorii* IX 3.2. 3, which uses the expression *instinctu*
  diabolicae fraudis in regard to a cleric keeping a concubine; see *Corpus iuris*
  canonici ed Aemilius Richter and Aemelius Friedburg 2 vols (Leipzig 1879–81)
  II 454. The Dominican has not been identified.
6 Hecuba was the mother of nineteen of Priam's fifty sons (*Iliad* 24.495–7), including Hector and Paris. In Euripides' play about her she is a tragic figure
  who takes horrific revenge on her malefactors.
7 Cf *Adagia* I ii 62. The septuagenarian suitor is probably Tilmann Limperger of
  Mainz, an Augustinian friar and former regent in theology at Freiburg, who
  was suffragan bishop of Basel since 1498. After coming under Oecolampadius'
  influence in 1523, he was forbidden to preach and, in 1525, was suspended
  from all ecclesiastical functions; but Bishop Christoph von Utenheim continued to pay him the salary of a suffragan bishop (CEBR II 330–1). The fact of
  his marriage is not otherwise known.

1884 / From Gervasius Wain   Paris, 9 October [1527]

This letter is in the Rehdiger Collection (MS 254 72) in the University Library, Wrocław, and is autograph throughout. It was first published in Enthoven Ep 54. Allen's year-date of 1527 is justified from comparison with Epp 1902–3, 1909, and 1911, from Ep 1827:15–16, which mentions Wain's visit to Basel, and from the reference in lines 13–14 below to Cardinal Jean de Guise's reception of the Chrysostom edition dedicated to him in Ep 1841.

Gervasius Wain, a native of Memmingen, studied arts in Paris 1505–c 1510 under Erasmus' friend Ludwig Baer, and then theology in 1510–11 in Freiburg-im-Breisgau. He returned to Paris, where he took the doctorate in theology in 1522. In a letter to Béda in 1525 (Ep 1581) Erasmus sent greetings to Wain. In February 1526, the Paris faculty of theology asked Wain to write a rebuttal of Oecolampadius' *De genuina verborum Domini ... expositione liber*; he did report on the book, but in the end it was Josse Clichtove who formally refuted it (Farge *Procès-verbaux* 126 141B). Erasmus took great pleasure in Wain's visit to Basel in 1527 (Ep 1827), and gave him letters to carry to Paris. Through the patronage of Margaret of Navarre (line 17) and Jean de Guise, cardinal of Lorraine, to whom Erasmus recommended him (Ep 1911:76–7), Wain entered the diplomatic service of King Francis I, and from 1531 to 1534 carried out at least seven missions to Germany aimed at strengthening the French king's influence with German princes against Emperor Charles v. On Wain see Farge BR 431–5 no 471.

Greetings. Your services towards me, most learned Erasmus, have put me so much in your debt, especially considering my complete unworthiness, that I can never make equal repayment; yet this is the only way I can express my appreciation.[1] And now once again I am most gratified to you for your letter,[2] a token of your affection for me, but more than that for your   5
congenial conversation. I count it one of my greatest blessings that in our every encounter[3] you never fail through your affable discourse to rid me of much of my ignorance. Wherefore I shall take diligent care, even if I cannot make adequate compensation, to ensure that you never find me lacking in my duties and devotion towards you, in those things that are within my   10
competence.

* * * * *

1884
1 That is, in conveying information about matters in Paris
2 Not extant but probably contemporary with Ep 1854
3 Thus the 1527 visit was not the first.

Gervasius Wain
A drawing of the image incised on his tombstone
Société archéologique d'Eure-et-Loir
Dalles tumulaires et pierres tombales du Département d'Eure-et-Loir
(Chartres: Imprimerie Garnier 1895) vol I
Library, Pontifical Institute of Mediaeval Studies, Toronto

I delivered both of your letters to court, where they were not received
with overwhelming favour.[4] The *Chrysostom* gave great pleasure to the lord
cardinal, especially since it came from you.[5] I should think that you have
placed this gift in the right hands, because he is universally acclaimed for   15
his probity and integrity. And you must not forget that he admitted me into
his household, and this at the suggestion of the queen of Navarre;[6] but I
have not yet decided to take up life at the court. I would like you to make
honourable mention of me in your letter to him;[7] this would greatly increase
my favour. I beg you to do this, if you can do so conveniently.   20

For the rest, lest I seem to have missed any opportunity either in time
or in place in my devotion to you, let me relate in a few words what Béda is
plotting against you. From the *Paraphrases* he has extracted I know not how
many thousands of heresies, as he calls them, to set before the faculty.[8] I
send you those that the faculty has already condemned as well as those it   25
is now examining.[9] You have nothing to hope for from the faculty save ill

* * * * *

4 Allen suggests Epp 1835 (to Germain de Brie) and 1840 (to Guillaume Budé).
  Brie was not unknown at court (Gilbert Gadoffre *La révolution culturelle dans
  la France des humanistes* [Geneva 1997] 193), but nothing in Ep 1835 could
  have met with a cool reception. Budé, who had professional obligations at the
  court, might expect to receive letters there, and Ep 1840 might well have been
  read with little enthusiasm. Erasmus' Ep 1854 to the king's sister Margaret of
  Navarre might, more likely than those to Brie and Budé, have met the cool
  reception of which Wain writes.
5 Jean de Guise, cardinal of Lorraine, to whom Erasmus dedicated his translation
  of St John Chrysostom's commentary on Galatians (Ep 1841). He was one of
  King Francis I's most trusted advisors, and was to become a patron to Wain.
6 Margaret of Navarre, sister of King Francis I; see Ep 1854 introduction.
7 A favour Erasmus will fulfil in Ep 1911:76–7
8 Noël Béda had finished his work on Erasmus' *Paraphrases* a year and a half
  earlier, and on 17 May 1526 the faculty had approved Béda's *Annotationes*
  against Erasmus – most of which were directed against the *Paraphrases* (Farge
  Procès-verbaux 137 no 152B). Having seen Béda's manuscript even before it was
  printed by Josse Bade on 28 May 1526, Erasmus composed a formal rebuttal,
  the *Elenchus in censuras Bedae*, which he sent to the Parlement of Paris on 14
  June 1526 (Ep 1721). A letter to King Francis I (Ep 1722) prompted the king to
  order Béda's *Annotationes* withdrawn from sale; but it was quickly reprinted
  in Cologne. Erasmus followed up his *Elenchus* with the hastily composed *Prologus in supputationem calumniarum Bedae* (Basel: Johann Froben, August 1526)
  and later with a longer, considered reply, *Supputatio errorum in censuris Bedae*
  (Basel: Froben, March 1527; LB IX 516–702).
9 Béda published nothing further on the *Paraphrases*. The only development in
  1527 that is recorded in the faculty minutes was an order of 14 September to
  review the *Paraphrases* again as well as Erasmus' pamphlets against Béda, and

will, dishonesty, and injustice.[10] So then, take care not to lose heart, since you
still have your pen. You are dealing with the most ignorant and impudent
of slanderers. There are not a few men of letters on the faculty, but they are
looked upon as worse than the Lutherans.   30

Paris, on the holy day of St Denis
Your Gervasius

1885 / To Francisco de Vergara   Basel, 13 October 1527

This letter was first published in the *Opus epistolarum* (1529). It fulfils the
promises conveyed in Epp 1875 and 1876 to answer Francisco de Vergara's
Greek letter (not extant) written that spring; see Ep 1814:552. For the addressee, brother of Juan de Vergara, see Ep 1876 introduction.

ERASMUS OF ROTTERDAM TO FRANCISCO DE VERGARA,
PROFESSOR OF GREEK AT ALCALÁ, GREETING
Verily, my dear young man, you recall to me the image of Virgil's Dares,
challenging Entellus, worn out with years, to the fight, when you invite me
to answer your pleasantly discursive letter couched in flawless Greek.[1] The   5
more modest your invitation the more fierce the challenge, and your words
are all the more forceful because you refrain from using force. As a result,
I have less freedom to refuse you, since in your extraordinary modesty you
allow me this option in spite of your fervent desire to hear from me; in a
word, you overcome love with love. But this analogy falls short in several   10
ways. For Erasmus was never in learning what Entellus was in boxing, and
the contest is waged not with knotted cudgels but with the pleasant flowers
of the Muses and light flourishes of the pen. The loser does not vomit forth

* * * * *

to excerpt from all his books anything that was 'perverse and unsound' (Farge
Procès-verbaux 177 no 209B–C). As a result, 8 additional censured propositions
would be added to the original 106 to comprise the 114 censured propositions
in the omnibus condemnation pronounced by the faculty on 16 December 1527
but not published until 1531.
10 The faculty did not have a similar view of Wain, since it asked him to refute Oecolampadius' book on the Eucharist; but Wain never carried out this
assignment. See the introduction.

1885
1 *feliciter graecissantibus*; cf Epp 1875:202 and 1876:7–8, where Erasmus expresses
the same opinion in Greek. For Entellus see Ep 1838 n5 and *Aeneid* 5.387–423,
469–70, 10.349, 11.646, the source of the images Erasmus goes on to use.

a stream of dark blood from his mouth but drinks in draughts of delightful
learning; he does not leave the fight, his limbs livid with bruises and swollen   15
with blows, but with his mind enhanced with an increase of knowledge.
The analogy is appropriate in the sense that an old man is being challenged
by a young man in the flower of youth, although it must be said that I
am anything but sedentary and inert; indeed I am sweating freely in the
thick of the fray, engaged in a very different kind of intellectual pursuit.   20
And yet as I see that I am being challenged to a triple contest, one of love,
praise, and learning, I recognize that I am pitted against three brothers, the
more invincible because they cannot be separated. It was in that manner that
Horatius defeated the three Curiatii single-handed.[2]

Your brother Juan's letter is written in a pleasantly humorous style,   25
but nothing prevents one from telling the truth while jesting.[3] He says that
Spain has its Geryon, but a monster of very good omen, possessing three
bodies but only one soul.[4] First then, as regards renown for learning, so
far am I from wishing to engage you in a contest that, even if I had the
time and were given back my youth, I should only express my personal   30
congratulations to you for your felicitous talent, which holds such promise
for the future, and publicly congratulate your country, Spain, which can
lay claim to its ancient reputation for learning now restored through your
marvellous accomplishments. Since it is a country that has always flourished
because of the beauty and fertility of the land, its rich output of men of   35
outstanding talent, and its prowess in war, what would be lacking to its
complete good fortune save that it add to these the ornaments of scholarship

* * * * *

2 A reference to the famous story of 'Horatio at the bridge.' When the three
  Roman Horatii brothers were pitted against the three Alban Curiatii brothers to decide the outcome of the war, two of the three Horatii were killed.
  Horatius, finding himself alone against three opponents, by running away
  managed to separate them and thus dispatch them one by one.
3 Horace *Satires* 1.1.24
4 In Ep 1814:558 Juan de Vergara described himself and his brothers Francisco de
  Vergara and Bernardino Tovar as 'a triumvirate proclaiming your praise.' Erasmus' response mentions a letter from Francisco in which he had referred to 'a
  Geryon in Spain, with three bodies and one mind, most unfavourable to Erasmus.' But Erasmus goes on to say that he takes pleasure in another Geryon,
  'three most distinguished brothers who with one mind cherish Erasmus' (Ep
  1875:209, 211–12), and he repeats this remark in his reply to Francisco's lost
  letter (Ep 1876:22–4). Here Erasmus not only attributes the jest about Geryon
  to Juan, not Francisco, but also attributes to him the identification of Geryon
  as 'a monster of very good omen.' At line 120 below he correctly attributes the
  allusion to the inauspicious Geryon to his correspondent, Francisco; cf line 191.

and religion? With God's grace it has so blossomed forth in both of these in the last few years that it can inspire the envy or the emulation of all other countries, however pre-eminent they may be in this type of distinction. 40

Although in your kindness, my dear Vergara, you would reserve some portion of this praise for me, I am not so shameless as to acknowledge the validity of this attribution. I have perhaps aided or stimulated the native talents of my own countrymen, although it must be admitted that the mere act of stimulation often constitutes a kind of help in itself. But, after the grat- 45 itude owed to God himself, you owe your success to that most glorious of queens, Isabella, and to the former archbishop of Toledo Cardinal Francisco Jiménez, and to the present Archbishop Alonso de Fonseca, and those like them whose authority protects and whose generosity promotes and sustains the study of the humanities.[5] So then in the calculation of debts of gratitude 50 I shall not allow any credit to be given to me. Rather I should most willingly join in the chorus of praise, and as an equal member, if you will permit me. In this respect, I have always been for the most part a man of stoic mind, not more drawn to one region than to another but considering the whole world to be my homeland; and so impassioned am I for the study of the 55 humanities that I consider all those who are devoted to them or especially gifted in their pursuit as my closest kith and kin.

Moreover there are two reasons for my taking particular delight in the good fortune of Spain: first, that together we glory in having Charles, lord of human affairs, as our prince; and, second, I have countless proofs of the 60 sincere and loyal support of Spanish men of letters. In this I am so much the more in their debt, knowing how little I merit it. From my own countrymen I think I certainly deserve some credit, for there are some from whom I might claim exceptional gratitude. But to complain about one's own country and to bring one's own family to court, as it were, would perhaps be a breach 65 of filial piety, even if one were in the right. In any event, what you say is clear beyond all doubt. I am learning by my own experience that Spain or, for that matter, any other nation is more grateful to me than my own; still, it is not my purpose to complain about them. This is nothing new; it's an old, old story, my dear Francisco, that those who by dint of Herculean efforts 70

* * * * *

5 Erasmus uses the form 'Elisabeta' for Isabella 'the Catholic' (1451–1504), queen of Castille, husband of Ferdinand of Aragon and grandmother of Emperor Charles v. On Francisco Jiménez de Cisneros, whose patronage and policies had a profound effect on the diffusion of humanism and more specifically of Erasmianism in Spain, see Ep 1814 n56. On Alonso de Fonseca see Epp 1813 introduction, 1874.

contribute some great advantage to the state must struggle against a huge serpent.[6] Let anyone who envisages anything of the kind keep his eyes fixed on eternity. What is more, this hydra usually hisses more fiercely at those who introduce some new or unfamiliar blessing, or restore and bring back one from the past. Therefore we deliver this monster over to you somewhat 75 more tamed; still, the more famous you become by your good deeds, as you have already excellently begun, the more savage, believe me, you will find the Lernean monster.

But Zúñiga made sure some time ago that my felicitations concerning your Spanish countrymen was vitiated by some canker,[7] and he was fol- 80 lowed by those who have staged a new melodrama there in Spain.[8] There has been no one up to now, either Hollander or Brabantine or Fleming or Zeelander,[9] who attacked my name with such a savage pen as Zúñiga has done so often and with such bitterness, without ever a word of provoca- tion from me and in defiance of the authority of popes and cardinals.[10] And 85 no man in any nation has dared attempt what certain mendicant tyrants[11] in that region are setting in motion, as I have been told. But this very fact proves that Erasmus has supporters there as nowhere else. For what is it that stirs up such tumults except the overzealous support of friends? Often my friends do me more grievous harm by their exorbitant praise 90

* * * * *

6 The second of Hercules' six labours pitted him against the hydra, a serpent or monster that inhabited the swamps of Lerna near Argos. Two heads sprouted up every time one was cut off. This same allusion became popular with certain Catholic apologists at this time to describe the proliferation of Reformation churches.

7 Juan de Vergara had corresponded with Diego López Zúñiga with the in- tention of preventing further polemic between him and Erasmus; see 'The Vergara–Zúñiga Correspondence' CWE 8 336–46. With Erasmus he exchanged Epp 1277 and 1312. For a full appreciation of the polemic that ensued between 1519 and 1522 see Rummel *Catholic Critics* I 145–77.

8 The inquisitorial proceedings in Valladolid in summer 1527

9 Erasmus had been attacked by a number of theologians from the Low Coun- tries, such as Nicolaas Baechem (Egmondanus; see Ep 1815 n4), Vincentius Theoderici (see Ep 1815 n3), Frans Titelmans (see Epp 1823 introduction, 1837A), and, earlier, Maarten van Dorp (see Ep 1860 n1). Jean Briselot, who was confessor to the future Charles V, was frequently alluded to in passing or without mentioning his name (Epp 597:5–16, 601:17, 628:21, 695:42–4, 739:23–4, 1040:10); cf CEBR I 202. Although Ep 641:4–5 has no note identifying the 'black monk, all belly and little else,' Briselot is the target of Erasmus' complaint.

10 For the same argument see Ep 1581:206–11 (to Noël Béda).

11 Erasmus uses the Greek, πτωχοτυράννους.

than the detractions of my enemies. Before the *Enchiridion* spoke the Spanish tongue, Erasmus was perhaps less celebrated and esteemed in Spain but also less exposed to hostility.[12] Putting aside my personal interests I could easily put up with hostility, but I fear that the wickedness of certain individuals may cast a dark cloud over the peace and serenity of your Spain.   95

So much for the contest in learning. I come now to the contest of praise, which in your kindness, surely extravagant in this case, you pour out so profusely upon me that were I to accept it I would be the most shameless of men. If I were to return it, though it would be unequal to what you deserve,   100
I fear my commendation might lack credibility; for if I returned praise for praise, it would seem that I wished to return compliment for compliment rather than express admiration for your fine qualities. Nevertheless, lest it seem that you praised me in vain, it was not that you commended me to myself, my dear Francisco, but that you commended yourself to me in no small   105
way with these encomiums. For your words demonstrate that you have a profound love of the honourable qualities that you think you see in me; and either you yourself are possessed of those very endowments that you eulogize in me or you have a predilection for them. It remains for me, first, to thank you for erring on the side of affection in my regard, then to congratu-   110
late a young man already adorned with so many gifts, and lastly to spur on the running horse,[13] as they say, so that in your diligent race in this fairest of stadiums you may daily outdo yourself.

Finally in the third contest, that of good will, I shall not allow myself to be outdone, for in this it is always the greatest disgrace for anyone to be   115
outdone, because everyone has it in his power to win. Besides, I should be entirely unworthy of the name Erasmus if I could not return the affection of such a loving friend. Your letter from beginning to end is an expression of pure good will, pure friendship, pure gratitude. Need I mention how delighted I was by your Spanish genius for eloquence? How cleverly it de-   120
picted that prodigious Geryon, a blend of sophist, pseudotheologian, and pettifogger![14]

In my case, for reasons of age alone I should have been granted a respite from these gladiatorial struggles, but the gods decided otherwise.[15]

* * * * *

12 The *Enchiridion* had been available in Spanish translation since 1526; see Ep 1814 n21.
13 *Adagia* I ii 47; cf III viii 32.
14 See n4 above and Ep 1875 n53.
15 Virgil *Aeneid* 2.428

Erasmus must die in the arena, although he was born for anything but con-   125
flict. For a long time now I have been involved in a war that has not been
without bloodshed with the phalanxes of those who think that the flourishing of belles-lettres will be the death of their tyranny. And it is not a
single army. There are those who were entirely opposed to any revival of
good literature at all lest they appear to have some gaps in their knowl-   130
edge. Others of more moderate views seemed willing at least to tolerate
the Roman tongue but were of the opinion that Greek and Hebrew should
not be allowed on any terms. There is also that other type of enemy that
has lately begun to emerge from their ambuscades. They take offence if the
name of Christ is mentioned in literary works, as if what is not pagan is   135
not elegant.[16] To their ears 'Jupiter, greatest and best' sounds more polished
than 'Jesus Christ, redeemer of the world,' and 'gentlemen of the senate'
has a more pleasant ring than 'holy apostles.' They praise Pontano to the
skies,[17] but they turn up their noses at Augustine and Jerome. But as far as
I am concerned I should prefer one ode of Prudentius hymning the name   140
of Jesus than a shipload of verses of Pontano, whom in other respects I do
not dislike either for his learning or his elegance.[18] People of this persuasion think it almost more disgraceful not to be a Ciceronian than not to
be a Christian; as if, indeed, if Cicero were to come back to life now, he
would not speak about Christian subjects differently than he spoke in his   145
own times, seeing that the chief component of eloquence is to speak ap-
positely. No one denies that Cicero excelled in the virtues of oratory, although not every type of eloquence is suitable for all persons or all subject
matters.

* * * * *

16 The Ciceronians; Erasmus was probably thinking about, if not already writing,
    the *Ciceronianus* (Basel: Hieronymus Froben, March 1528) along some of the
    lines he develops here. Cf Epp 1805:69–95 and n15, 1875 n45.
17 Giovanni Pontano (1429–1503), president of the Academy of Naples, was a pro-
    lific writer of both prose and verse. In the *Ciceronianus* (CWE 28 436–7) Erasmus
    censures him for his ostentatious style and for the non-Christian sentiments of
    his works. Earlier, in a letter to Budé, he had classed him with the Ciceronian
    apes (Ep 531:498).
18 Aurelius Clemens Prudentius (348–c 410) is considered the most important
    figure in Christian Latin poetry. His hymns, written during his retirement in
    Spain, enjoyed great popularity and were used for centuries in the liturgy of
    the church. His book *Psychomachia* was a major source for portraying vices
    and virtues in medieval art and literature. Erasmus wrote commentaries on
    his hymn 11 (for the feast of the Nativity) and hymn 12 (for the feast of
    the Epiphany), and presented them as a Christmas gift to Margaret Roper,
    daughter of St Thomas More, in 1523.

What is the meaning of this detestable flaunting of the name of Cicero?   150
I'll tell you in brief, but for your ears only. Under this disguise they conceal paganism, which is dearer to them than the glory of Christ. I am not
worried about being deleted from the list of the Ciceronians provided that
I am inscribed in the list of Christians. If I find someone who combines the
virtues of Ciceronian eloquence with Christian piety I would prefer him to   155
ten Ciceros. As for myself, I was always so far from copying the style of Ciceronian expression that, even if I could achieve it, I would prefer a more
rugged, more compact, more sinewy style, less adorned and more masculine.
In general, rhetorical embellishment has been of slight concern to me, even
though I do not reject refinement of language when it comes naturally. At the   160
present moment I have no time to polish what I write; in fact, often I cannot
even read it over. I'll grant that there are genuine Ciceronians who have the
leisure to spend three months on a single letter, and not even a long one at
that. I sometimes have to complete a book in one day. Let them reserve their
reproaches for the failure to imitate Cicero for those who strenuously affect   165
to do so but with little success. Finally, if the truth may be spoken, even
among those who have no other model than Cicero no one up to now has reproduced a faithful likeness of him. I have no regard for an empty veneer of
language and a dozen words borrowed here and there from Cicero. I look for
the spirit of Cicero in its totality. With these words, my dear Francisco, I do   170
not propose some other model in preference to Cicero for those who aspire
to eloquence. They are meant only to ridicule those apes who consider nothing beautiful that does not recall Cicero. There was never anything of such
perfect beauty that it left nothing to be desired. As the painter with form so
the orator with words should seek his absolute model from among many.   175

This matter could perhaps be laughed at; but who can contemplate
in his mind the turmoil caused by the new gospel without profound sadness? And in the midst of this universal upheaval not only are we not clever
enough to devise methods to settle these tragic and sinister disturbances but,
on the contrary, we all strain at the rope, each pulling it in his own direc-   180
tion, stretching it until it breaks.[19] We discover new seedbeds of contention
and, as the saying goes, pour oil on the fire.[20] If only the minds of rulers
could be united in Christian concord there would be some hope of quelling
the storm that rages within the church. At the moment I do not see what recourse we have save to din our constant prayers into the ears of God so that   185
he will appear like some deus ex machina and bring a happy dénouement

* * * * *

19 *Adagia* I v 67
20 *Adagia* I ii 9

to these tragedies.[21] If you wish to know how stalwart a gladiator I am, read
the two books of the *Hyperaspistes*. You will say that it is Esernius pitted
against Pacidianus.[22]

I shall end my letter with a brief reminder to you, although you are   190
already aware of it, that these Geryons[23] can best be overcome by unremitting diligence in teaching, by civility, and by cooperation. There are certain
people who have brought grave contempt upon the study of good letters
by their petulant tongues – made graver still by the suspicion aroused by
these new beliefs.[24] They expend greater efforts in attacking other people's   195
professions than in enhancing their own, and they use philology to disguise their impiety.[25] When belles-lettres will shine forth in all their glory
these empty illusions will vanish of themselves, and those who have experienced the benefits of literature will mute the hisses of envy, while those
who now make loud outcries will gradually join forces with the company   200
of the learned.

If you are desirous of knowing what I am doing, among other things
I have all of Augustine in preparation.[26] You would scarcely believe what
monstrous errors I found there. He will emerge with a different appearance,
I think. I would gladly have sent you the *Paraphrases* as a gift, but they could   205
not be sent except through a bookseller,[27] and no copies are available at this
time. Even this letter I commit to the winds.[28] Return my warmest greetings
to Bernardino Tovar.[29] I hear that Sancho has forgotten his old contentions
and is well disposed towards me.[30] If this is true, commend me to him with

* * * * *

21 *Adagia* i i 68; cf Ep 1875 n13.
22 A pair of well-matched gladiators; cf *Adagia* ii v 98. In the two books of *Hy-*
   peraspistes Erasmus answered Luther's *Servum arbitrium*; see Ep 1804 n10.
23 See n14 above.
24 The phrase 'by these new beliefs' is rendered in Greek.
25 This last clause is rendered mostly in Greek. Erasmus probably reverts here
   to his dislike for 'Ciceronians.' The meaning of the 'professions' they despise
   is not clear.
26 It appeared in ten volumes (Basel: Hieronymus Froben 1528–9); see Ep 2157.
27 Probably because the volume was too bulky to consign to an ordinary messenger or traveller. The *Paraphrases* on the Gospels had already been printed
   in Alcalá (Miguel de Eguía 1527).
28 An expression used in Epp 1674:87–9, 1675:29–30, and 1822:38–9, meaning he
   could not be sure the letter would reach Vergara at all.
29 Vergara's half-brother; see Ep 1814 n14.
30 Sancho Carranza de Miranda, the Spanish theologian who had overcome earlier doubts about Erasmus' orthodoxy and intervened in his favour at the Val-

all diligence. If I can know for certain that what a certain person wrote to   210
me is true, I shall make every effort to see that all records of our previous
differences be obliterated.[31] They will be imputed to fate, which, as Homer
wrote, throws all mankind into disorder.[32] In all else you will not find me
lacking in any duty of a true friend.

Given at Basel, 13 October in the year 1527   215

1886 / To Charles II, duke of Savoy   Basel, 14 October 1527

This letter was instigated by Ep 1852 from Claude-Louis Alardet, brother of the
secretary of the duke of Savoy. With its capital at Chambéry, Savoy had been
virtually independent since 1430, although it still operated jurisdictionally under the aegis of the empire. Duke Charles II had ignored Luther's invitation
in 1523 to join the Reformation movement (CEBR III 200–1).

ERASMUS OF ROTTERDAM TO CHARLES, DUKE OF SAVOY, GREETING
Although my spirit is sorely tormented, illustrious Prince, by these mad
tumults of wars and beliefs from which no part of the Christian world is
exempt, yet I take great pleasure in congratulating your land of Savoy which
– first by the grace of God, then by your exceptional piety and wisdom –   5
has to this point maintained itself so free of contagion of these ills that its
neighbours also enjoy the same blessing. To congratulate you on this good
fortune would have been perhaps a routine though not entirely disagreeable
duty, as I see it. But in point of fact I address your illustrious Highness in
this letter not merely to convey my congratulations but also in order that   10
what inspired my congratulations may last forever. I shall not detain you
with a long preface but explain the matter in brief.

From numerous letters of friends I have learned about a certain member of the Franciscan order in your dominion endowed with many outstanding talents for preaching the word of God (and on that account, of course,   15
I respect and congratulate him). But this same individual, not only at banquets and in conversations, which perhaps might be overlooked, but also
in sermons at mass rants impudently against my name, without measure or

* * * * *

ladolid conference in 1527. See Rummel *Catholic Critics* I 56–61 and CEBR I
273–4.
31 Probably Alonso Ruiz de Virués; see Epp 1814 introduction and 1838.
32 *Iliad* 19.91 and 129

limit.[1] First of all, such behaviour is contrary to the example of Saint Francis, who merited praise not by slanderous talk but by living a good life in the   20
sight of both God and men.[2] In the second place, it is contrary to my deserts, since I have adhered steadfastly to the teachings of the Catholic church and at great personal risk have joined in close combat with Luther. This cannot be unknown to my antagonists, since my *Diatribe* is in circulation, as is Luther's retort, the *De servo arbitrio*. Then there are my two books of the   25
Hyperaspistes in answer to that work.[3] Moreover he acts contrary to the opinion of popes and of the emperor, who have more than once imposed silence by their edicts and letters on such outbursts, and have borne testimony to my piety in very honorific letters and honoured me with magnificent gifts freely bestowed.[4]   30

Some people think they are true Franciscans because, like Francis, they walk around barefooted in their ash-coloured tunic with a cord around their waists. But if they disregard the authority of pontiffs and princes; if they think it a slight offence to run a fellow soldier through as he fights valiantly with the enemy on the same battle line, they should at least consider how in-   35
jurious their actions are to the public tranquillity of the church and the good of their own order, to which they think they are giving marvellous support – perhaps more than enough and with more zeal than wisdom. I am a man, and by the grace of God I have so far not been drawn away from communion with the church by any enticements or animosities. But what if human   40
frailty, vanquished by such persistent hatred, should turn to the worse side? do they not foresee what storms I could stir up against them? What do the followers of Luther desire more than to have Erasmus out of the way?

But if these persons think that Luther is the mortal enemy of their order, as he is, why do they act in a way that could not please him more? Does   45
he not attack the church itself who, in the midst of the fray, stabs a defender of the church in the back with barbed tongue, when he should have come to his assistance? Furthermore, their attempt to convince the world that I was secretly in accord with Luther has always been false, and now the facts

* * * * *

1886
1 Jean Gachi, a member of the Franciscan convent at Cluses, had published a treatise in French against Luther in 1524, and in 1527 he turned his attention to Erasmus. See Epp 1852:18–21 (the only one of the 'numerous' letters known today which mention Gachi) and 1891.
2 Francis of Assisi (1181/2–1226), founder of the Order of Friars Minor, later called Franciscans, whose special charism was poverty and humility
3 On Erasmus' controversy with Luther see Ep 1804 n10.
4 See Epp 1589, 1690 n10, 1717, 1747, and cf n10 below.

themselves prove it to be utterly false. False too is their widespread accu-   50
sation that there are things in my books that are opposed to piety. To the
present day no one has been able to produce even one sentence of impiety
from my books, although many, with hostile intent, have tried. And if anything of this nature did fall from my lips – something not even Jerome or
Augustine could avoid[5] – I should have been admonished rather than ex-   55
posed to public obloquy, since any intention of impiety was far from my
mind. None of them ever brought this to my attention either verbally or in
writing. Even if in the course of defending the cause of true piety in my
works I make certain recommendations that they interpret to be prejudicial
to their way of life and their interests, let them judge whether or not it is   60
just to put human interests and customs before the cause of Christ. On this
basis I should have incurred the hostility of priests, bishops, cardinals, pontiffs, and princes, since there is no class of men whom I do not criticize at
one time or another.

How is it that when all others are satisfied, and many even express   65
their gratitude, they alone raise an uproar? I never made the slightest attack on any religious order in my writings. I merely point out the absurd
opinions of the multitude, showing what true piety is, without injuring anyone's name, while they fulminate against my name. I sometimes condemn
those who put their trust in human ceremonies, neglecting those things that   70
according to the teachings of Christ truly lead to piety.[6] Perhaps I censure
those who give more importance to the rule of Francis than to the gospel of
Christ. I find fault with those who use their wiles to entice innocent boys
into embracing their way of life without the knowledge or consent of their
parents.[7] I castigate those who consider themselves safe from the claws of   75
demons if they are buried in the cowl of Francis, even if they never made
any effort to imitate the life of Francis.[8] These are the things that irritate
some of them, even though they promote piety and are necessary as a moral
admonition.

Let them suppose something that is not true, that I have spoken deri-   80
sively about them; what excuse is there that in order to avenge a personal
insult they abuse the word of God, the sacred dignity of the place,[9] and the

* * * * *

5 Cf Ep 1864:105–9 and n16.
6 As in the *Enchiridion militis christiani*, which was perhaps Erasmus' strongest
  plea for a gospel church free of human ceremony
7 Cf Ep 1805:27–8, 331–2 and n70.
8 See Ep 1805 n71.
9 That is, the preacher's pulpit in church

forbearance of the Christian flock? There are laws, there are judges, there are a thousand ways by which one may make rebuttal or seek compensation for an act of injustice. That place was consecrated for a far different purpose, 85 and it is not fitting to contaminate it with human – not to say shameless – passions. Although my writings make their way over the whole world and are passed from hand to hand, what pope, what bishop, or anyone vested with authority has pronounced a condemnation against me? On the contrary, several have praised them, such as Leo x, Adrian vi, and Clement 90 vii.[10] Since this is a well-established fact, where do they get this authority to make judgments before the credulous throng to their heart's content against whomever they wish? They deceive the populace with lies and infect them with the contagion of their hatred, envy, and detraction in place of the salutary nourishment of the gospel, injecting into their simple souls the poison 95 of hatred and discord.

From such initial phases grave conflagrations sometimes arise that are more difficult to extinguish since they have built up little by little from tiny beginnings, just as doctors say that fevers that have imperceptibly grown strong from minimal causes are less curable. It begins with secret calumnies, 100 then comes public outcry, and soon, as fanaticism builds up on either side, the fire breaks out. From such and even slighter beginnings this Lutheran conflagration has arisen, which we now see with great sorrow of spirit has consumed a great part of the Christian world. But if these people are allowed to do whatever they please, where, I ask you, will this campaign of 105 defamation break out next? I am afraid that in the end it will be turned against bishops and princes.[11]

So then I am pleading not only my own cause here, illustrious Prince, but also that of piety and of the authority of the Gospels, which is being undermined by such prattling, and of the public tranquillity on which I 110 congratulated your Highness and Savoy at the beginning of this letter, and on which I wish to continue to congratulate you. But if in your wisdom you judge that this matter does not pertain to you, I shall not refuse to pay back in full measure what I owe to you. But if you perceive that it is of no less importance for the integrity of the gospel and public tranquillity than for 115 my personal reputation, I implore you by your twofold sense of duty – that which you have to God and that which you bear towards your country – that you acquaint yourself precisely with those who know this situation; and

* * * * *

10 See Epp 338–9, 518–19 (Leo); 1324, 1338 (Adrian); 1438 (Clement). Cf n4 above.
11 Erasmus used the same charge of *lèse-majesté* against Noël Béda in his letter to King Francis I (Ep 1722:52–4).

by the authority of your position admonish this cleric that, mindful of his
calling, he preach the gospel of Christ with the integrity required of him   120
and cease to profane and sully by his arrant abuse the good name of his
neighbour, who is totally undeserving of it and indeed worthy of the fullest
gratitude. If he harbours something against me let him advise, instruct, and
convince me of it; then, if he is of such a mind, let him air his views in
public. I did not put faith in these reports rashly. What he is doing there   125
his confrères did in Spain, Poland, Hungary, and France;[12] thus it is clear
that it is a well-planned plot. They would be well advised both for the sake
of their reputation and their piety to help me in my untiring struggle for
the Christian cause rather than harass me with their slander, and to use
their shields to protect their fellow soldier who is joined in hand-to-hand   130
combat with the common enemy instead of turning their weapons against
him.

I should have liked to initiate my correspondence with your illustrious
Highness on a more pleasant subject, but this is the material presently provided us by this Franciscan. The Lord will favour us with a more agreeable   135
subject one day if some occasion should arise when I can oblige you in some
way. That is my chief desire, and I shall do nothing more willingly. I wish
your Highness the very best of health, and I devote and dedicate myself
entirely to you.

Given at Basel, 14 October in the year 1527   140

1887 / To a monk   Basel, 15 October 1527

This letter first appeared in 1529 in the *Opus epistolarum* and was reprinted
several times. It exists in a number of manuscript copies, some of which identify the addressee as a Carthusian. The letter reveals him to be a lifelong
friend of Erasmus and younger by eight or nine years. Allen believes him
to be a Netherlander but rules out both Levinus Ammonius, who was about
twenty years younger than Erasmus, and his brother Johannes – unless the
latter was ten years older than Levinus. Jan of Heemstede, to whom Erasmus
dedicated his *Deploratio mortis Ioannis Frobenii* (Ep 1900) is another Carthusian with whom Erasmus was in close contact; but he was perhaps too young
to be the person intended here. Allen prefers to identify him with Gabriël
Ofhuys at Brussels, to whom Erasmus had written earlier (Ep 1239) in the
same vein.

* * * * *

12 Cf Ep 1804 n43, Allen Ep 2126:125–8.

ERASMUS OF ROTTERDAM TO A CERTAIN MONK, GREETING

Your gifts were most gratifying to me. My health is what one might expect of an invalid old man, overwhelmed by excessive labours that a young man in good health could scarcely endure. While I congratulate you on your good physical state of health, I am all the more saddened by your protestations 5 about your poor spiritual well-being. For the health of the body does not depend on us, but the good health of the soul depends to a great extent on us. I fear you may let yourself be taken in by the chicanery of certain people who go about these days boasting in grandiose terms of evangelical freedom.[1] Believe me, if you had a closer understanding of the issue, you 10 would not find your way of life so tedious. I see a race of men springing up from whom my soul shrinks in horror; I see no one getting better, but all whom I knew well growing worse,[2] so that I am sorely grieved that I once preached freedom of the spirit in my books. And yet I did this in good faith, not suspecting in the least that people of this kind would appear. I wished 15 to depart in some manner from exterior observances so that there would be abundant increase in true piety.[3] Now they are cast off to such an extent that instead of liberty of the spirit an unbridled licence of the flesh has taken their place. Some cities in Germany are filled with vagabonds, deserters from monasteries, married priests, most of them hungry and naked. They 20 do nothing but dance, eat, drink, and fornicate; they neither teach nor learn; there is no sobriety of life, no uprightness. Wherever they are all the good disciplines lie prostrate,[4] together with piety. I would write further on this subject if it were safe to commit it to a letter.

For so many years you have lived in a praiseworthy manner in this 25 fellowship; and now, as you write, your life is drawing to an end. You are about eight or nine years younger than I. You are living in a very comfortable place in a very salubrious climate; you derive much solace from the conversation of learned men; you lack neither a plentiful supply of good books nor natural endowments. What could be more pleasant in this life than living 30

* * * * *

1887
1 Erasmus intends here those who, in the name of Christian liberty, were throwing off obligations incurred under canon law, for example the vow of celibacy.
2 Cf Ep 1901:30–7.
3 Cf Epp 296:79–81, 1886:58–61, 1891:197–206. Erasmus did this particularly in his *Enchiridion*; but there are many examples also in the *Praise of Folly* and many of the *Colloquies*.
4 Erasmus makes a similar statement in Ep 1901:19–21.

a leisurely existence amidst green swards – a foretaste of heavenly bliss, as
it were, especially in this day and age, in this century of unimagined chaos
and disorder. I know certain individuals who, deceived by illusions of liberty, have deserted their congregations. Changing their way of life, they took
wives; and now they are destitute, exiles, scorned by those to whom they   35
were once dear. In their present circumstances, even if there were those who
desire their welfare, it would not be safe to come to their aid. How this has
affected their conscience God alone knows, and how pleased they are in their
new state of life is for them to determine. What kind of liberty is it when
one is not permitted to say prayers, to offer the sacrifice of the mass,[5] to fast,   40
to abstain from meat? Is there anyone more to be pitied than such men, even
in this age? If one were young or rich he could enjoy the advantages of this
world for several years – if, that is, there are any advantages to be enjoyed
there. But to do this at an advanced age is more madness than stupidity.
'But rules, jealousies, and the like are irksome to me.'[6] These encumbrances   45
are inconsequential when one is of good heart. In the other alternative many
more woes must be endured. Therefore may God grant greater discernment
to those who trouble your peace of mind with tales of this kind.

My life upon it, if this poor body of mine only had enough strength to
go on living, I should prefer to live there with you than to be chief bishop in   50
the palace of the emperor.[7] But you are unaware of both your own happiness
and the misery of this world. And there is no reason to expect a council.[8]
It will come too late, since the discord of leaders stands in the way.[9] And
even if it were organized, they would be dealing for sixteen years with

* * * * *

5 Erasmus writes *sacrificare*. The idea of the mass as a sacrificial rite, linked to
  the sacrifice of Christ on the cross, was a facet of traditional Catholic theology
  rejected by the reformers. Cf Ep 1881 n6.
6 Probably a complaint the monk expressed in his letter
7 Similar expressions about finding tranquillity can be found in Epp 1075:2–6,
  1102:1–3, 1805:285–7. Erasmus counselled Maarten Lips (Epp 901:21–5, 1070:9–
  12) and Paul Volz (Ep 1075:8–11) not to leave their monasteries – the former
  with success, the latter not. But he advised Oecolampadius against entering
  Altomünster (Epp 1102:3–6, 1158:5–7).
8 That is, a general council of the church, to which many looked for reform of
  abuses and settlement of theological polemic
9 The wars and rivalries between Emperor Charles v and King Francis i were
  indeed a consistent block to the chance of convening a council that both would
  support; only after the Treaty of Crépy in 1544, which brought temporary
  respite from the wars, could the Council of Trent be convened.

far different matters than religious observances.[10] Accordingly, my dearest   55
brother in Christ, by our long-standing and indeed lifelong friendship and
in the name of Christ, I beg, beseech, and implore you to shake off this
weariness altogether from your mind and not to give ear to these ruinous
fables of men who will not be of help to you but rather will mock you
when they have lured you into the ditch. If you will despise the deceitful   60
allurements of this world with all your heart, devote yourself entirely to
Christ, and occupy yourself in sacred readings and in meditation on the life
hereafter, believe me! you will find solace in abundance, and these petty
aversions that you mention will vanish like a cloud of smoke. Listen to your
counsellor; and if you do not find what I say to be true, then remonstrate   65
with me. May the Lord fill your heart with every spiritual consolation, my
dearest friend and brother in the Lord.

Given at Basel, 15 October in the year 1527
Erasmus of Rotterdam, by his own hand

1888 / To Alonso Manrique de Lara   Basel, 15 October 1527

Written to accompany an 'advance copy' of the definitive version of *Apologia
adversus monachos quosdam Hispanos*, printed by Froben in 1527 but not yet
circulated publicly (Epp 1877, 1879, 1967), this letter first appeared in the *Opus
epistolarum* (1529). Erasmus also wrote at this date to Juan Vergara, but that
letter is not extant (Allen Ep 2004:1–2).

ERASMUS OF ROTTERDAM TO ALONSO MANRIQUE, ARCHBISHOP
OF SEVILLE, GREETING

Reverend prelate, I send you my *Response*, committed to print but not yet
published, unless by your authority you recommend otherwise. You have my
leave to publish it there also if you think fit. I saw there was need of several   5
exemplars so that those entrusted with this charge might judge the matter
with greater certainty, and I did not have a sufficient number of scribes on
hand. Therefore instead of a host of copyists I used a single printer.[1] I shall

* * * * *

10 Erasmus' estimate was quite close; the Council of Trent was in effect for eighteen years (1545–63), although it was in recess during several of them.

1888
1 Johann Froben; see Allen Ep 1967:27–9. Erasmus is subtly apologizing for
   printing the work before receiving approval from Manrique (see Ep 1877
   introduction).

never cease to marvel at the flights of fancy of these men who make themselves so troublesome both to my endeavours and to your Highness' affairs   10
and disrupt the peace of Christendom. They could do no worse disservice
to themselves.

A few days ago I wrote at greater length.[2] I presume that letter has
reached you by now, since I sent it in two exemplars. I am also quite astonished at the attitude of the emperor. After I exposed my life to every peril,   15
trusting in his authority, he now, in return for my services, all but throws
me to the beasts.[3] Because of the emperor I did not have to stand in fear of a
faction that was truly to be feared; but now the emperor fears those whose
fears I allayed at my own peril. Still, I shall not cease to do what it befits a
Christian to do. Your Highness will do what seems most advantageous for   20
Christian piety. I pray that you be granted every happiness in Christ, and
dedicate myself entirely to you.

Words cannot express the sorrow I experience when I see the wrath
of kings grow more savage;[4] where it will all end is uncertain. I recognize
divine wrath raging against us through the fury of kings, but we do not see   25
the light. This tortures my mind more than the stupid uproar of the monks.
May the Lord turn everything to a good end.

Given at Basel, 15 October in the year 1527

1889 / To Juan Luis Vives   Basel, 15 October 1527

This letter, an answer to Vives' Ep 1836, first appeared in the *Opus epistolarum*
(1529).

ERASMUS OF ROTTERDAM TO LUIS VIVES, GREETING
A bundle of letters, among which was one of Virués to you, which you
sent on the first of June, was delivered to me towards the beginning of

* * * * *

2 Ep 1877 was written 45 days earlier, on 2 September 1527.
3 This and subsequent statements do not appear to be borne out in the historical
   record. In Ep 1872:5–12 Erasmus had assured the imperial chancellor, Gattinara, that his books against Luther were bearing fruit and asked Gattinara's
   support against his traditionalist Catholic enemies; as recently as the previous
   day (Ep 1886:26–30) Erasmus had boasted of the emperor's support and good
   will towards him. Here and in the following two sentences, however, he implies that Charles v, fearing the Catholic theologians, has left him undefended
   from them.
4 A reference to the wars between Christian kings that Erasmus so abhorred

October.[1] You had probably entrusted them to the bookseller Franz, for
that is the way he usually looks after his friends' affairs.[2] You are right in 5
concluding that you are numbered among my truest friends. But there are
other reasons as well for my writing you less frequently than you would
wish. Often letters go astray, they are intercepted or held up somewhere,
so that it is useless to write letters when they are not delivered or arrive
late. Then also you are not always in the same part of the world; amphibi- 10
ous creature[3] that you are, at one moment you swim your way to Britain
in search of pasture,[4] and at another you are making your nest and laying
eggs in Bruges.[5] Furthermore, writing letters nearly kills me – or whatever
more drastic word could be used. Caught up in the immense press of my
work, I have barely glanced at your books, which are so often torn from 15
my hands.[6] On another occasion I shall write you a more definite opinion,
since you place this lion's skin upon Erasmus – I might almost say upon this
ass.[7]

Augustine is being printed in a very impressive edition.[8] But they say
that your volume will not go to press at this time because all the book deal- 20
ers still have too many copies to sell. If you wish to have something corrected or added, it can be done. But, my dear Vives, I should not wish you to

* * * * *

1889
1 The packet was actually sent on 13 June; see Ep 1836:20–4. For Alonso Ruiz de
 Virués see Ep 1838 introduction. His letter to Vives is not extant; see Ep 1836
 n4.
2 Franz Birckmann, whose trustworthiness Erasmus habitually criticized; see Ep
 1804 n76. The letters in question here had in fact been forwarded by Erasmus
 Schets (Ep 1847:114–15).
3 Greek ζῶον ἀμφίβιον; cf Ep 1830:1.
4 Greek τῆς νομῆς χάριν. Vives was highly regarded in England, where he had
 entry at court as a teacher of Princess Mary.
5 Greek καὶ ὠογονῶν. Vives was married to Margarita Valdaura, daughter of a
 wool (and perhaps gem) merchant. The reference to 'laying eggs' is possibly
 a general statement about their domestic situation. They were never to have
 children; but at only twenty-one years of age at this time Vives' wife would
 have had prospects of progeny.
6 Presumably by the pressure of his own work; on the volume of his correspondence cf Ep 1804 n12. For Vives' prolific output at this time see Ep 1792
 n8.
7 ταύτην λεοντήν. In the first of his labours Hercules killed the Nemean lion and
 cut off his skin. Together with his club, this trophy became his distinguishing
 attribute in art and in literature. See Theocritus *Idyll* 25.276–9 and cf *Adagia* I
 iii 6.
8 The 1528–9 Froben edition in ten volumes; see Ep 2157.

encumber the volume with superfluous material.[9] Alaard protests that the
book was not edited with enough care; but I know that fellow.[10] There are
some places where you nodded, but they are very few. You remember the   25
note on *typho*.[11] You can emend that, but do not add anything unless it is
noteworthy and pertinent to the subject. This will please the printers, delight
the reader, and bring more glory to you. You will be in time if you send the
manuscript for the Strasbourg fair.[12] I almost envy you, despite our friendship, your close familiarity with the Laurinus brothers.[13] I am growing old   30
or rather dying on this treadmill, although I am constantly contemplating
an escape.[14] Farewell.

Basel, 15 October 1527

1890 / To Conradus Goclenius   [Basel], 15 October 1527

In the *editio princeps* of this letter, the editors of the *Vita Erasmi* (Leiden 1607)
proposed that Erasmus wrote it while he was in Louvain. To accommodate
that hypothesis, LB changed the year date from 1527 to 1517. Allen restored
it to 1527 because the LB conjecture would have Erasmus writing to someone
living in the same town about events that had not yet taken place. He therefore
also changed the place to Basel, on the evidence of the first paragraph, which
seems to answer a letter (not extant) carried by Nicolaas Kan in July 1527 (Ep
1857:26–7). Henry de Vocht (CTL II 301–8) argued later that the letter really
belongs in 1524, and that Allen's dating renders lines 8–10 to be no more than
'an apparently absurd piece of news' or, at most, 'a thinly veiled excuse for
not writing' to other correspondents (CTL II 304). The date 1524, he argues,

* * * * *

9 A reference to Vives' 1522 edition of the *De civitate Dei*. Renaudet *Etudes
   érasmiennes* 34 says that Vives' long and elaborate explications of the numerous allusions to Platonism made the book costly and put off the reader (cf
   Ep 1271:12–21). Vives disputed the reports of poor sales and blamed Franz
   Birckmann and the 'greed' of 'illiterate' book dealers (Ep 1362:44–67). On the
   revisions, cf Epp 1531:41–6, 1613:11–13.
10 Probably Alaard of Amsterdam (CEBR I 19–21)
11 In his annotation on *De civitate Dei* 11.33 ('one [company of angels] ... enjoys
   God, the other swells with pride [$\tau\acute{\upsilon}\phi\omega$]'), Vives had confounded the Greek
   word $\tau\hat{\upsilon}\phi os$ 'vanity' with $T\upsilon\phi\hat{\omega}\nu$, a monster born of Tartarus and Earth when he
   commented, 'The giant Typhon, a son of this earth, was an abominable creature.'
12 Held every January and July. Like the Frankfurt fair it was an important channel of communication between scholars and their editors, and served as a
   forwarding post for letters.
13 See Epp 1848, 1870–1.
14 Cf Ep 1861:7–8; see also the invitation conveyed in Ep 1878.

makes the passage a significant comment on the mission to Rome undertaken that year by Nicolas Wary to defend the privileges of Louvain's faculty of arts. But, because the attribution of 1524 created difficulties in regard to other passages of the letter that could not have been written prior to 1527, de Vocht also had to conjecture that the letter was cobbled together from two or more unconnected fragments that happened by chance to refer to the same subject or subjects. The present edition retains the date and place assigned by Allen.

For Goclenius, who was the pre-eminent regent in Latin at the Collegium Trilingue, see Ep 1857, to which this letter responded. It will be answered by Ep 1899.

ERASMUS OF ROTTERDAM TO CONRADUS GOCLENIUS, GREETING

My life upon it if it does not give me more joy, now that Fortune is smiling on you from all sides,[1] than if similar good fortune fell to my own lot. It is not merely that I have your interests at heart, as might be expected, but also that I am devoted to the cause of good letters, which you have so enhanced 5 and furthered by your uncommon learning, your zealous teaching, and your fertile genius as to have almost no equal.

I wrote to Wary, the president of your college, in Froben's care,[2] because Quirinus had almost made up his mind to return to his wretched countrymen.[3] You would hardly believe how haplessly it turned out that 10

* * * * *

1890
1 Allen identifies this good fortune with the Antwerp canonry recently obtained by Goclenius. Henry de Vocht saw it as Goclenius' substantial increase in salary at the Collegium Trilingue after he refused to accept the position of private tutor to Robert de Croy, bishop-elect of Cambrai (Ep 1457:4–6; see CTL II 244–5). In Ep 1899:6–13 Goclenius himself interprets Erasmus' congratulations to apply to his success in teaching.
2 Froben carried Ep 1856 on his way to the Frankfurt book fair. Henry de Vocht's redating of this letter (see the introduction) necessitated seeing 'Frobenius' as a misreading of 'Ennius,' that is, Ennio Filonardi, who usually carried Erasmus' letters to Rome in 1524. The designation 'president of your college,' which would have been unnecessary in a letter to Goclenius, must have been added by the editors of the Vita Erasmi (1607). For Nicolas Wary see Ep 1806A introduction.
3 A jesting description by Erasmus of his fellow Dutchmen; cf Epp 996:45, 1238:51–3. Quirinus Talesius of Haarlem was a student of Goclenius who had lately become Erasmus' servant and messenger. Erasmus had expected to send most of his letters to the Netherlands by him. Henry de Vocht (see the introduction) interpreted 'Quirinus' to mean Pope Clement VII, perhaps because he dwelt in the Quirinal palace.

you did not send with Nicolaas at least the manuscripts of Augustine on
the Trinity that Dorp had collated.[4] At the present moment Froben has four
presses in full operation and perhaps one or two more.[5] Therefore I beg you
not to miss the occasion of sending them with the bearer of this.[6]

Frans van der Dilft is staying with us; I hope he is as happy with this   15
arrangement as I am delighted by his company. At any rate I shall do my
best, as far as my concerns allow, to see that he derive some benefit from
his life in common with us. I can scarcely express in words how incensed
I am with those who have sought to turn such a noble mind to worthless
pursuits.[7]   20

I have hired the bearer of this letter at my own expense, since he had no
other commission. Therefore do not let him return empty-handed. Negotiate
with him as if it were a matter that regarded Froben, which indeed it is.[8]

I am pleased with Dilft in every respect except his knowledge of philology,[9] which you had extolled in such glowing terms; I find him more de-   25
ficient than sufficient in it. He is thinking of moving into the household of
Carinus. I should prefer he be with someone else. You can easily guess the
reason.[10] As far as I am concerned, I shall never be lacking in the duty of
giving admonition.

* * * * *

4 In February 1525 (Ep 1547:10–14) Erasmus had complained about the failure
   of Maarten van Dorp, who died 31 May that same year, to send his collated
   manuscript of Augustine's *De Trinitate*. Erasmus had sent his manuscript edition to Dorp, with the request that he note any variants he found in a manuscript at Gembloux. Erasmus' manuscript had been returned by Goclenius
   after Dorp's death in 1525, but Dorp's annotations had not reached him. The
   reference to Nicolaas Kan as a courier would not be possible if this letter were
   written in 1524 (see the introduction), since Kan was at that time a student in
   Louvain and had not yet journeyed to Basel.
5 The printing of Augustine's *Opera*, in the works intermittently since 1520 (Ep
   1309 introduction), was in full swing in 1527. In Ep 1910:10 Erasmus says
   plainly that six presses are at work on the edition.
6 A man named Burchardus, an employee of Froben, who carried letters to the
   Netherlands for Erasmus (Epp 1897, 1899; cf CEBR I 221)
7 Dilft had stayed with Erasmus in 1524 and was once again living in his household (late 1527–February 1528); see Ep 1857. At this time, probably urged by
   his family, Dilft was contemplating marriage and entry into imperial service
8 Because the materials he was to carry were for Froben's Augustine edition
9 This whole clause is rendered in Greek, probably because of its mild censure
   of Dilft.
10 Erasmus writes about Dilft's move in Greek. Ludovicus Carinus of Lucerne
   shared many friends and humanistic colleagues with Erasmus; but their relationship would later turn sour (CEBR I 266–8).

Froben is planning to print Terence with commentary;[11] if you can as-   30
sist us in this project, please do so, but promptly. In any case have this messenger return with the book on the Trinity. There is need of it now.[12] It is
not always convenient to hire couriers at great expense. I have destroyed
what you sent.

Farewell. [Louvain],[13] 15 October 1527   35

1891 / To Jean Gachi   [Basel], c 17 October 1527

This letter, prompted by Ep 1852 from Claude-Louis Alardet, should be read
along with Ep 1886. It first appeared in the *Selectae epistolae* (Basel 1528).

   Gachi was a native of Cluses in Savoy and a Franciscan friar. He composed
in French verse the *Trialogue nouveau contenant l'expression des erreurs de Martin
Luther* (Geneva: Wygand Köln 1524). His sermons, described in Ep 1852, delivered notably in Chambéry, denounced Erasmus as a friend of Luther, and
his copy of Erasmus' Ep 1858 to Robert Aldridge, printed as *Epistola in tyrologum* (cf Ep 1858 n2), bears his annotations in this same vein (Geneva, Musée
de l'histoire de la Réforme F Ere 1). As chaplain to the Poor Clare nuns in
Geneva, he was expelled in 1536 by the Protestant Bernese troops. See CEBR
II 68–9. Erasmus apparently received a conciliatory reply (not extant) to this
letter from Gachi. Although not completely assured by it, Erasmus appears to
have considered the matter closed (Epp 2033, 2045, 2126, 2205).

DESIDERIUS ERASMUS OF ROTTERDAM TO JEAN GACHI, FELLOW
SERVANT AND FELLOW SOLDIER IN CHRIST, GREETING
The number of letters reaching me and the credibility of those who write
them are too convincing to leave any doubt in my mind that not merely
at banquets, public gatherings, and private conversations but also in public   5
and sacred sermons you constantly revile my name before the ignorant and
motley crowd. I know that one must not give hasty credence to rumours,
especially when they report things that would destroy fraternal harmony;
but since it is a known fact that members of your religious order in Spain,
Poland, Hungary, England, and France have begun to act out the same scene   10

          * * * * *

   11 The project was interrupted by Johann Froben's death several days after this
      letter was written, but was finished by his son Hieronymus in 1532. The com-
      mentary was that of the fourth-century Roman grammarian Aelius Donatus.
   12 See n4 above.
   13 See the introduction.

that you are said to be enacting there,[1] it is quite clear that this is a concerted
campaign. Up to now their efforts have been frustrated, since everywhere
they run into influential and grateful people who support my efforts. I have
won their favour not through personal ambition but by the labours that I
have long expended in promoting the study of languages, reviving humane 15
letters, and restoring the great works of the classical authors. They readily
acknowledge withal that they do not attribute this favour so much to a person as to the studies themselves and to Christian piety. But if your friends
continue in their calumnies I am afraid that the result may be worse than
even I, against whom they seem to have conspired, would wish. For it fre- 20
quently happens to those who despise their enemy that 'while they sink their
teeth into the softer part, they break them on the solid.'[2]

Although they imagine me to be their enemy, I am not. For while I give
my full support to all those who practise piety, I have always singularly
favoured your congregation, since, while others seem mostly to have fallen 25
away or are giving in to the standards of the world, your order retains some
trace of a more uncontaminated religion. Witnesses to this fact are all those
members of your order who have been on familiar terms with me.[3] None of
them, I dare say, will come forward to say that he has ever been injured in
a word by Erasmus. There are some who will not deny that they received 30
assistance from me in the form of minor services and even small sums of
money – although it is not seemly to mention such things, which one gives
not to men but for piety's sake. Moreover, I cannot, even if I wished, dislike
men who radiate true piety; that is my nature. And I was never so prejudiced
as to detest any religious order because of the wickedness of a few. Such is 35
the nature of human affairs that 'nothing is perfect in every way.'[4] Noah's
ark had only eight people aboard, but of those one was evil.[5] What was
holier than the family of Abraham? Yet the boy Ishmael was expelled from

* * * * *

1891
1 Gachi was a Franciscan; cf Ep 1886:14, 185–7.
2 Horace Satires 2.1.77–8
3 Earlier Erasmus had much admired the piety of Franciscans like Dietrich Kolde
   and Jean Vitrier; he enjoyed scholarly exchanges with the Franciscans Amandus of Zierikzee, Francis Frowick, Jan Bijl, and Conradus Pellicanus, but broke
   with the last when he passed over to the Reformation. Early Franciscan critics of his were Nicolas Bureau and Henry Standish. Franciscan critics at this
   time, apart from Gachi, were Frans Titelmans and Matthias Weynsen.
4 Horace Odes 2.16.27–8
5 Probably an allusion to Gen 9:20–5, where Noah curses his son Ham

it together with his mother.[6] Isaac had twin sons; of these one was pleasing
to God, the other displeasing.[7] What was more sanctified than the house of   40
Jacob? And yet one of its members had no scruples in committing incest
with his father's concubine.[8] The piety of the prophet David did not escape
this ill fortune: one of his sons defiled his sister by incestuous relations, the
other plotted his father's downfall in an impious rebellion.[9] The apostle Paul
complains of the troubles afforded him by false brethren.[10] Lastly the Lord   45
himself suffered one of that rare and elect number of his disciples to be a
traitor.[11] And so, since your order has so many thousands – I do not say of
members but of monasteries – what would be more unjust than detesting
the whole order, in which there have been so many examples of piety and
learning, because of the improper behaviour of a few?   50

And even in your case, my dear Gachi, I am told that you are endowed
with outstanding talents for preaching the word of God and are not a man
of rude manners, which leads me to suspect that the things you are doing
are at the instigation of others and not of your own accord. And that is my
principal reason for writing to you. If I thought you were like some others   55
I know, I would not have taken this trouble. Not only would it have been a
waste of effort but it would have exacerbated an irreparable evil. Even so,
I hope that what rumour and the letters of friends have conveyed to me is
nothing but idle chatter. If perchance the situation is different from what I
have been told, please take it as if this letter were never written to you. But if 60
the rumour that has made its way here is true, nonetheless, wishing to take
the view that your actions result from someone else's prompting rather than
any personal malice, I shall so temper my admonition that I shall appear to
be pleading no less the cause of piety and of your order than that of my

* * * * *

6 In a first account the slave girl Hagar was banished before her son Ishmael was
   born (Gen 16:1–12); in a different one the two were expelled together (Gen
   21:9–21).
7 Esau, the elder twin, whose birthright and paternal blessing fell instead on
   Jacob, fulfilling the prophecy, 'the older shall be servant to the younger' (Gen
   25:21–34, 27:1–40)
8 Reuben (Gen 35:22)
9 2 Sam 13:1–22 (David's eldest son Amnon); 2 Sam 15:1–19:33 (Absalom). Jerome
   and Augustine both called King David a prophet, probably because authorship of the Psalms was ascribed to him. In his *Postilla super Psalterium* Nicholas
   of Lyra referred to David as the most remarkable of the prophets (Allen Ep
   1381:145n).
10 Gal 2:4, 2 Cor 11:26
11 Judas; see Matt 10:4, 26:25, 27:3 and their synoptic parallels.

own reputation. It will be a mark of your wisdom, excellent sir, to take it in   65
good part if I express rather freely and openly what the case demands.

First, I should ask you to consider carefully, my brother, how alien it is
to the character and way of life of your humble father Francis[12] to use such
intemperate language against a neighbour's name in public and in private,
when not only has no one made any adverse pronouncement against him   70
but leading figures of church and state have publicly honoured him with
official tributes. I am astonished that this has escaped your attention when
letters from the emperor attest to it,[13] and testimonials to me from Leo x and
Adrian vi exist in print.[14] In any case many people who know me are aware
of, and most have seen, the great stacks of letters I have from the present   75
Pope Clement, from many cardinals, archbishops, bishops, kings, dukes, and
learned men, which speak of me in quite different terms than those which
you are said to employ.[15] And, lest someone say that the testimony of words
is of little value, they confirm their opinion of me with handsome gifts freely
given. Were I to mention even a portion of these tributes I should appear   80
to be evoking those figures from comedy, Thraso or Pyrgopolinices,[16] even
though my account would be far less than the actual facts.

But let us pass over this. By what merit of mine do they do these
things? Is it because I strive to assist the cause of Christendom by long
hours of study and self-sacrifice to the best of my powers – or, rather, be-   85
yond my powers? I do the same thing you do, but in another way. For the
gifts of the Spirit are varied,[17] as functions are also varied, although they all
look to the same end. Those who brought goatskins, those who transported
rubble for the laying of the foundation contributed to the building of the
temple of the Lord in the same way as those who gave gold and precious   90
stones.[18] What does your piety draw on when you teach the people? Does

* * * * *

12 Francis of Assisi, thirteenth-century founder of the Friars Minor, called Franciscans
13 Epp 1270, 1731; cf Ep 1690 n11.
14 Epp 338–9, 864 (from Leo x), 1324, 1338 (from Adrian vi); cf Ep 1805 nn77
   and 78.
15 Erasmus made a similar statement in Ep 1796:21–6; cf also Epp 1195 and 1197
   introductions. On letters from Clement vii, see Ep 1805 n78. On the 'great
   stacks of letters' cf Ep 1804 n12.
16 Both were braggart soldiers: Thraso from Terence's *Eunuchus* and Pyrgopolinices from Plautus' *Miles gloriosus*.
17 Rom 12:6–10
18 Neither account of the building of the temple at Jerusalem (1 Kings [Vulg 3
   Kings] 5–8 and 2 Chronicles [Vulg 2 Paralipomenon] 2–5:1) mentions goatskins.

it not come above all from the Gospels, the letters of the apostles, and the holy Doctors of the church? Did I not restore for you the pitifully corrupted text of Jerome? Did I not provide a much more correct version of Ambrose than existed previously? Did I not deliver to you St Hilary cleansed of its er- 95 rors at the cost of great labours? Did I not bring back to the light of day the lost texts of Irenaeus and Arnobius?[19] I am labouring at this same task now for all the works of Augustine, in which I have found so many errors that no one would believe it possible.[20] And I think it would not be easy to find someone to put up with this tedium. Have I not delighted your ears with 10 many things from Chrysostom and Athanasius?[21] Finally, did I not collate, emend, and elucidate the source of all Christian philosophy, the New Testament?[22] How many errors I eliminated there, how many difficult passages I resolved, how much darkness I dissipated!

Who will be able to estimate how many toils and nightly vigils were 10 expended in this task and at what cost to my health? And yet whatever praise it merits is owed to him without whom human industry can accomplish nothing. The magnitude of my contribution is recognized by those who are seriously engaged in these studies, who find wholehearted delight in the sources of sacred writings and in the fair meadows of orthodox texts; 11 not just anyone at all from the common crowd but bishops, cardinals, celebrated doctors of theology – in a word, those who by their published works courageously and effectively carry on the defence of God's church. And certainly I think that you do what is particularly worthy of you to do. What could be dearer to you who profess to be dead to this world[23] than those 11 books that inspire in you the spirit of Christ? And if this is so, how can you

* * * * *

Nor was rubble used, since the foundation is said to be of massive stones dressed in the quarry, not on the site of the temple. Erasmus perhaps refers to making the tent in the desert to house the Ark of the Covenant (Exod 25:3–7), where gold, jewels, goats' hair, and rams' skins are among the gifts deemed necessary and acceptable; but, again, rubble is not mentioned.

19 See Epp 396, 1465 (Jerome), 1855 (Ambrose), 1334 (Hilary), 1738 (Irenaeus), and 1304 (Arnobius).

20 See Ep 1889 n8.

21 For Chrysostom see Epp 1558 (the six dialogues on priesthood), 1563 (the Greek and Latin text of the *De orando Deum*), 1661 (the Latin translation of six sermons), 1734 (the Greek text, with Latin translation, of two homilies on the Epistle to the Ephesians), 1800 (the *Lucubrationes*), 1841 (*Galatians*), and 1856 (*Babylas*). *Athanasii lucubrationes aliquot* was published in 1527; see Ep 1790.

22 The first edition was in 1516 (Ep 384), the fourth in 1527; see also Ep 864, Allen Epp 1174:15n, 1571:19n, Ep 1878 n37.

23 By solemn vows of poverty, chastity, and obedience; cf Col 2:20, 3:3.

hate the man who zealously provides you with these tools? But if you do not hold these things dear, that very fact proclaims that you are drawn to this scurrilous behaviour not by love of piety but by the appetites of the flesh. If someone sends you a gift of a basketful of fish, or a garment, or a basket filled with bread or some cheese, he is loved and lauded to the skies;[24] yet one who bestows much better things is assailed with every manner of insult!

But even supposing that you despise these things, which no truly pious man despises, surely you should not have begrudged this benefit to others. The Wise Man rightly counsels us not to forbid anyone from doing good but rather to strive ourselves to do good if we can.[25] Not to do good to anyone may be considered as idleness, but to bring accusations against one trying to do good is pure malice. What name shall we give, I pray you, to the desire to rob many people of the benefits resulting from another man's good actions? Is it not the most deplorable spite that someone should neither wish to benefit others himself, nor allow another to be of use, nor yet allow the fruits of piety to reach the eager multitude? On the contrary, it would behove us to congratulate the people and assist another's efforts – if not by deeds, certainly by approval. I, for my part, give my sincere approval to your investing your talent in the service of the Lord, and not merely approve but lend assistance. Why should I, engaged in the same activity, be shouted down in all this din?

You will say that there are things in my books that are at variance with the orthodoxy of the faith. This no one has been able to demonstrate so far, although a good number have tried. But let us pretend that it is true; of what importance is it if I have suffered the same fate as Cyprian, Hilary, Jerome, and Augustine?[26] For so many years now my books have been perused by so many readers; why did none of you admonish me or advise me? Now after all this time you suddenly raise a hue and cry before the unsuspecting multitude, who do not understand these matters – nor does it matter whether they do or not.

You will say that I have been admonished by others. True, but by troublemakers and men totally devoid of theological knowledge. Lee was held in check by his own country of England, so unsuccessful was his campaign.[27]

* * * * *

24 As a mendicant order, the Franciscans lived by donations in kind.
25 Cf Prov 3:27.
26 Cf Ep 1864 n16.
27 For the controversy with Edward Lee, see Rummel *Catholic Critics* I 95–120. The numerous letters denouncing him are summarized in CEBR III 311–14. For Erasmus' recent complaints about him see Ep 1814 n39.

Zúñiga was condemned by his own homeland of Spain and repressed by   150
threats from Rome.[28] Recently Béda has conducted himself in such a way
that anyone in his right mind would take him for a madman.[29] This was
not admonishment but pure invective. Thus, if the authority of cardinals,
pontiffs, the emperor, and kings has imposed silence on them, how much
more do they condemn these tantrums that you have unleashed upon the   155
multitude, whence only quarrels, animosities, sedition and tumult can arise?
The madness of those others was more tolerable, yet it was not tolerated by
the leaders of the church. You and your confrères introduce a new tactic,
venting your fury upon anyone you please before the motley crowd. How
many times has Erasmus been branded as a heretic before them, how many   160
times was he called the teacher of Luther and more dangerous than Luther,
how many times has he been singled out with other reproaches? And this
evil example arises from you religious, who profess great forbearance and
supreme detachment from the world.

The Gospel tells us to speak well of those who speak evil of us,[30] but   165
you do evil in word and deed towards those who do good to you. For while
you make these denunciations of Erasmus he does not cease to provide you
with things of more value than quantities of cheese and eggs. If you are
judges, why do you not study the case in a legitimate manner and then
pronounce judgment? If you are not, whence comes this precedent of rant-   170
ing publicly against another man's reputation? If some buffoon were to go
about babbling against a decent man, calling him a drunkard, a glutton, a debauchee, a thief, and a pimp, no one would tolerate such unbridled licence of
speech; yet you apostolic men consider it sport to call someone a heretic and
a heresiarch even in public sermons? If you acknowledge the authority of the   175
Roman pontiff in exemptions, privileges, and indults that are to your advantage, why do you openly disregard him in this case, challenging the very person to whose judgment I have always submitted my works? More precisely,
why do you dare condemn publicly one whom he publicly praises? Can it be
that when papal authority serves your purpose it is sacrosanct and is as heavy   180
as lead, but in different circumstances it is lighter than straw? And in the
meantime where is that famed obedience of yours, which is always on your
lips, if whenever it is convenient you disdain the edicts of pontiffs, bishops,

* * * * *

28 See Epp 1805 n76, 1885 n7. The best overview of Erasmus' polemic with Zúñiga
   is CEBR II 348–9; for the issues involved see Rummel *Catholic Critics* I 145–77.
29 On Béda see Epp 1571 introduction, 1664 introduction and n1, and 1804 n14;
   Rummel *Catholic Critics* II 29–59; Farge BR 31–6 no 34.
30 For example Matt 5:43–5

and princes? And at this point, of course, the saying of the apostles is chanted
in response: 'We ought to obey God rather than men,'[31] although this saying   185
belongs as much to the Lutherans now as it does to you. But where did God
ever ordain that men, in disregard of the edicts and commands of princes,
should rant and rave against a man who has served religion well – if this is
to claim too much, then certainly against someone who in no wise deserved
it; if this also is too much, at least against one in whose books the authority   190
of the church has not to this day condemned a single statement?

But, you say, they contain elements that have given occasion to a certain
diminution of your popular esteem. I shall give a resume of the topics that
I have always treated in my books. I speak out courageously against war,
whose convulsions we see have been shaking the whole Christian world for   195
many years now. I tried to recall theology, which had sunk to sophistic quibbling, to its origins and pristine simplicity. I strove to restore to their former
splendour the sacred Doctors of the church, the living source of teachings
that some read in fragmentary form, not to say in bits and pieces. I have introduced Christian content into the study of good letters, previously all but   200
given over to paganism.[32] I assisted in the revival of the study of languages
as best I could. I transformed the wrong-headed views held by the general
run of men on many subjects. I roused the world from its sluggish observance of well-nigh Jewish rituals to a more authentic Christianity, but in
such a way that I never criticized the ceremonies of the church but merely   205
suggested improvements.

It would take a long time, excellent sir, to demonstrate how necessary
all this was. And yet it was carried out by me with such moderation that I
did no harm to any religious order or to anyone's name or reputation, nor
did I form any faction or incite rebellion. Indeed had not certain Dominican   210
and Carmelite pseudomonks (for your order was favourably inclined to me
at that time)[33] proclaimed to the people that someone had come forward
who was correcting the *Magnificat* and the Lord's Prayer and the Gospel
of John,[34] and equally ignorant and seditious accusations, the disturbance
would not have amounted to anything at all.   215

* * * * *

31 Acts 5:29; cf Epp 1875:52, 1902:97, 1904:21, 1909:50.
32 Cf Ep 1581:120–6. This will also be a major theme in *Ciceronianus* (Basel: Froben,
   March 1528) LB I 973–1026 / ASD I-2 606–709 / CWE 28.
33 On Erasmus' relations with the Franciscans see n3 above.
34 Erasmus' translation of these passages in his New Testament was criticized
   by the Carmelites Sebastiaan Craeys, Nicolaas Baechem, and an anonymous
   Dominican, among others. See Ep 948:108–13; Erasmus *Apologia qua respondet*

But some say that this Lutheran conflagration started from my writings. Yes, that is what some people say; but it is a boldfaced lie, since to the present day no one has been able to produce a single article of belief subject to official disapproval that I hold in common with Luther. Lastly the facts themselves proclaim what a shameless lie it is to accuse me of collusion with Luther. Yes, just as Hector colluded with Achilles. You will be able to judge this yourself if you read my *Diatribe* and Luther's response, the most antagonistic of all his writings, and also my answer to him in the two books of the *Hyperaspistes*.[35]

I am not unaware that there are those who proclaim that my works disparage religious orders. For my part I am strongly of the opinion that Christianity would be no worse off if there were not so many distinctions of rite, food, and titles, especially when we see that monasticism has sunk to such a low ebb that, if you remove the externals, monks would almost be more corrupt than the rest. Indeed a great number of monasteries are so lacking in any religious discipline that no place else would be less conducive to leading a religious life. And yet, up to now I have never written that; but what difference would it make if I wrote what everyone knows? I merely indicate what true religion is founded upon, criticizing those who through enticements, bugbears, and other reprehensible tricks lure simple and inexperienced youth who do not yet know themselves, let alone religion, into a net from which they cannot extricate themselves.[36] This is extremely prejudicial both to the young boys and to the order, for which it would have been more profitable to have a few sincere recruits than a great number of mediocre ones.

If these things are not true, it has not been entirely pointless for me to caution you against them. But if the world is full of such examples, some of which I would be ashamed to mention, then you will admit in your wisdom that my admonition was not only useful but necessary. One who advises that marriage is not to be contracted hastily does not condemn marriage: rather he is giving thought to the dignity of marriage. In some of my writings I criticize certain persons who live recklessly but are persuaded that they will be safe from the claws of evil demons if they are transported to

* * * * *

duabus invectivis Eduardi Lei CWE 72 37 and nn181-3 and his *Responsio ad annotationes Eduardi Lei* 243 CWE 72 347-8 and n766; Rummel *Catholic Critics* I 140-3.
35 On the controversy with Luther see Ep 1804 n10.
36 See Ep 1805 n70.

the grave clothed in the Franciscan habit.[37] If there are none who are adversely affected by this evil practice, then my warnings have been useless;   250
but if countless examples show not only that simple people are prey to this
superstition but even that members of your order foster it and promote it,
you should have been the last persons to put such an idea into the heads of
ordinary folk. Such actions, even if they provide some temporary gain, earn
for you the hatred of learned, sensible, truly pious men.   255

What more shall I say? Would your order collapse if Christians were
persuaded that the Franciscan habit will be of very little assistance in the
next life unless one has imitated the sanctity of St Francis? You will say,
'What was the use of these admonitions?' My retort would be, 'What was
the use of these practices? What was the use of preserving customs of this   260
sort?' If you wish to keep the reputation of your confrères in such excellent
repair, why do you engage in such mad and uninhibited accusations against
the name and reputation of another? Your calumnies do not have to do with
a religious habit but inflict the charge of heresy, the most heinous of all
crimes; and your accusation is false, while everyone is aware of the question   265
of the habit, since you yourselves are constantly peddling it. Then too it
almost seems typical of many members of your order to lash out with the
virulence of a cynic[38] against bishops, priests, pastors, abbots, poets, and
rhetoricians; and yet you cannot abide a few remarks directed against the
Franciscan habit, although out of the great tribe of Franciscans not a single   270
name is uttered. If you are so sensitive about your reputation you should
have seen to it that your confrères did not provide so much material for
popular gossip, quite often of a kind as to make me blush when I hear it. I
have never divulged any of these stories, although many of them have been
clearly substantiated. On the contrary, through my words and writings I   275
have restrained Luther and some others who were planning to spread them
among the people.[39]

For this courtesy of mine, my dear Gachi, see what disfavour some
have given me in return; and certain people number you among them.[40]

* * * * *

37 See Ep 1805 n71.
38 The Cynics in Greece held that virtue lies in self-control and independence; but
   they engaged in open diatribes on the streets before large audiences, attacking
   vice in vigorous and often vulgar terms.
39 Although no specific defence of the Franciscans made by Erasmus to Luther or
   to anyone else is known, some of the correspondence has not been preserved;
   see Allen Ep 1041:46n.
40 See Ep 1852:18–39.

Perhaps this was enjoined upon you by your superiors and for this you   28
even expect praise for your obedience. What if your superiors ordered you
to give me poison? Would you do it? And yet what some people do is even
more criminal. Poison takes the life of only one body; these slanders infect
thousands of souls. But let us imagine that I have behaved badly towards
some members of your order. Is there no way of taking vengeance except   28
by lying slanders and defamatory public speeches? Are there no laws in
the world, no judges, no legal representatives? This kind of vengeance is
warlike and seditious, not in the spirit of Francis. 'Let us all raise an outcry together, let us overwhelm the innocent with our cries.' But Christ was
overcome by such a holy tumult.[41] Do you like this example? If you do, may   29
you like the outcome as well. He who takes up the sword will perish by
the sword.[42] He who uses violence invites violence. The country folk are
no longer asleep;[43] moreover by these actions you make yourselves hated
by princes, bishops, and true believers, if you scorn the silent judgment of
decent people.   29

While this behaviour is entirely unworthy of your profession it is much
more pernicious to abuse the authority of the gospel, the place,[44] the Franciscan name and habit, and the religious patience of the Christian people
in perpetrating such a crime. You yourself know that there is no more sacred function than the preaching of the gospel, and you are not unaware of   30
how much religious respect is owed to that place; and you know perfectly
well what the people expect there. No one ought to approach that function
or that place unless he be prepared by the most fervent prayers for pardon
and, one might say, inspired by divine power. What sort of behaviour is
it, therefore, to make scurrilous attacks on another man's reputation from   30
this place, resorting to manifest lies? What if it were the custom now, as it
once was, for the people to signify their displeasure by hissing and stamping their feet? These antics of yours, I fear, would be rejected not only by
hissing but with rocks. This silence, this patience is accorded by the pious
throng out of respect for the majesty of the gospel and the holiness of the   3
place; and would you abuse matters of great sacredness for the most shameful purposes? It is as if someone were to administer the most deadly poison
under the guise of the Eucharist.

There is great reverence among some people for your name and profession, which ought to be used for the public good and not for impious   3

* * * * *

41 Cf Mark 15:10–15, Luke 23:13–23, John 19:4–7.
42 Matt 26:52
43 An allusion to the peasants' uprisings in Germany
44 That is, the preacher's pulpit in the church

calumny. What is the aim of all this clamour? That the people should have
a low opinion of Erasmus? Suppose you succeed in this. Will they thereby
have a good opinion of all of you, if they have a bad opinion of me alone?
On the contrary, my excellent friend, I fear that through this scandalous hue
and cry you are bringing great disfavour upon your own name and ren-   320
dering mine more illustrious. This is what we see has happened in several
countries, although I have not opened my mouth. If you wish to appease
this hatred that you have aroused you must return to that purity of life by
which you first won over the favour of good men. By your present strategy,
my dear Gachi, you are betraying your order much more than I could, even   325
were I to let fly the bloodiest shafts from my pen – which, however, I shall
not do. You can rest easy on that score; but what others will do is beyond
my control. That is up to you.

Now how is it that although my works touch quite often and rather
freely on the affairs of princes, kings, emperors, popes, cardinals, and bish-   330
ops, none of them is hostile to me? Only you, who should have been the
most tolerant of all, stir up these tumults. Do you alone have no need of
someone to counsel you? Are you alone free of all defects? Is it your reputation alone that must remain unsullied? Would that you might be the first
to ensure that! Even supposing that you can convince the ignorant of the   335
things that are said about me, what will the learned say, who because they
know my writings will immediately detect the impudence of your slanders?
But perhaps you flatter yourselves with the thought that with these outcries you will consign my books to oblivion. I fear your efforts may have
the very opposite result. I hear already that booksellers are boasting that   340
they owe it to your complaints that people are buying my books more than
ever.

Come now, let us imagine that you may do anything you like, and let
us suppose that no one will rise up to defend my innocence and quell your
insolence: do you not fear that avenger whose hand no mortal being can   345
escape? Or do you think that he will instantly account as holy that which
your cupidity induces you to regard as holy?[45] Far different, believe me, are
the judgments of God from those of men. But if the efforts of those who try
to bring about the restoration of good letters and a more genuine theology
with true piety seem to be harmful to your interests, I pray that your piety   350
will ponder the reason for this anomaly. For since you make profession of
an apostolic life, how can it be that you do not tolerate one who invites
you to apostolic simplicity? But if it is some human consideration that is the

* * * * *

45 Cf *Adagia* iv vii 16, as at Epp 1804:265–6, 1858:347, 1875:49–50.

stumbling block, then it is just, my good man, that human considerations
yield to divine ones.   355

Reflect also on this in your good judgment: whether your stratagems
come at a good time. You see how all these dissensions throw the whole
world into confusion. Why was it necessary to add new disturbances to the
old ones, running the risk that they may erupt into a more serious conflagration than you think? How often have we seen uncontrollable tempests 360
arise from the most insignificant beginnings! The Lutheran conflagration has
grown from frivolous beginnings to such proportions! At first it was a joke,
a diversion. Then Prierias wrote his response:[46] suddenly there were outcries from the monks to the people; there were articles, bulls, edicts, and
much more. What good it has done up to now I know not. How much more 365
prudent it would have been not to add evil to evil, but rather to devote one's
energies to restoring the church to its earlier tranquillity, even if there were
something in my writings worthy of criticism; everything has its proper moment. Do you think perhaps that Luther has been crushed and prostrated?
Would that the pestilence were exterminated! It has been dealt a serious 370
blow by edicts and articles, I admit, but it still holds sway in the minds
of men. What chiefly recommended it to men's minds was the wickedness
of certain monks. The battle cry of some of your confrères has not escaped
my notice. 'When Luther has been disposed of, we will attack Erasmus.'
Dispose of Luther, therefore; and then, if you see fit, attack Erasmus. But 375
when Luther was running riot unchallenged, you did no more than mutter protestations like snails inside their shells. I, on the other hand, at the
behest of the emperor, the pope, and other princes have joined in hand-to-
hand battle with Luther – and in a region bordering on the area where he
is most powerful. When the enemy was made weaker by my warfare, my 380
risks, and my wounds, you suddenly spring forward from the rear and attack one who is engaged in combat – for what purpose, I ask you? Do you
envy the Catholic church its victory? Do you wish to give comfort to the enemy? That is exactly what you are doing. You vent your rage upon Luther,
enemy of the church, in words; but in deeds you supply him with reinforce- 385
ments such as allies give to one another in war. If I merited your hatred
through some failing, your private feelings should have been subordinated
to concern for the public welfare, and you should have demonstrated your
favour to me at least as long as I was fighting untiringly in the ranks of the
church.   390

* * * * *

46 On Silvester Prierias see Ep 1875 n41; cf Ep 1909:128–31 and n27.

There are some people whose one ambition it is to assemble from my vast output of writings some things that I wrote in my youth or in times of peace or without a serious purpose and distort them to suggest similarity to Lutheran beliefs. Moreover they do this with insolence and slanderous intent. But how much better advised they would be to extract those passages   395
that prove I disagree with the unorthodox beliefs of Luther – if, that is, they sincerely favour the cause of the pope. Human emotions prevent some individuals from doing this. For that reason I advise you, my dear Gachi, brother in the Lord, that, harkening to my advice, you in turn advise your confrères not to put their trust in conspiracies[47] of this type, or in close-   400
ranked phalanxes, or in unseemly tirades and anonymous calumnies hardly befitting a man, or in the credulity of foolish women and the stupidity of the crowd, but that they fix the anchor of their hope in the Lord and in true piety. If you esteem your order, you will accomplish this best of all by a forthright way of life, and you will of course have my approval. If you foster   405
the tranquillity of the church, you will have me as your fellow soldier – not very robust perhaps, but loyal. Putting aside personal animosities let us accomplish the work of Christ together. And if our approaches are different, or our powers unequal, let our goal be the same. But if you are determined to continue in the path you have begun, no charge will be imputed to me.   410
This letter will acquit me before the sovereign judge. I shall repeat what I said at the beginning: if it was an empty rumour that reached me here, consider that this was not written to you but to those others who I know for certain are perpetrating such things. May the Lord impart to all of us his Holy Spirit. Amen.

415

1892 / To Amblard and Claude-Louis Alardet   Basel, 18 October 1527

This letter, which answers Ep 1852, was first printed in the *Opus epistolarum* (1529). It is closely tied to Epp 1886 and 1891.

For the brothers Alardet see Ep 1852 introduction and CEBR I 21–2. Erasmus will write again to them in 1529 (Ep 2084).

ERASMUS OF ROTTERDAM TO THE ILLUSTRIOUS BROTHERS AMBLARD AND LOUIS ALARDET, GREETING
To your eagerness of mind, distinguished young men, I am well aware that any letter, no matter how long, will seem all too brief; but in view of my

* * * * *

47 Erasmus uses the term *syncretismus*, on which see Allen Ep 1051:4n and *Adagia* I i 11.

pursuits even the briefest of letters cannot but seem long. I am ashamed, to 5
be sure, to have written but once or twice to you in such a careless fashion
and with such brevity,[1] since I recognize what is owed to your exceptional
loyalty towards me and to your distinction of intellect and the good fortune with which you are both abundantly blessed. No one would believe
the extent of my exertions, and yet I have scarcely a moment to devote to 10
the health of this frail body weighed down with age and sickness. Still I
have great fear that you may attribute the scantiness and unpolished style
of my letters to weariness or ingratitude. But I am certain that if you knew
the huge amount of work this puny creature has to sustain, you would be
astonished that I write anything at all. 15

I do not altogether approve of your advice that I should appeal to the
authority of the illustrious prince to counter the insolence of that preacher.[2]
I say this for various reasons: the matter is too insignificant to trouble such
a great leader about it. The malice of men like this preacher, when it meets
with resistance, usually becomes more swollen, like a torrent when obsta- 20
cles are thrown in its path, but when ignored dies away more quickly, either
because they are exhausted from their bellowing or because their listeners
grow weary. Even less satisfactory was your advice to silence the cleric with
a long letter of rebuke. I have already experienced that these people raise
their crests[3] if one deigns to write to them: thinking that they are more re- 25
doubtable than they are, they become more violent. If you write calmly and
temperately, they ascribe it to fear and take heart. But if you treat them as
they deserve, you are only stirring up a hornet's nest.[4] Nevertheless, since
I am convinced that in your wisdom you do not insist on this without good
reason, I have written to both of them, but with the understanding that it is 30
left to you to decide whether to deliver the letters or suppress them. You are
better able to decide what is expedient, since you are there on the spot and
are very well acquainted with the circumstances of the matter and the persons involved. Moreover, since my letter to the illustrious prince is rather
laconic, your eloquence will make up for whatever is lacking. Even if I had

* * * * *

1892
1 Letters not extant
2 In Ep 1852:52–8 Claude-Louis Alardet had advised Erasmus to write to Jean
  Gachi directly or to appeal to Duke Charles for support against his criticisms.
  Despite what he says here, Erasmus did so in Epp 1886 to Duke Charles and
  1891 to Gachi; cf line 30 below.
3 *Adagia* I viii 69
4 *Adagia* I i 60

the time I thought it would be more fitting and safer to address the monarch in a few words lest I doubly offend him by burdening him with a letter that was both displeasing and verbose. Since to gratify your wishes I could not remain silent altogether, and since the nature of the case precluded a pleasant tone, I thought it best to say as little as possible to the prince.[5] I recognize his exceptional wisdom both from what many people say about him and especially from the fact that in the midst of the sea of troubles that surrounds him he has continually preserved the peace and tranquillity of his principality, not exposing it to the fury of war or the contagion of impiety.[6]

For such good fortune I congratulate your native Savoy exceedingly, praying Christ that in his goodness and power he may allow similar congratulations to be extended to the entire world of Christendom. But I see all too clearly that unless the authority of princes restrain the malice of certain individuals these screeching jackdaws[7] will stir up more serious disturbances than these hawkers[8] of the new gospel have done. It was the assault upon belles-lettres that first gave rise to this tragedy, and if they continue as they have begun things will come full circle. But in my opinion those who cherish good letters will promote them more if instead of wasting their time in squabbling with these boorish blatherers they would spend it in stimulating, refining, instructing, and encouraging talents that show good promise. For that motley crew are totally invincible, whether in sheer numbers, battle array, conspiracies, malice, public outcries – and you may add, if you wish, pretence and trickery. They can only be held in check by cudgels or famine.

That was how that most worthy man Count Hermann von Neuenahr forced Jacob of Hoogstraten to make an abject and clownish retraction, of which I have a copy.[9] By what means? you will ask. Not by arguments, not

* * * * *

5 Erasmus employs in punning fashion three Greek words – ἥκιστα, ἥδιστα, and ἐλάχιστα – in this sentence.

6 A reference not only to the frequent wars between the French Valois and the imperial Hapsburgs but also to the religious unrest in the adjoining Swiss cantons

7 Greek κραγέται καὶ κολοιοί (cf Pindar *Nemean Odes* 3.82), referring to anti-Erasmian Catholics like Gachi

8 *praecones*, referring to evangelical reformers like Guillaume Farel and Otto Brunfels, whom Erasmus did not respect

9 Neither the document nor its circumstances are known. Neuenahr (c 1492–1530) had attended the universities of Cologne and Bologna before becoming archdeacon of the Cologne chapter and chancellor of the university in 1524. He was a strong supporter of humanism, especially in the Reuchlin affair (1514–17), and of Erasmus, especially against Edward Lee (CEBR III 14–15). On Hoogstraten see Ep 1821 n12.

by objective reasoning, not by warnings or threats or insults; all of these methods were attempted without success. By what means, then? By cheese and eggs. Hoogstraten's brethren were denied the right of collecting them in the territory under the count's dominion.[10] Similarly, as long as the peasants held the stage,[11] it's a marvel how these same monks drew in their horns, which they now lay bare so ferociously. They are so indifferent to the authority of princes that they would sooner give orders than obey them. They have been completely exempted from the jurisdiction of bishops through various bulls; and yet they usurp their functions by hearing confessions and preaching the gospel.[12] The Roman pontiff alone they occasionally obey, but only when it suits them. When that is not the case no one has stronger contempt for him than they. And in the meantime they vaunt that holy obedience, although they obey neither human nor divine laws.

These remarks, I admit, do not apply to everyone. There are some honest men even among them, but being so few in number they are so overpowered by the tyranny of the others that they cannot be what they are. Let others see to the repression of this breed of men: it is my task, surely, as far as it lies in me, to restore a purer Christianity and revive good learning. If they espouse this same cause they will be serving their own best interests as well as those of public tranquillity. But if they think their way of life ill accords with finer things, at least they are aware, I believe, that it is just that the worse yield to the better, the human to the divine. They prefer to be feared rather than loved,[13] and certainly they have achieved their goal; and on that account they behave in such a violent manner, failing to consider how fleeting is the law of fear. It is astonishing how they despise me; but why shouldn't they despise Erasmus when they fly in the face of emperors and archbishops? But if I had as much desire to return their insults as they to inflict them, perhaps it would have been better for them to provoke some monarch rather than the insignificant[14] Erasmus.

Perhaps I have lingered too long on this. Yet I thought it better to discourse at greater length on the subject so that you in your wisdom might ponder the measures to be adopted in dealing with these crows. I pray

* * * * *

10 Hoogstraten's religious order, the Dominicans, were obliged by their rule to beg for their food. In a letter to Wolfgang Capito Erasmus recounts a somewhat different version; see Ep 877:18–34.
11 The uprisings known as the Peasants' War of 1524–5
12 Competition between the secular, or parish clergy and the mendicant orders over the right to administer sacraments dated back to the thirteenth century.
13 See Ep 1870 n3.
14 μονόγραμμον 'drawn with a single line'

that the Lord will always keep from harm this amiable union of brothers
working together for the greater good of all.   95
    Given at Basel, the feast of St Luke in the year 1527

1893 / To Willibald Pirckheimer   Basel, 19 October 1527

> Erasmus published this letter in the *Opus epistolarum* (1529). It answers Pir-
> ckheimer's Ep 1880, and will be answered by Ep 1930. The letter is particu-
> larly noteworthy for Erasmus' insistence on his loyalty to the church defined
> broadly here as 'the consensus of the whole Christian people,' and his willing-
> ness to set aside personal theological interpretations or convictions and give
> absolute credence to its definitions of faith.
>   For Pirckheimer see Ep 1880 introduction.

Warmest greetings. I have never feared your pen,[1] my dear Willibald, since
I have long and direct experience of your discreet courtesy and unwavering
loyalty in the preservation of friendship. But I took it badly that Oecolampadius for no good reason included my name in his books, when I told him
myself that it is displeasing to me to be named by him, even more displeas-   5
ing to be adversely criticized, and most displeasing to be praised.[2] All the
same he never puts an end to it. For this I have never imputed any charge
to my dear Willibald. For many things cause us pain that we cannot blame
on anyone. If your silence, which has been more prolonged than usual, gave
me cause to doubt, this should not seem strange to you, since you know   10
yourself how fickle – you might say Euripus-like – the human mind can be;[3]
and you know too the many stratagems and the malice of tongues, especially in this day and age. I do not altogether regret having entertained this
tiny suspicion, insignificant though it may be, since it extorted a letter from
you that I much desired.   15
    In your efforts to dissuade me from writing *apologiae* I recognize a
wise and friendly advice;[4] and you are not the only one to do so, but almost

* * * * *

1893
1 For the context of this remark, see Ep 1880:24–40.
2 Ep 1538
3 Euripus was a strait in eastern Greece, between Euboea and the mainland,
   known for the suddenness and rapidity of its tides; cf *Adagia* I ix 62. Pirckheimer, partly under constraint, had changed his attitude towards Oecolampadius; see Ep 1880.
4 Cf Ep 1880:17–20 and n8. From his earliest defence of the *Praise of Folly* (Ep 337)
   against the criticism of Maarten van Dorp, Erasmus had invested an enormous
   amount of energy in defending his works against his critics' attacks, usually

all sensible men who wish me well do the same. But this is my destiny; yet I
have kept silent more often than I have answered. Certainly I always regret
that I answered Cousturier, but I did it at the instigation of a great friend.[5]   20
Dorp, who returns so often to his old self, I succeeded in vanquishing.[6] If
you were thoroughly acquainted with the tragic designs of Lee and the cha-
rades of Zúñiga, which because of their poor reception in Spain were transferred to Rome,[7] you would be less disapproving of my action. To keep
peace with Luther was made impossible by leaders of state.[8] Certain the-   25
ologians of Paris with one whom you know as intermediary, have long ago
staged their play.[9] Now with the same provocateur they have revived it,
grooming Béda for the role, to whom I have made answer.[10] All my friends
congratulate me that these things have come to light during my lifetime, for
my enemies were expecting my death with each passing day. Seeing that   30
I was more alive than they wished, they were overcome with impatience

* * * * *

from traditionalist theologians. He had just finished the latest, the *Apologia adversus monachos quosdam Hispanos*, in response to the accusations made against
him at Valladolid.

5 Nicolas Bérault advised him to dedicate *Adversus Petri Sutoris quondam theologi
Sorbonici nunc monachi Cartusiani debacchationem apologia* (Basel: Johann Froben,
August 1525), answering Cousturier's *De tralatione bibliae* (Paris: Josse Bade,
December 1524), to Jean de Selve, principal president of the Parlement of Paris
(Ep 1591 introduction). Erasmus, however, needed little persuasion to answer
Cousturier, whom of all his opponents he held most in contempt; cf Ep 1804
n65.

6 With *Ad Martinum Dorpium theologum epistola* (Ep 337) a response to Dorp's Ep
304. For 'returns ... to his old self' cf Terence *Hecyra* 113.

7 On the controversy with Edward Lee over Erasmus' *New Testament* see Rummel *Catholic Critics* I 95–120; on that with Zúñiga, ibidem I 145–77; cf Epp
1877, 1879. Zúñiga's later works were printed in Rome; Erasmus may also be
alluding to the more recent attacks from there by Alberto Pio.

8 King Henry VIII, Pope Adrian VI, and others urged Erasmus to write *De libero
arbitrio* (Epp 1419 introduction, 1643:43–8 and n10). Erasmus said the *Hyperaspistes* resulted from pressure applied by Charles V (cf Ep 1731) and from the
urging of friends (Epp 1815:61–2, 1835:7–9). For the 'repeated' promptings of
Duke George of Saxony, see the indexes in CWE 10, 11, 12, and this volume.

9 The first investigations of Erasmus' works by Paris theologians occurred
in June 1523 (Clerval *Procès-verbaux* 356) and January–February 1524 (Farge
Procès-verbaux 6–7 nos 5A, 6A–B; 14 no 13C; 17 nos 16A, 18C. Erasmus accused
Jacobus Latomus of stirring up theologians in Paris like Béda, whom he accused of arranging to have Lee's book printed there; see Ep 1804:232–5.

10 The *Elenchus in censuras Bedae* (June 1526), the *Prologus supputationis errorum
in censuris Bedae* (August 1526), and the *Supputatio errorum in censuris Bedae*
(March 1527); see Rummel *Catholic Critics* II 29–59 and Ep 1804 n14.

and bounded onto the stage, thinking they would finish their play with impunity once Erasmus was buried. That person in Spain whom I mentioned has once again, by concocting a deceitful booklet, stirred up so much confusion there that the matter is exasperating both the emperor and the court, the archbishops and the academies.[11] That is all that stupid little creature, born to create discord,[12] is worth. And yet he will not succeed there either, even though he has seven orders of monks on his side.[13] It is not that I devote much time or effort to these disputes. Much more time is given over to letters,[14] which sometimes are neither agreeable nor necessary. I readily believe what you say about clerics.[15] For I see a race coming into being from whom my mind recoils violently: I greatly fear the outcome. It is the death of concord, charity, faith, learning, morals, civility. What is left?

That vainglorious young man of whom you speak has brought a great evil upon himself, and he gives no sign of relenting.[16] After being the architect of the whole Hutten tragedy and abusing his familiarity with me, he is

* * * * *

11 That is, by the conference convened at Valladolid and attended by theologians mainly from the universities of Salamanca and Alcalá. Erasmus blamed Edward Lee, who was in Spain on a diplomatic mission, for stirring up opposition there and suspected that he was about to publish a new book; see Epp 1744:133–5 and n19, 1814 n39.

12 Cf Ep 1909:20–3. Erasmus often mocked Lee's small stature (for example Epp 906:494, 1026:14, 1061:496).

13 In Ep 1879:46–7 he enumerated six: Trinitarians, Dominicans, Franciscans, Carmelites, Augustinians, and Benedictines; he perhaps would add Carthusians here, because of Pierre Cousturier's membership in that order. Cf Ep 1805:139.

14 A frequent complaint; see Ep 1804 n12.

15 This subject is not raised in the fragment of Ep 1880 that has survived.

16 The incomplete draft of Ep 1880 does not mention Heinrich Eppendorf (1491–c 1551), a former friend (cf Epp 1122:10–11, 1125:57–60, 1283 n4, 1342:370, 1383:1–15, 1437:10–113). Erasmus considered him to have betrayed a confidence in his difficult dealings with Ulrich von Hutten and to have persuaded Hutten to write his *Expostulatio* as a means to blackmail Erasmus and his friends in Basel. Erasmus frequently criticized Eppendorf without naming him (as here); but sometimes he complained in great detail (see especially Allen Epp 1934 introduction, 1929:11n, 1940:19n). Erasmus' 1524 colloquy *Hippoplanus* 'The Cheating Horse Dealer' was generally thought to have been composed with Eppendorf in mind. A settlement arbitrated in 1528 in Basel by Beatus Rhenanus and Bonifacius Amerbach soon lapsed again into mutual recriminations, and Erasmus' 1529 colloquy Ἱππεὺς ἄνιππος, *sive Ementita nobilitas* 'The Knight without a Horse, or Faked Nobility' reflected his renewed antagonism towards Eppendorf.

astonished that I wrote to the prince pleading with him that he divert that talent from such foolishness to some honourable function.[17]

I am happy that your trouble with kidney stones has abated. Mine has changed into another malady, chronic but more tolerable. I bade farewell to 50 my doctors and entrusted myself to God.[18] I was thinking of celebrating the name of Albrecht Dürer myself. Nevertheless I am pleased to be reminded of it.[19] I curse that gout of yours for a selfish reason, that it prevented you from finishing your letter, since your longest letters are the ones I find most delightful. That the emperor honours you as you deserve gives me great 55 pleasure;[20] would that he could also take away your malady!

So much for your letter to me; now to the letter in which you as much as celebrate a triumph over Oecolampadius.[21] You did not wish me to be a judge of this affair. Nonetheless I took great delight in it, not only because it is brimming with clever pleasantries but also because it reveals that you 60 are in very good humour. I learned from it that I have been attacked by him again. I never stated that his opinion was substantially better. Among friends I said that I would go over to his side if the authority of the church gave him its approval, but I added that I could in no way dissent from the church's opinion. By the church I mean the consensus of the whole Chris- 65 tian people.[22] Whether the hypocrites you mention said the same I know

* * * * *

17 Several letters to Duke George of Saxony to this effect appear to have been intercepted, probably by Eppendorf himself. See Ep 1448 introduction.

18 The new ailment was an ulcerated bladder; see Ep 1729:20. Despite what he says here, Erasmus appears to have been satisfied with the care provided by Jan Antonin (Ep 1825:2), and held hopes of finding relief under the care of Paracelsus (Ep 1809).

19 A promise carried out in a eulogy of Dürer's skill in the *De recta pronunciatione* in 1528, only months before the artist's death (CWE 26 398–9 and nn139, 140 [page 597]; ASD I-4 40). Dürer made at least two charcoal sketches of Erasmus in 1520 (Ep 1376 nn1 and 2; see the reproduction in CWE 8 28) and the famous portrait engraving in 1526, reproduced in CWE 11 263, which Erasmus did not consider a good likeness (Ep 1729 264:11–13 and n9). Dürer was not mentioned in the incomplete draft of Ep 1880.

20 Pirckheimer had been appointed imperial councillor in 1526.

21 Pirckheimer's irreverent *De convitiis monachi illius qui graecolatine Caecolampa-dius, Germanice vero Ausshin nuncupatur, ad Eleutherium suum epistola* (Nürnberg np 1527). In changing Oecolampadius' name to 'Caecolampadius' he employs an oxymoron meaning 'blind brilliance'; cf his other mordant play on Oeco-lampadius' name in Ep 1880:2, 12. The expression 'celebrate a triumph' is rendered in Greek.

22 Cf Epp 1637:65–70, 1729:27–30.

not.[23] I at any rate said it without dissimulation and with all sincerity, and I never wavered with regard to the truth of the Eucharist.[24] I do not know what weight the authority of the church has for others, but as far as I am concerned it has such importance that I would agree with the Arians and the Pelagians if the church had approved their teachings.[25] It is not that the words of Christ are not sufficient for me; but it should not seem strange if I follow the interpretation of the church on whose authority I believe in the canonical books of Scripture. It may be that others have more native intelligence or more strength. I put my firm trust in the definitive pronouncements of the church. Reasoning and argumentation have no end. In your good judgment you will recognize to which words of your letter I am referring. I would like to go on at greater length, but it is simply out of the question. All of Augustine is being printed.[26] Although I always refused this burden it is nevertheless thrust upon my shoulders. Farewell.

Given at Basel on the day after the feast of St Luke in the year 1527

Your devoted Erasmus of Rotterdam

I had begun to write about the Eucharist against the opinion of Oecolampadius a year ago,[27] and I still have the beginning of it. But I thought it would be of no avail except to stir up agitation here. For at that time Oecolampadius was in power here, and he still has the support of the common people. Besides I heard that the bishop of Rochester and the Parisians had girded themselves for this task.[28] And there is

* * * * *

23 Perhaps a reference to Ep 1880:2, where Pirckheimer used the singular (hypocrite) to refer to Oecolampadius

24 Erasmus' views on the Eucharist are discussed at great length in Epp 1637 and 1640 addressed to Conradus Pellicanus. See also Ep 1708 introduction and n2.

25 For an extended discussion of the Arians, fourth-century Christians condemned for not accepting the divinity of Christ, see Ep 1877 passim. Pelagianism, a heresy that arose in the late fourth century, teaches that humans of their own initiative can take the initial and conclusive steps to gain their salvation. Erasmus' point is not to approve those heresies but to emphasize his trust and submission to definitive pronouncements reached by consensus in the church.

26 The ten-volume edition by the Froben press (Basel 1528–9); cf Ep 2157.

27 Erasmus abandoned his plan to respond to Oecolampadius' *De genuina verborum Domini: 'Hoc est corpus meum' . . . expositione* (np 1525); see Epp 1616:22 and n2, 1679:101–2 and n22, 1708:55–7 and n6. He did however compose a short pamphlet, *Detectio praestigiarum*, to refute arguments put forth by an unnamed author on this subject; see Ep 1708:15–30 and n2.

28 John Fisher published *De veritate corporis et sanguinis Christi in Eucharistia* (Cologne: Petrus Quentell, March 1527). On the response of the Paris faculty of theology see Ep 1884 introduction.

no lack of things for me to do without taking that upon myself. Again,
farewell.   90

Give my kind greetings to Dürer.[29] You have the complete loyalty of
Glareanus.[30] Baer and our suffragan also commend you.[31]

To the illustrious Lord Willibald Pirckheimer, counsellor of his imperial Majesty

1894 / To Nicolaus Vesuvius   Basel, 23 October 1527

This manuscript, hastily written, is autograph throughout. Allen, who was the
first to publish it, had transcribed it in 1911, just prior to its sale that same year
by the Huth Library at Fosbury to the auction firm of Maggs Bros Ltd, which
produced a facsimile of it in its catalogue no 269 (Summer 1911). The buyer
was not revealed, and its current location remains unknown. For Vesuvius see
Ep 1827 introduction.

Warmest greetings. I have written recently through the intermediacy of Anton the Swiss,[1] and I sent some books as well. I trust that they have reached
you. By the present traveller, who is about to set off in your direction, I
wish merely to greet you and all your friends, who are also mine. This
young man, Pierre Du Chastel, is remarkably well trained in languages and   5
in the liberal arts. He was my guest for several months.[2] Farewell. Basel, 23
October 1527

* * * * *

29 See n19 above.
30 The Swiss humanist Henricus Glareanus, who shared Erasmus' fears that the
   Reformation movement would upset the advance of learning; on him see Ep
   1821 n15.
31 Ludwig Baer, a native of Basel and graduate in theology of Paris, was a neighbour and friend of Erasmus, who valued his moderate and conciliatory theological positions. The two would both move to Freiburg-im-Breisgau to distance themselves from the reformed city of Basel. See Farge BR 23–6 no 23;
   cf CEBR I 84–6. Tilmann Limperger, suffragan bishop of Basel since 1498; see
   Ep 1883 n7. Nikolaus von Diesbach, coadjutor bishop with right of succession,
   had resigned on 21 February 1527; see Ep 1844 introduction.

1894
1 Probably Ep 1827, addressed in the *Opus epistolarum* to 'a certain medical doctor,' and carried by Anton Bletz of Zug. See Ep 1827 introduction.
2 Pierre Du Chastel, of Arc-en-Barrois (Haute-Marne), obviously carried the letter from Basel to Langres. While a house guest of Erasmus he worked for the

Yours, Erasmus of Rotterdam

To the most honourable master Nicolaus Vesuvius, chaplain to the
bishop of Langres 10

1895 / From Andrzej Trzecieski   Wrocław, 28 October 1527

Autograph throughout, this letter is in the Rehdiger Collection (MS 254 150)
in the University Library, Wrocław. It was first printed by Casimir von Mi-
askowski 'Beiträge zur Korrespondenz des Erasmus von Rotterdam mit Polen'
part 2 *Jahrbuch für Philosophie und speculative Theologie* 15 (Paderborn 1901)
212–13.

Andrzej Trzecieski learned Hebrew and Greek in Cracow and, by the time
he wrote this letter, had pursued these studies further in Leipzig and Erfurt.
Attracted to the Reformation, he became acquainted with Melanchthon and
made his home in Cracow a gathering place for religious reformers. He enjoyed the protection of Jan (II) Łaski, and became book buyer for the library of
King Sigismund II Augustus. For his prodigious literary output and activities
– among them supervision of a Polish translation of the Bible (Brest-Litovsk:
Bernhard Woiewodka 1563) see Allen's introduction; cf CEBR III 348.

Greetings. You will pardon me, most kind Erasmus, if I, a barbarian and
stranger to the Muses and the Graces, should dare to address you, a man
skilled in every branch of learning, in a most unlettered letter. This is owed
to your great kindness and benignity, by which you have won over to yourself men of every nation, so much so that they can never forget you. Thus it 5
was that when I heard your praises being sung at the home of Jan Antonin
of Košice,[1] an old companion of mine, and learned that you had written him
a very friendly letter and that you had been highly spoken of at the house

* * * * *

Froben press. In 1531 he would come back to Basel before travelling to Italy,
Egypt, Jerusalem, and then to Constantinople as interpreter for the French ambassador. In 1536/7 he entered the service of King Francis I as royal librarian
and accumulated several benefices. He was given oversight of the *lecteurs royaux* (the nascent Collège royal, later Collège de France). As bishop of Mâcon
he tried without success to protect the printer Robert Estienne from censure
by the Paris faculty of theology. He died in 1552 shortly after appointment as
bishop of Orléans; see CEBR I 409–10.

1895
1 On Antonin see Ep 1810 introduction.

of Krzysztof Szydłowiecki,[2] chancellor of our prince, and when a copy of
your *Lingua* arrived there, I made up my mind at that very moment to write 10
you a letter, inelegant though it might be. But my adverse health, which has
long debilitated me, did not permit me to do so. This has resulted from a
wound in the head received from a certain nobleman, whom I had not offended even in word, when I was returning to my lodgings after supper, as
my friend Antonin will well remember. It was through his medications that 15
I was called back from Orcus[3] when I was already almost mourned for dead.

Now, because of a ravenous plague that began to rage through all the
quarters of Cracow since the feast of St John,[4] I have betaken myself to
Leipzig and then to Erfurt to pursue the studies of Greek and Hebrew for
which I have always had a great passion; and if my impecunious state had 20
allowed it I would also have paid you a visit. Returning on the road to
Wrocław I came upon a messenger sent to you by the very reverend lord
Andrzej Krzycki, bishop of Płock, and other prominent men, distinguished
admirers of yours.[5] I did not wish to let him go without a letter of mine
to you. The burden of my letter is simply this, that you admit your faithful 25
Trzecieski into your friendship and give him your greetings in one of your
learned letters. It has always been and still remains his ambition that, if you
do not deem him worthy of your friendship, you admit him at least into
the number of your less important clients. Farewell, and if your occupations
allow it, please give reply.[6] 30

If there are any new things to report from this quarter, I think those
eminent gentlemen who have sent the present messenger to you will have
amply informed you of them. Otherwise I would have written about them.
Again farewell.

* * * * *

2 On Szydłowiecki, to whom Erasmus dedicated the *Lingua*, his treatise on vices
   of the tongue, see Ep 1820 introduction.
3 A name for the underworld in Roman mythology
4 The Nativity of St John the Baptist, celebrated on 24 June at the summer sol-
   stice, was a commonly used calendar reference; but Trzecieski might mean the
   feast of the Beheading of John the Baptist, which fell on 29 August. He probably does not intend the feast of St John the apostle and evangelist, which fell
   on 27 December.
5 Krzycki's letter, which is not extant, probably answered Erasmus' Ep 1822. The
   other letters were most likely from Krzysztof Szydłowiecki, Jan (II) Łaski, and
   Jan Antonin, answering Erasmus' Epp 1820, 1821, and 1825 (see also Epp 1824
   and 1826). Erasmus responded with Epp 1918, 1915, and 1916. The messenger,
   named George, will later carry Ep 1915 to Jan Łaski.
6 No reply is extant, nor is Trzecieski mentioned in other surviving letters.

Wrocław, 28 October. In the year 1527 from the redemption of the   35
world

My compatriot Johannes Rullus,[7] a man entirely devoted as no other
to your good name, sends his greetings.

Andrzej Trzecieski, a Polish knight

To Erasmus of Rotterdam, theologian, a man of unsurpassed abilities,   40
to mark the beginning of a friendship. In Basel

1895A / To the Pious Reader   Basel, October 1527

This letter is the preface to *Secundus tomus Operum D. Augustini* (Basel: Hieronymus Froben 1528), which comprised Erasmus' edition of St Augustine's correspondence. Peter Bietenholz noticed its absence in both LB and Allen, and printed it as an Appendix to his *History and Biography in the Work of Erasmus of Rotterdam* (Geneva 1966 103–5). The letter carries the month- and year-dates only, but it was undoubtedly written prior to 26 October 1527, the date of Johann Froben's death – an occurrence Erasmus would not have failed to mention here, given Froben's devotion to completing the Augustine edition.

DESIDERIUS ERASMUS TO THE PIOUS READER, GREETING

From the end of the second book of the *Retractations* as well as from the epistle prefaced to the *Catalogue of Heresies to Quodvultdeus* it is sufficiently clear that at the time of their writing neither the epistles nor the sermons to the people had been systematically arranged by Augustine.[1] That he did not   5
attend to this task afterwards can be proven by the fact that in this latter volume no account seems to have been taken of time, person, or subject matter. More certain proof was provided by the fact that immediately on first sampling it was detected that some letters had been mixed in that were not to or from Augustine, which we have identified with a note of critical appraisal;   10

* * * * *

7 Rullus (d 1532) came from an Alsatian family that had emigrated to Cracow. He studied there and later was a schoolmaster in Wrocław, where he belonged to the circle of young humanists centred around Leonard Cox. See CEBR II 178.

1895A

1 Erasmus' comment on the lack of system or arrangement in the two books by St Augustine is more easily recognized in the first, *Retractationum libri duo* PL 32 656 / CSEL 36 204:15–20. In the last of the four letters prefaced to *De haeresibus ad Quodvultdeum liber unus* (Ep 224) PL 42 19–20 / CCSL 46 281:35–45 / FCNT 32 118, Augustine comments that he has not found time to review his letters and homilies with a view to composing a third book of *Retractions*.

some were simply fabricated, such as those from Boniface to Augustine and
Augustine to Boniface.[2] We have not moved any of them from their position, however, except for one exceedingly prolix and remarkably illiterate
letter, and we would not even have done that if that same letter were not
contained in a later volume. I used such great precaution so that no one   15
might complain of my excessive diligence. Interspersed with these are some
letters that Augustine himself calls books in the *Retractations*. Although at
times it is rather difficult to distinguish a letter from a book, somewhere
in his writings Augustine suggests that it may be brevity or length rather
than literary style or type of subject matter that confers or removes the name   20
of letter, especially since we have the precedent from the apostles that any
kind of serious discussion could be committed to letters. For with the exception of the Gospels, under which term we include also the Acts of the
Apostles, they left nothing in writing besides the Epistles,[3] but these were
concerned with subjects that were not at all personal and that they wanted   25
to be read by everyone. Elsewhere Augustine thinks that nothing can be
deemed a letter that does not bear the name of the writer and the addressee.
And certainly there are some that you can truly call 'epistles,' which deal
with matters that are personal and resemble human conversation, but they
are very few.   30
   But concerning this matter each may have his own opinion. I should
like to emphasize that in no other work do his piety, charity, mildness, humanity, civility, devotion to the flock entrusted to him, and love of concord
and zeal of this saintly man for the house of God shine out more brightly.
How he exerts himself, how he strives, how he becomes all things when-   35
ever there was some ray of hope of attracting the pagan to Christ or the
heretic to the communion of the church.[4] How he humbles himself; how,
in Paul's words, he changes his tone,[5] seeking the opportunity to arouse
and propagate piety wherever he felt that some spark of a good mental out-

* * * * *

2 Erasmus perhaps thinks them to be spurious, anachronistic inventions of a
   correspondence between St Augustine and St Boniface (680–754), the English-
   born 'apostle to Germany,' who died three centuries after Augustine; but Augustine's actual correspondent of that name was a Christian governor in northern Africa during the reign of Honorius. He died in battle in Italy in 432 (FCNT
   4 Ep 189 n1).
3 Erasmus shared the opinion of many, even from patristic times, who denied
   the usual attribution of the Apocalypse, or Book of Revelation, to St John the
   Evangelist.
4 Cf 1 Cor 9:22.
5 Gal 4:20

look resided. What simple woman, what common man, what courtier, what   40
pagan, what heretic does he not answer readily, affably, and persuasively?
With what anxious solicitude does he make intercession for the wicked Circumcellians,[6] who deserved more than one death! Who pleaded with greater
fervour for his friends than he did for his enemies? With what great travail he brings all to Christ, how he congratulates those who return to their   45
senses, how anxiously he looks out for those in peril, how zealously he in-
structs those who go astray, eager to heal all, to lose no one! How desperately he is afflicted by any obstacle that arises! Truly you would see in him
the hen mentioned in the Gospel, solicitous and anxious to gather her brood
under her wings and protect them.[7] In some epistles one can also detect the   50
oratorical style that the Greeks call forensic, especially when he is arguing
against the faction of Donatus,[8] and the subtlety of his arguments does not
diminish his characteristic intensity. But whether he teaches or reproves or
fights with the most unredeemable enemies you will never fail to sense the
inborn sweetness of Christian charity, so that, if this could be considered   55
an appropriate comparison, he seems to recall the figure from comedy, Micio, who is gentle even when he is being most reproachful.[9] In this one man,
as in a mirror, one can contemplate the bishop as Paul depicted him: above
reproach, the husband of only one wife, temperate, sensible, respectable,
hospitable, a teacher; not a drinker or a brawler or one greedy for money,   60
but gentle; not quarrelsome, not a lover of money, not arrogant, not angry;
a lover of goodness, self-controlled, devout, just, holding firm to the sure
word, as he has been taught, able to give instruction in sound doctrine and

* * * * *

6 Circumcellians were fanatical fourth-century Christian bands in North Africa.
 Their name derived from their tactic of encircling the dwellings they attacked,
 but they referred to themselves as *Agonistici*, or soldiers of Christ. At first they
 too were orthodox in doctrine and concerned chiefly with social grievances,
 but they gradually allied themselves with the Donatists (n8 below), who were
 of special concern to St Augustine. Cf Epp 1902:179–81 and n31, 1906:51–5.
7 Cf Matt 23:37.
8 The Donatists arose in the fourth century when they refused to accept a bishop
 (or any priests ordained by him) who had been consecrated by a *traditor*, that
 is, someone who had denied his faith in Christ during the persecution of Dio-
 cletian. They were more schismatic and rigorist than heretical, but denied the
 validity of sacraments administered by most priests. Claiming to constitute
 the one true church, they rebaptized converts who joined them, for which
 they were repeatedly condemned by councils and synods.
9 Of two brothers in Terence's *Adelphi*, Demea is stern and authoritative in
 bringing up his son, while Micio, a bachelor who has adopted the elder of his
 brother's two sons, is more lenient and permissive.

to confute with all gentleness those who contradict it.[10] If bishops, and theologians who discharge the office of bishops,[11] were to contemplate them-   65
selves in this mirror, certain of them would be ashamed, I think, of their
haughty demeanour joined with ignorance and their harshness coupled with
impure morals.

From some of Augustine's books one can perceive what kind of person he was while still an infant in Christ,[12] from others how he was as a   70
young man, from still others how he was as an old man. From this one volume you will know the whole Augustine at one and the same time. That
great intellect would have given us more abundant fruit if he had happened
to be born in, or to live in, Italy or in Gaul. Africa was primitive, lustful for
sensual pleasures, inimical to study, interested in the exotic.[13] Thus his own 75
people frequently harass him with questions of a rather frivolous nature,
not very conducive to piety; and he is often compelled to adjust his style
to suit their temperament. But to cultivate such a thicket there was need of
such a farmer. He would have written things more worthy of reading if he
had governed himself according to the tastes of the Romans or the Greeks   80
and had made less allowance for the ignorance of the simple-minded. But
Christian charity gives greater priority to doing good to as many as possible rather than to receiving the approval of the elite, being more desirous
of the salvation of one's brother than of procuring one's own glory. Some,
especially women, were possessed by pious ambition, considering it a great   85
accomplishment to have succeeded in obtaining some written communication, of whatever sort, from the bishop. The result was that while the saintly
man was deferring to everyone's wishes he gave less satisfaction occasionally to the more discriminating reader. I think anyone would find it hard

* * * * *

10 Cf 1 Tim 3:2–4, Tit 1:7–9. The passage 'above reproach . . . those who contradict
   it' is written in Greek.
11 Erasmus doubtless means theologians who arrogated to themselves the power
   to determine good doctrine from bad. He may have in mind his Paris enemy
   Noël Béda, who led the Paris faculty of theology against Guillaume Briçonnet,
   the reforming bishop of Meaux. See 'L'autorité épiscopale contestée: Requête
   de Noël Béda . . . à l'encontre de l'évêque Guillaume Briçonnet' in Farge *parti
   conservateur* 67–78.
12 *qualis fuerit adhuc infans in Christo*: the operative concept is *in Christo*, since
   Augustine was baptized as an adult.
13 Africa's supposed interest in novelty was proverbial; see *Adagia* III vii 10.
   Augustine was born in 354 in Tagaste in present-day Tunisia and returned to
   become bishop of Hippo Regius in the same region in 395.

to believe how much toil went into the removal of errors and putting order 90
into a very confused style of writing. But the best kind of almsgiving is
that conferred on the person who is not conscious of it, and it is even more
generous when conferred upon one who objects to it. Our investment is in
Christ, not in men, whose incredible ingratitude we experience all too often.
Yet their malice will never deter us from the desire to do good; our dealings 95
are with a debtor worthy of the greatest trust.

Lest I omit anything: I have cut off from the end of this volume that
long-winded, appended text that goes under the name of Cyril, who suddenly begins to speak in Latin and writes a Latin worse than Augustine's
Greek: a shameless fabrication.[14] But if anyone has the desire to read it, 100
he will find it among those things that have been added to the tomes of
St Jerome.[15] Whoever takes delight in such things may find full satisfaction
there. Judicious reader, see that you read through these writings attentively;
you will not regret the time spent therein. Farewell.

Given at Basel, the month of October in the year 1527   105

1896 / From Richard Sparcheford   London, 3 November [1527]

Autograph throughout, this letter answers Ep 1867, with which Erasmus sent
Sparcheford his translation of Chrysostom in return for the Englishman's gift
of Thomas Linacre's book on syntax. The original is in the Rehdiger Collection (MS 254 139) in the University Library, Wrocław, and was first printed in
Enthoven Ep 162. For Sparcheford, see Ep 1867 introduction.

RICHARD SPARCHEFORD TO ERASMUS OF ROTTERDAM, CHAMPION
OF THE CATHOLIC FAITH
Often when I consider within myself, O truly Catholic sir, in what manner I
could reciprocate your generosity towards me, I see immediately that even

* * * * *

14 Bietenholz (see the introduction) emended *male* 'bad' to *peius* 'worse.' If *male*
were retained, the text would read, 'under the names of Cyril, who suddenly
begins to speak Latin, and of Augustine speaking bad Latin to a Greek.' All
later editors of St Augustine's letters, following Erasmus' lead, have omitted
this text altogether.
15 Because the letter purported to be from St Cyril of Jerusalem (c 315–86) is
entitled *De miraculis Hieronymi* 'On the Miracles of Jerome,' Erasmus included
it as the last item in his edition of Jerome's epistles (Basel: Hieronymus Froben
1537) IV 367–86. It carries a similar *censura*, or warning, to the reader about its
dubious authenticity.

if I had the wealth of Croesus it would prove of no avail.[1] For there is no   5
comparison between corporal benefits and those of the soul. You have indeed enriched my soul. It would not be equal recompense, it seems to me, if
it were within my power to load you down with all the riches of this world.
Another avenue must be attempted, which will be satisfactory to us both.
Spiritual things must be compensated by spiritual things. In the end, this   10
one thing I promise in good faith: that as long as I live and even after my
death (if the chance be given me) I shall not cease to call upon the good
and almighty God for the well-being of your soul and body. Accept in good
part, therefore, my sentiments of loyalty towards you; and I should be glad
if you have recourse to your friend Richard as to a son if he can be of any   15
use to you.

Farewell. From London, written impromptu, 3 November
Devotedly yours, Richard Sparcheford
To be delivered to Erasmus of Rotterdam, champion of the Catholic
faith   20

1897 / From Maximilianus Transsilvanus   Houtem, 6 November 1527

This letter (Ep 76 in Förstemann-Günter) is autograph throughout. It was in
the Burscher Collection at the University of Leipzig (on which see Ep 1254
introduction).

For Maximilianus Transsilvanus, see Ep 1802 introduction.

†

Burchardus delivered your letter to me here together with three bundles of
your letters.[1] I shall take diligent and faithful care that they be brought to

* * * * *

1896
1 Sparcheford likely seeks not only to thank Erasmus for the gift of the Chrysostom translations but to praise his works in general. Croesus, the last king
of Lydia (c 560–546 BC), completed the subjugation of the Greek cities on the
Asia Minor coast. His fame for wealth arose from his policy of replacing coins
made from electrum, a natural alloy of gold and silver, with coins of pure gold
and pure silver, a practice adopted in Greece in the fifth century BC.

1897
1 On the courier see Ep 1890 n6. Erasmus' letter to Transsilvanus is not extant. Among the other letters were Epp 1885 and 1888, accompanied by advance copies of the Apologia adversus monachos quosdam Hispanos; see Epp 1879,
1967.

Valdés[2] in Spain by the first courier who leaves from here, so that he may distribute them to their respective addressees. I think, however, that they will arrive too late, since that assembly in Spain which was to concern itself with you was dissolved on 13 August, not without great affirmation of your glory and immortality.[3] You will be able to verify this from the letter that Valdés sent to me and that I forward to you.[4]

I hear that the theologians of Louvain, whether it be because of a letter from the emperor or warnings from the chancellor and others or rumours of what has been going on in Spain, have become much more tractable and amenable and are no longer waging savage warfare against the cause of good letters.[5] I hope that you will soon overcome their hatred. This is all that is lacking during your own lifetime to make your happiness complete.

The emperor thinks only that he is maintaining a general peace.[6] Since you are closer to Italy you must know very well what the French are up to there.[7] I think Fortune is toying with both of them,[8] giving hope of victory now to one and now to the other, so that there would be no end to the war. Farewell, and think kindly of your Maximilianus.

From my country house, 6 November 1527
Your devoted friend Maximilianus Transsilvanus

†

To the illustrious Erasmus of Rotterdam. In Basel

* * * * *

2 Alfonso de Valdés; see Epp 1807 introduction, 1839.

3 The Valladolid conference; see Epp 1791 introduction, 1814 n37, 1846 introduction.

4 Not extant. An earlier letter from Valdés to Transsilvanus, dated 1 August 1527 and relating events of the inquisition and his opinion of some of the delegates, was edited by Caballero *Valdés* Ep 17 335–40.

5 On the emperor's letter to the University of Louvain, now lost, see the introduction to Ep 1784A, from Mercurino Gattinara to the University of Louvain. Valdés himself wrote a similar letter to the chancellor and theologians of Louvain on 12 February 1527; see Caballero *Valdés* Ep 8 321.

6 A subject much on Transsilvanus' mind and that of Valdés (Caballero *Valdés* 337, 345); cf Epp 1888:14–18, 23–6, 1907:55–9.

7 Despite the Peace of Madrid (1526), which left his sons as hostages in Spain, King Francis I ordered Marshal Odet de Foix (Lautrec) to invade Lombardy in August 1527. In early autumn 1527, Andrea Doria took the city of Genoa on behalf of the French. Transsilvanus could not at this time know that Lautrec, bypassing Milan, would take Parma on 7 November as a prelude to a planned march south to Naples – a campaign that ultimately failed.

8 That is, Emperor Charles v and King Francis I

1898 / From Jan Becker of Borsele   Louvain, 6 November 1527

This letter, Ep 77 in Förstemann-Günther, answers Ep 1860. The original, autograph throughout, was in the Burscher Collection at the University of Leipzig
(on which see Ep 1254 introduction).

For Jan Becker, tutor to Maximilian (II) of Burgundy, see Ep 1851 introduction.

Fervent greetings. A few days ago, dear Erasmus, most respected of all
teachers, I received your letter,[1] brought to me from Antwerp by a certain
bookseller. You wrote it there in Basel before the first of September. It gave
me all the more pleasure in that it was long awaited. But this pleasure was
augmented in no small way by the fact that in the midst of your arduous   5
and unceasing occupations you thought fit to write to Maximilian of Burgundy, my pupil in literature. However, almost all the joy engendered by
your letter to me was dispelled when I learned that the letter to Maximilian
had been intercepted or lost through someone's carelessness and neglect.
You can hardly imagine how this fine young man was overjoyed when he   10
learned from my letter that you had also written to him. He supposed that
it must have been included in a pile of letters sent to others all at the same
time. But when his hopes proved false, he could hardly hold back his tears,
and truly not a day goes by without his deploring his misfortune. I should
not have the audacity to ask such a favour of you again, but I thank you for   15
having expended your efforts in such a humble service this once.[2]

Since you indicate that you are not quite sure whether the young man
is the son of Adolph, prince of Veere, I shall tell you about him briefly.
Maximilian, a lad of thirteen, is the first-born son of Adolph of Burgundy,
lord of Beveren.[3] He is indubitably a boy of excellent natural abilities and   20
highest promise. This is the fifth year that I have looked after his education; but before the end of this year he will go to live at the court of

* * * * *

1898
1 Ep 1860
2 On Maximilian see Ep 1859 introduction. Because that letter failed to reach
   Maximilian, Erasmus wrote again (Ep 1927) in January 1528 to assuage the
   boy's disappointment.
3 Maximilian was actually the second son of Adolph, as his elder brother Philip
   III of Burgundy had recently died. In 1528 Erasmus would dedicate his *De
   pronuntiatione* to him (Ep 1984). On Adolph see Ep 1859 n1.

the cardinal of Liège,[4] and I shall return to my curacy in Zeeland[5] and ever remain, as long as I live, your most faithful and devoted servant. Farewell, most learned Erasmus, and I pray you to be mindful of me now and again.

Louvain, 6 November 1527

Jan Becker of Borsele, your most devoted servant

To Erasmus of Rotterdam, most learned in every field of study, teacher worthy of everlasting esteem above all others. In Basel

1899 / From Conradus Goclenius   Louvain, 7 November 1527

This letter was first published by Allen from the original autograph manuscript (Öffentliche Bibliothek of the University of Basel, ms Goclenii Epistolae 3). It answers Ep 1890. For Goclenius, a regent at the Collegium Trilingue, see Ep 1857 introduction.

Warmest greetings. You have demonstrated your sentiments towards me in such tangible ways that all verbal testimony is superfluous. Nevertheless I was extremely touched by your congratulations,[1] since they came so sincerely from your heart. Henceforth I shall be careful not to do anything unworthy of the favour of Erasmus, that is to say, the prince of universal learning. And yet in that very matter for which you especially congratulate me I must give due acknowledgment to you. For if through the diligence and industry of my teaching I have been of any help to the cause of good letters it was accomplished not only under your auspices but also by your assistance. It is with the aid of your writings and following your excellent counsel that I have served up to now in this campaign. The burden becomes sweeter now when I see that I am bringing home a rich reward from a highly lauded and unrivalled commander.

But enough of this; now I shall respond to the rest of your letter. First, concerning the manuscripts of Augustine on the Trinity which have remained here so long not through my fault but because of others who, perhaps because they objected to the weight, said that you would ask for them

* * * * *

4 Erard de la Marck (Epp 738 introduction, 746, 1030, 1038); cf CEBR II 382–5.
5 The deanery of Zanddijk or Zandenburg, near Veere

1899
1 See Ep 1890 n1.

when the proper moment came.[2] I readily gave credence to their words, because when I wrote to you on two occasions that I had them you gave no
answer – at least as far as I can remember, and I am not one to neglect your   20
orders.[3] It is only since the death of Dorp that you indicated your wishes to
me, and I have not rested until I got them back from the Carthusians.[4] In
this I was assisted by Pieter de Corte, director of the College of the Lily.[5]
Therefore I have now entrusted them to Burchardus, an agent of the Froben
firm, whom you sent here.[6] You need not doubt that the corrections were   25
made by Dorp, although you will not recognize his hand. They were copied
by his servant, Jacques Romeroie,[7] under Dorp's direction.

In Donatus' commentaries on Terence I emended innumerable passages
as far as was possible without the aid of ancient manuscripts.[8] I had decided
last year to write to you about this matter so that you might persuade Froben   30
to be kindly disposed, as he now seems to be of his own accord.[9] At that
very time a friend who was aware of my project brought me a short preface
of Johann Sichard, in which he aspires to the palm of praise for the complete commentaries of Donatus, which he claims he will soon publish from
ancient manuscripts.[10] Being perfectly aware that with any ancient manu-   35

* * * * *

2 That is, messengers who, like Nicolaas Kan, had declined or for some other
  reason failed to carry them the long distance to Basel; see Ep 1890 n4.
3 In Ep 1778:22–4 Goclenius acknowledged that Erasmus had asked Hans Bogbinder to recover this copy of the *De Trinitate* annotated by Dorp; but he apparently did not conclude from this that he should dispatch them to Erasmus.
4 Maarten van Dorp, who died on 31 May 1525, had probably collated Erasmus'
  manuscripts with those conserved at the abbey of Gembloux.
5 Pieter de Corte was director of the Lily and a candidate for the doctorate in
  theology. A staunch opponent of the Reformation, he was on good terms with
  Erasmus (CEBR I 344–5).
6 See Ep 1890:13–14 and n6.
7 An amanuensis of the late Maarten van Dorp (CEBR III 169–70)
8 Donatus, the most famous grammarian of the fourth century, numbered
  among his pupils St Jerome. He wrote commentaries on Terence and Virgil, and his *Ars minor* and *Ars major* became standard grammar texts in the
  Middle Ages.
9 See Ep 1890:30, where Erasmus solicited Goclenius' help with Froben's projected edition of 'Terence with commentary.' Goclenius could not yet have
  heard of Froben's death, which occurred on 26 October.
10 The claim appeared in the preface to an edition of annotations on Aulus Gellius
  by Petrus Mosellanus (Basel: Johann Bebel, August 1526). Sichard never produced the edition of Terence, but he did edit a small volume of grammarians
  that included the *Liber de orthographia* of Quintus Terentius Scaurus and some
  works of Donatus (Basel: Adam Petrus, August 1527). A distinguished teacher

script whatever many things can be restored of which there are no traces in printed books, and not doubting that he would fulfil the promises by which he had voluntarily bound himself before a tribune of scholars, I elected to keep silent for a while until I saw 'what this promiser would produce worthy of such mighty claims.'[11] I certainly would be most grateful to him if he made some advancement in the text of Donatus, an excellent authority on Latin. If not, I thought that my own work would still be valuable if, after Sichard had published his, I had made some conjectures that were more correct. But now that he claims to possess that ancient manuscript, I think it is preferable that Froben deal with him, especially since any ancient manuscript cannot but be more correct or at least more capable of being corrected than printed books. As far as I am concerned I would feel happy both for scholars and for Froben, although I'm sure that those who hope to carry off the prize in this affair would not be so ungrudging. But if they would apply themselves to the task with all due diligence and not just routinely, and would not keep us in suspense by long delays, I would wish them all the palms in Idumea,[12] if one palm is not enough for them. But if Sichard disappoints our hopes, as may well happen, and if Froben wishes to make use of what I have done, I shall send him a copy whenever he desires. But I think he must first make some arrangement with Sichard concerning that ancient codex. If he can obtain it he will have no need of my book, as far as I can see.

I am glad that our friend Frans van der Dilft's stay with you was pleasant. I hope that he will heed your advice and reflect seriously about the wisdom of such a long trip.[13] He speaks very highly of your kindnesses to him and solemnly promises that he will do all in his power to live up to my recommendations of him. That is all we can hope for; the rest lies in his own assiduity and in the lap of the gods.[14] I hope that by his services to you he will deserve your continued friendly disposition towards him. I shall therefore

* * * * *

and future rector of the University of Tübingen, Sichard wrote a *Praelectiones in libros codicis Justiniani* (Basel: Johann Michael Fickler 1565; repr 1586), and edited more than twenty volumes of Latin literature and legal texts (CEBR III 247).

11 Horace *Ars poetica* 138
12 The southern part of Judaea known in ancient times for its palm trees, *palmarum dives Idume* (Lucretius *De rerum natura* 3.216)
13 Perhaps a trip to Spain to enter imperial diplomatic service; or perhaps a metaphorical allusion to Dilft's contemplating marriage and abandoning scholarly pursuits – a move Erasmus regretted (Ep 1890:18–20); cf Ep 1857.
14 The phrase 'lap of the gods' is rendered in Greek.

cease commending him to you any further. In a letter I admonished him 65
forcefully not to let the present opportunity go to waste.[15]

Dirk Martens of Aalst sends effusive thanks for the epitaph.[16] He has
been suffering severely for several months from gout in his feet and in his
hands, and indeed he has been spared no form of the malady save for gout
of the tongue. But by I know not what benevolence of destiny, unless it was 70
brought about by your good genius, what usually is ill-omened and harmful to others has proved to be a most auspicious omen for Dirk. For as soon
as the epitaph that you composed for him was brought to him, still alive but
already at the point of death, he was seized with such joy that there was no
room left for the gout or any of its after-effects. In the epitaph, however, al- 75
though it was written by you, he noted one fault, namely that he has not yet
survived all his relatives, since there is still a daughter or granddaughter
of his who is a nun at Aalst. Your poem reads: 'Having survived my brothers, wife, offspring, and friends.'[17] 'Well then,' I said, 'do you want me to
write to Erasmus to correct such a grave error?' 'It is not necessary,' he said. 80
'Time will easily correct it. For I have no doubt that I will live longer than
she; because I see and interpret it as an omen from Erasmus.' And so your
epitaph restored both health and good hope to Dirk.

Here, as far as the tranquillity of studies is concerned, all is perfectly
calm. However, new storms would undoubtedly have arisen if the public en- 85
emies of good studies had had their way in Spain. For instance, at an assembly of leading men of the court of the emperor, a certain person lamented
the Louvain academy's demise (that is how they refer to its diminution of
revenue, while in very fact it has never been so flourishing or crowded with
students). He laid the blame openly on the Collegium Trilingue;[18] I cannot 90

* * * * *

15 The letter is not extant.
16 Dirk Martens had been printing books in Aalst since 1473 and in Louvain
since 1512. In 1518 Martens had lodged Erasmus in his own home and cared
for him, even though doctors had (mistakenly) diagnosed his illness as plague.
He printed fifty of Erasmus' books, and promoted the works of scholars at the
Collegium Trilingue. The epitaph was for Martens himself. Erasmus probably
composed it about this time; see Reedijk *Poems* no 115 / CWE 85–6 348–9, 708–
11 (notes) no 126. Engraved in copper, it was removed from Martens' tomb in
1784. *Pace* CEBR II 394–5, it is no longer displayed in Sint Maarten in Aalst, and
is presumed lost. (Information supplied by Alexandre Vanautgaerden, curator
of the Maison d'Erasme, Brussels.)
17 This is the third line of the epitaph.
18 On the Collegium Trilingue see de Vocht CTL. It was endowed in 1517 by
Jérôme de Busleyden. Goclenius was its Latin professor.

conjecture for what other intention it was done. This accusation was completely ignored by the others, but the Palermitan[19] did not think it should be
ignored. If the other leading men had assented to his remark, all the printing shops would have to shut down. Obviously this seemed to him to be a
very convenient method for remedying all the world's cancers, whose pus,   95
according to him, flows from that source. But now with the victory of your
cause in Spain,[20] the morale of the enemy seems to have declined. I think
you have been fully informed of his position through the letter that I had
forwarded to you with Christoph von Carlowitz, the German nobleman. He
left here for Basel on 26 October, partly to become better acquainted with   100
you and partly to enjoy the company of his old friend Ludovicus Carinus
by staying with him for a while.[21] In any event, if some unforeseen obstacles have delayed him on the way, you may be sure he will soon be
with you.[22]

I shall send your letter to Maarten Lips as soon as a messenger is avail-   105
able.[23] He will find it all the more agreeable because of the golden contents
of the letter. From Lips I also send you notes of various readings in several works of Augustine. You could have known of these from a letter of
his which I entrusted to Carlowitz along with the others.[24] I presume you
have heard from Ceratinus of the misfortune of Hadrianus Cordatus.[25] He   110

* * * * *

19 τῷ Πανορμίτῃ, referring to Jean (II) de Carondelet (on whom see Ep 1806 introduction). CEBR I 272–3 does not mention his siding with this unnamed critic
of the Collegium Trilingue.
20 The inquisitorial assembly at Valladolid had closed *sine die* on 13 August 1527
due to danger of plague.
21 Such a letter is not known; see also line 108 below. Formerly a student of
Petrus Mosellanus, Carlowitz had probably visited Erasmus earlier in 1524.
He studied with Goclenius in 1527, and would serve Erasmus intermittently
for the next two years before entering the service of King Ferdinand I and
Prince George of Saxony (CEBR I 269–70). On Carinus see Ep 1890 n10.
22 The ending of this phrase is conjectural: in beginning a new page, Goclenius
neglected to complete the sentence. Ep 1924 shows that Carolwitz had arrived
in Basel by December.
23 The letter is not extant; perhaps answering Ep 1837, it was probably contemporary with Ep 1890. Lips, a priest at St Maartensdal in Louvain, had been
transferred to Lens, near Liège, perhaps because of his advocacy for Erasmus.
See Ep 1837 introduction.
24 Not extant; perhaps the same letter mentioned above in line 98
25 On Jacobus Ceratinus, an accomplished scholar and an acquaintance of long
standing, see Ep 1843 introduction. Cordatus was a canon of St Peter's, Mid-
delburg, and vicar of West-Souburg, both on the island of Walcheren located at
the mouth of the Scheldt River. His misfortune was imprisonment on suspicion

is now paying a very heavy penalty for his unbridled tongue.[26] He is still in prison; although there is hope that he will soon be freed.

But I am ashamed of my lengthy chattering and shall not add another word,[27] save to mention that which you alone among mortals deserve above all and without ceasing: namely that you enjoy the best of health 115 and that through your immortal works you make this the most blessed of eras.

Louvain, 7 November 1527
Yours, Conradus Goclenius
To the distinguished Erasmus of Rotterdam 120

1900 / To Jan of Heemstede [Basel, ? November 1527]

This letter, a Lamentation on the Death of Johann Froben, was printed first in a volume containing the *Ciceronianus* and the *De recte pronuntiatione* (Basel: Hieronymus Froben, March 1528), and was reprinted with slight revisions in later editions and in other works.

Jan Symons, better known under the name of his native village of Heemstede (near Haarlem), was a painter and illuminator with humanist credentials who became a Carthusian in 1521 and was ordained a priest in 1522. His first contact with Erasmus involved an epitaph for the tomb of Maarten van Dorp in the Carthusian house at Louvain, which Erasmus sent with Ep 1646; that precedent likely inspired Erasmus to address this formal letter to Heemstede containing two epitaphs for Johann Froben (CEBR II 171).

ERASMUS OF ROTTERDAM TO JAN OF HEEMSTEDE, CARTHUSIAN, GREETING

Although I have reached this advanced age, most virtuous friend, I have learned from experience that I am not yet sufficiently known to myself. Yes, and I thought that through the precepts of philosophy and the long and 5 almost uninterrupted experience of enduring misfortunes I was sufficiently prepared for those common daily occurrences that we see can be borne stoically even by the frail female sex. But the unexpected death of my friend Johann Froben has so afflicted my spirit that no distraction has been able

* * * * *

of sympathizing with Luther – the same sentiments that Erasmus had at one time mistakenly attributed to Ceratinus.
26 Rendered in Greek; cf *Anthologia Planudea* (an expurgated selection of Greek epigrams) 4.89.6.
27 Cf Horace *Satires* 1.1.121.

to free my heart of this grief.[1] And time, which can assuage even the most   10
grievous of sorrows, far from alleviating my distress, has made it increase
a little more each day, as relentless as a slow and insidious fever that steals
upon us unawares. There is nothing more irremediable, they say. A visceral
anxiety consumed me despite my efforts to resist. How much more powerful are the bonds created by spiritual affinity and mutual sympathy than   15
are those of nature! How much have I struggled with myself! With what reproaches have I blamed myself! Where now, I ask myself, is that rhetorician
who with a brilliant display of words can ease or banish the sorrow of others? Where is that Stoic philosopher, the tamer of human emotions? Where
the theologian who used to teach that the death of pious men should be ac-   20
companied not by tears and mourning but by congratulations and applause?
Need I go on? Never was I more ashamed of myself. Never before have I experienced the force of sincere friendship and of the mutual bond that joins
kindred spirits. The death of my own brother I bore with resignation,[2] the
loss of Froben I cannot bear. I am not angry at my sorrow, which is most jus-   25
tified, but I am exasperated that it is excessive and too prolonged. Then too,
just as the love I bore him in life derived from no single cause, so the longing inspired by his death does not spring from any one single cause. I loved
him more for the sake of liberal studies, for the enhancement and progress
of which he seemed called by divine destiny, than for his predilection for   30
me or for his blameless life.

Who would not love a man of such character? He was an incomparable friend to his friends, so simple and sincere that even if he had wished
to pretend or dissemble he would not have been able to do so, since it was
contrary to his nature. He was so ready and eager to do good to everyone   35
that he took joy in bringing some advantage even to the undeserving. Thus
he was liked and appreciated by swindlers and debtors alike. If money was
stolen from him or withheld by debtors in bad faith he would mention it
with the same good cheer with which other men greeted some unexpected
windfall. He was of such incorruptible honesty that the saying 'You could   40

* * * * *

1900
1 Froben's death occurred on 26 October 1527 (Allen VII xxii, correcting the date
  given at line 6n of this letter). Successor to the Basel press founded by Johannes Petri and Johann Amerbach, Johann Froben was Erasmus' preferred
  printer and close friend, as he makes clear in this letter. On Froben and his
  press see A. Hernandez in Gewerbemuseum Basel *Johann Froben und der Basler
  Buchdruck des 16. Jahrhunderts: Ausstellung* (Basel 1960); CEBR II 60–3; ER II 451–4.
2 Pieter Gerard, whom Erasmus mentioned only rarely, was three years older.
  His date of death is unknown (CEBR I 441–2).

play morra with him in the dark'[3] fitted no one more than him. And just as he did not plot deceit against anyone so he could not suspect others of it, although he was frequently the victim of fraud. He was no more capable of conceiving what the disease of envy was than those born blind can imagine what colour is. He pardoned offences, even those deserving capital punish-   45
ment, before asking who had committed them. He was unable to remember a wrong done to him or forget the most banal service rendered him.

    And yet in this regard, it seems to me, he was more virtuous some-times than was expedient for a vigilant father of a family. I would advise him from time to time that he could conduct himself as he saw fit with true   50
friends but that with impostors, while he might be benevolent in words, he should be on his guard lest he suffer ridicule as well as loss. He would smile in a kindly manner, but I was singing my tune to deaf ears.[4] The kindness of his nature vanquished every admonition. And, as for myself, what snares did he not lay for me, what occasion did he not seek to thrust some gift upon   55
me? And I never saw him more happy than when he had succeeded either by cunning or entreaty to have me accept something. There was need of the utmost caution to avoid the traps he set. And never did I need my rhetoric more than in finding the right tone in which to refuse what he was forcing upon me without giving offence to a friend. For I could not bear to see him   60
sad. If it happened that one of my servants had to buy cloth for a garment, he would get wind of it beforehand and pay for it without my knowing it, and no manner of entreaty could induce him to accept reimbursement. I would have had to resort to similar ingenuity if I had wished to save him from some loss. Such was the contest that went on between us continually,   65
far different from the behaviour of the common crowd, when one person strives to make off with as much as possible and the other to give as little as possible. I could not prevent him from giving me something, but cer-tainly his entire family will bear witness, I think, that I availed myself of his generosity with the greatest moderation.   70

    Whatever labours I undertook were undertaken for the love of literary studies. Since he seemed born to give honour, distinction, and advancement to them and spared no toil, no vigils, thinking it reward enough if a good author could be put into men's hands in a fitting manner, how could I have played the predator with a man so highly motivated? Whenever he showed   75

* * * * *

3 *Adagia* I viii 23. Morra or mora is a game of Italian origin in which one player
   tries to guess the number of fingers held up simultaneously by another.
4 *Adagia* I iv 87

me and other friends the first pages of some great author, how filled with joy he was, what enthusiasm there was in his face, what an air of triumph! You would say that he had already reaped the fruit of all his labours abundantly and expected no other recompense. I shall not here extol Froben's merits by criticizing others. It is too well known what faulty and shoddy editions of   80
the authors are sent to us by certain printers, even from Venice and Rome. But from his house in a very few years what volumes have appeared, and with what elegance! And he kept his workshop free of contentious little books,[5] from which others derived no mean profit, to avoid contaminating literature and the learned disciplines with feelings of ill will.   85

He had printed Jerome twice.[6] When he wished to print Augustine again in similar fashion, several friends, myself among them, tried to dissuade him. But he had so set his mind upon it that he was often heard to say among his employees that he wished his life to last no longer than was necessary to complete the Augustine.[7] He saw the first and second volumes   90
to completion.[8] His wish was a pious one, and that desire was worthy of everlasting remembrance; but it was decided otherwise by divine wisdom,[9] whose designs are hidden, and it is not for us to question or criticize them.

He was rather advanced in years, but his health was so stable and vigorous that he never succumbed to any illness throughout his whole life. Six   95
years ago,[10] he fell from the top of a stairway onto a brick pavement. It was a fall that could easily have resulted in death. He recovered nevertheless but, as might be expected, some effects of the accident remained, no matter how much he tried to conceal it. He was of such noble spirit that he was ashamed to show pain. A year before he died he was seized by a terrible   100
pain in the heel of his right foot. Doctors rushed to offer assistance, which

* * * * *

5 In the case of Luther's early pamphlets, however, it was rather Erasmus' threats to withdraw his own works from Froben's press that prevailed upon Froben to cease. See Epp 904 20n, 1033:52–5, 1143:23–5 and n6, 1167:305–7, 1195:143–4.
6 Both editions in nine volumes, the first in 1516 (Ep 396), the second in 1524–6 (Ep 1465)
7 Froben's predecessor Amerbach issued the first Basel edition in 1506. The second edition (ten volumes), a burden on both the press and its editors, finally appeared in 1529.
8 The colophons of both bear the date 1528; but Erasmus' prefatory letter to volume II (Ep 1895A) must be dated prior to Froben's death on 26 October 1527.
9 Virgil Aeneid 2.428
10 Hence about the time of Erasmus' return from Louvain in late 1521

only served to aggravate the pain.[11] They disagreed about the nature of the malady and each attempted his own remedy; some even prescribed amputating the foot. Finally a doctor from another place arrived who alleviated the pain,[12] making it tolerable enough to permit him to sleep and to eat. In the end he recovered sufficiently to journey to Frankfurt twice on horseback.[13] The pain was confined to the toes of his right foot, which he was not able to bend. For the rest, he was in sound condition. I warned him repeatedly, as did his doctor, that he should go outdoors less frequently or dress more warmly to protect himself against the cold, but he did not listen. He considered it shameful to omit any of his former activities, since that would be an indication of his illness. By now the paralysis had extended to two fingers of his right hand, a prelude to the impending attack. Finally, while he was engaged in some work in a high place, seized probably by an attack of the illness, he fell head first to the ground and sustained a serious injury to the cranium. Carried to his bed, he never opened his eyes or gave any sign of consciousness, nor indeed any sign of life at all, except that he moved his left hand. The paralysis that he had concealed had immobilized his whole right side. After remaining in a coma for two days he regained consciousness just before dying. With difficulty he half opened his left eye, but his tongue remained paralysed. He did not survive more than six hours.

Thus our friend Froben, removed from the affairs of men, passed to a happier life, leaving his wife, children, and friends in bitter grief, and the whole city and all his acquaintances in deepest mourning.[14] At his death it behoves all those who cultivate good letters to shed tears and put on mourning; they should adorn his grave with parsley and flowerets, pour libations, and burn incense,[15] if such rites were of any avail. In any case, to express

* * * * *

11 Erasmus' opinion of doctors could sometimes be laudatory (for example Jan Antonin, Guillaume Cop, and Paracelsus) but was often negative (for example Ep 1729:21–2: 'The doctors are no more helpful than a swarm of flies'). See also Ep 1915:37–8 and n12.
12 Presumably Theophrastus Paracelsus; see Ep 1809:22–4. He is probably also the doctor mentioned in line 109.
13 In March and September 1527 (Ep 1875:26), proving Erasmus' fear in December 1526 (Ep 1769:16–17) that he might no longer be able to make the trip (his only comment at the time) to be wrong.
14 A native of Hammelburg (in Lower Franconia, Bavaria), Froben had acquired citizenship in Basel in 1492, and was a member of the distinguished 'Schlüssel' guild since 1522. His widow, Gertrud Lachner, would shortly marry Johann Herwagen. We know of two sons: Hieronymus, Froben's eldest son by his first wife, and Erasmius, his younger son with Gertrud Lachner.
15 Cf Virgil Eclogues 6.68.

our gratitude let us all offer fervent prayers for the deceased, celebrate his
memory with fitting eulogies, and give our support to the Froben press.
For not only will it not cease its activities because of the passing of its mas-   130
ter but it will strive with all its strength to improve what he instituted into
something greater and better.

You are receiving the epitaphs for Dorp later perhaps than you expected but with interest that will make up for the delay.[16]

EPITAPH FOR JOHANN FROBEN BY ERASMUS OF ROTTERDAM[17]   135

This stone marks Johann Froben's lifeless bones,[18]
Whose fame, undying, lives through all the world.
His life was pure, his gift to learning great,
Which, like an orphan, mourns its grievous loss.
He with devotion, riches, skill, and care   140
Rescued and graced the wisdom of the past.[19]
Grant him, O Lord, in heav'n eternal life.
With us on earth his fame will never die.[20]

* * * * *

16 Erasmus had already sent his epitaph for Dorp, who died on 31 May 1525 (Ep
    1646:22–44); cf Reedijk *Poems* no 113 / CWE 85–6 154–5, 546–7 (notes) no 71.
    He appended to this letter two epitaphs for Froben as 'interest.' When this let-
    ter was first printed with the *Ciceronianus* and *De recta pronuntiatione* (Basel:
    Hieronymus Froben, March 1528) it was followed by sixteen pages of epi-
    taphs: the two on Froben by Erasmus (as here) along with others on Froben
    by Henricus Glareanus and Hilarius Bertholf; then verses on Maarten van
    Dorp by Jacob Volkaerd, Conradus Goclenius, Frans van Cranevelt, Erasmus,
    Germain de Brie, and Alaard of Amsterdam, with prose laments by Adri-
    anus Cornelii Barlandus and Juan Luis Vives. There are as well four lines
    by Erasmus, never reprinted by him elsewhere, on Jacob Volkaerd (Reedijk
    Poems no 114 / CWE 85–6 156–7, 547 [notes] no 72), who died shortly after
    his friend Dorp. Later printings removed the epitaphs on Dorp but added
    three more on Froben by Andrea Alciati and Janus Cornarius. See Allen Ep
    1900:130n.
17 This Latin epigram and the Greek one which follows it, along with an epitaph
    in Hebrew, were engraved on Froben's tomb in St Peter's Church, Basel; see
    Alfred Hartmann *Basilea latina* (Basel 1931) 199–200. The Hebrew inscription is
    the only source confirming the date of Froben's death as 26 October 1527. The
    original metre of the Latin epigram is elegiac distich and of the Greek epigram
    trochaic tetrameter catalectic. The translation here is in iambic pentameter; for
    prose translations see CWE 85–6 156, 548 (notes) nos 73–4.
18 *arida ... ossa*, probably a reference to the 'dry bones' passage of Ezek 37:4
19 Cf Virgil *Aeneid* 3.102.
20 Ovid *Amores* 1.10.62

FOR THE SAME MAN BY THE SAME AUTHOR, IN GREEK

So here the printer Johann Froben sleeps.
To no one letters owe a greater debt.
Mourn not his death: his deathless soul lives on.
His fame lies in the legacy of books.

1901 / To Martin Bucer   Basel, 11 November 1527

The manuscript of this letter, autograph throughout except for the address in a
secretary's hand, is in the Parker Library at Corpus Christi College, Cambridge
(119 21). It was first printed, with slight variants, in the *Opus epistolarum* (1529).
   Martin Bucer, or Butzer (1491–1551), a Dominican friar and priest, was a
trained theologian who adopted a humanistic approach early in his studies.
In 1521 he obtained release from his vows in the Dominican Order and was
incardinated into his diocese as a secular priest. At about the same time he
became enthusiastic about Luther's movement, but by 1525 he had adopted
the more radical Eucharistic theology of Zwingli. By 1527 Bucer had become
the pastor of a reformed church in Strasbourg. The letter answers another (not
extant) in which Bucer had apparently asked Erasmus for an interview with
himself and other Strasbourg reformers who planned to pass through Basel
on their way to the theological disputation at Bern, but the interview did not
take place. The polite tone of friendship present here later dissolved, with
Erasmus and Bucer both publishing accusations against each other. See J.V.
Pollet *Martin Bucer: Etudes sur la correspondance, avec de nombreux textes inédits*
2 vols (Paris 1958–62); cf CEBR I 209–12; OER I 221–4.

Warm greetings. You plead the cause of Capito like a practised rhetorician;
but I see that despite your eloquence as an advocate you are not sufficiently
equipped for this defence. If I were to marshall my arguments and conclusions, you would see that you have to devise another speech. But I have had
my fill of disputes, and I am not easily stirred up against those whom I have
loved sincerely. What the knight Eppendorf has dared or not dared is his
business, except that he plays this game too often. I will not involve Capito
in this play, unless he involves himself in it again. He must not think that
I am so stupid as not to understand what is going on. But I have written to
him about these matters.[1] Furthermore, as to your pleading your cause and

* * * * *

1901
1 Erasmus' friendship with Wolfgang Faber (or Fabricius) Capito of Haguenau,
   a former Benedictine monk and humanist and, with Martin Bucer, an architect

the cause of your church,[2] I think it preferable to make no reply, because even if the situation were not dangerous it would require a very lengthy speech. I shall confine myself to a few select comments.

The man who conveyed information to me about the teaching of languages is a person whose reliability not even you would despise; and he does not have a bad opinion of you either.[3] Moreover, I never entertained any adverse opinion of you, at least as far as personal feelings are concerned. The people who live in your part of the world are the same ones who used to blather on here about all studies being the invention of evil spirits. Make no mistake, wherever this race of men is in power, whatever name they go under, all serious learning languishes and falls into abeyance.[4] At Nürnberg teachers are hired with funds from the public treasury, but there are no students.[5]

As for yourself, you are putting together many conjectures about why I did not enrol in your church. Well, you can be assured that first and foremost what kept me from allying myself with you was my conscience. If I could have been persuaded that these developments proceed from God, I would have been fighting in your camp long ago. A further reason is that I see that there are many in this flock who are estranged from any evangelical

* * * * *

of the Strasbourg reformed church, did not survive Capito's conversion to the Reformation and Erasmus' suspicion that he supported the attacks of Heinrich Eppendorf; see Epp 1368, 1374, 1485; CEBR I 261–4; and cf Ep 1893 n16. In Ep 1923:17 Erasmus tells Hieronymus Emser that Capito and other reformers were in Basel in connection with the theological disputations at Bern.

2 That is, the reformed church in Strasbourg. Erasmus had already refused to give it his approval (Ep 1485:7).

3 Allen (14n) infers that Bucer had objected to the report of an unnamed correspondent who told Erasmus that schools in reformed cities taught little else beyond 'dogmas and languages.' Observing a close connection between this and passages in Erasmus' *Epistola ad fratres Inferioris Germaniae* (Basel: Hieronymus Froben, 1 August 1530; cf LB X 1598A–B), Allen conjectures that this unnamed critic is Willibald Pirckheimer, a surmise borne out by Erasmus' 1531 letter to Helius Eobanus Hessus (Ep 2446 passim) in which Erasmus deplores trends in the Nürnberg schools on the evidence of letters (not extant) from Pirckheimer, and likewise assigns blame for similar trends in reformed universities to those who call themselves 'evangelicals' (Allen Ep 2446:101–14). Eobanus had himself earlier attributed the decline of education at Erfurt to the hostile positions of Protestant preachers, but he was himself now teaching at Nürnberg's St Aegidius Gymnasium, founded recently by Philippus Melanchthon; cf CEBR I 434–6.

4 Cf Epp 1828:30–3, 1875:152–4.

5 See n3 above; for this allegation about Nürnberg cf Allen Epp 2006:15–17, 2008:33–4.

sincerity. I am not speaking of rumours and suspicions but of things I have 30
learned from experience, and indeed my own bitter experience, not just
among the rank and file but even among those who seem to count for something, not to speak of their leaders. As for those I do not know it is not mine
to judge; the world is a big place. I knew some excellent men before they became involved with this movement; I do not know what they are like now. 35
It is clear that some have become worse and none better,[6] as far as human
judgment can discern.

The third thing that deterred me is the great dissension that exists
among the leaders of the whole affair.[7] Without even mentioning the prophets[8] and the Anabaptists,[9] just look at how Zwingli, Luther, and Osian- 40
der wrangle among themselves in their nasty little books.[10] I have never approved of violence in leaders, but the behaviour of certain individuals instigates it in this case; whereas, if what you boast of really existed among
you, it would have behoved them to promote the gospel by sanctity and tol-
eration. Let me give just one example from many: what was the purpose of 45
Luther's insulting behaviour towards the king of England when, with all
the world's approval, he had undertaken such a difficult enterprise?[11] Did
he not consider what role he was playing? Was he not aware that the eyes

* * * * *

6 Cf Ep 1887:12–13, 17–48.
7 The disparity in doctrine and dissension between various reformers would
   become a common counter-Reformation charge, especially with early Catholic
   polemicists like Johannes Cochlaeus and Florimond de Raemond and, a century later, Jacques Bénigne Bossuet.
8 Probably the so-called Zwickau prophets, upon whom Erasmus had commented as early as February 1522. See Ep 1258 n13; cf OER IV 318–19.
9 Anabaptists rejected the practice of infant baptism and preached the necessity to rebaptize mature believers. They were roundly rejected by mainstream
   reformers and by civil governments in general. Prominent early Anabaptists
   were Thomas Müntzer, Conrad Grebel, Georg Blaurock, and Balthasar Hub-
   maier. See OER I 31–5, II 260–2.
10 In the controversy over the mode of presence of Christ in the Eucharist, Andreas Osiander (c 1496–1552), the principal reformer in Nürnberg by 1522, took
   a middle position between Zwingli's symbolic interpretation and Luther's defence of a real presence. He would later develop independent views on Chris-
   tology and justification; see CEBR III 35–6, OER III 183–4.
11 Luther's *Contra Henricum regem Angliae* (Wittenberg: Johann Grunenberg, November 1522) and *Antwortt deutsch Mart. Luthers auff König Henrichs von Engelland buch* (Wittenberg: Nickel Schirlentz, August 1522) sharply attacked King
   Henry VIII for his treatise *Assertio septem sacramentorum* (London: Richard Pynson 1523; STC 13078). For this and all the polemic around it see Epp 1773 n7,
   1869 n1.

of the whole world were turned on him alone? And he is the director of the whole show! I am angry with him not so much because he has treated me so offensively but because he betrayed the cause of the gospel, turned princes, bishops, pseudomonks and pseudotheologians against good men and redoubled their servitude, which was already unbearable: this is what torments me. I can almost see before my eyes a bloody and bloodthirsty age once those he has provoked catch their breath again, which is clearly what is happening now. You will say that there is no large group of people that does not have its share of bad persons mixed in. Surely it was the responsibility of the leaders to make morals their chief concern and not deign even to speak to liars, perjurers, drunkards, and debauchees. Now I am told that the situation is quite the opposite, and I can almost see it with my own eyes. If a husband found a more obliging wife, or a teacher more obedient pupils, or a magistrate more docile citizens; if an employer found more loyal workers, or a buyer less deceitful sellers, this would be a strong recommendation of their evangelical teaching. But as things stand, the morals of certain ones among them serve only to cool the enthusiasm of those who first supported this movement through love of piety or hatred of pharisaism. Princes, even those who at the beginning had nourished good hopes, now stand aghast when they see emerging an unruly[12] populace of vagrants, fugitives, debtors, the unclad, the indigent, and every kind of villain.

I cannot relate these things without extreme sadness, not only because I foresee that a matter begun in the wrong way will end up worse but also because I will suffer for it in the end.[13] Certain ill-wishers impute it to my writings that in some quarters scholastic theologians and monks are less esteemed than they would wish, that rites are being abandoned, that the authority of the Roman pontiff is neglected, although it is no mystery from what source this evil has sprung. The monks have stretched the rope too taut, and now it is breaking.[14] They placed the authority of the pope almost above that of Christ; they measured piety by external observances, they bound men with enormous constraints in confession;[15] the monks reigned unchallenged, openly plotting the cruelest

* * * * *

12 Greek in the manuscript
13 *Adagia* I i 84, from Donatus' commentary on Terence *Eunuchus*
14 *Adagia* I v 67, an allusion repeated twice more in this paragraph
15 The theological basis for auricular confession was the Gospel text 'Whatsoever you shall bind on earth, it shall be bound also in heaven' (Matt 16:19, 18:18); cf Allen Ep 1976:69.

brutality.[16] Finally, as the proverb has it, the stretched rope broke. It could not have turned out otherwise. And I am desperately afraid that the same thing will happen one day to princes if they continue to stretch their rope beyond the limit. On the other hand, when the other side[17] began to enact   85
its part of the play there could be no other outcome than the one we behold. And would that we may witness nothing more terrible!

If the leaders of this affair[18] had Christ as their goal, they should have abstained not only from vices but from every form of evil; and instead of presenting a stumbling block to the gospel they should have zealously   90
avoided things that may be permissible but are of no profit.[19] Above all they should have avoided all discord. If they had handled the matter with frankness and moderation, they would have obtained the favour of princes and bishops, for not all of them are beyond hope. Nor should anything have been done away with arbitrarily without having on hand something better   95
to substitute for what was worse. As matters stand now, those who have rejected hourly prayers[20] do not pray at all. Many who put off their pharisaical garb[21] are worse in every other way than they were before. Those who ignore the constitutions issued by bishops[22] refuse to obey the commandments of God. Those who disregard the rules about fasting and abstinence[23] 100
now indulge the gullet and the belly. It is a long tragedy, which we partly hear about every day and partly learn from others. I never approved of the abolition of the mass, even if this sordid and mercenary tribe who perform priestly functions has always irked me.[24] And other things could have been

* * * * *

16 *phalarismum*. Phalaris was a brutal tyrant in Sicily; in *Adagia* I x 86 the Greek word is translated 'Phalarism.'
17 Those rising up against oppression, both in religion and in polity
18 That is, reformers such as Luther, Zwingli, and 'evangelicals' like Farel and Oecolampadius
19 Cf 1 Cor 6:12.
20 That is, the duty of praying the breviary at fixed times every day, imposed by canon law on clerics in major orders, which grew out of the monastic practice of prayer seven times a day. On the development of the Divine Office see Ep 1815 n5.
21 That is, the religious habits worn by different monastic and mendicant orders
22 Decrees issued at diocesan synods or provincial councils that became part of the corpus of canon law or of diocesan custom
23 Christian adults living in communion with Rome were bound by strict laws of fasting and of abstinence from meat during the forty days of Lent, on four three-day periods known as Ember days, and on other specified liturgical occasions. They had to abstain from eating meat every Friday of the year.
24 Erasmus objected to priests who demanded an offering of money to celebrate mass or administer sacraments to the faithful.

changed without upheaval. Now there are some who are not pleased with   105
anything that is traditional, as if a new world could suddenly be established.
There will always be things that pious men must put up with. If someone
wishes to abolish the mass altogether because many abuse it, then the sacred sermon – almost the only thing that you have retained – must also be
abolished. I feel the same way about the invocations to the saints and about   110
statues.

　　Your letter required a longer answer; but, considering my occupations,
this is very long. I hear that you are endowed with brilliant talents for
preaching the gospel and that you are a man of greater civility than many
others. Therefore I wish that in your wisdom you would strive from this   115
moment on through constancy, moderateness of doctrine, and integrity of
life to guide this movement, however it may have begun, to an outcome
worthy of the gospel. To this end you will have me as your helper to the
best of my ability. Now, despite the onslaught of the phalanxes of the monks
and of a few theologians using every device at their disposal, nothing shall   120
make me knowingly suffer the loss of this little soul of mine. It will be a
mark of your prudence not to spread this letter abroad lest it stir up some
commotion.[25] If I could see you in person I should say more. Farewell.

　　Basel. The feast of St Martin in the year 1527

　　I had no time to look this over.   125

　　Erasmus of Rotterdam, in my own hand. To Master Martin Bucer, pastor in Strasbourg. In Strasbourg

1902 / To the Faculty of Theology of Paris   Basel, 12 November 1527

　　Erasmus had last written to the faculty of theology of the University of Paris on
23 June 1526 (Ep 1723), at the same time as he wrote to the Parlement of Paris
and to King Francis I (Epp 1721 and 1722). Those letters arrived too late to affect the faculty's condemnation of the Colloquies (16 May 1526), but the letter to
King Francis provoked him to order Noël Béda's Annotationes against Erasmus
and Lefèvre d'Etaples to be removed from sale. This injunction notwithstanding, by December 1526 the faculty was conducting a full-scale investigation of
Erasmus' books without royal interference.

　　About 7 July 1527, however, Francis wrote to the University of Paris (that
is, the four faculties of theology, law, medicine, and arts convened together)
the letter translated immediately below from the French text (Simancas MS Est

* * * * *

25 Contrary to this plea, Erasmus himself would publish this letter, with slight
　　variations, in the Opus epistolarum (1529) after he had moved from Basel, which
　　embraced the Reformation, to the Catholic city of Freiburg-im-Breisgau.

2687 1). Allen erroneously labelled it 'From Francis I to the Theological Faculty at Paris' (which we have emended) and published it preceding Ep 1902. With this letter the king also sent a personal envoy to deliver to the university the small book, anonymously authored and printed, *Duodecim articuli infidelitatis magistri Natalis Bedae ex libro suarum annotationum excerpti, reprobantur & confutantur*, on which see Ep 1875 n30. It purported to disclose heresies and blasphemies in Béda's *Annotationes*. When the university convened, Béda tried to apologize for any trouble he might have brought on it; in any case, the four faculties cleared him of all blame and denounced not Béda but the *Duodecim articuli* as impious and dangerous, and they expressed complete confidence in whatever judgment the faculty of theology would make about it. The masters also decided to ask the king to forbid sale of this book, which carried, in their opinion, 'such a scandalous title' (Bibliothèque de la Sorbonne, Archives de l'Université de Paris, Reg 16 f 87r–88v). The theologians resumed their examination of Erasmus' works, and on 16 December 1527 condemned 114 propositions drawn mostly from Erasmus' *Paraphrases* on the New Testament and his books against Béda, but withheld publication of their condemnation until July 1531 (Paris: Josse Bade). A separate undated edition of these censures, thought by Philippe Renouard to be earlier but not prior to September 1529, is now judged to have appeared later in 1532 (Renouard *Imprimeurs* II no 774). Two later editions are known (Cologne: Melchior Novessanus 1543, and Venice: Aldine Press 1549). On 23 June 1528, Béda succeeded in getting the whole University of Paris to ratify the theologians' censures of Erasmus, including their earlier censure of his *Colloquies*. On these events, see Farge *Orthodoxy* 190–6 and CWE 82 introduction.

Allen, taking his cue from the salutation employed by the editors of the *Opus epistolarum* (Basel 1529), headed this letter 'To the Sorbonne.' Erasmus, who was living in Freiburg-im-Breisgau at that time, never uses the term 'Sorbonne' in the letter. He uses instead the general term *collegium* six times, but employs the more restricted term *facultas* four times. Ep 1922:40 makes it clear that Erasmus addressed this letter to the faculty of theology of the University of Paris, not to 'the Sorbonne' – a misnomer for the faculty of theology infrequently employed elsewhere by Erasmus and frequently used by historians today but never used in official documents of that time (see Farge *Orthodoxy* 3–4). We have retained the salutation used by the Basel editors in 1529 but have corrected the address to its proper form. Delivery of Erasmus' letter was delayed when it was confiscated in Alsace with a whole packet of his letters dispatched at the same time; see Ep 1922:40. Nothing in the faculty of theology's proceedings alludes to its reception or to the 'brief responses to certain articles' (line 13 below) that Erasmus enclosed with it. Those articles may simply be an advance copy of the *Apologia adversus monachos quosdam Hispanos* that Erasmus had already sent to Spain (Epp 1879 introduction) and would shortly send to Jan Łaski in Poland (Ep 1915 n21).

From Francis I to the University of Paris   Saint-Denis, [c 7 July 1527]

FROM THE KING

Dear and esteemed friends:[1] Soon after our return into our kingdom,[2] having been notified by learned men about a certain book composed and published by master Noël Béda,[3] doctor of theology, containing several errors, heresies, and blasphemies, we ordered the said book to be confiscated and withheld 5 from sale until such time as we would otherwise ordain.[4] But because, prior to our said ordinance or otherwise, the aforesaid book was distributed and published in divers places,[5] to the great scandal of several of our subjects and others, and, as is to be feared, is infected with the said errors and heresies, principally in that the said Béda, we have been told, maintains that his said 10 book was approved by our dear and esteemed friends the dean and faculty of theology,[6] and under this pretence remains pertinacious and obstinate in his said errors: to this end we send herewith a little treatise written against the said book, containing, as the title says, twelve articles of infidelity of the said

* * * * *

1 Translating freely the formulaic 'Chiers et bien amez,' or 'Dear and well-beloved'
2 From his captivity in Spain after having been taken prisoner on 24 February 1525 in the battle of Pavia. After signing the Treaty of Madrid and giving his sons as hostages until a ransom had been paid, Francis re-entered France on 17 March 1526. He made his way very slowly through France, lingering in the Loire valley and then at Saint-Germain-en-Laye, not making his official entry into Paris until 14 April 1527.
3 Francis had learned about Beda's *Annotationes* from Erasmus himself; see Ep 1722, dated 16 June 1526.
4 That Francis I forbade the sale of Béda's book because he thought it contained not simply unwarranted criticism of Lefèvre and Erasmus but also heresies and blasphemies is something we learn from no other source.
5 The king ordered Josse Bade's Paris edition to be withdrawn from sale and an inventory of all unsold copies to be made; but Bade reported to Béda that he had already sold or dispatched throughout Europe 600 of the 650 copies he had printed (Paris, Archives nationales x^{1a} 1529 f 371r–v). The book was then reprinted at Cologne (Petrus Quentell 1527).
6 The faculty of theology had approved Béda's book on 15 February 1526 after hearing the report from the three masters (Jacques Pasquet, Jean Gaillart, and Jacques Berthélemy) who had been delegated one month earlier to review it; Farge *Procès-verbaux* 126 no 141A.

A symbolic depiction of the court of King Francis I
Cabinet des Estampes, Bibliothèque nationale de France, Paris

master Noël Béda with the confutations of each, so that you may send to us   15
your advice and doctrinal opinion on this matter.[7]

And because the said Béda, as the syndic of the aforesaid faculty or otherwise, may have several disciples and devotees, and because the matter is
of great importance, we desire that in this matter you proceed according to
your customary manner of making decisions, and that all the doctors and mas-   20
ters or regents of the four faculties of our said university read attentively
and carefully the aforesaid twelve articles with their rebuttals contained in
the said treatise that we are sending to you;[8] and that after comparison of
the said book of the aforesaid Béda with the said articles and rebuttals and
after mature deliberation on them, setting aside every bias and intrigue, you   25
send to us the determination or conclusion that you shall have jointly decided about the said twelve articles, whatever it may be, along with your
reasons and motives, if you have thus decided that the twelve articles seem
to you to be true; as well the resolution of the arguments and reasons contained in the rebuttals of the same, should you find them not sufficiently   30
refuted, to this end: that we may give orders in the matter of these doctrines and their authors as reason dictates and without any doubt or scruple. For we have no intention of protecting any monsters in our kingdom,
but rather of extirpating from it all errors, heresies, and blasphemies, especially the most manifest and public ones, along with their authors, their sup-   35
porters, and their disciples; and so as not to commit on our account any action unworthy of our name and title with which among all other kings and
Christian princes we have been graced,[9] hoping that you, whose status and
office is to elucidate doctrines,[10] may also spare no labour in the exercise of

* * * * *

7 *Duodecim articuli infidelitatis magistri Natalis Bedae* (n p [Paris: Josse Bade] n d
   [1527]). The anonymous book has usually been attributed to Louis de Berquin,
   but he denied the charge. With the late Walter Bense Jr (cf Ep 1875 n30), this
   annotator believes that its author was the Paris theologian Jacques Merlin,
   whom Béda had pursued in the Parlement for several years because of his
   Apologia for Origen (Farge *Parti conservateur* 79 n3). Shortly after this, Merlin
   would be imprisoned for opposing the taxation imposed to ransom the king's
   sons in Spain. On Merlin see Farge BR 325–31 no 343.
8 The king's instructions notwithstanding, the three faculties of arts, medicine,
   and law decided to defer to whatever judgment would be rendered by the
   faculty of theology; see the introduction above.
9 That is, 'Most Christian King'; French kings had claimed this title since the
   fourteenth century. The kings of Spain were styled 'Most Catholic Majesty.'
10 The faculty of theology claimed this role for itself (Farge *Orthodoxy* 115). Pierre
   Lizet, king's counsel in the Parlement of Paris and later its *premier président*,
   confirmed that role when he termed the faculty of theology to be a 'permanent

your discernment, and thus that you act quickly to further our wishes and   40
desires, maintaining in this way the reputation which heretofore your school
has enjoyed over all those in other kingdoms and countries. In this we ask
and also command you most formally, and above all if you desire to do
us service, that for the good of the Christian religion you take great diligence in this matter, in such wise that we may speedily have your advice and   45
decision.

Given at Saint-Denis

ERASMUS OF ROTTERDAM TO THE SORBONNE COLLEGE, GREETING
I have learned by experience, illustrious fathers, how unsafe it is to believe
in rumours; but I have also learned by experience that it is not safe to ignore rumours when they first arise. It will therefore be a mark of your fair-
mindedness to consider that this letter was never written to you, should the   5
report that has reached me prove false. But if it is true, I appeal to your
sense of integrity to lay aside your personal feelings and consent to read
these words attentively. For unless I am entirely mistaken it does not so
much regard me personally as it does the prestige of your college and the
public tranquillity of education and religion.   10

So far is the matter from being secret that several friends have written me that it is common knowledge in Paris, and some have brought word
to me from Paris, that Noël Béda collected a great stack of articles from all
my writings and has brought them to your attention, and that some of them
were censured in an official pronouncement.[1] First of all I testify before   15

* * * * *

council in Gaul' and a 'college approved by law and delegated principally to
condemn all errors of faith, to extirpate heresies.' Lizet added that the Parlement 'has always sought and followed the advice and deliberations of the
faculty in all matters of faith' (Paris, Archives nationales x^{1a} 8342 f 255v–256;
cf Farge *Orthodoxy* 289). The king acknowledged this role of the faculty of
theology when it suited him and ignored it when it did not.

1902
1 Although the faculty approved Béda's *Annotationes* against Erasmus on 15
  February 1526, eighteen months prior to the writing of this letter (Farge *Procès-
  verbaux* 126 no 141A), no specific accusation of heresy appeared in the faculty's
  deliberations at that time. The final and general censure of Erasmus, decided
  on 16 December 1527 (but not published until 1531) accuses Erasmus of heresy
  in no more than a dozen of the 176 propositions deemed offensive on thirty-
  two different topics. See Argentré *Collectio judiciorum* II-1 53–77. Gervasius
  Wain, Louis de Berquin, or Germain de Brie are Erasmus' most likely infor-
  mants about the 'great stack of articles' being considered by the faculty and

God, who sees into the depths of the human heart, that I detest impiety and anything that detracts from the concord of the flock of Christ, and I shrink body and soul from those who join to themselves disciples who are not recognized by the church, the spouse of Christ. I believe I have affirmed this position consistently and with convincing arguments. In this present age companions and disciples would not have been lacking to me if I were not such a staunch foe of heresy and schism. Not to mention my personal services to the church in this affair, no one can doubt that, as my published writings make clear, I have shown myself to be a faithful and steadfast soldier in the defence of the faith. The fierce attacks against me by Alber, Otto, Leopold, and Luther himself proclaim this to all.[2] On my side there is my pamphlet on the Eucharist and the two books of the *Hyperaspistes*.[3] I should be surprised if they are unknown to you, since they are offered for sale there.[4] Since that is the case one might well wonder that I have merited the hatred of all enemy factions when I am not able to merit your sympathies. Against the evils of calumny nothing is safe, and it is possible that some impious word may have been let fall in my writings. This much is certain: my mind is free from impiety, and I am prepared to delete from them whatever would infringe the purity of religion. So those who conspire against me with such undivided loyalty are simply conspiring against their fellow soldier and the champion of the cause they claim to be defending. Whom do they gratify but those very persons they consider to be betrayers of the church, whose cause they are betraying because of personal animosities?

Furthermore, since in your wisdom you know how much falsity and venom the human tongue is capable of, especially in these times, you should put more trust in the facts themselves than in the murmuring of informers.

* * * * *

censured a month later. Erasmus published the faculty's censures along with his responses to them in *Declarationes ad censuras Lutetiae vulgatas* (CWE 82).

2 Erasmus Alber, a schoolteacher in Eisenach, wrote a book criticizing Erasmus' *Spongia* against Hutten (Ep 1466 n19). Otto Brunfels, like Alber, attacked Erasmus for his treatment of Hutten (Ep 1405 introduction). Leo Jud had written a refutation of Erasmus' *Detectio praestigiarum* on the Eucharist (Ep 1708 n1). Luther's 'fierce attack' is no doubt his *De servo arbitrio*.

3 On *Detectio praestigiarum* cf Ep1893 n27; on *Hyperaspistes* see Epp 1667 and 1853 and cf Ep 1804 n10.

4 In June 1526 Erasmus had enclosed copies of his *Detectio praestigiarum* and the first book of *Hyperaspistes* to the faculty with Ep 1723. As well, *Hyperaspistes* 1 had been reprinted in Paris by Pierre Vidoue in 1526 (Moreau *Inventaire* III 292 no 992). *Hyperaspistes* 2 was never printed in Paris, but copies of it could have reached there from Basel, where it appeared in August 1527.

Or if it is witnesses you seek, you ought to listen to those who know me more intimately, such as Ludwig Baer, certainly no enemy of mine, nor indeed of any man, but one most devoted to your community, and a man as pious as he is learned.[5] He knows from close hand what I am doing and what are my sentiments. Moreover, given the weighty authority of your status, your judgments must be characterized by greater fairness and clemency; and it is not in the least fitting that your position in society should serve the personal interests of stupid or wicked men. For my part I have never been at war with any class of men, nor shall I ever be, I hope – so far is it from my mind to take up arms against your assembly,[6] whose oracular pronouncements have always enjoyed the highest prestige.[7]

With regard to my responses to Béda,[8] I never thought that they concerned your august assembly; but it has been my conviction in the past and still is that in some way or other he extorted the permission to publish his book, and without your knowledge included his own spiteful feelings in it.[9] What are my grievances against this person? First of all, although I invited him most courteously in a letter of mine to settle the dispute between us with Christian moderation,[10] he published a book full of manifest calumnies, lies, and blasphemies. The matter is out in the open; there can be no concealing it. This action in itself is unbecoming for one who would like to play the role of theologian and official censor![11] If my response irritates

* * * * *

5 See Ep 1893 n31.
6 Erasmus uses the word *senatus*, a term usually applied to the Parlement of Paris; but he clearly intends the faculty of theology here.
7 See the letter of Francis I to the University of Paris (at the head of this letter) line 10 and n10; cf Farge *Orthodoxy* chapter 3: 'Consultant of Christendom?'.
8 By this time Erasmus had published four works to refute Béda's criticisms of him. See Ep 1804 n14.
9 The faculty approved Béda's book after it was reported to be 'very useful for refuting and putting down many perverse teachings and for defending truth and the laws and rites of the church'; see the letter from Francis I to the university lines 11–12 with n6 above. We can neither confirm nor refute Erasmus' accusation that Béda added 'spiteful' passages without the faculty's knowledge; cf Ep 1905:118.
10 Probably Ep 1571, dated 28 April 1525, the first of eleven letters exchanged between Erasmus and Béda. The correspondence became increasingly bitter and concluded with Ep 1906, written four days after this one.
11 For the quarrel between Erasmus and Béda about who was a theologian and about the role of theologians in society see James K. Farge 'Erasmus, the University of Paris, and the Profession of Theology' *Erasmus of Rotterdam Society Yearbook Nineteen* (1999) 44–5.

him, he should impute the blame to himself, since he was deterred neither by warnings nor pleas from resorting to this type of writing. To the charge of being unlearned, stupid, or foolish I will make no objection; but if I am 65 not impious, I will not allow myself to be called such; nor should I allow it, lest anyone become impious by my example.[12] And yet one could pardon this action to some degree as resulting from an outburst of wrath or fury; but when he was reminded by my response how far he had strayed from the duty of a Christian,[13] did he – I ask you – give any sign of shame 70 or repentance, did he try to be reconciled with his brother, whom he had thus betrayed? Even if the slightest offence existed between him and his brother, he would be obliged to leave his gift before the altar and be reconciled before making sacrifice.[14] The fact is that attacking one's brother in books such as these is no less grave an offence than murder and in some cir- 75 cumstances even graver, and yet in the meantime he frequently approaches the holy table of the Lord. Far from being reconciled with his brother, he heaps calumny upon calumny and tries to draw your authority into collusion with his excesses. It is as if he has not sinned enough up to now but must spatter his disgrace upon others. And yet, illustrious gentlemen, it be- 80 hoves your authority to cure men of such temperament, not to favour them; although to cure is to show true favour.

Therefore, since Béda is carried along by desire for revenge, you see the source of this trouble. Nor is it any secret to me where the oil comes from that is cast upon the fire.[15] Edward Lee has spread abroad in Spain a 85 book written against me, much more ignorant and slanderous than the previous one that he published in Paris,[16] not without Béda's cooperation, if I

* * * * *

12 See n39 below.
13 On their correspondence, see Ep 1804 n14 and n10 above, but no earlier letter could match the vehemence and lack of respect shown in Ep 1906.
14 Matt 5:23
15 Cf *Adagia* I ii 9.
16 Edward Lee, one of Erasmus' first critics, was now an ambassador for Henry VIII in Spain. Spanish theologians and churchmen had been aware of charges of heresy against Erasmus ever since the attacks launched by Diego López Zúñiga, and the recent translations of Erasmus' *Enchiridion* had stirred up anti-Erasmian sentiment even more. Erasmus blamed Lee for the onset of criticism there and, contrary to the opinion of many that Erasmus was wrong, Erika Rummel has shown that a serious attempt was being made to print in Spain a new edition of Lee's 1520 book against Erasmus. (See Epp 1744 n19, 1814 n39.) The Paris volume contained: an *Apologia contra quorundam calumnias Erasmi* addressed to the scholars in Louvain; a descriptive index to the annotations; a short prefatory letter (Ep 1037); the *Annotationum libri duo in*

mistake not.[17] This lent courage to certain monks, who stupidly imagine me
to be their enemy, when they are their own worst enemies. First they staged
a melodrama at the court of the emperor, but that attack was easily sup-   90
pressed.[18] Then the Franciscans staged the same thing at Salamanca, stirring
up the people with furious harangues. This uprising was put down with
difficulty by the church authorities.[19] Finally Pedro de Vitoria, a Dominican preacher in Burgos, whose brother is a member of your college, made
his appearance.[20] He stirred up such a tempest that his followers boasted   95
that they would not obey the edicts of the emperor or of the church, using
as their slogan, 'We must obey God rather than men.'[21] As a result, seeing
that the situation was heading towards rebellion and that there was no other
way of restoring order, the authorities permitted them to submit their articles to the archbishop of Seville to be examined by learned men consid-   100
ered to be above all suspicion.[22] Some excerpts from the book of Lee were

* * * * *

Annotationes Novi Testamenti Desiderii Erasmi (243 annotations on the 1516 edition of Erasmus' New Testament and 25 annotations on the second edition
prefaced by an index); and an Epistola apologetica to Erasmus (Ep 1061, answering Epp 998 and 1053). It was published by Gilles de Gourmont for Konrad Resch, Pierre Vidoue, and the widow of Berchtold Rembolt, probably c 15
February 1520; see Moreau Inventaire III 606 no 2386; CWE 72 xix n36.

17 This charge comes up frequently (see Epp 1861 n4, 1893 n9, 1903 n3, 1906 n4,
1915 n20). Although nothing in Béda's writings or actions in the faculty prior
to the publication of Lee's book indicates any concern about Erasmus, Béda's
1526 Annotationes against Erasmus and Lefèvre d'Etaples acknowledges his
having enlisted others to refute Erasmus and helping arrange the publication
of 'other sound works' against him. This was certainly the case with Pierre
Cousturier's De tralatione bibliae, but it also opens the possibility of his having
helped Lee to publish his book as well.

18 Cf Ep 1903:13–14.

19 Cf Epp 1903:17, 1909:39–45. More detail about this attack is provided in the
Apologia adversus monachos quosdam Hispanos (Basel: Hieronymus Froben 1529)
220–2; cf LB IX 1092D–1093A. This and similar charges against Erasmus set the
stage for the Valladolid Conference; see Ep 1791 introduction.

20 Pedro de Vitoria, also mentioned in Epp 1903:20, 1909:46, was the brother
of the illustrious Dominican theologian Francisco de Vitoria. (The accuracy
of this name has however been challenged; see CEBR III 407, and cf Ep 1836
n8.) Erasmus would shortly write to Francisco de Vitoria about this matter (Ep
1909). Because Erasmus would have known that no Dominican could belong to
the Collège de Sorbonne, his statement here that Vitoria 'is a member of your
college' makes it clear that he uses 'college' here as a synonym for 'faculty,'
not for the Collège de Sorbonne.

21 Acts 5:29; cf Epp 1875:51–2, 1904:21, 1909:50.

22 See Epp 1791 introduction, 1814 introduction, 1847:76–80.

presented,[23] of a stupidity and malice hardly to be imagined. I would have sent them together with my responses save that I thought them totally unworthy of your attention.

And this is the Lee whom Béda claims to be a consummate theologian,[24] although, as is clear, he never set foot in a school of theology. Not even Lee himself can deny that; and if he did deny it his writings are proof enough to the contrary. Although I replied to his tiresome reproaches, which he published against my advice,[25] in a far more moderate tone than he used to provoke me, he makes it his aim somehow to avenge the hurt – not by justifying himself, which he is unable to do, but by calling for a public stoning. His is a character destined to excite controversy. In the first disturbance that he stirred up in Louvain, he did not please my enemies and he severely displeased his friends in England. Such was the dénouement of that drama.[26] Of this present tempest I know not what the outcome will be. In any event various people write to me from Spain saying that the

* * * * *

23 See lines 85–7 and n16 above.

24 Erasmus' phrase *absolutum theologum* is stronger than Béda's single reference to Lee as a *doctus theologus* (*Annotationes* [Cologne 1526] f ccliii). The adjective *absolutus* could mean either a high level of learning ('consummate,' as translated here) or a person with a finished degree (a meaning preserved in the German *Absolvent* 'graduate.') Béda's use of *doctus* falls short of both meanings. But his description of Lee as *theologus* is inconsistent with his refusal to consider Erasmus as a fellow theologian. Paris, Louvain, and other northern universities did not recognize Erasmus' theology degree because it was granted *per saltum*, that is, 'by skipping over' the academic requirements (see Paul Grendler 'How to Get a Degree in Fifteen Days: Erasmus' Doctorate of Theology from the University of Turin' *Erasmus of Rotterdam Society Yearbook Eighteen* [1998] 40–69). Lee perhaps held a bachelor's degree in theology from Oxford, but he did not obtain the doctorate until 1531– and it too would be granted *per saltum*; see CEBR II 311–14. Thus, although Erasmus' *absolutus* exaggerates Béda's *doctus*, he correctly points out Béda's inconsistent and prejudiced recognition of Lee as a theologian, when he adamantly refused to apply that title to Erasmus.

25 Erasmus claimed that, to encourage Lee when he was a young student, he had suggested that he make notes on his *New Testament*, but that when he saw the result he advised against their publication. Probably not finding a publisher in Louvain, Lee sent his *Annotationum libri duo* to Paris, where Gilles de Gourmont produced them in February 1520; see n16 above. Erasmus responded with *Apologia qua respondet duabus invectivis Eduardi Lei* and *Responsio ad annotationes Eduardi Lei* and sought to stir up opposition to him from correspondents all over Europe. See Rummel *Catholic Critics* I 95–120.

26 *fabulae catastropha*; cf Ep 1875 n13.

monks there earn nothing for themselves except the odium of learned men and princes, and render my name more famous and celebrated. While I do not much like this celebrity, I wish they too would be deserving of es-teem. But they have made up their minds to conduct this whole affair with 120 violence, confusion, shameless behaviour, cajolery, and conspiracies. I, se-cure in the knowledge of a good conscience, have but this one regret: that I have been, if not the cause, at least the occasion of dissensions among Christians. If they arose through my fault I would await with a heavy con-science the last day, which cannot be too far off, and for which I prepare 125 myself daily. In the light of present circumstances, however, although the fault lies with others and I have offered my utmost resistance, I cannot help but be grieved at the public misfortune. But I bear up with it with more equanimity considering that these things come about by the will of God, who wishes that I be purified in this way and that their wickedness may 130 be made known to the world so that they may be more easily cured. In the meantime I will do what I judge to be pleasing to God, committing the is-sue to his will. And thus I have no doubt but that those who began these tumults spur Béda and his colleagues on to promote the success of their intrigues.   135

You see, most learned masters, the source and seedbed of this affair. What could come from it that would be worthy of Christian piety? And yet up to this point the reputation of your college has been such that the world would expect a judgment far different from what Lee and Béda have produced. I need not fear anything similar from you, unless my opinion 140 of you is entirely mistaken. And yet when I reflect on the kind of age we are living in, how much licence is given to audacious behaviour and ma-licious slander; when, furthermore, I can plausibly conjecture that sitting among you in that very assembly are those who either agree with Béda's opinion or cater to his hatred; or again that some through fear of unpop- 145 ularity or dislike of trouble keep their peace, and so it frequently happens that the worse part wins out over the better – for all of these reasons it did not seem inappropriate for me to take thought in this letter for your good name and my own tranquillity of mind, as far as it lies in me. But if this fear is groundless it cannot cause you any displeasure, since it proceeds 150 partly from a dislike of discord and partly from my esteem for your lofty station.

I beseech you again and again that as men of principle you will take it in good part if I seem to express my sentiments rather freely. I trust that you will interpret it as a sign not of arrogance but of frankness and a clear 15[5] conscience. Far be it from such a serious institution that to please men such

as Béda, Cousturier,[27] or pseudomonks (for I have always nourished a special affection for true monks) you have it in mind to crush Erasmus under
a great mass of articles – and especially without having read my response,
without considering the context, without taking into account the personage   160
whom I represent as the speaker, without comparing those passages with
what precedes and what follows, and without explaining why what I have
written appears to be impious.[28] For such is not the judgment of learned men
but rather a kind of public stoning. And if it were the prerogative of your
authority, it would still be far from the laws of Christian charity, which does   165
not break the bruised reed nor quench the smoking flax.[29] You see what tolerance Augustine used even against hopeless heretics. Towards those who
received false doctrines from the hands of their ancestors, or were lured
into error by artifice or led by persuasion to believe impious teachings, he
wishes every leniency to be shown, deeming that they should be taught, not   170
reprimanded.[30] But as for me, who have striven to the best of my feeble
powers to advance the cause of good letters and religion; who have steadfastly avoided all factions; who, for the good of the Catholic church would
have incited my most devoted followers to turn against me; who exposed
this frail body and this mind to every danger: to think they would unleash   175
these frenzied attacks against me – as Béda has done, soon to be joined by
others girding up for the assault – my God! how far this is from the example
of Christian mildness! how far from the opinion the Christian world has entertained of your college until now! Turmoil such as this is not invoked by
St Augustine even to put down heresiarchs, lest they claim that they were   180
conquered by force rather than won over by the truth.[31]

* * * * *

27 The Carthusian critic whose work the faculty approved; see Ep 1804 n65.
28 Erasmus will make these same points in Epp 1905:61–79 and 1909:143–65 and
     his formal response to the publication of the faculty's censures in 1531, the
     Declarationes ad censuras Lutetiae vulgatas (Basel: Hieronymus Froben, January
     1532; repr September 1532); cf CWE 82.
29 Isa 42:3; cf Matt 12:20; cf Ep 939:120–1.
30 In 1519 Erasmus had used the same arguments to urge the Elector Frederick
     of Saxony to show tolerance for Luther (Ep 939:114–24).
31 But Augustine grew weary and wary of the excesses of heretics, especially vi-
     olent ones like the Circumcellions (cf Ep 1895A:42–3), and in the end – basing
     his decision on St Paul, who numbered heresy with the fruits of the flesh (Gal
     5:19) – the bishop of Hippo advocated energetic intervention by civil authori-
     ties against them. For the full range of Augustine's writing on tolerance and
     intolerance see Joseph Lecler *Toleration and the Reformation* trans T.L. Westow
     2 vols (New York and London 1960) I 53–9.

Perhaps nothing is easier than to quash Erasmus, but you will not have a very brilliant triumph if so many great-souled heroes conspire together to crush an insignificant gnat, even if I am not so destitute of friends as certain people think. But truth is invincible, and Christ the defender of truth is unassailable. It is difficult to kick against the goad.[32] Your authority, your learning, your unanimity would be better put to use against those who openly despise your teachings, who take cities and regions away from you and gain them to their own cause. I am astonished that you take time away from those adversaries to dissect little phrases that are either ambiguously expressed or, if correctly stated, not in the language in use in the schools, or even many that are distorted. Erasmus is weak, I confess, but the truth is powerful; God forbid that you be in collusion against it. If such were to happen, it would pose greater danger for your reputation than for mine. For even if a thousand judges were to pronounce that a gold cup was made of bronze the authority of the judges would not be able to turn gold into bronze, and the owner of the cup would not feel the loss; but the judges would cause their authority to decline.

Do not, I beseech you, be moved to anger! I do not have such low esteem of you as to think that you would pronounce a judgment contrary to the obvious truth; although there are some members of your assembly who, like Béda, either do not understand what has been said through their ignorance of language or, corrupted by animosity, believe the most patent truth to be false. But I think even upright and learned men can be deceived if they attempt to pronounce judgment on a bare phrase excerpted from somewhere or other without reference to the context.

I shall give an example: 'Everyone should eat whatever he wishes according to the desire of the body, provided he do so moderately and sparingly, giving thanks to God for all of which he partakes.'[33] If someone were to set forth this statement by itself as being found in the works of Erasmus, at first one ignorant of the Latin language would take offence, thinking that with the phrase 'desire of the body' I meant 'the appetite' – that is, that

* * * * *

32 Acts 26:14
33 The passage, in which 'according to the desires of the body' translates *corporis affectu*, is from Erasmus' paraphrase on 1 Cor 8:8 (LB VII 887A), to which Béda had taken exception. Erasmus' reply is in the *Prologus supputationis* (LB IX 474C–E). St Paul was instructing the Christians in Corinth that, even though the Jewish law of abstaining from food offered to heathen deities no longer pertained, they should abstain nevertheless if there were danger of giving scandal (1 Cor 8:9-13). Erasmus uses this example again in Ep 1905:69–79.

everyone should eat what the body craves – whereas I mean by the word 'desire' the 'natural condition and health of the body.' This is made clear by what follows: 'for the well-being of the body.' Moreover, in the same chap-   215
ter I make exception at great length for the possibility of giving scandal to my brother. One who passes judgment on the simple statement is not aware of this. Besides, it is not Erasmus speaking here, but Paul. One who does not know this thinks that I am condemning the commandments of the church concerning abstinence from certain foods.[34] Such a person, no matter how   220
learned, will be misled into condemning what he does not understand. And yet that statement could have been made, without any charge of impiety, from the time of the apostles to the age of Augustine; since, as I believe, the church did not forbid any kind of food to anyone. Consequently, when the reader understands that this is said through the mouth of Paul and does not   225
pertain to our times, and when he sees that what I expound is handed down by the Apostle in many passages,[35] will he not say that it is absurd to accuse me of impiety for repeating something piously said by the Apostle? Will he not think it fair that either I be absolved with the Apostle or the Apostle be condemned with me? Since this is simple enough even for a sailor to un-   230
derstand, what will people think of that judge? obviously that he was either singularly ignorant or dishonest.

Paul says of himself and of Christians, 'We are of all men most to be pitied.' He also wrote: 'Let us do evil that good may come of it.' Again: 'Vain is our preaching, vain too is our faith.'[36] What is more irreligious than   235
these words if they are taken by themselves, without taking into account the persons speaking and without reference to the context? Yet it is no less shameful to lift excerpts from my writings, as anyone would readily agree. I really wonder what these people are thinking. Do they believe that instead

* * * * *

34 'Commandments of the church' were known to medieval preachers but were not defined in form or number by the church. The Council of Trent prescribed some of them, like attendance at mass, but its *Catechism* never treated them as a body of laws. In the mid-sixteenth century St Peter Canisius listed these: to observe the feast days appointed by the church; to attend mass reverently on these feast days; to observe the fasts on the days and during the seasons appointed; to confess one's sins annually; and to receive Holy Communion at least once a year (and certainly around the feast of Easter). Erasmus' *De esu carnium* was critical of canonical rules of abstinence.

35 For example Rom 14:20–3: 'Do not, for the sake of food, destroy the work of God. Everything is indeed clean, but it is wrong for anyone to make others fall by what he eats.'

36 1 Cor 15:19; Rom 3:8; 1 Cor 15:14; cf Ep 1905:65–72.

of men the world is inhabited by mushrooms,[37] and that men have lost all   24
common sense? Do they not see what kind of world we live in? Do they
think that everyone is immediately going to take it as a heavenly oracle when
they hear, 'Béda the theologian has judged it to be so'? Perhaps this is their
scheme: 'We will shout it out all at once, and by our shouts we will drown
out the little man. The race of monks is spread over the whole world just like   24
the humours in the human body. In public and in private, in secret and in
the open, they will invent accusations, they will shout him down, they will
denounce him. He is alone, and he speaks nothing but Latin; and if he does
answer, we will stifle him; if anything of his is read, it will be read only
by a few. With contempt for these few, we will win the day through sheer   25
numbers!' But I, with Christ to sustain me, will see that even the lowly
crowd will know of their malicious prejudice, as it has already begun to
know.

But let them suppose that Erasmus has been silenced. Do they think
that no one will rise up to defend innocence against such tyrannical mal-   25
ice? Though men may relax their efforts, do they not reflect that God sees
these things and often turns evil counsel back upon the head of its author?
God forbid that such a detestable thought should ever take hold of your sacred faculty. I merely caution you not to diminish your authority by serving
the interests of those who invent such conspiracies – authority which ought   26
to exercise its power for building up, not tearing down. You are learned
men, you are theologians; nothing is expected from you but what is truly
learned and worthy of God. Jean Gerson rightly advises the Roman pontiff
not to hurl the thunderbolt of anathema rashly and indiscriminately, lest he
draw scorn upon himself in two ways: through routine, if he hurls down his   26
lightning bolts too often, or through reproach, if he strikes the undeserving.[38] Up to now the phrase 'Such was the decision of the faculty of theology
of Paris' carried much weight. But this authority must be safeguarded by
the gravity and equity of the judgments, and all the more scrupulously in
this age, which is more inclined to despise human authority. As far as it lies   27
within my power nothing shall detract from the eminence of your assembly;
I would rather add to it. If you find anything truly impious in my works,

* * * * *

37 *Adagia* IV i 38
38 Jean Gerson, a master of theology and chancellor of the University of Paris in
   the early fifteenth century, was admired by scholastics and by many humanists. The reference is perhaps to his 'Sermo de officio pastoris in concilio Re-
   mensi' 2.2.2 *Opera omnia* ed Louis Ellies Du Pin (Paris 1706) II 552; cf *Oeuvres
   complètes* ed Palémon Glorieux 10 vols (Paris 1960–73) V 136–7.

I will be among the first to root out my error. But if your assembly pro-
nounces judgments like the majority of Béda's charges – uninformed, unfair, blind, breathing nothing but violent hatred and malice bent on doing   275
harm – I will consider it to be not the verdict of the faculty but of Bédaizers.

I cannot be a heretic unless I wish to be one.[39] Moreover, since I neither
am nor wish to be one, I shall make every effort not to be regarded as one,
and I am confident that Christ, as the undisputed defender of innocence, will
stand by me. If we join forces in defending the cause of piety, the immortal   280
spouse of the church will favour our efforts.[40] But if with mutual contempt
and mutual disparagement we tear each other to shreds, what will be left
to us but, according to the words of Paul, to consume one another tooth and
nail.[41] There are more than enough tumults in the world, enough division,
and the world is filled with defamatory articles to the extent that things   285
it was once forbidden to contemn are nowadays objects of contempt. How
much more honourable it would be to convert ourselves to true Christianity, putting up with one another and helping the weak rather than crushing them? Certain people have but one desire, to extract things from my
writings that can be twisted into Lutheran beliefs; and with perverse skills   290
they distort things that are diametrically opposed[42] to his doctrines. How
much more useful it would be for eliminating the Lutheran party if they
would extract those passages that openly contradict his dogmas, of which
there is a great plenitude throughout my writings! Then let them take those
statements that might have two meanings and interpret them in the other   295
sense. Perhaps it might be expedient to overlook certain things that slipped
by through carelessness.[43] There are some things that do no harm if they
are passed over, but if debated give rise to grave contentions. If you do not
think you should concede this much to my merits, then at least grant it for
the sake of the cause that is now at issue, for the prestige of your faculty,   300
for the sake of men's opinion of you. If it is not possible that there be no
Bédas among you, at least let the world know that you are not all Bédas – although I would gladly receive even Béda himself into Christian friendship

* * * * *

39 In canon law formal heresy implied both knowing and deliberately willing to
   deny a truth of the faith (*Decretales Gregorii* IX 5.7.1; cf Thomas Aquinas *Summa
   theologiae* II–II q 11 a 1).
40 That is, Jesus Christ. St Paul develops the analogy of the church as the spouse
   of Christ in Eph 5:23–33.
41 Gal 5:15
42 *Adagia* I x 45
43 Cf Epp 1828:18–19, 1864:143–4, 1879:25–6, 108–11.

if he would only apply himself to more serious pursuits. Too much energy
has been devoted to hatred and conceit.   305

Since therefore my petitions pertain not only to my own reputation
but to the public interest of the church and to the authority of your faculty,
do not allow yourselves to give more importance to the uncontrolled feelings of a certain few than to the impartial judgments of good and learned
men. What I ask is that, if possible, this matter be settled among us in pri-   310
vate, fraternal discussions. For if there is anything erroneous in my writings, no one can provide a more effective remedy than I myself, if I am
alerted to it. If that is not possible, then let your judgments be free of personal animosity and let them exhibit Christian charity; let your authority
serve the cause of Christ rather than the interests and advantages of men,   315
and do not show reluctance to read the passage from which Béda the clever
article-fashioner[44] takes his excerpts. Do not be reluctant to look into the
particular time and persons to which the words refer. Then take the trouble to read through the books I have written in response, and in this way
gain a thorough knowledge of the case before you publish your opinion,   320
lest an undiscerning judgment be issued, which will be a greater disgrace
to you than to me. If you find anything truly impious, I will be among the
first to repudiate the impiety. In that way I will not suffer harm, the cause
of piety will be justly looked after, and your authority will not be subjected
to malicious talk.   325

You see that what I ask is not unjust, nor would I ask it if I belittled
your authority, as do those who propose new dogmas. On the other hand
I should not make this request if I were not aware of how powerful the
obstinacy of the wicked can be even among men of worth. If you wish to
serve the best interests of the monks, tell them to abandon these malicious   330
schemes and devote themselves to that purity of life that gained them such
great favour in the eyes of the world. There is no surer way for them to
appease the hatred that they aggravate all the more by these turmoils. If
they are determined to despise the judgment of men and to carry on like
brawling ruffians, let them reflect that such tactics have not succeeded, not   335
even for kings. I have sent brief responses to certain articles,[45] which I hear

* * * * *

44 *articulifex*, a biting adaptation of *artifex*; cf Ep 1911:21. Béda and the faculty used
    the common scholastic approach of devising distinct articles to cover all aspects
    of a question. In dealing with something considered heretical, each different
    aspect would constitute a separate article followed by a refutation or response.
45 See Ep 1905:111–13 and n23, where Erasmus tells the Parlement of Paris that
    he is sending answers to several articles that, from what he has been told,

have already been submitted to your judgment, so that you may judge more
accurately concerning the others. I beg you to read them. I have also sent you
a book pointing out the relevant passages in order to save you the trouble
of searching them out.[46] I pray that the Lord Jesus will inspire in your minds 340
those decisions that will be both worthy of your sacred college and salutary
for the Christian people.

I shall repeat what I said at the beginning. If vain rumour has brought
these tidings here, consider this as not having been written. I have not been
lacking in my duty; if any tumults arise, the blame will fall on others. 345

Given at Basel, on the day after the feast of St Martin, in the year 1527

1903 / To [Gervasius Wain]   [Basel, c 12 November 1527]

Allen discovered the manuscript of this letter in the Staats- und Univer-
sitätsbibliothek Bremen (MS a 8 no 6). He assigned its date from its similarities with information about Spain in Ep 1902, and conjectured its addressee
to be Gervasius Wain, who had written to Erasmus on 9 October (Ep 1884)
and to whom Erasmus is known to have written at this time (Ep 1922:41–2; cf
Ep 1911:76). Drafted in a secretary's hand and bearing neither salutation nor
closing, this is the only extant page of several that must have comprised the
letter actually sent. If Allen's conjecture about its addressee is correct, then
Erasmus' letter was probably dispatched with others that were confiscated in
Alsace and that he eventually recovered and redirected (cf Ep 1922:41–2). Still,
we cannot be sure that its addressee actually received it.

Lee is enjoying a remarkable career[1] in Spain, completing the last act of the
farce he began long ago in Louvain. I have no doubt that he has likewise
played his part admirably in Paris in Béda's circle, even if he has not yet

* * * * *

the faculty was investigating; and Ep 1922:44–5, where he mentions sending
'two short pieces' (codicili) in his defence, one to the Parlement of Paris and
the other to the faculty of theology. The proceedings of neither the Parlement
nor the faculty mention reception of these responses.
46 Possibly the Supputationes (Basel: Froben, March 1527), an omnibus volume
containing the lengthy, newly composed Supputatio errorum in censuris Bedae.
But Erasmus' description of it as a 'short piece' on the same subject as the 'little
printed book for the archbishop of Seville' (Ep 1922:44–5) leaves some doubt.

1903
1 The phrase was written in Greek. On Lee and his supposed role in stirring up
the Spaniards against Erasmus see Ep 1814 n39.

been caught in the act.[2] About his performance in Spain I am very well informed through the letters of numerous important men, all bearing the same   5
message.[3] But the facts speak for themselves. It is the same play, the same
theatrics that went on in Brabant.[4] First he communicated his deceptions to
those initiated into such mysteries, especially evil-minded monks. Now he
will pretend that he has been inhibited by imperial law.[5] But in the meantime that cursed book passes through the hands of monks, especially the   10
mendicant tyrants.[6] As a result the first attack against Erasmus was made by
a certain ecclesiastic,[7] the confessor of the emperor, a man respected for his
holiness. He was held in check, however, by the authority of the grandees
at court and of the emperor. Rebounding from this obstacle the stormy seas
unleashed their fury with greater violence at Salamanca through the efforts   15
of the barefoot Franciscans.[8] It was played out in public in the midst of
great turmoil, to the point that it could barely be put down by the archbishops and the dignitaries of the court. In the end the evil flared up again
at Burgos through the agency of a Dominican with the auspicious name of
Pedro de Vitoria.[9] Here they began to fly in the face of the restrictions of   20

* * * * *

2 Erasmus always presumed Béda had sponsored the publication in 1520 of
  Lee's notes criticizing Erasmus' edition of the New Testament, and that he
  had even written much of it (1906:64–6; cf Ep 1902 n17). Edward Lee is never
  mentioned in contemporary documents of the faculty of theology of Paris. On
  Lee's *Annotationes libri duo* see Ep 1902 nn16 and 25.
3 For example Epp 1791, 1839, 1847 and others known to be lost
4 On the images from the theatre, see Ep 1875 n13.
5 No law or edict to this effect is known; but the imperial chancellor Mercurino
  Gattinara reported to Erasmus (Ep 1643) that Emperor Charles v had ordered
  the Louvain theologians to desist in their attacks on Erasmus, and Gattinara
  himself later wrote a similar letter to Louvain (Ep 1784A).
6 πτωχοτυράννων. In writing directly to Lee Erasmus used the Latin phrase *et
  mendici sunt et tyranni* (Allen Ep 998:60). On the supposed new book of Edward
  Lee against Erasmus see Ep 1814 n39.
7 Κυριακόν. The Dominican master general García de Loaysa (CEBR II 336–7) had
  succeeded the Franciscan Jean Glapion as Charles' confessor (Ep 1275). Loaysa
  denounced what he perceived to be heretical passages in the Spanish translation of Erasmus' *Enchiridion* but failed to prevent its publication in 1526. This
  'first attack' preceded the affair at Salamanca and thus took place in 1526 or
  earlier; cf Ep 1902:89–91. Ep 1731 from Emperor Charles v (dated 4 August
  1526) was perhaps written with these Spanish troubles in mind.
8 *Franciscanos* γυμνόποδας. The reform-minded 'Observant' and 'Spiritual' Franciscan friars were likely to go barefoot or, in winter, to wear simple sandals.
  On the dispute at Salamanca see Epp 1744:136 and n20, 1902:91–3.
9 See Epp 1836 n8, 1902 n20, and 1909:46–7.

princes, saying 'We must obey God rather than men.'[10] It spells the end of Christianity if the books of Erasmus get into the hands of the people.'

Since an edict prevented them from venting their fury upon me in public sermons,[11] they betook themselves to Alonso Manrique, the archbishop of Seville, who has supreme authority and jurisdiction over matters of faith.   25 There, after huge outcries, the archbishop forbade anyone to make mad accusations against me. They were ordered to submit their articles to the scrutiny of learned doctors. A day was set, and all was enacted with the proper formalities.[12] In this affair the book of Lee served a useful purpose, for those slaves of the belly[13] would never have read so many volumes. This meas-   30 ure was taken so that a permanent silence with regard to my books might be imposed upon them by legitimate authority. Things have come to such a pass in the affairs of men that the greatest princes stand in fear of men dead to the world,[14] and those who vaunt their vow of obedience do not obey even human laws. The letters of learned men testify how much zeal is be-   35 ing employed on the part of good men in my cause. I merely fear that these circumstances may give rise to some new troubles in Spain, something to which I should be so averse that I would prefer defeat[15] to such a victory.

1904 / From Alonso Fernández de Madrid   Palencia, 13 November 1527

An abridgement of a longer original, this letter was first published in LB III-2 1723 *Appendix epistolarum* no 343. The letter actually received by Erasmus is now kept in the Rehdiger collection at the University library in Wrocław (MS 254 6). Erasmus will answer it with Ep 1969.

Alfonso de Valdés, asked by Fernández to forward his letter to Erasmus, judged it to be prolix and its defence of Fernández' translation of the *Enchiridion* (about which Erasmus had mixed feelings) too ardent, and asked Diego Gracián de Alderete, his protégé at the imperial court, to make a careful abridgment and to obtain Fernandez' approval of it. The manuscript letter-book of Gracián (see Ep 1914 introduction) confirms this. The date is that of the original letter, not of the abridgement.

* * * * *

10 Acts 5:29; cf Epp 1875:51–2, 1891:185, 1902:97, 1904:21, 1909:50.
11 See n5 above for a similar decree directed at preachers in Louvain.
12 27 June 1527; see Epp 1791 and 1814 introductions. On Manrique de Lara see Ep 1846 introduction, and cf Epp 1877, 1879, 1888.
13 *ventres*. See Ep 1805 n53.
14 That is, those living under vows; see Ep 1891:115 and n23; cf Col 2:20, 3:3.
15 This word is rendered in Greek.

Fernández (1474–August 1559), a nobleman, was the archdeacon of Alcor in the diocese of Palencia and a renowned preacher with intellectual gifts. He chose to serve exemplary, or 'model,' Spanish churchmen. He also translated a wide range of works and edited liturgical and devotional texts (CEBR II 23–4 and CWE 12 526–7 'Letters of Juan de Vergara and Others Concerning Erasmus' no 3 introduction).

Best greetings. I sent two letters to you, most renowned Erasmus, at the end of October when the emperor was staying in Palencia, one carried by Valdés and the other by Martinus Transsylvanus.[1] I expressed in them the great love and good will I bear you. I think they will have reached you by now. I saw recently your letter to Luis Coronel written on the first of September,[2]   5 which was delivered to him while he happened to be my guest. I read it and reread it with great pleasure. Right from the beginning it savours of the purest Erasmus and contains nothing that does not plainly recall your pious and learned self.

There is one passage, however, that disturbed me. You say: 'As for those   1 who translate my books into Spanish, I know not whether they do so out of devotion to me; the truth is that they contribute greatly to my unpopularity.'[3] Up to now I have seen no book of yours put into Spanish except for the *Handbook of the Christian Soldier*, which by everyone's account was rather successfully translated by me. Its appearance was accompanied by such enthusi-   1 asm and approval of your good name and was seen to be of such usefulness to the Christian people that today no other book is so much in men's hands. In the palace of the emperor, in the cities, in the churches, in monasteries, even in hostelries and in the streets there is hardly anyone who does not have the *Enchiridion* of Erasmus in Spanish. Previously it was read in Latin   2 by a few experts in the Latin language and it was not entirely understood by them. Now it is read in Spanish by all without distinction; and those who had never heard the name of Erasmus have come to know it from this one book.

* * * * *

1904
1 Martinus Sydonius Transsylvanus, a colleague of Alfonso de Valdés, was probably attached to the imperial chancery at this time. He may have been kin to Maximilianus Transsilvanus (Epp 1802, 1897). Charles v was at Palencia 27 September–10 October 1527. Neither letter is extant.
2 Not extant. For Coronel, who had been vice-president at the Valladolid inquisitorial assembly, see Epp 1814 n64, 1836 n15.
3 Erasmus made the same comment to Vergara; see Ep 1875:55–7. On Fernández' translation of the *Enchiridion* see Ep 1814 n21; for his account of its reception, see his letter to Coronel CWE 12 526–9.

But enough of this. Now that you are aware of my good will towards you I thought it should be pointed out to you that in your book entitled 25 *Exomologesis* I would like to have seen a concluding section that would give a little more emphasis to auricular confession.[4] In its present form it has the approval of good and learned men, but with this addition it would satisfy even the unlearned and the prejudiced.

Farewell, O glory of letters. Palencia, 13 November 1527
Your most devoted Alonso Fernando, archdeacon of Alcor. 30
To the illustrious Master Erasmus of Rotterdam, in Basel

1905 / To the Parlement of Paris   Basel, 14 November 1527

Unlike Epp 1721 to the Parlement and 1722 to King Francis I, this letter was not copied into the registers of the Parlement. It was sent with a packet of Erasmus' letters that was confiscated in Alsace. Although Erasmus was able to recover and redirect them (cf Ep 1922:38–40), we cannot know whether the Parlement actually received this letter. It is known only from Erasmus' copy, published in the *Opus epistolarum* (1529).

The Parlement of Paris, the highest court in France, was a strongly conservative body composed of about 120 men divided into several different courts but they all met regularly together in what was known as the 'Conseil.' At this time, most of them shared the negative attitude of the faculty of theology towards the nascent religious Reformation and towards Erasmus. For documents illustrating its stance see Farge *Parti conservateur.*

ERASMUS OF ROTTERDAM TO THE SENATE OF PARIS, GREETING
If this matter[1] had to do only with me personally, honoured judges, it might rightly appear presumptuous to some of you that I, an insignificant creature with no good services to commend myself to you, should not be afraid to stand before this most august assembly, engaged as it is with so many grave 5

* * * * *

4 The *Exomologesis sive modus confitendi* (Basel: Johann Froben 1524) was Erasmus' treatise on the sacrament and practice of confession. See Ep 1426. Fernández' suggestion was not taken up by Erasmus in his second edition (Basel: Hieronymus Froben, March 1530); but he dealt with it at length in the *Apologia adversus monachos quosdam Hispanos*, objections 29–32 (LB IX 1062–4), which he was writing at this time.

1905
1 Undoubtedly the rumours that Béda and the faculty of theology were preparing a wide-ranging censure of Erasmus' works (see Ep 1902 n1).

affairs of state.[2] But since I am convinced that in your wisdom you will perceive that the subject of my letter pertains more to the public tranquillity of learning and of religion and to the prestige of the faculty of theology itself than to my reputation alone, I thought I had no other recourse but to your authority as to a sacred anchor and the last stronghold of justice.[3]   10

Not to detain you with a more lengthy preamble, Noël Béda – who, in a recently published book that was both ineffectual and unsuccessful,[4] lashed out against me with such fury that the Most Christian King, as soon as he learned of it, forbade the book to be sold and undoubtedly would have forbidden it to be printed if he had been informed in time[5] – this same Noël   15
Béda in an even more violent attack, as I learn, but by another method,[6] has begun to reenact the play that had such an inauspicious beginning. He is beside himself with anger because I dared to answer such shameless calumnies,[7] as if in deference to him I should admit to opinions and blasphemies that have never entered my mind even in a dream, whereas it is the greatest   20
impiety to acknowledge the charge of impiety unless you acknowledge your

* * * * *

2 Although most of the Parlement's business involved private litigation, it also claimed and exercised the prerogative of registering royal decrees and of remonstrating against those it judged to be unfounded in precedent. Its members had only recently incurred royal wrath in the *lit de justice* of July 1527 for measures taken to restrict royal authority during the captivity of Francis I.

3 Cf *Adagia* I i 24. The Parlement of Paris was indeed the supreme court of appeal in France.

4 On Béda, the syndic of the Paris faculty of theology since 1520, and his *Annotationes* against Lefèvre and Erasmus, see Ep 1804 n14. On his *Annotationum in Jacobum Fabrum Stapulensem libri duo, et in Desiderium Erasmum Roterodamum liber unus* (Paris: Josse Bade 1526) see further Walter Bense Jr 'Noël Beda's View of the Reformation' *Occasional Papers of the American Society for Reformation Research* 1 (December 1977) 93–107.

5 The Parlement knew very well that Francis I had prohibited the sale of the *Annotationes*; see Epp 1721–2, and cf the king's letter to the University of Paris (at the head of Ep 1902) lines 1–6. On the Parlement's support for Béda's book, despite the king's censure, see Farge *Procès-verbaux* 142 no 161A–B and *Orthodoxy and Reform* 261–2.

6 At the time Béda was mustering support in the whole University of Paris for the general censure of Erasmus that occurred on 16 December 1527 and was preparing several doctors of theology to harangue the king about the dangers of doctrinal errors held by Erasmus and Lefèvre d'Etaples. See Farge *Procès-verbaux* 158 no 179C.

7 Erasmus had already replied to Béda's *Annotationes*; see Ep 1902 (Erasmus' letter to the faculty of theology) n8.

guilt. Not even on this point, however, do I accuse the faculty, by whose permission the book was allowed to be printed, for I have no doubt that it was afterwards and without their knowledge that Béda added his venomous aspersions.[8] For that reason I tempered my response so that I would not knowingly utter a single word contrary to my conscience. But if I could not defend my innocence without exposing the falsity and impudence of his calumnies, he should have imputed the blame to himself, as the one who had provoked the issue and not to me, who did not have the option to be silent. This was especially so since I had invited the man in a very friendly letter to settle our dispute with Christian moderation, promising all that might be expected of a man devoted to the cause of piety and concord.[9] But now that his calumnies are too evident to be ignored he is planning to take vengeance in another way, and there are those who are spurring him on in his unusually roused state of emotion to make of him an instrument of their own revenge.

He has assembled a huge pile of articles,[10] exactly like those with which the book condemned by the king overflowed, which he did not himself extract from my books but took from extracts made by various petty masters. For he never read my writings himself, as can easily be surmised. These articles he delivered to the faculty of theology for examination, and I hear that some of them have been given to the censors.[11] As far as I am concerned, I am of the mind that if any impiety can be found in my writings I should not wish to be granted any indulgence for such an error. But what is written with such circumspection that it cannot be distorted by calumny, armed with cunning and hatred?[12] This good fortune did not fall to Augustine or to the apostles. Furthermore, unless Béda lacked all confidence in his cause, he would at least answer to certain passages that are so outrageously false and groundless that you can feel them, as they say, with your

* * * * *

8 See Francis I's letter to the University of Paris (Ep 1902 introduction) n6 and Ep 1902:55–6 and n9.
9 Probably Ep 1571. Ep 1581, though blunter in style, is still couched in respectful terms, but later letters make clear Erasmus' contempt for Béda; cf Ep 1902 n10.
10 Cf Ep 1902:13–14.
11 The faculty of theology had condemned certain articles from the *Colloquies* on 16 May 1526 (Farge *Procès-verbaux* 136 no 152A) and was now preparing the wider censure that would appear on 16 December 1527. It would be made public only in 1531.
12 Cf Ep 1864 n16.

hands.[13] But omitting what should have been his first concern, he resorts   50
to force and instigates the faculty to crush me under a multitude of articles and by the authority of its decisions. I do not have such a low opinion
of myself or of the most sacred[14] faculty that I should stand in fear of its
judgment. How could I do so when I have long demanded this of them?

But Béda himself has sufficiently revealed how blinded by hatred are   55
his views. And he has many followers in this assembly; some are silent out
of fear of unpopularity or through love of tranquillity (if anyone ever puts
forward something that smacks of fairness, he is quickly reputed as worse
than a Lutheran).[15] Some of them are unacquainted with polite learning and
do not understand what I write. Moreover, even honest and learned men   60
can still be deceived. They excerpt a single phrase that by itself seems sacrilegious but if joined to what preceded and what followed would be regarded as pious. They present things under the name of Erasmus that are
quotations from Paul or from the Gospels. It is applied to the church of our
time, when it is suited to the early church. For example, Paul says of him-   65
self and of Christians, 'We are the most miserable of men.' What could be
more blasphemous if you add nothing to it? But if you add what Paul added
– 'if there is no resurrection of the dead' – it is a pious statement.[16] Likewise
Paul, says, 'Food does not commend us to God.'[17] This was said without offence to piety by the Apostle in those times in which there was danger that   70
Christians might be corrupted by the Jewish prohibitions regarding foods,
and when the church had not yet forbidden any kind of food. They interpret this statement, which is explained in my Paraphrases in the person of
Paul but using different words, as if in defiance of the church's constitutions
Erasmus were now teaching that anyone can partake of any food whatso-   75
ever, a concept I never even dreamed of. One who is unaware of this will

* * * * *

13 Cf Cicero *Pro Sestio* 32.69.
14 The adjective *sacratissima* was an official title of the Paris faculty of theology, just as *saluberrima* described the faculty of medicine and *consultissima* the
   faculty of canon law.
15 This had indeed happened to the Dominican master Pieter Fabri in 1523 for
   questioning whether Jerome was the translator of the Vulgate Bible and urging
   wider use of vernacular translations (Clerval *Procès-verbaux* 379–80). A similar
   reaction greeted master Nicolas Maillard, who argued in 1524 that the study
   of Greek and Hebrew would be an advantage to theologians (Farge *Procès-
   verbaux* 30 no 27F).
16 1 Cor 15:13–19; cf Ep 1902:233–5. Erasmus' examples are not answers to charges
   made by Béda or the faculty.
17 1 Cor 8:8; cf Ep 1902:207–24.

condemn that statement, which is not mine but Paul's, and in so doing will
condemn the Apostle instead of me. From this example you will be able in
your good judgment to surmise the rest.

From these machinations, which have their source and seedbed in ha-   80
tred, anger, envy, and desire for revenge, what will be the result but tumults and dissensions, although there are more than enough of these evils
in the world already? It would be more fitting that they lend their support
to my efforts to protect the church as best I can and that the authority of that
college,[18] which has always been held in the highest esteem, should serve   85
the glory of Christ and not the passions of men like Béda, Cousturier,[19] and
certain persons who falsely lay claim to the name of monk. Since they have
placed all their trust in dishonesty they do not answer the refutations of their
glaring calumnies, but by hateful conspiracies and disturbances they go to
the attack, all the more hostile because I refuse to desert to the Lutheran   90
camp. Whatever madness has been perpetrated up to now by the likes of
Béda and Cousturier I considered as not pertaining to the faculty of theology, to whose authority I have bowed many times[20] and shall continue to do
so, if it is permitted me. But if they continue to suppress – I shall not refer
to myself, who am nothing – truth and piety with such methods as the Jews   95
once used against Jesus,[21] I shall see to it that the world understands that
what they condemn as impious is true Christian piety, and was either not
understood or maliciously distorted. I shall so present the plain and simple
truth to the eyes of men that it will be evident to weavers and weaveresses
alike. I do not know what accretion of glory will come to them from this   100
affair. I should wish that the situation is such that I can protect my own innocence without impairing their authority. No pious man can admit to the
charge of impiety. Even if it were permitted me to admit it, it is not expedient for others, who would be drawn into error or confirmed in their error
by this view.[22] In this matter, therefore, if your authority, than which there   105
is no greater in that kingdom after the king himself, were to impose silence
on these tumultuous and malicious intrigues, it would be in the best interests first of all of the peaceful pursuit of study and the tranquillity of the

* * * * *

18 That is, the faculty of theology of Paris
19 On Cousturier see Ep 1804 n65.
20 A rhetorical statement; no such admission or submission by Erasmus is recorded in fact.
21 This charge of using false evidence against Jesus is best supported in Mark
   14:55–9.
22 Cf lines 20–1 and 96–8 above, Epp 1879:54–5, 1902:32–3 and 322–4.

Christian religion and then of the prestige of the faculty of theology, if it
acts in a way worthy of your counsel.   110

Now, in order that you may acquaint yourselves with the whole question without undue trouble, I send answers to several articles which are being investigated in a session at the Sorbonne, as I am told.[23] At the same
time I send the book in which I respond to the calumnies of Béda, indicating the relevant passages so that they will be more readily discernible.[24] If   115
your authority holds these rowdy disturbances in check, it will be greatly
appreciated. But if these men ignore even that, I shall give an accurate portrayal of the spitefulness of this calumny in its true colours, and I shall
send it to the Most Christian King.[25] And I have no doubt that, being a sincere lover of true piety and a hater of discord, he will in some way im-   120
pose silence upon these men who, to please a few stupid pseudomonks under the guise of religion and piety, conduct themselves as true enemies of
religion and piety. May your august assembly flourish and be preserved
safe from harm by him through whom kings reign and judges render just
judgments.[26]   125

Given at Basel, 14 November in the year 1527

1906 / To Noël Béda   Basel, 16 November 1527

This is the last in the increasingly bitter exchange of letters between Erasmus
and Noël Béda, the syndic, or director, of the faculty of theology of Paris (Ep
1804 n14). Erasmus' previous letter to him (Ep 1679) was written nearly two
years earlier (6 February 1526), and Béda had replied to it on 29 March 1526
(Ep 1685). The present letter, which Erasmus published in the *Opus epistolarum*
(1529), is not a reply to Béda's Ep 1685 but is rather a summary denuncia-

* * * * *

23 The Paris faculty met twice a month in regular session at the church of Saint-
Mathurin, which belonged to the Trinitarian order. Additional or extraordinary meetings were usually convened at the Collège de Sorbonne. Allen suggests that Erasmus sent the *Prologus supputationis* (Basel: Johann Froben, August 1526); but since that was aimed at Béda's positions in his book of a year
and a half earlier, Erasmus may refer here to notes that anticipate his published response to the faculty's determinations (under consideration at this
time but published only in 1531).
24 *Supputatio* (Basel: Johann Froben, March 1527); cf Epp 1902 n45 and 1922:45–6.
25 There is no record of any letter from Erasmus to Francis I after his Ep 1722 (16
June 1526), which succeeded in convincing the king to ban the sale of Béda's
Annotationes.
26 Prov 8:15

tion of Béda and a final exhortation to him to reexamine his censures – or, as
Erasmus calls them, his calumnies. We cannot be certain that Béda received
this letter, which was sent with others that were confiscated in Alsace (see Ep
1922:38–40). Those letters – or some of them – were eventually recovered and
redirected, but this one does not appear with the letters from Erasmus that
Béda published in his *Apologia adversus clandestinos lutheranos* (Paris: Josse Bade
1529; repr Argentré *Collectio judiciorum* III-2 2–80); nor, however, did two other
letters from their correspondence appear there.

ERASMUS OF ROTTERDAM TO NOËL BÉDA, GREETING
I fear I may be undertaking this task in vain; nevertheless charity, which according to Paul hopes all things, has encouraged me to make this attempt to
see if I can win over my brother.[1] At this moment, my dear Béda, I wish to
see in you not the sort of person you have revealed yourself to be in your actions and in your writings,[2] but rather a brother in Christ and a colleague in
the priesthood and in the profession of theology.[3] I beseech you, what spirit
drives you to return to that old farce in order to please Lee, who has embarked on a similar venture in Spain,[4] and to avenge your suffering?[5] And
in your utter lack of principle, which you share with your accomplices, what
makes you so eager to rub off the stain of your reckless behaviour on your
college,[6] which has always been held in respect and veneration? Your blatant
calumnies are known to all, your manifest lies, the shameless slanders that
you showered upon your undeserving neighbour who invoked your friendship. Armed with flowery conceits like these, you strut about, not lying low
but shamelessly appearing in public, and you give no thought to reconciliation with your brother. Perhaps you even dare in this fratricidal frame of
mind – I shudder to mention it – to approach the sacred Eucharist and the

* * * * *

1906
1 Cf 1 Cor 13:7, Matt 5:22–5.
2 That is, in his active pursuit, as syndic of the faculty of theology, of humanists
  whom he regarded as heretics, and in publishing his *Annotationes*.
3 Erasmus resented Béda's and Pierre Cousturier's refusal to address him as a
  fellow theologian; cf Epp 1581:20–1, 1902 nn11 and 24.
4 Erasmus was convinced that Béda had encouraged Edward Lee to publish his
  critical book against Erasmus' New Testament annotations in 1520 and suspected that Lee was planning a new attack; cf Ep 1814:311–12 and n39, 1902
  n17.
5 Probably a reference to the royal suppression of Béda's *Annotationes*; see Ep
  1722 introduction.
6 The faculty of theology of Paris, not Béda's own Collège de Montaigu

communion table,[7] and in that mouth that stirs up such discord to receive
the heavenly symbol of peace. How can one reconcile such slanderous talk   20
with the Eucharist, or such violent hatred with Holy Communion?

It is human, says the poet, to sin,[8] and yet whether to sin in such a
way can be called human I know not. It is human to lapse into ordinary
defects. What you do knowingly and willingly, with perverse and obstinate
spirit, is more criminal than murder, more execrable than poisoning. Yet,   25
even admitting that it may be human to vent one's rage against your brother
once, under the sway of drunkenness or frenzy, surely it is diabolical to
continue to do so. But to add evil to evil, to heap worse upon worse! I adjure
you by your baptism, what name shall we give to that? If you had even an
ounce of shame you should at least have first purged yourself of lies and   30
calumnies too well known to be concealed before girding yourself for new
calumnies. Now so far are you from being dissatisfied with yourself·that
you even criticize the supreme power of the king, implying that it hinders
the administration of justice.[9] But if the king were to administer justice to
you, my fine friend, you would reap the reward accorded to calumniators,   35
trouble-makers, and enemies of public order.

My brother, I am in desperate fear for the salvation of your soul. And
although you pretend that I am your enemy, you – I know from certain
experience – are more than an enemy; yet, as Christ loves me, I take pity
on such an enemy. Examine your conscience, my brother, return to your   40
senses; it is better to retrace one's steps than to rush headlong over the
precipice. If you scorn men's judgments of you, if you spurn my solicitude
for your salvation, you should at least respect God, who sees into every
heart and avenges all evil machinations. Would that I possessed some rite
of exorcism or incantation to charm away this loathsome spirit from you!   45
An evil spirit sent by the Lord lay hold of Saul, yet at intervals it left him
when David played on his harp.[10] But you are so set on rushing headlong
into worse difficulties that I am afraid that not even David's harp could
soothe your raging spirit. Certainly I should like to have a miraculous lyre

* * * * *

7 Here and in line 21 Erasmus uses the late ecclesiastical Latin transliteration of
  the Greek σύναξις, appropriated directly into English usage as 'synaxis' in the
  seventeenth century to apply to the mass or Eucharist.
8 Terence *Adelphi* 471
9 Like its ally, the Parlement of Paris, the faculty of theology thought the policies
  of King Francis I to be too lenient towards humanists and heretics. The faculty made several attempts to urge the king to adopt more stringent measures
  against them or to give the Parlement free rein to deal with them.
10 1 Sam 16:14, 23

so that I could cure this great affliction of yours. For I see that you are in 50
the gall of bitterness and in the bond of iniquity.[11] When did Augustine, to
whom you seem to give great importance, ever rage with such fury against
the Donatists or the Circumcellions as you do against Erasmus, your friend
and brother, and one who at his own personal risk combats those whom
you detest as enemies of the church?[12] Nothing has ever yet been found in 55
his writings that could be called impious. It is only the manner of expression or words not understood or malicious distortion that provide food for
calumny.

And at this point the example of Lee commends itself to you, whose
first outburst of fury did not please even my enemies and was a cause of 60
great displeasure to his best friends in England. And there is still no one in
England who believes what he is doing in Spain. And you call him a perfect theologian, although he never set foot in a school of theology.[13] He is
so important to you for no other reason than that he hates Erasmus. And I
have reason to believe that his first book, printed in Paris, was in great part 65
from your hand.[14] Flatter yourself, call it zeal for the faith as much as you
like; believe me, it is pure madness, the work of Satan. The spirit of Christ
produces far different things – charity, joy, peace, patience, kindness, goodness, faithfulness, gentleness, faith, moderation.[15] How could such a mass
of calumnies, lies, and blasphemies issue from the heart of a man unless it 70
were possessed by the spirit of Satan? Just return to your senses, my dear
Béda. Merciful is the Lord and of great compassion.[16] If you call upon him,
he will impart his good spirit to you, who will lead you back on the right
path. As for me, I will readily pardon what has been done, interpreting that
the Lord commanded you to slander me, as he once commanded Shemei to 75
curse David.[17] Perhaps it seemed good to him to purify me in this way. And
if I wrote anything harsh against you I will not hesitate to beg your pardon
and make amends as best I can.

* * * * *

11 Acts 8:23
12 Undoubtedly, an allusion to Erasmus' three books contesting ideas of Luther:
   De libero arbitrio and the two books of *Hyperaspistes*. For the comparison
   with Augustine's opposition to the Donatists and the Circumcellions, see Ep
   1895A:42–3 with nn8 and 6; cf Ep 1902 n31.
13 See Ep 1902:105 and n24.
14 Lee's *Annotationes*; see Ep 1902:85–8 with nn16 and 17.
15 Gal 5:23; Erasmus' list is a slight enlargement of what are traditionally called
   the 'fruits of the Holy Spirit.'
16 Jon 4:2
17 2 Sam 16:5–6

All good men profess with one accord that no book has been of more profit to them than my *Paraphrases*, which is the work you single out for attack.[18] Don't you see that this is a suggestion of the serpent who envies man's salvation? Why do you not show yourself instead an instrument of Christ? You boast that you are the champion of the church. But by what means, I ask you, could you attack the church more vehemently than by crushing with your calumnies the man whom the church's adversaries consider their mortal foe and by stirring up new discords in the world? I know that your passions are prompting you to do this. But, believe me, there is nothing more deluding than hatred, nothing more empty than anger, nothing more deceitful than envy. Believe me, I repeat, my dear Béda, you are listening to the worst of counsellors. Take counsel judiciously with charity and the spirit of Christ, and you will perceive into what an abyss Satan is striving to carry you off, deluding your mind with the false image of piety. Do you not see how much discord there is in the world? And you, as if it were not enough, embark on this dreadful business.

If I should yield to the insults heaped upon me and defect to the enemies of the church, from whom would God demand an account of this wretched soul of mine but from you? That I have stood firm until now is not owed to my own strength but to divine assistance; and with that same support I shall hold out to the end, as is my hope. Who would not be wearied by such bitter and sustained abuse? If I were to give in, do you not see what havoc I could create? And do you not consider how widespread is the evil you are now fomenting? Erasmus is not so bereft of friends as you imagine. And, though he be the weakest of mortals, do you not reflect that truth is a powerful and invincible force? Do you not take into consideration that the great majority of men are prone to disregard both the authority of papal councils and that vested in you? What will they say when they see a swarm of accusations produced, to which I have already responded, as if no response had been made? or when they see verbal quibbling, distortions of the truth, and malicious suspicions? I for my part will do my utmost to avoid being the cause or even the occasion of such a calamity, if that is possible. To that end I conform myself to the

* * * * *

18 All fifty-eight pages of Béda's *Annotationes* against Erasmus contain references to alleged errors in the *Paraphrases*. His special attention to the paraphrase on Luke may have risen from the Parlement of Paris' request to the faculty to review it in order to ascertain whether or not the printer should be granted a *privilège*, or copyright for it (Farge *Procès-verbaux* 6 no 5A, 8 no 7E, 11–12 no 11A, 17 nos 16A, 18C).

norms of Christian tolerance and moderation. But if you remain deaf to all these admonitions and continue to fan the flames, knowing I am innocent of all impiety, I will vigorously rebut any charge of impiety made against me. The outcome will not be laid to my charge. This letter will acquit me before God and men. I shall pray to God that he give you a better frame of mind. If he hears my prayer I shall give thanks for his goodness, and I shall rejoice with you and shall have no desire to remember past evils.

Given at Basel, 16 November in the year 1527

1907 / From Alfonso de Valdés   Burgos, 23 November 1527

This letter answers one from Erasmus dated 28 August, but not extant, which Erasmus chose not to publish and which may have contained a sharp rejoinder to Valdés' suppression of certain letters of Erasmus (see Ep 1839:60–2). The present letter, autograph throughout and conserved in the Rehdiger Collection (MS 254 156) in the University Library, Wrocław, was first printed in LB III-2 1721–2 *Appendix epistolarum* no 342. It would be answered by Erasmus' Ep 2018, which is almost exclusively devoted to answering Valdés' query here about the meaning of Erasmus' motto, *Concedo nulli*.

For Alfonso de Valdés, a member of the secretarial staff of Emperor Charles v, see Ep 1807 introduction.

Cordial greetings. The letters that you sent on 28 August to the emperor and the chancellor and the two archbishops and then to me and the rest of your friends have finally arrived.[1] The emperor read your letter in Latin and in my translation into Spanish, and he will respond by the first carrier.[2] The archbishops and all the others will do the same.[3] Concerning the outcome of the drama staged by the monks, I have written you in duplicate copy and I have answered your letter of 18 September.[4] I presume they have all

* * * * *

1907
1 Epp 1873 (to Charles v, dated 2 Septemer), 1872 (to Mercurino Gattinara, dated 1 September), 1874 (to Alonso de Fonseca, dated 2 September), and 1864 (to Alonso Manrique de Lara, dated 26 August). The letter to Valdés was probably dated 28 August.
2 Ep 1920
3 The responses from archbishops Fonseca and Manrique de Lara are not extant. Erasmus replied to the latter on 21 March 1528 (Ep 1980).
4 Valdés' letter, which probably contained the accusatory articles that Erasmus refuted in his *Apologia adversus monachos quosdam Hispanos*, is not extant; see Ep

reached you. The archbishop of Seville took great pleasure in your letter and
declares his loyal devotion towards you.[5] We discussed your case at great
length. He says that he would like you to explain, for the benefit of the   10
weak, certain passages found in your works and to give clear expression to
your ideas, which he knows to be orthodox.[6] I answered that you would be
glad to do this as far as your honour and reputation would allow, which all
your followers wish to remain intact. We decided in the end that we should
await Luis Coronel,[7] who was absent at the time. He arrived yesterday and   15
bids me to send his best greetings. We will exert every effort to put an end
to this business without confusion and without prejudice to your authority.[8]

In the meantime be of good heart and do not let the wickedness of
the monks trouble you, at least no more than befits a good Christian. For as
far as you are concerned they cannot add to your glory in any better way   20
than by railing against you with their insolent abuse. I would prefer that
you suppress publication of your response to the articles of the monks and
make sure that it is not printed. This would certainly be a sign of your moderation, especially since the articles have not appeared in print anywhere. I
would also wish that you not mention any monk by name but rather that you   25
answer them all in general and that you secretly send your response to the
archbishop of Seville.[9] I would not wish, my dear Erasmus, that you drive
these hornets into a frenzy, since they are already more than a little stirred
up.[10] Although they are despised by nearly everyone, they command the admiration of some because of the insolent audacity they display in their public 30

* * * * *

1879 n16. Erasmus' letter to Valdés is not extant; but its contents were reported
by Diego Gracián in a letter to Alonso Fernández; cf Allen 7n.
5 Alonso Manrique de Lara, inquisitor (Ep 1864)
6 Erasmus once reported that Henry VIII had once asked Colet to rephrase his
opinions for the sake of clarity (Ep 1211:658–60). Manrique's and Valdés' desire for Erasmus to do likewise was shared by many of Erasmus' Spanish supporters like Virués, Tovar, Coronel, and Gratián, but Erasmus resented such
suggestions as unfriendly.
7 On Luis de Coronel, a secretary to Alonso Manrique de Lara, see Ep 1814 n64.
8 The Valladolid inquisition had been prorogued *sine die* on 5 August because
of an outbreak of plague.
9 On the articles see n4 above. Erasmus had already sent his *Apologia adversus
monachos quosdam Hispanos* to Manrique in a first draft on 2 September (Ep
1877) and then in a more complete version in October (see Epp 1879 introduction, 1888). Contrary to the advice of Valdés, he would publish it in 1529
(Basel: Hieronymus Froben).
10 Cf *Adagia* I i 60.

sermons, stopping at nothing, scorning princely authority and the decrees of the senate.[11] This they owe to their cowl and to the naivety of the Christian populace.

You need have no fears about your works, since you have distinguished defenders in Spain. Put the finishing touches on your book *De ratione concionandi*, the dialogues on Lutheranism, and all the other works you promise in your catalogue.[12] I see that you take a great task upon yourself in wishing to answer the letters of all your friends.[13] I praise your courtesy, but you could easily save yourself this fatigue if you wrote at greater length to one person and merely greeted your other friends in two or three words of salutation.

I am most grateful for the letter you sent to Virués.[14] His good will towards you deserves a similar friendship in return. He exercises great prestige in all circles. I hear the same about Luis Coronel and Juan de Vergara.[15] You could write to them occasionally as special friends and ignore all the others, whose sentiments are less a help than a hindrance. Besides, it is not worth your while to write long letters to those whom scarcely anyone else would deign to address.[16]

I wished to give you this friendly advice; take it always in good part. We are anxious to see the second book of the *Hyperaspistes*.[17] It has not yet

* * * * *

11 The identity of the 'senate' here is not clear. Valdés perhaps intends the same group of 'fathers' who convened Erasmus' critics prior to the more formal inquisition in Valladolid (see Ep 1814:145–50).
12 Valdés must have had in hand a copy of Erasmus' *Catalogus lucubrationum* (1523), which listed not only works completed but those that Erasmus intended to finish (Allen I 34:19–22 / Ep 1341A:1334–8). He finished the work on preaching, *Ecclesiastes sive de ratio concionandi* only in 1535 (Basel: Hieronymus Froben). The promised 'dialogues on Lutheranism' (Allen I 34:22–9 / Ep 1341A:1338–46) were never written. The colloquy *Inquisitio de fide* 'An Examination concerning the Faith,' produced in 1524, might be considered an alternate solution to this proposal, since in it Luther appears under the altered name of Barbatius.
13 Cf Ep 1804:69–70 and n12.
14 Not extant. It doubtless answered Virués' Ep 1838 and acceded to the appeal that Valdés had made on behalf of Virués (Ep 1839:104–5).
15 On Coronel see n7 above; on Vergara, Ep 1814 introduction.
16 Valdés certainly intends here Juan Maldonado, to whom Erasmus had sent the lengthy Ep 1805, which Valdés intercepted and for which he had already reproached Erasmus (Epp 1805 introduction and 1839:9–15, 49–62).
17 It had appeared in late summer (Basel: Froben, c August 1527); see Ep 1853.

arrived here. We have not seen the concluding part that you said you had written for the Babylas, and we do not know what Babylas you are talking about unless you explain it to us.[18] In addition, there are some who wish to know the meaning of that device you use to seal your letters with the inscription, 'I yield to none.'[19] There is a movement to establish concord among princes. The emperor desires it sincerely for the sake of public tranquillity, but I see others who are set on plunging the government into chaos.[20] If God in his goodness does not look favourably upon these matters, it will be all over for both sides.[21]

Farewell.

At Burgos, 23 November 1527

I have written this in haste, for the courier is here. I could add nothing more.

You recognize the hand of your friend Valdés.

* * * * *

18 The 'Babylas' was Erasmus' Greek edition of John Chrysostom's *De Babyla martyre* (Basel: Froben, August 1527), the life of the third-century martyr Babylas; see Ep 1856 introduction and n5. With it Froben printed at the end the *Epistola in tyrologum quendam impudentissimum calumniatorem*, a defence of Erasmus' theology of the Holy Spirit, which is published in this volume as Ep 1858 to Robert Aldridge.
19 Erasmus will later answer this query with Ep 2018, where he establishes that it is not he who speaks these defiant words but Terminus, the god of death. He explains that, upon receiving a ring bearing that god's image, and being about forty years old, he took this as a reminder of the inevitability of death. He subsequently had a seal made with the image of Terminus bearing the motto *Cedo nulli* 'I yield to none' (see CWE 2 150 *illustration*), and later had a medallion cast by Quinten Metsys bearing Erasmus' image on one side and Terminus and the slightly altered motto *Concedo nulli* on the other (see Epp 1092:5–6 and n2, with page 260 *illustration*; cf Epp 1408:34–8 and n17, 1452:32–42). This reminder that death yields to no one, he explains, exhorts him to live a better life; cf J.K. McConica, 'The Riddle of "Terminus"' *Erasmus in English* 2 (1971) 2–7.
20 Valdés' *republica* could possibly be interpreted as 'Christendom' or 'commonwealth.' However, given his position as imperial secretary and taking into account his deep concerns about the growing religious division in Germany, the political rifts among the German princes, and the rivalries between them and the emperor, Valdés probably refers here to the well-being of the Hapsburg empire. See also the following note.
21 Allen, seeing this in relation to Erasmus' use of *republica* in Ep 1872:20 to Gattinara, interprets this to mean the two polities of church and state. But see previous note.

1908 / From Juan Maldonado   Burgos, 29 November 1527

The autograph of this letter (first published as Ep 78 in Förstemann-Günther) was in the Burscher Collection of the University Library of Leipzig (on which see Ep 1254 introduction). Maldonado, unaware of Erasmus' letter to him (Ep 1805, which had been intercepted and suppressed by Alfonso de Valdés), writes here to inquire about Erasmus' reception of Ep 1742. For Maldonado and the circumstances of this correspondence see Epp 1805 introduction, 1839:10–14, 49–50, 78–81.

†

Cordial greetings. I wrote to you, Erasmus of Rotterdam, glory of our age, in the month of September 1526,[1] at greater length perhaps than I should have, since you apply yourself with such fervour to sacred studies that it seems a breach of piety to distract you even in the slightest. But while I gave in too much to the love I bear you and all that concerns you, I almost forgot   5
about the mass of sacred labours that weighs you down. I even thought that I would be doing you a favour if I recalled the devotion of my fellow Spaniards to you, if I disclosed to you the irritation of your ill-wishers and the sincerity of those who wish you well, if I revealed to you the melodrama enacted by the hooded bands.[2] Thinking all that was over, perhaps I made   10
you complacent about repelling the darts that were subsequently hurled against you with tragic fury. But who would have thought that these actors, who put on a show of piety, once ordered to be silent, would unexpectedly return to the stage? I shall not recount to you what went on recently in Valladolid at the crowded assembly of your friends and enemies;[3] I know   15
that you will have had a complete report. I read your letter to Valdés,[4] who is a forceful and effective herald of your praises. I also read the one to Virués,[5] a pious man and a theologian after your own heart. You make it

* * * * *

1908
1 Ep 1742
2 An allusion to the hooded cloaks worn by members of some religious orders
3 The inquisition into Erasmus' orthodoxy; see Epp 1791 and 1814 introductions.
4 Only Ep 1807 is extant. It is nevertheless puzzling that Maldonado read mail addressed to Valdés, who did not know Maldonado at all at that time, and who still considered him as someone whom scarcely anyone else would deign to address (Ep 1907:46–8).
5 No letters of Erasmus to Alonso Ruiz de Virués are extant; but see Epp 1814 n17 and 1907:42. Virués had written to Erasmus (Ep 1838).

sufficiently clear in these letters that nothing escapes you and that you are
already preparing your thunderbolts against these fierce giants who have   20
tried to thrust you down from the heavens.[6]

There is one thing, however, about which I shall not be silent. After the
postponement of the assembly that had been convened against you,[7] I approached a certain Dominican,[8] a man of great learning and one on whom
the faction of your rivals was principally dependent (I had some acquain-   25
tance with him through our common literary interests, and your works had
often elicited admiration from both of us). I asked him whether what I heard
was true, namely, that he had been a fierce opponent of yours in the assembly and that all the hopes of the monks hung chiefly upon him. I also asked
him whether he thought you were a true Christian or not. He began to   30
temporize and to admit in ambiguous words that you were a sincere and
Catholic Christian and that those who spread rumours to the contrary were
mistaken in their judgment. But he maintained that there were things in
your writings that should be eliminated and that their removal would not
detract in the least from your glory. And at the same time he cited one or two   35
passages in which, even if what you said were true, he said that you leave
a loophole for doubt concerning some very important aspects of Christianity. I shall not mention the many words we exchanged on this subject. In the
end we parted, with his declaring that if ten lines were to be removed from
your books, all that remained would be salutary for the Christian people.   40

When he left me, he immediately ran into citizens who are devoted followers of the monks, because they have not read your works. In their presence he condemned not only ten lines but recommended that all your writings be consigned to the flames. He did the same, I found out a little later,
in the presence of certain meddlesome nuns and other prominent women,   45

* * * * *

6 The mythical race known as Giants were defeated by the Olympian gods.
7 On 13 August 1527 because of the outbreak of the plague
8 Allen (21n) concluded that the Dominican intended here was Pedro de Vitoria, the Dominican brother of the illustrious Francisco de Vitoria – perhaps
  because at this time Pedro frequented Burgos, where Maldonado lived (cf
  Ep 1903:19–20 and n9), and because in Ep 1910:276 Erasmus asks Francisco
  to try to temper the criticisms of his brother. But Maldonado more likely intended here Francisco de Vitoria himself, who fits better Maldonado's description of his 'great learning' and of their 'common literary interests.' *Pace* Juan
  Luis Vives' opinion that Francisco de Vitoria was totally devoted to Erasmus
  (Ep 1836:25–36), we know that his opinions about Erasmus were mixed in the
  very sense described here by Maldonado. See Beltrán de Heredia *Cartulario* VI
  115–17. On the problem of identifying Vitoria's brother see Ep 1836 n8.

who in our country often lay down rules for their husbands in matters of religion. I relate this to you so that you may understand that the more intelligent among your antagonists are stirred up and inveigh against you and your works more through weakness of character, afraid to desert the common cause, than through sound judgment. They know full well how profitable your works are to Christianity, but they are reluctant to renounce their widespread tyranny, which they have no hope of retaining if your writings survive unscathed. When in the company of those who have read your writings without prejudice, they hang back, dissemble, and resort to every expedient. They are satisfied that if they prove you wrong even in one article out of so many then their frenzied attacks were not an act of impiety. But when they happen upon unlettered men who know no Latin, they exude their poison and reveal their true selves.

Valdés claimed and Virués confirmed that in one of your letters in which you named those to whom you were writing you mentioned my name. In any case no letter of yours reached me.[9] If you did write it I am most annoyed that it was not delivered to me, whether through my own ill luck or the carelessness of the letter carriers or those to whom you send bundles of letters. If you did not send it, I do not ask a reply. I prefer that you spend your precious time in sacred studies rather than diverting it to things that hold you back and are of no benefit to your studies. It will suffice if in some way I may know that my letter reached you. In the letters you write to Valdés or Virués, who are my close friends,[10] you may add in the margin that you received my letter; or even a simple greeting would be enough.

In Burgos you have a great number of friends, especially in Diego Osorio, a patrician of very noble birth.[11] He has such admiration for your writings and so identifies your cause with that of all Christians that he

* * * * *

9 Erasmus had actually addressed Ep 1805 to Maldonado through the offices of Valdés; but the latter, shocked at its tone and claiming not to know Maldonado, sent a copy to Juan de Vergara but did not forward it to Maldonado, reporting to the latter merely that Erasmus had sent his greetings; see Ep 1805 introduction. After reading this, Erasmus, ignoring the advice of Valdés, dispatched a copy of Ep 1805 to Maldonado, but there is no confirmation that he received it.

10 Surely an instance of 'name-dropping.' Virués knew Maldonado, but he had to explain to Valdés who Maldonado was: see Epp 1839:11–14 and Ep 1907:46–8.

11 A nobleman and long-time patron of Maldonado. Juan Luis Vives had already sent to Erasmus a copy of a letter from Maldonado to Osorio describing the meeting at Burgos between Pedro de Vitoria and Alonso Ruiz de Virués; cf Ep 1836:22–3.

never ceases to complain and lament daily to the archbishops of Toledo and
Seville[12] that they have listened to your critics without making a concerted   75
effort to make this clear: that you were indicted in absentia for all of Spain
to see and had to rely on friends to plead your cause; and that your adversaries, driven on by envy, struggled in vain and in the end were vanquished
by the testimony of truth and suffered the punishment that they deserved.
Thus they may serve as a warning to sincere and believing Christians that   80
they should not always put their faith in outward appearances and monkish garb. He therefore sends his greetings, not daring to write to you; for,
as he often says, there is in our day no style so polished that, compared to
yours, it does not leave one cold and provoke nausea. He is more a man of
piety and fairness than of ambition and desire for empty glory.   85

Farewell, from Burgos, 29 November, in the year 1527.

Your humble servant, Juan Maldonado of Burgos

†

To the excellent professor of Christian philosophy Desiderius Erasmus
of Rotterdam

1909 / To Francisco de Vitoria   Basel, 29 November 1527

Although line 46 of this letter reveals the identity of the addressee, Allen conserved the anonymous and misleading Latin salutation printed in the *Opus
epistolarum* (1529) – the same confusion of the Paris faculty of theology with
the Collège de Sorbonne that we saw in the salutation of Ep 1902. Vitoria held
his doctorate from the Paris faculty but had no connection whatever with the
Sorbonne. Erasmus makes the mistake himself in Ep 1922:41. In the text of the
present letter, however, he never uses the term 'Sorbonne' but employs instead the terms 'your college' (nine times) and 'faculty' (twice). Thus the misnomer 'Sorbonne' in the salutation may perhaps be attributed to the Basel editors, not to Erasmus, who was living in Freiburg-im-Breisgau when the *Opus
epistolarum* was published.

The letter does, however, betray Erasmus' mistaken presumption that Vitoria exercised influence with the Paris faculty of theology. This probably stems
from Juan Luis Vives' inaccurate report that Vitoria 'has defended your cause
on more than one occasion before a crowded assembly of theologians in Paris'
(Ep 1836:25–8). Although Vitoria remained in Paris for one year (1522–3) after
completing his doctorate in order to teach in the Dominican *studium*, he then

* * * * *

12 Alonso de Fonseca and Alonso Manrique de Lara

returned to Spain in 1523. He never took part in the deliberations of the faculty of theology – indeed there was only scant mention of Erasmus in the faculty meetings in that academic year. Believing Vives' report, however, Erasmus sent this letter to Paris with several others addressed to correspondents there, along with one to be forwarded to William Warham in England and at least one pamphlet to Spain (Ep 1922:40–5). Marcel Bataillon, knowing that Vitoria was in Spain and not taking into account Vives' report, speculated that Erasmus' real intention was that the letter be opened and read by interested persons in Paris (Bataillon *Erasme* [1991] II 97). On Vitoria see Ep 1836 nn9 and 10.

This letter draws together a number of Erasmus' criticisms of the Paris faculty, its syndic Noël Béda, and of scholastic theology in general.

ERASMUS TO A SPANISH THEOLOGIAN OF THE SORBONNE,
GREETING

God by his good favour makes right intentions prosper; the perverse plots of men he generally turns back on the heads of those who contrive them. For many years now certain monks (in name only, for in reality no one 5 could less deserve the title) imagine that I am their enemy. Their only motive is that the reflowering of good letters and the efforts of a new, spiritual Christianity to regain its primitive vigour detract from their privileges and authority. In fact there is hardly anyone who holds true monks, the purest of Christians, dearer than I do. These men have long been prejudiced against 10 me; and, as the proverb has it, the only thing lacking to the wicked was a convenient pretext.[1]

This was provided them in Spain, as letters of friends inform me, by Edward Lee, who was discharging a mission of peace there in the name of the king of England. But contrary to the intentions of his king he has ignited 15 a disastrous fire.[2] He did the same thing once before in Louvain,[3] infecting the whole university as far as he could with the poison of discord. The

* * * * *

1909
1 *Adagia* II i 68
2 Erasmus suspected Edward Lee, who served as Henry VIII's ambassador to Charles V from 1525 to 1530, of fomenting the recent opposition to him in Spain. See Ep 1814 n39. For accounts similar to the one in this letter, see Ep 1864:6–10, 1893:33–8, 1902:85–6, 1903:1–2.
3 Erasmus' troubles with Lee began in Louvain after the publication of his *Annotations on the New Testament* (1516), and he complained about Lee at that time in over seventy letters. On the controversy between them see Rummel *Catholic Critics* I 95–120.

venture came off so badly that it did not please even my enemies and gave
great displeasure to his best friends, except for a few unlearned persons[4]
who were swayed more by passion than by reason. His character seems to   20
have been created, fashioned, and sculpted for nothing else than the sowing
of discord. When I was forced in my apologies to expose the man's malice
together with his abysmal ignorance,[5] he repressed his resentment for several years, but in the meantime was preparing a book against me – not to
defend his own actions, for that would have been impossible, but to heap   25
new calumnies upon me. He went about this in such a clandestine manner that no one in England believes what I say about his activities in Spain.
Nor have I any doubts that in his trip through France he spread his venom
among his comrades in malice.

In Spain, certainly, when he encountered monks who were ill-disposed   30
towards me, he began to circulate a disturbing book much more idiotic than
the previous one, and he pretends that he wishes to publish it. But that he
will never do; I wish he had.[6] It contained alarming accusations against me
concerning the most holy Trinity, against the divinity, dignity, and glory of
Christ, and against the divinity of the Holy Spirit. In addition, there were   35
brief epitomes laying the subject matter before the reader with amazing du-
plicity. The monks took heart from all of this, and the first attack took place
at the emperor's court with the help of the Dominicans.[7] This was quashed
by the authority of the grandees. It was renewed again with such passion at
Salamanca by those Franciscans who are reputed to follow a more strict ob-   40
servance and who seemed determined either to win or to die in the attempt.[8]
They spoke out in public meetings, babbled on in private converse, posted
articles for all to see, and issued challenges to debate; you know the various stages of these melodramas. With some difficulty this disturbance was
calmed though not suppressed by the emperor and a few of the archbishops.   45

Finally there appeared on the scene the Dominican Pedro de Vitoria,
superior of the order in Burgos, who is active as a preacher; he is your

* * * * *

4 *Idiotae*; see Allen Ep 1153:171n.
5 On Lee's *Annotationes libri duo* and Erasmus' responses, see Ep 1902 nn16 and
  25.
6 See Ep 1814:311–12 and n39, and cf Ep 1864:6–9.
7 That is, by the Dominican master general García de Loaysa, confessor to Emperor Charles v; see Ep 1903:12 and n7.
8 Cf Epp 1902:91–3 and n19, 1903 n8. Vitoria, now living and teaching in Salamanca, would know these events in greater detail than Erasmus, who had
  them only second-hand from his Spanish correspondents.

brother, I am told.[9] He inaugurated the play with such fanaticism that the people cried out that in this world we must not listen to emperor or bishops but must obey God rather than men.[10] Need I say more? The situation was heading for open revolt. Whereupon the emperor and the bishops decreed that these rabble-rousers cease their outcries, submit whatever articles they considered to be contrary to the faith, and in the meantime refrain from public disturbances. They obeyed reluctantly but more than compensated for their silence by private grumbling. Seven orders of monks are engaged in this conspiracy.[11] The articles were exhibited and proved to be not only outrageous and completely unfounded but dangerous to deal with because of some blockheads, not lacking in Spain, tainted with Judaism or paganism.[12] Deliberations began, but the proceedings soon degenerated into mad confusion, and in the end a sudden outbreak of pestilence dissolved the assembly.[13] The fact that your brother is the ringleader of this episode does not make you any the less dear to me. Letters from friends assure me that you are a man endowed with singular learning and objectivity,[14] and I have the hope that with time you will recall your brother to saner judgment.

For the rest I do not doubt that those who are staging this drama have secretly sought the help of your college,[15] so that by joining forces with them they may crush Erasmus. How alien such intentions are to a Christian spirit you will readily perceive in your wisdom. As far as I am concerned, my loss will hardly be felt. But I fear this may be the origin of new discord, since I have always championed and preached the cause of peace and concord. Cousturier and Béda are persuaded that Erasmus is a figure of no importance.[16] But he has won the loyalty of many powerful personages through

* * * * *

9 Cf Epp 1836:20 and n8, 1902:93–4, and 1904:18–20.
10 Acts 5:29, cited also in the accounts in Epp 1902:97 and 1903:21
11 See Ep 1893:38.
12 Cf Epp 1858 n69, 1805 n15.
13 See Ep 1814.
14 For example Ep 1836 from Juan-Luis Vives (lines 25–36)
15 If (as seems likely) Erasmus thought Vitoria still to be in Paris, the use of 'your college' here would refer to Vitoria's alma mater, the faculty of theology of Paris. If he intended the letter to be forwarded to Spain, the reference is of course to the University of Salamanca, where Vitoria was teaching at this time.
16 On Cousturier, the Carthusian doctor of theology of Paris and author of the anti-Erasmian book *De tralatione Bibliae*, see Ep 1804 n65; on Béda see Epp 1804 n14, 1906.

his studies in all parts of the world. It may seem silly to mention it, yet it
must be said. My shelves are full of the most cordial letters from kings, the
emperor, cardinals, archbishops, bishops, dukes, men of high standing, and   75
scholars.[17] In fact, I have such fervent patrons in Spain that I have been compelled to write to them not to stir up fatal discord in their striving to show
me their devotion, but rather to abandon Erasmus to the deep, to be rescued
perhaps by some sea-monster.[18]

And from such insignificant beginnings, how many firestorms do we   80
see breaking out! In Spain things have been calm up to now and studies were flourishing in complete tranquillity.[19] Now, as people inform me,
the outrageous behaviour of monks, abetted by Lee, has brought on this
tempest. So far they have earned only the hatred and derision of good
men. What good can arise for Christianity from such polluted sources? Lee   85
plots revenge by whatever means he can. The same spirit animates Béda.
He fails to answer the questions he should have addressed, but rehashes
the same articles arranged in a different order, thinking that things will
turn out well if your censure condemns some of them.[20] He does not reflect how little importance the world gives nowadays to these kinds of cen-   90
sures, and would give even less if it saw through such malicious judgments
as those of Lee and Béda, whose madness your college should have cured
rather than appeased. What shame does a man have who gave the world
such a book to be read without waiting for the judgment of the college?[21]
Without permission to print it he printed it anyway, but he evaded the   95

* * * * *

17 Cf Ep 1804 n12.
18 Probably an allusion to Jonah and the whale (Jon 1:12–17)
19 Cf Ep 1805:386–8.
20 Many of the points raised by Béda in his *Annotationes* reappear in the censures
   of Erasmus by the faculty of theology (in 1526) and by the whole University of
   Paris (in 1527 and 1528). See Ep 1875 n26. Erasmus still hoped to forestall or
   soften an eventual general censure in Paris, of which he had received a most
   pessimistic outlook from Gervasius Wain (Ep 1884).
21 Erasmus' information is faulty. On 16 May 1526, when Béda asked the faculty's permission to publish his rebuttals of Erasmus' *Paraphrases,* he explained
   that several of the doctors present had studied the materials and could report
   on them. After hearing the report of those masters, the faculty deliberated and
   concluded formally that Béda's articles against Erasmus could be printed and
   diffused; see Farge *Procès-verbaux* 137 no 152B. Béda's censures of Erasmus
   were therefore appended to the book containing his more numerous censures
   of Lefèvre d'Etaples that the Faculty had already approved on 15 February
   1526. The *Annotationes* against Lefèvre d'Etaples and Erasmus was published
   28 May 1526 (Paris: Josse Bade).

king's edict by having it distributed in Germany and secretly sold among you.[22] Furthermore, when my *Supputationes* had exposed before everyone's eyes the ignorance of the man matched only by his malice,[23] instead of defending himself he selected some articles from his stack of calumnies, translated them into French, and sent them to the king's court.[24] The arti-   100
cles he selected were calculated to arouse everyone, from the leading cit-
izens to the simplest women – in a word, all of France, as he had previously done in maligning the title attributed to the king of England.[25]
Now he thrusts these same articles in your face, but arranged in a different order, of course, so as to appear new, as if no answer had been made   105
to them.

When such actions are carried out through evil intrigues and with perverse intention, what, I ask, can come of it but great harm? I shall, of course,
do my utmost to prevent it from happening; at any rate, I shall see to it that
the blame cannot be laid at my door. I shall not however repay evil with   110

* * * * *

22 See the letter from Francis I to the faculty of theology of Paris, at the head
   of Ep 1902, nn4–5. The Cologne printer Petrus Quentell quickly reprinted in
   August 1526 the edition that Francis I had just banned in France. There is no
   evidence that Béda himself arranged this, as Erasmus charges here. Printers
   in the sixteenth century commonly reprinted books without the permission or
   even the knowledge of the author.
23 On the *Supputationes errorum in censuris Natalis Bedae* (Basel: Johann Froben
   1527), the omnibus volume containing four books against Béda, see Ep 1804
   n14.
24 Obviously a confused report about the *Duodecim articuli infidelitatis Bedae*. This
   small book, purportedly translated into French, was an open attack not by
   Béda but against him. It was sent to the king; see Ep 1875 nn30–1 and the
   letter of King Francis I (at the head of Ep 1902) n7. Many false reports were
   circulating at the time. See for example Ep 1763, in which Levinus Ammonius mistakenly reported that the Parlement of Paris took an active role in
   suppressing Béda's *Annotationes* and that it ordered Béda to notify in person
   every bookseller in Paris about the ban.
25 In dedicating his *Paraphrases on Luke* (August 1523) to King Henry VIII
   Erasmus attributed to him the title 'most invincible king of England and
   France' (see Ep 1381), and this was maintained in the second edition
   (1523–4). Béda rightly commented that this offended French officials (see
   Divinationes ad notata per N. Beddam de Paraphrasi Erasmi in Matthaeum LB
   IX 489A–B), and Erasmus removed it in his 1526 edition. In that same
   year the Paris faculty of theology approved for printing Henry VIII's response to Luther's criticism of the *Assertio septem sacramentorum*, but insisted that the title *Rex Franciae* be excised (Farge *Procès-verbaux* 166 no
   188D).

evil, nor shall I avenge my personal grievance at the cost of public detriment to the church. Just as I will not commit the crime of impiety, so I will
not suffer calumny. But suppose I were neither willing nor able to put up a
struggle; there would still be no lack of those who would seize upon this as
an occasion and pretext for dispute. What then is Christianity, if there is no   115
peace? And where is peace if there is no charity? Where, in turn, is charity
when everything is conducted with such hatred, such spite, such outrageous
and ignorant calumnies?

We see from what meagre beginnings such tempests arise, how eas-
ily a dormant evil is awakened, and with what difficulty it is stilled once   120
set in motion. Whence did this ravaging fire spread by Luther take rise,
and how did it arrive at its present dimensions, if not from the kind of
indiscretions Béda is perpetrating? Martin had proposed that his theses
concerning papal indulgences be discussed. These indulgences were being
preached with no less impiety than impudence by certain mendicant tyrants,   125
who stop at nothing in hope of gain. To their excesses Luther opposed his
Problemata.[26] Those whose interests were at stake took offence. The *Problemata* were sent to Leo x. Silvester Prierias refuted them so successfully
that the pope imposed silence on him.[27] After this the monks made a great
hue and cry among the people, and could speak of nothing but heresies,   130
blasphemies, and schisms. I recount what I saw with my own eyes. Nothing

* * * * *

26 The *Resolutiones disputationum de indulgentiarum virtute* (Wittenberg: Johann
Grunenberg, May 1518), usually referred to by Luther as his *Probationes*. See
WA 1 522–628.
27 On Prierias, the Dominican theologian and master of the papal palace who was
the censor of books in Rome, his responses to Luther, and the controversy that
resulted, see Ep 1875 nn41 and 42. Allen 118n contends that Erasmus' irony
cannot refer to Prierias' *Errata et argumenta Martini Luteris recitata* (Rome: Antonio Blado, 27 March 1520) because it contains a commendatory brief from
the pope. He concludes that it must instead refer to Prierias' *In praesumptuosas
Martini Lutheri conclusiones de potestate papae dialogus* ([Rome: Jacopo Mazzochio
1518]), his first book against Luther which answered not Luther's *Problemata*
but his original *Ninety-five Theses*. On these works see also Friedrich Lauchert,
Die italienischen literarischen Gegner Luthers (Freiburg-im-Breisgau 1912; repr
Nieuwkoop 1972) 15, 23, whose argument that Prierias does not deserve his
negative reputation has been affirmed by Heiko Oberman, Carter Lindberg,
Remigius Bäumer, and Michael Tavuzzi. Lauchert (15) regards as a false rumour the statement that the pope silenced Prierias; cf Michael Tavuzzi *Prierias:
The Life and Works of Silvestro Mazzolini da Prierio, 1456–1527* (Durham, NC and
London 1997) 119–22, who argues convincingly that for the most part Erasmus' correspondence shows respect for Prierias both as a theologian and as a
person.

won more universal favour for Luther. But if there had been a sober discussion of the matter of indulgences as they were originally intended, this epidemic would never have taken hold of the world.

And in fact what was ever written by anyone with such piety and caution that it could escape the calumnies of the temperament that is revealed in the writings of Béda? I wrote not in a rhetorical but in a somewhat refined style;[28] not that I condemn the scholastic style - it too has its uses, but it is not everywhere appropriate and does not appeal to all readers.[29] I strove to attract scholars of belles lettres, as with a lure, to the love of sacred letters. Béda does not understand such language. This is borne out by the facts themselves; there is no need of proofs. Then in the *Paraphrases* I deploy a mode of expression proper to each speaker; I do not make allusions to our times, but try to give clear expression to what Christ and the apostles taught in their times. Béda examines what was said in a rhetorical style by the standard of scholastic – or rather Sorbonic – precepts, new ones proliferating there daily. He does not appreciate figures of speech, which character is speaking, or the times in which he lived. What is more wrong-headed than this desire for calumny? It is all the more pernicious when it excerpts my words from here and there, artfully omitting those that explain my meaning and preclude any occasion for calumny. Sometimes he substitutes his own words for mine, leaves things out, and adds things, in whatever way it serves the purposes of calumny.[30]

By way of example: St Jerome, exhorting the clergy to disdain riches, expresses himself in this way, 'He can have no part with the Lord who possesses anything besides the Lord.'[31] If someone were to interpret this maliciously, does he not seem to deprive all clergy without exception of any right to property? Similarly, who held marriage more in contempt than he?[32] What

* * * * *

28 Vives had alerted Erasmus to Vitoria's love of good style (Ep 1836:29–30). The Flemish humanist Nicolaus Clenardus praised Vitoria as one of the great stylists of the age; see *Correspondance de Nicolas Clénard* ed Alphonse Roersch, 3 vols (Brussels 1940–1) I 38, 225–6 and III 18–19, 191.
29 Erasmus' habitual criticism of scholastic style and theology is not infrequently tempered by statements like this; cf Epp 622 introduction, 947:42–3, 950:21, 952:49–51, 967A:16–18, 980:43–5, 950:21, and 1219:55–7.
30 See Ep 1911:21–3.
31 Jerome Ep 52.5 to Nepotian CSEL 54 421:17–20 / trans W.H. Fremantle *The Principal Works of St Jerome* (Oxford 1892; repr Ann Arbor, Mich 1975) 91
32 St Jerome's most extreme case against marriage, a commentary on passages from the Epistles of Peter and Paul, is in his treatise *Adversus Jovinianum libri duo* 1.4–14 PL 23 (1883) 224–231C / trans W.H. Fremantle (see preceding note) 350–1. The citation is not verbatim.

kind of good is that which is praised by comparing it with what is worse?
What blasphemies would my opponent intone if he found anything like that 160
in my writings? Likewise when Basil, exhorting the rich to generosity, said
they appropriated to themselves the goods of others,[33] what more subver-
sive statement could be found if you examine it not according to the rules of
exhortation but with dogmatic rigour? I could compile thousands of statements of this kind from tried and true authors, if circumstances required it. 165

But the most shameless part of all is that he charges me with things that
I neither wrote nor dreamed of. And you see how men's minds are stirred
up; gone is that simplicity of the common people. Once it was enough to
say, 'Such is the verdict of the venerable faculty.' Would that in our day they
would at least listen to the voice of reason and the Scriptures! You will say, 170
'With such people you must not use arguments but rods.' Perhaps that is
what human law prescribes, but the law of charity dictates otherwise.[34] It
does not easily despair of anyone. Many err innocently, many are so slightly
infected that they can easily be cured.[35] And if there were no hope for the
leaders, nevertheless for the sake of the others who have not yet been given 175
up for lost it would be useful to refute their leaders with sure and evident
proofs and telling passages of Scripture. I for my part might have wished
that the authority of the Roman pontiff had more influence for the edifica-
tion of the church, but you see how low it has fallen. And none did more
harm to that authority than those who shamelessly exalted it. The same can 180
be said of the monks. They deprived themselves of what was their due when
they demanded more than was their due. So, according to the proverb, the
rope that is stretched too taut breaks.[36] The world expects something exceptional and superhuman of you. This idea was inculcated in everyone's
minds first of all by the fame of your college, then by the many years dedi- 185
cated to the study of philosophy and to sacred letters. Now, now is the time,
O men of God, to manifest that exceptional and superhuman quality. This
storm requires expert pilots; this disease demands outstanding doctors; do
not waste your time in frivolities.

* * * * *

33 Basil of Caesarea *Sermo de divitiis et paupertate* 2.5 PG 32 1170. For a study of this
letter see Yves Courtonne ed *Saint Basile: Homélies sur la richesse* (Paris 1935).
Erasmus did not include these sermons in his 1532 Greek edition of Basil; they
were first edited by Simon de Maillé, archbishop of Tours (Paris: Guillaume
Morel 1556–8).
34 Cf for example Christ's admonition to turn the other cheek (Matt 5:39).
35 Cf Ep 1555:75–8.
36 *Adagia* I v 67

This faculty should fight under Christ's banner and not serve the per-   190
sonal interests of men. Put to use your skill and authority against those who
attack the citadel of your prestige[37] openly and deliberately and have shaken
it in the eyes of many, expressing in printed books a loathing for your dogmas. Do not turn your energies against one who defends the same things
you do to the best of his ability, fighting a bloody battle, one who is pre-   195
pared to excise mercilessly anything really irreligious that might be found
in his works. In war the soldier who has performed his duty well usually
receives a reward from his commanders. Will it be my reward, after carrying out my duties with all earnestness, to be crushed under the calumnies and lies of men like Cousturier and Béda? This battle must be fought   200
with the sword of the gospel and the spirit of Christ,[38] not with the cunning of mischief-makers. Wisdom conquers malice. Malice does nothing but
produce malice. God forbid that your authority be at the service of any
man's malice in opposition to pious zeal. By this time the world and its
rulers understand for the most part that this confusion is the work of pseu-   205
domonks, whose purpose in suppressing Luther is to deal a death blow to
the study of languages and literature as well. As they never learned these,
they have an aversion for them and are ashamed of their ignorance. Even
if both their aims were pious, they are hurrying the second one on prematurely.[39] Their other target, Luther, is still alive, not to say reigning in   210
many people's hearts. He has on his side those who profess his teachings,
those who defend them, those who make light of your authority and expose it to scorn before the public, eager to espouse whatever has been condemned by your decisions. Show your manly courage against them rather
than against Erasmus, who is serving in your camp under the same banners,   215
who is fighting not without bloodshed those whom you consider to be your
mortal enemies.

    And yet it may happen that in my struggle against impiety I myself
may at some point fall into some impious belief. This happened to Jerome
and Cyprian and Ambrose and Augustine,[40] if you subject them to severe   220
scrutiny. If such were the case, it may be ascribed to ignorance or imprudence, but not to malice. If anyone could prove and demonstrate any impiety in my writing, I will gladly suppress it like a spurious offspring; if

* * * * *

37 Presumably the Paris faculty of theology
38 Eph 6:17; cf Matt 10:34.
39 That is, attempting to destroy good learning before they have finished with
   Luther and his followers
40 Cf Ep 1864 n16.

something is not well understood, I will explain it. That will be accomplished without undermining Christian charity, for the greater benefit of   225
all concerned, and lastly to the honour of your order, whose good name
must be preserved intact in all respects in the best interests of Christianity. This approval is best won by sound arguments, not through hatred and
calumny.

There are those who pretend that I show little regard for the esteem   230
owed to theologians, because here and there in my writings I recall them
from their immoderate preoccupation with petty questions, or because I exhort them to scriptural sources and the study of languages. And Béda, I
suppose, was thinking of their reputation when he published such a book!
I refer specifically to the book he wrote against me; for the others I leave it   235
to others to judge.[41] It would have been in keeping with the prestige of the
college first of all that there were no Bédas in it and next that they did not
wield such power.[42] If it has been resolved to defend all his actions whether
right or wrong, then everyone will know that the matter is being conducted
with bias rather than sound judgment. Would to God that this will not oc-   240
cur. You swore to achieve consensus,[43] but in honourable causes. You swore
a mutual defence of honour, but by such methods as these your honour is
greatly damaged. If it is the honour of tyrants and not of theologians, it
is anything but honour. Perhaps the matter does not concern everyone, but
everyone's reputation will be affected. Wherefore men of integrity should   245
take all care that nothing be issued under the name of the college that does
not correspond to its reputation.[44]

* * * * *

41 His *Annotationes* against Lefèvre and Erasmus. For the list of Béda's books,
    see Farge BR 35.
42 Béda was the syndic, or director in charge of the faculty's agenda and enforc-
    ing its decisions, from 1520 to 1533. He had proposed revival of this office,
    which had fallen into desuetude in the fourteenth century, and was elected its
    first holder. But he had also tried three or four times, without success, to be
    relieved of its burden. See Farge *Orthodoxy* 41–2. In effect the faculty found
    Béda indispensable in carrying out its decisions.
43 Faculty decisions were arrived at not by counting votes but by consensus after
    deliberation. Rarely was a decision taken or published without a sense of con-
    currence of 'the larger and better part' of the members.
44 Probably an attempt on Erasmus' part to forestall publication of the faculty's
    common verdict against him, which was arrived at first on 16 May 1526 and
    later expanded and renewed in December 1527 and June 1528 (Farge *Orthodoxy*
    190–1); cf Ep 1875 n26.

I am not familiar with the present state of affairs of the college, but partly from the tenor of the times and partly from other sources I can easily hazard a conjecture.[45] In every deliberative body there have always been   250
those who by their ambitions and unscrupulousness arrogate supreme control to themselves, and it is not easy for the better part to win. First this ambitious faction decides on a course of action in private. Next, they exclude men of integrity and bring in those they consider suitable. At first they commit themselves to consensus, but then come the threats. 'Now,' they say, 'we   255
shall see who belongs to the Lutheran faction.' If anyone tries to speak impartially, he is called worse than Luther by the murmuring assembly. There are men of mild temperament who prefer to keep their peace rather than start an argument with such men; others set their convictions aside for some private reason. There are those who nurture some fear or hope, and for that   260
reason suppress their better judgment; others do not understand what is set forth plainly and simply. There are those who are blinded by the same passions as Béda; others, as we know, no matter how sensible, are roused to frenzy by the clamour and tumult of those around them. And so a decision of the whole is not decided but extorted. When it is published those   265
who extorted it introduce their own prejudices without the knowledge of their colleagues or with their connivance. And this is called a decision of the college.

I would never have written these things to you if I had not been persuaded by the letters of learned men[46] that you are a man of great and sound   270
judgment and that you will see to it that proper procedures will be observed there.[47] In me, you may be sure, no duty expected of a Christian will be lacking. Spiteful calumnies I will not tolerate even if six Roman pontiffs

* * * * *

45 For example Ep 1884 from Erasmus' friend, the Paris theologian Gervasius Wain, written 11 October 1527, which Erasmus had recently received and in which Wain reported Béda's 'plots' and the faculty's 'ill will, dishonesty, and injustice' regarding Erasmus. In what follows Erasmus expands Wain's report (lines 250–68).
46 Notably Ep 1836:25–36 from Juan Luis Vives
47 These lines confirm the conclusion in the introduction that Erasmus mistakenly thought Vitoria to be in Paris and to have influence in the deliberations of the faculty of theology. In fact, even if Vitoria were still in Paris, his being a Dominican would work against his having influence in the faculty. See James K. Farge 'Les dominicains et la Faculté de théologie de Paris' in Les dominicains en France devant la Réforme 1520–1563 Mémoire dominicaine. Histoire. Documents. Vie dominicaine 12 (Paris 1998) 21–36.

were to give corroboration to your verdict. For neither papal authority nor
that vested in you should have any power to suppress truth and innocence.   27:
Make this same intercession with Pedro de Vitoria, your brother.[48] In that
way, you will both have a splendid victory,[49] if Christ triumphs, if charity wins the day; and you will render a much greater service to your college and your brother than to Erasmus. May the heavenly Spirit infuse into
your souls all that is pious, holy, and conducive to Christian friendship.   28(
Farewell.

    Given at Basel on the vigil of the feast of St Andrew. In the year 1527

1910 / To Germain de Brie   Basel, [c 29 November 1527]

> First published in the *Opus epistolarum* (1529), this letter replies to another (not
> extant) in which Brie laments the death of a good friend. Erasmus' previous
> letter to him (Ep 1835) answered Brie's Ep 1817. This letter contains a number
> of Greek words and phrases. It was among those confiscated in Alsace (Ep
> 1922:43).

ERASMUS OF ROTTERDAM TO GERMAIN DE BRIE, GREETING
Yes, you would surely say that Erasmus outdoes Atlas if you knew what a
mass of toils and troubles this puny little man carries on his shoulders.[1] If
I dedicated myself to nothing else I could scarcely keep up with the letters
that speed their way to me from all parts of the world,[2] not always pleasant   5
nor of the kind that can be answered in a few words. How much time do
you think I have lost in *apologiae*?[3] not to mention the time I have spent in
revising old works[4] and printing new ones. At the present moment all of
Augustine, a writer of obscure subtlety and not very pleasing prolixity, is

    * * * * *

48 See n9 above.
49 *victoria*.The play on the surname of the brothers Vitoria is more successful in
   Latin.

   1910
1 Atlas was a mythic Titan, guardian of the pillars of heaven. In later lore he
   himself holds the heavens up, a role that made him a favourite subject in
   Hellenistic art.
2 Cf Ep 1804:69–73 and n12.
3 That is, Erasmus' polemical works against Lee, Zúñiga, Pio, Cousturier, Béda,
   Luther, and more recently against the Spanish monks; cf Ep 1893:16–28.
4 Notably the *New Testament*, the *Adages*, and the *Colloquies*

being rushed through six presses.[5] You will be pardoned for your laconic   10
brevity if you can report a similar excess of work.[6]

I wonder who this dear friend can be whose passing drove you into
exile, as you write;[7] when you really value something you are loath to let it
go.[8] I hope, my dear Brie, that you can fulfil your wish, at your convenience,
to betake yourself here to lift your own spirits and to pay me a visit. The   15
consolation will be mutual, for it is not many days since Johann Froben took
leave of us,[9] a man of true nobility if ever there was one. But I am afraid you
will say that you did not see Erasmus even if you saw him: what you will
see is a cicada just at the point of shedding its skin.[10] Here comrades are few
but faithful: Beatus Rhenanus, Bonifacius Amerbach, Henricus Glareanus.[11]   20
You know them all from their writings, I imagine. That is my triumvirate.
They sustain my old age with their reassuring words. I assure you that you
will receive a warm welcome from them, and I am not afraid of the ruin
that the proverb portends.[12]

I can scarcely say how many curses I invoke upon these wars because   25
of which we are cut off not only from Italy,[13] which you say you pine for, but
practically from the whole world. And day by day, it seems to me, the anger
of princes grows more ferocious. What an eclipse we have witnessed of the

* * * * *

5 Cf Ep 1890:12–13. See also Ep 2157, the preface to the ten-volume edition
   (Basel: Hieronymus Froben 1529), and Ep 1895A, the preface to its second volume of letters. For an extensive treatment of the Augustine edition see Allen
   VIII 145–7.
6 Rendered in Greek, πολυπονία
7 As the letter is not extant, the identity of the friend remains unknown.
8 Horace *Epistles* 1.10.31–2
9 See Ep 1900, a eulogy of Froben, who died on 26 October (n1).
10 τὸ σύφαρ
11 Erasmus' friendship and collaboration with Beatus Rhenanus dated from 1514.
   In 1527 it had become somewhat strained, partly from a divergence of interests but more over the Eppendorf affair. Beatus left Basel in 1527 to settle
   permanently in Sélestat; see Ep 1821 n4. For Bonifacius Amerbach see Ep 1914
   introduction. The Swiss humanist Glareanus remained faithful to Erasmus all
   his life, and followed his lead in opposing reformers like Oecolampadius and
   Zwingli. Like Erasmus he moved to Freiburg-im-Breisgau to distance himself
   from the Reformation in Basel, but stayed to promote a reformed Catholic
   church in Freiburg after Erasmus returned to Basel. See also Ep 1821 n5.
12 Cf *Adagia* I vi 97: 'Stand surety, and ruin is at hand.' Erasmus uses the name
   of the goddess Ate for 'ruin' (ἄτη) in the adage.
13 Erasmus expresses a similar sentiment in Ep 213:2–3.

Roman sun by the Spanish moon!¹⁴ But the fates themselves prod us to turn
willy-nilly to philosophy, and teach us detachment from human affairs.   30

Before I received your letter, Balista came to see me on his way back
to France.¹⁵ I have never seen a more amiable person. He asked no other
service of me. As for the Babylas, I shall leave it to your decision.¹⁶

Farewell, at Basel, in the year [1528]

1911 / To Jean de Guise, cardinal of Lorraine   Basel, 30 November 1527

Having seen merely ephemeral results from his letters to French authorities
and institutions a year earlier (Epp 1721–3 and 1741), Erasmus attempted again
in Epp 1902, 1903, 1905, 1909, and this letter to forestall the censure of his
works in Paris. With those other letters dispatched at the same time and in
the same direction, this one was confiscated in Alsace, although Erasmus was
able to recover and expedite them again. He published this letter in the *Opus
epistolarum*.

For Erasmus' relations with Jean de Guise, cardinal of Lorraine, see Ep 1841
introduction.

ERASMUS OF ROTTERDAM TO JEAN, CARDINAL OF LORRAINE,
GREETING
I shall not detain your Excellency with preambles. While I continue to do
all in my power to end the discord within the church and restore it to tranquillity, Noël Béda foments new disorders.¹ The man is livid with resent-   5
ment, first of all because the book he wrote against Jacques Lefèvre was suppressed by a royal edict, although it has not in fact been suppressed, and
then because in my response to him I exposed my innocence and his shamelessness so clearly to everyone's view that it could not be better reflected

* * * * *

14 That is, the eclipse of the pope by the emperor, since the sack of Rome in May
   1527
15 Brie's letter is not extant. Allen identifies Balista with Girolamo Fondulo (Fun-
   dulus), an Italian teacher and friend of Brie, who enjoyed the patronage of
   French royalty and of humanist churchmen (see CEBR II 42).
16 Erasmus' Greek text of St John Chrysostom's *De Babyla martyre* appeared at
   the Froben press in August 1527; cf Ep 1856. Erasmus' comment here might
   relate to Brie's proposal to translate it into Latin (cf Epp 1817:44–8, and Ep
   1835:11–12).

1911
1 For a more extended disparagement of Béda, see Ep 1909:86–106, 135–53.

in a mirror.[2] Therefore he is preparing revenge with a gladiator's spirit[3] –   10
not by justifying himself, which is not possible, but by heaping up the same
calumnies once again in a different form. He has allies in the Sorbonne college[4] – 'like lips like lettuce'[5] – no exception here. The others are either ter-
rified by threats or keep silent to avoid confrontation. Meanwhile Béda and
his henchmen continue on their merry way to their hearts' content. The farce   15
is being acted out under the name of Erasmus, not of Lefèvre, although both
are their targets. He has a host of propositions taken from the *Paraphrases*, a
work that he despises for no other reason than that it incites many people
to piety. These, they say, he is delivering to the faculty, and I hear that they
have already pronounced judgment against several of them.[6]   20
    But how does this trickster[7] present them? He omits those parts that
clarify the matter and leave no room for calumny,[8] and adds things of his
own that lend themselves to calumny. He presents statements of the evangelists or the apostles that pertain to the early church as if I made them in
reference to our own times; and so under my name the teachings of Christ   25
and Paul are condemned. And this is not without a purpose; for nothing is

* * * * *

2 Béda's *Annotationes* contained two books of censures against Lefèvre and another against Erasmus. The Paris edition was suppressed, although its printer
   Josse Bade explained to authorities that 600 of the 650 copies printed had already been sold or shipped elsewhere, and the Cologne edition came out very
   quickly, a fact about which Erasmus complained several times, as he does
   here. For the withdrawal from sale of the Paris edition by the king and its
   reprint see Epp 1721 and 1722 introductions, 1763, 1902 introduction (the letter from Francis I to University of Paris 1–13 and n5), 1905:13–15, 1909:95–7;
   for Erasmus' response see Epp 1902 n8, 1905:113–15, 1909 n23.
3 *Adagia* I iii 76; cf Ep 1815 n19.
4 Erasmus may mean the Collège de Sorbonne itself, but more probably the
   faculty of theology. Neither Béda nor most of his associates in that faculty had
   any connection whatsoever with the Collège de Sorbonne.
5 Cf *Adagia* I x 71: *Similes habent labra lactucas* 'Like lips like lettuce.' Béda (a
   donkey, with rough lips) and his cohorts (thistles) are well suited.
6 Cf Epp 1884:24–6, 1905:41–2. On 16 December 1527 the faculty condemned
   114 propositions drawn mostly from Erasmus' *Paraphrases* and from his *Colloquies*. The proceedings of the faculty reveal that members from several different colleges had been delegated to examine propositions drawn from the
   Paraphrases, but there is no evidence of a judgment rendered until 16 December 1527 (Farge *Procès-verbaux* 137 no 152A–B, 177 no 209B, 178 no 210A, 179
   no 212B, 180 no 214A). For the final censure, not recorded in the *procès-verbaux*,
   see Argentré *Collectio judiciorum* II-1 53–77.
7 *artifex*; cf Ep 1902 n44.
8 The account that follows echoes Epp 1902:224–8, 1905:69–76, 1909:143–5.

more opposed to the aims of Béda and his cronies than the purity of the gospel teachings. Through such trickery even learned and honest men can be fooled. And although I gave very clear answers to most of his objections, he still presents his criticisms as if I had never answered them. By such stratagems he hopes that when my books are forbidden he will be looked upon as God.

The driving force behind these secret goings-on is the pseudomonks,[9] who hate good letters more than any heresy or magic, however much they try to conceal it. From these intrigues, which originate in the worst of sources and employ the worst of methods, what else could result but a great disaster for the world? As the tree, so is the fruit.[10] The root of this tree is contaminated by jealousy, hatred, and a mad desire for revenge. Its branches are shamelessness, perversity, calumny, insolence, falsity. How can it bear anything but poisoned fruit?

To accomplish his goals without any risk Béda tries to involve the authority of the college of theology in his outrageous behaviour, although the most sensible part of that college would condemn and repudiate the man's unruly excesses, if everyone were free to say what he thinks. And if the whole college were to issue judgments like those of Béda, it would not do so without grave loss to its own prestige. I should not willingly diminish the high esteem in which this college is held, but no pious man should suffer the charge of impiety. To the degree that his royal Majesty will impose silence upon wicked conspiracies of this sort, he will at the same time be safeguarding the tranquillity of his kingdom and of scholarship and of the church. These interests will be best preserved if the college issues judgments worthy of the most learned and best theologians. And as for myself, I would prefer to devote my precious time and efforts to other things. For I am hard at work on Augustine so that a more correct text worthy of him may be made available.[11]

If your Excellency will grant me this service, the greatest fruit of this kindness will redound to the state. His royal Majesty may be informed in

* * * * *

9 Although this was likely true in Spain, it is less applicable to Paris, where doctors from mendicant orders had little influence in decisions of the faculty of theology. See James K. Farge 'Les dominicains et la Faculté de théologie de Paris' in *Les dominicains en France devant la Réforme 1520–1563* Mémoire dominicaine. Histoire. Documents. Vie dominicaine (Paris 1998) 21–36.
10 Matt 12:33
11 See Ep 1910:8–10.

the following manner: at the present moment the world is everywhere torn apart by discord, even if we do nothing to make it worse. We should do all we can, using every honest expedient, to put these evils to rest, rather than provoke new disturbances through our personal animosities. So renowned a faculty would be better advised to use its resources against declared enemies than against its comrades-in-arms, and to heal all those it can rather than alienate those who are of sound health. Its authority should serve the glory of Christ, not the private ambitions of Béda. The faculty itself will have most to gain. There is no end to calumny, especially if anger and jealousy are brought to bear in its decisions. Finally, a book in which some error is found should not immediately be condemned, since many errors are found in the most respected Fathers of the church.[12] It is best to overlook certain human failings, for, once stirred up, they break out in some worse form. Your Highness would rightly be angry with me if I were acting in my personal interest. But I am certain that in your zeal for true piety you will not neglect the common good. I wish you every success in this undertaking.[13]

If you wish to be more fully informed about these matters you will be able to learn the whole story from Gervasius, the theologian.[14] He is a man of uncommon learning and impartial judgment.

Given at Basel. The feast of Andrew the apostle, in the year 1527

1912 / From Johann von Vlatten   Speyer, 30 November 1527

Autograph throughout, this letter was in the ill-fated Burscher Collection in the University Library, Leipzig (on which see Ep 1254 introduction). It was first published as Ep 79 in Förstemann-Günther.

Johann von Vlatten was a cleric from the duchy of Jülich-Cleves. After legal studies in both Orléans and Freiburg-im-Breisgau, he matriculated at Bologna in 1526 and received a doctorate in civil and canon law that same year. Ten letters from Erasmus to him and nine from Vlatten to Erasmus are extant, several of them during the Diet of Augsburg (1530), which Vlatten attended. Ep 1390, the dedicatory letter to Vlatten in Erasmus' *Tusculan disputations* (Basel:

* * * * *

12 Cf Ep 1864 n16.
13 We know not whether the cardinal of Lorraine exhorted the king along these lines; but no royal measures against Béda or the faculty took place at this time.
14 Cf Ep 1884:18–20, Gervasius Wain's request that Erasmus mention him to Guise, his patron; cf also Ep 1903.

Johann Froben, November 1523), is of great importance for revealing Erasmus' understanding of Cicero and of classical antiquity in general; Erasmus also dedicated to him both editions of the *Ciceronianus* (Epp 1948 and 2088; cf CWE 28 337–41). Vlatten may well have been instrumental in Erasmus' completion of his treatise on preaching, the *Ecclesiastes* (1535): see Epp 2804, 2845, 3031. See also Ep 1390 introduction; CEBR III 414–16.

Greetings. Last year, most learned Erasmus, I sent you from Rome the medical works of Hippocrates, printed from a manuscript by Minutius Calvo,[1] so that with him as your guide you might be able to look after your health more satisfactorily. If you received them, my desire and expectation in this matter will have been amply satisfied. If not, seeing that these wicked 5 times are so fraught with danger and intrigue that any transferral from one place to another involves some risk,[2] you must write to inform me of it. I wrote to you from Regensburg during the recent assembly of nations concerning various subjects that I wished you to know about.[3] I entrusted delivery of the letter to envoys from Strasbourg;[4] I have thus far 10 had no answer. But at the present moment, when I learned that these excellent young men, sincerely devoted to your cause and dear friends of mine, were on their way to see you, I did not wish that such loyal followers should arrive there without a letter from me.[5] I wished neither to

* * * * *

1912
1 Vlatten visited Rome shortly after receiving his doctorate in Bologna. From 1510 to 1512 Marco Fabio Calvo transcribed the works of Hippocrates from Greek manuscripts, but the Latin translations appeared only in 1525 from the Roman press of Francesco Calvo (who in 1518 or 1519 had changed his middle name from Giulio to Minuzio, after his native town of Menaggio, near Como; cf CEBR I 245). The two Calvos, translator and printer, are apparently not related, although Erasmus confused them earlier in 1527 (see Epp 1810 n18, Ep 1825:33–4 and n13). Prior to the collaborative work of the two Calvos, when only a few works of Hippocrates had been available in Latin, the Greek physician Galen, who had settled in Rome in 164 AD, had been considered to be the best medical authority. See Marie-Laure Monfort *First Printed Editions of the Hippocratic Collection at the Bibliothèque Interuniversitaire de Médecine of Paris (BIUM)* http://www.bium.univ-paris5.fr/histmed/medica/hipp_va.htm.
2 War continued between papal and imperial forces, even after the sack of Rome in 1526.
3 The imperial diet convened briefly in Regensburg in May 1527.
4 The letter is not extant.
5 One of them was probably Christoph von Carlowitz, who left Cologne on 26 October 1527 for Basel, where he was a member of Erasmus' household until February 1528; see Ep 1899 n21. His companion has not been identified.

have them accuse me of discourtesy nor have you think that I had com-   15
pletely forgotten your numerous good services to me, which I do not imagine I shall ever be able to repay. You need not respond to this missive
unless you have nothing else to do, lest I seem to hold you back in any
way from your Christian apostolate – something I know is done by many
troublesome individuals who burden you with bundles of letters every   20
day.

Your magisterial volumes on free will gain the unanimous approval of
the most critical minds here,[6] although even they fear that controversies of
this kind with this type of person may some day be harmful to your venerable old age and to Christianity as a whole. For if you become involved in   25
these tragic calamities and dedicate yourself entirely to them, many splendid religious works from the past, which await from you and you alone elu-
cidation, elegance of style, and defence against egregious errors, will despair
that it is all over for them, and not without reason. Imagine, in your great
wisdom, what an enormous loss to literature and to religion this would en-   30
tail! My dear Erasmus, by the living God, apply yourself therefore to this
task, using the gifts that Christ has given you. It will bring not only glory
to you but concord and well-being to the state. This you will do if you ignore the insipid treatises of your adversaries and never cease to elucidate
the ancient sacred writers.
                                                                         35
I was inspired to write you these things more out of love of the Christian commonwealth than because I thought you needed my advice and encouragement. Therefore in your innate kindness take in good part this counsel of a young man. There are some eminent men of our social rank, Erasmus, who are eager to speak to you personally some day, who see you as   40
a man born for great and honourable things and successfully engaged in
the work of religion, and who want to express their sincere devotion to you.
These men, I assure you, not only champion your great merits but spread
your fame in a very visible manner. If I can steal away secretly for a few
weeks next spring, I shall come to visit you. Farewell, glory of our land, and   45
remember this most devoted follower of yours kindly, as I do you.

Speyer, in the year 1527, on the feast day of St Andrew the apostle
Johann von Vlatten, scholaster of Cologne, your most loyal servant in
every necessity

To the eminent Master Desiderius Erasmus of Rotterdam, his most re-   50
spected friend

* * * * *

6 Since Vlatten uses the plural he must intend not only the *De libero arbitrio* but
   also the two volumes of the *Hyperaspistes*, all directed against the theological
   positions of Martin Luther.

1913 / From Diego Gracián de Alderete   [Burgos? 1 December 1527?]

Allen was the first to print this letter, which is on f 1 of a seventeenth- or
eighteenth-century manuscript copy of the letters of Diego Gracián that is in
the library of the Casa de Alba at the Palacio de Liria in Madrid (ADA.C. 136
no 26a 158). Because the volume had suffered damage in a fire, Allen had
to interpolate a number of conjectural readings (not signalled below) and to
indicate one lacuna (marked here as an ellipsis). The text ends in the middle of
a page without a conclusion. The copyist's notation, *Deest nonnihil* 'something
is missing,' reveals this to be a defect in the original, not the result of damage
in the fire.

Diego Gracián de Alderete studied in Paris and in Louvain under Juan Luis
Vives. A protégé of Alfonso de Valdés, he served as secretary and translator
to a number of diplomats, bishops, nobility, and court figures, among them
Emperor Charles v. See Ep 1904 introduction and CEBR II 122. Erasmus will
acknowledge reception of this letter with Ep 1970 (15 March 1528) without
making any specific reference to Gracián's attempt to console him. Gracián's
drawing on the *Historia scholastica* instead of the Bible contravened much of
what Erasmus was working to accomplish by his biblical scholarship.

DIEGO GRACIÁN TO ERASMUS OF ROTTERDAM, GREETING

After taking leave of Maximilianus Transsilvanus, I sent you two letters,
most learned Erasmus, in which I made known to you what great efforts he
was exerting in behalf of your distinguished self at the court of her Serene
Highness Margaret of Austria.[1] Nor were my own frequent recommenda-   5
tions lacking to spur him on in his zeal and affection for you. Subsequently
I went to Spain, where at the court of the emperor a melodrama was being enacted very much like the one in Belgium.[2] Another Maximilian came
forth here also, namely, Alfonso de Valdés,[3] the emperor's secretary, who
undertook to defend your cause with great loyalty. Do not let men's wicked-   10
ness trouble you, my dear Erasmus; it is nothing new for good men to be

* * * * *

1913
1 Margaret, the daughter of Emperor Maximilian I and aunt of Charles v, had
   been regent in the Netherlands since 1517. The letters from Gracián are not
   extant; see Allen Ep 1970:3–4. On Transsilvanus see Ep 1802.
2 The attack on Erasmus by Spanish theologians, which Gracián compares to
   the hostility in Louvain of Vincentius Theoderici and the Carmelite Nicolaas
   Baechem
3 See Epp 1807 and 1907.

afflicted by adversity. For from the beginning it was ordained that in this perverse world the good man would undergo persecution.

Glance at the history of the world: how many examples you will find to support your cause. Abel's innocence was not tolerated by his   15 impious brother.[4] Abraham, the only one who worshipped God, was exiled by the Chaldean idolaters.[5] The mild and guileless Jacob, fearing the threats of his wicked brother, left his paternal household.[6] As for his son Joseph, his evil-minded brothers tried to destroy him.[7] Moses, who was destined to be the bearer of the divine law, was expelled by the Egyp-   20 tians into Ethiopia.[8] David, already destined to rule by the will of God, was persecuted by the king, who resisted the divine will.[9] Elijah, for having brought about the death of the pseudoprophets, was driven into exile by Jezebel.[10] Manasseh, unable to abide the reproaches of Isaiah, dared to kill

* * * * *

4 A reference to his murder by Cain; cf Gen 4:4–8.
5 One biblical account (Gen 11:31) relates that Abraham freely chose to leave Chaldea for Canaan, while another (Gen 15:7) says that he was led by God to do so. Gracián's version that Abraham was exiled by the pagan Chaldeans comes not from the Bible but from the late twelfth-century *Historia scholastica* of Petrus Comestor (PL 198 1091B / CCCM 191 80:36–9). This text, often used in place of the Bible itself during the Middle Ages, omitted some biblical texts and conflated or expanded others with materials from patristic commentaries, Midrash, the secular historian Josephus, and apocryphal legends. Erasmus and humanists in general objected to this kind of manipulation of the authentic biblical text.
6 Gen 27:43–5
7 They sold him to a passing caravan of merchants (Gen 37:18–28).
8 Neither the book of Exodus nor its parallel version in the *Historia scholastica* mentions Moses going to Ethiopia or being exiled by the Egyptians. As a young man he had fled to save his life to Midian, where he married the daughter of a local priest (Exod 2:11–15). The book of Numbers (12:1) relates that Moses' brother and sister reproved him for marrying a 'Cushite' woman, while the *Historia scholastica* relates that Moses married an Ethiopian princess (Liber Exodi 6 PL 198 1144). Gracián's reference to Ethiopia may also arise from the fact that the translators of the Septuagint, the Vulgate, and of versions stemming from them have confused the Cushites (the people of the ancient kingdom of Nubia in today's northern Sudan) with the people known to ancient Greeks and Latins as Ethiopians, following the sense of the word for 'dark' people; *Dictionnaire de la Bible* (Paris 1895–) II 744, sv 'Chus.' Departing from all biblical accounts, the *Historia scholastica* further relates that Moses led an army of Hebrews who saved Egypt from an invading army of Ethiopians.
9 King Saul; 1 Sam 16:13, 18:8–11
10 3 Kings (Vulg 1 Kings) 19:2

him.[11] Jeremiah was stoned by the Jews for making evil prophecies against   25
them.[12] The Babylonian captives banished <. . .> Ezechiel.[13] A method was
sought out to do away with Daniel because he would not submit to the spiteful terms of the Persian satraps; therefore he was thrown to the lions, with
whom he led a safer life than with his enemies.[14] The Baptist perished also,
victim of an incestuous woman's treachery.[15] St Paul, though he preached   30
the truth, was not listened to.[16] The Son of God made man, who came to
rescue the world from ruin, was rewarded with an ignominious death,[17]
which only added to his glory. When virtue is attacked it shows its true
mettle, like gold tested in the fire. Virtue can be shaken, but it cannot be
submerged.   35

1914 / To Bonifacius Amerbach [Basel? December 1527?]

This original autograph note (Öffentliche Bibliothek of the University of Basel
MS AN III 15 93), first appeared in the *Epistolae familiares* (Basel: C.A. Serin 1779).
Allen's dating is based on the reference (line 3) to a letter written recently to
'the cardinal' – possibly Ep 1911 to Jean de Guise, cardinal of Lorraine – and
to the message included there for oral delivery to King Francis I (lines 48–50;
cf line 1 below). If, instead, the king is Henry VIII (Ep 1878) and the cardinal
Thomas Wolsey (Ep 1998) then the date must be moved forward to June 1528.

Erasmus had known Bonifacius Amerbach, legal scholar and youngest son
of the Basel printer Johann Amerbach, to whose firm Johann Froben had succeeded, since at least late 1521, when he moved to Basel. He designated Bonifacius as his legal heir and the executor of each of his three wills, the first on

* * * * *

11 Not in the Bible; but the *Historia scholastica* (PL 198 1414B–C) relates that according to Jewish tradition King Manasseh exiled Isaiah, who then died of
   thirst on the site of the pool of Siloe.
12 Although the biblical text of Jeremiah records several plots against him, there
   is no mention in them of his being stoned, but a Christian tradition, probably inspired by Heb 11:37, presumed that Jeremiah died by stoning. See Tertullian *Adversus Gnosticos scorpiace* PL 2 (1878) 160A / CSEL 20 part 1 161:2;
   cf Jerome *Adversus Jovinianum libri duo* 37.2 PL 23 (1883) 350C. These accounts
   may also have stemmed from the apocryphal work known as IV Baruch,' where
   Jeremiah, as he is being stoned, predicts the coming of Jesus Christ after a
   lapse of 477 years. See *The Rest of the Words of Baruch: A Christian Apocalypse of
   the Year 136 AD* ed James Rendel Harris (London 1889) 17.
13 The lacuna in the text makes it impossible to identify the passage.
14 Dan 6:13–22
15 Matt 14:1–11
16 For example Acts 18:12, 19:8, 22:22; 2 Tim 2:15 4:9, 4:14
17 Matt 26, 27; Mark 14, 15; Luke 22, 23

22 January 1527 (CWE 12 538–50), the others in 1533 and 1536. Bonifacius saved all his notes and all the letters he wrote or received, so that the volume of his correspondence rivals that of Erasmus. It forms the kernel of the Amerbach papers in the University Library, Basel, and of the ten-volume *Amerbachkorrespondenz*. See CEBR I 42–6.

Greetings. Kings do not wish to suffer the torment of bad handwriting, and I have no secretary. I wrote to the cardinal in my own hand. If you come over after lunch, I shall give you a copy of the letter. Farewell.

1915 / To Jan (II) Łaski
Basel, c 9 December 1527?

Erasmus published this letter in the *Opus epistolarum* (1529). Allen's conjectural date is based on similarities with Epp 1916, 1917, and 1918. The letter which it answers is alluded to in BRE 265. Łaski will answer this letter with Ep 1954. On Łaski see Ep 1821 introduction.

ERASMUS OF ROTTERDAM TO JAN ŁASKI, PROVOST OF GNIEZNO, GREETING

I admire your prudence on this point,[1] my most distinguished friend. It is no ordinary man who can put men of evil character to good use and draw something worthwhile from harmful creatures. There are some people who 5
have a strong attachment to me, sometimes to my great detriment. I would prefer those who choose their friends more wisely.

Concerning the letter to the king I am happy that your advice brought me good fortune,[2] and my joy will be more abundant if it proves to be of equal profit to the state. Your show of devotion towards me cannot but in- 10
spire great gratitude in me; however, I should not cease to warn you lest your zealous support of me win you unpopularity. I cheered Glareanus when I showed him part of your letter. He is busier than ever; therefore the kindness of your gift was not misplaced.[3] As regards Beatus, do not be concerned;

* * * * *

1915
1 The letter from Łaski that occasioned this remark is not extant. Cf Allen Ep 1954:1–8, where Łaski attributes the prudence to Erasmus.
2 Erasmus wrote Ep 1819 to King Sigismund I of Poland at Łaski's behest. The 'good fortune' is not clear. Sigismund had not yet acknowledged Erasmus' letter, and did so only in February 1528, sending him a gift of 100 Hungarian ducats at that time (Allen Epp 1952:33–4, 1954:13–20).
3 Probably in acknowledgment of *De geographia* (Basel: Johannes Faber Emmeus 1527), which Glareanus dedicated to Łaski; cf Ep 1821 n5. As a result, Glareanus wrote to Łaski, eliciting a response on 20 February 1528, printed in

what is said of him is true, but he will not refuse a token of your affection   15
for him.[4] He can scarcely believe that the little book you mention has been
printed there in Poland, while sorely hoping that what you say is true.[5]

I would reprimand Hieronim for his courage, if it were not already too
late.[6] My anxiety was doubled by the precarious state of your health, and I
will not rest content until a letter from you brings me more cheerful news.   20
While it will give me great pleasure to see you, I am somewhat preoccupied
about how Spain will treat you. Not a few men have met their death there.[7]
Nor must it seem strange if I have anxious fears for so precious, so dear,
and so rare a possession.

I would not wish that there be any improper dealings with the king   25
concerning a gift,[8] lest I seem to have been hunting for it; for I know this
would delight some people. With regard to the two hundred florins[9] you

* * * * *

Lasciana ed H. Dalton (Berlin 1898; repr Nieuwkoop 1973) 18. On Glareanus
cf also Ep 1910 n11.

4 In acknowledgment of Beatus' dedication to Łaski of *In C. Plinium* (Basel: Johann Froben, March 1526); see Ep 1821 n5. Beatus Rhenanus was in Basel; see
Ep 1910:20. He wrote to Łaski at this same time (BRE 265, 15 December) and
was answered by Łaski on 20 February 1528: see *Lasciana* (n3 above) 114–15.

5 Beatus was correct in doubting that the Cracow printers had produced a complete Pliny. Łaski had probably alluded to the edition of book 1, followed by
an index of the whole work, published in Cracow by Marcus Scharffenberg on
22 November 1527.

6 Hieronim, Jan Łaski's elder brother. Like Jan he had been a paying guest in
Erasmus' house in Basel for six months. Erasmus dedicated the *Modus orandi
Deum* to him (Ep 1502; cf Epp 1622, 1751, 1805). Alternate forms of his name
are 'Hieroslai' and 'Hiaroslai.' Maria Cytowska (CEBR II 297) uses the Slavic
form 'Jarosław' when writing about the father of the three brothers, Hieronim,
Jan, and Stanisław Łaski. Erasmus clearly intends in this case Hieronim, the
brother, not Jarosław, the father. Like the Łaski family in general, Hieronim
was no friend of the Hapsburgs. After the defeat at Mohács (1526) he had
thrown his lot in with John Zápolyai, their Hungarian rival for the throne. Jan
Łaski was apparently unaware that Hieronim was in Constantinople when he
replied to Erasmus (Ep 1954) on 20 February 1528.

7 Several of Erasmus' friends or patrons had died in Spain or on voyages to
Spain, for example Jérôme de Busleyden, Jean Le Sauvage, Pedro Ruiz de la
Mota, and Jean Glapion; see Allen Ep 1926:1. In Allen Ep 1954:29 Łaski will
advise Erasmus that he has not yet committed himself to going to Spain.

8 That is, from King Sigismund I in return for Erasmus' Ep 1819

9 Almost certainly a reference to Łaski's purchase of Erasmus' library. In Erasmus' first will, dated January 1527, he stated that Jan (II) Łaski had agreed
to purchase his library for the sum of 400 'gold pieces,' while allowing Erasmus its use until his death, and that he had already received 200 of them from

may do as you think best. Nothing has reached me yet. I am grieved to learn that the study of literature is declining in your country while it is flourishing in Brabant and Spain. Of wars I see no end, so violent is the wrath of princes. The cruel rumour that Rome has been captured again is circulating here.[10] I hope that it is false.

Here the pestilence has carried off numerous victims once more, but it is milder than last autumn. Johann Froben, my friend beyond compare, was taken from us by a stroke of paralysis.[11] At first he was tormented for a long time by severe pain in his right foot so that a crueler death could hardly be imagined. The pain was tranquillized rather than eliminated by a doctor who was more daring than learned.[12] He began to regain a little strength; and, although his friends counselled him to stay at home and avoid the cold, he gave them a friendly smile but did not listen to them. So it happened that as he was trying to retrieve something from a high place a seizure of the malady threw him to the ground. The fall itself was enough to cause his death; after two days he could barely open one eye, already breathing his last. This man's passing has greatly affected me, especially since several presses are busily at work with all of Augustine.[13]

I shall gladly do what I can for Hosius.[14] But for the moment I do not have the time to write. I think your other friends will write to

* * * * *

Łaski. See CWE 12 542 with n20, which gives the value of these Rhenish gold florins. This sum is far too large to be seen (as some have done) as an expected reward from Łaski's uncle Archbishop Jan (I) Łaski for the dedication of the edition of St Ambrose (Ep 1855).

10 Imperial troops had entered and sacked Rome on 6 May 1527. Since only 70,000 of the 400,000 ducats ransom could be paid, the second pillage by imperial forces began on 25 September, and they remained in Rome until mid-February 1528, when most of the sum had been paid. The sum of 400,000 ducats was then worth £133,333.333 *groot* Flemish, £910,000.000 *tournois*, and £93,333.333 sterling.

11 See Ep 1900. The account of this illness parallels lines 95–121 there.

12 Perhaps the doctor called Vendelinus Hock of Brackenau, said to be Beatus Rhenanus' own doctor; see Allen Ep 1769:16n.

13 Epp 1890:12–13, 1910:8–10. The edition would appear in ten volumes in 1528–9 (Ep 2157).

14 The young humanist Stanislaus Hosius of Cracow was at this time a protégé of Piotr Tomicki and of Łaski. In Leonard Cox's edition of Statius' *Sylvae* (Cracow: Matthias Scharffenberg 1527) Hosius published a long poem describing Łaski's travels in western Europe and his association with Erasmus. He also published Erasmus' Ep 1819 to King Sigismund I (Cracow: Matthias Scharffenberg 1527). Later, as a bishop, Hosius would attend the Council of Trent,

you.[15] What I sent you at the time of the last fair seems not to have arrived.[16]
The same is true of my letter, which I entrusted to Severinus Olpeius, who
said he was setting out in your direction.[17] I dedicated Ambrose to your   50
uncle.[18] Whether my mind was influenced by an adverse fate[19] in so doing
I wish to know from you, for I was of two minds about it for a long time.
Someone more venomous than a viper has stirred up a tragic fuss against me
in Spain. Béda composed the prelude for it,[20] and now he wants to add the
dénouement, as you will learn from the enclosed letters and little book.[21] I   55
trust that in your prudence you will not spread any word of this in advance.
I had convinced your messenger George to remain here,[22] but he preferred
to hurry back to you rather than waste time idly here. Farewell, from Basel
in the year 1527.

1916 / To Jan Antonin   Basel, 9 December 1527

Published in the *Opus epistolarum*, this letter recounts much of the contents of
Ep 1915. For Antonin see Ep 1810 introduction.

ERASMUS OF ROTTERDAM TO THE PHYSICIAN ANTONIN, GREETING
Although your devotion, greater than that of Pylades,[1] surpasses all
kingly gifts, nevertheless you do not cease to rival them with new

* * * * *

direct the Counter-Reformation in Poland, and actively promote Catholicism
in Germany and Sweden; see CEBR II 206–7.
15 That is, Glareanus and Beatus Rhenanus (lines 12, 14–15 above).
16 Via Froben who went to the Frankfurt book fair in September; cf Ep 1916:11.
These letters apparently accompanied the edition of Ambrose (lines 50–1
below).
17 On Severinus Olpeius see Epp 1810:52–4, 1916:10–11. None of the letters carried by him at that time are extant.
18 Jan (I) Łaski, archbishop of Gniezno; see Ep 1855.
19 *Aeneid* 2.54
20 On the charge that Noël Béda had sponsored the 1520 publication of Edward
Lee's *Annotationes* against Erasmus cf Epp 1902:87 and n17, 1906:64–6 and n14.
Erasmus also suspected that the recent attacks on him in Spain and in Paris
were related; cf Ep 1902:85–6, 1903:1–3, 1906:7–8, 1909:92.
21 Probably an advance copy of the *Apologia adversus monachos quosdam Hispanos*;
see Epp 1877, 1879, 1888, 1967. On Edward Lee and the 'tragic fuss' in Spain
see Ep 1814 n39 and the references given there. On the images from the theatre, see Ep 1875 n13.
22 The messenger mentioned in Ep 1895:32

1916
1 The mythical faithful companion of Orestes

gifts[2] and threaten me with something so grand and extravagant that I will
not be able to overlook it. I wish I could convince you, Antonin, that your 5
affection is more precious to me than three royal kingdoms. George[3] delivered everything faithfully. I pray that Hieronim Łaski's courage will meet
with success; but I fear that he may be taken into custody.[4] Alexius Thurzo
has rendered me ample satisfaction if he took my challenge in good part.[5]
Severinus Olpeius left here in the month of September, laden down with my 10
letters.[6] I had also given letters to Froben on his way to the fair.[7] Whether
they were delivered or not I am not yet certain.

That the sagacious king was not displeased with my letter gives me
reason to rejoice; I neither approve nor disapprove its publication.[8] I am sure
you can make a good case for your decision. I would prefer that the prefaces 15
and verse be omitted,[9] for the simple reason that the praise contained in
them might excite jealousy. I do not want any efforts made to extort a gift.
For it will seem that this was all I was after, although in reality it was the
least of my concerns. In this matter I complied with the wishes of Jan Łaski,
who repeated the same message to me again and again. 20

It is too late now to take thought for Johann Henckel.[10] All we can do
is pray that what has been done will turn out well. I have had no correspondence from Paweł Krassowski.[11] I merely know of his good will from

* * * * *

2 Perhaps the gilt cup bearing the inscription *donum Antonini medici* that Erasmus still had in his possession in 1534. For documentation about it see Allen
   2n. For an earlier gift from Antonin see Ep 1698:16.
3 The messenger; cf Ep 1915:57.
4 That is, by the Turks, whom he approached on behalf of John Zápolyai, the
   anti-Hapsburg claimant to the throne of Hungary; see Ep 1915 n6.
5 Thurzo was a loyal supporter of the Hapsburg cause in Hungary, where King
   Ferdinand appointed him lord chief justice in 1527. In Ep 1572 Erasmus dedicated his Latin translation of two treatises of Plutarch to him; in the dedicatory letter Erasmus attempted to alert Thurzo to the ill effects of anger and
   of bearing a grudge (lines 78-99). Apparently he had not yet made any gift in
   acknowledgment of Erasmus' dedication. Cf Ep 1810 n13.
6 See Ep 1915 n17.
7 See Ep 1915 n16.
8 Ep 1819 to King Sigismund I of Poland; see the introduction.
9 See Allen Ep 1819 introduction.
10 His former service to Mary of Austria, queen of Hungary, left him in disfavour with John Zápolyai, who refused him permission to travel with Antonin to visit Erasmus but offered him a bishopric instead, which Henckel
   refused; cf Ep 1803:48–52 and n13, 1810:41–51.
11 A canon of Lvov and secretary to King Sigismund I, he published in 1528
   two of Erasmus' translations of Chrysostom with a dedication to Chancellor
   Krzysztof Szydłowiecki (Cracow: Hieronim Wietor 1528); cf CEBR II 273.

your letter, and I welcome it gladly. The same can be said of Zambocki, Hosius, Georg Werner and Lange,[12] some of whom were recommended to me 25 by Łaski. To all of them at another time I shall show my reciprocal feelings. At the present moment I neither have the time nor is it expedient to write further. The road is long and I am not certain of the reliability of the messenger.

I cannot tell you, my dear Antonin, how happy I am that you have such 30 a kind and good-natured patron, especially in these troubled times. I wrote him a brief note,[13] although it went against my sense of modesty. You must take the blame for my impudence.

Béda is so unabashed by his madness that he is plotting a tragic farce much more insane than the last one.[14] Unless some extreme fate is urging 35 them on, I do not know what the theologians' intentions are. I admire greatly Johannes Leopolitanus for his sincerity;[15] would that many more would imitate him. I am afraid that a translation of 'The Funeral' would not have success.[16] It would only irritate those whom we cannot silence. Whatever melodramas are enacted in France or in Spain arise from this source. We 40 must also take care that no potential danger recoil upon those who brought this about or who were privy to it. For your excellent spouse I pray for every happiness.[17] The linen cloth you sent me was appreciated more than

* * * * *

12 Erasmus is probably referring to the Jan Zambocki who served at this time as secretary of Piotr Tomicki and would in 1528 become secretary to the king; see CEBR III 467. On Stanislaus Hosius of Cracow see Ep 1915 n14. A Silesian Pole living in Hungary, Werner had at first been a partisan of John Zápolyai, but about this time switched his allegiance to Ferdinand of Hapsburg. Some of his poems were printed by Hosius with Erasmus' Ep 1819 to King Sigismund (Cracow: Hieronim Wietor 1527); see CEBR III 438–9. Johann Lange of Karvinà was at this time a schoolmaster in Złotoryja (Silesia), and would later serve in the court of Ferdinand of Hapsburg; see CEBR II 290.

13 Ep 1919 to Piotr Tomicki is dated two days later; on Tomicki see the introduction.

14 That is, the impending general censure of Erasmus by the faculty of theology of Paris; see Epp 1875 n26, 1902 introduction, 1906.

15 Jan Leopolita (Jan of Lvov), a newly licensed doctor of theology at the University of Cracow and preacher of the chapter of St Florian in Cracow, was an avid reader of Erasmus' works; see CEBR II 325.

16 The colloquy of this name (CWE 40 762–95) was first published in February 1526. A German translation had already appeared (Magdeburg: Johannes Knappe, 1527), but no translation into Polish at this time is known.

17 Antonin had married Anna, daughter of the Cracow goldsmith Jan Zimmermann (CEBR I 63).

gold, rendered agreeable to me both by the affection of the sender and by its very novelty. If your Josephus comes I shall be most anxious to see him.[18]　　45

Here the pestilence has broken out again; Johann Froben passed away recently, seized by an attack of paralysis.[19] The disease had given some symptoms of its presence; but a man of such robust health felt ashamed to be sick. Farewell, Antonin, dearest of mortals.

At Basel, the morrow of the Immaculate Conception in the year 1527　　50

1917 / From Caspar Ursinus Velius　　　　　Gran, 10 December 1527

The manuscript of this letter, written in the hand of a secretary but corrected and signed by Ursinus, is in the Rehdiger Collection (MS 254 64), Wrocław. It was first published in LB III-2 1723–4 *Appendix epistolarum* no 344.

For Velius see Ep 1810 n6. At the time of this present letter he was in the retinue of Ferdinand I on his Hungarian campaign.

From your letter to Faber,[1] a man of great learning and a very good friend of mine, it was easy for me to understand that some memory of Velius still resides in your heart. For a while I had the suspicion that it had been completely obliterated, since you have failed up to now to do what you promised in a letter last year, namely, that you would write to King Ferdinand and warmly recommend me to his Highness.[2] My favour with the king would have undoubtedly been increased by a simple commendation from you. Leading men at the court and Faber himself were instrumental in winning over his sympathy towards me some time ago. Thanks to their support I was introduced into the court, and from the shelter of the scholastic life I immediately had the courage to move on to the military camp. Bidding farewell　　10

* * * * *

18 Josephus Tectander (c 1507–c 1543), Antonin's brother-in-law, had accompanied him earlier to Basel and would do so again in August 1535. He was at this time at the court of King John Zápolyai; see CEBR III 313–14.
19 See Ep 1900:120–1.

1917
1 Not extant, presumably written to Johannes Fabri of Leutkirch (CEBR II 5–8), who, like Ursinus, was in the service of Ferdinand I of Hapsburg at this time. The most recent extant letter from Fabri was Ep 1771. He would write again on 17 June 1528 (Ep 2000), and Erasmus answered with Ep 2006.
2 The letter is not extant. As far back as 18 February 1522 Ursinus had tried to get a recommendation to Ferdinand from Erasmus; see Allen Ep 1917:4n.

to the Muses I began to cultivate Bellona and Gradivus whom, fiercest of all the gods, I have found propitious.[3]

You will perhaps say, 'What has the poet to do with the court?' Do not call me by that name in future, as I have suddenly changed from a poet to an historian,[4] not by my own temerity and wilful audacity but through the judgment of others and the pressure of friends. I have already written a book on the brilliant and heroic exploits of the king,[5] who has obtained astonishing and almost unbelievable success in this kingdom. In this regard I am quite perplexed that in your letter to the king of Poland you did not think fit to call him king, while you did not hesitate to bestow that title on the count, that parricide and betrayer of his country.[6] I was shocked, I must admit, by the indignity of it all, especially when I read in that same letter the name and title of a certain satrap (longer than an inscription celebrating the triumph of an emperor).[7] Whether this was all presented on purpose or by accident, you have surely incurred the reprehension of many people. But you will pardon me if I urge you, not by way of reproof but in the spirit of friendly advice, that in any future mention of Ferdinand, king of Pannonia and Bohemia, in your works and writings you do not defraud him of his due honour.[8] If you bear in mind that these are still only the virtuous deeds of a young man,[9] you would not be wrong to prefer him even to kings of more mature and advanced years.

* * * * *

3 Bellona was the Roman goddess of war; 'Gradivus' was a title of the god Mars.
4 Cf Allen Ep 1935:71.
5 That is, Ferdinand I of Hapsburg. Erasmus will mention Ursinus' work, *De bello pannonico*, in Allen Ep 1977:45–6 to Willibald Pirckheimer. It remained in manuscript (Vienna, Österreichische Nationalbibliothek MS Lat 7688) until it was edited by Adamus Franciscus Killarius as *De bello hungarico* (Vienna 1762).
6 See Ep 1819:153 and n24. John Zápolyai, *voivode* of Transylvania since 1512, claimed the throne of Hungary after King Louis II was killed at Mohács in 1526 (cf Ep 1810 n8). Because of contradictory orders from Louis, Zápolyai's army did not advance to reinforce the royal forces at that disastrous battle.
7 See Ep 1819:154–6. On Krzysztof Szydłowiecki, the castellan of Cracow and chancellor of Poland, see Ep 1820.
8 Erasmus told Jan Antonin that he neither approved nor disapproved of Hosius' publication of the letter containing the phrase which friends of Ferdinand I found offensive (Ep 1916:13–15). When Erasmus himself published Ep 1819 in the *Opus epistolarum* he changed the offending passage about Zápolyai to read 'who has usurped the title of king'; and in writing to Ferdinand himself (Ep 2005) he addressed him as 'king of Bohemia and Hungary.'
9 Born on 10 March 1503, Ferdinand was twenty-four at this time.

But I shall leave these matters aside for now. To treat them as they deserve would require not a letter but a huge book. To return to myself and my personal interests, I am still of my long-standing conviction that be- 35
cause of the violent and insane interpreters of the gospel who have sprung up helter-skelter in Germany and have stirred up dreadful disturbances, a man of pious and upright training can live anywhere else but in that nation in these tempestuous times. For that reason I left Basel for Vienna; then, after putting together travel and living expenses for the next two years, I 40
withdrew from there to Italy. Then before a year had elapsed, I was called back by a letter from Ferdinand; as well, driven away chiefly through fear of the plague, which was raging fiercely in almost all the towns and in the big cities, I returned to Vienna.[10] There for the past three years I have lived comfortably and agreeably, since that pernicious heresy which breaks out every 45
so often and tries to diffuse its poison has been effectively crushed through the merits of the glorious Ferdinand. Although he has not yet succeeded in destroying altogether this many-headed hydra,[11] yet to the best of his powers and with his inborn greatness of spirit he has subdued and weakened it, warded it off from many places it was threatening, and eradicated it from 50
places where it was already taking root.

Furthermore, with regard to that heresy which has embedded itself in the very heart of Germany and holds sway over those who are partly improvident, partly wicked and impious, I think it will collapse before long of its own exertions and will leave behind to the nation, in addition to the mas- 55
sacres and horrible dissensions and the reappearance of a savage barbarity,[12] an everlasting disgrace in the eyes of other nations and their inexpiable hatred. In my opinion, if the Turks should come to know of the wicked crimes of these depraved men, they will attack Germany if not through desire of pillage then to prevent this contagion from overrunning regions under their 60
control.

* * * * *

10 Ursinus left Basel c January 1522 prior to the real manifestations of heresy, and before going to Vienna stayed in Freiburg-im-Breisgau to study under Udalricus Zasius. He was in Rome during the winter of 1523–4 and returned to Vienna early in April.
11 The many-headed serpent or monster of Greek mythology slain by Hercules, each head of which when cut off was replaced by two others. The metaphor was thus already being applied to the Lutheran phenomenon at least two years prior to Johannes Cochlaeus' *Septiceps Lutherus* (Leipzig: Valentinus Schumann 1529).
12 The Peasants' War of 1524–6

The books of Protagoras, who entertained unorthodox opinions about the immortal gods, were publicly burned by order of the Athenians, and their author was punished with exile.[13] What kind of reward do you think this kind of men deserve from their fellow citizens when, after impiously overturning divine and human laws, they establish new laws of their own under the impulse of anger and hatred? To the great detriment of the public good they offer a deceptive foretaste of liberty and dispel any sense of impending disaster from the simple-minded.[14] Yet they promise the salvation of the soul! This is what they and their like – not I, certainly – believe: that there will be a place among the blessed for those who in the manner of brute beasts lead inhuman, godless, rebellious lives, casting away all fear of law and of God. But I am being carried away too much on this point; I am confiding it to you, who I know will not make it public. With anyone else I would not dare permit myself such licence, for it would be stupid to pour oil on the fire.[15]

Give my greetings to Rhenanus, Bonifacius, Froben,[16] and your other friends. The best of health to you, most honourable friend. Faber,[17] who is most devoted to you, sends his greetings. Piso, who had lost all his possessions, died at Wrocław in March, the victim of grief, I believe. It must have been difficult and bitter for a man who had dwelt in Italy among men of elegance to live here in a ravaged country, especially at such an unfavourable moment.[18] But our life is pleasant compared to the grim religion of the Germans. Once again, farewell. Please do not show this letter to anyone.

Gran in Pannonia,[19] 10 December, in the year 1527

* * * * *

13 The trial and punishment of Protagoras, an early Sophist (c 485 BC) and author of the dictum 'Man is the measure of all things,' is dismissed by many as an invention or error of later writers.
14 Ursinus is here adapting a sentiment of Livy from the preface to the second book of his history (Livy 2.1.3), where he comments that if Lucius Junius Brutus had acted earlier to expel the kings from Rome the liberty attained would have been premature and detrimental to the republic.
15 *Adagia* I ii 9
16 Beatus Rhenanus, Bonifacius Amerbach, Johann Froben. Ursinus would not yet know of Froben's death (Ep 1900).
17 Cf n1 above.
18 Jacobus Piso, a long-time friend of Erasmus (Epp 216, 850, 1206), had been the teacher of King Louis II of Hungary, who fell at Mohács; he had been the Hungarian ambassador in Rome from 1507 to 1514.
19 Gran is located on the right bank of the Danube, about 37 km north-west of Budapest.

Your Ursinus Velius
To Erasmus of Rotterdam, peerless prince of theology and eloquence

1918 / To Krzysztof Szydłowiecki   Basel, 12 December 1527

Erasmus published this letter in the *Opus epistolarum* (1529). For the addressee
see Ep 1820 introduction.

ERASMUS OF ROTTERDAM TO KRZYSZTOF SZYDŁOWIECKI,
KNIGHT PALATINE AND CASTELLAN OF CRACOW,
CHANCELLOR OF THE KINGDOM OF POLAND, GREETING
Outstanding virtue is not wanting in praise or due recompense, even if its
brilliant efforts are not crowned with success, which is in the hands of God   5
alone. Nevertheless we would have been happier if the seductions of power
had not prevailed over reasonable and right counsel. Experience confirms
the utter truth of what Homer wrote thousands of years ago: 'Of food and
drink, of song and dance, and all things sweet by nature man has satiety: of
war alone, cruellest of life's evils, he has no fill.'[1] What else can I say, my   10
excellent friend, except that God, unfavourably disposed towards us, puts
into the minds of certain princes an insatiable passion for war? Are there any
evils lacking in our times? What region of the world is not either undergoing
or preparing itself for war? Where does pestilence not rage? Where is need
not felt? And yet, afflicted in all these ways, we do not acknowledge that   15
God is spurring us on with floggings to regain our senses; but rather, as
if everything were normal, we feast, join in marriage, cross swords, and
contend in battle to extend the boundaries of our kingdom. I hope, however,
that through your efforts and the efforts of men like you and through the
ability of King Sigismund human affairs will some day be restored to a   20
more tranquil state.

　　You write that my letter found great favour with the king and all the
leading men at court. I greatly rejoice that Jan Łaski's advice and my compliance with it were not without success. You need not in your great kindness
concern yourself about a gift.[2] I have long since obtained what I desired if it   25
found favour and promoted the cause of peace. I am most grateful for your

*　*　*　*　*

1918
1 *Iliad* 13.636–9
2 King Sigismund I of Poland, urged by Szydłowiecki and Andrzej Krzycki,
  acknowledged Ep 1819 and sent 100 gold ducats in February 1528; see Allen
  Epp 1952:33–4 and 1954:13–20.

devotion to my friend Antonin.[3] Indeed I am so obligated to this man for his many merits that whatever friendly office your Excellency may render to him I shall gladly consider as conferred upon me. May the Lord preserve you in excellent health.

Given at Basel, 12 December 1527

1919 / To Piotr Tomicki   Basel, 12 December 1527

This letter of self-introduction, written at the suggestion or with the approval of Jan Antonin, who was Tomicki's physician, was first published by Erasmus in the *Opus epistolarum*, and is the first of many letters exchanged with Tomicki. It will be answered by Ep 1953.

Piotr Tomicki held a doctorate in canon law from the University of Bologna. After several diplomatic missions for King Sigismund I he was appointed royal vice-chancellor and bishop of Cracow. He was staunchly pro-Hapsburg, and opposed a policy of peace with the Turks and an alliance with France. An adamant opponent of Lutheran ideas, he succeeded in prohibiting the importation of books from Germany (1523) and the attendance of Polish students at German universities. In the royal chancery he formed a generation of Polish statesmen and diplomats with high standards of Latinity, and was a generous patron of humanist scholars and of the ideal of *trilinguitas*. See CEBR III 327–9.

ERASMUS OF ROTTERDAM TO PIOTR TOMICKI, BISHOP OF CRACOW, GREETING

I had neither the time nor a suitable subject on which to write to you, most distinguished prelate, and was restrained also by a sense of propriety. But your friend Antonin[1] painted such a vivid and affectionate portrait of your spirit and character that if I should say that you are unknown to me I should be clearly lying. Moreover, I should be devoid of all feeling of piety and humanity if I did not entertain sentiments of respect, admiration, and sincere affection for such a prelate. I am no less happy for my friend Antonin that he has found a patron under whose auspices he can lead an honourable and peaceful life in these tempestuous times. For I am so fond of this utterly guileless soul that I am more cheered if any good fortune has befallen

* * * * *

3 Jan Antonin of Košice, Erasmus' physician in Basel in 1523–4 and now physician to King Sigismund I; see Ep 1810 introduction.

1919
1 Jan Antonin; see Ep 1810 introduction.

Piotr Tomicki
Stanisław Samostrzelnik
Institute of Art, Polish Academy of Sciences, Warsaw
Photo courtesy of Department of Art History, Jagiellonian University, Cracow

him than if it had fallen to me. It would be of little consequence for me to
congratulate you on your high office, which you owe not to fortune but to
your outstanding endowments of intellect, nor shall I account you fortunate   15
because you are among those most preferred and acceptable to his Serene
Highness, since he does this more out of good judgment than through feelings of personal sympathy. It is our age and the realm of Christendom that
I should congratulate. If it were blessed with more bishops like you, this
tempest in the affairs of men would more quickly return to a state of calm.   20

This letter delivered to your Highness is more than laconic; yet you
would avow that it is prolix if you knew what toils beset me. I pray for
every blessing and prosperity for your most reverend Highness.

Given at Basel, 12 December in the year 1527

1920 / From Charles V   Burgos, 13 December 1527

Allen based his edition of this letter, which answers Ep 1873, on the rough
draft and fair copy preserved at Simancas (MS Est 1554 fols 577, 583). Erasmus never published the letter, even though it presented a kind of imperial
stamp on his orthodoxy. Both letters, however, were published in Spain as the
preface to three different translations of selected *Colloquies* of Erasmus; see Ep
1873 introduction. The imperial secretary Alfonso de Valdés wrote this letter
in the emperor's name in an attempt to assuage Erasmus' anxieties about any
resumption of the inquisition into his writings in Spain. Valdés also made the
Spanish translation that is printed with the Latin text in Allen VII 276–8. On
this letter see Bataillon *Erasme* (1991) I 298–9.

CHARLES, BY THE GRACE OF GOD ELECTED AUGUST EMPEROR
OF THE ROMANS, ETC
Honourable, devoted, and beloved friend! Your letter brought us the greatest delight, on two counts: that it came from you and that from it I understood that the madness of the Lutherans is on the decline. The first cause   5
of our joy you owe to the singular good will we bear you, the second we
and with us all of Christendom owe to you, since through you alone was
accomplished that which emperors, popes, princes, universities, and hosts
of learned men failed to attain.[1] Wherefore we are most pleased to see that
undying praise among mortal men and eternal glory in heaven will ever be   10

* * * * *

1920
1 Erasmus had claimed that Lutheranism was on the decline, partly from his
own efforts (Ep 1873:13–14).

yours, and we sincerely congratulate you on your success. All that remains to be done is that you strive with all your powers to bring to completion this mission that you have so felicitously begun. We on our part shall never be lacking in aid and support to your most godly efforts.

But as to what you write about the way your works are treated in this   15
country, we are greatly disappointed. For you seem somehow to lack confidence in our sentiments of good will towards you, as if any declaration could be made in my presence against Erasmus, whose Christian piety is above all suspicion. The investigation into your books that we have authorized poses no threat,[2] save that if any human failing be found in them, you   20
yourself, harkening to friendly advice, may either correct it or so explain it that you leave no room for scandal to the weak. In that way you will procure immortality for your writings and silence your detractors. But if nothing worthy of criticism is found, you can see what glory you will achieve for yourself and your writings. We wish therefore that you be of good heart   25
and be assured that we will never cease to do all in our power to safeguard your honour and reputation.

There is no reason for anyone to doubt that we have acted vigorously to the best of our ability thus far to promote peace in public affairs. What we are doing now and what we will do in the future we prefer to exem-   30
plify in deeds. One thing we ask of you, that in your prayers you cease not to commend all our actions to Christ, who is all good and all powerful. Farewell.

Given in our city of Burgos, the thirteenth day of December in the year of our Lord 1527, the ninth year of our imperial rule   35
By order of the emperor. Alfonso de Valdés

To the honourable, devoted, and beloved Desiderius Erasmus of Rotterdam, our councillor

1921 / To Henri de Bottis   Basel, 22 December 1527

This letter responds to another, not extant, that Bottis had written perhaps to a third party upon hearing a false rumour of Erasmus' death. It first appeared in the *Opus epistolarum* (1529).

Henri de Bottis had been a student in Paris at the Collège de Montaigu, where Noël Béda was principal until 1514. After taking degrees in civil and canon law he became the official of the bishop of the short-lived diocese of

* * * * *

2 The inquisition in Valladolid opened on 27 June. It was prorogued on 13 August 1527 on account of an outbreak of plague but never officially concluded.

Bourg-en-Bresse (at that time in the duchy of Savoy). He termed himself
a 'young man' in the preface of his only published work, *Tractatus de syn-
odo episcopi et de statutis episcopi synodalibus* (Lyon: Vincent de Portonariis and
Jean David 1529). This book was cited by the Calabrian archbishop Giovanni-
Baptista Castaneus during an intervention on episcopal jurisdiction at the
Council of Trent in 1562; see *Concilium Tridentinum* IX (Freiburg-im-Breisgau
1923) 119. In Ep 1963, which answers the present letter, Bottis recalls instances
of corporal punishment of students at the hands of Béda. Erasmus will reply
(Ep 1985) with a further denunciation of Béda; see CEBR I 176–7.

ERASMUS OF ROTTERDAM TO HENRI DE BOTTIS, DOCTOR OF LAWS,
OFFICIAL OF BOURG, GREETING

Dearest friend in the Lord, while your singular devotion to me gives me
reason to rejoice, I am at the same time saddened that you are afflicted by
a groundless sorrow. I am borne in funeral procession so many times, and   5
each time I survive. I for my part am prepared for either eventuality, as the
Lord will see fit.

Johann Froben, a man destined from birth to give lustre to the world
of letters, has left us, to my great sorrow;[1] but when I reflect upon the
nature of his illness (it was paralysis), when I think of the troubled times in   10
which we live, I feel more like congratulating him on being taken from us
rather than mourning his loss. He had begun at great expense the publication of all of Augustine, and wished no longer life than was necessary to accomplish that task.[2] But God has reserved for him, I hope, something better than what he desired.[3] His son Hieronymus and I are man-   15
aging the press. *De ratione concionandi* has not been published yet; something always comes up to thwart our purpose and direct our attention
elsewhere.[4] And you can hardly imagine how much trouble the Augustine
is giving.

Now I not only have to deal with the Spanish phalanxes,[5] but I have a   20
more deadly war on my hands with others. Béda leaves no stone unturned

* * * * *

1921
1 See Ep 1900.
2 See Ep 2157.
3 Cf Heb 11:40.
4 For Erasmus' treatise on preaching, *Ecclesiastes sive de ratione concionandi* see
   Ep 1804 n28.
5 See Epp 1791, 1814:115–288 and n39, 1879. For an account in a recent letter of
   the troubles in Spain, see Ep 1903.

to spoil his image as a good man.[6] And yet I am glad to be forewarned.[7] For you and all those who love me in Christ I wish the best of health.

Given at Basel, the day after the feast of St Thomas the apostle, in the year 1527

25

1922 / To Georg Schmotzer   Basel, 27 December 1527

This letter, which illustrates the risks taken in dispatching letters at that time, was published by Erasmus in the *Opus epistolarum* (1529). Bonifacius Amerbach wrote a similar letter (AK III Ep 1221; cf Allen's introduction to the present letter) to someone, perhaps Schmotzer, in Ensisheim, likewise asking for the return of Erasmus' packet. Allen Ep 1965:1–3 shows that Erasmus did recover the intercepted letters and was able to send them off again, although at least one of them (to William Warham) he had in the meantime dispatched in duplicate on 4 January 1528.

Georg Schmotzer had been a professor of law at Freiburg and was at this time an imperial councillor in Ensisheim; see CEBR III 227.

ERASMUS OF ROTTERDAM TO GEORG SCHMOTZER, DOCTOR OF
CIVIL AND CANON LAW, GREETING

Illustrious Doctor, while I am more than a little distressed that this has happened, I am happy that a chance occurrence allowed me to find out about it. Ruffus, the guardian of the Franciscans at Rouffach,[1] wrote to his former   5
confrères that a packet of my letters was discovered in a public hostelry at Thann and was delivered into the hands of the senate of that town. When I learned of this I dispatched my own messenger thither. Through him I was informed that the letters were given by the senate to the provost,[2] who was to see if there was anything in them that was connected with the state. The   10

* * * * *

6 On Noël Béda; see Epp 1804 n14. Epp 1902 and 1905 are concerned with Erasmus' ongoing dispute with him; cf also Ep 1906.
7 Allen (17n) thought this passage refers to the troubles in Spain; but Bottis' position in Bourg-en-Bresse was more likely to provide him news about Paris and about his former principal Béda.

1922
1 Johannes Ruffus Fabri was formerly a member of the convent in Basel. Rouffach is located about 12 km north of Ensisheim in upper Alsace (CEBR III 177).
2 Probably Jakob Rieher, provost of Thann between 1523 and 1536, although he never formally took up residence there; cf CEBR III 261. Thann is about 23 km south-west of Rouffach.

said provost – he is here present – asserts that nothing at all was found in them which concerned the affairs of princes in any way. Nonetheless the letters were sent to the council of Ensisheim.[3] Whether this was done because of antipathy towards me, excess of zeal, or sheer ignorance I shall not discuss for the moment. I send so many bundles of letters and writings to   15
England, France, Spain, Poland, and Brabant every day and in turn receive them from the emperor, who regards me as one of his sworn councillors, from King Ferdinand, from the king of England, from archbishops and cardinals;[4] yet never has such an inauspicious incident taken place. For I am not in the habit of committing anything to a letter that would in any way   20
disturb the interests of the state.

Consequently, since I myself am not unknown and those to whom I write are indeed well known, it would have been a mark of courtesy when they saw that the letters came from me to send them back to me and not to present them for examination to extraneous persons. At the least, after   25
scrutinizing them, there was no need to send them to you, thereby doing an injustice both to me and to my correspondents. For the circumstances are such that it is of great importance to me that my letters reach their destination. If they ended up in the hands of others it would be of no advantage to them, but it would be a great disadvantage for me. Even in the midst of war   30
there is a certain respect for private letters, especially if they contain nothing that is of interest to the enemy. But no matter how these things came about at Thann, I beg you with all earnestness to be kind enough to ensure that my messenger is not detained there too long and that he carry back to me all papers, duly sealed, so that another messenger may take them to their   35
proper destination.

From the words of the provost of Thann it is not quite clear which letters they were, but I presume that it is a packet of letters that I recently entrusted to a certain Anton Bletz of Switzerland.[5] In it there was one letter to the Parlement of Paris, one to the faculty of theology, one to Noël   40
Béda, one to a Spanish theologian of the Sorbonne, one to the theologian

* * * * *

3 The local government representing the Hapsburg empire in Alsace, with its seat in the town of Ensisheim, which is about 22 km north-east of Thann
4 For references to similar comments about letters to and from all parts of the world, see Ep 1804 n12; for letters from the emperor, kings, archbishops, and cardinals see Ep 1874:49–72 and the notes there. On Erasmus' appointment as councillor to (then) Prince Charles see Allen Ep 370:18n.
5 Anton Bletz of Zug; see Epp 1827 introduction. The packet was most likely destined for Paris, from where some of the letters would be dispatched to Spain and others to the Low Countries.

Gervasius, one to the cardinal of Lorraine, one to the honourable Louis de Berquin, one to Germain de Brie, one to Lieven, a former servant of mine, one to the archbishop of Canterbury;[6] and there was a little printed book for the archbishop of Seville.[7] There were two short pieces on the same sub-   45 ject, one to the Parlement of Paris, the other to the faculty of theology,[8] and a few copies of letters from others, if I remember correctly. I beg you to re-turn them all to me, at least those that are in your possession. If there are some others, I ask that they be sent here, since I know that I wrote noth-ing that concerns you. You will put me much in your debt by this service.   50 And if anything arises in which I can render you a similar kindness you will find that I am not one to forget my obligations nor slow to return a favour.

I added this letter to the first one because I learned that the president had taken leave of you.[9] If that is true, I trust that in your readiness to help   55 this will be taken care of, especially since, as far as you are concerned, it is a matter of no great consequence. Farewell.

From Basel, the feast of John the Evangelist, in the year 1527

1923 / To Hieronymus Emser   Basel, 29 December 1527

Allen was the first to publish this letter, the original autograph of which is pre-served in the Rehdiger Collection (MS 243) in the University Library, Wrocław. Allen reports that a contemporary note on the verso indicates that it was proba-bly received at Dresden on 4 February 1528. The year-date is further confirmed

* * * * *

6 Epp 1905 (to the Parlement of Paris), 1902 (to the faculty of theology), 1906 (to Béda), 1909 (to Francisco de Vitoria; see the introduction there on why Eras-mus sent the letter to Paris), 1903 (to Gervasius Wain; the salutation 'theolo-gian of the Sorbonne,' applied in error to Vitoria, would have been appropri-ate in Wain's case, as he was a *socius*, or fellow, of the Collège de Sorbonne since 1516 and was prior of the Sorbonne in 1521–2), 1911 (to Jean de Guise), 1910 (to Brie). The letters to Berquin, Lieven Algoet, and Warham are not ex-tant. Algoet (see Ep 1848 n5) was living in Paris at this time. The letter to War-ham, though not extant, reached him along with a duplicate sent on 4 January 1528; see Allen Ep 1965:1–2.
7 An advance copy of the *Apologia adversus monachos quosdam Hispanos*, appar-ently sent in duplicate (cf Epp 1879, 1888) to Alonso Manrique de Lara
8 See Ep 1902:336–8 and nn45–6.
9 That is, the president of the council at Ensisheim. His identity is not known. The first letter is not extant; or perhaps Erasmus is referring to the letter writ-ten the day before by Amerbach (AK III Ep 1221, edited in Allen's introduction to the present letter).

by Emser's death in Dresden, of which Erasmus had not yet received news, on 8 December 1527 (Allen Ep 1928:7).

For Hieronymus Emser see Ep 553 introduction; cf CEBR I 429–30.

Greetings. At the time of the last fair I sent you a letter jointly with a letter to our illustrious prince, in which I had referred to certain aspects of the Heinrich Eppendorf affair,[1] with regard to whom I now know for certain that through someone in the confidence of the prince he procured a letter that I had previously written to his Highness.[2] What purpose he had in mind 5 I know not. At any rate it was entirely unjustified. And I can well imagine that it was done without the knowledge of the prince. Shortly afterwards, two men arrived here bringing a letter from you that contained little more than a salutation.[3] Since they were unknown to me and considering how often we are deceived, I had made up my mind not to send an answer back 10 with them; but since they insisted I gave them a bit of money and entrusted them with my reply.[4] I should like to know whether this has reached you, and am curious to know also what the illustrious prince thinks of the second book of the *Hyperaspistes*.[5]

Lee is putting on a marvellous show in Spain.[6] He has the strong sup- 15 port of Béda and his followers in these histrionics.[7] You will hear of the outcome before long. Capito, Bucer, Urbanus and I don't know who else are present here,[8] en route to Bern, where they will hold a conference and make

* * * * *

1923
1 The letter to Emser is not extant. Some of its contents with respect to Eppen- dorf can be divined from Allen Ep 1940:11–25. The letter to Duke George of Saxony is Ep 1869. On Eppendorf, see Epp 1893 n16, 1901 n1.
2 The letter is not extant, but it was answered by Duke George with Ep 1448. Erasmus was suspicions of Otto von Pack, who was in the service of Duke George and who in January 1528 attempted to betray his master to Landgrave Philip of Hesse; see Allen Epp 1934:85n, 1951:13–18; CEBR III 39.
3 Not extant
4 Also not extant
5 It had appeared in the late summer, in time for the autumn Frankfurt fair; see Ep 1853.
6 Edward Lee, one of the first critics of Erasmus' biblical annotations. Now an ambassador in Spain, Erasmus saw him as the root of his troubles there; see Ep 1814 n39.
7 Noël Béda, syndic of the Paris faculty of theology; see Epp 1804 n14, 1902, 1906.
8 On Wolfgang Faber Capito, the Strasbourg reformer, see Ep 1901 n1. On Mar- tin Bucer see Ep 1901 introduction. Urbanus Rhegius (1484–1541), a priest and

some formal pronouncements concerning the abolition of the mass and the
services for the dead.[9] They had several public meetings here. May God   20
bring it to some good end, for it looks like it will lead to grave uprisings.

The bearer of this was sent by Christoph von Carlowitz,[10] a young
man of singular talents and profoundly devoted to study. You will be able
to entrust safely to him whatever you wish to write. I wish you perfect
happiness in the Lord.   25

Given at Basel, the day after the feast of the Holy Innocents. 1527[11]
Erasmus of Rotterdam in his own hand. To the most eminent scholar
Hieronymus Emser. In Dresden

1924 / To George, duke of Saxony   Basel, 30 December 1527

Erasmus chose to publish this letter in the *Opus epistolarum* (1529), despite
Duke George's displeasure about the criticism Erasmus' expresses here of the
use of violence against heretics. Vexed by this criticism, the duke refused to
answer this letter personally. But Erasmus wrote again on 16 January 1528
to express his pleasure at the duke's satisfaction with the second book of the
Hyperaspistes (Ep 1929).

ERASMUS OF ROTTERDAM TO GEORGE, DUKE OF SAXONY, GREETING
Illustrious Prince, there was nothing of such great importance at the present
time that merited my disturbing your Highness, but I was moved to write
by the availability of a trustworthy courier who would soon be returning

* * * * *

humanist, had adopted Lutheranism definitively in 1524 and married in 1525.
He was nevertheless allowed to remain in Augsburg until 1530; see CEBR III
151–3.
9 The council of the city of Bern had opted for a reformed Catholicism in 1525,
but this did not satisfy the more radical reformist opposition. After the Disputation of Bern, theological discussions between reformers and then between
reformers and Catholics, which took place 6–26 January 1528, the formal and
legal basis for the Reformation mandate was adopted for Bern on 7 February 1528; see OER I 143–5 and Irena Backus *The Disputations of Baden, 1526, and
Berne, 1528: Neutralizing the Early Church* Studies in Reformed Theology and
History 1 no 1 (Princeton 1993).
10 See Epp 1899 n21, 1912 n5, 1924:43–51, 2010.
11 Allen writes 1528, on the basis that in the manuscript an 8 appears to be written over a 7. He dated the letter 1527/8, but included it with letters of 1527,
probably because Erasmus would surely have heard of Emser's death, which
occurred on 8 December 1527, by December 1528.

this way. Such an opportunity presents itself all too rarely for me to allow 5
it to be missed. At the time of the last fair I sent your Highness the second
book of the *Hyperaspistes* together with a letter.[1] I have not yet been able to
know for certain whether they arrived or not.[2] It is difficult to put in words
how much dishonesty and treachery exists among men these days in these
matters. Therefore if it is not inconvenient to your Highness I should be 10
most grateful if you would deign to indicate to me in a few words whether
what I sent reached you and whether it met with your approval, to which
I attach great importance. The same man cannot bring forth and pass judgment, as Plato has Socrates say.[3] This one thing I know, that I have never
found anything so troublesome as replying to such a prolix recital of abuse 15
and bombast,[4] the reading of which itself required a strong stomach.

This new type of disturbance calls for someone of exceptional ability who by his wisdom, authority, and intelligence can quell these uprisings. I am both astonished and aggrieved that no such person has yet come
forth. Theologians, armed with their arsenal of syllogisms and problems, 20
are theologians, it would seem, only within the walls of the schools.[5] If ever
there were a time to put into play that mysterious wisdom greater than
ordinary human ken, surely it is now. Certain bishops seem to be occupied with other matters, and most monks are more concerned with their
bellies than with the gospel.[6] The emperor and King Ferdinand seem to 25
look to severity as if it were a sacred anchor,[7] and undoubtedly they are

* * * * *

1924
1 Ep 1869
2 Less than three weeks later Erasmus wrote again to Duke George, saying that
  he had learned of the duke's reception of this letter and his approval of the
  book (Allen Ep 1929:1–3).
3 *Theaetetus* 150C–D. This is a loose application of Socrates' metaphor of mid-
  wifery, in which he claims that, although he himself was not able to bring
  forth wisdom, he could extract knowledge from others. Here with Socratic
  irony Erasmus says he has brought forth a work but it is up to another (Duke
  George) to estimate its worth.
4 Luther's *De servo arbitrio*. On the whole controversy see Ep 1804 n10.
5 An old charge of Erasmus, much vaunted in his *Antibarbari*, the *Praise of Folly*,
  and the *Paraclesis*
6 Not monks but mendicant friars; cf Ep 1805 n53.
7 *Adagia* I i 24. Erasmus makes the same criticism of imperial policy a few days
  later in his letter to Hermann von Neuenahr (Allen Ep 1926:17–18) and on 20
  March 1528 to Willibald Pirckheimer (Allen Ep 1977:46). On 24 March 1528 he
  will defend but clarify his criticism by reminding Duke George of St Augustine's cautions about violence against heretics (Allen Ep 1983:9–30).

driven to this by those who in the name of the gospel want to be permitted to do whatever they please. But I am afraid the situation is going to deteriorate. Desire for plunder will incite many even against the innocent, and whoever has any possessions will be exposed to danger. Those who have nothing will fare well from other people's misfortunes, as happens in time of war. And this will lead to universal confusion. If the evil cannot be extirpated at once, it must at least be skilfully mitigated for the time being until the disease will yield to a healing hand. It is hard to use amputation and cauterizing when the greater part of the body is affected by the disease. It is a baleful medicine that loses more patients than it saves. If the diseased part in both camps could be removed with prudent moderation through the authority of rulers acting together, the affair would have a less bloody outcome. I pray that he who knows what is good for mankind would deign to inspire princes with plans of action that will restore true piety and concord; for I see that nothing is left to us but prayer.

Christoph von Carlowitz is active here,[8] a young man who in addition to his noble lineage is distinguished by an uncommon learning and the maturity of judgment characteristic of an older man, to such an extent that aside from his years and appearance there is nothing young about him. So dedicated is he to higher studies that the pleasures other young men seek out in banqueting, gambling, and love affairs he derives entirely from books. On which account, since he gives singular promise of himself, I am pleased to congratulate your dukedom. It was he who sent the bearer of the present letter. The same courier will carry back to me whatever your illustrious Highness wishes me to know. May God keep you well and flourishing.

At Basel, 30 December. In the year 1527

1925 / To the Nuns of Denney [Basel, 1527 or 1528]

Thomas Grey, an Englishman whom Erasmus had tutored in Paris in 1497–8, visited Basel in late 1525, where he sought Erasmus' recommendation for his son's reception at the Collegium Trilingue in Louvain (Epp 1624:20, 1641; CEBR II 129–30). At the same time he persuaded Erasmus to send a letter to the Franciscan nuns at Denney (near Cambridge), where Grey's sisters were members. To express their pleasure at receiving the letter (not extant), the nuns sent Erasmus a gift, which never reached him. In the present letter he thanks

* * * * *

8 See Epp 1899 n21, 1912 n5, 2010.

the sisters, and sends as a return gift the *Epistola consolatoria in adversis* (Basel: Hieronymus Froben 1528), which constitutes the greater part of the present letter. Erasmus reprinted the whole with slight changes as an appendix to his *De pueris instituendis* (Basel: Hieronymus Froben, September 1529). Because of its nature as a spiritual text Allen included only short excerpts from it. In the same way, since its full text with introduction and annotations appears in CWE 69 185–201 (*Letter of Comfort in Adversity*), we publish here only its opening and closing sections, which are in an epistolary style.

DESIDERIUS ERASMUS OF ROTTERDAM TO THE NUNS OBSERVING
THE RULE OF ST FRANCIS, SERVING BENEATH THE BANNER
OF CHRIST NEAR CAMBRIDGE, GREETING

The Lord gives us good advice, beloved sisters in Christ, when he urges us to lay up for ourselves treasure in heaven, where the moth does not destroy   5 and the thief does not steal.[1] The gift you kindly sent me may have been stolen, but no one, however thievish, could purloin your love or your devoted prayers, in which you so generously commend me every day to your Bridegroom. So let us take care to enrich ourselves in the kind of wealth that makes the one who imparts it, by sharing it with one in need, not poorer but   10 richer, and which cannot be stolen from the one on whom it is bestowed. To receive little things so gratefully and eagerly means surely to long for a greater gift.

The letter that Thomas Grey insistently urged me to write – I cannot refuse him anything – was dashed off on the spur of the moment rather than   15 composed; but since I understand that it gave you such pleasure, I have decided to send you together with the letter a little flower culled from the ever-verdant garden of Isaiah, which may at the same time refresh and invigorate your hearts with the fragrance of the Holy Spirit.[2] And certainly if the scent of an earthly flower not only gives pleasure but also reinvigorates   20 the senses, how much more will flowers of this kind, germinated and nourished by the breath of the Holy Spirit, increase the gladness and strength of the soul, if they are set before our minds. For there cannot be anyone who is not occasionally overcome by grief and a kind of weariness when he contemplates the evils that abound everywhere in these times, or so strong in   25 spirit that he does not undergo some degree of mental anguish in the midst of such great disagreements over doctrine. Here than is the little flower from

* * * * *

1925
1 Matt 6:19; cf Luke 12:33.
2 Cf *Virginis et martyris comparatio* CWE 69 159.

Isaiah for you, to give you joy instead of weariness, and to strengthen and uphold your hearts with the power of faith: 'In quiteness and trust,' he says, 'shall be your strength.'[3] ... So have no fear, little flock,[4] be brave, because he who has undertaken to protect you has conquered the world.[5] 30

I do not think it necessary to encourage you, most devout lady,[6] on whom the charge of the community of sisters is laid, or to remind you of your duty; I would rather congratulate you, if that were not unsafe in view of human weakness, or a source of embarrassment to your singular modesty. 35 I simply pray that you will continue your practice of remembering me in your prayers to the Lord, and that you will convey my particular greeting to the sisters of Thomas Grey. May the Lord preserve you all from harm. At the same time pray in your charity for the thief,[7] so that he may turn from a kite, or rather harpy, into a dove,[8] and may at last stop playing Cretan[9] 40 and stealing anything, in case he should provoke the hand of Christ against him, and so that his name may be changed.

* * * * *

3 Isa 30:15
4 Luke 12:32
5 John 16:33
6 The abbess of Denney was Dame Elizabeth Throckmorton, whose family was prominent in Tudor politics. After the dissolution of her convent in 1539, she retired to her family home, Coughton Court in Warwickshire, where with two or three other nuns from Denney she attempted to live the Franciscan rule until her death in 1547. For sources on her see CWE 69 186 n4.
7 See n1 above.
8 Horace *Epodes* 16.32
9 *Adagia* I ii 29. From Homeric times the Cretans were known as liars. St Paul (Titus 1:12) quotes the early Greek poet Epimetheus as saying 'Cretans are always liars.' The saying, 'to lie like a Cretan' is still sometimes used in current English.

TABLE OF CORRESPONDENTS

WORKS FREQUENTLY CITED

SHORT-TITLE FORMS
FOR ERASMUS' WORKS

INDEX

TABLE OF CORRESPONDENTS

WORKS FREQUENTLY CITED

This list provides bibliographical information for works referred to in short-title form in this volume. For Erasmus' writings see the short-title list following. Editions of his letters are included in the list below.

AK
Die Amerbachkorrespondenz ed Alfred Hartmann and Beat Rudolf Jenny (Basel 1942–) 10 vols to date

Allen
Opus epistolarum Des. Erasmi Roterodami ed P.S. Allen, H.M. Allen, and H.W. Garrod (Oxford 1906–58) 11 vols and index

Argentré *Collectio judiciorum*
Charles Duplessis d'Argentré *Collectio judiciorum de novis erroribus ... qui in ecclesia proscripti sunt et notati* 3 vols (Paris 1725–36; repr Brussels 1963)

ASD
Opera omnia Desiderii Erasmi Roterodami (Amsterdam and Leiden 1969–) 11 vols in 37 vols to date

Augustine ... 21st Century
The Works of Saint Augustine: A Translation for the Twenty-First Century (Hyde Park, NY 1990–) 35 vols to date

Bataillon *Erasme* (1991)
Marcel Bataillon *Erasme et l'Espagne* rev ed, text by Daniel Devoto, ed Charles Amiel (Geneva 1991) 3 vols. This posthumous edition replaces the original French edition (Paris 1937) and two editions of the Spanish translation, *Erasmo y España* (Mexico City 1950 and 1966).

Beltrán de Heredia *Cartulario* VI
'La Conferencia de Valladolid en 1527 en Torno a la doctrina de Erasmo' in *Cartulario de la Universidad de Salamanca* VI *Ultimos documentos* ed Vicente Beltrán de Heredia OP (Salamanca 1972)

BRE
Briefwechsel des Beatus Rhenanus ed Adalbert Horawitz and Karl Hartfelder (Leipzig 1886; repr Hildesheim 1966)

Caballero *Valdés*
Fermín Caballero *Alonso y Juan de Valdés* (Madrid 1875; repr Cuenca 1995)

CCCM
Corpus christianorum continuatio medievalis (Turnhout 1966–) 229 vols to date

CCSL
Corpus christianorum series Latina (Turnhout 1953–) 176 vols to date

CEBR	*Contemporaries of Erasmus. A Biographical Register of the Renaissance and Reformation* ed Peter G. Bietenholz and Thomas B. Deutscher (Toronto 1985–7; repr 2003) 3 vols
Clerval *Procès-verbaux*	Jules-Alexandre Clerval ed *Registre des procès-verbaux de la faculté de théologie de Paris* (Paris 1917)
CSEL	*Corpus scriptorum ecclesiasticorum Latinorum* (Vienna, Leipzig, and Prague 1866–) 122 vols to date
CWE	*Collected Works of Erasmus* (Toronto 1974–) 50 vols to date
DTC	*Dictionnaire de théologie catholique* ed A. Vacant, E. Mangenot, and E. Amman (Paris 1899–1950) 15 vols in 30 and index
Enthoven	*Briefe an Desiderius von Rotterdam* ed L.K. Enthoven (Strasbourg 1906)
ER	*Encyclopedia of the Renaissance* ed Paul F. Grendler (New York 1999) 6 vols
Farge 'Berquin'	James K. Farge 'Les procès de Louis de Berquin: Episodes dans la lutte du Parlement de Paris contre l'absolutisme royal' *Histoire et Archives* 18 (2005) 49–77
Farge BR	James K. Farge *Biographical Register of Paris Doctors of Theology, 1500–1536* Subsidia Mediaevalia 10 (Toronto 1980)
Farge *Orthodoxy*	James K. Farge *Orthodoxy and Reform in Early Reformation France: The Faculty of Theology of Paris, 1500–1543* (Leiden 1985)
Farge *Parti conservateur*	James K. Farge *Le parti conservateur au XVIe siècle: Université et Parlement de Paris à l'époque de la Renaissance et de la Réforme* (Paris 1992)
Farge *Procès-verbaux*	*Registre des procès-verbaux de la faculté de théologie de l'Université de Paris, de janvier 1524 à novembre 1533* ed James K. Farge (Paris 1990)
FCNT	Fathers of the Church: A New Translation (Washington, DC and New York 1948–) 118 vols to date
Förstemann-Günther	*Briefe an Desiderius Erasmus von Rotterdam* ed Joseph Förstemann and Otto Günther XXVII. Beiheft zum *Zentralblatt für Bibliothekswesen* 27 (Leipzig 1904; repr Wiesbaden 1968)

GCS	*Die griechishen christlichen Schriftsteller der ersten Jahrhunderte* (Leipzig and Berlin 1897–) 75 vols to date
LB	*Desiderii Erasmi Roterodami opera omnia* ed J. Leclerc (Leiden 1703–6; repr 1961–2) 10 vols
Moreau *Inventaire*	Brigitte Moreau *Inventaire chronologique des éditions parisiennes du XVIe siècle d'après les manuscrits de Philippe Renouard, 1501–1535* (Paris 1972–) 5 vols to date
NPNF	*A Select Library of Nicene and Post-Nicene Fathers of the Christian Church* 1st and 2nd series (New York 1886–99; repr Grand Rapids 1974) 28 vols
ODCC	*Oxford Dictionary of the Christian Church* ed Frank Leslie Cross and Elizabeth A. Livingston 3rd ed (Oxford 1997)
OER	*Oxford Encyclopedia of the Reformation* ed Hans J. Hillerbrand (New York and Oxford 1999) 4 vols
Opus epistolarum	*Opus epistolarum Des. Erasmi Roterodami per autorem diligenter recognitum et adjectis innumeris novis fere ad trientem auctum* (Basel: Hieronymus Froben, Johann Herwagen, and Nicolaus Episcopius 1529)
PG	*Patrologia cursus completus. . . series Graeca* ed J.-P. Migne (Paris 1857–66; repr Turnhout) 161 vols. Indexes F. Cavallera (Paris 1912); T. Hopfner (Paris 1928–36) 2 vols
PL	*Patrologiae cursus completus . . . series Latina* ed J.-P. Migne, 1st ed (Paris 1844–55, 1862–5; repr Turnhout) 217 vols plus 4 vols indexes. In the notes, references to volumes of PL in which column numbers in later editions or reprints differ from those in the first edition include the date of the edition cited.
Reedijk *Poems*	*The Poems of Desiderius Erasmus* ed Cornelis Reedijk (Leiden 1956)
Reeve *Annotations*	*Erasmus' Annotations on the New Testament: Facsimile of the Final Latin Text with All Earlier Variants* ed Anne Reeve and M.A. Screech (London 1986; Leiden 1990–3) 3 vols
Renaudet *Préréforme*	Augustin Renaudet *Préréforme et humanisme à Paris pendant les premières guerres d'Italie (1494–1517)* 2nd ed (Paris 1953)
Renouard *Imprimeurs*	Philippe Renouard *Imprimeurs et libraires parisiens du XVIe siècle: ouvrage publié d'après les manuscrits de Philippe Renouard* (Paris 1964–) 6 vols to date

Rummel *Annotations*   Erika Rummel *Erasmus' Annotations on the New Testament: From Philologist to Theologian* (Toronto 1986)

Rummel *Catholic Critics*   Erika Rummel *Erasmus and his Catholic Critics* (Nieuwkoop 1989) 2 vols

Rummel *Jiménez*   Erika Rummel *Jiménez de Cisneros: On the Threshold of Spain's Golden Age*, Medieval Texts and Studies 212 (Tempe, Ariz 1999)

SC   *Sources chrétiennes* (Lyon 1942–   ) 531 vols to date

STC   *A Short-Title Catalogue of Books Printed in England, Scotland, and Ireland and of English Books Printed Abroad, 1475–1640*, ed A.W. Pollard, G.R. Redgrave (London 1926); 2nd ed rev W.A. Jackson et al (London 1976–91) 3 vols

de Vocht CTL   Henry de Vocht *History of the Foundation and the Rise of the Collegium Trilingue Lovaniense, 1517–1530* (Louvain 1951–5) 4 vols

WA   *D. Martin Luthers Werke, Kritische Gesamtausgabe* (Weimar 1883–   ) 73 vols to date (with indexes)

WA-Br   *D. Martin Luthers Werke: Briefwechsel* (Weimar 1930–78) 12 vols

ZW   *Huldreich Zwinglis Sämtliche Werke* ed Emil Egli et al, Corpus Reformatorum 88–101 (Leipzig and Zürich 1905–59; repr 1981) 14 vols

SHORT-TITLE FORMS FOR ERASMUS' WORKS

Titles following colons are longer versions of the same, or are alternative titles. Items entirely enclosed in square brackets are of doubtful authorship. For abbreviations, see Works Frequently Cited.

Acta: Acta Academiae Lovaniensis contra Lutherum *Opuscula* / CWE 71

Adagia: Adagiorum chiliades 1508, etc (Adagiorum collectanea for the primitive form, when required) LB II / ASD II-1–8 / CWE 30–6

Admonitio adversus mendacium: Admonitio adversus mendacium et obtrectationem LB X

Annotationes in Novum Testamentum LB VI / ASD VI-5, 6, 8, 9 / CWE 51–60

Antibarbari LB X / ASD I-1 / CWE 23

Apologia ad annotationes Stunicae: Apologia respondens ad ea quae Iacobus Lopis Stunica taxaverat in prima duntaxat Novi Testamenti aeditione LB IX / ASD IX-2

Apologia ad Caranzam: Apologia ad Sanctium Caranzam, or Apologia de tribus locis, or Responsio ad annotationem Stunicae . . . a Sanctio Caranza defensam LB IX

Apologia ad Fabrum: Apologia ad Iacobum Fabrum Stapulensem LB IX / ASD IX-3 / CWE 83

Apologia ad prodromon Stunicae LB IX

Apologia ad Stunicae conclusiones LB IX

Apologia adversus monachos: Apologia adversus monachos quosdam Hispanos LB IX

Apologia adversus Petrum Sutorem: Apologia adversus debacchationes Petri Sutoris LB IX

Apologia adversus rhapsodias Alberti Pii: Apologia ad viginti et quattuor libros A. Pii LB IX / CWE 84

Apologia adversus Stunicae Blasphemiae: Apologia adversus libellum Stunicae cui titulum fecit Blasphemiae et impietates Erasmi LB IX

Apologia contra Latomi dialogum: Apologia contra Iacobi Latomi dialogum de tribus linguis LB IX / CWE 71

Apologia de 'In principio erat sermo' LB IX

Apologia de laude matrimonii: Apologia pro declamatione de laude matrimonii LB IX / CWE 71

Apologia de loco 'Omnes quidem': Apologia de loco 'Omnes quidem resurgemus' LB IX

Apologia qua respondet invectivis Lei: Apologia qua respondet duabus invectivis Eduardi Lei *Opuscula* / ASD IX-4 / CWE 72

Apophthegmata LB IV

Appendix de scriptis Clithovei LB IX / CWE 83

Appendix respondens ad Sutorem LB IX

Argumenta: Argumenta in omnes epistolas apostolicas nova (with Paraphrases)

Axiomata pro causa Lutheri: Axiomata pro causa Martini Lutheri *Opuscula* / CWE 71

Brevissima scholia: In Elenchum Alberti Pii brevissima scholia per eundem Erasmum Roterodamum CWE 84

Carmina LB I, IV, V, VIII / ASD I-7 / CWE 85–6

Catalogus lucubrationum LB I / CWE 9 (Ep 1341A)

Ciceronianus: Dialogus Ciceronianus LB I / ASD I-2 / CWE 28

Colloquia LB I / ASD I-3 / CWE 39–40

Compendium vitae Allen I / CWE 4

Conflictus: Conflictus Thaliae et Barbariei LB I

[Consilium: Consilium cuiusdam ex animo cupientis esse consultum] *Opuscula* / CWE 71

De bello Turcico: Utilissima consultatio de bello Turcis inferendo, et obiter enarratus psalmus 28 LB V / ASD V-3 / CWE 64

De civilitate: De civilitate morum puerilium LB I / CWE 25

Declamatio de morte LB IV

Declamatiuncula LB IV

Declarationes ad censuras Lutetiae vulgatas: Declarationes ad censuras Lutetiae vulgatas sub nomine facultatis theologiae Parisiensis LB IX

De concordia: De sarcienda ecclesiae concordia, or De amabili ecclesiae concordia [on Psalm 83] LB V / ASD V-3 / CWE 65

De conscribendis epistolis LB I / ASD I-2 / CWE 25

De constructione: De constructione octo partium orationis, or Syntaxis LB I / ASD I-4

De contemptu mundi: Epistola de contemptu mundi LB V / ASD V-1 / CWE 66

De copia: De duplici copia verborum ac rerum LB I / ASD I-6 / CWE 24

De esu carnium: Epistola apologetica ad Christophorum episcopum Basiliensem de interdicto esu carnium LB IX / ASD IX-1

De immensa Dei misericordia: Concio de immensa Dei misericordia LB V / CWE 70

De libero arbitrio: De libero arbitrio diatribe LB IX / CWE 76

De praeparatione: De praeparatione ad mortem LB V / ASD V-1 / CWE 70

De pueris instituendis: De pueris statim ac liberaliter instituendis LB I / ASD I-2 / CWE 26

De puero Iesu: Concio de puero Iesu LB V / CWE 29

De puritate tabernaculi: Enarratio psalmi 14 qui est de puritate tabernaculi sive ecclesiae christianae LB V / ASD V-2 / CWE 65

De ratione studii LB I / ASD I-2 / CWE 24

De recta pronuntiatione: De recta latini graecique sermonis pronuntiatione LB I / ASD I-4 / CWE 26

De taedio Iesu: Disputatiuncula de taedio, pavore, tristicia Iesu LB V / CWE 70

Detectio praestigiarum: Detectio praestigiarum cuiusdam libelli Germanice scripti LB X / ASD IX-1

De vidua christiana LB V / CWE 66

De virtute amplectenda: Oratio de virtute amplectenda LB V / CWE 29

[Dialogus bilinguium ac trilinguium: Chonradi Nastadiensis dialogus bilinguium ac trilinguium] *Opuscula* / CWE 7

Dilutio: Dilutio eorum quae Iodocus Clithoveus scripsit adversus declamationem suasoriam matrimonii / *Dilutio eorum quae Iodocus Clithoveus scripsit* ed Émile V. Telle (Paris 1968) / CWE 83

Divinationes ad notata Bedae: Divinationes ad notata per Bedam de Paraphrasi Erasmi in Matthaeum, et primo de duabus praemissis epistolis LB IX

Ecclesiastes: Ecclesiastes sive de ratione concionandi LB V / ASD V-4, 5
Elenchus in censuras Bedae: In N. Bedae censuras erroneas elenchus LB IX
Enchiridion: Enchiridion militis christiani LB V / CWE 66
Encomium matrimonii (in De conscribendis epistolis)
Encomium medicinae: Declamatio in laudem artis medicae LB I / ASD I-4 / CWE 29
Epistola ad Dorpium LB IX / CWE 3 / CWE 71
Epistola ad fratres Inferioris Germaniae: Responsio ad fratres Germaniae Inferioris
    ad epistolam apologeticam incerto autore proditam LB X / ASD IX-1
Epistola ad graculos: Epistola ad quosdam imprudentissimos graculos LB X
Epistola apologetica adversus Stunicam LB IX / Ep 2172
Epistola apologetica de Termino LB X
Epistola consolatoria: Epistola consolatoria virginibus sacris, or Epistola consolatoria
    in adversis LB V / CWE 69
Epistola contra pseudevangelicos: Epistola contra quosdam qui se falso iactant
    evangelicos LB X / ASD IX-1
Euripidis Hecuba LB I / ASD I-1
Euripidis Iphigenia in Aulide LB I / ASD I-1
Exomologesis: Exomologesis sive modus confitendi LB V
Explanatio symboli: Explanatio symboli apostolorum sive catechismus LB V /
    ASD V-1 / CWE 70
Ex Plutarcho versa LB IV / ASD IV-2

Formula: Conficiendarum epistolarum formula (see De conscribendis epistolis)

Hyperaspistes LB X / CWE 76–7

In Nucem Ovidii commentarius LB I / ASD I-1 / CWE 29
In Prudentium: Commentarius in duos hymnos Prudentii LB V / CWE 29
In psalmum 1: Enarratio primi psalmi, 'Beatus vir,' iuxta tropologiam potissi-
    mum LB V / ASD V-2 / CWE 63
In psalmum 2: Commentarius in psalmum 2, 'Quare fremuerunt gentes?' LB V /
    ASD V-2 / CWE 63
In psalmum 3: Paraphrasis in tertium psalmum, 'Domine quid multiplicate' LB V /
    ASD V-2 / CWE 63
In psalmum 4: In psalmum quartum concio LB V / ASD V-2 / CWE 63
In psalmum 22: In psalmum 22 enarratio triplex LB V / ASD V-2 / CWE 64
In psalmum 33: Enarratio psalmi 33 LB V / ASD V-3 / CWE 64
In psalmum 38: Enarratio psalmi 38 LB V / ASD V-3 / CWE 65
In psalmum 85: Concionalis interpretatio, plena pietatis, in psalmum 85 LB V / ASD
    V-3 / CWE 64
Institutio christiani matrimonii LB V / CWE 69
Institutio principis christiani LB IV / ASD IV-1 / CWE 27

[Julius exclusus: Dialogus Julius exclusus e coelis] Opuscula / CWE 27

Lingua LB IV / ASD IV-1A / CWE 29
Liturgia Virginis Matris: Virginis Matris apud Lauretum cultae liturgia LB V /
    ASD V-1 / CWE 69

Luciani dialogi LB I / ASD I-1

Manifesta mendacia ASD IX-4 / CWE 71
Methodus (see Ratio)
Modus orandi Deum LB V / ASD V-1 / CWE 70
Moria: Moriae encomium LB IV / ASD IV-3 / CWE 27

Notatiunculae: Notatiunculae quaedam extemporales ad naenias Bedaicas
Novum Testamentum: Novum Testamentum 1519 and later (Novum instrumentum
    for the first edition, 1516, when required) LB VI / ASD VI-2, 3

Obsecratio ad Virginem Mariam: Obsecratio sive oratio ad Virginem Mariam in
    rebus adversis, or Obsecratio ad Virginem Matrem Mariam in rebus adversis
    LB V / CWE 69
Oratio de pace: Oratio de pace et discordia LB VIII
Oratio funebris: Oratio funebris in funere Bertae de Heyen LB VIII / CWE 29

Paean Virgini Matri: Paean Virgini Matri dicendus LB V / CWE 69
Panegyricus: Panegyricus ad Philippum Austriae ducem LB IV / ASD IV-1 / CWE 27
Parabolae: Parabolae sive similia LB I / ASD I-5 / CWE 23
Paraclesis LB V, VI
Paraphrasis in Elegantias Vallae: Paraphrasis in Elegantias Laurentii Vallae LB I /
    ASD I-4
Paraphrasis in Matthaeum, etc LB VII / ASD VII-6 / CWE 42–50
Peregrinatio apostolorum: Peregrinatio apostolorum Petri et Pauli LB VI, VII
Precatio ad Virginis filium Iesum LB V / CWE 69
Precatio dominica LB V / CWE 69
Precationes: Precationes aliquot novae LB V / CWE 69
Precatio pro pace ecclesiae: Precatio ad Dominum Iesum pro pace ecclesiae LB IV,
    V / CWE 69
Prologus supputationis: Prologus supputationis errorum in censuris Bedae LB IX
Purgatio adversus epistolam Lutheri: Purgatio adversus epistolam non sobriam
    Lutheri LB X / ASD IX-1

Querela pacis LB IV / ASD IV-2 / CWE 27

Ratio: Ratio seu Methodus compendio perveniendi ad veram theologiam (Methodus
    for the shorter version originally published in the Novum instrumentum of
    1516) LB V, VI
Responsio ad annotationes Lei: Responsio ad annotationes Eduardi Lei LB IX /
    ASD IX-4 / CWE 72
Responsio ad collationes: Responsio ad collationes cuiusdam iuvenis geronto-
    didascali LB IX
Responsio ad disputationem de divortio: Responsio ad disputationem cuiusdam
    Phimostomi de divortio LB IX / ASD IX-4 / CWE 83
Responsio ad epistolam Alberti Pii: Responsio ad epistolam paraeneticam Alberti
    Pii, or Responsio ad exhortationem Pii LB IX / CWE 84
Responsio ad notulas Bedaicas (see Notatiunculae)

Responsio ad Petri Cursii defensionem: Epistola de apologia Cursii LB X /
    Ep 3032
Responsio adversus febricitantis libellum: Apologia monasticae religionis LB X

Spongia: Spongia adversus aspergines Hutteni LB X / ASD IX-1
Supputatio: Supputatio errorum in censuris Bedae LB IX

Tyrannicida: Tyrannicida, declamatio Lucianicae respondens LB I / ASD I-1 / CWE 29

Virginis et martyris comparatio LB V / CWE 69
Vita Hieronymi: Vita divi Hieronymi Stridonensis *Opuscula* / CWE 61

Index

This Index contains the names of persons, groups of persons, places, and literary works. An index of subjects covering all volumes of the Correspondence will be published after completion of the series.

384; on qualities of a bishop 409; heresy as a fruit of the flesh 443; church as spouse of Christ 447n; was not heeded 492; quotes Epimetheus about Cretans 517n

Paul III (Alessandro Farnese), pope, and Reginald Pole 114n

Paul of Samosata 335n

Paulinus of Milan *Vita sancti Ambrosii* 238n

Pauvant, Jacques, executed for heresy 314n

Pavia: French defeat at 36n, 73n, 123n, 132n, 134n, 154n, 234n, 433n; Nausea at 159; Pirckheimer at 346

Pelagius, Pelagians: St Augustine refutes 15, 270, 329; Jerome attacks 195n; Erasmus adheres to church condemnation of 403

Pellicanus, Conradus (former Franciscan) xvi, 19, 20, 352, 382, 403

Pentheus, king of Thebes 83

Perseus 103n, 277n

Peter, St, apostle: Ciceronians spurn the name of 31–2; accommodates Judaizing Christians 105–7, 195–7, 266; alleged error in faith of 196; Epistle of 477

Peter Abelard 33n

Peter Lombard 33n; *Sentences* 330

Peter the Chanter 33n

Petit, Guillaume, OP, confessor of Francis I 189n

Petit, Jean, bookseller in Paris 24n, 37n

Petrarch, used spectacles 158n

Petreius, Johann, printer in Nürnberg 347n

Petri, Johannes, printer in Basel 421n

Petrus, Adam, printer in Basel 418n

Peypus, Friedrich, printer in Nürnberg 347n

Pfefferkorn, Johann, attack on Reuchlin and Hebrew books 131n

Phalaris, a tyrant of Agrigentum (Sicily) 430n

Philip the Arabian 248n

Pigge, Albert: papal letter to theolo-

gians of Louvain 34, 137, 283; reports sack of Rome 223

Pilate, Pontius 267

Pindar 188; source for *Dulce bellum inexpertis* 122n; *Nemean Odes* 397

Pio, Alberto, prince of Carpi 25n, 179n, 191, 316n, 400n; *Ad Erasmi Roterodami expostulationem responsio accurata et paraenetica* 25; the colloquy *Exequiae seraphicae* satirizes burial of 44; close to Aleandro 191; Erasmus' response to 482n

Pirckheimer, Willibald: realigned with Catholicism 347; lost letter from 347n; bookplate of 348 *illustration*; counselled moderation in polemical works 349

– works: *Adversus convicia Ioannis, qui sibi Oecolampadii nomen indidit, Responsio secunda* 427n; *Apologia seu podagrae laus* 347n; *De vera Christi carne et vero eius sanguine* 347n

– letter from 346–50

– letter to 399–404

Piso, Jacobus 502n; reports on events in Hungary in a lost letter 60, 62n; his circle of humanists in Buda 62n; death of 502

Pistorius, Christophorus: tutor to Albert II of Brandenburg 351n; and the Eucharist 352–3

– letter from 350–3 (mentioned 229)

Plato: and civil war 119; and process of fair judgment 514

– works: *Laws* 135; *Republic* 119n; *Theaetetus* 514

Plautus, works: *Miles gloriosus* 69, 386; *Persa* 85–6, 98, 99

Pliny the Elder (Gaius Plinius Secundus) *Naturalis historia* 9, 117; Froben's edition of 129n, 296; Cracow edition of book 1 494n; cited 9n, 117, 263

Pliny the Younger (Gaius Plinius Caecilius Secundus), writes about his family 214

Płock, bishops of: *see* Krzycki, Andrzej; Leszczński Rafał